D0269878

FREUD ON BROADWAY

Freud
On
Broadway

A HISTORY OF PSYCHOANALYSIS AND THE AMERICAN DRAMA

W. DAVID SIEVERS

HERMITAGE HOUSE   •   NEW YORK, 1955

For
SAM and PAULINE

Preface

The material upon which this book is based was first gathered and presented as a doctoral dissertation at the University of Southern California in 1951. I cannot but express the deepest gratitude to the members of the committee which guided that research, steering it—I hope successfully—through treacherous waters between the Scylla of pedantry and the Charybdis of exuberant discipleship. The chairman of the committee, Dr. Milton Dickens, participated with invaluable encouragement and assistance in the "birth trauma" of the study. To Dr. Lee Edward Travis, lay analyst and professor of Psychology and Speech, I shall remain forever indebted for his contributions and influence, which extended far deeper than this book indicates. Professor William C. deMille, whose own contributions to the theatre are a part of the history of the maturing American drama, proved an unfailing source of support with his sagacious wit and keen insight. Dr. James H. Butler's scholarly knowledge of Greek drama and its deeper implications enriched the study, as did the astute criticism of Dr. William B. McCoard.

To the thirty-three American playwrights who responded to my questionnaire I must express special gratitude, for without them such a study would have been purely subjective. The generosity of such authors as Thornton Wilder, Paul Green, Elmer Rice, S. N. Behrman, Clifford Odets, Arthur Miller, Robert Sherwood, George Kelly, Samson Raphaelson, and many others, is appreciatively acknowledged.

I am indebted, too, to Kenneth Macgowan for invaluable information, to George Freedley for making available the scrapbook collections of dramatic criticism in the New York Public Library, and to the Los Angeles Institute for Psychoanalysis for making accessible its

7

library. The arduous task of indexing was most capably done by Ruth Boorkman. My thanks, too, go to Robert C. Wylder, my colleague in the English department of Long Beach State College for finding time to read and correct the manuscript along with his other freshman compositions, to Dr. Thomas G. Macfarlane of our Psychology department for his reading and critique of the manuscript, and to my patient wife. I should not fail to mention my three children, without whom this book would likely have been completed several years sooner but with considerably less understanding of psychology.

W.D.S.

Contents

FREUD ON BROADWAY

CHAPTER I

Introduction

When this book was first planned, it was my intention to call it "From *Suppressed Desires* to *A Streetcar* of the Same Name." As the study progressed, however, it became clear that Susan Glaspell's entertaining little satire was not the first nor Tennessee Williams' *Streetcar* the last of the dramas which derived their themes from psychoanalysis. To obtain a full picture of Freud's impact we must trace the whole development of the American psychological drama from its tentative beginnings a decade before *Suppressed Desires* to its most recent manifestations in the work of Arthur Laurents, William Inge and Arthur Miller.

On the occasion of Sigmund Freud's eightieth birthday celebration in 1936, Thomas Mann was invited to give the principal address. Referring to the influence which Freud has had upon literature, he said:

> I realized this connection only at a time when his achievement was no longer thought of merely as a therapeutic method, whether recognized or disputed; when it had long since outgrown his purely medical implications and become a world movement which penetrated into every field of science and every domain of the intellect; literature, the history of art, religion and pre-history; mythology, folklore, pedagogy. . . .

Yet the psychological play is as old as the drama itself. The mystery of human motivation was the subject matter of the earliest extant dramas of Aeschylus, Sophocles and Euripides. At least five centuries before the Christian era, audiences were responding to the stories of Oedipus, who inadvertently slew his father and married his mother, and Electra, whose destiny it was to avenge her father's death by causing the murder of her mother. Rooted deeply in an archaic, savage period of man's prehistoric development, these Greek legends became fresh revelation in the hands of master playwrights who "saw life steadily and saw it whole." And today, as a result of Freud's work, this Sophoclean vision of the wholeness of man's inner life has been rendered as accessible as a pocket book edition, and Oedipus and Electra have become prototypes familiar to every literate person.

The influence of literature upon Freud's own thinking has been made clear in his writings. Although, as his biographer tells us, Freud attended the theatre "only very occasionally," it was to the Greek dramas, to Shakespeare and to Goethe that he turned for reinforcement when his psychoanalytic theories were under attack—for supporting evidence derived intuitively by the great poets. When Thornton Wilder, who knew Freud and used to call upon him during his later years, asked him why psychoanalysis had appeared relatively so late in human culture, Freud's answer was: "Yes, but the poets have always known it."

Wilder's quotation of Freud was taken from a questionnaire sent out in connection with this study to some sixty American playwrights, in an effort to obtain evidence as to the actual extent of Freudian influence upon the drama. The provocative and varied answers of the thirty-three who returned their questionnaire will be referred to throughout the chapters to follow.

It is far from the purpose of this book, however, to test a play against Freudian dogma and to rule upon the results, judging as the best plays those which adhere most closely to orthodox psychoanalytic theory. We have ample evidence from the Marxian dramatic criticism of the thirties to indicate the dangers of a dogmatic approach. It is not even necessary to concede any validity to the theory of psychoanalysis itself in order to recognize that the ideas of Freud and his colleagues have had a vast influence upon the drama of the last forty years. On guard against the temptation to "project" Freudian motives where none was intended, we have drawn our evidence principally from the plays themselves—from the stated or hinted clues provided by the dramatist to his characters' psychology.

It must be remembered, too, that the fact that a playwright denies any influence of Freud upon his thinking does not necessarily indicate that there has been no influence. If Freud has taught us anything, it is the role of the unconscious in human behavior. The ideas of psychoanalysis may have reached a particular writer from a multitude of sources while it was "in the air" of the times, from cocktail conversations, popular magazines, even from the work of other playwrights; it is impossible to pinpoint the genesis of an idea (to say nothing of the matter of "resistance," which several important playwrights may have been reflecting by their unwillingness to discuss the influence of Freud upon their work). We can only conclude, as Miss Lillian Hellman has so ably expressed it in her note to the author: "You absorb what is of your time to absorb."

In his eloquent appreciation of Dostoevsky's *The Brothers Karamazov,* Freud wrote: "Before the problem of the creative artist, analysis must, alas, lay down its arms." In antiquity, as Freud knew, the dramatic poet was the world's first psychologist. With the rise of inductive science in the 19th century, a chasm between the poet and the scientific psychologist began to open and it reached its widest cleavage by the late 19th century. It is clear that the recent trend in the drama has closed the gap and promises to restore this classic unity of poet and psychologist. In his letter Lynn Riggs quoted a psychoanalyst who said to him, "You're doing the same thing I am." Mr. Riggs concluded, "I suppose that is so of any writer whose concern is with the nature and meaning of people."

The chapters to follow will trace in detail the growth of this movement in the American drama which, although no novelty in its larger outline, has as yet not been described in all its particulars. We have heard, for example, of Freud's influence on O'Neill, but his comparable impact on Philip Barry has been generally ignored. We know of Odets' interest in proletarian problems but we have not known his indebtedness to Freud's psychological world-view. *Our Town* has moved a generation of playgoers but assumes greater interest after Thornton Wilder's statement of conscious application of Freudian concepts. The work of Behrman, too often dismissed as "drawing room comedy," becomes, when viewed in its breadth, a sizeable contribution to psychoanalytic drama. And so it is with Elmer Rice, Lillian Hellman, Samson Raphaelson, Robert Sherwood, Rose Franken and a host of others. The names of authors whose work was found to parallel the theories of psychoanalysis becomes a roll call of the American dramatists since 1920. Yet each author treats the ideas in his individual way, as we shall observe, adding flesh and blood from his own experience. Paul Green has ably expressed the obligation of the creative artist to go beyond mere textbook application of Freudian psychology:

Freud's pioneer work no doubt is of world stimulating effect, but if the dramatist fails to pass beyond Freud into
the realm of freedom and self-responsibility, then I for one
think he would likely be a half-baked dramatist.

We had the half-baked ones too, as the chapters to come will show.

For those who are not entirely at home in psychoanalytic theory,
Chapter II is a necessary preface to the rest of the book. It attempts
very briefly to give some definitions and Freudian viewpoints. It is
inevitably inadequate, of course, and the reader is referred to one of
the excellent summaries of psychoanalysis: Clara Thompson's *Psychoanalysis: Evolution and Development;* Patrick Mullahy's *Oedipus—
Myth and Complex;* Ives Hendrick's *Facts and Theories of Psychoanalysis;* and the numerous individual works of the Menningers,
Reik, Brill, Horney, and Fromm. It should be made clear, too, that although we refer to "Freudian" concepts, we must not underestimate
the contributions of Jung, Adler and others whose work is a part of
this history. In spite of the countless intramural divergences within
the psychoanalytic fraternity and recent non-orthodox refinements of
both theory and practise, the name of Sigmund Freud has become
the chief identification for the entire movement, and is so used in
this book.

Viewed half a century after his first publications, the significance
of Sigmund Freud for the drama lies not in the specifics which may
or may not prove obsolete, but rather in his pioneer accomplishment
of opening gates so that others might enter to explore with a variety
of techniques. In the perspective of his times Freud seems a unique
combination of scientist and intuitive genius, daring iconoclast and
patient researcher, humanitarian and high priest. His introspective
honesty was that of a creative artist, yet his medical training taught
him to respect a dispassionate, clinical method. He founded a new
aesthetics as well as a new practise of medicine and psychology. His
book on wit is as rich a contribution to literature as his paper on paranoia is to psychiatry. His theories have been watered down and
adapted until today it is virtually impossible to read a popular magazine—from a report on narcotics addiction to a brassiere advertisement, to listen to a radio "soap opera" or to watch a television mystery drama, without coming into contact with ideas derived from
psychoanalysis. The second Kinsey Report takes for granted most
of Freud's insights while quarreling with some of his specific hypoth-
eses. Though we still stand far from a complete understanding of
the human organism and the forces that motivate it, we are much

nearer to that understanding than we were before the work of Freud. He was truly the great opener of doors.

There are still those, however, who would belittle Freud's influence. One of the criticisms frequently heard is a statement such as this: "Shakespeare did pretty well with *Hamlet*, and he had never read Freud. How do you explain that?"

Freud himself offered the explanation. In analyzing the differences between Sophocles' *Oedipus the King* and Shakespeare's *Hamlet*, Freud wrote:

> But the whole difference in the psychic life of the two widely separated periods of civilization, and the progress, during the course of time, of repression in the emotional life of humanity, is manifested in the differing treatment of the same material. In *Oedipus Rex* the basic wish-phantasy of the child is brought to light and realized as it is in dreams; in *Hamlet* it remains repressed, and we learn of its existence as we discover the relevant facts in a neurosis only through the inhibitory effects which proceed from it.

The significant phrase, "the progress of repression . . . in the emotional life of humanity," explains away the dilemma. The three hundred years between *Hamlet* and Freud were marked by an even more pronounced growth of repression in the emotional life of the western world than in the two thousand years between *Oedipus* and *Hamlet*. The insights of a Sophocles, a Shakespeare, a Goethe were nowhere to be found in the American drama during the 19th century. Since cloying sentimentalism rose in the 18th century it had been gradually choking out Restoration frankness in favor of "middle class morality." It is no historical accident that Freud, Havelock Ellis, and their convention-smashing colleagues came at the climax of a most severe period of Puritan repression, associated with the reign of Queen Victoria. Although "poets have always known it," they have not always been free to express the deepest truths in their art. The progress of repression in the race made it necessary for someone to rediscover what the Greeks had candidly faced, what Shakespeare had intuitively known, and what Anglo-Saxon Puritanism had preferred to "forget" (in quotes because nothing repressed is ever truly forgotten). It was to be Sigmund Freud's role in the history of literature to recall to the world's consciousness what a Victorian *super-ego* had chosen to taboo. To become fully aware of the tremendous changes which have resulted in the American drama since the advent of psychoanalysis, however, we must examine briefly the drama that immediately preceded Freud.

CHAPTER II

Backgrounds...
Psychological and Dramatic

CLYDE FITCH AND INHERITED FACULTIES

During the years when Sigmund Freud was formulating his concepts, what was the state of the American drama? Let us look, for example, at Clyde Fitch's popular hit, *The Moth and the Flame*, written in 1898, three years after Freud's first major publication. In this play, an unwed mother brings her child to the church to prevent her seducer from marrying another woman. She exclaims to her more fortunate rival: "And think what it is to . . . watch your child, your own flesh and blood, day and night, all its life, terror-stricken . . . lest you find *some trace of his father in him.*"

Arthur Hobson Quinn has said that Fitch was the finest realist of the turn of the century; his "studies of human characters who are endowed with a shining virtue or possessed by one absorbing vice" made the earlier writers of American melodrama, Bronson Howard, James A. Herne and William Gillette, seem contrived and sentimental. "The real inspiration of Clyde Fitch," wrote Quinn, "came from his unremitting study of men and women in their social and personal relations." Fitch must be taken as the high water mark of American realism before Freud, beyond which the drama could not move without a fundamental change of psychology.

Fitch's *The Girl With the Green Eyes* (1902) illustrates 19th century "faculty psychology," which assumed that specific character traits were inheritable. The heroine, Jinny Tillman, is governed by one obsessive vice, jealousy, which she is supposed to have inherited from her parents. Her irreproachable husband attempts to help Jinny's inherently weak brother out of a marital difficulty, and Jinny assumes that her husband is unfaithful. When she later learns of his noble motives, she turns on the gas, only to be rescued and reconciled with her husband at the end. Another of Fitch's heroines, Becky Warder in *The Truth* (1906), is a pathological liar, again as a result of heredity. In Eugene Walter's famous success of 1909, *The Easiest Way*, we see another lady struggling in vain with her inherent trait of "waywardness."

This suggests the state of the serious American drama at the turn of the century. Concepts of human motivation seemed, by today's standards, naive and one-dimensional. Plots were largely a matter of intrigue and contrivance in the French manner of Eugene Scribe. Characters behaved from *conscious* intent only, superficially motivated by the various moral virtues or lack thereof. Dishonesty, alcoholism, profligacy, cruelty, weakness, all were taken as static character traits which resulted from "hereditary taint." The pressures of environment, the dynamics of childhood, the interplay of drives and restraints were not taken into account. A woman was either chaste or she was "fallen." For a lady to acknowledge sexual needs was still twenty-five years away. Moral judgment was a substitute for psychological analysis.

Most American playwrights were tailors who cut their cloth to fit the great stars of the stage. The best box-office attraction was the safest and least offensive play. *The Old Homestead* (1878) by Denman Thompson, *Hazel Kirke* (1880) by Steele MacKaye, and *Secret Service* (1896) by William Gillette made the tears flow and the box-office coffers fill during the years when the new movement in literature was having its birth pangs in Vienna. True, James A. Herne had dared in 1890 to show upon the stage in *Margaret Fleming* the wife of a philandering husband tenderly offering her breast to a hungry infant, the child of her husband and the other woman. As Quinn has observed, "Audiences of 1890, however, were not ready for the shock which arises from the relapse into the primitive."

This, then, was the cultural environment in which Freud's theories were first offered. True, there had been hints in the European drama of things to come: Shelley's daring play of a father's incestuous love for his daughter, *The Cenci* (1819), is a solitary monument of closet drama. In Germany, Heinrich von Kleist anticipated Freudian drama by almost a century, and out of morbid, introspective romanticism created two unique dramas; *Das Käthchen von Heilbronn* (1810), a study of masochism in a heroine who will endure every humiliation and indignity which her lover can heap upon her; and *Penthesilea* (1808), a study of the Amazon queen who murders her lover with uncontrollable sadism. Gassner has called this strange, brooding romantic playwright "the unrecognized father of modern psychological drama, the forerunner of Strindberg and O'Neill." This father, however, left no literary descendants among the American playwrights of the period.

In Europe, where the playwright was not under such direct pressure to show a profit at the box-office, the romantic tradition generally gave way more quickly to the realistic and scientific attitude as the 19th century progressed. The same realistic attitude which produced the work of Ibsen, Gorki, Tolstoi, Becque and Hauptmann also produced a revaluation of concepts within the medical profession and stimulated the scientific study of psychology. It is interesting to note that it was not until 1879, the year of Ibsen's *A Doll's House,* that the profession of experimental psychology may be said to have been begun by Wilhelm Wundt, who established the first laboratory at Leipsig.

THE ORIGIN OF PSYCHOANALYSIS

The immediate predecessor of psychoanalysis, however, was not the scientific laboratory, but the romantic and mystic phenomenon of hypnotism. Interest in hypnotism dates from about 1760 when an Austrian medical student, Anton Mesmer, began to cure paralysis and convulsions by "drawing out" the disease with a magnet and later with passes of his hand before the patient's eyes. King Louis XVI of France appointed an investigating committee (which included Benjamin Franklin) to determine whether Mesmer was a charlatan. The committee concluded that the cures were genuine but discredited the idea of "magnetic fluid."

The American playwright, Anna Cora Mowatt, author of *Fashion,* tells in her *Autobiography of An Actress* that she was mesmerized as early as 1842 for the treatment of illness. By the middle of the century, a French country doctor named A. A. Liébault was successfully using Mesmerism in treating patients who suffered from paralysis, hysteria, blindness and tics, merely by telling them under the hypnotic trance that their symptoms would disappear. The term "hypnotism" was introduced around 1843 by James Braid, an English surgeon who borrowed the Greek word for sleep (*hypnos*).

During the same years Jean Marie Charcot began to study nervous and mental illness through the use of hypnosis at the Salpêtrière Hospital in Paris, and affirmed the radical motion that men as well as women might suffer from hysteria (a logical impossibility because the Greek word *hysteron* meant womb, and hysteria was thought to be an ailment of the uterus).

Conservative physicans scorned Charcot's concepts and attempted to find an organic cause for every illness. If none could be found, it was assumed that there was a "degoncracy" in the brain itself, thus attaching a stigma to mental illness which implied both moral and physiological degeneration. Treatment generally consisted of hydrotherapy, electrotherapy, and drugs, some of which gave temporary relief, probably because of suggestion.

Emil Kraepelin helped to standardize the diversified psychiatric terminologies by classifying cases of insanity as *manic-depressive* or *dementia praecox* (deterioration occuring early in life—now known as *schizophrenia*). But these diseases were considered things apart from and unrelated to normal behavior—and of course incurable. A borderline case was called "neurasthenic" and the patient was told to go home and "forget about it" or take a "rest cure." Working to free psychiatry from this dilemma were Charcot and his pupils.

Two of these pupils were later to become famous. The first, Pierre Janet, found that hysterical patients could recall when hypnotized certain events forgotten in the waking state. He developed the theory of "dissociation" to account for this apparent internal division within the personality. Hysterical individuals were susceptible to being "split," he believed, because of a congenital mental weakness; he reunified them by suggesting through hypnosis that disturbing events in their lives were over and done with.

The other of Charcot's distinguished students was an Austrian physician, Sigmund Freud. Freud was born in 1856, was graduated from the Vienna Medical School in 1882, and remained on to study neurology and anatomy until 1885, when he made the crucial decision to go to Paris and study psychiatry with Charcot.

Freud soon became a member of Charcot's inner circle and translated his book on hypnotism into German. Freud returned to Vienna and began to practise as a neurologist in 1886. When he spoke before the august body of the Vienna Medical Society and attempted to expound Charcot's views, he was scorned and ridiculed—to such an extent that he withdrew from the learned societies and pursued further explorations in isolation. It is one of history's little ironies that the President of the Vienna Medical Society at the time of Freud's rebuff was the eminent professor Richard von Krafft-Ebing, whose name was to be so closely linked with Freud's in the public mind in the United States. The latter's *Psychopathia Sexualis* (1886), however, reflected the older viewpoint that sexual deviation was a form of degeneracy which could be scientifically described but not accounted for.

After a second period of study in France with Liébault and Bernheim, Freud sought out Dr. Josef Breuer, a respected Viennese family practitioner, who had once told him of a novel therapy he had used with a hysterical patient (the now famous case of Anna O.). While Anna O. was in a self-induced hypnotic stupor, she would mumble to herself. Breuer soon discovered to his amazement that after talking about incidents of her early life which she could not recall when awake, she would awaken from the trance calm and free from anxiety. Dr. Breuer soon formalized this technique which Anna O. had herself named "the talking cure." Each day Breuer hypnotized her and led her to talk about a different symptom until one by one they all disappeared. Breuer concluded that something had been drained off—some residue of painful memories that were released in a "catharsis."

Freud tried the Breuer "cathartic method" and found that he could accomplish the same results even without hypnosis. He merely asked the patient to lie down on a sofa and relax completely. Seating himself at the head of the sofa where the patient could not see him, he would ask the patient to report anything and everything that came into his mind without reservation, reticence or censorship. Thus the technique of *free association* evolved: first hypnosis—then talking it out under hypnosis—then talking it out without hypnosis. This process of candidly reporting to the therapist everything that occurs to the patient remains to this day the core of psychoanalysis.

During these years when the excitement of scientific discovery seemed to be a part of the very air in Vienna and the other European capitals, Freud urged Breuer to collaborate with him on further experiments with the "talking cure," but Breuer had abandoned his method after his one application of it and was reluctant to reopen the problem. Finally, in 1893, Freud prevailed upon him to publish in collaboration a paper which truly marks the beginning of a new era in psychology: "On the Psychical Mechanism of Hysterical Phenomena."

PARALLEL LINES—ARTHUR SCHNITZLER

The same year, another Viennese physician and friend of Freud's, Dr. Arthur Schnitzler, made perhaps the first application of scientific hypnotism to the drama—in his little one-act comedy *Questioning Fate* (part of the *Anatol* cycle). Anatol, anxious to learn if his current mistress is faithful to him, hypnotizes her and is about to ask the fateful question when he loses courage to do so and prefers not to hear what her subconscious might reveal. The *Anatol* episodes, first translated into English in 1903, were not professionally staged in New York, however, until 1912.

Schnitzler's career in Vienna interestingly parallels Freud's. He was graduated from the Vienna Medical School three years later than Freud, served in a hospital as a resident psychiatrist, and himself began experimenting with hypnosis and suggestion. Schnitzler wrote reviews for a medical journal, among which was one on Freud's translation of Charcot's *Hypnotism*. Schnitzler also wrote a research paper on Loss of Voice or Aphonia and Its Treatment by Hypnosis. Gradually, however, Schnitzler abandoned medicine for literature. His *Anatol* cycle is best known in this country but in other plays too he paralleled psychoanalytic concepts closely enough to warrant the title "first Freudian dramatist": *Paracelsus* (1898), a one-act (admired by Freud) which treats hypnosis and the subconscious from the point of view of Paracelsus, a 16th century forerunner of Mesmer; *The Veil of Beatrice* (1900), which recognizes the dream as wish-fulfillment; *The Lonely Way* (1904), in which a character has the uncanny psychological power of "deja-vu" (the sensation of having seen a new sight before); *The Call of Life* (1906), in which a girl who is wasting her life nursing an invalid father finally gives him an overdose of sleeping pills and goes out to her lover; and most significant of all, *Hands Around* (*Reigen*, 1897). In the latter play variations in attitude toward the sex act are analyzed on every level of society with the clinical naturalism of a surgeon and the precision of a Kinsey; it was not written frivolously, but out of deep melancholy concerning the hypocritical and brutalizing role which sex occupied in society. Schnitzler finally permitted the book to be privately printed in 1900, but did not authorize a production until 1920, when Max Reinhardt staged it expressionistically but did not thereby avoid riots and front page scandals over it. In New York the premiere in 1923 was closed by the Society for the Suppression of Vice. The recent French film version, *La Ronde*, met a better fate.

During these same years another physician was similarly exploring the individual psyche. Anton Chekhov's little farce, *The Marriage Proposal* (1889), predates Freud and Schnitzler, showing a reluctant suitor attempting to propose and suffering from assorted twitches, chills, humming in the ear, heart murmurs and feet going to sleep as he fearfully faces the woman of his choice.

Wedekind also preceded Freud in his expressionistic protests against the secrecy and suppression surrounding the adolescent's curiosity about sex. His remarkable pioneer work, *The Awakening of Spring* (1891), could be acted in New York as late as 1917 only to a closed membership meeting of the sponsors of *The Medical Review of Reviews*—and then the city authorities tried to stop it!

PSYCHOANALYTIC DEFINITIONS

In the case of Anna O., a girl was forced to devote some years of her life to nursing her ailing father (the situation Schnitzler used in *The Call of Life*). During this time she developed paralysis of the arm. Breuer traced the cause of the paralysis back to shattering or *traumatic* emotional experiences which she had not dared to confess to her father and hence had banished from her conscious attention. These feelings (mainly related to her wish for freedom) did not die or dissipate but underwent *repression*, continually striving to return to consciousness. To block these unwanted impulses from consciousness or "dam them up," the girl was forced to exert energy, which set up a conflict within her between the repressed impulses and the restraining forces. The energy thus thwarted had to work its way to the surface on some wrong nerve pathway—and it chose the innervation of the arm. The symptom of paralysis was accordingly produced by *conversion* of energy, leading Freud and Breuer to term the illness *conversion hysteria*. Other examples of conversion hysteria are tics, twitches, pains, and numbness. Freud and Breuer thus began to refine the old catch-all term of "neurasthenia" and to note varieties of neurosis. In addition to conversion hysteria, they found *anxiety neurosis* (often associated with hypochondria, irritability, and hypertension) and *compulsion neurosis,* which included obsessions, doubts, guilts, and fears.

When Freud and Breuer enlarged their paper in 1895, the resultant *Studies in Hysteria* contained the hypothesis that there exist in the human personality two levels, the *conscious* and the *unconscious*. Freud of course did not invent the unconscious. The German philosopher, Edouard von Hartmann had written *The Philosophy of the Unconscious* in 1868, and as far back as 1816 Johann Herbart had discussed "the subconscious." But whereas the unconscious was to Herbart and von Hartmann a theoretical concept and to Schopenhauer a form of Will, to Freud it was a scientifically observable function of personality—that part of the mind which controls behavior without the conscious ego's awareness of its true motives. "The ego is not master in its own house," Freud later proclaimed, recognizing what a shock this discovery was to the pride of man. When he was hailed on his seventieth birthday as "the discoverer of the unconscious," Freud corrected the speaker and said: "The poets and philosophers before me discovered the unconscious. What I discovered was the scientific method by which the unconscious can be studied."

Freud distinguished precisely between the unconscious and the vague term subconscious, which he preferred not to employ. Similarly, Freud's translator, Dr. Brill, distinguished between *repression*, which is an unconscious process, and *suppression*, which is a *conscious* disciplining of one's impulses as required by civilization. (Susan Glaspell's satire should rightly have been called *Repressed Desires*.)

When *Studies in Hysteria* was reviewed in the Viennese medical literature of 1895, only one writer apparently grasped the full implications of this first tentative formulation, and he was not a medical reviewer, interestingly enough, but a dramatic critic and director of the Imperial Theatre of Vienna. In an article entitled "Surgery of the Soul," Alfred von Berger wrote: "We dimly conceive the idea that it might one day become possible to approach the innermost secret of the personality of man." Von Berger noted the similarity of the new psychology to that used by poets. He may be said to have anticipated even Freud in applying psychoanalysis to the interpretation of drama. Lady Macbeth, von Berger observed, had repressed from consciousness her anxiety and horror at the murder of Duncan and Banquo, and as a result developed a defensive neurosis.

The parting between Breuer and Freud came shortly after the publication of *Studies in Hysteria*, and was occasioned by the growing belief in Freud's mind that the cause of hysteria could generally be traced back to sexual maladjustment. Breuer himself saw no sexual etiology in the case of Anna O., and withdrew from further research with Freud apparently out of embarrassment at the implications of their discovery.

Freud was not, of course, the first writer to treat sex scientifically. Havelock Ellis had published on sex before Freud, the first volume of his monumental *Studies in the Psychology of Sex* appearing in German the same year as the *Studies in Hysteria* (1895). As Ellis has pointed out, Freud's own private life was entirely conventional, and he did not personally participate in the revolution that was beginning against entrenched Victorian morality. But his manner of expressing himself on sex and his attitude toward its importance were completely revolutionary, shocking both those who viewed sex as sacred and those who held it to be indecent.

MESMERISTS AND *DOPPELGÄNGERS*

The ferment created in intellectual circles in Vienna and Paris by the work of Charcot and Janet actually preceded Freud to this country and was referred to under the catch-all title of "the new psychology." William James, America's leading psychologist, was interested in the subconscious, as well as in spiritualism, which had seen a revival as a movement around 1848 and had spread to England, where the Society for Psychical Research crystallized popular interest in communication with the dead, exchange of souls, thought-reading or telepathy, automatic writing, and survival after death. These phenomena are of interest here only because James and others considered the "subconscious" or "subliminal self" as scientific proof that the spirit world existed and that communication between spirits was possible. Another movement allied to the "new psychology" was that of "faith healing" or the "mind cure," which had grown up in this country around 1867 and had given rise to the Christian Science religion. The Mental Hygiene movement, too, was rooted in these years. The crusade of Dorothea Lynde Dix to reform the barbarous "insane asylums" began in 1841, but it was not until after 1908, when Clifford Beers published his work, *A Mind That Found Itself,* that the movement for preventive psychotherapy and the enlightened handling of the insane gained momentum.

The two American psychologists who were most influential in popularizing the theories of Charcot and Janet were Dr. Morton Prince and Dr. Boris Sidis, both of whom practised scientific hypnotism. It was Prince's *The Dissociation of a Personality* (1906) which popularized Janet's concept of the subconscious splitting or dissociation of personality; this was one of the first books on "the new psychology" to be widely read in America and to influence the writing of a Broadway play. In spite of the efforts of Dr. Prince to win scientific acceptance for the therapies of Charcot, Janet and Bernheim, hypnotism at this period was still linked in the popular mind with black magic and the occult. Dramas employing hypnotism and "spells" were of course too numerous to deal with here; our concern is only with the use of hypnosis as a therapy to release unconscious conflicts or to reveal repressed material. In this interpretation Schnitzler led the way with his *Questioning Fate.* Gerald Du Maurier's best-selling British novel, *Trilby,* however, became the first hypnosis-play to achieve outstanding popularity, although it was based upon the older interpretation of hypnotism. It was first dramatized in 1895 by Paul M. Potter and played with great success by Wilton Lackaye in the role of the sinister hypnotist, Svengali. Trilby is shown as an artist's model who loves an English painter but falls under the spell of Svengali, a musician who discovers that she has a fine voice. Under his hypnotic power she becomes a famous concert singer, but when Svengali dies she is unable to sing again. Dr. A. A. Brill, Freud's American translator and exponent, tells what a tremendous impression *Trilby* made upon him as a young man, fostering in him the interest in hypnotism which ultimately led him to Zurich and Vienna.

The subject of the split personality also reached our drama by way of a British story, derived from German romanticism. In the 19th century "Gothic" melodrama of Germany, the theme of the *doppelgänger* or double-personality was a popular one. In the plays of Tieck, Werner, Büchner and Grillparzer as well as the tales of E. T. A. Hoffman, there are gruesome, necrophilic episodes of the transmigration of souls from one body to another, vampires, werewolves that combined human souls and animal instincts, and the splitting of the individual into the dual role of the good-and-bad twin brothers.

A British version of the *doppelgänger* theme which proved highly popular on the American stage was Robert Louis Stevenson's *The Strange Case of Dr. Jekyll and Mr. Hyde.* Dramatized by T. R. Sullivan, it was played in the repertory of Richard Mansfield from 1897 through 1905 and became the classic symbol of the split personality. The virtuous Dr. Jekyll tells his fiancée, Alice: ". . . in every man there are two natures, one of good and one of evil—and he who has them under such control that the good always balances the bad is indeed blessed." Jekyll is not thus blessed, and frequently feels a change coming on—he writhes in agony, and assumes the hideous and twisted shape of Mr. Hyde, a fiend who would kill Alice. Eluding police by changing back to Dr. Jekyll, he is finally trapped and kills himself. Despite the play's naive melodrama and far-fetched claptrap, its theme is the psychological dualism of man's nature, which was not explained scientifically until Freud explored the origin of hostile impulses in man.

George Sylvester Viereck and Edgar Allan Woolf tried to capitalize on this theme in *The Vampire,* which was seen in New York in 1909. *Dracula,* which did not reach Broadway until 1927, illustrates the same split-personality motive in Gothic melodrama; the monster is one of the "undead" who sleeps by day and walks the earth by night searching for human blood to suck. The heroine believes herself the victim of horrible nightmares until the two red spots on her neck confirm the presence of the vampire. The evil genius by day proves to be the suave Count Dracula who uses hypnosis over his victims to prepare them.

The Jekyll and Hyde theme persisted through the war years in *The Masquerader,* Guy Bates Post's famous vehicle by John Hunter Booth (1917), in which a poor but honest man changes place with a famous member of Parliament (his exact double) who is a dope fiend, and in *One* (1920) by Edward Knoblock, in which twin girls possess only one soul between them, and can communicate with each other across the Atlantic by pressing a red rose or a red ribbon against their breast. One sister has to die in order for the other to acquire a complete personality and her sweetheart. Although twins do in fact often develop a sense of incompleteness without each other, it is evident in this play that the older generation of playwrights were not able to divorce the new psychology from the hocus-pocus of 19th century melodrama. In the psychological climate which immediately preceded the Freudian era, the "subconscious" embraced a multitude of sins. It was a vague and mystic area which accounted for the irrational and inexplicable: split personality, "doppelgängers," hypnotism, telepathy, automatic writing, vampires, werewolves, and spirit transference. It did not as yet, however, include sex.

Sex was still the object of strict taboo on the Broadway stage—in fact the producer of Shaw's now-tame *Mrs. Warren's Profession* and his leading lady were arrested in 1905 for staging the play in New York. The next year saw the production of possibly the first hint that a new order was on the way. William Vaughn Moody's *The Great Divide* (1906) dared to show a woman learning to love the man who had violated her. Although buried deep in sentimentality, there is in this drama the germ of the new spirit of freedom for woman to find sexual fulfillment (symbolized by the West) in conflict with the moral Puritanism of New England.

AUGUSTUS THOMAS

The first American playwright to introduce the "new psychology" of the subconscious in a Broadway drama was Augustus Thomas. In 1907, his milestone, *The Witching Hour,* began its long run of 212 performances in a season which included Nazimova in *The Master Builder* (in which Ibsen, by the way, as early as 1892 had given strong hints that he accepted the possibility of thought transference).

Augustus Thomas, whose earlier plays *Alabama* and *In Mizzoura* were certainly not psychological studies, tells in his autobiography of an early interest in telepathy and spiritualism. After working as publicity agent for a "thought-reader," Thomas went on to read the psychic books of Dr. Thomas Hudson, William James, Charcot and Janet and to write a one-act sketch, *A Constitutional Point,* based on the concept of telepathy between living and dead. On several trips to Paris, Thomas tells of going to hear lectures by Charcot: "when a kindred subject was on the calendar during my stay in Paris I would go to the indicated *salle* of the Sorbonne and hear some lecture on psychology."

The Witching Hour, the first fruit of these lectures on psychology, combines as many psychic and subconscious elements as Thomas could compress into four acts. Jack Brookfield is a gambler with mesmeric and telepathic powers, which his niece, Viola, may have inherited from him. He meets Helen Whipple, whom he loved years ago and who would have married him had he but given up his gambling. Now she is a widow with a son, Clay, who has a phobia concerning a cat's-eye scarf pin which causes him to stab to death a man who teases him about it. She goes to a Supreme Court Justice (who dabbles in telepathy and hypnosis) and explains to him that her mother, whom the judge had once been in love with, also suffered from a phobia for a cat's-eye jewel and that Clay must have inherited it. The justice promises to get them a new trial on the strength of this evidence, and is firmly convinced that the spirit of the dead woman he loved "was in this room tonight and directed a decision of the Supreme Court of the United States."

Jack tries by telepathy to influence the jury while it is out. Hardmuth, the vindictive prosecuting attorney, is threatened with exposure by Jack and comes to kill him. But in a famous scene Jack saves himself by hypnotizing Hardmuth, who has a gun against Jack's stomach: "Stop! You can't shoot—that—gun! You can't pull the trigger! You can't—even—hold—the—gun!" The gun drops from Hardmuth's hand. (Never did hypnotism work so well for Freud!) Jack then cures Clay of his phobia by making the boy look at the cat's-eye and face it down. Realizing that a murder-wish in his own mind was transferred to the mind of the murderer, Jack repents sufficiently to win Helen as his wife.

Quite a lump of "new psychology" to digest in one play! When Daniel Frohman read the script of *The Witching Hour,* he rejected it with the words, "Forget it, Gus; go out West and give us one of your wholesome *Arizonas.*" But Thomas did not forget it. He took the play to Lee Shubert, who put it immediately into rehearsal. In reviewing the play, Walter Prichard Eaton demonstrated a better grasp of the new psychology than did Thomas, pointing out that Bernheim in his research at Nancy had found that people could not be hypnotized against their will, as was the villain of Thomas' drama. The real interest for Eaton was Thomas' thesis that "our thoughts are dynamic as well as our words."

Thomas said that in his research for *The Witching Hour*, "I got a fund of information that would have served for fifty plays." Only two out of the fifty materialized, however. His next play, *The Harvest Moon* (1909), has as its *raisonneur* a Monsieur Vavin, who is supposedly a friend and colleague of Charcot. A young girl (who later proves to be his daughter) is suspected of having inherited "wayward tendencies" from her mother. Vavin dramatizes the newer point of view which rejects inherited vices and virtues, pointing out the influences of environment in the girl's life: having heard from childhood that her mother was wayward was a sufficient mental suggestion to make her touchy on the subject. To illustrate the power of mental suggestion, Vavin in five minutes persuades a very healthy man that he is quite ill. As a final dividend from Charcot's lecture notes, Thomas has Vavin reunite the lovers through the use of a theory of various colors which, according to Charcot, invariably produce certain emotional reactions while the subject is under hypnosis.

Thomas wrote one further "mental suggestion" play, *As A Man Thinks* (1911), which adds some "new thought" to an otherwise hackneyed plot of double moral standards and infidelity. The wise old Jewish physician, Dr. Seelig, realizes perhaps more clearly than any character up to that time in an American play, that "what a man thinks" may affect his physical health. He comes close to speaking words Freud might have written when he advises his patient who would avoid discussing her husband's infidelity: "In surgery we sometimes find a condition where a wound has healed too quickly and on the surface only. The treatment is to re-open it entirely. A mental trouble has its analogy. Better talk of it."

Following this play, Augustus Thomas did heed Frohman's advice and gave us some more *Arizonas: Rio Grande* and *The Copperhead*. If his plays were ill-digested hodge-podges of "new psychology," and surely not "an example of Ibsen in America," as Walter Prichard Eaton called *The Witching Hour*, at least Thomas had seized upon a significant new field from which to draw subjects for the drama. A number of other playwrights were quick to follow suit: Edward Locke's *The Climax* (1909) shows a young doctor so much in love with his sweetheart, who is about to leave him for an operatic career, that he pretends to have an operation performed on her throat, then hynotizes her into believing her voice is gone. In the end the girl recovers her voice and is willing to forgive her somewhat impetuous medical swain.

Two plays by Charles Klein also include unwilling victims of hypnosis. In *The Third Degree* (1909), the police take advantage of a ray of light reflected from the barrel of a gun to hypnotize an innocent man into confessing a crime. This incident was purportedly based on ". . . an anecdote related by Prof. Hugo Munsterberg in 'On the Witness Stand,' and the play itself, the Professor assures us, might be actually a transcript from life." Klein's next play, *The Next of Kin* (1909), contains a malevolent, Svengali-like hypnotist who almost succeeds in convincing a "lunacy commission" to commit an heiress to an insane asylum, thereby permitting him to inherit her fortune. In their search for novelty, Broadway playwrights such as Thomas, Locke and Klein were thus quick to sense the theatrical possibilities of the "new psychology," although these early treatments were necessarily based upon superficial understanding.

HYPOCHONDRIA

In the years between 1895 and 1909, while Broadway was having its first glimpse of the new psychology, Freud was enlarging his theoretical grasp of unconscious motivation and formulating most of the theories for which he is known. As the world's first professional listener sat at the head of his couch, Freud soon realized that everything which entered the patient's mind was somehow related to his symptoms, that nothing could be dismissed as inconsequential. The meaning of these *free associations*, as he termed them, was often distorted or disguised because they had to pass the scrutiny of the patient's own inner censorship before they could be verbalized. The psychic censor which Freud assumed to be at work repressing unwanted or forbidden thoughts from reaching consciousness was later to be renamed the *super-ego*. Because so much of the activity of the *super-ego* is unconscious, the individual is rarely aware of his defense mechanisms, conversion symptoms and rationalizations. Some re-evaluation may be necessary to acquaint the patient with himself. This is the purpose of psychoanalysis, which may be defined as the interpretation of dreams and free associations in terms which the patient's conscious ego can assimilate, in order to free or purge him of the control which unconscious impulses exerted upon his behavior. The term psychoanalysis was in use by 1898 and was soon enlarged to mean not only the therapeutic technique devised by Freud but the resultant psychological theory of unconscious motivation as well.

Freud soon observed obstacles which stood between the psychoanalyst and the patient. One was *resistance,* the psychic force which prevents the repressed idea from being recalled. A patient may be quite sincere in saying that he cannot remember, for the repressing mechanism long ago may have withdrawn the painful associations from consciousness. A second obstacle to psychoanalytic cures, Freud soon found, was the phenomenon of *transference.* Early in his practise Freud discovered that his women patients entertained amorous or hostile thoughts toward him. Freud concluded that patients were transferring to him the emotions aroused by a parent in an earlier period. The analyst thus became a "father-image" or "mother-image," and the patient unconsciously responded as though he were a child again. Transference places a heavy moral responsibility upon the analyst, who must not imagine that the patient actually loves or hates him as a person. These strong emotions are merely being relived, and may be used by the analyst to help effect the cure—by showing the patient his tendency to transfer emotions from a more childish period into situations where they are not applicable. The final stage of psychoanalytic therapy must inevitably be the dissolution of the patient's dependence upon the analyst and the development of self-reliance.

Another form of resistance is *hypochondria,* or as Freud termed it the "secondary gain of illness." When a patient unconsciously utilizes a physical symptom in order to gain sympathy, attention, or control, there is a strong resistance to being cured. This is a newer interpretation than the conventional theatre hypochondria of *Le Malade Imaginaire* or that favorite dramatic illness of 18th century plays, "the vapours." Freud believed that the illness was not imaginary at all but very real to the patient, although its origin was in emotional conflict rather than germ or virus. In this new approach to hypochondria lies the kernel of a revolution in the practise of medicine. The modern study of psychosomatic medicine has found unconscious emotional conflict as a contributing factor in asthma, allergy, ulcers, tuberculosis, headaches, obesity, and even, it has been conjectured, cancer.

The first American play to champion this new interpretation of hypochondria was *The Mollusc* (1908) by English-born Hubert Henry Davies, a San Francisco drama critic. His play treated the psychological parasite who, like a marine biological organism, clings to someone else in that dependency which is the source of her power. Suspecting that the heroine's illness is a device for maintaining authority over her husband, the lady's brother tells her: "It may have been a plot, or suggestions may have arisen like bubbles in the subconscious caverns of your mollusc nature." The analogy of the subconscious being submerged or under water was a favorite one with psychoanalysts during these early years. There is in *The Mollusc* also a brief discussion of the meaning of dreams, although the brother's dream of arriving in England "with no baggage and nothing on but my pajamas" is not analyzed.

An early play to capitalize on the current interest in mental healing was Mrs. Frances Hodgson Burnett's *The Dawn of a Tomorrow* (1909), followed the next year by a more mature and serious-minded study of the influence of the mind on the body, William Vaughn Moody's *The Faith Healer*. Michaelis, the healer, cures a paralytic woman, believing his power to be supernatural. But a doctor interprets the cure as based on natural causes, a "jog of the mind" (the nature of which the doctor little understands). This and Michaelis' growing physical desire for a young girl, Rhoda, cause him to doubt his supernatural powers. Through Rhoda's belief in him, however, he finds his own faith again to continue to help the sick.

The same season saw a conventional and farcical treatment of mental healing and hypochondria, *Her Husband's Wife*, by A. E. Thomas. The wife is sure she is going to die young because her parents did. Though doctors can find nothing wrong with her, she consumes pills and powders and finally, as a gallant dying gesture, picks out a second wife for her husband. She selects some one dowdy and unattractive, but the girl improves her appearance and proceeds to vamp the husband, until the wife is forced to relinquish her plan to die and win her husband back.

FORMAL INTRODUCTION OF FREUDIANISM IN THE U. S.

The year 1909 is significant as the beginning of the formal introduction of Freudian psychology into America. A year before, Dr. A. A. Brill, one of Freud's inner circle, returned to America and began the practise of psychoanalysis in New York, and in the same year another disciple, Dr. Ernest Jones of Toronto, began publishing in the psychological journals a series of articles on Freud's theories. Then Professor G. Stanley Hall, President of Clark University, at Worcester, Massachusetts, invited Freud to speak at the 20th anniversary celebration of the founding of Clark. The meetings in Worcester in 1909 were attended by many eminent American psychologists, including William James. Freud brought with him some of his most distinguished disciples—Carl G. Jung, Sandor Ferenczi, and Ernest Jones. As Freud spoke in German, there was little popular reaction at first, but Freud to his amazement found his theories known and taught at Clark. (A student at Clark shortly thereafter was S. N. Behrman.)

Carl G. Jung, whose name was to be linked with Freud's and who later because the spearhead of the revolt against the orthodoxy of Freud, was assistant chief of psychiatry at the Burghölzli clinic at Zurich. Jung and his chief, Bleuler, were the first regular psychiatrists to apply Freud's theories in the treatment of institutionalized patients.

Jung made two significant contributions to the mainstream of psychoanalysis: he began to give association tests to his patients and to interpret the findings psychoanalytically, the first laboratory verification of psychoanalysis. The patient was read a list of words and asked for the first "reaction-word" that came into his mind, while his reaction-times were checked with a stop-watch. Then the test would be repeated and the patient asked to recall his original words. Any prolonged reaction times or lack of responses would indicate "that the stimulus word has touched a complex and thus retarded or completely inhibited the reaction."

In this way Jung used the term "complex" to indicate a cluster of ideas about which the patient had a strong emotional blockage or response. Jung noted such clusters as "religion complex," "sex complex," and "death complex." In his Worcester speech Jung described the association test and how it had been used to discover a theft by a nurse in the hospital—the forerunner of the lie detector.

Freud soon took over Jung's term "complex" and made use of it in his next great publication, *The Interpretation of Dreams* (1900), which became one of Freud's most widely read books. From his clinical experience with patients, Freud concluded that "wish—fulfillment is the meaning of every dream." (This wish is not confined to sex, as some opponents of Freud have charged.) The unfulfilled wish has been repressed from consciousness until some *daytime stimulus* or event on the day preceding the dream reawakens it, and thus aroused it threatens to disturb the person's sleep. These wishes form the *latent content* of the dream, but the psychic censor forbids them to pass undisguised; hence there is a process, called the *dream-work*, in which the latent wishes are disguised into acceptable impressions which are called the *manifest content*. The forms of disguise include *condensation*, or compressing many associations into one image; *dis-*

placement, or substitution of cause for effect, "it is," for "would it were," several people for one person, or one person for several; *symbolization,* or the use of a kind of shorthand, which when interpreted on the basis of folklore, mythology, idiomatic phrases and proverbs, becomes a key to the unconscious life of the dreamer (within a few years Freud, Stekel and other psychoanalysts had assembled general classes of symbols which were found to be common to many dreamers: weapons, snakes, neckties, pillars and shafts represent the male genital; caves, boxes, pockets and shoes symbolize the female genital; swimming was thought to symbolize human birth, mounting the stairs sexual intercourse, and the severing of any limb of the body or the cutting down of a tree castration); finally, *secondary elaboration,* or the disguise by which dream plots are amplified, tied together and complicated in order to further obscure the true meaning.

In *The Interpretation of Dreams,* too, is the first statement of one of the most controversial of Freud's teachings, later to be known as the *Oedipus complex.* Freud had found that fantasies of sexual seduction by a parent often lay at the root of hysteria. He concluded that these fantasies represented a repressed wish for union with the parent of the opposite sex. Freud turned to the drama of *Oedipus The King* by Sophocles for the classic illustration of this tendency which he believed to be universal among men—the urge to achieve union with the mother and to kill the father who is the chief obstacle to the goal. Of King Oedipus, Freud wrote:

> His fate moves us only because it might have been our own, because the oracle laid upon us before our birth the very curse which rested upon him. It may be that we were all destined to direct our first sexual impulses toward our mothers, and our first impulses of hatred and violence toward our fathers; our dreams convince us that we were. King Oedipus, who slew his father Laius and wedded his mother Jocasta, is nothing more or less than a wish-fulfilment—the fulfilment of the wish of our childhood.

In this one stroke Freud began a new aesthetics and a new theory of the relation of the audience or reader to the work of art.

Because Freud found these incestuous and murderous wishes prominent in the unconscious fantasies of his patients, he concluded that the way each individual handles his feelings for his parents (the so-called *family romance*), will determine his later potentialities for neurosis. Although civilization insists on the taboo of incest, the infant very logically seeks security and bodily comfort (diffused rather than specifically genital) from the body of the mother. In puberty

the normal development is for the boy to identify himself strongly
with the father and to relinquish this dependency upon the mother.
That Sophocles himself understood these dynamics, and saw his play
as deeper than legend, is suggested by Jocasta's lines:

> For many a man hath seen himself in dreams
> His mother's mate, but he who gives no heed
> To suchlike matters bears the easier life.

From Sophocles Freud turned to Shakespeare, pointing out similar Oedipal wishes in *Hamlet* and thereby beginning the psychoanalytic study of Shakespeare which has in subsequent years become so impressive a field of literary criticism.

Between 1908 and 1910 a considerable body of Freudian theory
was made available in English. Dr. Brill's translations of Freud began
with *Selected Papers on Hysteria* in 1909, and the Clark University
lectures were reprinted in 1910. By then the literary magazines,
too, had discovered Freud and had begun his popularization. *Current Literature, Forum, McClure's, The American Magazine, Century, Dial* and *The Nation* all treated psychoanalysis, with titles such
as:

Masters of the Mind
Remarkable Cures Effected by Four Great Experts
Without the Aid of Drugs or Surgeon's Tools

The book for which Freud "incurred the displeasure of the
world," was *Three Contributions to the Theory of Sex* (1905), which
appeared in English in 1910. In it Freud introduced the word *libido*
with his special meaning, the broad psychosexual drive (later called
"the pleasure principle"), which manifests itself in all pleasurable
body sensations, including affection, friendship, self-esteem, love for
parents and children, and even satisfaction in work—all, in short,
that is comprised under the word "love." The normal adult takes as
his sexual aim that of union with the opposite sex. There are many
other directions, however, in which the libido may be deflected. The
first two Freud described were *fixation* and *regression*. Fixation, although loosely used in popular jargon, meant to Freud that for some
traumatic or environmental reason a portion of the libido is stunted
in its development and remains bound at an infantile level. In later
life, when the individual finds himself frustrated in the forward
movement of the libido, it tends to flow back over the previous stages
and return to the point of fixation. This flowing backward to less
mature patterns of reaction Freud called *regression*.

Freud also analyzed *perversions* or *inversions* for the first time from a dynamic point of view, interpreting them not as degeneracy but as fixations of the libido at childhood levels of sexuality. Neurotics, unlike homosexuals, however, have too strong a *super-ego* to accept these outlets and hence must struggle to repress their inverse tendencies, causing hysteria and anxiety, even paranoia. Other fixated impulses may result in a *sadist*, who derives gratification from inflicting pain on others; a *masochist*, whose pleasure is derived from having pain inflicted upon him; a *voyeur*, or peeping tom; a *fetichist* (who projects his libido onto inanimate objects); or an *exhibitionist*.

In *Three Contributions*, also, Freud is said to have destroyed the "innocence of childhood" concept by describing the sexual outlets to which infants and children have recourse—the *oral* area of gratification by nursing at the breast or thumb-sucking (which gives rise to "oral regressions" in those adults whose infantile sucking pleasures were interrupted); the erotic area of the *anal* region, associated with retention (and when fixated, with sadism and miserliness); and finally the *genital* region (in which exhibitory or masturbatory behavior provides childhood gratification). Memories of childhood sexual practices are usually associated with shame and guilt and are repressed as the child grows older, until the adult has so-called *infantile amnesia* concerning his childhood. *Castration fear* in boys and *penis envy* in girls were also found to be frequent factors in the unconscious life of the child. As the child reaches adolescence, his choice of a sex object is often based upon a reawakened childhood memory of the mother or father, which he "projects" onto someone else. These contributions to the theory of sex first suggested to the world the critical importance of the infant and child's emotional needs for later adult adjustment and motivated the scientific study of the child which was to produce a revolution in pedagogy and education.

Viewed in the light of the Victorian era from which psychoanalysis emerged, it is little wonder that many people reacted with shock and anxiety as Freud's ideas became known. His writings were called "obscene" and "immoral," and he was attacked for his emphasis upon the "animal instincts" rather than the "spiritual" in man; and there were frequent misinterpretations of his famous phrase, "In a normal sex life no neurosis is possible."

The first of his disciples to break with Freud was Alfred Adler (in 1911), who felt that Freud had over-emphasized sexuality as a primary cause of neurosis. Adler believed that sex was a *symptom* of neurosis as well as a *cause*, and stressed the *inferiority of the organs* which gave some individuals an *inferiority complex* and caused them to strive for *superiority* as a compensation. The *will-to-power*, which manifested itself as *aggression* or *ego-striving*, was the key to Adler's psychology, and he made a more detailed contribution to the psychology of parent-child relationships than did Freud. Adler's therapy was based upon adjusting the individual's goals to those within his capacity to achieve. His books began appearing in English in 1917 and had considerable influence because of their less technical language. Adler settled in this country, where he taught from 1932 until his death in 1937.

Freud's books continued to appear in English; *The Interpretation of Dreams* in 1913 and *The Psychopathology of Everyday Life* in 1914. The latter was of considerable influence in its explanation of unconscious motives as the cause for everyday forgetfulness, "slips of the tongue" and "slips of the pen," now known as "Freudian slips." Freud cites an example in Shakespeare, Portia's speech to Bassanio:

> One half of me is yours, the other half yours,
> Mine own, I would say; but if mine, then yours,
> And so all yours.

O'Neill was to make significant use of the slip of the tongue as the crisis of *Mourning Becomes Electra*.

These, then, were the principal contributions of Freud, summarized as concisely as one dares. (The task is somewhat like preparing a five-minute recording of the principal themes of Beethoven.) After 1912 Freud's work tended more to revision and modifications, philosophic-analytic papers, and applications of psychoanalysis to aesthetics and literature, while the younger psychiatrists, such as Karen Horney, Erich Fromm, the Menningers and Harry Stack Sullivan freed psychoanalysis from orthodox dogma and applied their revisions of Freudian insights not only to the individual but to the social and political forces of our times.

Freud's interest in the drama, however, continued. He wrote rather sketchy interpretations of *The Merchant of Venice* and *King Lear,* and more thorough and scholarly studies of *Richard III, Macbeth,* and one contemporary drama, Ibsen's *Rosmersholm.* Freud set the precedent for psychoanalytic studies of literature which were carried on by Dr. Ernest Jones with his studies of *Hamlet,** by Otto Rank, Hanns Sachs, Fritz Wittels, C. P. Oberndorf, Theodor Reik, and S. E. Jelliffe, until there is today a considerable bibliography of literary analyses by psychiatrists. Some of it is conjectural and sub-

---

* *Time Magazine,* Aug. 10, 1953, states that Dr. Ernest Jones, Freud's disciple and author of notable books on Hamlet's mother-fixation, coached Sir Laurence Olivier in his interpretation of the role.

jective, giving the analyst's projections into the drama which may or may not illuminate the playwright's conscious intent—as when Mark Kanzer interprets the Sacred Grove to which the blinded old Oedipus is led by his daughter Antigone as symbolic of the female genital.

DAVID BELASCO DISCOVERS SEX

David Belasco, New York's leading showman, was one of the first to sense which way the wind was to blow in the new century. As early as 1898 he had produced *Zaza*, which depicted a French prostitute (albeit one who reforms in the end). The year of Freud's Worcester lectures (1909), Belasco brought to Broadway two relatively daring plays. The first, Eugene Walter's *The Easiest Way*, however, still reflected the moralistic viewpoint which had little tolerance and no understanding—and was, in fact, deeply pessimistic of human nature. The smug hero expects a kind of impossible nobility from his fiancée and when she slips from the straight and narrow, throws her over, exclaiming, "Laura, you're not immoral, you're just unmoral, kind o' all out of shape, and I'm afraid there's not a particle of hope for you." The novelty in *The Easiest Way* lay in the fact that it did not have a happy ending or a glib conversion of the fallen woman, but rather let the heroine, rejected by the man she loves, exclaim, "I'm going to Rector's to make a hit, and to hell with the rest."

The first drama to turn away from the moralistic viewpoint and to deal with the theme of sexual frustration in anything resembling an unembarrassed manner was Belasco's adaptation in 1909 of a French play, *The Lily*, by Wolff and Leroux. It showed a tyrannical father who keeps his two daughters from marrying. The elder is a subdued old maid, but the younger becomes the mistress of an artist. The elder defends her sister's conduct on the grounds that "any fate for woman is preferable to that of an enforced celibacy." These bold words apparently marked the first recognition in the American theatre of the sexual needs of woman, and stirred the critic for *The Nation* to call the play "pernicious from the moral and silly from the social point of view." In spite of *The Nation*, *The Lily* bloomed, however, for 164 performances on Broadway.

Eugene Walter's next play, *Just A Wife* (1910), brought together a husband, his wife, and his mistress for a relatively frank discussion of sex. Belasco meanwhile made other contributions to the new drama of psychology. In 1913 he produced a play written by "a dangerous maniac," Roland Molineaux, who had been imprisoned and then acquitted of murder; his play entitled *The Man Inside*, was apparently the first in American drama to champion prison reform and a psychological rather than a punitive approach to penology.

As was his wont, Belasco altered the play, adding melodramatic complications, until he had to bar the "madman author" from rehearsals for fear he would attack him. Molineaux was a year later committed to an asylum. The incident, however, reveals Belasco as something more of a man of courage in the theatre than he is often depicted. In 1913, too, he undertook to produce a play which everyone assured him would fail because of its morbid heroine. It was *The Secret*, from the French of Henri Bernstein, and proved to be the first psychological study of perverse, sadistic malice in a woman.

Belasco's most popular play, however, and one which succeeded as no play had since *The Witching Hour* in making new psychology pay at the box-office, was *The Return of Peter Grimm*, which began its long run of 231 performances in 1911. Belasco derived the idea for his play from a compact supposedly made between the psychologist, William James, and a friend, that whichever died first would attempt to communicate with the other to test the validity of spiritual telepathy. There is, as well, a suggestion in the play that Belasco might have had a cursory acquaintance with Freud's theories as publicized after the Worcester lectures.

After making a compact with a friend similar to that of James, old Peter Grimm dies at the end of Act I. Soon after death, however, he realizes that Frederick, the man he had made his ward, Kathrien, promise to marry, is a scoundrel. He therefore tries to "get through" to the living from the next world, but fails to communicate until a child who is ill and feverish becomes a "sensitive" for his telepathy. Unseen by the living, Peter's spirit walks the stage as Thornton Wilder's Emily Webb was to do a quarter of a century later. Peter tries to make the child name Frederick as his illegitimate father in order to provide cause for breaking his engagement to Kathrien. Almost like a psychoanalyst talking to a patient, Peter speaks to Frederick:

> . . . you can remember many things tucked away in your childish brain—things laid away in your mind like toys upon a shelf. Come: pick them up and dust them off and bring them out again. It will come back. When you lived with Annamarie . . . there was you . . . and Annamarie . . . and . . .

In a dramatic moment the boy names his Uncle Frederick as the man who had come to visit his mother.

Doctor: Are you sure you remember that? Weren't you
too small?
William: No: I *do* remember . . . I always did remember,
only for a little while I—I forgot . . .

This scene might almost be considered a fairly vivid dramatization
of the Freudian "return of the repressed" were it not vitiated by the
spirit of Peter Grimm hovering onstage to prompt the boy. Walter
Prichard Eaton was astute in sensing that Belasco did not commit himself as to whether he was borrowing from psychology or
spiritualism:

Now whether this was due to Peter or a sudden rising to the
'threshold' of his consciousness (as Professor James would
say) of a subconscious memory, is a moot point, very
cleverly left by Mr. Belasco as a loophole of escape from
any charge that he accepts a spirit phenomena as proved.
At any rate, the child's confession frees Kathrien from her
hateful marriage, and Peter has accomplished his purpose.

If *The Lily* and *The Return of Peter Grimm* represent two tentative steps forward in the direction of new psychology for David
Belasco, he may be said, like the Sabine soldiers, to have taken one
step backward the next year. His production of Edward Locke's second hypnosis-play, *The Case of Becky* (1912), reflected all the theatricality and contrivance of the older drama along with the superficial naturalism of stage setting for which Belasco was famous. Just
as *Peter Grimm* claimed William James for authority, so Belasco
was guided in rewriting and producing *The Case of Becky* by "the
most advanced scientific theories of multiple personality," derived
from Dr. Morton Prince's *The Dissociation of Personality*. Prince describes in detail the case history of a Miss Christine L. Beauchamp,
whom he treated for her inner conflict among three personalities,
saintliness, deviltry and common sense. It was estimated that more
than a hundred plays based upon the case of Miss Beauchamp were
submitted to Broadway producers, and Belasco was sued for plagi-
arism when *The Case of Becky* opened. He succeeded in establishing,
however, that he had taken his story from Prince's book rather than a
similar play.

In *The Case of Becky*, the schizophrenic heroine, Dorothy, is
gentle and pleasant until she reverts to her other self or *doppelgänger*, Becky, a hateful spitfire. To make the Becky half of her re-
cede into oblivion, she is hypnotized by a psychiatrist, Dr. Emerson,
whose work is interrupted by a travelling hypnotist, Balzamo. By a

theatrical coincidence, Balzamo had seduced Emerson's wife some
years before by means of hypnosis. Now Dr. Emerson overcomes
Balzamo with the help of a whirling hypnosis-machine in his "scientific" laboratory. He also learns that Dorothy is his own daughter,
her split personality caused by the fact that she was conceived and
born while her mother was under hypnosis!

The Case of Becky may have been taken seriously in 1912, but
there were already some who saw the humorous implications in the
direction which the modern drama was taking. Perhaps the first playwright to express a satiric amusement at the psychological drama
was Percy MacKaye in his drama Anti-Matrimony (1910).

Anti-Matrimony is a rather keen lampoon not only of the morbidity of modern psychology but of Ibsen, Nietzsche and "free-love."
A young playwright, Morris, and his wife keep their marriage a secret
because they prefer to be thought modern "anti-mats" living in beautiful free-love. His brother and sister-in-law are shocked, and try to
win them back to conventionality by themselves feigning an even
more daring modernity. The sister-in-law pretends to be a frustrated
dancer:

> All my life I have concealed it. Only occasionally, at picnics
> and birthday parties, I have given way to the divine in-
> stinct, and dazzled my bewildered partner in the two-step.
> At all other times my imprisoned genius has struggled like
> a captive faun for freedom. But what hope has an artist with
> a husband at home!

Mildred is, in short, the first of many American heroines to protest, "I
have repressed my personality."

Morris is writing a modern drama entitled Hosmer's House
which turns out to be MacKaye's satiric potpourri of Ibsen. Morris
chooses his plot devices from a catalog of the modern masters: "Suicide—pistols, coal-gas, drowning (mill-race preferred). Desertion,
divorce, insanity, general disintegration, cataleptic hysteria . . ."

> Morris: . . . the Hero, Hosmer, is an artist philosopher; a
> super-man, born with all the tragic advantage of genius.
> He is the last of an ancient house, and inherits a noble
> neurasthenia and subtle melancholia of character.
> Mildred: Neurasthenia, I understand, is the foundation of
> tragedy.
> Morris: Absolutely. (He goes on to explain that the other
> characters in the play will be:) . . . a morphine patient,
> an inebriate pastor, a suicidal doctor, a tubercular poet,
> a kleptomaniac and some others.

Mildred: Are none of them—quite well?

Morris: Only the wife, for contrast. Undiseased persons are essentially undramatic. . . . My characters have only those highly artistic diseases adapted to modern technique. . . . Inheritance is the modern form of fate, you know. But the minor persons still puzzle me. Which do *you* prefer—death by paranoiac insanity or pistol shot?

Not until they think Morris' brother has shot himself in the millrace "with a brace of the General's pistols" do the anti-mats "come to their senses" and revert to conventionality. But MacKaye was certainly being more prophetic in his catalog of modern dramaturgy than he himself could have realized in 1910.

Less than four months after *Anti-Matrimony,* another play by Percy MacKaye opened, this one in complete contrast with his philistine raillery at new psychology. *The Scarecrow,* with its gentle and imaginative story, belongs surely among the modern dramas which *Anti-Matrimony* meant to satirize. Derived from Hawthorne's story of *Feathertop,* it brings to life a scarecrow who poses as a nobleman until he is betrayed by a magic mirror which reveals the inner self. This symbolic and tender tragedy dramatizes the discrepancy between our real selves and the image of ourselves to which we prefer to cling—which Freud was to call the *ego-ideal.*

MacKaye's catalog of neurasthenic heroes fairly well summarizes the new drama by 1910, but omits two main tendencies which are apparent by now: "Subconscious" phenomena which included in one lump hypnotism, telepathy, spiritualism and split personality (represented in at least eight plays); and "mental healing" (found in at least five plays). The three plays by Augustus Thomas marked the first effort to exploit the "new psychology," although his understanding of mental suggestion in relation to somatic health was relatively naive. David Belasco was less sure of his content but more successful in satisfying the public palate with something new and psychological. *The Mollusc* marks the beginning of a comedy of character derived from insight into unconscious needs. But the concepts of Freud had not yet been differentiated from the general influence of "new psychology" on the drama, an influence which first reached America from the French school of Charcot and Janet. It might be said that curiosity about the subconscious had preceded Freud to America, but it remained for him to tell us what was to be found therein.

CHAPTER III

First Freudian Plays

☆   ☆   ☆   ☆

ARTHUR HOPKINS IN THE ROLE OF PROPHET

By 1912 the American drama was ready to take a new direction. True, it lagged behind the European theatre, which had already seen the major works of Wedekind, Schnitzler, and Strindberg. But the seed of psychological honesty was not as new in Europe as it was in the Puritan soil of this country, and the germination took longer. The influence of Wedekind, Schnitzler, and Strindberg was, curiously enough, not as pronounced as the direction set by Augustus Thomas, Belasco, and Klein in defining the new drama.

Credit for the first application of a psychoanalytic—as contrasted with a pre-Freudian—concept of psychiatry in American drama rightly belongs to Arthur Hopkins, whose play *The Fatted Calf* opened on February 19, 1912. Lacking a published text, we can only assume from available reviews that it dealt with the use of psychotherapy in the actual cure of paranoid symptoms; although it ran only eight performances, one critic prophetically called Mr. Hopkins "the latest—undoubtedly not the last—to conduct a tour through the country that Augustus Thomas rediscovered."

The Fatted Calf concerns Helen Pemberton, a young girl whose parents have, with the best of intentions, unwittingly cultivated the impression that she is insane until they—and she—are thoroughly convinced of it. A Dr. Winter tells the parents that the trouble with

46

Helen lies not in her but in their attitude toward her. Indignantly the parents order the doctor out of the house. When Helen's brother Roland returns unexpectedly from Europe (where presumably he absorbed the new psychology), he tries to help his sister, partly because the high eugenic standards of his fiancée won't permit her to marry into a family with suspected insanity. Roland calls the doctor back and they play along with Helen in her conviction that her parents have poisoned all the food in the house, and that she is a prisoner in her home. Fearing that she might commit suicide, the mother objects to freeing her with the familiar words, "I love my daughter. . . ." Roland answers with the most startlingly new lines in modern drama:

> The mother-love of the twentieth century is a product of woman's unoccupied mind. The new mother-love has resolved itself into a grim warning finger pointing day and night to catastrophies which might befall the child. It is no longer mother-*love* but mother-*fear*—and fear hews down more victims every day than all the pestilences of the earth combined.

Dr. Winter uses hypno-therapy on Helen's paranoid fantasies of persecution, and gradually she responds to the suggestion that she is healthy and normal; with the help of her brother and Dr. Winter she finally elopes with the young man she loves and whom her parents have refused to let her see. The parents are overwhelmed by the implications of what they have done (out of motives yet to be explored by later playwrights) in planting suggestions of inadequacy in their daughter since childhood, and the father needs a sanitarium himself at the end of this curiously modern play.

Except for a collaboration, *Burlesque,* Arthur Hopkins wrote only one other play, *Conquest,* which dealt with the Hamlet theme, and he produced the memorable Freudian *Hamlet* with John Barrymore in 1922.* Hopkins later went on to become one of Broadway's most distinguished producers of serious theatre. As early as 1918 he had published his superb essay, *How's Your Second Act?,* in which he brings to bear his knowledge of psychoanalysis in evolving a theory of Unconscious Projection in play direction, the use of which will, like hypnotism, "still the conscious mind" in order that the play may speak to the unconscious mind of the audience. Hopkins deserves great credit for *How's Your Second Act?* and for his influence

---

* There is some evidence that Robert Edmond Jones, designer of the *Hamlet* sets, as well as Arthur Hopkins and John Barrymore were psychoanalyzed by Dr. Smith Ely Jelliffe.

as a major force in bringing the new psychological realism to American audiences, for whom, as he writes, "All the repressed desires burst forth into flame in the theatre, and for a few hours they have full sway, to be silenced again until dreams have their sway." The season after *The Fatted Calf*, Hopkins produced *The Poor Little Rich Girl*, forerunner of post-war Freudian expressionism and a significant milestone in the development of the dream play.

THE DREAM PLAYS BEGIN

The dream in drama is hardly a novelty. Aeschylus used it brilliantly in *The Eumenides*, and Shakespeare's dreamers include Richard III, Queen Katherine, Brutus, and Lady Macbeth. But the nineteenth century romantics tended to employ the dream prophetically or as a dramaturgic excuse for fantasy. Beginning in the romantic tradition, Gerhart Hauptmann reflected a curiously persistent interest in dreams and was undoubtedly the father of the modern dream play. At one period of his career he kept a notebook in which to record his dreams, and in 1888 he studied in Zurich with Dr. Auguste Forel, a psychiatrist, hypnotist, and director of the Burghölzli clinic where Jung was later to practice psychoanalysis. Hauptmann's *The Assumption of Hannele* (1893) marked the first attempt to create a modern dream play entirely out of the elements of the dreamer's inner life. In the feverish dreams of the adolescent girl, Hannele, there is wish-fulfillment, anxiety, identification of her nurse with her dead mother, a self-pitying projection of her own funeral, and a romantic fantasy with the kindly schoolmaster, whom she finally identifies with The Saviour. The last act, as written by Hauptmann, was suppressed because of its erotic fantasy as a doctor bends over Hannele with a stethoscope.

Strindberg also preceded Freud's publication of *The Interpretation of Dreams* in his use of characters who split, recur, and disappear with the inconsistent logic of the dream. His *To Damascus* appeared in 1898, and a year after Freud's book Strindberg wrote *The Dream Play* (1901). Hauptmann and Strindberg had little effect upon the American drama, however, until after 1909, when Freud's discussion of the dream at Worcester was given wide publicity. Then a veritable wave of dream plays hit Broadway. *Hannele*, first seen in 1894, was revived in 1910, followed a month later by Marie Dressler in a musical comedy burlesque entitled *Tillie's Nightmare*. The following season saw at least five dream plays, some of which merely used the explanation that "it was all a dream" to account for impossible happenings.

Hopkins' production of *The Poor Little Rich Girl* (1913) by Eleanor Gates, was the most elaborately inventive American dream play to date, and one which suggested the influence of Maeterlinck's *The Blue Bird*. The little rich girl, neglected by her parents and abused by the servants, has a fantastic dream based upon daytime associations. The maid, for example, is two-faced and appears with two faces; a candle burns at both ends; a bear appears because the girl's father was at the mercy of Wall Street bears; a bee frightens her because someone had said that her mother ". . . had the society bee in her bonnet . . ." (according to a little bird, who also appears). There is distortion and displacement in the dream, but it is rather pun-visualization than repressed wish-fulfillment. The one wish which is fulfilled in the dream—to go fishing—was conscious to the girl before she fell asleep. The parents change their attitude in Act III (as though they had been able to see their daughter's dream) and permit her to join her fishing companion. It is possible that this play represents some superficial contact with Freudian dream psychology, or at least that its long run reflects a heightened interest in the meaning of dreams resulting from Brill's translation of *The Interpretation of Dreams*, which appeared the same year.[*]

It remained for Alice Gerstenberg, two years later, to give Broadway its first really authentic glimpse into unconscious life. Her dramatization of Lewis Carroll's *Alice in Wonderland* and *Through the Looking Glass* did not enjoy as long a run as did Eva Le Gallienne's version in 1932 when audiences were better able to identify Freudian symbols. But *Alice in Wonderland*, as well as the neurotic life of its author, later proved of interest to a number of psychoanalysts. Charles Dodgson preceded James Joyce in his use of "portmanteau" words; he was a minister and a mathematician, a stutterer and a lifelong celibate who sublimated his sexuality into a spiritual preoccupation with little girls. Although *Alice in Wonderland* (1865) preceded Freud, Schilder has pointed out the themes of sexual symbolism and severe anxiety which run through it—as in the dreams of neurotics, Alice finds constant threats in her dream. Most of her anxieties center around oral repressions, changes in the size of

---

[*] By the 1913-15 seasons there was a rash of musicals using the dream motif, including *When Dreams Come True* and *Miss Daisy*. At least four dream plays appeared during 1914-15, including Belasco's production of Molnar's *The Phantom Rival* in which a wife dreams of her first lover, projecting him into a variety of glamorous careers, only to be disillusioned on meeting him as the prosaic person he has become. Edward Knoblauch's *My Lady's Dress*, in which a woman with a new dress dreams of the various operations that went into the making of it, is in a curious way the forerunner of the documentary drama.

her body from eating things which make her larger or smaller, and sadistic (castration) threats—"off with her head." Space is distorted with constant changes, juxtapositions and secondary elaboration which would delight a surrealist. Not all of these symbols could have been meaningful to 1915 audiences, but *Alice in Wonderland* carried insight into the unconscious several steps beyond that of *The Poor Little Rich Girl*, and Alice Gerstenberg's next play, *Overtones*, was to carry it even farther.

THE CRITICS DISCOVER FREUD

The 1913 season saw the production of the first American play which reflected an interest in the consequences of sexual repression. There had been a British drama, *The Blindness of Virtue*, by Cosmo Hamilton the previous season which made a passionate plea for frank discussions of sex between parents and children. But in *The Smouldering Flame*, William Legrand faces for the first time the problem of a woman's frustration and thwarted maternal impulses. Mathilda Thomas, a neglected spinster who is old before her time overhears her attractive young cousin arranging a midnight rendezvous with her fiancé, and contrives to substitute herself in the darkness. Ten years later Mathilda has an "adopted child" whom, thanks to the long arm of coincidence, the father acknowledges in the end.

Less far-fetched in its manner of dealing with the dangers of denying sexual needs was Alice Brown's *Children of Earth* (1915), in which a woman who has given up her chance to marry in order to care for her father for twenty-six years finally has her freedom. She almost runs away with a young married farm hand, only to give him up to his wife in the end. A minor character, the old village idiot, is the symbol of the author's thesis that unless the individual fulfills his sexual life he may become, like this old man, "love-cracked." The fact that *Children of Earth* was selected as the winner of a $10,000 prize offered by Winthrop Ames indicates a significant change in attitude.

When *The Boomerang* opened in 1915, this review in *Current Opinion* might have led one to believe that at last an American play had made profound application of psychoanalysis:

> Psycho-analysis and the theories of Professor Freud have done yeoman's duty these last few years in the laboratory and in the pot-boiler's workshop, but it is doubtful if they

were ever called upon for more fruitful service than when Winchell Smith and Victor Mapes tapped them for the inspiration of 'The Boomerang.'

The plot of *The Boomerang*, however, is far removed from psychoanalysis. The authors satirize the hero, "an over-educated young physician who returns from special study in Europe" (which audiences apparently identified with psychoanalysis). He is much more interested in golf than medicine, hires an attractive young nurse, Virginia, and examines his first patient, Budd, a "restless, sleepless, nervous, depressed" young man with an over-anxious mother. When Budd's pulse leaps at the mention of Grace Tyler, the doctor assumes that he suffers from unrequited love. He administers a hypodermic "to fight your nerve bugs," but this is only water to take his mind off his jealousy. The nurse expresses surprise that jealousy can be treated by a doctor, to which he replies: "Not by the family physician! But a modern doctor can treat anything!"

Thereafter *The Boomerang* is a routine love story. The doctor advises Virginia that "love is a game" (strange advice from a psychoanalyst), and it proceeds to boomerang as he falls in love with the nurse and ultimately wins her. The sleepless patient and his over-anxious mother, later to become familiar types in the psychoanalytic drama, were here characterized in an entirely conventional way. The incredible success of such a flimsy play (533 performances) leads to the conclusion that audiences were able to recognize the "modern doctor" as related to the new psychology, and were ready to enjoy seeing him satirized.

The more discerning who failed to find psychoanalytic concepts in *The Boomerang* did not have long to wait, however; Alice Gerstenberg's one-act play, *Overtones*, was first presented by the Washington Square Players on November 8, 1915, and later played in vaudeville. Except for the dream plays, it marks the first departure from realism for the purpose of dramatizing the unconscious. There are four actors to represent the two characters in the play;* Harriet and Margaret are both cultured women, while their respective "primitive selves," Hetty and Maggie, are mysteriously veiled and swathed. Hetty says to Harriet, "I am the rushing river; you are the ice over the current." (The metaphors suggest Jung.) Hetty represents the self of basic, passionate urges which reproach Harriet for missing the chance to marry John, the love of her life. Margaret has married him instead, and is now a struggling artist's wife living in such poverty

* It was later expanded into a full-length play and presented in Chicago (1922) but not on Broadway.

that for Maggie the basic inner want is food. Margaret comes to persuade the wealthy Harriet to commission a portrait from John. The amusing struggle is between the two women and their inner selves which yell and fuss at their respective outer selves, but do not hear each other. In this entertaining sketch Miss Gerstenberg has sought to dramatize the psychoanalytic concept of the dual instincts of *ego* and the suppressed inner wants which Freud later called the *id*. Although rejected, these needs were known to the cultured selves, and hence *Overtones* cannot be considered a study in unconscious repression as much as in conscious hypocrisy and the duality of man's personality.

In the same season, *Any House,* by Owen and Robert H. Davis, employed the same device of two actors to represent the individual and his "better self" (although the influence of *Overtones* was denied). This modern morality play, without being Freudian, reflects a current interest in split personality and inner conflict.

A third play of the 1915-16 season contained a non-realistic device for the dramatization of guilt-feelings. *The Devil's Garden,* by Edith Ellis, from a story by William B. Maxwell, suggests a greater awareness of psychoanalytic mechanisms than *Overtones* or *Any House*. The hero has murdered a man under extenuating circumstances—for having seduced the hero's wife—and the crime goes undetected. For ten years he acquires wealth and reputation, but suffers from guilt-feelings, which are intensified when he learns that his adopted daughter has fallen in love with him (the first implication of an Electra relationship on Broadway). In the dark of his room, the voice of his conscience speaks to him until he breaks down and writes his confession; *The Devil's Garden* is thus a transitional link between the medieval morality play, the romantic melodrama of guilt such as *The Polish Jew,* and the schizophrenic drama of O'Neill.

"SUPPRESSED DESIRES" AND THE PROVINCETOWN

From 1916 the story of the psychological maturing of the American drama is closely interwoven with the history of the "Art Theatre" or "Little Theatre" which spearheaded the revolt against the hackneyed commercial theatre of Thomas, Klein, and Belasco on what had been called "The Great Trite Way." The Little Theatres, inspired by the work of Gordon Craig, Adolphe Appia and Stanislavsky, began to spring up between 1912 and 1915 in various parts of the country—through the efforts of Maurice Browne in Chicago, Sam Hume in Detroit, the Vagabonds in Baltimore; in New York City the

Neighborhood Playhouse, the Washington Square Players, and the Provincetown were part of the intellectual ferment out of which grew the new American theatre:

> The little theatres were manned largely by the pre-war younger generation, who held memories of repressed Victorian childhood and had been the intelligent minority at college. They had been stirred by Isadora Duncan, had listened to Eugene Debs, had discovered Krafft-Ebing, and had wondered why professors of dramatic literature damned Strindberg as decadent and Schnitzler as immoral. It was a restless time. Values were being questioned; dozens of new schools and movements in art were springing up. Cubism was fighting it out with Futurism, and everybody wrote free verse. *The Little Review* was printing Ulysses in installments, Gertrude Stein had discovered a new language, the old *Masses* was blazing away at injustice, *The New Republic* was in the first flush of its youth, Stieglitz was making magic with the camera. The International Exhibition had brought modern art to America, and a set of new text-books had appeared: *Sister Carrie, The Harbor, Spoon River Anthology.*

Alice Gerstenberg, associated with the Chicago Little Theatre, gave the new movement impetus with *Overtones* and *Alice in Wonderland.* But it was the summer of 1915 before a group of serious young artists and writers, who found themselves vacationing at Provincetown, Massachusetts, met to do something about the lamentable state of the American drama. All were amateurs in the theatre, but all had the passionate conviction that the theatre could and should be a medium of serious artistic expression. Meetings were held and it was decided to produce some one-act plays. On the first bill, given at the home of Hutchins Hapgood, was *Suppressed Desires,* by Susan Glaspell and her husband, George Cram Cook.

Suppressed Desires struck upon a most timely and lively topic, although still a localized one in New York (for Cook had submitted his play to the Chicago and other little theatres only to have it rejected as "too special"). In Greenwich Village, according to Parry, psychoanalysis was an intriguing new fad:

> The intellectuals would rather 'psych' each other than eat. They were so fascinated by 'this lingo about the libido' that Susan Glaspell was to exclaim in despair, 'You could not buy a bun without hearing of someone's complex.'

Suppressed Desires is an ingenious and delightful satire on the

effects of amateur psychoanalysis in the hands of a giddy faddist. At
breakfast Henrietta (first played by Susan Glaspell) hounds her
husband Stephen (played by George Cram Cook) with her newly
found hobby, psychoanalysis. The sympathy of the audience is with
Stephen, for Henrietta is depicted as a silly and nagging wife who
would go so far as to wake Stephen up at night to find out what he
is dreaming. Mabel, her sister, who is visiting them, is warned by
Stephen not to reveal her dreams. "If you do, she'll find out that you
have an underground desire to kill your father and marry your
mother." But Mabel doesn't even know what psychoanalysis is:

> Mabel: It's something about the war, isn't it?
> Stephen: Not that kind of war.
> Mabel: I thought it might be the name of a new explosive.
> Stephen: It is.

Henrietta tries to scare Mabel with the cases of people who are
ready for the insane asylum because of a suppressed love, but
Mabel replies, "I don't believe they have them in Chicago."

A Freudian slip and a drop of a plate give away Mabel's subconscious wishes which Henrietta would interpret as a suppressed
love for one Lyman Eggleston. (She has dreamed of someone shouting "Step Hen," and she associates this with "Egg-leston.") Two
weeks later, however, Stephen has secretly been psychoanalyzed
(the fastest analytic therapy ever recorded) and confronts Henrietta
with his unconscious desire to be free of their marriage. Henrietta
cannot forgive her psychoanalyst for that: "And I've sent him more
patients . . . " Mabel, too, has been given a two-week going-over
and the psychoanalyst has discovered that her suppressed desire is
none other than Henrietta's husband: "Step-Hen" in the dream
meant Stephen, and his last name, Brewster, meant "Be Rooster."
To hold her husband, Henrietta must eat her words and admit that
one need not follow every suppressed desire to avoid the insane
asylum. Raising a tear-stained face, Henrietta moans, "Look at all
I've done for psychoanalysis and what has psychoanalysis done for
me?" Henrietta is forced to let Stephen sleep undisturbed at night,
to burn her *Journals of Morbid Psychology*, and Stephen, in return, is
willing to remain with her.

> Mabel: But what about me? What am I to do with my
>   suppressed desire?
> Stephen: Mabel, you just keep right on suppressing it.

Although based more on puns than genuine psychoanalytic insight, *Suppressed Desires* was apparently the appropriate combina-

tion of timeliness and raillery, for it was repeated during that summer of 1915 in an old fish house on a wharf owned by Mary Heaton Vorse and with that performance was born America's most famous experimental theatre, the Provincetown.

Another group of serious minded amateurs, the Washington Square Players, later to become the Theatre Guild, must be given credit for beating the Provincetown to Broadway (they had been playing since February, 1915, with a repertoire that included works by Maeterlinck, Andreyev and Chekhov). The Provincetown, however, devoted itself to native American drama by its own members. The next summer, 1916, they returned to the fish wharf at Provincetown, revived *Suppressed Desires*, formed a subscription audience, and acknowledged Cook's leadership in the attempt to create a playwright's theatre. In their search for native playwrights they were introduced to a shy, dark, twenty-seven-year-old boy who, when asked if he had written any plays, handed them a one-act entitled *Bound East for Cardiff*. The Provincetowners promptly produced it. Thus it was that Eugene O'Neill and the Provincetown Players found each other early in their respective careers and reinforced each other's efforts.

Suppressed Desires and *Bound East for Cardiff* were first seen in New York in November of 1916 when the Provincetown moved from the Cape to Greenwich Village and institutionalized itself. The hysteria of war moved one Greenwich Village literary light, Bobby Edwards, to attack *Suppressed Desires* because of the Austrian origin of psychoanalysis, exclaiming: "It is the only blot on the record of the little theatre movement that this most foul and insidious of German propaganda should have been innocently distributed by them."

WARTIME THEMES

With hysteria at fever pitch, it is no wonder that little of literary merit emerged from the war years. Nevertheless, it is worth dwelling for a few moments on some of the themes and plots which were reflected in the playwriting of the war period, to pay brief tribute to the first groping efforts that paved the way for the masterpieces of O'Neill, Rice, Barry, and Miller, who finally compacted the world of the unconscious into theatrical form.

Suppressed Desires cannot accurately claim to be the first formal introduction of psychoanalysis to Broadway audiences. A month beforehand, Clare Kummer's comedy *Good Gracious, Annabelle,* had opened its long run with apparently the first mention of Freud's

name in a Broadway play. An otherwise conventional comedy, *Good Gracious, Annabelle* utilizes association tests in crime detection.*
A house detective, Wickham, has been studying "the association of ideas," and is able to apply his own skill when some shares of stock are stolen:

> Wickham: In this case, I use the Freud system.
> Wimbledon: Fraud system—what's that?
> Wickham: By the simple saying of words placed in a certain order or disorder, I can detect the guilty party.

He subjects his suspects to words like "periscope, altruistic, Stockbridge, oblivious," but fails to catch the criminal, and his efforts are called off. This play marks the first of many uses in American drama of word association tests and lie detectors, which more correctly should be attributed to Carl Jung than to Freud.

The war years 1917-19 saw the obvious pattern of anti-German, patriotic, and spy plays. Interest in psychology was apparently satisfied with superficial plays on amnesia, such as Eugene Walter's *The Knife* (1917).†

The European importations of these years reflected a more mature effort to deal with psychological themes than did the jerry-built Broadway pieces. The Danish writer Hjalmar Bergstrom in *Karen* (written 1907, presented in New York 1918) depicts a Tennessee Williams-like character whose mind breaks under the tyrannical discipline of her fanatical father, and who consequently runs nude through the streets. Her sister, Karen, is a "new woman," defying her father and championing a single standard in sexual morality. Her clergyman father would rather she bring ten illegitimate children home than to employ birth control, but the wise and tender mother understands the root of the difficulties of both her daughters. The closest an American play came to such a theme at this time was H. Austin Adams' *'Ception Shoals* (1917), in which a

---

* Several seasons before, in 1913, Robert H. Davis had begun the vogue for psychological criminology in his one-act play, *The Guilty Conscience*, which introduced a character of a detective whose methods were based on psychology.

† The other amnesia plays included Hopwood's *Judy Forgot* (1910), and *De Luxe Annie* (1917) by Edward Clark, in which a respectable wife suffers a blow on the head causing amnesia, and she becomes a notorious criminal until her innocence and social rank are restored by a surgical operation on the brain. *Another Man's Shoes*, by Laura Hinkley and Mabel Ferris (1918), also dealt with a man struck on the head (the somatic origin of mental illness was a persistent feature which died hard), who becomes a different and successful man and is struck on the head again and reverts to the day of his first blow, forgetting all in between. The next season saw *The Net* by Maravene Thompson again depicting an amnesia victim from a blow on the head who is cured by a "far-seeing neurologist."

girl (played by Nazimova) imprisoned in a lighthouse goes mad and leaps to her death.

Even British importations were more frank than ours—witness Miles Malleson's *Youth* (1918), in which a precocious young author talks at great length about repression and "the denial of sex" and falls in love with an ingénue who knows:

> . . . that love is everywhere and *is* everything, and that you're part of it and it's part of you . . . that our bodies and their passions—the things they hush up—and our souls and their yearnings are different expressions of the same great thing. . . .*

The perennial farce and melodrama now began to have the name "psychoanalysis" tacked on to give old situations a modern slant. Mark Swan's bedroom farce, *Keep It to Yourself* (1918), for example, shows a man hypnotized and put to bed in a hotel room, whereupon the hotel changes his room in order to accomodate a newly-wed couple, with ensuing complications as the hypnotized man follows his unconscious impulses in the absence of the bridegroom. Even more remote from actual psychoanalysis was *Three Wise Fools* (1918) by Austin Strong, in which one of the three old bachelors is a brain specialist who has been reading "A Psycho-Analysis of Mental Grooves." He is apparently the first medical man to pursue psychoanalysis on Broadway, though wherever he and the author got their information on psychoanalysis, it was assuredly not from Freud. The doctor is interested only in getting the three old doddards out of their ruts, and that is accomplished not by Freud but by cops and robbers, romance, and sentimental complications out of Scribe and Pinero.

WISH-FULFILLMENT

If the war years of 1916-1919 produced any conspicuous tendency

---

* Another freely speaking modern woman occurs in J. Hartley Manners' *The Harp of Life* (1916) in which Lynn Fontanne appeared. Other conventional plays incorporated psychological elements—for instance, Willard Mack and Lou Tellegen's clap-trap *Blind Youth* (1917) introduced a son despised by his mother because he resembled the father she hated; *The Invisible Foe*, by Walter Hackett (1918) showed a villain betraying himself by unconsciously writing his brother's name as a forged autograph; *A Cure for Curables* by Earl Derr Biggers and Lawrence Whitman (1918) and *The Three Bears* (1917) by Edward Childs Carpenter dealt with hypochondria; George M. Cohan's obviously contrived *The Miracle Man* (1914) dealt with faith healing, as did *The Very Minute* (1917) by John Meehan, in which a drunkard is cured by spiritual power and the shock of his father's death.

in the Broadway drama, it was toward wish-fulfillment by fantasy. Freud had written that not only night dreams but day dreams as well were the converted products of the wish. Playwrights of course were prone to treat exclusively non-sexual wishes at first, but in exploring the mechanism of wish-fulfillment these early writers laid the foundations without which *The Adding Machine* and *Dream Girl* would not have been likely. War years would naturally lead us to expect escapist drama. But some of the dramas of these years were more than mere *divertissement;* for the first time there was an awareness of the mechanism of escape and a consciousness that the individual uses the day-dream to counteract his daily pressures. So although the playgoer could escape the current grim realities, he could also learn something of the psychological mechanism which made him do so.

The best known wish-fulfillment plays of the period include *His Majesty Bunker Bean, Magic, The Willow Tree, Eyes of Youth, Barbara, April, Jonathan Makes a Wish, The Happy Ending* (produced by Arthur Hopkins) and Sir James M. Barrie's *A Kiss for Cinderella.*

His Majesty Bunker Bean, which Lee Wilson Dodd adapted from the successful novel by Harry Leon Wilson, shows a mousy, insignificant typist who day-dreams of being a millionaire and marrying the boss' daughter. Timid and ashamed of his name, he would have had an "inferiority complex" had he appeared a few years later in American drama. Bean finds an outlet for his frustrations in the psychic fad and goes to a fake psychic medium who soon has him filled with self-confidence. His delusion of grandeur lasts long enough for him to make a fortune on the stock market and to elope with the boss' daughter, only to collapse when he learns of the fakery. The advice of a wise old baseball player to rely on himself—plus liberal amounts of whiskey—restores Bean's inner security. The dynamic point of view that personality—even as timorous a one as Bean's—can be changed is the major thesis of psychoanalysis. But the metamorphosis was generally too easy in these dramas, by-passing the long and arduous course of therapy necessary and reducing change to a pat formula or a "thirdactic" conversion.*

The hero of *The Willow Tree* was even more out of touch with reality than Bunker Bean. In this fantasy by J. H. Benrimo and George C. Hazelton, an Englishman escapes his materialistic sweet-

---

* The wish-fulfillment plays did not crowd out the conventional dream plays such as *The Barton Mystery* (1917) by Walter Hackett, Mark Swan's *If,* Monckton Hoffe's *Anthony in Wonderland* (1917), and the highly successful *Forever After* (1918) by Owen Davis, in which the flashback was used to reveal the past.

heart and lives in a garden in Japan, hanging his verses on the willow tree. In analyzing this play, a Jungian psychoanalyst, Dr. Smith Ely Jelliffe, has pointed out the maternal symbolism in the wish to live beneath the embracing branches of the willow tree:

> All mythology attests to the unconscious association of the mother with the heart of the tree and her localization there. Myths of birth from the tree confront us in the legends of such remote lands and cultures as those of ancient Greece and the islands of Oceanica.

An old Japanese tells the Englishman how he may call forth the Princess of the Willow Tree and when she is summoned from his own fantasy—according to Jelliffe a projection of the mother-image—he proceeds to fall in love with her lovely and untouched innocence.

When his real sweetheart arrives from England the escapist is forced to choose between reality and fantasy. News of England's entry into the war rouses him to accept his adult responsibilities rather than live as an auto-erotic self-seeker. He cuts down the willow tree and returns to a real world. In Jelliffe's interesting essay, one of the first psychoanalytic studies of a non-Shakespearean drama by an analyst, he points out prophetically that beneath the clean, trim prettiness of Japan is the daily weariness, poverty, and frustration of basic impulses that must erupt just as do its volcanoes.

Another drama of wish-fulfillment by the supernatural, *Magic*, by G. K. Chesterton, had its Broadway run abruptly terminated by President Wilson's call for American entry into the World War. Playgoers did not have long to wait, however, for the choice bit of wish-fulfillment of the period, *Peter Ibbetson* (1917), adapted by John N. Raphael from the novel by George DuMaurier. *Peter Ibbetson* tells of an unhappy young architect who has been raised by a cruel uncle, Colonel Ibbetson. In a reverie flashback Peter remembers his youth in France with his mother and an adored companion, Mimsey. Mimsey believed in dreams and tried to teach Peter, her "Gogo," to "dream true" (done by going to sleep with your feet crossed and your hands behind your head). As an adult, Peter meets the unhappily married Duchess of Towers, and they recognize each other as the childhood playmates, Mimsey and Gogo. But Peter hears Colonel Ibbetson insinuate that he had been intimate with Peter's mother and in a fury Peter kills him, out-Hamleting Hamlet in hatred for his uncle. For this crime Peter must go to prison; but thanks to Mimsey's instruction he can "dream true." Mimsey's fantasy-visits to Peter sustain him in prison for twenty-five years until he dies, freed at last to join his sweetheart-mother-image in the spirit world. (Surely it is no coincidence that Mimsey rhymes with whimsey.)

Jelliffe, who also found this play material for literary psychoanalysis, points out that the play takes its audience into the inner fantasy of a prison psychosis. The fact that audiences could seriously watch this drama seems a regression in the psychological maturity of the theatre, or at least proof that wish-fulfillment of the unattainable perfection of childhood and the mother-image is a deeply rooted yearning—especially of a people in war.

The British school of sentimental wish-fulfillment dramas reached its best expression in Barrie's *Dear Brutus*, in which there is a mysterious character of whom Jelliffe wrote:

> Lob . . . his little simple name rings its changes through many tongues—is no forgotten and discarded past. Lob, love, life, libido, belongs to the measureless unconscious life of man, the preservation of its power, impulse, striving, and he moves and flits and plans and makes things come to pass out in the external conscious world as well.

When the characters awake from the dream-second-chance which Lob has given them, each retains some insight, some self-knowledge from the dream (as may happen in psychoanalysis). In the dream the drunken artist had created for himself a beloved daughter named Margaret (the name of Barrie's own mother) and in her famous speech to the moon, Jelliffe points out the unconscious erotic elements referred to in Sadger's study, *Sleep Walking and Moon Walking*.

The most promising of all the wish-fulfillment plays—at least the one with the freshest observation of character rooted in valid psychology—was *Barbara* (1917), written by an early pupil of George Pierce Baker, Florence Lincoln. Barbara, hemmed in and victimized by two aunts, finds escape in fantasy and creates three children of her imagination. She gives them names, prepares toys for them, and after suffering a shock awakes to believe in the complete reality of her delusions. Her "pathologic disposition to maternity" is cured again by the surgeon rather than the psychoanalyst, and she adopts three live children. A critic, reacting to the newer style of realistic and underplayed emotion, called the acting "positively Ibsene." *Barbara* may suggest an early Laura from *The Glass Menagerie*, but the pre-Freudian cure by surgical rather than emotional therapy dates the play.

Not unlike Barbara's dissociation from reality was that of the childlike heroine of Charles Rann Kennedy's *The Army With Banners*

(1918), in which a girl blissfully dresses as a bride to await the momentary visit of the Lord and mistakes a callow revivalist preacher for Him.

Finally Stuart Walker's *Jonathan Makes a Wish* (1918), in spite of a rather innocuous and mild style, manages to achieve some sense of the terrors of an anxiety dream. A young boy dreams in his delirium of falling, of masochistic punishment by being humpbacked, and seeing people he knew well who fail to recognize him. Walker touches as well on the tyranny of parents in restricting the free development of children and their choice of careers. Employing sentimentality rather than the vigor of a Rice or Lawson, Walker nevertheless succeeds in this play in depicting perhaps the most accurate dramatic version of an anxiety dream so far seen on the American stage.

Clearly the work of Walker, Florence Lincoln, Arthur Hopkins, Susan Glaspell, William Legrand, and Alice Gerstenberg had set the stage. It awaited only the end of the war with its new freedom in the arts to ring up the curtain on the great period of psychoanalysis in the American drama, a period prophesied as early as 1921 by Kenneth Macgowan when he wrote that the play of tomorrow ". . . will attempt to transfer to dramatic art the illumination of those deep and vigorous and eternal processes of the human soul which the psychology of Freud and Jung has given us through study of the unconscious, striking to the heart of emotion and linking our life today with the emanations of the primitive racial mind."

CHAPTER IV

The Post-War Era—Transition

ENTER THE MOTHER

The ink was hardly dry on the Armistice before it was clear that the playwrights, seeking for new themes to replace the war, were turning to psychoanalysis as a major topic. With the exception of *The Fatted Calf*, American plays had been skirting the main issues of psychoanalysis and dangling before the public only the more superficial and palatable of gleanings. Beginning with the 1919 season, however, the critics themselves noted the new era. Heywood Broun proclaimed in his review of *La Malquerida*, Benavente's powerful Spanish drama of an inverted relationship between a man and his step-daughter:

> Into the Freudian aspects of the play we cannot go because it would open up a field which would require columns and columns of twisting and turning. Moreover, it is at least three volumes ahead of us. If things keep up this way no dramatic critic will be properly equipped for the theatre until he has become a highly trained neurologist.

Broun's prophecy was not far wrong, and it was soon apparent that critics *were* delving into their three volumes to catch up with the changing concept of human relationships. A week later opened an amusing example of the new playwriting, for which several critics had their volumes of Freud on hand. Oliver Morosco had offered a prize for the best play written in George Pierce Baker's classes at

Harvard, and it was won by Rachel Barton Butler with her *Mamma's Affair* (1920), of which Alexander Woollcott wrote:

> It requires at least a surface knowledge of the Freudian explorations to write this play and playgoers with a bit of that knowledge will have the time of their lives as it unfolds. It is true that the Freudian playgoer lies in wait for the slightest lurking excuse to descend into the subconscious—discovering clues and symptoms of which playwright, producer, and players are blissfully unaware. He sees an inhibition at every turn and with the slightest encouragement would talk about the Psycho-Anabasis of Xenophon. But *Mamma's Affair* really invites his special attention.
>
> It is all about the Oedipus complex. Or what is it called when the ingrowing bond is between mother and daughter? The Medea Complex? Well, no matter—for after all, the common, unread run of us can relish the new piece at the Little Theatre and, as its somewhat uncomfortable story develops, will wriggle and chuckle with many a spasm of recognition.

This recommendation promises considerably more insight than *Mamma's Affair* has to offer; it deals with an amusing hypochondriac mother, a distant forerunner of Mrs. Phelps, who keeps her daughter hovering over her and ministering to her. The doctor called in recognizes that the mother has tried to gratify "an abnormal sentimentality" by keeping the daughter close to her, and proceeds to fall in love with the daughter himself and free her from the anaemic young man she was expected to marry. The doctor's therapy is merely a "rest cure" for the girl away from her mother, and all ends happily as the mother realizes that the marriage will give her a doctor in the family.

Not too far removed from the frivolity of *Mamma's Affair* was *We Girls* by Frederic and Fanny Hatton (1921), in which a giddy widow claims to be forty-six, uses baby talk, bobs her hair, and is kept from marrying a boy of twenty-two only when her twin brother arrives looking at least sixty. Her daughter is one of the first flaming youths of the twenties, discussing sex freely with the butler and the maid, and learning from the butler all about psychoanalysis and the Freudian approach to love. Similarly, *Red Geranium,* by Ruth M. Woodward (1922), goes back to the Restoration for the plot of the country girl coming to Greenwich Village and learning about free love, Freud and a hero who presents each mistress a red geranium when he tires of her.

By now some of the main patterns of psychoanalytic drama have emerged: (1) in *We Girls* and *Red Geranium* flaming youth uses Freud as a rationale; (2) in *Mamma's Affair* the possessive mother ruthlessly holds onto her grown children for her own selfish needs. The so-called Oedipal pattern of an older woman's relationship with a younger man was first given serious treatment by Eugene O'Neill in *Diff'rent* (1920) and by Frederick Lansing Day in *Makers of Light* (1922), in which a shy seventeen-year-old pupil falls tragically in love with his schoolteacher; (3) in *True to Form* by Augustin MacHugh (1921) the father joins the mother in trying to suppress their daughter until a rebellious son-in-law has to carry his wife away from the inhibiting influence of her parents. Among the other new themes derived from psychoanalysis were guilt feelings and the influence of childhood, latent homosexuality, and sex suppression. But the mother-son relationship was leading the field by 1923 with at least seven plays on Broadway.

Although plays of wish-fulfillment declined after the armistice,* the vogue of dream-plays begun in 1913 continued unabated. While some were run-of-the-mill dreams which merely provided the dramatist an excuse to extricate himself from some inexplicable happenings, the freshest as well as the most successful of the dream plays was the British writer Walter Hackett's *Captain Applejack* (1921), in which the hero dreams of himself in the swashbuckling role of one of his ancestors. Although Woollcott called the play "good fun as well as good Freud," the truth is that except for the conversion of real life characters into other roles less inhibited than in reality, *Captain Applejack's* dream is no more Freudian than it is a dream. If our dreams were only constructed in such well-made plots, we could all become playwrights overnight.

In addition to dreams, many a psychic spirit hovered close above the Broadway playhouses during the 1919-20 season. The ectoplasm which proved most commercial was derived from the British author Allan Langdon's *Smilin' Through*, which had just the right combination of psychological return-of-loved-ones in flashback and sentimental treacle over the spirit sweetheart, Moonyeen, to console a bereaved nation.

THE PSYCHOANALYTIC ERA BEGINS

The growing sophistication of the audience and its respect for psychoanalytic thinking rendered obsolete the psychological potpourri

* There was only Arthur Richman's *Not So Long Ago* (1920) in which the little seamstress conceives of an entirely imaginary love affair which of course is later materialized.

of the pre-war period, and the theatre was now ready for the first
major talent whose work is rooted in psychoanalytic soil—Eugene
O'Neill. Although O'Neill's unique gifts did much to further the
Freudian drama, it is evident that there would have been a psychoanalytic period in the American drama even had there been no
O'Neill. O'Neill's first success, *Beyond the Horizon,* opened and won
the Pulitzer Prize the same year that *Smilin' Through, Mamma's
Affair* and *Five O'Clock,* a heavy-handed rejection of Viennese
psychiatry in favor of "common sense," were playing. Little wonder
that O'Neill appeared to historians of the theatre as the herald of a
new American drama. The chapter devoted to O'Neill will trace his
interest in psychoanalytic themes; although he stands alone among
his contemporaries in the breadth and originality of his talents,
O'Neill was in his subject matter conspicuously a part of a larger
movement rather than the isolated Freudian which he is too often
considered. The season of *Beyond the Horizon* also saw Elmer Rice's
For the Defense, with the character of a psycho-hypnotist, thus
reflecting another promising young writer's interest in the new
psychology. Within the next five years, the ranks were joined by
Theodore Dreiser, Lewis Beach, Susan Glaspell, Owen Davis, John
Howard Lawson, Martin Flavin, Maxwell Anderson, J. C. and
Elliott Nugent, George Kaufman, Marc Connelly, Philip Barry, Dan
Totheroh, and Sidney Howard.

Taken together, the drama of O'Neill's contemporaries serves
to establish beyond a doubt that the period of the twenties in American drama must be called The Psychoanalytic Era. The change in
the theatre was amusingly summarized in *The Harlequinade,* by
Dion Clayton Calthrop and Granville Barker (1921), in which the
history of Harlequin is traced through various centuries. The
published version ends with a tepid satire on Harlequin thrown out
of work by Ibsen's problem plays. In the Broadway production,
however, Harlequin ends up watching the Bronx Art Theatre present *Inhibitions, The Fourteenth Freud Complex Series.* Cried the
critic for *The Sun* indignantly (but in vain):

> Keep Freud and Jung and the horrors of their psychoan-
> alysis, their subconscious repressions, their complexes and
> inhibitions off the stage, and let them flourish on the printed
> page, where they belong.

Psychoanalysis had penetrated the musical comedy field* by 1919;

---

* Another musical play to attract considerable attention was the sensuous
and daring spectacle, *Aphrodite* (1919) by Pierre Louys, produced by Ray Comstock and Morris Gest, with ballet by Michel Fokine.

Nothing but Love, by Frank Stammers and score by Harold Orlob, dealt with dual personality and a water-phobia.

Paralysis was cured by psychotherapy in *Pagans,* by Charles Anthony (1921), which dealt with a shell-shocked and partially paralyzed artist who dies in the end from no apparent cause (except that, as Kenneth Macgowan, then critic for *The Globe,* speculated, the leading man, Joseph Schildkraut, wanted to play a tragedy for his first American vehicle). Framed in voodoo, Mary Hoyt Wiborg's *Taboo* (1922) shows a mute child recovering its speech at the psychological moment to save an innocent Negro accused of murder.

In contrast with this, there was a naturalistic study of the Negro as early as 1921 in Ernest Howard Culbertson's *Goat Alley,* which depicted the poignant tragedy of a slum girl and indirectly made a plea for birth control. On opening night, Dr. Victor Robinson of the *Medical Review of Reviews* made a preliminary speech, quoted Freud, and begged for an unprejudiced hearing of the play.

As in former periods, European writers were less fettered than Americans in the handling of their themes. The Viennese writer, Paul Frank, in *The Mandarin* (1920), created a portrait of an insatiable Baron, a sensualist who dreams that a Chinese mandarin doll comes to life and possesses supernatural power to get him any woman he craves. Even more candid was *The Children's Tragedy* (1921) by Carl Schoenherr, a German writer who tells the story of three children who spy on their mother from their attic bedroom as she has an affair with a forester. Freud believed that nothing human should be alien to man, and the Zola naturalists had proclaimed even before Freud that our theatre must depict life as it truly was. But true naturalism—not the surface pictures of Belasco —had yet to make its fight to be accepted in New York, and it was with the subject matters introduced by psychoanalysis that the fight was made. To this cause the novelist Theodore Dreiser lent his weight.

THEODORE DREISER

The first American play with a thoroughly unembarrassed treatment of sex was Theodore Dreiser's *The Hand of the Potter* (1921), the most trenchant piece of naturalism until *Dead End* some fourteen years later. In a play that is still timely during our present wave of sex killings, Dreiser draws a clinically observed picture of a sexual psychopath with the authentic detail that places him among America's great novelists. Aaron Berchansky is a tired old Jewish father living in a New York tenement with his family, which includes a

pathetic boy of twenty-one who has just completed a prison sentence
for assaulting a little girl. With a twitch in his left shoulder and an
oddly malformed head which makes him repugnant to girls, Isadore
is obsessed with desire for sex. We see him first trying to kiss his
flashy sister, then his niece, and finally, when left alone in the
tenement to write letters applying for a job, an eleven-year-old
neighbor girl who walks in. He is gentle with her, showing her a pair
of opera glasses, until she brushes against him and causes him to
lose all control of his "fierce, demoniac hunger." When the neighbor
girl's body is discovered and Isadore is missing, the evidence is soon
found. At the trial the family would shield Isadore, but the harassed
father breaks down on the stand and tells how his son "hasn't been
right" since he was twelve. Meanwhile, Isadore hides out in a
furnished room, and with masterful character development Dreiser
shows his progressive panic, disintegration, and hallucinations. He
begins to see red and black spots before his eyes, and he twitches
uncontrollably, both valid symptoms of converted sexual energy.
When the landlord comes for rent, his little daughter stays behind to
talk to Isadore, and almost suffers the same fate as the other girl;
but Isadore somehow makes himself release her, and after writing
a note explaining how little girls stimulate him, he commits suicide.

The last scene brings in newspaper reporters who discuss the
case. Dreiser's *raissoneur* is Quinn, an Irish reporter who knows his
Freud, Ellis, and Krafft-Ebing:

> I've been readin' up on these cases for some time, an' from
> what I can make out they're no more guilty than any other
> person with a disease. Did ye know, ayther ave ye, that
> there's something they've called *harmones* which the body
> manufactures an' which is poured into the blood streams of
> every waan ave us which excites us to the m'aning ave
> beauty an' thim things—'sensitizes' is the word they use
> . . . This felly could no more help bein' what he was than
> a fly can help bein' a fly an' naht an' elephant, an' that's
> naht at all. Nature is deeper an' stronger than anything we
> know . . . It's more luck than anythin' else, an' that's true,
> too. Now we were sayin' a while ago that ye can't under-
> stand why a man like that would be attackin' a little girl,
> unless he were a low, vile creature, even if he wasn't bal-
> anced quite right—but I can. If ye'd ever made a study ave
> the passion ave love in the sense that Freud an' some
> others have ye'd understand it will enough. It's a great
> force about which we know naathing as yet an' which we're
> just beginnin' to look into—what it manes, how it affects
> people.

Dreiser gave great credit to Freud for influencing his philosophy of life through his friend, Dr. A. A. Brill. Of Freud's influence, Dreiser wrote:

> I shall never forget my first encounter with his *Three Contributions to the Theory of Sex,* his *Totem and Taboo,* and his *Interpretation of Dreams.* At that time and even now quite every paragraph came as a revelation to me—a strong, revealing light thrown on some of the darkest problems that haunted and troubled me and my work. And reading him has helped me in my studies of life and men.

Dreiser wrote no other full-length plays, and his loss to the theatre renders it all the poorer.

HARRY WAGSTAFF GRIBBLE

In a more whimsical mood the same year was *March Hares* by Harry Wagstaff Gribble, about which Heywood Broun wrote: "It is rather like the annual college show of the pupils of Dr. Freud in a year when they had chosen farce." The March Hares are mad with the brilliant, inverted wit of people who use humor as a defense mechanism against their emotions. Although attractive to women, the hero, Geoffrey, behaves very much like one himself. His ménage is smart and chi-chi and the zany behavior of the household is apparently usual. He lives with his fiancée and her mother, but the arrangement is proper enough. He has never kissed the girl because she wouldn't tolerate it. Love, to Geoffrey, is "a state of mind at which two people arrive simultaneously for the purpose of not annoying each other." Each of them brings "an affinity" home, and in addition, the maid, Ethel, is in love with Geoffrey. Janet's mother observes that Geoffrey "dreams feverishly enough in the daytime. The thought of what his nightly dreams must be like brings tears to my eyes." Geoffrey curls up on the sofa and tells Fuller, the man Janet brought home, to ask him questions till he falls asleep. This is the clearest hint of latent homosexuality in the play. The brilliantly contrived plot unravels satisfactorily, with Janet wishing "God would send a red-blooded man to this house," until Geoffrey, piqued at last, arouses himself to something like virility for the final clinch with Janet.

With its facetiously effeminate wit and precocity, *March Hares* is a twentieth century comedy of manners in the best Restoration tradition of Wycherley or Congreve. After *March Hares* Gribble and Wilton Lackaye adapted Louis Verneuil's French farce, *Oh Mama* (1925), in which a step-mother and step-son fall in love. The critics were grateful that after a somber season which had included *Desire*

Under the Elms, the same theme was here handled with Gribble's "flagrant hilarity." Only one other of Gribble's plays falls within this study and that was altogether devoid of hilarity. *Revolt* (1928) was a serious study, akin to *Elmer Gantry* and *Bride of the Lamb,* of a fanatic, bigoted preacher who attempts to suppress the emotions and twist the minds of his three daughters, Faith, Hope, and Charity. He forbids warm food on Sunday and brands as prostitutes girls who like to dance. His son is ridiculed by his college mates when they find out who his father is, and in a mock Temptation in the Wilderness, the son is forcibly baptised and a nail driven through his hand. The children finally rebel against the shell-backed religion of the father, and his own lust for a girl betrays him as he is in the act of baptizing her. He shoots himself at the end of *Revolt,* a play Robert Littell called "good, tight and often exciting theatre."

SUSAN GLASPELL AND GEORGE CRAM COOK

The year 1921 also saw two unusual and sensitive plays by a man and wife who contributed much to the growth of the native American drama during these years—George Cram Cook and Susan Glaspell. After their amusing one act collaboration, *Suppressed Desires,* they each wrote a psychological drama in 1921. Cook's was entitled *The Spring,* and when its production and reception were disappointing at the Provincetown, Cook bitterly left the group, believing that he had been slighted in favor of O'Neill whom he had himself helped so greatly to encourage. This led to Cook's departure for Greece where he later died.

The Spring, viewed in its historical perspective, appears a little out of date even for 1921. Referring to Frederic Myers, William James and Janet, the play treats hypnosis, telepathy, long-distance hypnosis via telepathy, and automatic writing (dictated by the subconscious). A somewhat narrow-minded professor of psychology is worried for fear his daughter will go insane because of her occult powers to read others' minds. A "Professor of Nervous Diseases" also behaves most un-Freudianly and is about to carry the girl off by force to an asylum. With a definite suggestion of Jung's influence, the young hero urges the girl to be his "sensitive" for his experiments to verify that there is an "underground or wireless connection between minds. . . . We may not be the disconnected islands we supposed. The islands join beneath the sea." He seeks something more than the old spiritualist doctrine:

> I want the subsconscious to reveal its own source of knowledge. Instead of suggesting to *your* unconscious: 'Reveal

the spirits of the dead,' I want your writing to be born of the suggestion: 'Reveal yourself.'

The promise contained in this sensitive attempt to express the collective unconscious is never realized, however. The hero re-hypnotizes the girl and brings her out of her psychic trance, but he must go to jail for striking and killing the doctor who would have committed her. The girl assures him she will be with him in prison (through the same mental telepathy that reunited Mimsey and Peter Ibbetson four years before). *The Spring* is thus a strange and original evocation of mysticism, Indian survival of the spirit, thought-communication in the great universal unconscious, as well as an attempt to assimilate Jungian psychoanalysis. Mystically, Cook wrote of *The Spring,* "The music of water went all through the play. It will hypnotize the audience and make it easier to reach that deep level where I am you and you are me." Awed by the frontier to which the new psychologists had pushed human insight, Cook spoke to his wife of a great spiritual communion based on the unconscious oneness of man:

> Do you know what this means? It means that you and I, before we die, may turn the thought of the world as sharply as Darwin did—but inward. This is a voyage greater than Columbus!—for what we seek is—the unknown hemisphere of the soul! You and I are going to set sail into ourselves; for there, in the ocean of the unconscious, is the shore of our new world.

If others who sailed those seas kept better contact with the shore, none expressed the challenge of the voyage more eloquently than this little-known Greenwich Village poet who made a very real contribution to the American drama in founding and guiding the Provincetown Players.

The play by Cook's wife, Susan Glaspell, was entitled *The Verge,* and is one of the truly remarkable pieces of psychological literature of our times. The author draws a terrifyingly real portrait of maniac-depressive psychosis. The heroine, Claire, has brilliant flashes of rationality, but in Act I is obsessed with a desire to cross-breed plants in a hothouse. She is strangely troubled with the compulsion to break out of molds—to be something that has never been before. This compulsion begins symbolically as an expression of rebellion against social molds of Puritan convention, against her monotonous pattern of marriage with an inept first husband, a happy-go-lucky second husband, and against a run-of-the-mill daughter. But it grows perilously close to psychosis as she believes she has grown a new species of perverted plant which has found "otherness."

She names the new species "The Edge-Vine." Even the conventional pattern of an egg (perhaps as a sexual symbol) violently upsets her. When her daughter arrives, Claire is agitated with loathing for her, and retires to brood in a strange tower—a room shaped in curves with a bulging window like a womb. This apparently marks the first expressionistic distortion of scenery in our theatre for a subjective effect—that of unconscious "regression to the womb."

During her depressive cycle in the second act, Claire remains in the tower, where a neurologist is brought to treat her. At the other extreme of her cycle, she has an ecstatic love scene with the symbolically named Tom Edgeworthy. In Act III, she returns apparently rational again, but is soon at manic intensity offering herself to Tom. But he makes the mistake of saying she is beautiful (the loathed mold of convention), and her grip on reality is loosened. Saying, "I'd rather be the steam rising from the manure than a thing called beautiful," she embraces and passionately strangles him to death. Gently singing "Nearer My God to Thee," Claire has completely lost touch with reality as the curtain falls on this haunting experience within the mind of a psychotic individual, whose oversensitivity—and possibly her unconsciously homosexual wish to be "other" than woman—drove her past the verge of insanity. *The Verge* is possibly the most original and probing play that had been written in America by 1921, and brings to mind Dr. Daniel Schneider's theory that creative writing is a process of turning inside out or objectifying the life of the unconscious.

Susan Glaspell wrote three other plays, the first a trivial comedy, *Chains of Dew* (1922), in which a fancied poet believes himself a martyr to a shallow wife and a possessive mother. His Greenwich Village companions go home with him to help him break the ties, only to discover that the wife and mother are far more sympathetic than he painted, and that he is held to them only by "chains of dew." More significant is Miss Glaspell's next play, *Alison's House,* which won the Pulitzer Prize in 1930. A muted, static play of mood, Chekhovian without the Russian's humor, *Alison's House* is a fictionalized biography of the 19th century American poetess, Emily Dickinson. Although dead many years, she is very real to her family. The flip young son of the family is writing a theme on Alison for English and wants to know if she was a virgin; but the family is strangely reluctant to talk of Alison's love life. Although there is little specifically Freudian, the general theme is the return of the past, the importance of reminiscence, and the sublimation of unfulfilled love into great poetry. The family, who would withhold her poetry from publication, is a repressed and rigid clan of Puritans for whom Miss Glaspell has nothing but scorn. Although Alison does not enter, we feel her as a gentle, spiritual soul who had infinite wisdom born of her frustration in an unsensitive family. It was her brother, we finally learn, who had sent away her lover, a married man. *

In Susan Glaspell's last play she returned to psychoanalytic concepts at a deeper level of insight. With a most misleading title, *The Comic Artist* (1933), written with her second husband, Norman Matson, shows a young comic strip artist, Karl, suffering in the shadow of his older and more successful artist brother, Stephen, and obsessed with the fear of being a carbon copy. Karl is married to Nina, a former mistress of Stephen's, who is beautiful, petted, cruel. An erotic sadist and masochist, Nina still loves Stephen so passionately that she sobs, "Hit me, Stephen! Hit me! . . . When I try to do right I am wicked. I try to say good things and toads come from my mouth. Hold me, Stephen."

Stephen senses that he has become the father-image for his younger brother—their father had died many years ago. Stephen's wife, Eleanor, quietly tries to win her husband back and save Karl, but is accused of selfish motives:

> Karl: Stephen tells you your motives are selfish?
> Eleanor: They don't (*with a little laugh*) feel that way to me. But perhaps they never do. We don't seem to know much about motives. They come from places we don't— turn a light on.

Karl comes to realize that at first he loved Nina only because she was Stephen's. Stephen is finally able to relinquish Nina, but Nina pretends to be committing suicide in the surf and Karl is actually killed trying to save her. Although *The Comic Artist* has gotten us ahead of our story by a number of years, this incisive character study of sadism and latent homosexuality derives its wisdom at least in part from Freudian concepts and clearly illustrates the distance Susan Glaspell and the American theatre itself had come in the two decades since the superficial ridicule of psychoanalysis in *Suppressed Desires*.

THE 1922-23 SEASON

No fewer than five plays of both distinctive literary quality and Freudian content reached Broadway during the 1922-23 season. For

---

* By contrast with *Alison's House*, a recent treatment of the Emily Dickinson story, *Eastward in Eden* (1947) by Dorothy Gardner seems literary and mawkish. Where Miss Glaspell's poetess remained offstage but was suggestively quite real, Miss Gardner's heroine is physically real but psychologically unrealized.

the first time a conspicuously Freudian play reached the "smash-hit" category and set a record with 648 performances—*Rain*, by John Colton and Clemence Randolph. Another proved to be one of the most enduring of Elmer Rice's work, *The Adding Machine*. A third, Owen Davis' *Icebound*, won the Pulitzer Prize, and John Howard Lawson's *Roger Bloomer* marked the high point in American expressionism. A *Square Peg* by Lewis Beach completes this quintet of notable dramas with psychoanalytic influence. *Icebound, The Adding Machine,* and *Roger Bloomer* will be discussed in succeeding chapters.

Known only by a previous one-act, *The Clod*, done by the Washington Square Players in 1915-16, Lewis Beach nevertheless created a special niche for himself in the American drama by *A Square Peg*, a naturalistic classic. In it a family is dominated by a driving, selfish woman, Rena Huckins, who was never intended by nature to be a mother—"she drifted into the profession by mistake. She is a square peg in a round hole." She is depicted coldly and clinically in the style George Kelly was later to employ; she is more ruthless and less devious than Howard's Mrs. Phelps, and without her education, humor, or gentility. Her husband, James T. Huckins, is a passive-dependent male—a complete mouse. A fresh creation in American playwriting and one whom we shall meet frequently, particularly in the work of Odets, Huckins would rather keep quiet than have an argument with his wife, and hasn't slept with her since their youngest child was born. Rena bosses her children around, thwarts her daughter's one good chance for marriage, and to top it all, brings her whining, sniveling old maid sister to live with them. The playwright hints at Rena's frigidity as part of her trouble, and the daughter knows that "She wouldn't be the person she is now if she'd been where she belonged. Or if Father had been different. But suppression, Gene, has ruined her."

The father has been quietly embezzling money from his employer in order to buy a farm in Canada and escape his family, but must use the money instead to help his son pay off a blackmailing floozie. When the father is trapped and confesses to his embezzlement, Rena is selfishly interested only in saving her own face. There is a tender scene in which father and daughter talk intimately for the first time. She offers to wait till he is released from prison and then keep house for him, a fine, sensitive handling of the theme of the return of the repressed Electra-complex. Although the father is actually relieved at the prospect of prison, Rena fixes it up with the bank to repay the money so he won't have to go to prison. This the father can't face, and he commits suicide. Rena's only reaction is:

"Like that . . . all my work . . . gone."*

Beach's second major work, *The Goose Hangs High* (1924), is relieved by more humor than *A Square Peg*. It concerns the Ingals, who have, according to the old Granny, raised their children to be "rotten spoiled" because they are accustomed to wealth and self-gratification. They chatter about Freud like typical moderns of the flapper age: Lois urges her brother to get married, "Simply to keep you a normal, human being. You'll have all sorts of complexes if you don't hurry up."

When, however, Mr. Ingals loses his job, the children prove themselves unselfish and unspoiled. They rally around Dad, giving up college and marriage in order to support the family. They even find Dad a chance to pursue an old hobby, horticulture. Even when he has a chance to get his job back, Dad stays at the thing which, for the first time in his life, satisfies him. The theme of self-realization is well contrasted with the older convention of "self-sacrifice for the sake of the children" as practised by parents like Rena Huckins. Beach apparently intended the play as a rebuttal to the charge that permitting children their own way and their own fulfillment necessarily "spoils them."

Perhaps the most celebrated of the psychoanalytic quintet of 1922-23 was *Rain* by John Colton and Clemence Randolph, adapted from Somerset Maugham's story *Miss Thompson*. A sincere and moving drama which was Freudian not only in superficial details but in its thematic core, *Rain* tells the story of a fanatic missionary, Reverend Davidson, who proselytizes for the early Christian denial of sex (the psychoanalytic term for his fanatic aversion to sex is *reaction-formation*). On his wedding night he had told his wife that theirs would be a spiritual marriage only, and she has in consequence become as warped, meddlesome, and frustrated as he. He has come to Pago-Pago Island in the South Seas to teach the happy pagan natives to stop dancing and enjoying life, to put clothes on—in short, to teach them what sin is.

When Miss Sadie Thompson arrives on the island, fleeing from a San Francisco frame-up and a Honolulu red-light house, she and a Marine sergeant are attracted to each other; but Davidson tries to get Sadie sent back to the States. The Marine offers to help her escape and even to marry her, but Reverend Davidson, who takes a more-than-spiritual interest in Sadie, devotes himself to urging her to repent and go back to San Francisco and atone in prison. Mrs.

---

* A recent television production of *A Square Peg* confirmed its theatrical vitality and its psychological universality, in spite of the omission of the blackmailing wench and the unhappy ending.

Davidson tells the sagacious Dr. McPhail that her husband had a strange dream the night he had been praying with Sadie in her room —he had dreamt of the mountains of Nebraska. The Doctor interprets the dream, pointing out that the mountains of Nebraska are rounded and smooth—"Didn't it strike you they were curiously like a woman's breasts?" This appears to be the first true example of Freudian dream symbolism to be used in a Broadway play.

Dr. McPhail comments with restrained sarcasm that Mrs. Davidson derives a vicarious pleasure out of condemning the pagan dances and erotic customs of the natives. "We live in the day of the new commandment," he observes. "Thou shalt not enjoy thyself . . . Too bad man couldn't develop a soul without losing the Garden of Eden."

Modern anthropologists have paralleled Maugham's interest in primitive cultures and their apparent freedom from the neuroses and psychosomatic illnesses of civilization. Dr. McPhail is acutely aware of the contrast between the pagan's mental health and ability to integrate sex in his life, and the neurotic conscience of "civilized" man which cannot face a function of his own body and therefore must ironically send missionaries to teach the remaining primitive cultures a sense of "sin." Even the derelict trader is on the island as an escape from an oppressive conscience or *super-ego,* personified to him as his ancestors, who instilled in him too exacting standards and a sense of his own unworthiness: "Man, they used to rise out of their winding sheets every night to sit on my chest and tell me unless I up and did something I'd be damned." At least one psychoanalyst, Ives Hendrick, has praised the accuracy of the motivation in *Rain.*

The climactic scene comes when Reverend Davidson, feverishly at work trying to convert Sadie (and almost succeeding), seduces her instead and then commits suicide in overwhelming shame. Sadie is freed of her new load of guilt and relieved to know that Davidson was just like all other men. She will go to Australia to wait for her Marine.

With its psychoanalytic interpretation of the dream of the rounded hills of Nebraska and its insight into the conversion of repressed sexual energy into religious fanaticism, *Rain* marks a considerable step forward in the American drama toward the frank and mature handling of psychoanalytic themes. With *Rain, Roger Bloomer, A Square Peg, Icebound,* and *The Adding Machine,* as well as the early work of O'Neill (*Beyond the Horizon, Diff'rent* and *The Emperor Jones*), Dreiser's *The Hand of the Potter,* and Glaspell's *The Verge,* Freudian drama may be said by 1923 to have come of age in the American theatre.

CHAPTER V

The Freudian Twenties

☆　　☆　　☆　　☆

MATRIARCHY RAMPANT

It has been said that the villain in drama was abolished by
Freud. It is true that the all-black Squire Cribbs species of villain
has been superseded in melodrama by a villain whose evil derives
from unconscious childhood influences which can be understood if
not condoned. On a higher level the villain in tragedy has become
the inner man, the villain within who splits the individual and
makes of him an ambivalent figure such as O'Neill's Dion Anthony
or Williams' Blanche DuBois. But while Freud in one sense inter-
nalized the villain, his dramatic followers in the twenties created a
new "heavy"—the Mother.

According to the psychoanalytic point of view, it is the mother
who all too often in our civilization reduces her children, especially
her sons, to dependency, ambivalence, and psychic impotence. (Jung
enthroned the Earth-Mother as the primal force in unconscious life,
while to Freud the father assumed more significance as the obstacle
who stood between the son and his unconscious objective of reunion
with his mother; from either point of view, the Oedipus complex or
mother-son-father relationship was of focal importance in the origin
of neurosis.) The drama of the twenties makes vividly clear that one
of the most striking changes in American *mores* brought about by
psychoanalytic concepts has been the desentimentalization of the
role of mother. Philip Wylie gave her the final *coup de grace* in his
Generation of Vipers.

76

Of all the psychoanalytic themes that appeared in the drama of the twenties, the Oedipus complex was the most frequent one, appearing in at least fifty plays between 1923 and 1934. Its most characteristic form was that of the dominating mother and fixated son whose life was warped by her jealousy of his sexual partner. *The Silver Cord* best illustrates the category, but Howard's play had many predecessors, including Maurice Clark's *Tragic Eighteen* (1926), and Jesse L. Williams' *Lovely Lady* (1925), in which the son, so devoted to his mother that he does not drink or go with flappers, falls in love with an elderly matron who becomes a mother-image through the psychoanalytic mechanism of identification. Other plays in which a man projects onto an older woman his unconscious need for maternal protection include O'Neill's *Dynamo* and *Desire Under the Elms,* as well as Lulu Vollmer's *Dunce Boy* (1925).

A characteristic picture of matriarchy occurs in *Your Uncle Dudley* (1929) by Howard Lindsay and Bertrand Robinson, in which a ruthless mother drives her daughter into a concert career because she had herself been frustrated along those lines. She treacherously ruins a rival's chances in a musical competition, and then when it appears that her daughter will elope to Europe, pretends to drink lysol and stages a fainting fit. Mother's brother, Uncle Dudley, is a lovable, easy-going benefactor of the town whose eyes are finally opened to the human relationships around him. So familiar had the pattern of matriarchal dominance become by 1929 that in reviewing *Your Uncle Dudley,* Robert Littell felt constrained to cry out, "There ought to be a closed season during which playwrights are not allowed to paint mothers black and then shoot them. It's too easy."

The Oedipus theme was used for everything from farce to melodrama. In between were delightful comedies such as Preston Sturges' *Strictly Dishonorable* (1929), in which an eager but virginal young girl breaks with the callow young man who is under his mother's wing and virtually throws herself at an Italian opera singer who is taken aback by her starry eyed efforts to get into bed with him. The singer, however, proposes marriage only after he has cabled Italy to get the permission of his old mama.

Even history was not immune to Freudian interpretation, and in *Young Alexander* (1929) Hardwick Nevin depicts a chaste and pure young Alexander who worships his mother and falls in love with the ideal, unattainable beauty of Helen of Troy from reading Homer, only to be confronted with the very real wife of Darius who comes to his tent in the guise of Helen. He had been hypnotized and when he awakes in the morning is confident he has spent the night with Helen. Robert Sherwood's *The Road to Rome* is a similarly tongue-in-cheek pseudo-Freudian interpretation of history.

A popular farce by Dorrance Davis, *Apron Strings* (1930), burlesqued the silver cord theme by setting up a priggish young man who is married to a modern young lady whose mother says of her:

> Barbara is looked upon by all her young friends as a recognized authority on suppressed desires. She knows her *Freud* from cover to cover—and she can and does discuss Havelock Ellis with the best of them. I've heard her do it many a time out there on our front porch, until I was obliged to shut the living room windows in self-defense.

The young man, however, suffers from a violent mother-fixation: although his mother is dead, he must consult a trunk full of her letters of instructions which she left him for every occasion—after two weeks of marriage he has still not consummated it because his mother's letter advised him to treat the bride reverently at first. A friend finally manages to get him drunk and contrives to get the trunk of letters stolen: only then is the bride able to seduce her husband.

Among the more serious treatments of the Oedipus complex there were at least two attempts to retell the Hamlet story with Freudian interpretation. Zoe Akins in *The Furies* (1928) depicts a son who suspects his mother of murdering his father and who moans, "Mother, you have my father much offended." The son had been reading too much Shakespeare, however, and it turns out that the mother was innocent; she ends up locked in a pent-house with the real killer, a madman whose mad sister wildly plays the violin in the next room. *The Furies* is notable also as one of the few attempts in serious drama to depict subjective forces in external staging. Miss Akins used the technique introduced by O'Neill in *Strange Interlude* (which had opened one month before) of having the characters freeze while each in turn speaks his inner thoughts. Scenically also the author attempted to visualize the warped mind of the killer by having the walls of his room sloped, the table legs fantastic, and the candles and staircase surrealistically contorted.

The other reworking of the *Hamlet* material was by Arthur Hopkins. In *Conquest* (1933) he followed Shakespeare's story rather literally, transposing it to a rich Connecticut dynasty. The wife of the industrialist destroys her husband by selling his corporate stock to her lover. The son later avenges his father by ruining the lover through stock manipulation; at last free of his Oedipal fixation, he rebuilds his father's firm and is free at the end to express his love for the young lady of the play. The plight of a young man compelled to punish his mother for his father's death received its most superb handling, however, by O'Neill in *Mourning Becomes Electra*.

William Bolitho humorously summarized the new attitude toward motherhood:

> The mother today, it is no use to deny, is in great disfavor. It is she, above all, who has to sustain the weight of the new psychoanalytical attack on things as they are. Mother's Day is the great fast, the Yom Kippur of the new psychological learning. Mother-fixation is the most dreaded disease of the times, supplanting the old bogies of constipation, smallpox and appendicitis.

From this period on, mother's motives were suspect and no man dared blink his eye while mentioning his mother, lest Freudian-minded playgoers smile knowingly.

FLAMING YOUTH

Next to the Oedipus complex, the psychoanalytic concept found most often in the drama of the twenties was the theme of sexual suppression and frustration. Youth turned to psychoanalysis as a rationale for rebellion from the standards of their parents. With flasks on their hips and words like "inhibited" and "suppressed" on their lips, the younger generation was depicted as violating the pre-war moral codes in the name of self-expression and individual freedom.

One of the earliest of these interpretations was *The Changelings* (1923) by Lee Wilson Dodd,* an interesting transitional play constructed on the older playmaking lines of Fitch but generously sprinkled with Freudian terminology which was only superficially understood. Two middle-aged couples, the Aldcrofts and the Fabers, are old friends, and the Aldcroft daughter, Kay, has married the Faber son, Wicky. Wicky, a college instructor (playwrights were a trifle hard on this profession during the twenties), is losing his wife because he is too hard at work on his thesis to notice her discontent. Wicky comes to his parents and flings himself into his mother's arms like a little boy. In the ensuing fight over Kay and modern woman's right to be free of convention, the older couples split apart. Mrs. Faber sides with Mr. Aldcroft and Mrs. Aldcroft finds herself in Mr. Faber's arms for consolation just as her daughter, Kay, enters; Kay is so shocked she leaves for the apartment of a notorious Lothario.

In the best Pinero tradition they all rush off to the man's apartment. Mr. Aldcroft fights the man who would have seduced his daughter and is comforted in his bruised condition by Mrs. Faber,

---

* Dodd also satirized the Freudian influence on literature in a book of criticism, *The Golden Complex: A Defense of Inferiority*. 1927.

who loves him and finds that it is reciprocated. They will not run off, however, choosing to sacrifice their own desires for their children's happiness. Sadly he asks her:

> Wally: What is this new-fangled lingo for being decent?
> Dora: (Smiling sadly up at him, and gently withdrawing her hand) Inhibited, Wally. We are—*inhibited* . . .

In championing the side of conventional morality, the author sees no middle ground between being "a sensual, self-worshipping little beast" and being morally inhibited and finding God. Wally says to his daughter:

> It's impossible to understand the human heart, Kay. . . . It's as if there were hidden forces—great black reservoirs of hidden forces. . . . There they lie in us, quiet and deep and—terrible . . . until some shock comes . . . and they well up and transform us . . . change everything.

The "terrible shock" of Kay's going to a man's apartment proves enough to reunite the young couple as well as to untangle the older changelings, but the reunions and rediscovery of each mate's virtues are a little sudden and far from convincing.

There were a number of other anti-Freudian plays, such as *Helena's Boys* (1924), a heavy-handed satire of psychoanalysis by Ida Lublenski Ehrlich from a story by Mary Brecht Pulver, in which a mother whose sons have embraced "the gospel according to Greenwich Village," tries to cure them by posing as herself addicted to Freud, a liberated vocabulary, liquor, and free love. The sons are, of course, shocked and see the error of their ways.

Israel Zangwill created in *We Moderns* (1924) a similar portrait of giddy youth. Helen Hayes played a nineteen-year-old ingénue who exclaims, "Ain't psychoanalysis wonderful!" and is torn between an upright young engineer and "a snaky poet who writes free-love verse and is addicted to seduction." One kiss from him sends her back to her noble-minded engineer.

A leading playwright of the anti-Freudian point of view was Rachel Crothers, who created in *Expressing Willie* (1924) one of the most acidulous attempts to ridicule the entire school of self-expression and the faddists who turned to Freudianism among the other unconventional *isms* of the twenties. The Willie who needs expressing is a *nouveau riche* yokel whose mother is his driving force, warding off all females who would marry him. Now a divorcée named Mrs. Frances Sylvester is after Willie, and so Mama in defense invites Willie's old home-town sweetheart, a mouse of a spinster named Minnie, to come and visit. Minnie arrives amidst Willie's absurdly affected friends—a phony painter who urges Minnie to "free yourself"—and Mrs. Sylvester, who comes from her psychoanalyst raving:

> Oh, I've just had the most inspiring experience of my whole life. You *must* go to this new man. He probed to the very depths of my being and *oh* the things we brought up out of my subconscious! I'm reborn. He's given me wings and flight.

When they mock Minnie and her piano playing, she takes the painter's advice to let herself go, and within an hour has remade herself. Seductively dressed and free of all repression, she plays the piano passionately and another guest follows her to the piano, singing, "Express Yo'self—Don't suppress yo'self." Now Minnie would help Willie free himself too, urging: "There *is* greatness in you. *Get it out!*" She goes to his bedroom at night, hides in the closet as Frances Sylvester also comes to woo Willie, saying seductively as she puts her hand on his, "Of course, I don't believe that sex *is* the basis of all things. Not at all—at all—*at all*. I believe the spiritual is the fountain—the source of life." The next morning, with mother's help, Willie realizes he loves Minnie. "If we were all running around without any *suppressions,*" mother concludes, "we might as well have tails again." Willie offers to marry Minnie and also give her a musical career, while the self-expression faddists are brushed aside. *Expressing Willie* can hardly be taken seriously as criticism of psychoanalysis because the faddists are so outrageously caricatured.

Although Miss Crothers has contributed a number of other comedies of American manners—there was *Let Us be Gay* in 1929, again with the outcome favoring conventionality as opposed to daring youth—only once, in *Susan and God* (1937), so poignantly played by the late Gertrude Lawrence, did she achieve real depth of insight into human emotions. Instead of psychoanalysis, Susan's fad was the Oxford movement, and she returns from England raving about it in almost the same words that Mrs. Sylvester used to extoll psychoanalysis. Although the Oxford movement bears elements of Jungian philosophy, the part that intrigues Susan is the public confession to God of one's errors, and she begins to meddle into the "depths" of her friends.

Challenged to apply some of her glib preachment to her own life and her marriage, Susan has to eat her words. She ends up, however, restoring her alcoholic husband's self-confidence, making a happier home for her adolescent daughter and finding her own fulfillment through helping others. Miss Crothers created in *Susan and*

God a delightful comedy utilizing the same special talent for deflating affectation which she applied less maturely to *Expressing Willie.* In answer to the author's questionnaire, Miss Crothers wrote that she believed all good playwrights deeply understand human nature, but that few have been at all influenced by psychoanalysis.

Miss Crothers' comment notwithstanding, the list of plays dealing with flaming youth and newfound Freudian freedom is long: *Forbidden* (1923) by Sydney Rosenfeld, *Sinner* (1927) by Thompson Buchanan, *These Modern Women* (1928) by Lawrence Langner, *The Great Necker* (1928) by Elmer Harris, *Nice Women* (1929) by William A. Grew, and *Borrowed Love* (1929) by Bide Dudley suggest the general category. To such an extent was Freud's name associated with the wildness of the twenties that Channing Pollock in his moral allegory, *Mr. Moneypenny* (1928), named his wicked resort "Club Libido."

SELF-REALIZATION

Beneath the superficial, naughty (and therefore intriguing) exposés of "flaming youth," there lay, as many playwrights realized, a serious need for new understanding of the individual, new tolerance for his uniqueness, and new respect for his search of self-realization. Many of the fine plays of the twenties dealt with this theme of individual fulfillment—*Strange Interlude* being perhaps the most eminent.

Often the villain who stood between the individual and his fulfillment was big business or the mechanized rut of industry. Such was the case in *Behold This Dreamer* (1927) by Fulton Oursler and Aubrey Kennedy, the hero of which, Charley Turner, is a slightly mad young artist with dreams of fame. He moons around the house until his wife grows furious. His father-in-law, who manufactures brushes, tries to get him into that reputable occupation, but Charley replies:

> Charley: There's not enough sex in the brush business for me to work too hard.
> Strickler: Sex in the brush business!
> Charley: Yes. There must be something sexual in a man's work before he can succeed.
> Strickler: Sex in the brush business!
> Charley: We conceive in ecstasy and bring forth in agony.
> . . . Sex is at the root of everything in life—including your brush business. Love is an energy—and a man must love his work as he loves his mistress. It is an energy that makes us create, children or books, music or brushes. It is

not enough to love wife, children, home, and the Lord
God Almighty. We have thought of love too long as a
thing of man, woman and child. It is the creative energy
—it is God Himself in his richest garments. Think that
over, old brush man.

This delightfully Freudian definition of psycho-sexual energy is
enough for the father-in-law to get Charley committed to an asylum,
where he makes friends with a group of whimsically mad characters
and a melancholy girl, Melodie. While under her inspiration, he
paints a surrealist painting entitled "Nude with a Pineapple" which
wins an art prize and brings Charley the reputation of genius. He
leaves the asylum, only to find he misses Melodie, can't get along
with his wife any better than before—she is in love with an insurance
man anyhow—and finally returns to live in the relative sanity of the
asylum. The connection between psychoanalysis and surrealist painting which expresses the individual's unconscious was also the subject of Ernest Pascal's *The Amorous Antic* (1929).

The theme of *Behold This Dreamer*—that madmen are the only
sane ones—was given another and more entertaining variation by
Maurice Clark in *Button Button* (1929), which is perhaps the most
amusing of the satires on psychoanalytic faddists who use Freud as
an excuse to meddle in other people's lives. Mrs. Patience Boynton-
Woodhouse, whose newest fad (following antiques and numerology)
is psychoanalysis, has a brother-in-law, Button, in a sanitarium for
the feeble minded; she gets him taken out and put in her care in
order to practice psychoanalysis on him. Button turns out to be a
thoroughly delightful, rational man whose only aberration lies in
hating the aggressive, money-making Babbittry of his brother. Prod-
ding him to take up basket weaving and to confide in her, she proceeds to give a superb misunderstanding of the meaning of repression:

First conscious thoughts upon arising. Repressions. Tell me,
are there any incidents in your life which stand out with
particular vividness?

When she urges him to tell his dreams, he relates a dream which
provides one of the neatest moments in all of psychoanalytic satire:

Button: Last night I dreamed that it was away back in the
year 1840 and I was a young man taking my sweetheart
to the Little Church on the hillside.
Mrs. W.: (Writing) How lovely.
Button: She had on hoop skirts—I can see just as plainly
how her skirts stood out all about her . . . just then we

came to a stile and she started to climb the stile, and I
looked up and saw the sun streaming in my window, and
I knew it was daylight and I was safe and sound in my
own little room.
Mrs. W.: (Glares at him) Hum. (She slowly tears up the
chart.)
Button: I warned you.
Mrs. W.: This sort of thing takes the heart out of me. Must
I remind you that you are a gentleman?

Ultimately all ends well for Button, who escapes marrying Mrs.
Boynton-Woodhouse's choice, the daughter of a modern poetry faddist, and runs off with the maid who loves him. Although broad in
its comic effects, *Button Button* provides some delightful satire of
giddy matrons for whom psychoanalysis is only a hobby.

As Button's withdrawal from the practical world was used for
comic effect, psychotic regression from the real world formed the
basis of serious drama in John L. Balderston's *Berkeley Square*
(1929), the plot of which was allegedly suggested to him by Henry
James' *The Sense of the Past*. Balderston shows a modern young man
reading eighteenth century family journals until England of 1784
becomes more familiar to him than his own time and place. Gradually Peter Standish regresses until he is an eighteenth century gentleman, deriving humor from the fact that he knows ahead of time
how the other characters will behave—taking for granted that Kate
is destined to marry him and therefore forgetting to woo her. At
the end, Peter is completely out of touch with present reality and
breaks with his modern sweetheart in order to remain alone with
his ghost-sweetheart, a century and a half older than he is. Dr. A. A.
Brill, Freud's pioneer American exponent, gave an interesting interview on *Berkeley Square* in which he pointed out that Peter's malady
is an accurate clinical picture of schizophrenia. Peter was unable,
according to Brill, to attach his libido to a woman of flesh and
blood, very likely because of a childhood mother-fixation. He must,
therefore, create a love-object out of unconscious memory, and
gradually, as in schizophrenia, he loses himself in the past. Karl
Menninger, however, interpreted *Berkeley Square* as an illustration
of the *deja vu* phenomenon—illusion of having previously done an
action.

Also guilty of neurotic withdrawal from the real world (shown
symbolically rather than fancifully) was the heroine of *The Boundary
Line* (1930) by Dana Burnet. Unique in its treatment of frigidity
through symbolism, *The Boundary Line* depicts a poetic, idealistic
writer who is married to a hard, emotionless, sterile woman, obsessed

with the desire to fence in their property. The fence becomes the symbol of defense against the intrusion of emotion into her life, for it is built at the expense of an old neighbor who pleads for access to a creek. The husband finally leaves her and finds his fulfillment by joining a caravan of gypsies. Possessive and retentive enough to suggest the Freudian anal-erotic character type, this wife is first cousin to Kelly's Harriet Craig.

A number of imported dramas treated the theme of self-realization in various ways: a forerunner of *Berkeley Square* was Molnar's *Launzi* (1923) adapted by Edna St. Vincent Millay, in which a young girl suffers from schizoid withdrawal from life, imagining herself dead and an angel. Franz Werfel created in the symbolically powerful *Goat Song* (1926) an allegory of the animal or *id* in man caged up and hidden by the repressive force of civilization. Georg Kaiser's *The Phantom Lover* (1928) depicts a neurotic girl developing an imaginary love affair with an officer who is ignorant of her existence. Italian drama reflected a parallel interest in psychiatric themes in Pirandello's *The Living Mask* (*Henry IV*, 1924) and Rosso di San Secondo's *Puppets of Passion* and *The Stairs* (1927), both with a view of life that humans are "mannikins gesturing feebly upon the wire of sex."

EXPRESSIONISM

The term "expressionism" has been given to plays which distort or depart from objective reality in order to express a truth about an inner state of mind or feeling. The term has of course larger implications than psychoanalytic drama and often was applied to social criticism or anti-war plays as well as satires on the mechanization of twentieth century society. The influence of Toller, Kaiser, Strindberg, and Evreinov pointed the way in form and staging, with some indebtedness to the angular, grotesque movement of modern dance. But if the precedent in form came from German and Scandinavian drama, it was not until it drew upon the subject matter of Viennese psychiatry that expressionism made any headway in the American theatre.

Although we have seen the seeds of expressionism growing in the pre-war dream plays, Eugene O'Neill's experiments in form gave expressionism its impetus, notably in *The Emperor Jones* (1920) and *The Hairy Ape* (1922). By the time O'Neill's *The Great God Brown* brought expressionism to its most striking psychological application in 1926, Lawson's *Roger Bloomer*, Rice's *The Adding Machine* and Kaufman and Connelly's *Beggar on Horseback* had explored various ways of externalizing the subjective life of man. With *Strange Inter-lude* the form seems to have reached its apex in the hands of a master who could make it subservient to content. After that expressionism began to decline, although Sophie Treadwell used it effectively in *Machinal* to explore a fresh psychological type. The period of expressionism lasted roughly from 1923 to 1929—although at no time did it rival realism in quantity. During the depression it dropped off sharply—life itself was distorted enough, apparently. There is evidence from recent plays such as *Dream Girl, Death of a Salesman,* and *The Seven Year Itch,* however, that expressionism is far from dead as a useful vehicle for psychological statement.

Less concerned with sex than *Roger Bloomer,* but more imaginative and entertaining, *Beggar on Horseback* (1924), by George S. Kaufman and Marc Connelly, is the American theatre's most famous Freudian dream play. It was based on the German of Paul Apel but was given an American setting and theme, satirizing the Babbittry of business men and their attitude toward the arts.

A struggling young composer, Neil McRae, is in love with Cynthia, but is sought by the rich and giddy Gladys Cady, who brings her patronizing father and mother and fatuous brother Homer to inspect him. After they leave, Neil falls asleep and dreams of what his marriage with Gladys might be.

In Neil's mad, expressionistic dream, the mechanisms described by Freud were amusingly employed—for example, the daytime stimulus. Mr. Cady had mentioned they have two butlers, and in the dream two butlers appear, then four, then six, then eight, twelve, etc. There are other elements of secondary elaboration, such as trains leaving for nonsensical towns and incongruous associations freely distorted. His wedding takes place in a railroad station, just as they leave on their honeymoon, to express her haste in marrying him. Next, the inlaws all move in with them, and Mr. Cady has a telephone attached to his chest, buying eighteen holes of golf just as he would stock in the market. Neil resents the insinuations that he only married Gladys for her money, and goes to work for Mr. Cady's firm. He has a fantastic experience of anxiety trying to get through a requisition for a pencil at the office, and the satire on mechanized office efficiency is delightful. Another dream mechanism is the displacement of one individual into two, as when Mr. Cady dictates to two stenographers, Miss Hey and Miss You. Neil tries vainly to compose on the side, but Gladys tears up his great symphony and in fury he kills her, her parents, and Homer.

The next part is his trial. Homer is the district attorney and Mr. Cady becomes the Judge, a projection of the father-image onto a figure of authority. The satire on our courts is sharp and incisive. A newspaper has reported the results of the trial even before it takes place. Gladys would go dancing with the jury; Neil's defense is to play his music for the court, and there is an interlude of a ballet pantomime, "A Kiss in Xanadu" (which is most unFreudian). The court's verdict is to condemn Neil to "Cady's Consolidated Art Factory," where he sits in a cell mechanically producing works of art to order, while a guide takes tourists through the factory as if it were a zoo. Neil finally rebels and goes to die with Cynthia, while his best friend acts as executioner. When Neil awakes, he knows it is Cynthia he loves; Gladys has found someone else she would rather dance with anyhow, so all ends well.

The Freudian elements in the dream, it may be seen, include displacement, condensation, distortion, masochism, anxiety, identification of father with authority figure, free association, and wish-fulfillment (hence its title, derived from "If wishes were horses . . ."). Neil's dream is free of childhood or sexual elements, however, and instead is anticipatory, as Jung believed dreams to be. In writing and staging, the originality and unhackneyed Freudianism of *Beggar on Horseback* made it one of the most successful pieces of expressionism of the twenties.

A year later George S. Kaufman kidded the vogue of dream plays to which he had contributed. In his *The Butter-and-Egg Man*, a zany play which the butter-and-egg man is being induced to finance on Broadway includes a delirious dream with angels coming down the aisles and a judge who turns out to be the father and ultimately to be God. Five years later Kaufman, Morris Ryskind, and George Gershwin used the dream device again in *Strike Up the Band* (1930) to satirize the self-made business man and the folly of war.

Among the more successful of the dream plays derived however remotely from Freudian psychology was *The Devil in the Cheese* (1926) by Tom Cushing. A father who finds his daughter bewildering to him eats some magic cheese, sleeps and dreams that a god gives him one wish. He wishes that he could see inside his daughter's mind. This he and the audience proceed to do. The daughter is seventeen and in love with a steamship steward. The play becomes a dream-within-a-dream as the girl fantasies her boy friend shipwrecked with her on a desert isle and nurses him through illness; he ends up, of course, in the White House. There are two actors playing the father, one as he sees himself and one as the daughter sees him, decidedly more heartless and shriveled.

This device of two actors to play one individual was found in at least seven plays during the psychoanalytic period. In three of these the splitting was between the primitive and controlled selves, as in *Overtones, Any House,* and *Days Without End.* One actress played a number of subjectively seen aspects of herself in Howard and Sheldon's *Bewitched,* and *Beggar on Horseback* showed butlers multiplying in a fashion typical of anxiety dreams; finally in *The Wisdom Tooth* two actors were used to depict both the adult and the child within the grown-up.

This play (1926) by Marc Connelly is a delightful study of an "inferiority complex" in a young clerk, Charlie Bemis—the epitome of non-entities in the tradition of Rice's Mr. Zero. He wishes he had courage to tell off the boss for firing a pretty secretary, but he only can do it in the washroom when the boss isn't there. His girl is disappointed in him for being such a namby-pamby, and he begins to reflect on his childhood, his Grandma and Grandpa who thought he was destined to be President. As he day-dreams, in walk his grandparents and he proceeds to re-live his childhood. With a child actor playing himself as a boy, Charlie sees himself as a fearless and righteous youth who once saved a horse from being burnt to death. His girl assumes various shapes through the mechanism of identification—she is a circus queen and a childhood playmate. He fantasies telling the boss off—and this time the boss appreciates him the more for it. Regression to his childhood restores Charlie's confidence and he says "Gee, I certainly was a nice little kid."

Connelly never tells us just what changed Charlie from a nice, courageous boy into a Mr. Zero. After the dream, however, he is miraculously a new man; he tells the boss off in reality, and although he is fired for it, it does not devastate him—and Sally's love is reborn. One of the foremost neurologists of the country wrote to Alexander Woollcott his interpretation of *The Wisdom Tooth:*

> Connelly's *The Wisdom Tooth,* aside from whether it is dramatic or appealing, contains one of the most profound and sound psychological ideas I have seen on the stage. It is the exact converse of Barrie's *Peter Pan!* There infantilism is extended into adulthood. Here is the age-old idea of the rebirth of the hero. A dilapidated "yes-man" goes back into the past and recovers his boy soul, and under the magic of the eternal feminine the adult non-descript dies and is born again as the boy-man. Fortunately he is kept as no more than the reborn infant-hero without the Satevepost miraculous immediate ascension to the throne. He is still a failure, he is still in the manger, but a star is in the sky, and a wise woman holds him up. Observe it from this angle and wonder that how a wisecracker intuitively plumbs the depths.

And yet if curing an inferiority complex were literally that simple, psychiatrists would soon be unemployed.

Distorted or expressionistic scenery has never truly taken root in our non-musical theatre. We have noted the first apparent use of subjectivism in stage design in the womb-like tower to which the heroine retreats in Glaspell's *The Verge*, followed by visual distortions in Rice's *The Subway*, and *The Adding Machine*, in Lawson's *Roger Bloomer*, and in Zoe Akins' *The Furies*.

One striking attempt at visualizing psychology in scenery was Austin Strong's *A Play Without a Name* (1928). Reminiscent of Evreinov's *The Theatre of the Soul*, the scene is set inside the brain of his hero and resembles:

> . . . the cavernous regions of the young man's subconscious. These regions are uniquely huge and revue-like, with much papier-maché and chiffony gauze for bones, and eerie glares and Bengal lights and traffic signals and gleaming switchmen making frenzy of each sentence. . . .

A motion picture screen shows the turbulent images in the hero's brain while voices in choral speech intone his inner thoughts; a strange figure at a switchboard controls the hero's actions, and two other figures pull levers releasing or inhibiting him, with the black form of Fear in a corner under his ear. The play achieved its interest by showing a scene objectively and then repeating it as seen subjectively in the hero's brain. The plot concerns the husband's philandering while his conscience urges him to return to his patient wife. The critics felt, however, that the staging became a curiosity which distracted the audience from any emotional response to the story. Unlike *Strange Interlude*, there would be no play, as Richard Lockridge pointed out, without the novelty of the form.

One of the few other plays to use motion pictures for psychological effect was *Damn the Tears* (1927) by William Gaston, which traces the mental breakdown and growing psychosis of a former athlete. Purportedly a true story of a Harvard baseball player, the play shows a baseball hero who fails his team in a crisis and is disgraced. When he learns that he has failed his examinations for law school, his mind cracks. He is sent to a sanitarium, and when he is finally released, he is a wandering and broken man, groping his way by night to the baseball field that was the scene of his many triumphs. He goes to sleep and dreams of the last shameful game, which returns to him in distorted, brilliant detail. A policeman wakes him up to arrest him as a vagabond. Losing touch with reality, his mind wanders to the gentle calm of a garden with his dream girl playing celestial music for him, and he falls gratefully at her feet, a child again. Using puppets as well as motion pictures, a chorus of off-stage voices, and a dream, *Damn the Tears* was not a Broadway success, although it was an interesting attempt to utilize the resources of the modern stage for the psychological study of character in disintegration.

The dream device was used for virtually every theatrical purpose—for farce comedy in Harry Delf's *Atlas and Eva* (1928), in which one Elmer Nebblepredder carries everyone else's troubles on his shoulders like Atlas, until in his delirious dream he sees himself being refused admittance to Heaven until he stops worrying; as left-wing propaganda in *Singing Jailbirds* by Upton Sinclair, in which an I.W.W. organizer, jailed in solitary confinement has a delirious dream of his trial as a mockery of justice; and for pseudo-Freudian interpretation of the Bible, in Bertram Bloch's *Joseph* (1930), which turned for its subject to the first great dream interpreter, Joseph, as played in modern vernacular by George Jessel.

Before leaving the dream play, we should note a delightful and unique play by F. Scott Fitzgerald, the only contribution to the drama by this distinguished American novelist of the twenties. In *The Vegetable* (1929) Fitzgerald turns his satiric genius upon the Horatio Alger success formula that "Any American who doesn't have ambition to be president of the United States is no better than a vegetable." His hero proves to be just that—for he goes to sleep on bad bootleg gin and dreams of being President, much to his discontent. His expressionistic dream includes displacement and identification of real characters—his deaf and senile old father turns up as Secretary of the Treasury and burns up all the federal currency; his bootlegger becomes a foreign ambassador who tries to buy the State of Idaho, and a comic-opera General Pushing is ousted from power so that the President can wear the uniform himself. When "the Vegetable" finally awakens, he realizes that it is essential to do only what will fulfill his deepest wishes. His is a childhood ambition to be a postman, which an expert "analyzer" has found out by analyzing him in Act I. His shrewish wife finally concedes that to be the best postman in the world is just as important as to be the President of the United States.

Among serious plays, a distinguished example of the fusion of expressionism and Freudianism in the American drama was Sophie Treadwell's *Machinal* (1928). In the style of *Roger Bloomer* and *The Subway*, but without the dream, Miss Treadwell explores the unconscious processes that might motivate a young girl such as figured in the famous Ruth Snyder murder case. The heroine, simply named

The Young Woman, is a gentle, tender, sexually baffled creature in a hard, mechanized civilization teeming with sexual threats which arouse her anxiety. Craving emotional satisfaction yet having been brought up to view sex as loathsome, the Young Girl is in constant panic at her libidinous urges which threaten to break through wherever she turns, in her mechanized office or the closely packed subway train. Her boss has fat, flabby hands which she fears, and her mother has a drab mind that can discuss only garbage and potatoes while the Young Girl probes her about love and marriage. The Young Girl marries the boss only because it represents escape from her mother and the tenement. Her honeymoon with an earthy, lusty man is a magnificent depiction of embarrassment, sexual panic and hysteria; she undresses in the bathroom and cries for her mother as her husband approaches her.

In the hospital after she has had a baby, she can't endure her husband's visits and projects death-wishes toward her baby. Associating God with her fat-handed husband, she identifies herself with the Virgin Mary and mumbles that "I'll not submit" to any further relations with him.

In a barroom scene that veritably crawls with sex in a variety of forms—a woman needing an abortion, men waiting for pick-ups, and a homosexual trying to seduce a young boy—the Young Girl accepts a man's offer of an affair. Alone with him, she relaxes and finds new freedom. In a tender and warm love scene that is not expressionistic, repressed memories of her childhood return to her—nursery rhymes and childhood images which purify her. Her lover, who has killed two men in Mexico, gives her the hint that leads her to kill her own husband with a bottle filled with pebbles. But her lover signs a deposition betraying her and she confesses in court that she killed her fat-handed husband to be sexually free of him. Just before the execution she again fights "submitting" to the barber who would shave her head, and she goes to her death as an escape from a life that had been a sexual hell. Miss Treadwell's portrait of an emotionally starved woman driven to murder by her fixated loathing of sex is a full-blown psychological study, although the others in the play have less dimension. *Machinal* shows the origins of frigidity in the mother's own disgust with her marriage which she conveys to the daughter. In form the play is notable for the free-association soliloquies which attempt to project the kind of unconscious turmoil from which crimes of violence erupt.

Miss Treadwell wrote a number of other plays including a study of Edgar Allan Poe, *Plumes in the Dust* (1936), and a somewhat inept drawing room satire on psychoanalytic faddists, *Ladies Leave*

(1929), in which she depicts a bored wife having an affair with her psychoanalyst and following him back to Vienna in what one critic called "a doorslam louder than Nora's." There was another unhappy lady in the play who couldn't eat or sleep until after she was psychoanalyzed, and then ". . . my dear, she went right out and divorced her husband and opened a tea room." Unlike *Machinal*, the other works of Miss Treadwell were not departures from realism.

INFERIORITY AND GUILT

The Adlerian "inferiority complex" came in for some entertaining treatments during the twenties—Connelly's *The Wisdom Tooth* and Philip Barry's *The Youngest*, for example. The most famous, however, was *The Poor Nut* (1925) by J. C. and Elliott Nugent. A long-run hit on Broadway, it told in comic terms the story of the worm who turns. The worm, in this case, is a college bookworm, Phi Beta Kappa, and student of botany, who is so shy that he can't face people. He is in love with Margie, and her friend Julia decides to psychoanalyze him. She decides he is an "emotional introvert" with an inferiority complex. Reluctantly he agrees to be psychoanalyzed, the process taking little more than one page in the script. Julia analyzes his dream of watermelon, discusses his "noodle soup phobia," and decides that his libido is turned inward. Then the plot goes off literally on another track—a track competition between the poor nut and the biggest athlete on campus. The poor nut beats the great athlete in the track meet (because the coach tells him to go out and feel superior). He concludes, "My libido is turned outward."

The phraseology is Jungian but the psychological change is purely "thirdactical." Superficial and thin as satire, the play nevertheless illustrates the ease with which playwrights of the twenties could provoke the laughter of recognition by the use of familiar psychoanalytic types and terminology.

Hallucinations arising from a guilt complex proved particularly popular because of the ease by which they could be realized on the stage. There was, for example, *Conscience* by Don Mullally (1924), in which a man who has strangled his wife has obsessive visions as he hides in a lonely cabin during a storm; in *The Undercurrent* (1925) by William H. McMasters, a business man's guilty conscience causes tortured hallucinations of the trouble he has caused his workers, until he repents and becomes a benevolent employer.

A metaphysical twist to a psychoanalytical idea formed the basis of Henry Myers' *Me* (1925) in which a tramp kills a man and assumes his personality, later restoring the heroine's sanity by recreating the repressed incident of terror. The heroine is glad to settle for the imposter who is at least alive.* Myers was apparently intrigued with "doppelgängers" and used the theme again in *The Other One* (1932) to show twin sisters, one suppressed by the other. Another revival of the "doppelgänger" device had a field day in *Brothers* (1928) by Herbert Ashton, Jr., in which two doctors debate the influence of heredity versus environment—a debate as ancient as Terence's *The Brothers*. They decide to experiment by splitting a pair of orphaned twins, one to a rich home and one to a slum home. The rich son turns out to be a brilliant lawyer but a dope fiend, while the poor son is a piano player in a dive, but good to the core. Wrongly accused of a crime, the poor brother is unknowingly defended by his rich brother—who goes to pieces afterwards and is committed to a sanitarium while the poor brother impersonates him for the sake of their poor old mother with heart trouble. The two doctors conclude that they don't know just what their experiments proved. (We know, however; it proved that melodramatic claptrap with a sprinkling of psychology was good for 255 performances on Broadway.)

Perhaps the most effective study in guilt was written by Kenneth Britton and Roy Hargrave in *Houseparty* (1929), which depicts college fraternity life, centering around a boy who accidentally kills a girl who was trying to blackmail him. Haunted by guilt feelings, the boy dreams of the event and is about to commit suicide when his close friend—so close, in fact, that there is a strong hint of latent homosexuality—saves the boy and is willing to give up his own girl and go abroad with the boy to help him get over the event.

HOMOSEXUALITY

The element of latent male inversion in *Houseparty* was first suggested in Gribble's *March Hares* (1921), and O'Neill's *The First Man* (1922) and *The Great God Brown* (1926), as well as Noel Coward's *The Vortex* (1925). The earliest hint of latent Lesbianism was in Glaspell's *The Verge* (1921), followed by Lawson's *Roger Bloomer* (1923). From 1923 on, the theme was treated with increasing frankness, culminating in 1926 in a translation of Edouard Bourdet's *The Captive*, which depicted a well-bred married woman struggling in vain against her inverted relationship with another woman. *The Captive* was closed by order of New York City authorities along with

* A great many other assorted fears and phobias cropped up in plays of the period, such as *Yellow* (1926) by Margaret Vernon, *Cock O' The Roost* (1924) by Rida Johnson Young, *What's the Big Idea* (1926) by Martha Hedman and Henry House, *Not Herbert* (1926) by Howard Irving Young, and *The Dark* (1927) by Martin Brown.

two pieces of commercial pornography, *Sex* with Mae West, and *The Virgin Man*—plays of the sort which vitiated the cause for a mature, adult examination of what Freud, Ellis and others found to be not uncommon as a form of human relationship. Under threat of the passage of a state censorship law, the producers of *The Captive* decided not to appeal the closing of the play, but Bourdet's play nevertheless did much to aid the cause of dignified study of inversion.

Although the search for thrills that would shock the box-office into the profit column occasionally resulted in such lurid trash as Mae West's *Pleasure Man* (1928), which dealt with female impersonators and homosexuals, most of the dramatic treatments of sexual deviation were high minded in their intent. There were portraits of effeminate young men in *The New Gallantry* (1925) by Merlin and Marlow, in Lawson's *Loudspeaker* (1927), and in Sophie Treadwell's *Machinal*. The two most perceptive studies of Lesbianism of the twenties by American authors were *These Days* (1928) by Katherine Clugston and Thomas H. Dickinson's *Winter Bound* (1929). The former anticipated Hellman's *The Children's Hour* in its girls' boarding school setting, and shows young girls driven into unnatural "crushes" with each other because of the frigid, warped influence of the old-maid head-mistress who teaches the girls that an interest in boys is disloyalty to the school. *Winter Bound,* by Thomas H. Dickinson, is a more somber and mature study of two girls who spend a winter together in a secluded Connecticut farmhouse to get away from men and to find spiritual peace. One is essentially assertive and masculine, the other feminine. A male neighbor intrudes, falls in love with the more feminine girl, and leads her to see for the first time the inverted sexual undercurrent of her supposedly sexless retreat. She finally is able to choose the man in preference to the woman, who is left alone lamenting that the world will better understand her predicament in a hundred years. It is interesting to note that *Winter Bound* was the last production of the Provincetown Players which had begun with *Suppressed Desires* fourteen years before, and which was about to obtain a subsidy when the stock market crash of 1929 put an end to its very real contributions.

Paralleling the growing candor in treatments of homosexuality was an increasing frankness in the Freudian theme of incest. Perhaps the first play to hint at an inverted father-daughter relationship was Dan Totheroh's play *Wild Birds* (1925). That same year Maxwell Anderson treated the subject more frankly in *Outside Looking In.* Although never as prevalent as the mother-son theme, father-daughter relationships occurred in a number of plays in 1929, beginning with a serious and perceptive farm tragedy of the inar-

ticulate, *The Earth Between* by Virgil Geddes, produced by the
Provincetown Players under the direction of James Light and with
Bette Davis in her professional debut as the girl. With a quiet
naturalism and integrity of characterization, Geddes tells a simple,
threadbare story of a widowed farmer's love for his daughter who
had taken her mother's place. His efforts to get rid of the young
hired hand who loves the girl form the only plot complication, and
result in the young man's contracting pneumonia in the drafty barn
where the father forced him to sleep. There are poignant moments
in *The Earth Between*, as there are in Geddes' later treatment of
a father-daughter relationship, *Native Ground* (1937). Here a farm
man and woman are in love, only to learn that he is actually her
father. They go through with the marriage and live together pla-
tonically. Believing that the girl's mother was merely being vindictive in thwarting them, he persists in urging sexual relations upon
his wife-daughter, driving her into an affair with a hired hand. The
second play of this projected trilogy was to deal with the love affair
and the third play with the daughter of this union. In his conception Geddes thus attempted to capture the Greek feeling for the
majesty of a struggle with the hereditary curse of evil within a
family. If he lacked O'Neill's mastery of his material, Virgil Geddes
at least prompted Maxim Gorki to prophesy that "The hope for drama
lies in America."

DEUS EX CLINICA

Far more numerous than plays of incest were those in which a
doctor of sorts prescribed or practised therapies resembling psychoanalysis. Psycho-therapy had been performed on Broadway since
The Fatted Calf in 1912, and hypnotism long before that. As late
as 1923 the old master showman, David Belasco, was still interested
in psychological themes, collaborating with Tom Cushing in an
adaptation of Fausto Martini's Italian play, *Ridi, Pagliaccio*. As
Laugh Clown Laugh with Lionel Barrymore, the play had as
therapist a "nerve specialist" who was called in to treat two men,
one who laughs incessantly because he is in love with no one, and
a clown who cries incessantly because he is in love with his ward.
The two men become friends in the psychoanalyst's office, but come
to grief when they both find themselves in love with the same girl.

The parade of psychologists across Broadway's boards continued
with *Tiger Cats* (1924) adapted by Karen Bramson from the French
of Michael Orme, in which "an eminent neurologist" struggles with
the problem of a man hating a woman intensely and yet bound to

her by passion. And it took no less than four doctors to "plumb the subconscious" in Abraham Goldknopf's *In The Near Future* (1925).

It remained for a physician, Dr. Louis E. Bisch, to bring to the stage the first actual attempt to dramatize psychoanalytic therapy itself. In *The Complex* (1925), his method of treating the heroine's neurotic fear of spending a wedding night with her husband is the same as Barry was later to develop—to let her see the father to whom she is so unconsciously attached for what he is in reality—a blackguard. The critics found elements of genuine drama in *The Complex* —though perhaps more melodrama than is usual in real life psychoanalysis. Dr. Bisch wrote only one other psychoanalytic play, *Killers* (1928) in collaboration with Howard Merling, which attempted to prove that within each man are the instincts of the killer.

A wide variety of therapies were prescribed during the twenties by the practising members of the Actors Equity Association. More sexual experience is the recommended remedy in *The New Gallantry* (1925) by F. S. Merlin and Brian Marlow, as well as in *What The Doctor Ordered* (1927) by Caesar Dunn. Arthur Richman was probably the first in dramatic literature to use a "truth serum" to probe his character's unconscious, in his play *All Dressed Up* (1925). Bewhiskered psycho-therapists struggled to cure "shell-shocked war veterans" and amnesia victims in a number of plays, although Mary Roberts Rinehart managed to create a relatively authentic study of an amnesia victim in *The Breaking Point* (1923). Even faith healing was with us in plays like William Hodge's *For All of Us* (1923).

Many years before he joined Richard Rodgers to create psychological music-drama, Oscar Hammerstein II employed a unique and original form of therapy which suggests the later work of Moreno in psychodrama. In collaboration with Milton Herbert Gropper, *Gypsy Jim* (1924) shows a gypsy walking into a household of neurotics and proceeding to straighten out their lives. The gypsy proves to be a rich philanthropist who has hired some actors, upon the advice of a psychoanalyst, to create new human relations for the emotionally impoverished family. The trick works—each has his faith restored through finding himself needed and loved again.

Most of the cures were, naturally, too easy. In *How's Your Health?* (1929) by Booth Tarkington and Harry Leon Wilson, for example, the doctor gives Jungian advice while prescribing gallons of colored water for the hypochondriac with good farce results. The work-a-day play carpenters, it seems, developed their own forms of therapy with a grateful nod toward Freud—the only requirement of the Forty-second Street and Broadway Medical College being that sanity and mental health must be restored by eleven P.M.

CHAPTER VI

Freud, Jung, and O'Neill

With the background of the psychoanalytic twenties in mind, we are in a position to evaluate the playwright who epitomizes the Freudian period—Eugene O'Neill. His unique theatrical animation, his provocative experiments with masks, asides and dinner intermissions, and above all, his preoccupation with sex and neurosis, fascinated playgoers of the twenties and gave the American drama its most distinguished dramatist.

O'Neill himself attempted to depreciate the influence of Freud upon his work. Complaining of critics who were wont to condemn his plays as "case histories from a Freudian textbook," O'Neill wrote to Barrett Clark:

> . . . they read too damn much Freud into stuff that could very well have been written exactly as it is before psycho-analysis was ever heard of. Imagine the Freudian bias that would be read into Stendhal, Balzac, Strindberg, Dostoievsky, etc. if they were writing today! . . . And I am no deep student of psychoanalysis. As far as I can remember, of all the books written by Freud, Jung, etc., I have read only four, and Jung is the only one of the lot who interests me. Some of his suggestions I find extraordinarily illuminating in the light of my own experience with hidden human motives.

Although O'Neill was unable to answer the questionnaire sent him, his earlier reply to an inquiry on Freudianism contributes some of the same information:

There is no conscious use of psychoanalytical material in any of my plays. All of them could easily have been written by a dramatist who had never heard of the Freudian theory and was simply guided by an intuitive psychological insight into human beings and their life impulsions that is as old as Greek drama. It is true that I am enough of a student of modern psychology to be fairly familiar with the Freudian implications inherent in the actions of some of my characters while I was portraying them; but this was always an afterthought and never consciously was I for a moment influenced to shape my material along the lines of any psychological theory. It was my dramatic instinct and my own personal experience with human life that alone guided me.

I most certainly *did not* get my idea of Nina's compulsion from a dream mentioned by Freud in "A General Introduction to Psychoanalysis." I have only read two books of Freud's, "Totem and Taboo," and ". . . and the Pleasure Principle." The book that interested me the most of all those of the Freudian school is Jung's "Psychology of the Unconscious," which I read many years ago. If I have been influenced unconsciously it must have been by this book more than any other psychological work.

It is not difficult to understand O'Neill's reluctance to acknowledge indebtedness to any source but original creativity or to identify himself with psychoanalysis during the years when the very name of Freud was cause for embittered polemics. With the perspective of a few years, however, the ways in which the writings of Jung and Freud illuminated O'Neill's own experience with hidden human motives can be viewed more objectively.

THE EARLY PLAYS

With the exception of *Diff'rent*, O'Neill's early period was not conspicuously Freudian. There were, however, consistently neurotic and even psychotic heroes in the early one-acts, portrayed with a frenzied emotional intensity. *Abortion* (1914), written when O'Neill was 26, does suggest some superficial acquaintance with Jung's concept of the archaic racial unconscious. A mawkish, youthful melodrama, the play deals with an idolized college athlete who is responsible for getting a poor townsgirl pregnant and then obtaining an abortion for her so that he could marry a rich society girl. Father and son have a friendly, man-to-man talk about what he has done and the son says that he hardly understands it: "It was the male beast who ran gibbering through the forest after its female thousands of years ago." The father answers, "That is pure evasion. You are responsible for the Mr. Hyde in you as well as for the Dr. Jekyll. Restraint—." The father concludes, however, that "We've retained a large portion of the original mud in our make-up."

O'Neill's first treatment of insanity, in *Ile* (1916), shows a fairly conventional, pre-Freudian handling of mental breakdown in the wife who wants to go home after two years on a whaling ship. The author's final picture of her madly playing the organ leaves us without insight into the unconscious forces contributing to her breakdown.

The portrait of Smitty in *The Moon of the Carribees* (1916-17) may be taken as somewhat autobiographical. Sensitive, searching, introspective, Smitty, like his creator, turned to the sea, to vagabondage, to drink, as forms of escape from unresolved inner conflicts. A hint as to the origin of some of these conflicts lies in the father-son relationship, which is frequently depicted in the early plays as a hostile one; in fact, the overbearing father may be considered O'Neill's most typical character—until he later purged himself of father-hostility in *Ah, Wilderness!* An intimate friend of O'Neill's has called him a curious dichotomy of God the Father whom he hates and the Earth-Mother whom he loves.

From available evidence it would appear that the conflict in young O'Neill stemmed from his relationship with his father, the famous actor, James O'Neill ("the Count of Monte Cristo"). O'Neill was bitterly hurt when his father sent him to a county tuberculosis institution when he could well have afforded a private sanatorium. O'Neill Senior did, however, send his son to Harvard in 1914 where he studied playwriting with George Pierce Baker. The best of the one-acts came after this exposure to the 47 Workshop and at least two of them, *The Rope* and *Where the Cross is Made*, deal with father-son hostility.

Before Breakfast (1916) is a monologue of despair and suicidal depression, which James O'Neill was called in to direct at the Provincetown, with unhappy results:

> Father and son, in a perfect Freudian pattern, disagreed on every point. O'Neill Senior tried to instill in Mary Pyne some of the histrionic technique of an era which the Players had no wish to revive, while O'Neill Junior stalked up and down, muttering his displeasure.

Except for a sympathetic old Negro Mammy to whom a young tough returns to die in *The Dreamy Kid,* O'Neill was unable, in these early plays to depict a tender and lovable woman. He captured

superbly the virility of men at sea; but his women were the loose
sluts of the waterfront or oppressed, self-pitying hags. O'Neill's own
mother was frail and ill—and he felt that she had been abused by his
father. But O'Neill was not yet ready to transmit these feelings
toward the mother-figure into dramatic form.

The raw emotion of a father's curse upon a rebellious son, as
shown in *The Rope*, was enlarged into O'Neill's first full-length
play to reach Broadway, *Beyond the Horizon* (1920). Augustus
Thomas, Moody and Hopkins had done their spadework; the critics
were now prepared to acclaim *Beyond the Horizon* as the curtain-
raiser to a new era in American psychological realism.

Although no Freudian terminology is used, *Beyond the Horizon*
is a sketchy outline of Freudian figures which O'Neill was later to
fill in. Failure at self-realization, he seems to say, is man's greatest
tragedy. He shows us three lives blighted by the drive of love which
is misunderstood and mishandled. It drives both Rob and Andy to a
wrong career, and Rob's ineffectuality makes of Ruth an emotionally
impoverished, frigid wife. Rob had been a sickly, pampered boy
with an over-protective mother. O'Neill remains here on the descriptive rather than the probing level, but his portrait of the passive-dependent, tubercular Rob is a powerful one.

The autobiographical elements of tuberculosis and a hostile
father reappeared in *The Straw* (1921) but without the universality
which is requisite for tragedy. There is a suggestion that TB may be
curable by faith and the power of love (as, in fact, recent studies of
psychosomatic medicine tend to confirm), but the unrelieved morbidity of the story caused Louis De Foe to say that compared to this,
Beyond the Horizon, Diff'rent, and *Anna Christie* were "things of
joy."

Anna Christie (1921) is not entirely flawless in its overwrought
fusion of psychological naturalism and conventional rejuvenation
of the "woman with a past." The unconscious magnetism of the
sea which was beyond Rob's horizon (and which in psychoanalytic
symbolism is often equated with the amniotic fluid and the return-
to-the-womb motif) recurs in *Anna Christie*. It is "dat ole davil, Sea"
which the father, Chris, blames for his own unfulfilled life and his
daughter's fall from innocence—a classic illustration of the defense
mechanism of rationalization. It was from O'Neill's own background
rather than any psychoanalytic textbooks that he drew for the
naturalistic setting of Johnny-the-Priest's waterfront saloon and flop-
house. It was in just such a dreary dive, later to reappear as Harry
Hope's saloon in *The Iceman Cometh*, that O'Neill himself lived
for a time as a young man, and to which he returned somewhat later

to attempt suicide. (O'Neill had gone to the real Jimmy-the-Priest's, as the incident was told, with two prostitutes and two bottles of rye in order to be caught by detectives and establish evidence required to get a divorce. When he awoke the next morning to find himself with the two prostitutes, he felt so depressed that he went out and bought veronal—a poison which could be purchased in small amounts. Two of his friends found him waiting for the veronal to take effect, and walked him around until the poison wore off. They wired O'Neill's father—but instead of coming to get Eugene, he merely sent $50. The two friends used the money to get drunk, then decided they had better take Gene to Bellevue Hospital in a taxi. Upon arrival, O'Neill was found free of the effects of the veronal—but the two friends were thrown in the alcoholics ward.)

FIRST FREUDIAN EXPERIMENTS

Diff'rent (1920), was O'Neill's earliest specific treatment of sexual frustration. His portrait of Emma, a hysterical girl with an obsessive revulsion for sex, could, of course, have been created without acquaintance with psychoanalytic literature, and we cannot be sure whether O'Neill had begun to read Freud by this time. We may only say that the available evidence and the date of the composition of *Diff'rent* strongly suggest that O'Neill consciously or unconsciously selected a character and treated a theme in a way which psychoanalysis had made timely and meaningful—as well as permissible on the stage.

Emma suffers from a "reaction-formation," rigid, irrational disgust with sex, which psychologists recognize as a defense mechanism against her strong unconscious preoccupation with sex. This Emma betrays with her hunger for the details of her fiancé's affair with a native girl in the South Sea Islands. Her haste in calling off the wedding without even verifying his infidelity suggests that Emma sought an excuse to avoid marital intimacy. Compulsively Emma insists on a fiancé who is "diff'rent" from her father and brother—who are earthy, sexual men.

Thirty years later Emma has become a pathetic, withered figure of a Freudian old maid, coquettishly attempting to regress to her youth and to act out with Caleb's nephew the fulfillment she had denied herself with him. She is over-rouged and over-dressed. O'Neill has selected effective details such as her wetting her lips feverishly as she prods the callow nephew for details of his sexual escapades in Paris during the war. The nephew exploits Emma's physical desire for him in order to get money from her and his uncle, who has become miserly and bitter during his thirty years of celibacy. Caleb apparently still loves Emma and would yet marry her, a fidelity which seems a little far-fetched. Not until he and Emma have gone to the barn to hang themselves is the oppressive tension released.

Although the theme is the tragedy of stifled sexual impulse, O'Neill in a published statement preferred to stress its symbolic, universal implications:

> *Diff'rent,* as I see it, is merely a tale of the eternal, romantic idealist who is in all of us—the eternally defeated one. In our innermost hearts we all wish ourselves and others to be diff'rent! We are all more or less Emmas—the more or less depending on our talents for compromise. Either we try in desperation to clutch our dream at the last by deluding ourselves with some tawdry substitute; or, having waited the best part of our lives, we find the substitute time mocks us with too shabby to accept. In either case we are tragic figures, and also fit subjects for the highest comedy, were one sufficiently detached to write it.

O'Neill's statement identifying himself with the Emmas of the world is revealing, implying that it is not the Emmas who are neurotically out of touch with reality, but rather the real world which is at fault for not being able to accept its eternal, romantic idealists. Although one may wonder how he came to choose such an unfortunate symbol as Emma for the eternal idealist, O'Neill seemed to be groping, as is Tennessee Williams, toward a new theory of tragedy based upon the discrepancy between our introjected *ego ideal* and the disillusioning light of reality.

This same discrepancy is the basis for tragedy in *Gold* (1921) which, like *Ile* is a chronicle of the sea and mental aberration. Unlike Emma, whose neurosis progresses before our eyes, *Gold's* Captain Bartlett is already heat-and-thirst crazed when we meet him in Act I on a South Sea island—making empathy with him more difficult. He suffers intense shame that his whaling voyages produce so little revenue although a rival whaler has found the treasured ambergris. When he finds a chest of pasteboard trinkets, he is overwhelmed with wish-fulfillment—the will to believe that the jewels are real. He permits (but not actually instructs) his cohorts to kill the men who deny that the jewels are real.

Back at home, he suffers from nightmares, murmuring that he "spoke no word" to order the death of his two men. He relives in his dreams the scene of the finding of the treasure and the murders. Freud has called these anxiety dreams "repetition-compulsions." The dreamer seems compelled to relive a painful memory (apparently in conflict with Freud's earlier theory that all dreams were wish-fulfillment; in *Beyond the Pleasure Principle* Freud later assumed that the wish was for punishment appropriate to the guilt-feelings).

The last act, years later, shows Captain Bartlett suffering from delusions that the ship he sent after the buried treasure will return momentarily. His son Nat's reason is so shaken that he too is about to see the hallucinatory ship, when his sister persuades Captain Bartlett to unburden his soul before he dies and thereby save Nat's mind. Free at last of his burden of guilt and wish-fulfillment, Bartlett dies at peace. The psychology of this theatrical melodrama is relatively conventional—there are no childhood components in Captain Bartlett's psychosis, although we find the familiar over-powering father and weak, ambivalent son.

Where the Cross is Made is a one-act treatment of the same story, which according to Barrett Clark, was written after the plot of *Gold* was conceived. This time, however, O'Neill plays a theatrical trick on us. He lets the drowned sailors enter carrying their chests of gold, slimy and dripping with seaweed. Nat, as well as the audience, sees these hallucinations, but the half-credulous doctor and the sister do not. When the hallucinations vanish, Captain Bartlett is dead of heart attack, still clutching a map one of the dream figures handed him. The psychological aspects of *Gold* are gone and in their place is melodrama.

Another of O'Neill's unsuccessful plays, *The First Man* (1922) might be called a case history in male hysteria, although it is doubtful that O'Neill saw his hero in this particular light. Curtis Jason is depicted as completely passive-dependent, allowing his wife to be of all kinds of help to him. They are about to leave on an anthropological trip to Tibet when he learns she is pregnant. "You have blown my world to bits," he cries, swearing not to love the child. When the wife dies in childbirth he hysterically refuses to see the child. Learning that relatives suspect the child of not being his, he changes his mind, goes to kiss it, and then leaves it in an aunt's care while he hurries off to Tibet. There are perhaps autobiographical elements in the theme of the misunderstood genius among a world of crass materialists. There is also a suggestion of latent homosexuality between Curtis and his best friend Bigelow, whom he suspects of being the father of the baby. Though O'Neill tries to portray the relatives as harpies and vicious scandal-mongers, our sympathy is as much with them as with the hysterically immature hero. There is little reason to believe *The First Man* reflects Freudian influence as much as the author's individual emotional experience in the Strindbergian battle of the sexes.

In *The Fountain* (1925) O'Neill returned to the *Diff'rent* theme—
the tragedy of unfulfilled emotional needs which are repressed until
too late. In terms of this concept O'Neill interprets Juan Ponce de
Leon's search for the fountain of youth in order to make himself
young in the eyes of a girl he loves and who can only look upon
him as "a father." This rather beautiful and neglected play contains an interesting use of a masked woman who appears as a vision
to Juan in his wounded delirium. With this exception the treatment is
romantic and not complex.

In 1924 O'Neill produced his most Strindbergian play, *Welded*,
and paid eloquent tribute to Strindberg's influence in a program
note for the production at the Provincetown of Strindberg's *The
Spook Sonata* by the triumvirate of O'Neill, Robert Edmond Jones
and Kenneth Macgowan. Calling Strindberg "the precursor of all
modernity in our present theatre," O'Neill coined the term "behind-
life plays" for Strindberg's intuitive insight into the pressures behind
human behavior. In *Welded*, O'Neill began his own search for the
forces behind the surface of life.

Welded is important only historically, however, marking
O'Neill's first attempt to use the aside to get beneath the surface of
the individual personality and to dramatize the unconscious forces
that determine behavior (although a similar device was used earlier
by Rice in *The Adding Machine*). At the end of Act I of *Welded*, the
two married people sit facing the audience and speak their inner
thoughts, each oblivious of the other. Like the wife in *The First Man*,
Eleanor rebels chiefly at her husband's possessiveness, wanting her
soul as well as her body. The furious intensity of his love for her is
expressed in the homosexually derived wish "to become you. You've
become me."

The husband, Michael Cape, is a playwright (whose plays must
contain precious little humor or psychological insight). He is making
love to his wife and about to carry her up to bed when he is frustrated by a knock on the door. The entire act seems little more than
a bawdy joke taken too seriously. He projects suspicions into his
wife's apparent relief at being interrupted, and he storms out to
destroy their love once and for all. They each seek another person
—Michael, a prostitute, whom he ends up calling "sister" and kissing
tenderly on the forehead; Eleanor goes to an older man, a father-
image. Each returns, however, realizing that they are welded inevitably together, that their ambivalent hostility and love are but
reverse sides of the same coin. At the end when the husband leads
her upstairs there is no interruption; they join their outstretched arms

to form a cross, a symbolic gesture suggesting the unconscious association of sexual union with religious sanctity.

As in *The First Man* and later in *Days Without End,* O'Neill here treats marriage in terms of the hatred caused by the awareness of dependency upon the partner. *Welded* is more than a little naive and typifies O'Neill's major weakness—a tendency to take himself too seriously.

THE INFLUENCE OF JUNG

Carl G. Jung's early contributions to psychoanalysis included, as we have seen, the term "complex" and the use of association tests. Jung, however, broke away from Freud in 1912 over the issue of the divine or spiritual aspect of the libido, which Freud felt to be unscientific. Freud had erroneously limited his analysis to a regressive search into the patient's past, Jung believed. The progressive, forward-looking line toward spiritual and creative expression was more significant to the Jungians—and The Mother, as symbol of this, was more universal to them than Freud's primal tyrant of a father. Impressed with the universality of unconscious symbols, Jung formulated the theory of the *racial* or *collective unconscious,* by which he postulated that "each individual inherits a residue from the significant memories of the human race," including its animal origin. Freud's Oedipus complex, Jung felt, was merely a "symbol of the desire for the unattainable"; sexual libido was only one form of the primal libido, the other form being spiritual energy. This dichotomous view of the libido was first advanced in Jung's *Psychology of the Unconscious* (1912, translated 1917). This work, which O'Neill has stated that he read, is an amazingly erudite collection of evidence from Greek, Latin, Sanskrit and Germanic myths indicating the close primitive connection between sexual symbolism and the divine strivings out of which man created a "father-archetype" called God.

O'Neill has stated that Jung was the only one of the psychoanalysts who particularly interested him. The internal evidence is persuasive that it was Jung's theory of the racial unconscious which influenced O'Neill's *The Emperor Jones* (1920). The hallucinations that appear to Brutus Jones during his wild night in the forest are at first personal memories, then become racial memories as he regresses deeper and deeper into his primitive past under the pressure of fear. The personal memories are of the Pullman porter whom he killed in a crap game, the chain gang from which he escaped, and "Little Formless Fears." The racial memories are of a Southern slave auction in which he is for sale, a slave ship in which Negroes are being brought from Africa, and finally of a Congo witch-doctor who demands Jones' sacrifice. In a hypnotized state he crawls on his belly toward a crocodile at the command of the witch-doctor and finally uses his silver bullet to shoot the crocodile. The use of the childhood phallic symbol of the crocodile climaxes this masterpiece of flashback dramaturgy. Each racial memory, of course, might be explained as part of the folklore a Negro child could have heard from his mother; but the thematic basis for the play is apparently Jung's regression to the primitive—to the racial unconscious. A religious rite in the Congo, where a drum is first used at the normal rate of the heart beat and then intensified with the growing frenzy of the pulse, was the basis of the theatrical device used so grippingly in this play. The Jungian psychoanalyst, C. P. Oberndorf, endorsed O'Neill's application of Jung's concepts:

> The archaic unconscious of Jung postulates a very far distant heritage which nevertheless persists in every person as a vital influence—the racial unconscious. Eugene O'Neill has relied upon this theory for the fears which grip a pursued Negro in his drama The Emperor Jones. Here the threats to which his successive ancestors were subjected from the primitive jungle in Africa to slave days in America rise up before the terrified Negro as he gropes his way through the darkness of a tropical jungle night.

The return of the racial unconscious also formed the basis of The Hairy Ape (1922). Magnificently O'Neill portrays the disintegration of Yank when he loses his sense of "belongingness" in the stokehole of an ocean liner. O'Neill is clearer now as to the symbolism of the sea than he was in the earlier plays—Paddy laments the old days when clipper ships sailed with "fine strong men in them—men that was sons of the sea as if 'twas the mother that bore them." O'Neill explains Yank's hunger for group identification in terms of his brutalizing childhood.

Under the traumatic shock of being called a filthy beast and discovering a clean, neat world which excludes him, Yank regresses to his primitive, animal unconscious; he is able to find belongingness again only at the zoo in front of the ape's cage. In this work, O'Neill found a striking symbol and an impelling, expressionistic form in which to clothe his Jungian theme (although Strindberg's The Dream Play, in which the two coal-heavers sit in despair at their rejection by the rich, may also have been influential).

Two years later, in All God's Chillun Got Wings, there is further evidence of Jungian influence. The play is a study of a white girl's marriage to a Negro and her schizophrenic regression to childhood as her emotions of love clash with her racial memory of hatred for Negroes. Her unconscious fears are symbolized by a Congo mask which grows larger and more menacing until she is driven to stabbing it with a knife.

The Negro she marries is ambitious to be a lawyer, but painfully shy in a white class at law school. His sense of inferiority (not developed in clearly Adlerian concepts) is derived from his childhood sensitivity about his color. As children the white girl and the Negro boy had played together, innocent of color barriers. After she has suffered her mental breakdown, the girl would return to the happy security of childhood and invites her husband to play with her again as they did as children—"Pretend you're Painty Face and I'm Jim Crow"—a poignant dramatization of psychotic regression. Perhaps the most Freudian element in O'Neill to date is his use of the childhood scene at the beginning of the play as a preparation for the later regression. At the Provincetown première, there was an attempt to suppress the play because of its theme of intermarriage, and the City of New York withheld permits for the child actors to play. Rather than cut the first scene which was felt to be psychologically integral, the stage manager, James Light, read the scene to the audience. The play disappointed critics such as Heywood Broun who hoped that a message of interracial understanding would emerge. Yet it proved an effective study of the disintegration of an ego under the conflicting pressures of love and guilt feelings—of alternating gratitude to Jim and shame for having married him. Ella's moments of reality and irrationality are perhaps compressed for dramatic effect, but highly effective is the schizoid debate which she conducts with herself: "No, he didn't hear you. Yes, he did too . . . What are you lying about? I'm not!" In this way, *All God's Chillun Got Wings* marks an original use of soliloquy in O'Neill's search for ways to dramatize the unconscious.

MASKS

Of all Jung's intriguing and quasi-scientific concepts, none was more widely known than his two character-types, *introverts* and *extraverts*. The introvert, according to Jung, turns in upon himself, is absorbed in his inner world; the cause is ". . . a turning inward of the libido whereby . . . interest does not move towards the objective but recedes towards the subject." The extravert, on the other hand, turns his libido outward and expresses a positive interest in objects of the outside world. An individual, however, is not at all times exclusively

an introvert or extravert. Jung developed the phenomenon of char-
acter-splitting, based on Janet's views of dissociation, pointing out
that an individual may appear very different to others in a social
situation than he actually is in his private *soul* or *animus* (the feminine of the spirit is *anima*). The words of Jung which particularly
illuminate O'Neill's handling of masks are these:

> Through his more or less complete identification with the
> attitude of the moment, he at least deceives others, and
> also often himself, as to his real character. He puts on a
> mask, which he knows corresponds with his conscious in-
> tentions, while it also meets with the requirements and
> opinions of his environment, so that first one motive and
> then the other is in the ascendant. The mask, viz. the ad hoc
> adopted attitude, I have called the *persona*, which was the
> designation given to the mask worn by the actors of an-
> tiquity.

O'Neill first made use of the mask in the 1922 production of *The
Hairy Ape*, which utilized a group of masked and expressionistically
caricatured churchgoers in the Fifth Avenue scene. The mask was
already enjoying a considerable artistic popularity under the influence of Gordon Craig, and was used by Robert Edmond Jones in
his designs for Hopkins' production of *Macbeth*. O'Neill, Macgowan
and Jones used masks at the Provincetown for Strindberg's *The Spook
Sonata* and for O'Neill's version of Coleridge's *The Ancient Mariner*
(1924) in which a masked chorus of six old sailors appeared as
drowned men pantomiming the story. In *The Fountain*, O'Neill used
a mask for Death in the delusions of Juan Ponce de Leon, and again
in *All God's Chillun* the Congo mask appears as omnipresent symbol
of the Negro race.

These uses of masks, however, were relatively traditional. It
was not until *The Great God Brown* (1926) that a playwright used
the mask in the sense that Jung visualized—to dramatize the discrepancy between the private *animus* of the individual and the social
personality which he must put forth for others to see.

The close parallel with Jung's *persona* is indicated by O'Neill's
own *Memoranda on Masks* in which he states:

> . . . for certain types of plays, especially for the new mod-
> ern play, the use of masks will be discovered to be the
> freest solution of the modern dramatist's problem as to how
> . . . he can express those profound hidden conflicts of the
> mind which the probings of psychology continue to dis-
> close to us. He must find some method to present this inner

drama in his work, or confess himself incapable of portraying one of the most characteristic preoccupations and uniquely significant spiritual impulses of our time. . . . What at bottom is the new psychological insight into human cause and effect but a study in masks, an exercise in unmasking?

O'Neill's first exercise in unmasking was *The Great God Brown,* a brilliant, original *tour-de-force* in the history of the drama. As much in debt to Nietzsche as to Jung, O'Neill names his leading character Dion Anthony, representing: "Dionysus and St. Anthony—the creative pagan acceptance of life, fighting eternal war with the masochistic, life-denying spirit of Christianity as represented by St. Anthony."

When we first meet Dion he is masked, his own spiritual, child-like faith in life hidden by the mocking, defiant expression of a sensual young Pan:

> (The mask) . . . which he puts on as a boy is not only a defense against the world for the super-sensitive painter-poet underneath it, but also an integral part of his character as an artist. The world is not only blind to the man beneath it but it also sneers at and condemns the Pan-mask it sees. After that Dion's inner self retrogresses along the line of Christian resignation until it partakes of the nature of the Saint while at the same time the outer Pan is slowly transformed by his struggle with reality into Mephistopheles.

Pitted against Dion is Billy Brown, successful in business but inwardly resourceless. The plot is the struggle between Billy and Dion. Without creative power himself, Billy covets the things that Dion possesses. First it is the girl, Margaret, whom Billy loves; but Margaret, removing her mask, confides to the Moon that she loves Dion. Her stream-of-consciousness asides foreshadowing *Strange Interlude,* she thinks out loud even as Billy makes love to her: "Dion is the moon and I'm the sea. I want to feel the moon kissing the sea . . ." Symbolically akin to Goethe's Marguerite, on whom O'Neill modeled her, Margaret is Earth-Mother, wife and daughter to her men, and croons, "Dion is my Daddy-O!" She fails to comprehend Dion's sensitive inner nature, however, and when Dion removes his mask she recoils from him in horror. O'Neill achieves poetic eloquence as Dion cries out his need for ego-defenses: "Why am I afraid of love, I who love love? . . . Why was I born without a skin, O God, that I must wear armor in order to touch or to be touched?" Secure once again in his mask, Dion marries Margaret.

Seven years later Dion is a drunken failure at painting and his

mask has turned Mephistophelean. Bergler, a more recent psychoanalyst, might term his inability to function as an artist "painter's
block." O'Neill here uses the first specifically psychoanalytic terminology in his dramas as Dion, starting to turn to the Bible, stops
himself with: "Blah! Fixation on old Mama Christianity. You infant,
blubbering in the dark, you!" Then Margaret goes to the successful
Billy Brown to plead for a job for Dion. Needing his genius to save
his own architectural work from being pedestrian, Billy hires him.
Having bought his talent, Billy even covets the prostitute Cybel, "an
unmoved idol of Mother Earth," to whom Dion has turned for
mothering and sympathy. A memory of his father, whose business
Billy bought out, causes Dion to take off his mask and soliloquize in
the most revealing psychoanalytic speech of the play. Of his father,
Dion says:

> What aliens we were to each other! When he lay dead, his
> face looked so familiar that I wondered where I had met
> that man before. Only at the second of my conception. After
> that, we grew hostile with concealed shame. And my
> mother? I remember a sweet, strange girl, with affection-
> ate, bewildered eyes as if God had locked her in a dark
> closet without any explanation. I was the sole doll our ogre,
> her husband, allowed her and she played mother and child
> with me for many years in that house until at last through
> two tears I watched her die with the shy pride of one who
> has lengthened her dress and put up her hair. And I felt
> like a foresaken toy and cried to be buried with her, be-
> cause her hands alone had caressed without clawing . . .
> so I shrank away, back into life, with naked nerves jump-
> ing like fleas, and in due course of nature another girl called
> me her boy in the moon and married me and became three
> mothers in one person. . . .

If this explanation for the super-sensitive Dion and his need for
the mask of Pan had come earlier and had in fact been dramatized
rather than soliloquized, our empathy with Dion might have been
considerably increased. As it is, Dion is rather inexplicable when we
first meet him—an unsympathetic weakling rather than a tragic hero.
Nor is the psychology of Billy explored at a very deep level, although
we are told he has an aloof mother and a father who is frustrated
professionally by Dion's father.

There are other unmistakably Freudian derivatives in this mask-
play. Dion kisses his own mask at one point, saying, "Peace, poor
tortured one, brave pitiful pride of man, the hour of our deliverance
comes"—a striking dramatic realization of the concept of Narcissism!

At another point Dion recalls a repressed memory of himself at four years of age, and Billy destroying a picture Dion was making in the sand because he couldn't do as well. The latent homosexuality in the ambivalent relation of love and hate between the two men is made clear when Billy confesses loving Margaret and Dion replies:

> No! That is merely the appearance, not the truth! Brown loves me! He loves me because I have always possessed the power he needed for love, because I am love!

For that Brown calls him a drunken bum and chokes him until Dion dies. Brown then removes Dion's mask and puts it on his own face. When Margaret enters, Billy passes himself as Dion, and kisses her so passionately she exclaims, "Why Dion? Aren't you ashamed? You haven't kissed me like that in ages." Later the homosexual theme is confirmed as Billy kisses Dion's mask, saying to it, "I love you because she loves you! My kisses on your lips are for her."

The psychological concept of introjection, by which one individual takes another's personality within him and unconsciously plays that role is nowhere in drama more stunningly theatricalized. And yet on the literal level, the play grows far-fetched at this point, asking us to believe that Billy, role-playing as Dion, could live with Margaret and convince her and the three sons that he is Dion. In order to deceive the office personnel, Billy-Dion does much running in and out, changing masks and contriving—to the point that the play comes dangerously close to ribald farce. Had the entire story been told in more expressionistic grotesquerie as Toller, Strindberg or Evreinov might have done, the concept of changed roles might have been successful. In the framework of psuedo-realism, however, it is nearer to the absurd.

By Act IV, even Billy finds the pretense too incredible to continue, and announces that Brown is dead—the mask of Brown being carried in as if it were a body. By this point, an expressionistic symbol has run away with the play.

In his "Memoranda on Masks," O'Neill said that Goethe's truth for our psychoanalytic century is that "Mephistopheles and Faust are one and the same—are Faust." This same truth is articulated by Cybel, the Earth-Mother, in whose arms Billy dies. She somehow senses that Dion and Brown were in fact one man. "Go to sleep, Billy," she murmurs. Billy answers the prostitute: "Yes, Mother. It was dark and I couldn't see where I was going and they all picked on me." His death is a regression to childhood, and Cybel reports to the police captain that his name was "Man."

In spite of its shortcomings, the originality of conception in *The*

Great God Brown makes it unique in American drama. If O'Neill
uses the masks more for Jungian introversion-extraversion than for
Freudian conscious-unconscious, he is on the road that is to lead him
to his masterworks; it is likely that O'Neill himself sensed the theatrical trickery of the masks, for he used them only once again and then
abandoned them. In *The Great God Brown,* however, Goethe, Nietzsche, Jung and Freud converge in moments of magnificence.

O'NEILL'S PRIMAL FATHER

Freud's first major book after his break with Jung was somewhat
indebted to Jung for the concept of the racial unconscious. *Totem
and Taboo* (1913) drew anthropological data from Frazer's *The
Golden Bough* in order to show the similarities between the obsessive
practices of neurotics and the rituals of primitive peoples. The universal taboo against incest among savages led Freud to suspect an
unconscious Oedipal drive toward incest—otherwise why would the
taboo have been so universally necessary? Linked with this was the
taboo against killing the sacred or totem animal or bird, except when
the tribe as a whole kills and eats it as a ritual.

It was Freud's hypothesis that the "primal horde" in the pre-
history of man consisted of a cluster of females dominated by an all-
powerful male ruler who drives away his growing sons. The sons
ultimately kill and eat the primal father. Then, to atone for their
guilt and prevent further strife over the females, they agree not to
enjoy the spoils but to seek women outside the tribe. The death of
the father is absolved by a commemorative feast in which the totem
animal, a substitute for the father, is ceremoniously eaten by the
whole tribe, shared equally as their guilt is shared. "Thus they
created two fundamental taboos of totemism out of the *sense of
guilt of the son,* and for this very reason these had to correspond
with the two repressed wishes of the Oedipus complex."

This concept of totem and taboo has been applied directly in
literature by Thomas Mann in his Biblical novels, *Joseph and His
Brothers,* and *Young Joseph.* The parallel is so strong that Engel and
others have concluded that *Totem and Taboo,* which O'Neill is
known to have read, furnished the germ of the theme for his *Desire Under the Elms* (1924).

O'Neill sets the stage for *Desire Under the Elms* with this use
of psychoanalytic symbolism:

> Two enormous elms are on each side of the house. They
> bend their trailing branches down over the roof. They ap-
> pear to protect and at the same time subdue. There is a

sinister maternity in their aspect, a crushing, jealous ab-
sorption. They have developed from their intimate contact
with the life of man in the house an appalling humaneness.
They brood oppressively over the house. They are like exhausted women resting their sagging breasts and hands and
hair on its roof, and when it rains their tears trickle down
monotonously and rot on the shingles.

The elms are the only soft things on this rock-ribbed farm, however.
In Ephraim Cabot, O'Neill creates the prototype of the primal
father, hard, all-powerful, ruthless. Cabot brings home his third
wife, Abbie, and thereby revives the hostility of his three sons,
Simeon, Peter and the youngest, Eben, a brooding neurotic who
violently hates his father for driving his Maw with whom he has
identified into her grave. Eben goes to the same village prostitute
whom his father has patronized, and with this introduction of the
sexual jealousy motif, we are prepared to watch the growing hostility
between the new Maw and the boys. The older two, in a kind of
mawkish, leering defiance, taunt their father and leave for California (the rebellion of the sons). The dialogue here is charged with
the *Totem and Taboo* motif, as Simeon says to his father:

Simeon: (With his sardonic burst of laughter) Ha! Eben's
    a chip o' yew—spit'n image—hard 'n bitter's a hickory
    tree! Dog'll eat dog. He'll eat ye yet, old man!
Cabot: (Commandingly) Ye git t' wuk!
Simeon: (as Abbie disappears in house—winks at Peter and
    says tauntingly) So that thar's our new Maw, be it?
    Whar in hell did ye dig her up? (He and Peter laugh.)
Peter: Ha! Ye'd better turn her in the pen with the other
    sows. (They laugh uproariously, slapping their thighs.)
Cabot: (so amazed at their effrontery that he stutters in con-
    fusion) Simeon! Peter! What's come over ye? Air ye
    drunk?
Simeon: We're free, old man—free o' yew an' the hull
    damned farm! (They grow more and more hilarious and
    excited.)
Peter: An' we're startin' out fur the gold fields o' Californi-a!
Simeon: Ye kin take this place an' burn it!
Peter: An' bury it—fur all we cares!
Simeon: We're free, old man! (He cuts a caper.)
Peter: Free! (He gives a kick in the air.)
Simeon: (in a frenzy) Whoop!
Peter: Whoop! (They do an absurd Indian war dance about
    the old man who is petrified between rage and the fear
    that they are insane.)

> Simeon: We're free as Injuns! Lucky we don't skulp ye!
> Peter: An' burn yer barn an' kill the stock!
> Simeon: An' rape yer new woman! Whoop! (He and Peter
>   stop their dance, holding their sides, rocking with wild
>   laughter.)

They throw rocks that penetrate the window of the room where Abbie is, and caper off.

The plot then centers on Abbie's possessive struggle for the farm which Eben regards as his. Abbie's way of dominating Eben is to tempt him seductively, though Eben fiercely fights her off. Lusting for Eben, Abbie tells Cabot that Eben has attempted to seduce her—an illustration of the classic Phaedra mechanism of projection.

To prevent Eben's getting the farm, Abbie realizes she must bear Ephraim a son. In a scene of powerful sexual undercurrents, O'Neill shows us the two bedrooms simultaneously—Eben alone and brooding in his, and the married couple in theirs—the father strangely excited by the thought of another son and Abbie fiercely concentrating on the sounds from Eben's bedroom. Ephraim tells in a highly revealing speech how he punished himself by a life of farming in rocky, forbidding soil, his pleasure in hard work a masochistic denial of his repressed sexual needs. Now, however, Abbie is so unresponsive to him that he goes down to the barn:

> Down whar it's restful—whar it's warm—down t' the barn.
> I kin talk t' the cows. They know. They know the farm an'
> me. They'll give me peace.

Eben is torn between his desire for and his resentment of Abbie, but she finally leads him to the parlor that hadn't been opened since his mother died. Eben strongly feels the presence of his mother in the room and talks to her. He senses that his mother would approve his union with Abbie—as a way of revenging herself on Cabot. Acting the role of Eben's mother-image, Abbie externalizes for him his infantile wish to return to his mother. Their kisses are but momentarily pure however and then surge into fierce passion. After their night of love, Eben is bold, confident and at peace with himself, his Oedipal feelings purged; now his mother can sleep in her grave. Ephraim too slept peacefully with the cows and is even able to smile with his son. The old primal hatred of father and son seems worked out. Eben chuckles, "I'm the prize rooster o' this roost."

When Abbie bears a son, however, Ephraim taunts Eben that the farm now belongs to the new child. Hamlet-like, Eben goes into a state of shock at his betrayal by Abbie; but Abbie is sincerely in love with Eben now—and is desolate at his thought of leaving for

California. To prove that her love transcends her materialistic grasping for the farm, she smothers her baby. Eben goes voluntarily with Abbie and the Sheriff who comes to get her at the final ironic curtain of this masterful exploration of the dark and murderous impulses confined within the Cabots' rockbound environment.

Kenneth Macgowan had let O'Neill read the manuscript of Sidney Howard's *They Knew What They Wanted* just before O'Neill began to write *Desire*, and O'Neill may have been unconsciously influenced. In both plays a woman marries an older man—a landowner—and bears a child by a younger man. But there the comparisons cease—or should, unless Howard's play is to suffer thereby. For where his play is photographic, O'Neill's throbs with brooding passion and pervading Jungian mystery—the elms, the cows and Abbie herself all as maternal symbols. To Freud's primal father O'Neill has added Jung's primal mother—and derived a tragedy from the clash of the two. O'Neill's personal resources fused with the savage impulses laid bare in Freud's *Totem and Taboo* for the pattern of his primitive masterpiece.

That the same pen which wrote *Desire* could also turn out the elegantly satiric treatment of Marco Polo in *Marco Millions* (1928) is a mark of versatility. There is little that is specifically Freudian in *Marco Millions* except the general theme that the Babbitts and merchants have always been too busy making money to achieve fulfillment of love. Only one Jungian symbol was allowed to slip in—a reference to a Chinese dragon-god, "our ancient symbol of Yang, the celestial, male principle of the Cosmos." Marco also at one point catches himself almost succumbing to the enchanting princess who loves him, and apologizes:

> My only excuse is, I forgot myself. I guess I'll have to stop overworking or I'll suffer a nervous breakdown. I felt like one of these figures in a puppet show with someone jerking the wires. It wasn't me, you understand. My lips spoke without me saying a word.

STRANGE DARK INTERLUDE

The "lips that spoke without me saying a word" brought O'Neill to the outstanding example in drama of the conflict between words and feelings. O'Neill's search for dramatic devices to penetrate the conscious surface of the personality culminated in 1928 in his masterpiece, *Strange Interlude*.

There is a conspicuous change in O'Neill's work beginning with *Strange Interlude*. To account for this we have evidence that O'Neill himself underwent psychoanalysis in 1927—the year in which he was at work on *Interlude*. He had been drinking heavily for some years without being able to stop. His marital difficulties (out of which *Welded* grew) weighed heavily upon him. His attitude toward sex, as reflected in all his plays from *Diff'rent* on, suggests a strongly guilt-ridden *super-ego* which splits sexuality into conflicting sensual and tender impulses—not to be united in an attitude of acceptance until *Strange Interlude*. Dr. Gilbert V. Hamilton, a Freudian psychiatrist, had obtained a grant to study six individuals through psychoanalysis, and O'Neill is reported to have been one of the six. During psychoanalysis Dr. Hamilton cured O'Neill's alcoholism and very likely saved his life thereby. (The findings of Hamilton's study were privately published for doctors under the title *Research in Marriage* and later popularized by Kenneth Macgowan and Hamilton as *What is Wrong With Marriage?*) The Freudian analyst, Gregory Zilboorg, has praised the insight of *Strange Interlude* and its effective dramatization of the stratification which makes us all ". . . in our 'normal' daily life go on unsuspecting that we are but a sort of endless dynamic battlefield rather than a compact whole."

The nine acts of *Strange Interlude* began at 5:30 p.m. and featured intermission for dinner. (Woollcott waggishly commented in his review that one first-nighter brought a different lady after dinner.) In *Interlude* O'Neill hit upon a group of characters as appealingly normal and identifiable as his Dion, Eben and Michael Cape were atypical. Purged of the anxiety and guilt that characterized the American drama's first reaction to psychoanalysis, *Strange Interlude* for the first time rises to post-therapeutic insight and acceptance, achieving tragic universality. Nina Leeds is Everywoman, and her story is based upon the psychoanalytic idea that tragedy consists of searching for—and not finding—emotional wholeness or awareness of self. Nina had been in love with Gordon, an aviator during the war. Although they urgently wanted to get married before he went overseas, Nina's father, Professor Leeds, persuaded Gordon to wait. When he is killed Nina suffers a traumatic shock and later becomes a nurse at a veterans' hospital, giving herself compulsively and promiscuously to men as a form of masochistic punishment (or "undoing") for having denied herself to Gordon. Professor Leeds feels equally guilty over his motives and finds release only by confessing to Nina that in his own loneliness since his wife's death he had blocked Nina's marriage from unconsciously incestuous motives.

Hovering in the background of Nina's life is Charlie Marsden, with an "indefinable feminine quality about him . . . ," a writer of superficial novels that never dig beneath neat surfaces. Marsden has

a hauntingly persistent memory—of his one experience with a
woman, a dollar prostitute who disgusted him and made him
shamefully remember his mother, to whom he is pathetically attached. When Nina's father dies, Marsden finds himself stepping
into the role of father-image to Nina, experiencing blended sadistic
and erotic feelings toward her as she confesses her promiscuity to
him. Dr. Ned Darrell of the veterans' hospital sizes Marsden up
as ". . . one of those poor devils who spend their lives trying not
to discover which sex they belong to!" Cynically, Marsden thinks to
himself of Darrell's professional interest in psychiatry:

> I hope not psychoanalyst . . . a lot to account for, Herr
> Freud! punishment to fit his crimes, be forced to listen eter-
> nally during breakfast while innumerable plain ones tell
> him dreams about snakes . . . pah, what an easy cure-all!
> Sex the philosopher's stone. . . . "O Oedipus, O my king!
> The world is adopting you!"

Although O'Neill avoided making Darrell a psychoanalyst, he
sounds very much the analyst when he advises Nina to marry Sam
Evans: "She needs normal love objects for the emotional life Gordon's death blocked up in her." Nina does achieve security and
poise in her marriage to Sam, a boyish, superficial and dependent
young man. When she proudly expects a child, her happiness is
shattered by Sam's mother who reveals that there is hereditary insanity in Sam's family and that they must never have children. This
is a tenuous element in the plotting, for psychiatrists have been unable to verify that psychosis (with a very few exceptions such as
Huntington's chorea) is hereditary.

Nina is forced to have an abortion without Sam's knowledge
of her pregnancy, and he begins to feel himself a failure as a husband because they do not have a child. Darrell counsels Nina to bear
a child by some other man and let Sam think the child is his—to
preserve his mental health. Darrell, always attracted to Nina, is, of
course, the one she chooses, and though he pretends that it is in the
interest of science, they find themselves very quickly entangled in a
passionate and deeply satisfying love affair.

Marsden's mother dies and he is utterly bereft—the wide-eyed
dollar prostitute recurring compulsively in his thoughts now in a
rather deep level reflection of the death and sexuality theme as discussed by Freud in *Mourning and Melancholia*. Darrell struggles
to resist Nina's hold on him lest it destroy the objectivity needed in
his profession. He abruptly goes to Europe to free himself.

Nina names her son Gordon, and Sam finds a new life for himself in the role of father. But on his return, Darrell's love is un-diminished and Nina, the Earth-Mother, gathers around her Darrell, Marsden and Sam, saying:

> My three men! I feel their desires converge in me! ... to form one complete beautiful male desire which I absorb ... and am whole ... they dissolve in me, their life is my life. ... I am pregnant with the three! husband! ... lover! ... father! ... and the fourth man! ... little Gordon! he is mine, too! that makes it perfect!

Unable to pry Nina away from Sam and her son, Darrell goes off to the West Indies to bury himself in biological research. He re-turns when young Gordon is eleven, and the boy grows hostile with Oedipal anxiety when he glimpses his mother kissing Darrell. As the years pass, Nina's loathing for the now successful and fatuous Sam has grown; her death-wishes toward him are more frequent, and she is overly possessive about her grown son, Gordon. Jealous of the girl Gordon loves, Nina is about to tell the girl that she can never marry him because of the hereditary insanity; but Darrell prevails upon her not to. When Sam dies of a heart attack at Gordon's boat races, Darrell almost reveals by a Freudian slip of the tongue that he is Gordon's father, but finds that he cannot destroy Gordon's high conception of his mother, and returns to the peace he has found in his obscure research—with a young assistant as son-substitute. As Gordon soars overhead in a plane with his sweetheart, Nina feels her own helplessness, the inadequacy of motherhood and her in-ability to hold onto her son:

> My having a son was a failure, wasn't it? He couldn't give me happiness. Sons are always their fathers. They pass through the mother to become their father again.

Nina thus reverses the Jungian image which had been funda-mental throughout the play—that God was a Mother. Now she re-gresses to childhood and finds security curled up in the arms of Charlie Marsden, whom she marries. God proves to be a Father after all, and Nina concludes:

> ... our lives are merely strange dark interludes in the electrical display of God the Father.

It is the triumph of Freud's Father-God over Jung's Mother-Goddess at the end of this life-cycle of woman—a monument of psycho-analytic literature.

O'Neill tells his saga by means of asides and soliloquies—old in the drama but new to realism and never before used for the purpose of getting beneath the surface of consciously articulated speech to the deeper level of what Freud called "the pre-conscious," if not the truly unconscious. At times, it is true, O'Neill's asides are merely conscious thoughts that another character should not be told. At other times, as Brooks Atkinson has pointed out, the asides are merely repetitious and retard the action, saying nothing that couldn't be revealed in dialogue: "But when the 'aside' shows contrast, and when it releases a smouldering passion that cannot burn in the normal dialogue, it is impregnated with the very stuff of drama." In the production, the other actors on the stage simply stood still or "froze" while the person spoke his asides in a lower and more intimate voice. Perhaps himself sensing that the device could run away with the play as the masks did *Brown*, the asides grow less frequent as the play progresses. Many of the asides and soliloquies are truly free associations such as might be produced on the psychoanalyst's couch, disconnected, telegraphic, associative.

It would not be entirely accurate to call these speeches "Stream of Consciousness." The term coined by William James describes rather the *continuity* or *unbroken line* of mental processes. Clearly this is broken and disjointed, as is the flowing association of ideas. They have been called by some "Interior Monologues," and O'Neill termed them "thought asides." But "Stream of the Unconscious" or "free association soliloquies" would be more descriptive—the degree of freedom depending on the activity of the psychic censor. With this play O'Neill found a new dramatic form equal to the challenge of modern psychology, returning to our theatre that breadth of insight into the tragic maelstrom of human motives which has been only too rare since Sophocles, Shakespeare and Goethe. *Strange Interlude* won the Pulitzer Prize, ran 426 performances in New York, and occupies a unique place in the history of the American drama.

ELECTRICAL DISPLAYS

If there is a key to O'Neill's *Lazarus Laughed* (1926) it is not Freud but Nietzsche. Unproduced on Broadway, this play is built around Lazarus as a symbolic figure, representing the triumphant victory of Yea over Nay, affirmation over despair and denial. The tedious Zarathustran debates are the farthest that O'Neill has gone in the direction of mysticism and abstract metaphysics. But every playwright should be entitled to one closet-drama.

In spite of the Yea repeated and chorused throughout *Lazarus Laughed*, the victory was only a theoretical one for O'Neill. His next

play, *Dynamo* (1929) reflects none of the Dionysian ecstasy one
might expect from a Yea-saying Superman. Instead it depicts a guilt-
ridden neurotic, Reuben, for whom Nietzsche would hardly care to
claim credit.

Dynamo is a fantastic lightning-flash illuminating a nightmare.
Reuben is the son of a primal, tyrannical father, a sin-obsessed
preacher. Next door to him lives Ada with her father, who is a cynical atheist, and her mother, a mooning cow of Cybel's clan. Reuben
is passive-dependent, fearfully guilty over sex, and as frightened
of lightning as of his symbolically named father, Light. In wooing
Ada, Reuben identifies her with his mother, who in her Oedipal
jealousy calls Ada a harlot, a projection of her own guilty desires.
Reuben is stunned when his mother betrays his secret love for Ada to
the wrath and punishment of his father, who belts his son as Mrs.
Light watches in sadistic delight. Reuben flees from his home during
an electrical storm, taunting God to strike him dead with lightning
if there is a God. When nothing happens, Reuben overthrows God
and substitutes Electricity, a deity for whom he has been purged of
his fear.

Fifteen months after his mother's death, Reuben returns home
bluff and arrogant. He has found himself sexually now, and is able
to make love casually; he seduces Ada on his first night home. His
father confesses with shame that he destroyed each letter the mother
wrote to Reuben. The son now sublimates both his maternal longing
and father-hatred into his new religion of Electricity, and goes to the
generator room of the electric company where he apostrophizes the
dynamo:

> . . . a great dark idol . . . like the old stone statues of
> gods people prayed to . . . only it's living and they're dead
> . . . that part on top is like a head . . . with eyes that see
> you without seeing you . . . and below it is like a body
> . . . not a man's . . . round like a woman's as if it had
> breasts . . . but not like a girl . . . not like Ada . . . no,
> like a woman . . . like her mother . . . or mine . . . a
> great, dark mother! that's what the dynamo is! . . . that's
> what life is!

This startling, original symbol of the generator as the Earth-Mother
is Jungian mysticism projected into modern technology.

Still obsessed with guilt over his erotic dreams of Ada, Reuben
beats himself masochistically to suppress them, but without success.
By the end, he is completely psychotic, talking to the dynamo as a
son-suppliant, worshipping the elements as a neo-savage. Sure that

he has conquered his physical lust for Ada through his faith in dynamo, he would test himself and Ada with a pure kiss; but his passion is soon out of control and he possesses her on the floor of the dynamo room. Feeling that he has betrayed his mother, he calls Ada the harlot that his mother had called her, shoots Ada and throws himself against the high-voltage dynamo to die in a loving consummation of the wish to return to the womb.

The two themes of guilt over sexual desires and twentieth century worship of scientific materialism are both challenging ones; but neither is given adequate realization in this mawkish piece of playwriting. The author of *Strange Interlude* here uses the same asides and stream of the unconscious, but admitted in later memoirs that it was a mistake.

Even more serious a shortcoming was O'Neill's tendency to take far too seriously the transparent problems of his hopelessly neurotic hero and his compulsive parents—sorry spectacles in need of immediate psychiatric help rather than elevation to the heights required in the tragic drama. Adolescent preoccupation with sex-guilt may be given serious and poignant treatment as did Wedekind, Lawson and Rice, or it can be given delightfully humorous treatment as O'Neill was soon to do in *Ah, Wilderness!* But the electric current that could bring his *Dynamo* to life was apparently short-circuited, for it produced neither heat nor light.

Profiting from his mistake in *Dynamo*, O'Neill brought the psychoanalytic drama to its fullest fruition in *Mourning Becomes Electra* (1931). Deleting in the final version the masks and thought-asides used in earlier drafts, he nevertheless managed to achieve a pervading sense of unconscious motivation in this modern retelling of a Greek legend.

He tells in his work diary how he sought to get ". . . modern psychological approximation of Greek sense of fate into such a play, which an intelligent audience of today, possessed of no belief in gods or supernatural retribution, could accept and be moved by." O'Neill turned to the legend of Electra and her tragic relationship with her father, mother and brother—a story second only to the Oedipus saga as a source of psychoanalytic archetypes. O'Neill carried the story beyond the Greek dénouement—and if one may venture to hazard a judgment—improved on it, by developing the character of Electra beyond the ending of Euripides:

> In Greek story she peters out into undramatic married banality. Such a character contained too much tragic fate within her soul to permit this—why should Furies have let Electra escape unpunished?

O'Neill tells in this remarkable document of literary creativity how he selected the Civil War period for a "mask of time and space" and how he chose as background a wealthy New England house built with a Grecian façade—"grotesque perversion of everything Greek temple expressed of meaning of life . . . Puritan conviction of man born to sin and punishment—Orestes' furies within him, his conscience—."

Again employing the dinner intermission, *Mourning Becomes Electra* is a trilogy of three full-length plays, *The Homecoming, The Hunted* and *The Haunted*, which correspond to Aeschylus' *Agamemnon, The Choephori,* and *The Eumenides.* Agamemnon becomes Ezra Mannon, a victorious general returning from Grant's army. Gone is the legendary Iphigenia motif; instead the hostility of Ezra and his wife, Christine, is deeply rooted in the New England tradition of stern repression and ensuing guilt over sex, which perverted Christine's romantic love for her husband into loathing of his lustiness and the sublimation of her tender impulses upon her son, Orin (Orestes).

During the men's absence at war, Christine has taken a lover, Adam Brant (Aegisthus), whose motives stem partly if not wholly from revenge. His mother had been a nurse girl of the Mannons, and his father Ezra's uncle who was disinherited for the love affair. For modern audiences this is an improvement over the Atreus-Thyestes feud.

The most effective addition in O'Neill's reworking of the story is the magnificent speech he gives Ezra in *The Homecoming,* in which he humbly begs Christine to make a fresh start with him. This sets up the audience's empathy with Ezra to a far greater degree than we would feel for Agamemnon, bringing home as he did a concubine, Cassandra. In New England of the Civil War period, Cassandra had to go.

It is too late for fresh starts, however, and Christine contrives the death of Ezra. Her daughter, Lavinia (Electra), whose love for her father has inverted into abnormal intensity, must prove to Orin that their mother is guilty of adultery with Adam before Orin will conspire to avenge his father's death. When he has seen her aboard Adam's ship, he is ready to undertake the punishment; unlike the Aeschylean matricide, Orin and Lavinia kill only Adam and thereby drive their mother to immediate suicide. But Orin takes her death upon his conscience, becoming obsessed with his domestic Furies, the torments of guilt and psychic masochism. The psychoanalyst, Fritz Wittels, has pointed out that with the changed status of women since antiquity, Lavinia could become the driving demon and Orin the weaker of the two; he felt that the character bore resemblance not to a Greek model but more to the Austrian writer, Hugo von Hofmannsthal's *Electra*, "written about 1910 and directly inspired by Freud's investigations."

After the deed, the tormented brother begins to identify his sister with his mother and through the Freudian mechanism of transference, to fall in love with her.

Cut off from a possible marriage and trapped by Lavinia, he is ultimately goaded into suicide. Apparently free at last, Lavinia almost achieves happiness in marriage with Peter (Pylades). But her unconscious betrays her and in speaking to Peter she blurts out the name of Adam. She realizes that her unconscious love for Adam forever vitiates her revenge of her father's death and condemns her to relinquish Peter and retire alone to the ominous Mannon home, to live with the Mannon curse and expiate her guilt—as Wittels phrased it, ". . . to bury herself alive in the house of the Tantalides."

Through the dramatic use of the Freudian slip of the tongue, O'Neill creates the climax of his trilogy. Lacking the benign goddess, Athena, of Aeschylus' trilogy who ultimately purges Orestes of his guilt, there is no mitigation for the neurosis-ridden Mannon family of O'Neill's drama.

A number of psychologists have found interest in *Mourning Becomes Electra*, including Ives Hendrick, Joseph Jastrow and Fritz Wittels. The latter felt that the play showed "a profound knowledge of Freud's incest complex" and was unquestionably a masterpiece.

In form, the play is as sternly restrained as O'Neill's earlier work was effusive, using soliloquy occasionally and making use of the portraits of ancestors on the walls to symbolize the oppressive power of the super-ego, the life-denying sterility of the Puritan conscience. If O'Neill had told his story with a greater command of poetic language and variation from the oppressive monochrome of morbidity (which the Greeks achieved through spectacle, dance, and the lyric chorus), there would be no doubt that *Mourning Becomes Electra* belongs with the Greeks, Shakespeare, and Goethe. Even with its shortcomings, it is probably one of the two most important tragedies written in America.

The marshalling of a musical language, lacking in *Mourning Becomes Electra*, was the principal asset of a version of the same legend by the California poet, Robinson Jeffers. In *The Tower Beyond Tragedy*, written in 1924-25 but not seen in New York until 1950, Jeffers uses the incest theme "to symbolize the plight of introverted humanity." Aware of the connection between his approach and the dream-studies of Freud and Jung, Jeffers develops the incestuous brother-sister love of Electra and Orestes to the point where she exhorts him to physical intimacy—a symbol for the ultimate in the degradation which Jeffers believes all sex to be. Using a loudspeaker by which Cassandra speaks with the voice of the dead Agamemnon, *The Tower Beyond Tragedy* proved to be lifeless in the theatre. A third version of the same material, Robert Turney's *Daughters of Atreus* (1936) sacrificed psychological analysis to its anti-war theme.

TWO SIDES OF THE COIN

While O'Neill was at work on his next play, *Days Without End,* an idea for a comedy was said to have come to him in a dream, and he put the tragedy down, completed *Ah, Wilderness!* in six weeks, and then resumed work on *Days.* Whether this is true, *Ah, Wilderness!* does suggest that this tragic writer had suddenly had a flash of insight that caused him to say, "I've been taking these things too seriously—this Oedipal hostility of father and son, adolescent guilt over sex, and outgrowing mother-love—it should be with a smile and not a sob." In a kind of day dream of wish-fulfillment, O'Neill creates in *Ah, Wilderness!* an idealized picture of boyhood (for his had had little of the gracious charm of the Miller family). With humor and delight in average people he resolves the father-son conflict with a chuckle and with the adult insight that was so lacking in his toosober treatment of Michael Cape, Curtis Jason, Dion Anthony, Reuben Light—and also, unfortunately, in the character then being born for *Days Without End,* John Loving.

Adolescent Richard Miller suffers guilt feelings over his curiosity about sex, and would be a radical as well. O'Neill sees that Richard's radicalism is an unconscious rebellion against all authority and particularly that of his father. Contrasted ways of raising children are shown, with the girl's father practising secrecy and suppression.

Uncle Sid, one of O'Neill's most rounded characters, drinks too heavily, and Lily, whom he loves and who loves him, has been unable to marry him because, like her prototype, Emma of *Diff'rent,* she was revolted by his taking up with "bad women" sixteen years ago.

There are many other fingerprints of the old O'Neill, but they are light touches only—Muriel is "tied to her father's apron-strings" and afraid even to kiss Richard. Nat has a "reminiscent obsession" to recount the story of his saving a boy from drowning at the age of twelve. There is one long soliloquy at the start of the beach scene, in which Richard thinks aloud in free association, remembering the prostitute, Belle, and transfers his erotic thoughts to Muriel.

Nat's lecture to his son on sex is a priceless bit of embarrassment and confusion. Drawing the line of duality between "nice girls" and whores, he can get as far as to urge his son to protect himself: "I mean, there are ways and means—" and can get no farther. He concludes, "But hell, I suppose you boys talk all this over among yourselves and you know more about it than I do." Nat and his devoted wife, Essie, conclude that ". . . no matter what life will do to him, he can take care of it now," and the curtain falls on a nostalgic scene of affection between the couple in the autumn of their lives.

Days Without End (1934), however, belongs in the sequence of O'Neill's development as a tragic writer seeking to enlarge our drama with new forms to express unconscious motivation. From *Welded*, to *The Great God Brown*, to *Strange Interlude* the line culminates (and terminates) in *Days Without End*. Here O'Neill uses two actors to represent one individual—the inner and outer nature of the hero, John Loving.

A number of interesting themes occur in the play—the death wish from *Mourning*, *Interlude* and *The First Man*, the question of the extent to which an author's work is consciously or unconsciously autobiographical, and the religious theme—which caused some critics to jump to the conclusion that O'Neill had espoused the Catholic Church. Although this is O'Neill's first formal approach to religious drama, critics who followed his career with a psychoanalytic eye should not have been surprised—there is latent in many of his earlier plays the unconscious search for Godhead and the need for the security of the omnipotent Mother- or Father-image.

The hero of *Days Without End* is an author, John Loving, with an ambivalent nature: John is the well-intentioned, sincere husband, and Loving, played by the second actor, is the cynical *defensemechanism* or reaction formation, sneering at all decent sentiments and wishing his wife would die. Loving, treated at a relatively conscious level, represents a blocked *Id* drive, distorted into a "sneer of scornful mockery." The debates between them suggest the medieval morality plays with the inevitable struggle between Vice and Good Deeds. When Loving makes snide remarks, others can hear them and John treats them as slips of the tongue—(a rather extreme slip as it is another tongue).

An uncle, priest and father-surrogate, Father Baird, tries to find an *end* (in the Adlerian sense of goal or objective) for John's aimless days. Balked in the novel he is writing, John confesses that he is haunted by fear that his beloved wife Elsa might die—yet in the novel the wife is made to die. The novel is, of course, autobiographical; it deals with a man who adored his parents, lost them in a flu epidemic, and gave up his faith in God as a result of his unfulfilled prayers.

Adoring Elsa as he does, John has been unable to prevent his cynical other self from a tawdry affair with Lucy Hillman at a drunken party. Dr. Martin W. Peck, a psychoanalyst, has written an interesting interpretation of this play in which he attempts to explain the basis of such experiments in adultery by apparently devoted husbands:

> In his youth death had rudely deprived him of parental love. To his anxious mind, a happy marriage brought with it the danger that this early sorrow and anguish would be repeated. On the basis of well-established facts in medical psychology, this sense of danger precipitated the hatred which may be understood in the nature of self-defense against a new injury.

In other words, Loving's compulsion to destroy love comes from the fear and panic at the thought that Elsa might be lost to him through death or infidelity on her part. When Elsa learns of her husband's infidelity (through a tightly structured scene in which details in his novel parallel the story of Lucy's affair) Elsa goes for a walk in the rain to struggle with her wounded pride and her awareness of her husband's death-wish toward her. She returns in a fever which makes her gravely ill. Now the thing John had dreaded and Loving had unconsciously willed is threatened. In panic John rushes to the church and flings himself at the foot of a cross, praying for Elsa's recovery. Behind him Loving rages and storms in Mephistophelean mockery—until news arrives of Elsa's improvement. Loving sees he cannot fight the power of God, and sinks to his knees, dead. Spiritually exalted, John Loving is now whole, one individual no longer split by inner conflict. Yea-saying John Loving proclaims, "Life laughs with God's love again! Life laughs with love!"

Little wonder that critics were baffled to see the old iconoclast, O'Neill, finding solace in the arms of the church. Dr. Peck points out a more psychoanalytic explanation, however, to the effect that John Loving attains a unified personality reconstructed by a release of aggression to which he had been a slave. For the first time he is able to achieve a love relationship without doubt, protest or reservation. Future biographers of O'Neill must necessarily pay great attention to *Days Without End* as the key to O'Neill's lifelong struggle between the yea-saying forces of love and the nay-saying forces which compulsively destroy love lest love be destroyed. If John Loving found his spiritual end in life, however, it was a short-lived reconciliation for O'Neill, whose next play was the most deeply pessimistic and anti-religious of any he wrote.

MISBEGOTTEN SOULS

Broadway was without a new O'Neill play for twelve years between *Days Without End* and *The Iceman Cometh*. O'Neill chose not to try to cope with the depression or World War II. His general reaction to both cataclysms was, however, contained in the shattering cynicism of *The Iceman Cometh* (1946).

For the summing up of his philosophy, O'Neill goes back to the early roots of his experience—back to Jimmy-the-Priest's saloon and flop-house which served as setting for the first act of *Anna Christie*. Here he assembles a grotesque and motley assortment of human driftwood. The theme of the play is stated symphonically at the outset and then developed with variations: "The lie of a pipe dream is what gives life to the whole misbegotten mad lot of us, drunk or sober." If for the words "pipe dream," we read "ego-defense," the play becomes valid as psychoanalytic drama.

Harry Hope's saloon is a dead end of hopelessness; yet each of the characters O'Neill places there lives with his private pipe dream or rationalization; there are two prostitutes who prefer to think of themselves as "tarts" rather than as "whores," and are particular that no one call them the latter; there is a Negro who had unconsciously been striving for "whiteness"—for acceptance by the majority group; there is a bartender who thinks of himself as a "protector" of the girls rather than as "pimp"; there is a couple who bicker their lives away while planning to get married, and several alcoholics who have various alibis for their weakness; there is a guilt-ridden young son of a famous free-thinking woman anarchist and IWW, now in prison, who has come to win acceptance and absolution from the man who was his childhood father-image and the lover of his mother. Finally, there is Harry Hope himself, who was formerly a ward heeler but hasn't been out of his saloon in twenty years from grief over his wife's death.

To this collection of failures living on the narcotic of illusion, O'Neill brings Hickey, a salesman formerly famous for the drunken parties he threw at Harry's. This trip, however, Hickey comes as a sobered and reformed man, having just lost his beloved wife. Hickey has learned that he could find peace only by accepting himself and rejecting the lies and defense mechanisms he had set up. One by one he tries to convert the others to face themselves honestly and accept their roles without sham. They respond to Hickey and one by one try to sober up and pull themselves back to reality. A brilliant Harvard law student whose father was in prison for graft shakes himself out of the alcoholic doldrums and goes to see about getting his old job back. The bickering couple go off to be married, and Harry Hope goes for a walk in the ward for the first time in twenty years. The Negro has a resurgence of pride in his race and stops pretending he is "white." Two old drunk army officers also unburden—one was a coward in battle and one used regimental funds to get drunk on. By the end of the third act, all the derelicts have thrown away their psychic crutches and gone out to restore their contact with reality. The suspense is real as we wait to see if their conversion lasts.

In Act IV each of them comes back to get drunk again, broken and defeated. The couple didn't marry, the colored man couldn't get backing for his Negro gambling parlor, and the law student couldn't get his job back. Harry Hope was so frightened by the first auto as he crossed the street that he scurried back to the saloon for cover. The guilt-ridden son masochistically retches out the confession that he hated his mother and informed on her to get money to spend on a floozy. A drunk who claimed his wife's infidelity drove him to drink is able to admit that he drank before her infidelity and that his inadequacy as a husband drove her to infidelity. The young son kills himself, and even Hickey confesses his own burden—that he killed his wife because she had been so loving and forgiving for all his escapades and infidelities. He couldn't stand her pipe dream of him and her inevitable forgiveness. By the time Hickey calls the detectives to arrest him, the others have all agreed they cannot face life honestly and have all gone back to the security of their alcoholic pipe dreams.

This cheerless picture of human frailty is an antidote for all the easy and glib conversion plays. Comparison with Gorki's *The Lower Depths* is inevitable, but the Russian playwright held out real hope at the end of his exploration of the depths; degradation is man-made and can be changed. Only the weak need illusions—the strong find their religion in truth. Especially through children can progress be made, Satine exclaims: "A man is born to conceive a better man." By contrast with this optimism, O'Neill's play is less psychoanalytic than Gorki's. Only two of O'Neill's characters appear to be the product of childhood influences on their personality—Hickey as a strict minister's son and the son of the anarchist woman whose ambivalence and guilt feelings stem from the insecurity of seeing a parade of assorted men coming home to make love to his mother. For the rest, O'Neill has no psychoanalytic explanation to offer—rather he intends the characters symbolically to represent humanity itself—but the symbols are unflattering, to say the least. The title derives from Hickey's mordant joke—that he found his wife at home in bed with the iceman—who is Death.

The weakness of the play is its interminable length and the lack of plot complication. The psychological truth which he chose to illustrate is done an injustice by the characters he uses as evidence. O'Neill's adamant denials of indebtedness to Freud are doubly ironic when we read *The Iceman Cometh*, so bereft of the dynamic promise of betterment for the human race which modern psychotherapy envisions. O'Neill's life-long pursuit of faith here reached a dead-end. If *The Iceman* (Death) *Cometh* is the summation of his quest for meaning, then his days have been truly without end.

A year after *The Iceman Cometh*, O'Neill's *A Moon for the Misbegotten*, the first of a projected cycle of plays, was tried out on the road and then abandoned. In 1952, with no prospects for its production, it was made available in a published version eagerly awaited by O'Neill's admirers. It contains a number of surprises and rewards.

For the first time since *Strange Interlude*, O'Neill has built a play around a woman character who is appealing in her universal humanity. For the first time since *Desire Under the Elms*, he has created a powerful peasant drama of primitive emotions. But *A Moon* is mellowed and enriched with the humor which was missing in *Desire Under the Elms*. There is a character that strongly suggests autobiography, and a new psychoanalytic element that O'Neill has not previously used—the concept of *kidding* and raillery as a defense mechanism.

The leading character of *A Moon for the Misbegotten* is Josie, a unique and superbly drawn character. She is oversized, 5'11", powerful, but womanly in proportion. She is the daughter of a tenant farmer, Phil Hogan, a primal father gone sarcastic, shrewd and crafty. The part cries out for Barry Fitzgerald in its tangy, ingratiating Irish humor.

Josie's brother Mike hates his father and escapes to town with Josie's help, leaving the stage free for the main action just as did the brothers in *Desire Under the Elms*. The seemingly autobiographical character is James Tyrone, Jr., a drunken son of a famous actor, who is groping to find himself and waiting a sizeable legacy from the estate of his recently deceased mother. He is a more cynical and worldly version of Reuben Light, Orin Mannon and Eben Cabot, with Dion Anthony's Mephistophelean dissipation on his face.

Josie has been promiscuous, and her father has ". . . a strange, embarrassed look" when the subject is mentioned, which suggests that the unconscious bond between father and daughter is the Electra-Agamemnon relationship. Phil even says that he is glad Josie is promiscuous—otherwise she might have married and he would not have her company and help on the farm.

Now Phil urges Josie to set her cap for Tyrone, who is their landlord and who may sell the farm out from under them. A rich and pompous land-owning neighbor comes to upbraid Phil for letting his pigs get to the icepond, but the raucous, mocking going-over which the neighbor gets at the hands of Phil and Josie is one of the comic classics of the modern drama. They turn the tables by accusing the neighbor of plotting to give their pigs their death of cold at the pond, and Josie's leering "Meet me tonight as usual, down by the pigpen" is the final straw that sends the neighbor running out reeling under the Hogans' salacious wit.

The plot then settles upon Phil's efforts to get Josie to keep Tyrone from selling the farm to the rich neighbor. Phil would even go so far as to walk in on them in bed and blackmail him into giving them the farm. Josie finds herself alone with Tyrone, knowing that she is very much in love with him, and yet torn between tenderness and revenge. When Josie is her bawdy self, Tyrone is revolted, and clings to the "life-giving illusion" that Josie is actually a virgin and her reputation only stems from men who dare not admit that all they got from her was a slap.

In a magnificent love scene, the two lives of quiet desperation come close to merging, each struggling with the ambivalent emotions of sensual and tender feelings. To Tyrone, Josie is ". . . beautiful and healthy and clean and fine and warm and strong and kind. . . ." Gradually Tyrone's psychic burden of guilt is poured out in Josie's maternal arms; the Oedipal fixation upon his mother, his hatred for his father; his giving up his drinking to please his mother; his violent relapse when his mother got sick; and his guilty death-wish toward her, hoping she would die so she would never know how drunk he was.

But his mother did see his stupor before she died, loading her son's *super-ego* with so great a guilt that at her funeral he could not cry. As he brought her coffin east on a train he sank to depths of alcoholic and sexual degradation, sleeping with a blonde "pig" for $50.00 a night. The blonde has subsequently haunted his guilty fantasies and represents a recurrence of the motif of desecrating love as a defense against being hurt by it. Tyrone wishes that there were some truth in spiritualism so that he could contact his mother:

". . . If I could tell her it was because I missed her so much and couldn't forgive her for leaving me. . . ." Freud has written of the frequent conflicts in neurotics between sensual and tender feelings toward women, and O'Neill has nowhere more ably dramatized this conflict than in *A Moon for the Misbegotten*. Josie is sympathetic to Tyrone's confession, and in her strong love for him would take him to bed. But he cannot, needing to keep Josie "diff'rent" from the sensual blonde pigs, to keep her a projection of the tender mother-image.

Purged by his confession, Tyrone sobs rackingly on Josie's breast and she forgives him on his mother's behalf. He falls peacefully asleep in the moonlight, a misbegotten soul regressed to the embracing, Jungian Earth-Mother at the end of a tremendous, suspenseful and dazzling act of drama.

The final act finds the sleeping Tyrone still in Josie's arms as Phil enters the next morning. He had fallen asleep and forgotten to surprise them according to the blackmail plot. Tyrone has assured Josie he was only kidding about selling the farm out from under them, and Josie perceives that her father knew Tyrone was only kidding but chose to exploit Josie's sincere love for him. Josie is so furious at her father that she too is ready to leave the farm. But when Tyrone wakes up, there is no mention of marriage or of Josie going away with him. Quietly he leaves, telling Josie he loves her. Josie knows that he can hope for peace only in death. In his own words, "Whether it's the bottom of a bottle, or a South Sea Island, we'd find our own ghosts there waiting to greet us." After he leaves, Josie goes back to cooking breakfast for her father, rationalizing: "Sure, living with you has spoilt me for any other man, anyway. There'd never be the same fun or excitement."

Until such time as a director can assemble the ideal cast, with an over-size Josie and an irascible, magnificently sardonic old Irishman to play the father, the final judgment on *A Moon for the Misbegotten* cannot be given. But it is worth hazarding the prediction that it will prove to be one of O'Neill's finest dramas. It is redeemed by humor as few of O'Neill's other plays are. It is theatrically playable and constructed with the suspense that derives from character. It confounds the critics who carped that he was too bookishly Freudian. It has veritable giants of characterization, subtle, original and deeply felt, surely no cases from a psychology text. Josie and her father are superb dramatic figures, joined in a kind of mental marriage of two vigorous, keen wits—an intellectual Electra complex. The bedevilled Tyrone has more compassion and universality than was manifest in Reuben, Orin, Dion and Eben. But it is Josie, rather than

Tyrone, who emerges as a truly tragic figure in the Aristotelian sense; her struggle and her yearning for fulfillment are decent and deserving, and at the end she achieves some insight, some *Anagnorosis* or objective awareness of herself and her two men. She is thwarted partly because of her size and most particularly because when she did find a man who could stand up to her as a Promethean equal, he proved to be a misbegotten figure, tragic in his schizophrenic split, gnawing away at himself with guilt and recriminations, and fated as surely as were the Greek heroes not to achieve the peace that Josie might offer him because of his own inner flaw . . . the tragic and modern flaw of Oedipal guilt-feelings.

O'NEILL IN RETROSPECT

When Eugene O'Neill died in 1953, with three Pulitzer Prizes and the Nobel Prize for Literature to his credit, he left behind three other manuscripts of the *Misbegotten* cycle, which may not be produced until twenty-five years after his death. Whatever will be the verdict of time upon his drama, there can be no doubt that he was the most important dramatist the American theatre had produced, and the first to achieve international esteem. In his eloquent eulogy, Brooks Atkinson spoke of O'Neill as "A giant writer . . . a great spirit and our greatest dramatist."

Among the psychoanalytic *leit-motifs* which recur throughout his work, those which derive from Jung include the concept of the mask, the Earth-Mother, regression to the racial unconscious, and escape to the South Sea Islands as a form of regression. From Freud seem to have come O'Neill's primal father and passive-dependent, hating sons, the theme of sexual denial and frustration, the discrepancy between the *ego ideal* and outer reality, the compulsion to degrade love, the Electra relationship, death wishes, latent homosexuality, guilt feelings, and the duality of sensual and tender love.

A variety of other sources, including Strindberg and Nietzsche, contributed to the fertility of O'Neill's psychological perception— perhaps the most influential of which was his own personal *weltzschmertz* and neurotic background. His early plays actually reflect only a superficial use of Freudian psychology, although a generation of playgoers and drama critics in the first flush of discovering Freud read into O'Neill more Freud, perhaps, then justified. It is only after O'Neill underwent psychoanalysis in 1927, that his most mature and most Freudian plays were written, *Strange Interlude* and *Mourning Becomes Electra*. Some of his most important plays owe more to

Jung than to Freud, to the mystic rather than the clinical approach to human behavior. If there is one persistent theme in O'Neill, it is the search for Godhead—male or female.

O'Neill's less successful plays, *Welded, Dynamo, Lazarus Laughed, All God's Chillun Got Wings, The Great God Brown,* and *The Iceman Cometh,* are those in which the psychic pressures playing upon the author were too great to be compressed into an objectified, controlled pattern. At times his plays seem to suffer not from too much Freudian influence but from too little. O'Neill often seemed unable to test reality in the case of his tragic heroes and to see them as the emotionally stunted individuals they were. The most autobiographical of them, Dion Anthony and James Tyrone, Jr., are less tragic to the audience than they must have seemed to O'Neill. Dion's mask depicts suffering but the audience has not participated in that suffering and hence cannot empathize with it. O'Neill, perhaps more than any other dramatist, illustrates the subtle interplay between external influences and the inner experiences, conscious and unconscious, which compel his material to assume certain forms. The role of psychoanalysis in O'Neill's plays was clearly that of providing illumination, suggestion, direction. But the flesh and blood of the characters, the emotional agony, is O'Neill's own. It happened that O'Neill reached the theatre during the era when Freudian psychology was first making its tremendous impact felt, and the interrelation of the two combined to make O'Neill seem to be, for a generation of playgoers, the epitome of Freudianism in the American theatre. It remained for Arthur Miller to pick up where O'Neill left off and pierce even deeper beneath the surface of the tragic *persona* than did O'Neill.

If O'Neill is something less than a master dramatist, he was nevertheless the finest theatre craftsman of his times; with his father's feeling for showmanship, he occasionally created stage magnificence. His compulsion to express deeper-than-surface reality led him to enrich the drama with new and renewed techniques. With the exception of *Ah, Wilderness!* which falls in a class by itself, O'Neill's finest work—if not the masterpieces of the modern American drama—may very likely prove to be those plays in which his psychoanalytic insights were deepest and his mastery of form greatest: *Desire Under the Elms, Strange Interlude, Mourning Becomes Electra,* and *A Moon for the Misbegotten.*

CHAPTER VII

O'Neill's Allies in Analysis

OWEN DAVIS

If one had to name the three playwrights who most consistently reflected psychoanalytic insights in a number of plays, the trio would consist of O'Neill, Philip Barry and S. N. Behrman. But the big three were not alone. Virtually all the serious American playwrights of the twenties reflected Freudian thinking to some extent, expressing playgoers' preferences, if not their own, for clinical case histories in complex human relationships. Some, like William Hurlbut, John Howard Lawson, George Kelly, Sidney Howard and Maxwell Anderson felt the need to unburden themselves of only one or two conspicuously Freudian plays, while others like Elmer Rice, Robert Sherwood and Martin Flavin reveal psychoanalytic attitudes as the very core of their approach to human motivation in the drama.

The prolific playcraftsman, Owen Davis, dabbled in psychoanalytic themes during his comprehensive career as he had in most of the other topics current in the twenties and thirties. His various treatments of Freudian subjects are in fact almost a miniature history of psychoanalysis in American drama. He began with a naive and theatrically inept attempt to dramatize the "new psychology" of the unconscious in *Any House* (1916); he went on to real maturity and insight in *Icebound;* took time out to poke satiric fun at psychology in *The Nervous Wreck* (1923) and *The Haunted House*

134

(1924), and after the giddy twenties ended utilized the residue of
Freudian insights in such a substantial theatre piece as *Ethan Frome*
(1936).

The *Nervous Wreck* (1923) was an apparently hilarious (though
there is little hilarity in the text) farce based on the familiar routine
of a hypochondriac's medicine bottles, pills, hourly nervous crises
and imaginary pains. The "nervous wreck" manages to give vent to
his "suppressed but virile ego" sufficiently to hold up a party of
tourists and an Arizona sheriff, later employing "the association of
ideas" test in order to catch the real criminal. Each suspect is given
a plate to hold and the guilty party is expected to drop his dish
when the key word is spoken; the scene was reputed to be the "most
original and convulsing situation" of the play.

Advertised as "a farce in three complexes, psychoanalyzed by
Owen Davis," *The Haunted House* (1924) shows no greater sparkle
in its satire of psychoanalysis and scientific criminology than did
The Nervous Wreck. The leading character is an author of detective
stories who turns detective himself, solving the crime by a psychoanalysis of sorts. The humor ran to such heavy-handed gibes as
the diagnosis that a tramp found with a bottle of milk must as an
infant have been deprived of his milk. Because the psychoanalysts
are supposed to have discovered that back of every crime "is a sex
impulse," the detective sleuths around trying to "cherchez la femme,"
using a séance and finally a truth serum without catching any
criminals. The only truths the serum unearths are the comic confes-
sions that the author's wife has secret contempt for his books, and
a newlywed's revelation of another love affair. Numbers of playgoers apparently responded to the dare in the advertisement, "Have
you been psychoanalyzed by Wallace Eddinger? See *The Haunted
House*," for it ran over a hundred performances. Davis made one
other equally successful attempt to poke fun at nervous wrecks, *Easy
Come, Easy Go* (1925), this time satirizing hypochondriacs who en-
slave themselves to a rigid schedule on a health farm, only to be
cured in ample time for the final curtain.

Although he adapted and co-authored many plays, including
such psychological novels as Fulton Oursler's *Sandalwood* (1926)
it was with *Icebound* that Owen Davis proved himself an original
and serious writer of some psychological depth. Winner of the
Pulitzer Prize for 1922-23 in competition with *Rain, The Adding
Machine* and *Roger Bloomer, Icebound* represents a compromise between a contrived, well-made plot and the stark naturalism of
O'Neill. It begins with a remarkable gallery of portraits of hard,
emotionally icebound New Englanders who sit waiting for their

domineering old mother to die. Henry, the oldest son, is a weakling who constantly borrows money. The women are all unfulfilled and gossip maliciously. Ben, the youngest son, is a black sheep who started a fire in a barn and is wanted by the police. The mother upsets the scheming family by leaving her money to a distant cousin, Jane. Jane takes over in a quiet, masterful manner, and makes a man of Ben by bailing him out and giving him work on the farm. Turning down the sniveling requests of the family, Jane encourages only Ben, who develops a new love for the farm, a feeling of closeness to the animals and their young ones. (Ephraim Cabot in *Desire Under the Elms* felt this same sublimated tenderness for his cows.) In France during the war Ben had glimpsed a different way of life—one in which emotions were expressed rather than repressed and there was a joy of living. Jane buys a dress like the one the French girl wore, and she and Ben finally acknowledge the attraction which they feel for each other. Icebound no more, Ben says of his mother, "I always thought a lot of her, in spite of our being relations." The characterizations are real and the symbol of icebound for emotional repression and frigidity is familiar in psychoanalytic literature.

Davis' other notable drama also dealt with frustration and icebound New England folk. Adapted by Owen and Donald Davis from Edith Wharton's novel, *Ethan Frome* depicts a tightlipped, laconic farmer who is unconsciously passive-dependent upon a woman, first his mother and then after her death the woman who had nursed her, Zeena, whom he married without love for fear of loneliness and insanity after his mother's death. Zeena becomes a nagging, whining hypochondriac who saps the vitality of Ethan and gives nothing of herself in return. Ethan is driven into the arms of Mattie and their tragic love is discovered by Zeena. The lovers are driven to attempt suicide sledding down a hill into a tree. The attempt fails and Mattie lives on, a hopeless cripple herself. Ethan is doomed to a life of caring for the two wretchedly helpless women on whom he had himself been dependent.

Owen Davis epitomizes the successful, working play-craftsman of our theatre, a type more prevalent in the American theatre before O'Neill than it has been since. Even Davis, however, could not remain impervious to the appeal of psychoanalysis as a theatrical subject.

WILLIAM HURLBUT

Although less successful and well known than Owen Davis, William Hurlbut paralleled his career in many respects. Like Davis,

he wrote a large number of hack theatre pieces to order for stars
and managers, and then like Davis he "got religion"—the new religion of psychology. He wrote one play of genuine literary and
psychoanalytic merit, *Bride of the Lamb* (1926), which considerably
startled the critics who had come to expect only frivolity or melodrama from Hurlbut. In this play he studies the unconscious mechanism whereby sexual energy is converted into religious fanaticism.
He creates a character (suggested perhaps by Billy Sunday) of an
itinerant evangelist preacher who had been an actor and carnival
barker before "being called," who calls himself "a go-getter for the
Lord," and whose frenzy of orgiastic preaching clearly has a sexual
basis.

He comes to a small town where the devout Ina Bowman lives
with her alcoholic husband and her asinine daughter. Out of the
frustration of her empty existence, Ina is given to erotic fantasies
of wish-fulfillment—imagining a rich and gracious life with a "kind
gentleman." She goes to the movies for vicarious sexual experience
but is righteously indignant at immorality in real life. When the
evangelist, Reverend Albaugh, arrives in town for a week of tent
revivals, he is invited to be the house-guest of Mrs. Bowman. She
is passionately drawn to him, first in religious exaltation and then in
transparently physical desire. The Reverend Albaugh tries at first
to deny her importunities and leaves her kneeling on the floor in a
writhing paroxysm of sensuous and sacred invitation:

> Our Father in Heaven—Blessed Jesus—Thy Son—Take me
> —take me—Amen—Jesus walking in light—Jesus the son—
> take me—fill me—Thy blood—wash me in the blood—Praise
> God the Lamb—the blessed Lamb—The Son of Man—Jesus
> the Lamb—bathe me in the fountain of the Lamb—the Bride
> of the Lamb—Thy Bride—beautiful Jesus—strong in spirit—
> strong—take me into Thy arms—Jesus my bridegroom—my
> bridegroom—Fountain of Blood—fountain of love—fill me—
> spray over me—Thy love—fill me—fill me—Take me—bride-
> groom—bridegroom—

Unable to resist, Reverend Albaugh returns and finding her in this
trance of sexual ecstasy, bends down to her on the floor and takes
her.

The next morning Ina reveals that she has had a familiarly
Freudian dream:

> I dreamt I had to go along a road to get to church—it was
> the church tower I had to get to—the steeple, a great high
> steeple,—and right across my way was a log across the road

—an awful big log—it was bigger than any log I ever did see
actually, and I was struggling to remove it, and knowing I
had to get to the church tower—I woke up in a perspiration!

Ina later interprets her own dream for Reverend Albaugh, the two
phallic symbols of the steeple and the log representing respectively
the Reverend and her loutish, drunken husband who lies in the path
of her fulfillment. Her daughter, who is also converted by Albaugh's fervor, is blissfully polishing her shoes for church when Ina
formulates her fiendish plot to kill her husband with shoe polish. Just
after she murders him, the wife of Reverend Albaugh catches up
with him after some years and Ina suffers a traumatic shock. When
the Sheriff finally arrives to arrest her, Ina has become psychotic in
her disassociation from reality; dressed in bridal clothes, she mistakes the Sheriff for her bridegroom, Mr. Christ, and walks out
proudly arm in arm with him, while the repentant Albaugh sinks
to his knees crying, "God forgive me—God forgive me!"

If the structure of *Bride of the Lamb* bears some of the fingerprints of the contrived dramaturgy of Hurlbut's earlier period, the
play nevertheless possesses genuine theatrical power and psychoanalytic insight. The character of Ina is depicted with the frenzy of
an O'Neill and the fine line of demarcation between religious ecstasy
and unconscious sexual excitement is nowhere better dramatized. If
Miss Shirley Booth is looking for vehicles she should revive *Bride
of the Lamb*.

The same season saw another study of religio-libidinal energy,
The Virgin, by Arthur White and Louis Bennison, and two years
later Sinclair Lewis' *Elmer Gantry* was dramatized to become perhaps the most famous portrait of a stage evangelist in the twenties.
In the thirties, *Tight Britches* treated the conflict of sex and religious
calling in a mountain boy.

The success of *Bride of the Lamb* (109 performances on Broadway) encouraged Hurlbut to explore further in Freudian fields and
his next play, *Hidden* (1927) delves into the hidden passion of a girl
for her sister's husband. She develops shooting pains across her eyes
when she sees her brother-in-law as Marc Antony in Roman undress
with bare legs, and almost faints in excitement when she comes upon
him in the bath. After she has finally seduced him and driven her
sister away in shame, she commits suicide. As Alexander Woollcott
pointed out, however, "If what ails the girl can be said to be hidden,
then so is the Woolworth Building." Apparently Hurlbut's flair for a
dramatic effect here exceeded his ability to create living characters
one dimension richer than a clinical case history.

Hurlbut's next play, *Paradise* (1927), again dealt with a woman's frustration and psychotic wish-fulfillment—this time a girl who is taunted by her two married sisters because she can't get a husband. Her defense against these jibes is to go to New York and write back that she is married—later that her husband has died, and to send a borrowed corpse home to prove it.

Two years later, with *A Primer for Lovers* (1929), Hurlbut returned to his earlier style, that of the bawdy bedroom farce. Only one other play of Hurlbut's need be noted, *Recessional*, a remarkable study of the psychological basis of miscegenation—a theme so bold that the play has never been produced on Broadway. Christine Farraday is the heroine of *Recessional*, a smart, wealthy widow who moves in an intellectual set which has adopted as a "fad" the entertaining of Negro artists. When someone brings a Negro boxer to an interracial party, Christine is strongly attracted to him. In order to control her desire, however, she stops entertaining Negroes, and urges her white suitor, Brooks, to have an affair with her. Brooks, however, idealizes Christine and prefers her on a pedestal. When he has left, Christine is unable to suppress her aroused desire and unlatches the door to admit the Negro as her lover.

Brooks has been writing a psychological study of the Negro, heavily borrowed from Jung. He explains the attraction which Negroes have for whites of the opposite sex as an unconcious regression to the primitive.

When Christine finds that she is powerless in the grip of her passion for the Negro, she murders him. Unable to conceal the fact that he was in her bedroom, she claims at first that she shot in self-defense against rape. Throwing aside all his Jungian psychology, Brooks becomes the leader of the posse who would drive all the colored people out of town. The only way she can stop him from his frenzied plans to do violence to innocent people is to tell him she was the Negro's mistress. He would still lead the mob, however, so that Christine is forced to appear before the mob and tell them her secret. Brooks stands by her loyally as she realizes that she was the victim of "Something waiting in me——A survival throughout the ages . . . I was attacked—yes, but from within."

Why Christine was the victim of this impulse to regress to the primitive is partially explained by reference to her childhood environment with a Negro settlement across the river from her home; in her own stultifying environment she had been acutely aware of the passionate music and song with which Negroes are able to abandon themselves. Hurlbut thus makes a rather striking combination of Jungian psychology and melodramatic theatricals. Perhaps we are better prepared for an O'Neill to challenge public narrowness than we are for a Hurlbut. The contrast with *All God's Chillun* would find Hurlbut's play lacking in compassion and depth of characterization, lacking the insight into the throbbing pressures of the unconscious which must be felt by author and audience empathically rather than merely explained by quotations from Jung.

JOHN HOWARD LAWSON

Expressionism had taken root in Europe but until 1922 had left the American drama relatively untouched. As far back as 1915 *Overtones* had used dual actors to portray one individual; but it was not until 1922-23 that Broadway saw in three plays the possibilities of purposeful distortion for the sake of expressing unconscious meanings. O'Neill's *The Hairy Ape* in March of 1922 used the device of grotesque movement and masks to suggest the imperious indifference of the Fifth Avenue crowd to the hairy ape, Yank. Then in March, 1923, within two weeks of each other, opened John Howard Lawson's *Roger Bloomer* and Elmer Rice's *The Adding Machine*, together representing the high-water mark of expressionism in America.

Roger Bloomer depicts the guilty torments of an adolescent growing into manhood unable to confide in his money-minded father and his empty-headed mother. Caustically, Lawson satirizes the self-made business man and his friend whose son, Eugene, goes to Yale. Eugene has seen a naked woman, and so disturbs the less sophisticated Roger, whose soliloquy of erotic adolescent fantasies is a magnificent free association of ideas ranging from Shelley to frightening advertisements about "Loss of Manhood."

Taking his College Entrance Board Examination, Roger becomes panicky at the Examiner in cap and gown, an authoritarian figure who piques his own inadequate sense of manhood. Roger so embarrasses a sales girl in his father's store that she quits, and he follows her, trying fumblingly to make love to her. "There's something between us," he tells Louise, "we both hate my father." All men disgust Louise, however, and she plans to go to New York. Roger gets her address and steals off that night.

In New York, Roger is a most disturbed young man. A fat landlady with flabby breasts invites him to make love to her but he is disgusted. He finds Louise, who works in a mechanized office which is expressionistically satirized with five men monotonously repeating each other's words. Her boss refuses Roger a job, a streetwalker rejects him for being broke, and Roger takes rat poison. Louise cares for him and nurses him back to health, but is upset

when Roger's friend Eugene comes and offers her an illicit weekend
at the shore. Disturbed by ". . . a dirty thing called Sex, made to
laugh at," Louise exclaims, "what's in a girl that makes men's eyes
pop? Am I dirty?" She is even frigid with Roger and confesses that
she wishes she could cut her hair short, put on trousers and be a
man, an indication of latent homosexuality derived from her hysterical aversion to men. Instead she takes poison and dies, saying
that they were, "Just two children, caught by this terrible Sex joke."
Roger is accused of her death and is taken to court. The Judge
resembles the College Board Examiner and again Roger's manhood
wilts. In his prison cell Roger has a nightmare which is the occasion
for most of the expressionism of the play.

If *Rain* first used a dream symbol in a play, *Roger Bloomer* was
the first American play actually to stage a Freudian dream in all
its fantastic distortion. A monument of Freudian symbolism, the
dream is in three movements, danced as a rapid ballet accompanied
by half-chanted words. The authoritarian figures return to taunt
Roger, the Judge and the College Board Examiner. Then there is a
procession of bird-like creatures with enormous flapping wings and
claws, resembling demons in some of Goya's etchings. Freud has
written of a dream in which similarly grotesque birds were analyzed
as symbols of sexual intercourse. The dreamer tries hysterically to
protect the corpse of Louise from the bird-like figures, but their
wings drop off and they become solemn people in black, singing a
hymn, a vivid dramatization of what Freud has called condensation
in the dreamwork. The fat landlady chases Roger and old women
taunt him with the epithet, "Straw man" (which Eugene had called
Roger in a previous scene), until they pull forth a straw figure and
tear it apart, strewing the stage with sawdust and straw. Then Roger
lunges at an old woman with a sword but it goes right through her.
He next stabs the prostitute and she wriggles on the sword, doing
an Oriental dance. When he tries to pull the sword out, it becomes
a big green writhing snake. (Freud has described both swords and
snakes in dreams as male phallic symbols.) Then Roger's mother
appears and protects him with her mother love, but she cannot save
Roger from women with whips and men with swords who fall on
him. In the confusion Louise stands beside him, radiant as an angel,
banishing the visions and saying softly that she too must go:

Louise: In yourself you must find the secret.
Roger: But I can't bear to be alone.
Louise: Oh, the passions of childhood were easy, but a
  man's thought is another thing.
Roger: I can't bear it, don't go. . . .

Louise: Go it alone, Roger; are you ready now? . . . I've given you yourself, take it. . . . Face the music; what music, falling about you like rain; what splendor of broken chords, brass trumpets braying in the morning and whisper of harps in the dusk . . . and far off, listen, the tread of marching people singing a new song. . . . Goodbye . . . a man's luck, Roger.

The prison attendant appears to wake Roger up and release the yawning, dazed young man, saying, "Come on, you're free, there's the world out there."

Roger Bloomer was apparently intended as an indictment of society for forcing youth to grow up in the atmosphere of secrecy and smut which surrounds sex. Lawson has perhaps weighted his scales a little too heavily, for his father is the bare outline of a money-mad Babbitt (until the end when he visits Roger in prison) and Roger himself has unusually severe manifestations of neurotic guilts and fears. But Lawson has inventively explored the troubled mind of an adolescent who takes the world too seriously, and has created a unique play in the modern American theatre. The imaginative form of the play includes telegraphic, clipped dialogue, soliloquies, the use of authoritarian figures who resemble each other, multi-scene staging, office mechanization, and a superb nightmare-fantasy which preceded by almost twenty years the Dali Surrealism of the Ballet Russe, *Bacchanale.*

The marching feet Louise heard at the end of *Roger Bloomer* indicated the direction Lawson was to go, and more and more he interested himself in socio-political problems, although often treating them with Freudian insight. In *Processional* (1924), he created a blatant, expressionistic backdrop of labor violence, Ku Klux Klan and social turbulence which made little use of psychoanalysis. In *Nirvana*, however, (1926) he baffled the critics again with an expressionistic exploration of sex and religion in which everyone seemed to go around asking "What is sex?" Lawson intended the play as a "comedy of the uncertainties and aspirations of the thinking man as he confronts the enlarging universe. . . . Freud has dragged strange monsters from the bottomless sea of the unconscious. . . . Einstein has deposed the straight line." Man seeks a new religion. Lawson wrote, ". . . a new and bitter realization of man's relation to the electric void through which he walks."

A year later Lawson tried expressionism again in *Loudspeaker,* a satire on political campaigns with a millionaire running for Governor while his wife dabbles in psychology under the influence of a bearded hypnotist and the daughter, Clare, a wild flapper, in search of a thrill, telling her mother: "Don't you even know, mother, that everybody's thoughts are obscenely vile? That's psychology." There is an effeminate reporter who says, "I don't smoke. I'm very ambitious and my mother, bless her, told me to keep away from all bad habits." The millionaire recalls a girl he once took to Atlantic City, and she appears, a visualization of his erotic fantasy. When Clare would defend her father, the mother says:

> Mrs. Collins: You take his side just because you've read so much Freud.
> Clare: I'm not thinking of Freud, I'm thinking of the election.

In the end Clare marries the swishing reporter and spends an unsatisfying honeymoon. If Lawson again failed in *Loudspeaker* to crystallize his concepts in an objective pattern which audiences could grasp, his brash, impertinent, jazzy attempt at expressionism, nevertheless, seem to capture perhaps better than any other drama, the mood of the Freud-and-flapper twenties.

Lawson's work in the thirties illustrates the conflict between the demands of the individual for realization and the growing social pressure to make a better society. *Success Story* (1932) creates with a wealth of psychoanalytic insight a portrait of a neurotic, East Side New Yorker who sells out his social ideals in an obsessive drive for power and money. The works of Alfred Adler which Lawson is known to have read may have enriched this portrait of the striving for superiority described by Adler as rooted in childhood inferiority. In his business and romantic life, Sol Ginsburg is bristling with hostility and aggression as a defense mechanism against racial sensitivity and inadequacy. He has paranoid suspicions that everyone is plotting against him, including his sweetheart, Sarah Glassman, whom he accuses of sleeping with the boss—a projection of his own repressed wish. In his relationship to Sarah he is sadistically compelled to hurt her:

> Sarah: I can't stand your going on like this—I'm the one you hurt—you like to hurt me, you like it . . .
> Sol: Protect! . . . thicken your skin, kid, you need a thick skin, you're too soft.
> Sarah: So are you; you're soft and emotional like a woman.
> Sol: Aw hell!
> Sarah: You don't look it, but I know.
> Sol: Maybe I was soft, but I'm gettin' over it fast.

The second act shows just how fast he rejects his sensitivity. He has risen in the Merritt advertising firm by writing copy he despises

for Glamour Cream. He is obsessed now with the desire to have
Merritt's mistress, Agnes, a frigid blonde who hasn't experienced a
love-relationship since she was 16. To his agonized supplication,
Agnes answers, "No, you want it too much—it's more fun to have you
all in a fever wanting something that's just a joke to me—that's the
kind of a cold potato I am." Sol's pursuit of Agnes is symptomatic
in the Adlerian sense rather than basic—sex as Adler saw it was a
secondary manifestation of the drive for power over others; to the
struggling East-Sider, the sure sign that he had arrived in the capi-
talistic world he despised was to acquire a flashy mistress. By the
third act he has married Agnes and is deteriorating emotionally, oppressed with his inability to satisfy Agnes, whose only outlet is
spending his money. Distracted to the point of contemplating suicide, and unable to give up Agnes though he hates her, Sol is reunited with Sarah, who has also been rising in the firm. Faithful
and still loving him, Sarah has been giving him her money to invest,
and he has sadistically withheld from her the accounting of it although it has vastly increased. He begs her to pull the trigger and
shoot him, saying:

> I got a demon in me makes me twist and turn people . . .
> I live in a series of contrivances like a picture in the funny
> papers . . . that's the curse on me, the desire eating me,
> to be a great man, leading armies, plotting for the earth
> . . . this feller Christ took me up to a high mountain and
> showed me the earth, you know the story? . . . Look at us
> in this office! Two men with a poisonous loving hatred, Mer-
> ritt and me, both in love with a woman's soul, which is you
> —and in turn we possessed a woman's body—a cheap thing
> —a rotten thing to buy with money—

This ambivalence of loving and hating, this latent homosexuality
which drives the two men to want a mistress in common suggests
O'Neill's similar treatment in *The Great God Brown*. Sol's Christ-
complex or identification with a Martyr is also a frequent symptom
of paranoia. At last realizing that only with Sarah could he find fulfillment, he begs her to go off with him but she refuses, saying
masochistically:

> It's no good, it hurts too much . . . bitter . . . it cuts into
> you, makes your flesh sore. . . . Hold me tighter, tighter!
> Crown me with thorns, burn me with kisses, tear me down,
> limb from limb . . . tear my body, trample me, make me a
> wilderness—we been walking in a wilderness, walking in the
> dark—show me the light——

Sarah shoots him as he had begged her to do, and when the others arrive, only Agnes is calculating enough to put the pistol in his hand so it would look like suicide: "Tell the police it's a suicide, tell 'em he had a nervous breakdown . . . too much work . . . too ambitious. . . ."

Thus in *Success Story*, Lawson comes close to a Freudian-Marxian synthesis in which a man is destroyed by unconscious pressures which derive from social forces, poverty, economic frustration and the warping influences of the slums. *Success Story* which ran for 121 performances in its Group Theatre production, preceded by five years Odets' treatment of a similar subject in *Golden Boy*.

Lawson's farewell to Freud came in 1934 with *Gentlewoman*, in which he depicts a rich woman whose husband was under a psychoanalyst's care for "Acute melancholia—bitter jealousy—accusations against himself—the sense that he was no longer adequate—psychic impotence—" He had compensated by his hobby of building model boats—perhaps a phallic symbol. When the husband commits suicide, Gwen, the wife, turns to a poor and crude young man from the coal mines, part radical and part fake. While she lives with him, he is unfaithful and drives Gwen to the psychoanalyst for help. But by now in his development, psychoanalysis is to Lawson the symbol of personal evasion of social responsibility. To Gwen's leftist lover their love affair means "to hide away in a corner of chaos and play a pornographic game." He leaves her to go to Iowa where there are farmers on strike, and Gwen lets him go without telling him she is carrying his child.

Further evidence of Lawson's development away from Freud is seen in *The International* (1927) and *Marching Song* (1936), which contain little of psychological interest. Lawson, who is known to have read much of Freud as well as Jung and Adler, seemed to develop a curious case of literary split personality; on the one hand he sensed the dramatic possibilities of unconscious motivation but on the other hand condemned the Freudians for seeking to adjust the individual to the world—a world which is sick and should itself be remade. Because unconscious motives are irrational and unpredictable, Marxians find them unsuitable for inclusion in their world-system based on voluntary surrender of the individual ego for the benefit of the mass. It remained for S. N. Behrman to see a sick social order in terms of the sick individuals who made it. Perhaps Lawson will yet find a synthesis between the demands of society and the right of the individual to fulfillment.

The psychoanalyst in *Gentlewoman* hinted at but did not develop the idea that our best avenue of understanding the psychology of radicals may come from psychoanalytic exploration of their unconscious motives. "The safety of America," he concludes, "lies in its sense of humor—as long as we can laugh at revolutions, we're safe."

ELMER RICE

To return to the vigorous days when the American theatre was first growing into long pants, Elmer Rice's *The Adding Machine* reached Broadway just two weeks after Lawson's *Roger Bloomer* in 1923 and remains perhaps the most successful example of American expressionism. A young graduate lawyer, Rice first made theatrical history as early as 1914 with *On Trial* and its novel device of the flashback. In 1919 he again utilized his legal background in *For the Defense*, the villain of which is a hypnotist who uses his power over young girls to bend them to his will.

Although Rice's early work was relatively naive in psychological foundations, Rice stated in a letter to the author that he had begun reading Freud nearly forty years ago—at the very beginning of his career (around 1913). He has read Jung, Adler, Ferenczi, Stekel and others as well and thus summarized his consciousness of psychoanalysis:

> The influence upon my thinking and my outlook upon life has certainly been very great: both in attaining a better understanding of myself and a better perspective upon the behavior of others. Undoubtedly, the effect upon my work has been considerable, though it would be hard for me, without a lot of digging, to be specific about it. I have never consciously set out to apply analytic theories, but the concepts of the unconscious, of childhood conditioning, of compensatory behavior, of the significance of dreams have unquestionably entered into the choice of subject and the treatment of character.

Rice was particular to distinguish the importance of psychoanalytic theory from its therapeutic application. His conclusion upon the efficacy of Freudian therapy was that it was still too undeveloped and too experimental, too unsure of its own methodology and too fraught with internal bickering to have scientific reliability. In spite of this impression, Rice would rank Freud with Darwin and Marx, "as one of the great contributors to intellectual progress, in the last hundred years (though I have as little respect for the behaviorists and eugenists and for the Communists, as I have for the couch-tenders)."

Rice apparently first applied his admiration for psychoanalytic theory in 1921 in a collaboration with Hatcher Hughes, *Wake Up, Jonathan*, an entertaining comedy based on changing concepts of child psychology. A fresh and uninhibited family of children are awaiting the arrival of their long-absent father, when an old sweetheart of the mother's accidentally arrives instead. He is a gentle dreamer and idealist, unsuccessful materially but rich in his inner security; it is he who wins the hearts of the children. When the real father, Jonathan, arrives, he proves to be a fatuous authoritarian and Babbitt who ridicules "self-expression" but who is finally awakened to the new day in pedagogy before the final curtain. Aside from talk of "the submerged part of the personality," there is little psychoanalytic terminology, but *Wake Up, Jonathan* follows the tentative beginning of Stuart Walker's *Jonathan Makes a Wish* (no connection between Jonathans) in reflecting the changing attitudes toward discipline of children.

When the Theatre Guild (already dubbed "The Theatre Guilt" for its interest in psychological drama) produced Rice's *The Adding Machine* in 1923, the American drama made a large step forward both in content and form—in depth of insight into character, and in technical means with which to dramatize it. Mr. and Mrs. Zero are symbolic of the nonentities to which our mechanized civilization reduces the individual. Rice is more interested in the society which makes zeros of humanity than he is in the particular family pattern which produces a Mr. Zero.

Mrs. Zero is a nagging shrew and Mr. Zero suffers from repressed erotic wishes toward the girl who leaves her shades up across the courtyard. At work he talks sharply to Miss Daisy Diana Dorothea Devore, and Rice anticipates *Strange Interlude* in using the aside to dramatize the stream of suppressed thoughts as each speaks aloud, oblivious of the other, strongly attracted to each other and yet despairing of ever achieving happiness. In a powerful and valid theatrical handling of free association, Mr. Zero reveals a deathwish as he recalls the eighty-seven dollar doctor bill when his wife had pneumonia and he thought she would die. He then makes a Freudian slip of the tongue in calling out "$87" instead of the figures he was adding. Zero indulges in wish-fulfillment as he imagines the boss calling him in to congratulate him on 25 years with the company. Instead, the boss calls him in and fires him to modernize the office with adding machines. His reaction is shown by the floor of the stage beginning to revolve, slowly, then more rapidly until with mounting sounds building up to a climax of thunder and a red flash of light, Mr. Zero's world blacks out.

To a party of the Zeros' friends, the Twos and the Threes, all cast from the same mold, Mr. Zero reveals that he killed the boss. His trial is one long soliloquy of free association, to which the Jury does not listen. The speech is a masterpiece of insight into the human mind, showing Zero's lifelong frustration, erotic longing and the conversion of this sexual frustration into racial bigotry toward Negroes and Jews.

After Zero's execution he arrives at a strange and expressionistic heaven reminiscent of *Liliom*. There Zero meets Shrdlu, who surprises Zero (but not the Freudian-minded audience) because he is in heaven even though he killed his beloved and saintly mother—whom we suspect of being viciously over-possessive. In Rice's heaven there are surprisingly few "good" mothers and few preachers —so few that when he finally meets Daisy and wants to marry her, the only ministers to perform the ceremony are Dean Swift and the Abbé Rabelais. In these Elysian Fields one can be forever free to seek one's own fulfillment, a kind of Freudian heaven. This is too much for Zero; a bundle of inhibitions, he does not know what to do with his freedom, and is sent by the heavenly Lieutenant back to earth to a monstrous adding machine. The mark of the slave was on him from the first, says the Lieutenant. He will be a baby again and will learn all the wrong things and learn them all in the wrong way.

His destiny is to operate a super-hyper-adding machine that requires only a slight pressure of the great toe of his right foot—the final triumph of the evolutionary process of the human race. An imaginary blue-eyed blonde vamp is summoned up to take him back to earth, and Mr. Zero dashes off with pathetic eagerness to chase an erotic phantom, symptom of his eternal and hopeless inadequacy. Rice's deeply thoughtful cry of protest against "what man has made of man" is an incisive and original work of art. Rice was perhaps not yet sure just what the wrong things were which the babies were being taught or how the insights derived from psychoanalysis might perhaps give us a generation of something better than Zeros. Yet some years before the work of Erich Fromm, Rice described as the thesis of his play his fear that a nation of Zeros might be easy prey for dictatorship:

> In *The Adding Machine* I have tried to show how the Zero psychology reacts to this ideal of freedom. Unless I have hit very wide of the mark, the Zero psychology is the slave psychology. And the one thing that the slave hates and fears beyond all other things is liberty. For the slave senses unconsciously that authority means not only exemption from thought, but security. The power which enslaves him

protects him as well. Thrown upon his own devices, he would not long survive. The demand for laws, for policemen, for armies is actuated almost always by a consciousness of inferiority. . . .

Written the same year as *The Adding Machine* was produced but not seen in New York until 1929 was an even more expressionistic study of unconscious psychology, *The Subway*. By 1929, however, *Machinal* and *Strange Interlude* had reached Broadway and had somewhat taken the edge off Rice's originality in *The Subway*.

The subway is perhaps the symbol for the seething underground of the unconscious which Rice here explores. Sophie Smith is a clerk in a mechanized office as depressing as Mr. Zero's. Her boyfriend leaves town to make good in Detroit, and Sophie finds herself in a pathetic state of sexual anxiety. On her way home in the crowded subway, she grows hysterical at being hemmed in by men—who seem to her animals. Rice here uses masks to visualize her loathing of men, and we see the hideous, grotesque masks of a pig, a dog, a monkey, a rat, a wolf closing in on her as the lights in the subway black out. This marks one of the very rare efforts by any playwright other than O'Neill to employ masks for psychological comment.

In Sophie's miserable family, the characters free associate from their unspoken wishes, with no one hearing the other in their lonely isolation. A young artist named Eugene had helped her when she fainted in the subway, and her erotic fantasies now center on him. In her bedroom she kneels and soliloquizes. She has had a typical anxiety dream—someone is chasing her and she can't run away—her legs are stiff and she can't move. Psychoanalytic literature has many cases of these dreams in which the wish to escape a man and the forbidden wish to be caught by him are condensed into this strange inability to run. Sophie's soliloquy is full of guilt over her erotic feelings, full of death-wishes and punishment. She resolves to go to Church on Sunday:

> My heart isn't clean . . . that's what's the matter with me
> . . . I've had bad thoughts . . . hating people . . . hating
> my own sister and brother . . . Forgive me! I know I've
> been bad but I'll be good, I'll be good . . . I'm always
> thinking about boys . . . but I won't anymore. And those
> other things I think of sometimes. . . . Where do my bad
> thoughts come from? Oh, I'm so ashamed, so ashamed . . .
> Forgive me, dear Jesus . . . Comfort me . . . I love you
> so . . . Make me like you . . . make my heart as clean as
> yours . . . I'm all alone . . . Love me . . . dear Jesus

. . . Take me to your heart . . . Love me . . . Love me
. . . I'm so lonesome . . . so lonesome.

Eugene takes Sophie to the movies, and in a remarkable scene
they sit watching the screen, speaking their inner (but not unconscious) thoughts, she aware of his hand near hers, touching hers; he
aware that he must not rush her; she finally lets him hold her hand,
but in panic at his touch, thinks: "I can feel his nails. They're digging
into me. Go on! Hurt me some more." Finally they rush out of the
movie in an erotic frenzy without waiting for the end of the picture.
After they have been lovers, Eugene is tortured by his *super-ego,*
dramatized as a toneless, impersonal voice calling out "Liar! Liar!"
because although he sincerely loves Sophie, he does not want the
responsibility of marriage. As in *Roger Bloomer* one whole scene
is devoted to a nightmare, but Sophie's is not visualized as Roger's
was: it is rather a montage of offstage voices in the darkness. She
hears the taunts of her friends, Eugene's passionate wooing, the
gloomy intoning of a preacher's "Thou shalt not commit adultery," her
mother's accusation that: "She was always a bad girl" (the only
hint of childhood etiology of Sophie's neurosis), a chorus of voices
calling her a "Nobody," fantasies of a Judge in Court calling her a
Bad Girl, masochistic images of jail and punishment as the chorus
builds to a climax shouting "Bad Girl." She next fantasies dying
of an abortion, as the gossipy voices of girls and boys call her unborn child, "You little bastard." An arm shoots out of the blackness
with forefinger pointed accusingly at her, then other arms until the
whole stage is a surrealistic cage of condemning arms. This is the
only visual effect in the dream. Sophie is distraught, and at the subway platform a friend of Eugene's tries to pick her up. In a final
orgiastic outburst, she throws herself under the subway train. Although *The Subway* is a bleak, almost skeletal play, Rice achieves an
exceptional intensity of expression in depicting both Sophie's love
and her guilt. One is tempted to speculate that if only Sophie Smith
had met Roger Bloomer, there would have been a marriage indeed!

In 1931 Rice was represented on Broadway with two penetrating and well constructed realistic plays: *Counsellor-at-Law,* which
depicts the ethical struggle of a driving, successful lawyer without
delving into psychological mechanisms other than his loyalty to his
old immigrant mother; and *The Left Bank,* which is full of psychoanalytic terminology and chatter. While not too fond of psychoanalytic therapy, Rice here uses its insights to explain the forces that
motivate Americans to become voluntary exiles in Paris during the
era of F. Scott Fitzgerald. To them America is a wasteland, a

Puritan, repressive prison from which they had to make a complete break. Rice shows us such an *avant-garde* couple living in Paris while their son is in a psychoanalytic-directed school in England because of his neurotic hatred for his father and his violent mother-fixation. As the husband explains to the man who is currently trying to seduce his wife:

> John: It's a well-known school for maladjusted children. Teddy has a neurosis.
> Alan: Golly, do kids have them now, too?
> John: Nearly all neuroses begin in childhood.
> Alan: Well, I think I'll have my dog psycho-analyzed. She seems to have an acute case of nympho-mania. Anytime you want a puppy, Claire——

Lillian, a soured elder sister of John's—who raised him on "smother love" so cloying that he married mainly to escape her—arrives and would take the son out of the "progressive" school where he is "running wild" and undisciplined.

Claire's niece and her husband arrive from the states, and each proceeds to have an affair with the other's spouse. The young man feels a trifle guilty making love to Claire, but Claire understands the difference between guilt and freedom:

> Claire: We've been taught for centuries to believe in the mortification of the flesh and to look for heaven anywhere except on earth. You can't enjoy the good things of life if you're ashamed of your appetites and have to be a little furtive about satisfying them.
> Waldo: Well, an awful lot of us seem to be trying to get over it.
> Claire: Yes, I know. Kicking off the lid and making whoopee. But most of that is nothing more than putting your morality in reverse. To be a real pagan, you have to swap your conscience for a palate.
> Waldo: And how do you go about doing that?
> Claire: Ah, that's the problem we emancipated Puritans are all trying to solve. I'm beginning to think it can't be done. I think that maybe you have to be born with the palate—and without the conscience.

Rice sees clearly that their "kicking off the lid" was a reaction and protest. The theme of the play, as stated by Claire, is that: ". . . all this sex business and the way we all talk and think and carry on, nowadays, is all part of a larger problem, a basic problem of adjustment and self-realization." Claire in the end achieves a kind of self-realization, and goes home to the states to accept the responsibility of raising her son, leaving John in Paris with Susie. *The Left Bank* is one of the most skillful of the studies of the lost generation in rebellion against themselves.

There is one play remaining in Rice's psychological period, a little-known and under-esteemed domestic drama, *Black Sheep* (1932). Without specifically psychoanalytic terminology, Rice creates a picture of an Oedipal mother-son relationship. The son, Buddy, has been a ne'er-do-well, away from home for seven years and forbidden by his father to cross the threshold. The very day a rich society lady tells them about her new fad, a fascinating new writer of the South Seas, the black sheep son returns and proves to be the famous writer. Now all prejudice against him vanishes, and he rules the roost. His mother is effectively portrayed as a sentimental, cloying, superficial woman who never understood Buddy, who tried to make him conform until he rebelled, and who now takes credit for encouraging his talent. Buddy brings a mistress back with him, captivates the maid as well, and pretty well demoralizes the household. Buddy is excellently characterized as a passive-dependent son, the victim of Oedipal mother-domination. He seeks women casually and promiscuously and yet requires the domination of a strong-minded woman to keep him writing and progressing. The mother is not drawn as insidiously as Howard's Mrs. Phelps. She is merely silly and unperceptive, while the father is a good-natured, golf-playing dolt. *Black Sheep* is Rice's delicious, quiet slap at the hypocrisy and blindness with which parents muddle through the business of human relations.

As the thirties progressed, Rice grew increasingly preoccupied with the social and political upheavals of the decade, and wrote such memorable dramas as *Street Scene* (1929), *We the People* (1933), *Judgment Day* (1934), *American Landscape* (1938) in which ghosts of former generations of American patriots return to the troubled citizens of the present, and an original approach to anti-Nazi drama, *Flight to the West* (1941).

Still troubled by American business men who wanted to do business with Hitler, Rice in 1943 wrote *A New Life,* a panegyric to the courage of youth in the debâcle. Turning his genius for realistic reporting of detail to the obstetrical ward of a hospital, Rice puts on the stage as harrowing a child-birth scene as the drama has known. *A New Life* is *Wake Up, Jonathan* brought up to date—with the same incredibly pompous business man trying to dominate the lives of his children and grandchildren. Rice depicts a millionaire business magnate and his snob of a wife trying to obtain control of their grandchild from the humble girl their soldier-son married during a two week leave. They would lavish their wealth and domination on the child as they had on his father and thereby make him passive and dependent. The son is painfully unable to choose between his wife and his parents, until the final curtain when he matures enough to make the choice of cutting the gilt-edged umbilicus. But the play is weakened by the tin-type of a heartless business man which Rice sets up and spends three acts knocking over. It remained for Arthur Miller to humanize this stereotype and give the business man three dimensions of inner reality. Rice has been eminently more successful in expressionism than in realism—in a form where it is desirable that characters be compacted with all the traits of their species rather than individualized. With the exception of the naturalistic *Street Scene*, Rice's plays give one the feeling that he compels his characters to serve as mouthpieces for his indignation at the state of the world—they *illustrate* a theme rather than exist in their own psychological world.

At any rate, it was to expressionism and psychoanalysis that Rice returned for his next play, *Dream Girl* (1945). The distance the play-going public had traversed in its understanding of psychoanalysis since *The Subway* (1929) is vividly illustrated by contrast with *Dream Girl*. Mr. Rice's heroine here is no morbid, guilt-ridden neurotic, but rather a "perfectly healthy, normal person" who has read considerably in psychiatry and knows all about "that damned little psychic censor" which gets in the way of dream interpretation (though she knows the obvious dream symbols—Maypoles and church steeples). When we meet Georgina Allerton in a memorable first-act soliloquy as she wakes up and prepares to face another day, she is ambitious to have a literary career, troubled over her love for a married man—her brother-in-law, Jim, and preoccupied with sex in a delightfully frank way. "Of course I suppose that up to a certain point there's nothing abnormal about virginity. But the question is, how can you ever be sure you haven't passed that point?" Georgina suspects that she has, and is mulling over a graciously illicit offer made her by George Hand.

The structure of the play is the reverse of Rice's first hit, *On Trial*—here we flash forward into Georgina's day dreams and see her wish-fulfillment fantasies—first what it would be like to bear her brother-in-law Jim's child as her sister is now doing. But Jim, the object of Georgina's wishes, is a mooning, impractical idealist who passively permits himself to be pushed around by Mrs. Allerton. Among Georgina's assorted fantasies are a scene in which her mother dies (a projection of Georgina's death-wish) while Georgina stands

Electra-like in her father's arms. Georgina clashes with the brash, smart-aleck book reviewer, Clark Redfield, but finds herself drawn to him in spite of herself because his impertinence and virile self-assurance are so unlike Jim's (and her own father's). In her fantasy Clark becomes a sadistic monster who twists a cat's tail for pleasure. Georgina imagines she shoots Clark and is defended in court by Jim, who behaves like a hero of a 19th century melodrama. One of Rice's most effective expressionistic devices to externalize inner psychological mechanisms is to have the actor playing Georgina's father also play the Judge, the obstetrician and other authoritarian figures in Georgina's fantasies—the same defense mechanisms of identification which was used in *Beggar on Horseback*. When she fantasies a Mexican love affair with George Hand, the face of Clark Redfield appears on a Mexican singer. Debating whether to take George's offer, she enjoys a masochistic fantasy of herself as a fallen woman leaning on the inevitable lamppost, rejected by Clark and Hand, and taking poison, to the remorse of Clark. She next goes to dinner with Clark and to the theatre, where she imagines that she is called upon to substitute in the leading role of Portia and wins great acclaim. Georgina and Clark's carping romance progresses and she finally knows she has met her master. Clark brings her to a closer grip with reality, pointing out that day dreaming is her form of escape from the real world. She sees Jim finally in his true light, not as the romantic martyr she had made him, and lets him go out of her life (to Reno, to get the divorce from Miriam so she can be near her obstetrician). The last scene shows Clark and Georgina being married by a sleepy justice of the peace who is also a projection of her father, and phoning her parents who seem relieved to learn that Georgina has come out of her dream life into reality. *Dream Girl* represents one of the most amusing and successful treatments of the inner life of wish-fulfillment and day dream, taxing the resources of modern stagecraft to keep pace with the free associations of a delightfully "normal, healthy" modern girl.

Apparently believing that playgoers had finally caught up with Freud, Rice produced in 1951 an earlier play, *Not for Children*, which had been written in 1935. A Saroyanesque piece of surrealist buffoonery, *Not for Children* attempts to castigate our theatre, but proved to be for neither adults nor children. A professor of psychology who had been fired for seducing a graduate student sits at the theatre with an actress, commenting on the play within the play which is no play at all.

At the end of *Not for Children* Rice kills himself off in a masochistic gesture of bravura, willing his millions to the actress and the professor of psychology on condition that they found the truly great American theatre. While we may agree with Rice's prophecy that the great theatre of the future will be born of the union of psychology and theatricality, *Not for Children* hardly derives from such a union.

Rice's recent play, *The Grand Tour* (1951), retains one charmingly expressionistic touch of the old Rice in an otherwise realistic play. The young lovers "do" France in stylized movements around the stage, absorbing all the wonders of the old world at Cook's tour tempo. By contrast with Laurents' *Time of the Cuckoo*, however, *The Grand Tour* is unexciting and actually not dependent upon its European milieu. Both plays begin as eager American girls go to Europe in search of long-postponed romance. Rice's heroine is a schoolteacher, a talkative, slightly annoying young lady, who verbalizes her emotions as a compensatory mechanism. She picks up a young man on the boat as he attempts suicide, and they fall in love. When they are about to go to a little hotel together, it turns out that he was at this same hotel on his honeymoon and their affair is temporarily postponed. He turns out to have embezzled some money from his bank in good melodramatic fashion, and in the end the girl uses her legacy to buy him out of the embezzlement trouble and then gives him up to his wife. At the end, she is back at her classroom telling her students about the glories of Europe, too noble a heroine to breathe the smoggy air of this Freudian century.

Although *The Grand Tour* is undistinguished, it is for Rice's grand tours of the unconscious life in *The Adding Machine*, *The Subway*, and *Dream Girl* as well as his photographic tours of the external world in *Street Scene*, *Judgment Day* and *Counsellor-at-Law*, that he will be chiefly remembered in the American drama.

MARTIN FLAVIN

One of the imaginative talents of the American theatre whose contributions have been somewhat neglected is Martin Flavin. As in the work of Philip Barry, the form and structure of Flavin's drama was dictated by the content, often resulting in original and unhackneyed dramaturgy. Like Barry, too, Flavin was indebted to psychoanalytic sources.

Flavin has stated in reply to the questionnaire that he was no greater student of Freud than the average creative worker of the present day. "But certainly," he wrote, "my plays and novels, to say nothing of my life and thinking, have been conditioned by the broad concepts of Freudian psychology . . . it seems to me impossible that they could have escaped it." Flavin felt that no one conversant

with the intellectual climate of the modern world could plead ignorance or deny the influence of Freud's theories:

> Freud is the origin of modern psychology—of a rational ap-
> proach to investigation of the human mind; and if there be
> at this time, or if there has been for the past thirty years,
> any other system worthy of serious consideration, I have
> been blissfully unaware of it. . . . Like Einstein's Relativity,
> the impact of it is not to be averted.

In 1919, Dr. J. Sadger, a disciple of Freud, published his interesting study, *Sleep Walking and Moon Walking,* in which he suggests that sexual and repressed Oedipal wishes are latent in the
obsession to gaze hypnotically at the moon and to walk in one's
sleep during the full moon. Sadger cites cases in which the full moon
aroused repressed memories of the light carried by the parent into
a child's room at night. Flavin's play, *Children of the Moon* (1923),
if not based upon Sadger's analyses, at least suggests a striking parallel in the handling of the subject of moon-fixation. The plot concerns
the efforts of a highly neurotic, possessive mother to break up her
daughter's love affair with an aviator. Her sadistic scheme is to tell
her then-perfectly-normal daughter that there is lunacy (literally—
the ancients also believed that the moon caused insanity) in the
family. Her grandfather is an old man who babbles insanely and
stares at the moon through a telescope. The moon to him is a maternal symbol and he suggests the Freudian motif of return to the
womb as he says:

> . . . do you realize that from the Moon we came? That to
> the Moon we must return? Do you realize that we are all
> of us children of the Moon?

The girl's brother, moreover, has been killed during the war
when he was on a night mission and flew off toward the irresistible
light of the moon. From these hints that she has the strain of lunacy
in her, the daughter soon breaks down and stares tremblingly at the
moon; it is not entirely clear, however, whether Flavin attributes
this to hereditary pychosis or to the oppressive force of the mother's
malicious suggestion. At any rate, the daughter and her lover fly
off toward the moon themselves in a pact of suicide.

Flavin's next play was an even deeper excursion into the realm
of insanity. This time he was on sounder ground, and in *Lady of the
Rose* (1925) he created a fine and gripping play which paints a dev-
astatingly accurate picture of psychosis. John Meredith, a playwright,
has invented an imaginary woman, wonderfully tender and gentle.

For years he lives in fantasy with her, speaking to his dream-lady of the rose who actually appears on the stage when he is alone. He has married a woman who resembled his fantasy, but she turned out to be a hard, shrewish, cynical opportunist. And so he sits alone in his retreat, brooding and dissociated from reality.

He has written a play around his dream-lady of the rose, and unknown to him the wife persuades a producer to stage it, so that she can star in it. It is a great hit, but the playwright secretly watches it and comes away in a state of shock, for the wife's coarse performance has killed the lovely image in his mind. He retreats further from reality, virtually fasting until at last the lady of the rose returns to him, speaking for the first time lines that he hadn't written in his play. Now the lady does not run away when outsiders come—which suggests the extent of his psychosis. He dies gently forgiving his wife.

Although Flavin does not refer to the origin of the lady of the rose, the clinical etiology of such a wish-fulfillment fantasy is apparent: the childhood idealization of the memory of the mother. *Lady of the Rose* ranks with *The Verge* and *Berkeley Square* as a powerful attempt to explore the psychotic mind. It is unique in American drama, however, in its subtle and tender evocation of the ideal mother-mistress-wife; the hero's psychosis is interpreted as the wish to return to the secure embrace of this lady of the rose, a wish so over-powering that it breaks down the reality-testing faculty of the mind. *Lady of the Rose* strikes so deeply into the unconscious subsoil that the reader or spectator is more ready to respond to the reality of the lady than he would likely care to admit.

In a lighter mood, Flavin returned with *Broken Dishes* (1929) to this theme of projecting idealized figures with whom to live in wish-fulfillment. This time his setting is an ostensibly normal family, but one in which there is almost as little contact with reality as in *Lady of the Rose*. Jenny, the mother has romanticized her former suitor, Chester Armstrong, and painted such a rosy picture of what her life with him might have been that she and her two older daughters are in love with this fantasy of projected wishes, while the mousy father, Cyrus (made famous by Donald Meek), has a permanent inferiority complex from comparison with the mighty Chester Armstrong. Jenny is a shrewish, fanatic matriarch and her two daughters have become nagging grouches because they have found no suitors who could compare with Chester. The youngest daughter (played by a young actress named Bette Davis) is in love with a humble working boy in town, but the mother would part them. While mother and the older girls are at the movies, the lovers con-

trive to get married, and persuade (with the help of some cider) the
timorous father to give his reluctant blessing. There is a gentle scene
of recognition of the unconscious bond between father and daughter,
who would pass up her honeymoon night to stay home and defend
her father against the mother's wrath. But the young husband insists that she break with her home—as he is resolved not to be the
kind of passive-dependent father Cyrus has become. Then in the
manner of Barry, Flavin makes his characters face the past and
purge themselves of it: into the domestic crisis walks the legendary
Chester Armstrong. Unlike the idealized conception of him, he turns
out to be a jailbird wanted by the police for a swindle. Jenny collapses from the trauma of having her wish-fulfillment fantasy destroyed, and confesses that the real Chester Armstrong was never
as she described him:

> Jenny: He was the butcher boy. He used to bring our meat.
> (Still sobbing). Father wouldn't have him in the house. I
> really didn't care for him myself until he went away, and
> then—(A pause).
> Cyrus: (Gently) Yes, Jenny?
> Jenny: I thought perhaps he'd got along. I used to think
> about it all so much—and then I just believed he had.
> Cyrus: Yes, I see.
> Jenny: He came to stand for all the things I'd wanted all my
> life.

Broken Dishes shows the light of reality effectively demolishing
the pathetic little ego-defenses which arise as compensations for
painful truth; the play proved to be one of the more enduring comedy dramas of the period.

In the same year, Flavin made one of the first and most significant attempts to apply the insights of psychoanalysis to a sociological problem, in this case, penology. *The Criminal Code* (1929) studies
the case of a decent young boy who accidentally kills a man in a
tavern brawl for insulting his girl. Because of political pressure, the
district attorney has to make an example of him, and he gets ten
years for manslaughter. In prison six years later, he has been on good
behavior but is undergoing mental breakdown. The same district
attorney has now been "kicked upstairs" and is the warden. The
prison doctor is psychoanalytic-minded, but knows how helpless he
is to alleviate the prisoners' sex starvation:

> You are not sick—Do you understand? You say you have no
> appetite—you cannot sleep—you have bad dreams—Humph!
> Physically you are not sick. . . . You are neurotic—Outside,

I would prescribe a change—the mountains or the sea. Hum!
It is not medicine you need. You understand? . . .

The doctor's influence helps the boy land the job of chauffeur to
the warden, and he proceeds to fall in love with the warden's daughter. There is a prison break, however, and the boy happens to witness
the shooting of a stool-pigeon. For political reasons the warden must
get the name of the killer from him; but he sticks to the criminals'
own code not to betray each other. When the daughter confides in her
father that she wants to marry the boy, the warden eases up his third-
degree methods even at the risk of political repercussions over the
prison break . . . too late, however, for the boy has killed a guard
in solitary, and another potentially useful member of society is lost
forever.

From prison frustration Flavin turned to a more symbolic and
allegorical handling of Freudian concepts, setting his play *Achilles
Had a Heel* (1935) in a zoo. In this play, Flavin creates a droll set
of symbols: the plodding elephant represents man's Conscience or
super-ego, and the lusty, scampering monkeys represent sexuality
or the *Id* drive. The hero of the play is a Negro elephant-keeper who
is attached to his pachyderm. He is a war hero, and his white commanding officer is now the monkey-keeper, resentful of his humiliating job. In revenge, he sets a mulatto prostitute to seduce the Negro.
The elephant-keeper is sorely tempted, but as he makes love to her
his elephant stamps and trumpets as a warning. To buy her a monkey
coat, he risks and loses his money in a crap game; he is disgraced
and his rival, the monkey-keeper, is given charge of the elephant.
The girl throws him over and he locks her in the cage with the
monkeys, concluding that she is nothing but lust and stupidity. The
loyal elephant at last kills the villainous monkey-keeper.

In the teeming bestiality of the zoo, a Lesbian nursegirl picks
up a girl whom a man was trying to seduce. There is also heavy-
handed humor based on a Prussian veterinarian, who would treat
the animals in the zoo psychosomatically. When a baby monkey has
no appetite, he gives a Freudian diagnosis: "Because he iss already
now a nerfous wreck." His father is a fool and his mother a strumpet,
he concludes, and with such a bad home environment, they decide to
send the baby to a circus. When the mother and father monkeys are
upset and the father stops eating, the doctor observes: "Dot's all up
in his head—She turns him down und he ain'd got no sense . . . Sex!
Sex! Sex! It's chust der same mit eferyvun. You always got too much
or—nod enough . . . It's a case for Jung or Freud."

Achilles Had a Heel proved either too obvious or too obscure in its Freudian symbols for the New York playgoer, and in spite of an impressive performance by Walter Hampden as the elephant-keeper, the play ran only a week on Broadway.

Flavin's final contribution to psychoanalytic drama was *Tapestry In Gray* (1935) which was a dramatization of a psychoanalysis itself. Dr. Marius is the psychoanalyst who asks Stephen and Iris to recall (face to face, not on the couch) any incidents which relate to her husband, Erik, who is mentally ill. The structure of the play is thus a series of free association flashbacks as repressed memories return to the surface. Sensing the need for a fluid staging to dramatize the rapid flow of associations, Flavin calls for a master setting in the psychiatrist's office and wagon stages of constructivist, semi-fantastic appearance for the remembered episodes.

In spite of the psychoanalytic basis of the plot, the play appears somewhat melodramatic. The tapestry of these three gray lives is gradually patched together—as a medical student, Erik had been a sexual sadist, sublimating his sadism by becoming a great surgeon. Iris had a traumatic early experience when a ballet teacher made passes at her and convinced her she would never be a great dancer. She then became a nurse and after Erik performs a great plastic operation on Stephen, she ruins the operation by loosening the bandages and leaves Stephen scarred for life. Erik later finds Iris as she is about to commit suicide, and has an affair with her, admitting he would like to cut into her. After Iris and Erik are married, she becomes jealous because he spends so much time with Stephen, and is obsessed with the fear that Stephen will discover that she was the careless nurse who ruined his life. Then their son is hurt and Erik operates at Iris' insistence, only to fumble the operation because he is so unnerved. The son dies and Erik's faith in himself as a surgeon is destroyed. Before the arrival of the psychiatrist, Erik commits suicide, knowing that Iris loves Stephen and that she had ruined his life by sapping his creative strength in her attempt to possess him. By the time she has dredged up all these guilty memories, Iris knows that she is in fact the psychiatrist's patient. She is overwhelmed with fear that she will destroy other lives as she has Erik's. At the end, Dr. Marius has shown her the true perspective that absolves her from her guilt; but she must send Stephen away and try to be self-reliant at last rather than to draw her strength from others. In spite of the rather text-bookish plot, *Tapestry in Gray* is the first true effort to dramatize a psychoanalytic therapy, later to be more successfully managed by *Lady in the Dark,* and *Home of the Brave.* Although in 1929-30 Flavin had three plays running on Broadway— two of them hits—*Criminal Code, Broken Dishes,* and *Cross Roads*—

he has since 1936 abandoned the theatre in favor of fiction, where the chance for success is less weighted against an author.

GEORGE KELLY

George Kelly is an anomaly in the modern theatre. During the psychoanalytic period in which playwrights were extracting drama from the emotional seething of living people, Kelly's portrait gallery consisted of coldly calculated and generally bloodless figures, observed clinically with detachment and not a little disdain. Conservative in his attitudes, Kelly points out the follies and ludicrous behavior of his times with a crabbed cynicism that would do credit to Ben Jonson if it did not lack Jonson's raucous gusto.

His first Broadway play, *The Torchbearers* (1922) as well as *Philip Goes Forth* (1931) satirize the impulse to self-expression in amateur theatricals and playwriting. In 1924, however, he created a forceful and realistic comedy of character, *The Show Off*, which depicts in Aubrey Piper a classic portrait of a latter-day *commedia dell' arte* boaster, while studiously avoiding any reference to the unconscious mechanisms responsible for compensatory "showing off" which Adler described as the "superiority complex."

His next play, the Pulitzer Prize winning *Craig's Wife* (1925) remains perhaps his most famous work. There is mature understanding in his masterful study of a selfish, frigid wife who finds her own release in dominating her husband, putting every bit of bric-a-brac in place, allowing no visitors nor smoking in her living room, and making of her home a thing as cheerless and coldly correct as she herself is. Without using Freudian terminology, Kelly achieves a valid picture of the mechanism of reaction-formation, the explanation for which is suggested by childhood factors. For twelve years after her mother died of a broken heart, Harriet Craig lived with a stepmother and felt a desperate need for independence. "I saw what happened to my own mother," she tells her husband, "and I made up my mind it 'ud never happen to me." Harriet's sexless, sterile life is not explained in terms of repressed drives, but rather by her attempt to substitute a home for a husband. She had married a home because that was what she needed, and the husband merely went with it as a concession she had to put up with. Satisfying the drive for security left Mrs. Craig emotionally impoverished for any honest marital relation, and audiences were virtually ready to stand up and cheer when the long-suffering Mr. Craig finally turns on his wife, smashes her favorite ornament and shows her up for what she is.

Judging by the popularity of the play, Craig's wife must have proven
a recognizable type of American woman.

Again in 1936 Kelly treated in *Daisy Mayme* woman's inhu-
manity to man, particularly to her own family. He depicts a generous
and easygoing bachelor who doesn't marry while he has to support
his mother and widowed sister. But when he finally wishes to marry
Daisy Mayme, he finds his sister insidious in her darkly motivated
attempts to keep him single. Without delving into the unconscious
factors governing the sister, Mrs. Fenner, who is sprung from Mrs.
Craig's family tree, Kelly is content with merely describing in realistic and meticulous detail the end product of human character. He
might be called a behaviorist in drama rather than a psychoanalyst.
Like *Craig's Wife*, however, there are living theatrical elements in
Daisy Mayme, as a recent television production confirmed.

In *Behold the Bridegroom* (1927) Kelly circles mothlike around
the periphery of psychoanalytic motivation without ever once dipping
into the center. He creates in Tony Lyle the portrait of a neurotic
young woman of the smart set who has been spoiled and sophisticated in her manners and bored by a surfeit of lovers. Kelly approaches her, however, with the moralist's disapprobation rather than
the analyst's perception. With Kelly's unique ability to name his
characters originally, there is a Gehring Fitler who loves Tony, and
a Mr. Train who is so different from her smart set males that she
picks him as her candidate for bridegroom. Fitler ultimately kills
himself when she firmly but gently rejects him as too prosaic. After
his suicide, Tony goes into a hysterical coma, and a conventional
physician calls it "psychological." When asked to account for it, he
sidesteps with a speech which was dated even for 1927:

> . . . there are a great many ways, Mr. Lyle; but unfortu-
> nately, they lead us into considerations of psychology; and
> the medical profession has probably thought it wiser to
> avoid those considerations.

There is also reference to a "nerve specialist" or "brain specialist" to
whom a character goes for treatment and finally elopes with, but
who does not appear in the play.

There is some hint that Tony's hysterical *aboulia* is derived from
her relationship to her father, of whom she had been too fond. The
father would remarry if only Tony would get married; but she
doesn't want to, and the father jokingly says that the two of them
would get along fine if they went off by themselves. Love for a young
engineer is found to be the cause of her coma, and when he finally
reaches her arms she is a humbler and wiser girl. Mr. Kelly has

merely chastened and slapped the wrists of his heroine, not released or purged her from her neurotic pressures. *Behold the Bridegroom* lacks the warmth of living characters, and the play bogs down in a mass of trivia realistically detailed.

Maggie, the Magnificent (1929) again raised more psychological problems than Mr. Kelly could successfully resolve. The conflict between mother and daughter is here treated with sympathy for the younger generation. The mother's transition is from stormy shrew in the beginning to a humbled, helpless and reserved mother in the end; but again it is accomplished without insight into motivating causes. After the failure of Kelly's next play, *Philip Goes Forth* (1931), Kelly retired from the theatre for 14 years, to emerge only once with a comedy, *Reflected Glory* (1936), concerning an actress who found that she too could not retire from the stage which had its hold upon her.

In 1945, Kelly produced *The Deep Mrs. Sykes;* the emotions depicted are anything but deep, however, and all Kelly manages to do is create in Mrs. Sykes another sister of Mrs. Craig, a thoroughly hateful and yet recognizable type of insecure woman who must resent security and success in other women—particularly in their relations with men (although a man is the last thing for which Mrs. Sykes would consciously acknowledge a need). The characters are a cold lot, moving mechanically through a meticulously plotted play with every stage cross and every extinguishing of a cigarette specified by the playwright. Mrs. Sykes is "an egotistic woman" about whom Kelly observes: ". . . they say they're really much deadlier than the male; because their egotism usually passes for mere feminine jealousy." She is emotionally impoverished, living a frigid marital relationship and disrupting a number of other lives because of her intuition that flowers sent to a woman across the street must have been sent by her own husband. The shoe of suspicion fits elsewhere, too, however, and the drunken wife of a doctor also is convinced it is her husband who is philandering. After a series of Aristotelian reversals, it proves to be Mrs. Sykes' married son who is the silent admirer of the lady across the street. But Mr. Sykes also has a mistress, though Mrs. Sykes for all her intuition fails completely to guess who it is. If Mrs. Sykes was at all deep, her author never got out of shallow water with her. Kelly seems rather an intellectual puppeteer pulling the strings of his studied and finely etched characters without passion, comedy relief or potential empathy.

Only in his most recent play has Kelly deviated from his affinity for frigid and hard-shelled women. In *The Fatal Weakness* (1946) he created, with help from the glowing acting of Ina Claire, a portrait of a charmingly sentimental and helpless woman, Mrs. Espenshade, who is such an incurable romantic that she goes to the weddings of people she doesn't even know. Her husband is having an affair with a woman osteopath which interests her so much that she participates in it vicariously and can't find it in herself to be jealous. Her daughter, too, is having marital difficulties, which Kelly ascribes to the influence of "self expression" and new thought which she gets from a child psychologist, "Dr. Bajarian in the Ziegler Building, a perfectly fascinating person," who apparently epitomizes the superficial dabbling in psychology which irritates Kelly. The daughter has been taking her son, Punchy, to him and has learned that Punchy loathes his grandmother:

> You've never seen anything like it. A perfect Oedipus complex in reverse; and once removed, of course.

The daughter views marriage as "an arrestment of the spirit," an anachronism that seems to smack of the early twenties rather than 1946. Surely this daughter is not representative of the postwar young married set. Although the daughter has just left her husband, she tells her mother with nice Electra-complex irony that "it would be perfectly *monstrous* if you were to leave papa." With the help of a snooping friend who has nothing to do but follow the clandestine lovers for whatever unnamed satisfaction she derives from it, Mrs. Espenshade finally accumulates enough evidence to warrant divorcing her husband. Reluctantly she does so, and then goes to the wedding of her husband and the other woman. Although thin and trivial, there is at least in *The Fatal Weakness* more warmth and affection for his characters than was to be found in Kelly's previous plays.

Kelly represents the dilemma of a twentieth century writer who would be a realistic recorder of human behavior without reference to the insights of the psychoanalytic movement. In his finest work, *Craig's Wife,* he parallels most strongly the concepts of Freudian psychology and creates the prototype of the frigid woman so familiar to psychoanalysts. But Kelly seems less curious about the deeper sources of human motivation than in depicting with objective, behavioristic eyes the everyday trivia that make up the human comedy.

In his answer to the author's questionnaire he indicates a guarded attitude toward Freudianism and a hint that the creative writer is an analyst in his own right. Stating that he had read none of the works of the Freudians, Kelly expressed doubt that "the mentalists" have contributed or will ever contribute much to a dramatist possessed of "the spark." He observed that psychological diagnosis, however valid, cannot by itself hold the attention of an audience in the theatre: "life is never so logical as that—it glints in patterns of conduct that only the intuitive eye can follow—mere intellectual tracings are not nimble enough." Kelly has perhaps diagnosed the weakness of some of his own plays, which tended to seem mere intellectual tracings.

SIDNEY HOWARD

The paradoxical Sidney Howard—who did everything from organizing a post of the American Legion to writing bitterly anti-war plays, *Paths of Glory* and *The Ghost of Yankee Doodle*—presented no more ambivalent attitude than his approach to psychoanalysis. On the one hand, he has given us *The Silver Cord*, perhaps the most famous and successful of the mother-fixation plays, and on the other hand he is known to have had a violent disagreement with the Theatre Guild because its directors insisted, during the rehearsals of *The Silver Cord*, upon interpreting it in Freudian terms. Joseph Wood Krutch has called this ambivalence symptomatic of Howard's ". . . temperamental antipathy to intellectual formulas, of his impatience with anybody's ideas even though they happen to be also his own."

Howard proved to be a somewhat eclectic writer, contributing a number of capable adaptations from a variety of sources: *Dodsworth*, from the Sinclair Lewis novel; *Yellow Jack* from the Paul de Kruif book; *Marseilles, The Late Christopher Bean* and *Ode to Liberty* from French writers, and *Lute Song* from the Chinese. Among his original work, *They Knew What They Wanted* (1924) was his first success, with its warm and affectionate portrait of an Italian winegrower in Howard's native California who obtains a wife by mail order and devotedly urges her to stay even though she becomes pregnant by a young hired hand. That same year, Howard collaborated with the older dramatist, Edward Sheldon, in *Bewitched*, which reflects an early interest in the psychological mechanisms of projection and identification. An American aviator spending the night in a French chateau has complicated dreams—of an evil hypnotist who casts a spell on him and of the girl he loves (who appears in the dream in six or seven different forms—as his mother, an old flame, the goddess of love and as the granddaughter of the sinister mesmerist). Howard explained the play in a letter to Barrett Clark:

> Then Sheldon and I did a real job called "Bewitched," which is a Freudian Fairy Tale. We can't find any actress

who isn't horrified of the part. She plays a young sorceress, an American girl of the boy's past in the beau monde, the boy's mother, a symbolic figure of sex appeal as such, and a young French girl. I can't make the notion very clear in summary but it is this—that a man expects the woman he loves to embody all the appeal of all kinds of women, flame, mother and mistress . . . and still to meet him on his own ground and if she can't do that, she bores him. So that, though you never see the real girl until the last page of the play and have no notion of how she will fare with the 100% male, you meet all the appeals to him in sequence and (in the sorceress) in combination. I should almost be inclined to send you that along with *Swords,* for it is a much more original play and much more my line.

Howard was too mercurial to follow *Bewitched* with another Freudian fairy tale, however, and in 1925 he wrote a realistic study of a dynamic and successful night club proprietor, *Lucky Sam McCarver.* The year of *The Silver Cord* he wrote a study of a daughter who "takes after" her father, *Ned McCobb's Daughter,* but the taking-after cannot be interpreted in terms of an unconscious father-daughter complex. Instead, he concentrates upon external and conscious problems centering around Prohibition rum-runners who tangle with the capable if not mannish daughter of Ned McCobb. When *The Silver Cord* arrived on Broadway in 1926, there had been only a hint of Howard's interest in the drama of unconscious motivation.

It is little wonder that Sidney Howard wanted no part of labels or "isms" when critics were prone to evaluate *The Silver Cord* in such terms as these:

> In *The Silver Cord* Howard has taken that old wheeze, the "Oedipus Complex," and dressed it up as literally as a fundamentalist parson dresses up his Genesis.
>
>   R. Dana Skinner, *Our Changing Theatre*
>
> . . . an embattling study of two sons in the coils of an Oedipus Duplex. . . . He makes straight for Freud, and lets you have in frank, infuriated biologist's terms just what it was that Mother wanted.
>
>   Gilbert W. Gabriel, *New York Sun*
>
> . . . Without calling openly upon Freud and Krafft-Ebing, Howard illustrates dramatically how the frustrated mother knew what she wanted. She wanted to exalt her sons into romantic images or ikons of what their father might have been. . . . If this play were represented by heraldry, the

device would show mother-love rampant and two sons couchant.

New York Telegram, December 21, 1926

In spite of Mr. Howard's denial that the theme was Freudian, *The Silver Cord* represents to a generation of playgoers the most palatable and civilized presentation of the possessive-mother-and-passive-son relationship. The play ran over one hundred performances on Broadway and has been included in many anthologies as illustrative of the Freudian drama. It is distinguished chiefly in its portrait of the mother, Mrs. Phelps, who, as notably played by Laura Hope Crews, must have been more than a little identifiable for the playgoers of the twenties. Her "unselfish" devotion to her sons is keenly dissected and revealed to be composed of intolerance, sexual jealousy of the sons' girls, and ruthlessness to preserve her matriarchy. We first meet Mrs. Phelps at her charming, gracious best as she receives her son, David, returning from Europe with his bride, Christina. From her first discourtesy to Christina at the introductions, however, she reveals herself obsessed by her grown sons to the exclusion of everyone else. Her first skirmish is in an effort to keep David at home rather than accepting an attractive job in New York. Next she persuades her younger son, Rob, to break off his engagement with Hester. When Christina announces she is pregnant, Mrs. Phelps is so stunned that she spills her cocktail on her dress (one might be tempted to call it a Freudian spill).

When Rob spinelessly breaks his engagement with Hester, she hysterically tells Mrs. Phelps what she thinks of her; leaving the house, she crosses a dangerous pond and slips through the ice. The boys run out to rescue her but Mrs. Phelps calls them back, concerned only lest her boys catch pneumonia.

Mrs. Phelps has contrived to have Christina and David sleep in separate rooms, but both the mother and wife come visiting during the night to recapture the wavering David. Mrs. Phelps is not above eavesdropping, and when found out plays the tragic martyr with feigned heart trouble. Christina brings David's ambivalence to a sharp focus and forces him to choose between his mother and his wife. The show-down scene as Christina and Mrs. Phelps confront each other is a memorable one in the theatre. Howard fairly gives Mrs. Phelps the best possible defense of her life—she had been left a widow after an unhappy marriage, and had sublimated all her emotional life in her sons. Christina's answer is the classic rebuttal to all of the "nobility" and self-sacrificing sentimentality of motherhood:

. . . It's a pity she didn't marry again. Things would have

been so much better for both of you if she had. . . . But the
fact remains, Dave, that she did separate you and me last
night and that she separated us because she couldn't bear
the thought of our sleeping together. And she couldn't bear
that because she refuses to believe that you're a grown man
and capable of desiring a woman. And that's because,
grown man that you are, down, down in the depths of her,
she still wants to suckle you at her breast!

Christina shocks David into awareness and he finally is able to make
the reluctant choice to go with his wife rather than stay with his
mother. But Robert remains, engulfed forever in the inverted and
sterile envelope of mother-love.

After *The Silver Cord* made his reputation, Howard followed
the play with another treatment of a psychoanalytic theme, *Half
Gods* (1929). As if in unconscious protest against being labelled a
Freudian, Howard here struck out against psychoanalysis in a satiric
attack on an omniscient psychoanalyst who is only a "half-god," and
of whom the words of Emerson express Howard's hopes:

> Heartily know,
> When half-gods go,
> The Gods arrive.

A tedious story of a married couple who feud and fuss even though
sexually attracted to each other, *Half Gods* shows the wife going to a
psychoanalyst (apparently a Jungian who uses face-to-face analytic
sessions). The extravagances of Jungian vocabulary are the target for
Howard's satiric barbs, as Dr. Mannering tells the wife:

The image has become clouded by a too vigorous projection of the anima and the subconscious rising in irresistible
revolt the consciousness can function only in confusion. But
distance will clarify, the adaptation to reality will follow
and the stream of the libido will flow on. Yes.

The giddy wife is thrilled to learn that psychoanalysis teaches each
wife to have a lover, and says, "Why, I think women ought to go
down on their knees to Freud and Jung."

Howard's grievances against psychoanalysis include all those
heard most often during the twenties: that it is a refuge for giddy
and empty-headed women with nothing else to occupy their time,
that it is outrageously expensive, (the husband gets an $800 bill for
his wife's therapy) and finally that it sanctions extra-marital experience. As Howard wrote to Barrett Clark, he meant the play to express ". . . some of American womanhood's revolt against marriage,

kidded, of course, but still pretty much as I see it." Of the ridicule of psychoanalysis, Howard wrote:

> For instance, the psychoanalyst scene which I balled up badly will be one long piece of horseplay at the expense of those gents, and I trust, very funny in the way it leads Hope further and further from the straight and narrow.

This heavy-handed satire is not the entire play, however, and the husband and wife undergo other complications before they are finally reunited. As the wife is about to leave for Reno, a somewhat arrogant doctor tells the husband:

> If you had courage, conscience or conviction, you would put your foot down on this woman's nonsense, carry her up those stairs this minute and impregnate her again.

By the end of this tasteless play, we gather that the husband will follow the doctor's advice.

Howard's hostility to psychoanalysis was only partially consistent, however, for in 1933 he wrote *Alien Corn*, which manifests, intentionally or not, considerable psychoanalytic insight. He depicts a close father-daughter relationship between a brooding old Viennese maestro and his pianist daughter, Elsa, created by Katherine Cornell. Julian, a neurotic introvert with a Ph.D. degree, is in love with Elsa, as is Conway, the married son of the founder of the college where Julian and Elsa teach. Among other symptoms, Julian suffers from what a Freudian might diagnose as castration panic:

> I think if I'd had brothers I might not have grown up such a neurotic worm. All kinds of things seem to set me off. Sounds, colors, the way people have of pronouncing words, anything with a sharp point on it! I can never look at anything sharp without feeling faint.

He also reveals amusingly the distracting influence which co-eds have during his lectures and examinations:

> You know that blonde Lathrop girl? Well, she was one of the last to finish just now. It's bad enough trying to lecture to that bosom of hers, but this afternoon, walking around to keep an eye out for cribbing . . . Well, every time I passed that girl and looked down . . . God!
>
> Phipps: Ever hear of the academic sex, Julian?
> Julian: No, what is it?
> Phipps: It's the sex that gets all its fun out of looking down.

Encouraged by Phipps to outgrow the academic sex, Julian turns like
Hedda Gabler to the manly hobby of pistol shooting. Several bulls'
eyes with these symbolic phalluses make a new man of Julian, and,
freed of his inferiority feelings, he says of his pistols:

> Julian: All right, my Freud and Jung. Put Lohengrin to bed.
> He's served me well . . . I *have* found my manhood.
> Phipps: These sudden changes of sex aren't good for you.

Julian's discovery of himself is too sudden to be lasting, however, and
when Elsa decides to go away with Conway, her lover and benefactor, Julian takes his own life. In the end, Elsa finds that she must
reject Conway, who would have her give up her career, and go to
Vienna alone and independent of any man.

Alien Corn reflects more maturely the influence of psychoanalysis than does the more famous *Silver Cord*. At his untimely death in
1939, Sidney Howard left a substantial body of drama, including an
unfinished play on Woodrow Wilson. Another play left in first draft,
Madam, Will You Walk?, was given a capable off-Broadway production in 1953 by Jessica Tandy and Hume Cronyn. It proved to be
a fitting summary to the philosophy of Howard as well as a return
to his early fantasy style of *Bewitched*. Militantly humanitarian, brilliant, and iconoclastic, Howard revealed himself in *Madam, Will
You Walk?* as still attracted by psychoanalytic concepts without permitting himself an open and admitted indebtedness. He uses instead
the framework of time-worn Faustian supernatural, complete with
red smoke pots, mysteriously moving chairs and a devil who appears
by magic. The devil, however, raises some astringent questions concerning the nature of good and evil, which arouse the expected cen-
sure from conventional church and bench. This ingratiating devil's
formula is to remove the repressive lid from the cauldron of humanity
and encourage people to release their deeper nature. Principally this
results in a taxi driver becoming a successful dancer. The *animating
force,* represented by this most humanitarian of devils, turns our
repressive stereotypes upside down and almost lands the young
heiress played by Miss Tandy in a mental institution. Howard is not
entirely successful in dramatizing his philosophy (which he calls
anthropocentric), but is at least clear that the conventional religious
and legal pillars stand in the way of man's fulfillment. The girl who
finds her fulfillment by helping others to realize themselves falls in
love with the dancing taxi driver and even has to ward off the amorous advances of the animating force or devil himself—who finally has
the good taste to disappear at the end and leave the lovers to their
destiny. Howard manages in *Madam, Will You Walk?* to intrigue an

audience with provocative discussion as well as sure-fire theatre necromancy and turns conventions upside down with Shavian or even Pirandellan zest. If the play left some critics unclear as to its purpose, it nevertheless made the Freudian commentary that an un-bridled curiosity and impatience with human stagnation may be not devilish but in the highest sense humanitarian.

Some of the scenes in *Madam, Will You Walk?* including a row-boat scene on a foggy lake and a court room trial of the devil are among the most inventive writing of this generally conventional writer. More a man of the theatre than a probing psychologist or con-sistent philosopher, Howard tried to express various aspects of his "man-centered" yearning that ". . . there be decency and justice in the world." It is perhaps ironic that the author of the most famous psychoanalytic play of his decade should have picked up and dropped psychoanalysis as he did many other current topics without ever giving the feeling that his themes had, as with Lawson and Rice, burned through to the heart and compelled expression.

MAXWELL ANDERSON

Striding amongst our realistic and psychological playwrights in his Elizabethan doublet and buckler, Maxwell Anderson today stands almost alone in our theatre as a champion of elevated language. We cannot hope to do him full justice in this study, as the majority of the work of this prolific and versatile writer lies outside the psycho-analytic field. There is, however, evidence in his early writing of a definite interest in the psychoanalytic drama which is significant for a full understanding of Anderson's work.

Anderson's first play is revealing. *The White Desert* (1923) was called by a contemporary critic ". . . the kind of thing for which the way has been made at once easier and harder by the work in the theatre of Eugene O'Neill and the authors of *Rain*." It was in verse and dealt with a spirited young girl, isolated on a wintry North Da-kota farm with her mean-minded, guilt-ridden husband whose reac-tion-formation against sex is so strong that even though he and his wife had been intimate before marriage, he forces her to confess to him that once as a child she had evil, erotic thoughts in church, and that the glance of a man passing her in the street had once given her a thrill. He curses her for her wantonness, and leaves her to go to town. In his absence there is a blizzard, and the girl staggers to the barn, hardly knowing whether she wants to feed the stock or commit suicide. A neighbor man finds her there, carries her home, and makes love to her. She confesses her infidelity to her husband when he returns, and he murders her for it. The theme of obsessive guilt-feelings concerning sex was Anderson's only link with O'Neill and the authors of *Rain*, however. Critics praised the young author's integrity of characterization and high purpose, but found the play too wordy.

Anderson's second play, written with Lawrence Stallings in 1924, proved to be an historic stepping-stone in the American theatre's progress toward naturalism. *What Price Glory?* was an anti-heroic, candid record of the reactions of hardened men to war. It extended the theatre's amount of permissible profanity to include, "God damn every son-of-a-bitch in the world who isn't here!" It shocked even urbane first nighters in its unvarnished picture of Sergeant Quirt and Captain Flagg drinking and playing a game of blackjack to determine who shall possess Charmaine. Although the authors were less concerned with subtleties of motivation than with an honest, photographic impression of war stripped of its patriotic glamor, the significance of *What Price Glory?* lies in its accurate portraits of the cynicism, the callousness and the completely unsentimental, animal need for sexual outlet, which are man's defense mechanisms against war.

After two other plays with Stallings, Anderson on his own adapted Jim Tully's *Beggars of Life* for the stage as *Outside Looking In* (1925). Again in a powerfully naturalistic idiom, Anderson depicts life among the hoboes who ride freight trains. This play combines two of Anderson's persistent themes, an ironic comment on social injustice and an awareness of the eruption of gross sexuality where environmental conditions are debasing. Two hoboes refer to incest, one telling of a girl who was seduced by her step-father, and the other of a boy who remembers an erotic experience with his sister.

There is also a reference to incest in Anderson's next play, *Saturday's Children* (1927), which was a study of love in poverty, anticipating the depression by several years in its picture of economic as well as emotional frustration and the resultant ruses a girl is forced to use to get and hold her man. The older sister has been reading articles on psychology in popular magazines, while the father acts as psychological advisor to the family, telling his daughter not to have a baby. He apologizes: "Anyway, fathers shouldn't confide in their daughters. It isn't hundred per cent——. No doubt it would be considered a kind of intellectual incest." Here and elsewhere, Anderson seems to reflect a kind of fear of psychoanalysis and its implications. Yet his unconscious preoccupation with incest is also manifest in the demented Judge Gaunt's limerick in *Winterset*:

Marmaduke behind the barn
  got his sister in a fix;
He says damn instead of darn;
  ain't he cute? He's only six!

Anderson's most Freudian play was *Gypsy* (1929), a character
study of Ellen, a "new woman," modern and promiscuous, with an
"ancient infantile fixation" on her feminine independence. Ellen is
married to David, with whom she had lived before marriage and had
wed only reluctantly, fearing marriage as a restriction on her freedom. She has been an emotional gypsy in her romantic wanderings,
and now is flirting with a writer, Cleve. David can forgive a past
love affair as long as she is honest with him and conceals nothing.
She must finally tell David, therefore, that she has been intimate with
Cleve, and moves out to live with him.

The crucial scene is between Ellen and her mother, also sexually
liberated and now on her third husband. Although reluctant to hurt
her mother, Ellen is unconsciously jealous and resentful of her. A
memory returns to Ellen—apparently not too deeply repressed—of a
summer before her father died, when Ellen was ten and she and her
mother spent a few months with some relatives:

Ellen: . . . it was rather crowded and there was only one
  room for us and one bed?
Marilyn: Yes.
Ellen: And there was a man there I didn't like, but you
  seemed to like him for some reason?
Marilyn: Who was it?
Ellen: I don't know his name—I just remember there was an
  odor about him I didn't like—and one night I woke up
  shuddering—and that odor was in the room. . . .

The mother denies the accusation, and apparently neither Ellen nor
Anderson realizes that she has stumbled upon what psychoanalysts
call the memory of a "primal scene." Case histories of patients in
analysis have furnished examples of the traumatic effect which may
be caused by a glimpse or even, as in this case, a vague sensory
impression of sexual relations between the parents. Ellen's Electra
jealousies and unconscious identification with the abused father
as well as the loss of childish idolatry for the mother must have had
a devastating effect upon her and contributed to her later masochistic
sexual restlessness. She does not derive any insight from the memory,
however, and instead confronts her mother with bitter recriminations: "Why am I that way? Who put it in my blood? You! You! Do
you wonder you make me hate myself?" Anderson, like the gypsy,

apparently seems to give greater place to inheritance than does modern psychology, and in spite of the rather deep level memory of the primal scene, he has not appreciated its dynamic role in Gypsy's psychology nor the influence of the mother-rivalry, but reverts instead to the now-obsolete psychology of inherited faculties of "the blood."

In the end, both her husband and lover walk out on Ellen, the latter for fear she would soon desert him. In the Broadway version she turns on the gas and commits suicide—the reader has his choice of a revised ending in which a new man who has been trying to date her telephones; she turns off the gas and goes out with him. Either way, Anderson's picture of the modern, liberated woman has not been a flattering one, and has reflected an incomplete understanding of the deeper forces that might contribute to a girl's rebellion against fidelity. While *Gypsy* placed Anderson in the current psychological swim, he barely got his head under water.

If we did not know of Anderson's distaste for psychoanalysis it might be tempting to find Freudian parallels in *Night Over Taos* (1932), but we have Anderson's statement as a restraint:

> If I was influenced by Freud it must have been at second hand, for I have never read him, and have only a vague notion of what he was trying to say. However, I notice that the Athenians of the 5th century B.C. wrote some Freudian plays, and probably were aware of some of the theories which are now known as Freudian.

Whether it was second hand or coincidental, Anderson does create in *Night Over Taos* a picture of a primal father who vies with his two sons for the possession of women in the pattern described in Freud's *Totem and Taboo*. Don Pablo Montoya is a powerful Spanish grandee ruling the little colony of Taos in New Mexico, isolated when Mexico broke away from Spain in the last century. Montoya has three wives, one of whom had been loved by his eldest son, Federico, but is now rejected. Montoya is about to take another wife, the young Diana, who is beloved of the younger son, Felipe. When the brothers think that Montoya has been killed fighting the Americans, they make peace with the enemy, split the estate, but come to blows fighting over Diana. Federico has betrayed his father to the Americans, and Felipe too is beset with "death-wishes" toward his father, that he might enjoy Diana. But the father returns, and ruthlessly puts Federico to death. To Felipe and Diana he offers a poisoned cup according to the ancient Spanish code of honor. In the end, Montoya drinks it himself, however, realizing that the old order of autocratic Spanish rule, with its contempt for the *peons* in favor of the *ricos,* is doomed to extinction. Like Paul Green, Anderson is able to extract some majesty from the spectacle of a dying order, and his primal father, Montoya, is for all his tyranny a more vital figure than his treacherous and weakling sons.

Night Over Taos was written in verse for the specific talents of the Group Theatre acting company, and pointed the direction Anderson was to take in his next plays. Championing the theatre as a cathedral of the spirit, Anderson expressed the need for exalted speech which was lacking in our realistic idiom. His cycle of three queens, *Elizabeth the Queen, Mary of Scotland* and the more recent *Anne of the Thousand Days* are lusty, swashbuckling, poetic plays in the Shakespearean manner, finding heroic tragedy in his queens' historic decisions without any considerable psychological penetration. There is in the latter play, however, a strong suggestion of the ambivalent loathing-grown-to-love which Anne Boleyn feels for the insatiable King Henry VIII. No woman had ever said no to the rapacious Henry, and Anne is shown astutely vaulting herself into the Queen's throne by denying Henry. Anderson humanizes history to the extent of suggesting that the English Reformation was what it was because of one man's libido and one girl's insistence on a wedding ring. Although the scenes of sexual flare-up between Anne and Henry have a kind of electric vitality, the later scenes add little to our understanding of the inner nature of a King who could put to death the one woman he had loved, or a woman who could choose martyrdom in order to safeguard the throne for her daughter.

In 1935 Anderson turned from historic to modern dilemmas and created in *Winterset* perhaps his most significant play, his first to use poetic language in a contemporary setting. *Winterset* treats the aftermath of the Sacco-Vanzetti case, upon which he had based his earlier play, *Gods of the Lightning,* and shows the son of a hypothetical Vanzetti torn between the tragic choice of love or avenging his father's death. On the track of the one witness who could clear his father, Mio meets Miriamne, the sister of the witness. Of the idealized attraction which springs up between them, Mio says, "This men called love in happier times, before the Freudians taught us to blame it on the glands."

Hearing her face likened to the transfiguration on the mount, Miriamne offers him her innocent young love and body, exclaiming:

This I can give you. And so forever the Freudians are
   wrong.
Mio: They're well-forgotten at any rate.

Whether or not this represents Anderson's mature evaluation of Freudian psychology, he stretches psychological credibility considerably when Mio recalls in clear, conscious detail the execution of his father which happened when Mio was four. Mio's famous speech is poetically eloquent but psychoanalytically dubious. Avoiding analysis of the complex personality of such a buffeted young man, Anderson casts his Mio in the heroic, Aristotelian mold, with one compulsive goal ruling his life. Like Hamlet, Mio proves to be more of a talker than a doer. But unlike *Hamlet*, it is destiny (externalized in Miriamne) rather than "tragic inner flaw" which brings him to death.

Like the demented King Lear holding court in the hovel, and with the hobo for fool, Judge Gaunt obsessively re-tries the case in the basement tenement of the Esdras family; but he cannot absolve his own guilt for what he knows to be a wrong sentence and instead his reason breaks under the pressure. At the end of *Winterset*, Mio and Miriamne face death together, and the old father, Esdras, magnificently states Anderson's stoic faith that man's conscious ego can, merely through an act of will, rise above darkness and chaos—within and around the individual:

> . . . yet is my mind my own,
> yet is my heart a cry toward something dim
> in distance, which is higher than I am
> and makes me emperor of the endless dark
> even in seeking!

If Anderson preferred the older mold of Shakespearean tragedy to Freudian dissection of motives, we must, nevertheless, be grateful to him for giving us in *Winterset* as pungent speech as the modern theatre has heard.

Wingless Victory (1936) is a retelling of the Medea legend in terms of 19th century New England intolerance which keeps a family from accepting the South Sea princess the sea-captain brings home. Here again Anderson seemed more concerned with extracting glowing poetry and heightened emotional expression from his story than in retelling a Greek legend for its psychodynamic relationships as O'Neill had done.

Anderson turned to fantasy in two following plays. If A. A. Brill is valid in his interpretation of *Berkeley Square* as a study of schizophrenia, then the same analysis applies to Anderson's *High Tor* (1937), a portrait of a maladjusted young man who is obsessed with the idea of holding onto his mountain against the inducements of a trap rock company, and who even turns down his sweetheart, Judith, for urging him to sell out.

Alone on his mountain, Van creates out of his unconscious need a set of characters who once roamed these hills, Hendrick Hudson's Dutch sailors and the Captain's wife, Lise, a phantom-sweetheart with whom he proceeds to fall in love. (Although Van is presumed to be dreaming, the phantoms are visible to the other modern characters as well.) With his head securely on Lise's maternal lap (and the very mountain itself perhaps unconsciously a maternal symbol), Van has regressed to a level which represents security. But Lise gently brings him back to reality, knowing she must leave him. When the real Judith returns, Van is ready to sell his mountain, and allays Judith's jealousy of Lise by saying:

> Was there a Lise?
> I think she was my dream of you and me
> and how you left the mountain barren once
> when you were gone.

The dissociated hero learns to accept his adult role, but only after Anderson's point had been made that the past to which Van regressed and in which his individuality was unfettered was somehow preferable to the crass commercial exploitation of the present.

Anderson's other fantasy, *The Star-Wagon* (1937), assumes a rather unoptimistic view of human adjustment potential, and with the elaborate invention of a time-machine, makes possible a second chance for his characters as Barrie did in *Dear Brutus*, only to conclude that they were destined to behave no other way than what they did.

As in *The Time of Your Life* and *The Gentle People*, Anderson's answer to the spectre of Fascism in Europe was the assertion in *Key Largo* (1939) that man must at last take affirmative action against the forces of evil. There is more psychological interest in this play than in any previous work since *Gypsy*, however; its hero, King McCloud, suffers from a severe guilt complex ever since he deserted three of his buddies during an attack in the Spanish Civil War. To absolve his guilt he compels himself to go to the families of the three men he left to die and to abase himself with masochistic recriminations. When he comes to the last family, he finds the blind old father and beautiful sister, Alegre, virtual prisoners of a gangster. After some rather tedious philosophical discussion of man's place in the universe, King is able to throw off his pattern of skin-saving and go to his death, taking the gangster with him. Again Anderson's psychological implication is not a hopeful one; drawing his analogy from experimental neurosis in rats who bang their heads against the doors where they had previously found food, Anderson sees man banging himself against the doors of assorted illusions—religions, Communism, social security and sex—until finally all fail to hold meaning: "the girl holds out her arms, and she's made of sawdust, and there's sawdust in your mouth." As in *Winterset*, the sensitive, poetic young man talks big to the gangster who holds the gun, and is converted from the philosophy of despair to a stoic courage to die without insight or *anagnorosis* into the forces that brought him to his tragic destiny.

Anderson's wartime plays, including *Candle in the Wind*, *The Eve of St. Mark* and *Storm Operation*, made effective contributions with their lyric odes to man's courage and vision of a better world, which sustain him through the trials of war. Because this was more of a civilian army than that of *What Price Glory?* there is less profanity, more dignity of purpose, and closer contact with the folks back home, "Mom" and the chaste sweetheart who is worth waiting for. Soldiers in this war, an officer who anticipated Kinsey has explained in *The Eve of St. Mark*, fall into statistics of sexual activity:

> Buscemi: Twenty percent of the men in an army camp will refuse all temptations to sexual intercourse because they've got wives or sweethearts and so they don't want to play. And then another twenty percent will take anything they can get. You know, the way it is with you, Mulveroy.
> Mulveroy: They got to have shoes. I draw the line there. They got to go home and get their shoes.
> Buscemi: But then he goes on and says, there's sixty percent in between that maybe will and maybe won't depending on the temptation. . . . There we can save a lot of boys from contamination.

Going away to war from naive, sheltered environments and with too rosy ideals, it was inevitable that Anderson's young people would suffer post-war disillusion and maladjustment; this he depicts in *Truckline Café* (1946). The heroine, a gentle person unable emotionally to stand the shock of the loss of her husband, has turned to drink and promiscuity, and is a waitress at a trucksters' café in California. She learns that her husband is alive after all, and upon his return feels such guilt for what she has done that she would avoid a reconciliation. But events change her mind: first, the fact that her husband had also had an affair while overseas, and secondly, the tragic case of a soldier who had described his mistress to a buddy in the South Pacific only to have the buddy recognize her as his wife and return to kill her. Shocked into awareness by these events, the wife decides to try and rebuild her marriage and her life.

In that rather pedestrian version of Joan of Arc as seen from backstage, *Joan of Lorraine* (1946), Anderson discusses the necessity for faith in the modern world as well as in Joan's time, and dismisses psychoanalysis as a form of dogma which must be taken on faith:

> You look hard at yourself, any of you, and you'll find you're living by something you can't explain—maybe a formal religion, maybe a crazy-quilt philosophy you made up for yourself out of odds and ends, maybe a cause, maybe the S.P.C.A. or the Baconian theory or Freud or scientific research or communism or Christian Science or anti-vivisection, or somebody you're in love with, or an institution that needs cherishing—like our poor old theatre here on Manhattan. . . .

Again there is Anderson's rather consistent stoic theme that human life may be of dubious value but that death with dignity represents man's final triumph. In his two most recent plays, Anderson restated his old social indignation—first a compassionate study of racial intolerance, *Lost in the Stars* (1949) based on Alan Paton's novel, *Cry the Beloved Country,* and less successfully in a portrait of that Athenian of the 5th century B.C. with whom Anderson would be most apt to feel a stoic kinship—Socrates, in *Barefoot in Athens* (1951).

If Anderson's persistent search for subject matters in the past seems a regressive tendency, he defends it with the examples of the Greeks, Shakespeare, Corneille, and Racine. If he does not achieve the poetic genius of these writers, he has nevertheless enriched our theatre with something of its pre-twentieth century majesty and elevation. If he has shown less use for introspective analysis of unconscious motives after his first efforts in *White Desert* and *Gypsy* than for a philosophic approach to man's destiny, he has at least reflected twentieth century frankness coupled with an Elizabethan lustiness in dealing with sex, more often sensual than tender. While many of Anderson's colleagues might have enriched their work with some of Anderson's mouth-filling, flamboyant verse, it may be conversely true that Anderson's plays lack only his Freudian colleagues' acknowledgment of pressures deeper than consciousness. Maxwell Anderson proved to be the only major American playwright to chart his course counter to the prevailing theatrical winds during the psychoanalytic period.*

---

* Anderson's latest play, *The Bad Seed* (1954) may be good theatre but weak psychology, presupposing that the seed of homicidal tendencies can be transmitted by heredity.

ROBERT SHERWOOD

That the distinguished author and advisor to President Franklin
Roosevelt, Robert Sherwood, was influenced by Freudian psychology is apparent both in his plays and from his questionnaire.
His work spans the period from the twenties to the fifties, reflecting
an interesting shift in the handling of psychoanalytic materials. In
the amusing first blush of psychoanalytic awareness, *The Road to
Rome* (1927) is a delightfully tongue-in-cheek Freudian interpretation of Roman history. Gassner has called it:

> . . . a summation of the effervescent theatre of the twen-
> ties by virtue of its irreverence toward historical reputa-
> tions, anti-heroic outlook, and Freudian concern with re-
> pressions and compensation mechanisms, with sex the object
> of the suppression and the drive to power and glory as the
> compensation.

The road to Rome is, in the play, being besieged by the army of
Hannibal; while the Roman senator, Fabius Maximus, is preoccupied
with defending Rome, his charming wife, Amytis, is sexually unfulfilled and eager. Fabius Maximus is too much dominated by his
mother to be an adequate husband, and although Amytis wants a
child, Fabius has been thus far inadequate. When Amytis wants
him to take her to see a play called *Oedipus Rex,* he objects and
his mother, with a most un-Aristotelian prudery, calls it "probably
one of the coarsest plays ever written." Amytis is intrigued with the
rumors of Hannibal's army raping the women, and confesses, "I was
just wondering what it would be like to be despoiled."

To satisfy her curiosity Amytis slips into Hannibal's camp, but
is disappointed to find Hannibal a driving leader with a one-track
mind which disapproves of his soldiers' philandering. When it looks
as if Amytis might be put to death, she contrives instead to seduce
Hannibal, and by morning she had made him see the folly of despoil-
ing Rome. Proud that he has seen how to rise above senseless war
and devastation, Hannibal orders his army away from Rome. Why
not, asks Sherwood, account for a historical fact with "cherchez la
femme?" Before he leaves, Hannibal wishes prosperity to Amytis
and Fabius and their son:

> Fabius: Thank you—but I have no sons.
> Hannibal: You may have. . . .

Also in the twenties Sherwood wrote a light-weight "worm-turns" comedy, *The Queen's Husband,* showing the Queen as matriarch and the King as the worm. *Reunion in Vienna,* although produced in 1931 was also still in the spirit of the twenties, with its carefree, debonair approach to sex. In the play, Professor Doctor Anton Krug is a world-famous psychoanalyst in Vienna, but his portrait and that of his wife, Elena, the exuberant and intriguing former mistress of Prince Rudolf Maximillian von Hapsburg, could hardly be based upon Sigmund Freud and his conventional, straight-laced family life (at least not as played by the radiant Lynn Fontanne and Alfred Lunt). There seems to be contentment but little warmth between Krug and Elena—he is a cold and formal physician, busily leading people back through their past to the thing they were avoiding or magnifying out of proportion; by helping them to face it for what it is in reality, its hold upon them is thereby lessened. Dr. Krug soon has a chance to test his theory upon his own marriage when the dashing Rudolf von Maximillian returns secretly to Vienna for an anniversary celebration among the ex-aristocracy. Anton applies his face-down-the-past formula and urges Elena to go to him, see him for what he is—a shabby, penniless exile, and realize that she had been romanticizing him in her imagination.

What Elena finds is not that at all, however, but a still fascinating and desirable male who is completely confident that she will spend the night with him. In a delicious seduction scene, Elena manages to resist him, however, and he is saved from the police only because of Anton's influence in Austria. While he goes to intercede with the police, Rudolf spends the night at their home and Elena finally succumbs to her desire for her old lover. The next morning Elena is serene and pleased with herself for her night with Rudolf, who must leave Austria. By not playing the jealous husband, Anton has held his wife, but it has not been a total victory—in fact Anton has been made to eat his words about "facing the past"—Elena faced it and was recaptured by it. But Anton, like Fabius Maximus, "may have a son," and we gather that he may in the future make more of an effort to be an adequate husband for Elena. Although the play is a delightful starring vehicle, the scales are perhaps tipped too far in Rudolf's favor. But Sherwood is perhaps implying that psychoanalysts are just human enough not to be able to apply their insights to their own lives. At any rate, there is good humor in seeing, as Sherwood expressed his theme, "science hoist with its own petard . . . ," the same theme Philip Barry was to treat more sympathetically in *Tomorrow and Tomorrow.*

In his questionnaire, Sherwood stated that Freudian psychology was most influential in *Reunion in Vienna,* and to a lesser extent in

The Petrified Forest (1935). No play of the thirties more effectively expresses the intellectual despair of the depression years than does this latter play. If we may respectfully differ with Mr. Sherwood, his application of psychoanalytic concepts in *The Petrified Forest* is not less than *Reunion in Vienna* but actually deeper and better integrated with his characters. His hero, Alan Squier (so memorably played by Leslie Howard), symbolizes futility and the abdication of the intellectual in favor of the ego-mad fascist and gangster, symbolized by Duke Mantee. Squier falls spiritually in love with a rare and fresh young girl, Gabby (Gabrielle), who works in the desert filling station run by her father, an early prototype of the American fascist. But Squier has such impotence of will that he cannot fight for Gabby, and has for spiritual and material sustenance only: "Shirt, underwear, socks, toothbrush, passport, an insurance policy, and a copy of *Modern Man in Search of a Soul*, by Dr. Jung."

In his questionnaire Sherwood said that he had read a few psychoanalytic books, including *Modern Man in Search of a Soul* and Beatrice M. Hinkle's Jungian study, *The Re-creating of the Individual* (which Sherwood recommended as particularly interesting for writers). Like Sherwood, Alan Squier has drawn a philosophy with which to face the spectacle of a world on the road to a second world war from the words of Jung:

> Disruption in the spiritual life of an age shows the same pattern as radical change in an individual. As long as all goes well and psychic energy finds its application in adequate and well-regulated ways, we are disturbed by nothing from within. No uncertainty or doubt besets us, and we *cannot* be divided against ourselves. But no sooner are one or two of the channels of psychic activity blocked, than we are reminded of a stream that is dammed up. The current flows backward to its source; the inner man wants something which the visible man does not want, and we are at war with ourselves.

Squier did not read enough Jung, however, for both Jung and Hinkle leave the reader not with despair, but with a kind of hope for mankind through spiritual rebirth. Instead, Squier, who had been married to a rich woman who made him feel like a gigolo, sees himself as one of T. S. Eliot's *Hollow Men*, on whom it is a supreme joke that the intellectuals thought man's conscious reason could conquer Nature. Squier's words parallel Jung's:

> Squier: They've dammed it up (Nature) and used its waters
>   to irrigate the wastelands. They built streamlined mon-

strosities to penetrate its resistance. They wrapped it up in cellophane and sold it to drugstores. They were so certain they had it subdued. And now—do you realize what it is that is causing world chaos?
Gabby: No.
Squier: Well, I'm probably the only living person who can tell you. . . . It's Nature hitting back. Not with the old weapons—floods, plagues, holocausts. We can neutralize them. She's fighting back with strange instruments called neuroses. She's deliberately afflicting mankind with the jitters. . . .

Squier has no will even to make love to Gabby, and leaves her on the verge of submitting to the hulking ex-football player who wants her. But all of their plans are arrested by a fleeing desperado, Duke Mantee, who brings Squier back along with a society couple, the Chisholms, whose car he had commandeered. Mr. Chisholm also suffers from the disease of the times, impotence, and Mrs. Chisholm breaks down under the tension, crying out to her husband:

You haven't the remotest conception of what's inside me, and you never have had and never will have as long as you live out your stuffy, astigmatic life. (*She turns to Gabby*) I don't know about you, my dear. But I know what it means to repress yourself and starve yourself through what you conceive to be your duty to others.

She had wanted to be an actress and had undergone psychoanalysis in Salzburg. But her parents forced her to return and marry respectably. Now, however, she advises Gabby to find fulfillment and is herself ready to give herself to Duke, who at least suffers no paralysis of the will. Even Squier admires Duke for his aggressiveness, though he says of him that the cause of crime "has something to do with glands." Squier's inability to find a meaning for living leads to what was called by Freud the "death-wish." He makes out his insurance papers to Gabby so that she will be assured of means of going to France where her mother is, and where "They can understand everything—like life, and love—and death——." When the shooting begins, Squier and Gabby take cover flat on the floor, huddled together in a tender love scene. She will get to Paris, but Squier feels that she must go unencumbered by him. He calls upon Duke to kill him as he had promised before making his escape.

The Petrified Forest presents no clearly defined philosophy of hope for modern man, and its effective catharsis comes from a mystic, Jungian optimism that somehow in Gabby, as the Mother-symbol, the race of men will find its faith reborn. Out of conflict between *introvert* (Squier) and *extrovert* (Duke Mantee), Sherwood has powerfully extracted the despair of the thirties in a drama that is alternately tender and brutal as it shifts from the aggressive and the degraded to the sensitive and the spiritual.

Sherwood's despair at the insanity of war was even more sardonically expressed in his next play *Idiot's Delight* (1936). Then, in the face of universal neurosis in Europe, Sherwood turned for a faith as did so many writers, to our own American heritage, and created in *Abe Lincoln in Illinois* (1938) a monumental biography which, while staying within historical fact and not attempting to psychoanalyze Abe Lincoln, was remarkably able to suggest the ambivalence, the brooding feelings of inferiority and failure, the preoccupation with death, the deep, even masochistic humility, the "civil war going on inside" of the man who has been most hero-worshipped by Americans. Sherwood shows him as fearfully avoiding his political destiny and listening instead ". . . to the whispers of the women behind him—his dead mother—," until a strong-willed Mary Todd entered his life as a mother-image to drive him to greatness. Perhaps in this ambivalence and passive dependency which Sherwood has seized upon lies the key to the fascination which Lincoln, like Hamlet, has had for his audiences.

In *There Shall Be No Night* (1940) Sherwood continues his effort to extract a faith from a world growing progressively psychotic—in which even Russia, where many liberals had looked for hope during the thirties, had betrayed its admirers by attacking Finland. His leading character is again a psychiatrist, but unlike Dr. Anton Krug, this one is a warmly portrayed humanitarian who is Sherwood's mouthpiece. Dr. Valkonen represents the epitome of European civilization which was then under attack by Germany, Italy and Russia—he is a Nobel Prize winner and personal friend of Pavlov, Freud, the Mayos, Jung, and Carrel. At the beginning of the play he makes a radio address which gives Sherwood an opportunity to reveal his own philosophy at some length. Dr. Valkonen's book, *The Defense of Man,* suggests Jung's rather than Freud's influence, quoting Jung's statement that, "There is no coming to consciousness without pain," to account for the present pain in the political world. Perhaps, Dr. Valkonen suggests, medical science has conquered so many illnesses of man that man's capacity to struggle, to overcome pain, has been weakened and has permitted man to grow up without adequate defenses (the term is used not in Freud's sense of neurotic defense-mechanisms but rather social and political defenses against evil). The result is to grow passive as the democracies did at Munich.

Dr. Valkonen sets out to illustrate in his conduct this theory of the need for toughness. He will not flee from the Russian army, but rather becomes a medical officer in the fight to defend Finland:

> Freud left Vienna after the Nazi occupation. He went to London, and he was welcomed there, he was honored. But —he couldn't speak. He knew that if he told the truth, it would be printed, and his own people, still in Austria, would be made to suffer for it, horribly. . . . So Freud was technically free—but he was silenced. What did he then have to live for? Nothing . . . So he died . . . No—I will not leave.

Dr. Valkonen finds himself in a school room converted into an ambulance station at the end of the play. His son, Erik, has been killed and his daughter-in-law has gone to the United States where she will bear Erik's child in safety. As with Gabby, the Jungian symbol of hope for the world is in the recurring cycle of Mother and child. Dr. Valkonen sends his autographed pictures of Freud and the other men of science to his daughter-in-law and stays to face death himself, knowing that although war may be temporarily necessary to stop a tyrant and gain time for man, the forces of light are slowly coming to consciousness and there shall be no night there:

> We have within ourselves the power to conquer bestiality, not with our muscles and our swords, but with the power of the light that is in our minds. . . . The true defenses of man are in man, himself. . . .

Sherwood's moving play expresses a double-barreled challenge: first for man to understand and conquer his own aggressive behavior (a newspaper reporter had said that he thought the Nazis derived a sexual thrill from bombing the innocent, "from that display of devastating power"; second—and this had the greater political effect on audiences of the time—the need for the sensitive, the pacifists, the ineffectual Alan Squiers, even the Harry Vans of *Idiot's Delight* who were preoccupied with their personal sex life while the bombs fell, to toughen up and to meet force with force, not because it is morally right but because it is necessary to give mankind time to find the final answer to living at peace with one's neighbors.

There Shall Be No Night was one of the most effective plays of the war years, although Sherwood's *The Rugged Path* (1945) again powerfully depicted the rebirth of the man of feeling who occasionally vaccilated in his pre-war pursuit of his ideals but who finally saw the need to fight and die as a part of the struggle to make a

better world. After the war, Sherwood revised and brought to the
stage Philip Barry's last play, the psychologically probing *Second
Threshold.*

Sherwood has paid due credit to the influence of Freudian-
Jungian concepts upon his thinking. When asked if he had ever
sought for dramatic devices to dramatize for the audience the working of the Unconscious, he replied, "I'm sure every creative writer
does this."* Sherwood's applications of psychoanalytic thinking have
always been distinctly original—distilled out of his own political and
social ideals and his awareness of the times in which he was writing.
He was sensitive, however, to the danger of too literal application of
psychological theories: "I have found," he wrote, "that study of
Freudianism is helpful. But, in some cases, too much of it has
tended to atrophy the creative impulse." He ably summarized a point
of view with which most of the authors replying to the questionnaire
would agree:

> I feel sure that most modern, creative writers have been in-
> fluenced to greater or lesser extent by Freudianism. It is my
> belief that the work of those who have accepted it as abso-
> lute dogma has been damaged thereby.

Sherwood's latest play derives from this same distaste for dogma,
and is reported to deal with the Mormons, who were oppressed and
persecuted until they finally found a home in the wilderness and
proceeded to persecute any new minority that appeared in the area.

* A good many playwrights disagreed with him, however. This question
proved to be one of the most controversial on the questionnaire. Those who an-
swered yes: Leopold Atlas, Moss Hart, Paul Osborn, Samson Raphaelson, Lynn
Riggs and James Thurber as well as Sherwood. Those answering no: Mrs. Colin
Clements, Paul Green, George Kelly, Emmet Lavery, Clifford Odets, Howard
Lindsay, Mark Reed, William Saroyan, and the Spewacks.

CHAPTER VIII

The Psychodramas of
Philip Barry

Eight years younger than O'Neill, Philip Barry was second only to
O'Neill in the contribution which he made to the modern psycho-
logical drama. Like O'Neill, he had the benefit of George Pierce
Baker's instruction in playwriting at the Harvard '47 Workshop; but
Barry took much more seriously than did O'Neill his roots in the
Catholic faith, and the resulting emotional conflicts over such ques-
tions as divorce furnished him with poignant dramatic themes.

We know that Barry's interest in psychoanalysis dates from
his earliest playwriting venture. Rejected by the army in World War
I, Barry went into the State Department and served in England
doing code work at the American embassy. It was while he was in
London that he wrote his first three-act play, *No Thoroughfare*,
which dealt with psychoanalysis. On his return, he submitted the
play to Elsie Ferguson, but it was rejected and has never been acted
or published. Its significance lies in the direction to which it pointed.
Although much has been written about Barry as a master of frothy
high comedy of manners, he has not been adequately evaluated as a
serious, Freudian-minded dramatist. It is clear that Barry's major
work cannot be fully understood without reference to psychoanalysis.

Barry's first New York production, *You and I* (1923), tentatively

187

states what was to become a major theme in Barry's work—the search for self-realization. The father in the play, a successful advertising agency huckster finds that he wants most to be a painter and resigns his job in order to follow his artistic bent. But when his son is on the verge of abandoning his own search for fulfillment and settling for a meretricious job in order to support a wife, the father finds that he must relinquish his own plans after all to insure the younger man a chance to find himself.

Barry's second play was perhaps more typically a young man's play than his first. *The Youngest* (1924) has the stamp of thinly disguised autobiography about it. It is the Cinderella or "the worm turns" legend of a youngest son with a fairly severe "inferiority complex" (though Barry just misses using that term). The youngest even stutters in the opening act, and is ordered about by his brothers, sisters and mother who ridicule his desire to be a writer. Because of an unexpected provision in his father's will, the youngest inherits everything, and suddenly enjoys new status in the household. He finally gains greater confidence in himself and wins the girl who first gave him encouragement, concluding that ". . . a man's greatest victory is over *his own family.*"

In *The Youngest*, too, we find an early statement of another of Barry's major themes—the regression to infantile pleasures. The girl's deepest unfulfilled wish of childhood was for a forty-two dollar Mother Goose book. Balloons fill the stage in one scene, suggesting that to be free and have fun means to regress to childhood pleasures. We will see this concept grow in the work of Barry.

THREE PSYCHODRAMAS

In a Garden (1925) was the first of Barry's three major psychoanalytic plays (the others being *Hotel Universe* and *Here Come the Clowns*), all fantastic in form and all dealing with the repressed past which is exhumed and faced down.

In a Garden depicts a famous and successful playwright, Adrian Terry, who resolves to stop writing and enjoy his life with Lissa, his wife, whom he dearly loves. But into this serene picture comes Norris Bliss, a diplomat back from China. Just before leaving he had made love to a girl in a garden. Compton, a writer friend, holds the pet theory that "Every wife is at heart another man's mistress"—the one who first made love to her. Somewhere there is a wife who has not forgotten that night in the garden with Norris. Adrian, who prides himself on his knowledge of human nature, has a psychoanalytic solution for the problem: —put the two lovers back into the original setting, the garden, and let them reenact their love and thereby get over it.

Adrian is jolted out of his smugness, however, to learn that it was his beloved wife, Lissa, whom Norris wooed in the garden. Now Adrian is stuck with his remedy and must go through with it. He stages the whole thing literally, making an *ersatz* garden in his library to recreate exactly the evening Lissa and Norris met. He is confident of the outcome, believing that human nature is always predictable: "Dig deep enough into anything, and you'll come on a substratum of unconscious motive."

In the garden, however, it turns out that Adrian has been anything but correct in analyzing his wife's emotions. She has resented her husband's superiority complex and feels suppressed by his omniscience. She yearns to do crazy, unpredictable things that somehow express her and proclaim her independence from her husband's benevolent domination. She agrees to meet Norris and go off with him.

Adrian realizes that his garden therapy has failed. He painfully learns that he not only underestimated his wife, but didn't even understand the motives of his faithful secretary, Miss Mabie, who with a few drinks and the mood of the garden talks uninhibitedly about sex. She has been reading about sexual symbols and the Italian spring festival of fertility. Leaning across the table confidently, she says, "I presume you all know the origin of the Maypole?" When Lissa and Norris leave, Miss Mabie is sure Lissa will return, and Adrian is a sadder, wiser playwright in the knowledge that human nature is infinitely more devious than the pat little motives he attributed to his stage characters.

In a Garden states a psychoanalytic theme in Barry's original, unhackneyed way, adding to it the fanciful conjecture that "Every wife is at heart another man's mistress" (which can hardly be credited to Freud). There is much that is subtle, tasteful, almost precious in Barry's handling of the motif of regression to a happier state. The garden may be intended symbolically as all happy states of wish-fulfillment. In a sense, the conclusion is anti-psychoanalytic, for Barry tests the proposition that to face down the force of the past will free one of its repressive power; as in *Tomorrow and Tomorrow* and *Reunion in Vienna,* the Freudian formula fails to live up to expectations. Clinically, of course, the test is over-simplified, insufficient and inadequately evaluated to produce insight. But Barry seems indeed to be criticizing all pat formulas for human nature rather than psychoanalysis itself. Lissa, he seems to be saying, had to find her own individuality and throw off the cloying protectiveness and unthinking suppression of her husband. It will take more than an evening in a stage-garden to determine if she and Adrian can readjust to each other on a mature basis, or if she can find happiness with Norris to whom she remains an illusion of youth. That Adrian's experiment failed is his own fault for attempting to be both clinician and participant, and for failing to help Lissa interpret the experience in a way which would contrast the reality of his present love with the memory of a romanticized one.

There are, to be sure, flaws in the motivation of *In a Garden*. Lissa's discontent is not entirely credible after the first-act picture of her married life and Adrian's offer to retire and take her away. She hardly commands our sympathy as a Nora Helmer. The motives of Norris, too, remain somehow unexplored in his clinging to an adolescent experience throughout his mature life. *In a Garden* is of considerable significance for the drama, however, as the first modern attempt to incorporate into a play the concept of psychodrama. A psychiatrist, Dr. Jacob L. Moreno, pioneered in the clinical use of psychodrama, in which patients act out improvisationally their disturbing situations and play various roles to enlarge their insight. Moreno did not begin publishing in English until 1928 and whether or not Barry knew of Moreno's previous work in Vienna with the "Theatre of Spontaneity" cannot be ascertained. At any rate, Barry was the first to see the aesthetic as well as clinical possibilities of acting out a past experience as a means of freeing the individual of its oppressive influence.

In 1930 (still anticipating Moreno's major publications, although there had been several articles on psychodrama by Moreno and Trigant Burrow in psychological journals), Barry transmuted the same materials of *In a Garden* into one of the truly original masterpieces of the modern American drama, *Hotel Universe*. That it should have baffled so many of the New York critics is strange, for its meaning is readily accessible with the key of psychoanalysis. But most of the metropolitan reviewers found it "vague," "off the deep end," "confused," and "mystic."

In one long act of irresistibly heightening mood, Barry assembles a group of characters in an old house in Southern France that used to be "Hotel de l'Univers," a mysterious, formerly deserted château where the past keeps cropping up in an unreal juxtaposition of people, places and time. Although the group has come to cheer up Ann, an old friend who is forced to devote herself to nursing her old father, their efforts produce anything but cheer. For they are a group of neurotic, anchorless souls, each with a drive or need which is barely understood on the conscious level.

Barry undertakes to release these bewildered and representative humans from their neurotic drives and bring them to consciousness by the use of psychodrama. Tom Ames remembers his improvised dramatic experiences from childhood, playing "Under the Piano" and giving free play to the fantasy. Now under the subtle and brilliant guidance of Barry, all of the characters find themselves in turn "Under the Piano" to relive and work out in catharsis the traumatic episodes of their lives, with each playing subsidiary roles (or "auxiliary egos," as Moreno calls them) for the others.

Pat Farley is the most Barryesque of the characters, with the bantering wit and cynicism of Nick Potter in *Holiday*. But Barry now sees this surface sarcasm and flippancy as a defense mechanism against deep-rooted despair and melancholia, growing to suicidal proportions as Pat's *leit-motif* of the "death-wish" is subtly developed. Pat and Ann had formerly been sweethearts, but then he had fallen in love with Mary, an English girl, whom he was forced to relinquish by his snobbish and authoritarian father. When Pat broke the engagement, Mary took her own life, and Pat has suffered traumatic guilt feelings over his weak submission to his father's will. As a result, he is "in love with death," and planning to take his own life on an Alpine skiing trip.

Pat is not the only one who harbors death-wishes. Lily half-jokingly makes a survey and finds that four out of the six others have also contemplated suicide. Tom Ames, Pat's Catholic friend, is equally rootless, and is on the way to Rome to seek absolution from the Church for the guilt he feels. A publisher, he had quit business because he felt the irony of printing books on the meaning of life when he could not find a personally satisfying answer. By now his will is so paralyzed that he cannot even get to Rome, and his wife, Hope, is worried about him. She is a frigid, unaffectionate wife, who unconsciously looks upon Tom just as she does her children. Although she claims that all she wants is to mother her babies, we know that her relationship with her children would be "smother-love."

The psychodrama role-playing begins as Tom and Pat mockingly impersonate Norman Rose, a wealthy Jewish financier who is one of the unhappy party. The role-playing begins to move backward to repressed memories after this "warm-up," however, and Tom begins to play himself as a boy, climbing upon a wall and calling to his wife, "Look, Mummy! Look where *I* am!" He thus projects onto Hope, his wife, the role of his mother. The dominant drive of his childhood was his identification with a Father Damien, a priest who went to the South Seas to treat lepers and contracted leprosy himself. In a rush of masochistic identification with the martyr-priest, Tom is sure that he too has the dread disease. As a childhood friend, Norman would play with them, but is cruelly rejected with the thoughtless anti-semitism of children. Norman's sensitive wish to be accepted by Christians without sacrificing his own religious integrity is seen to be a powerful component of his unconscious drives, as he claims that he preferred sardines to the ham sandwich he was offered. Tom soon turns on Pat too, as a Protestant heretic, and the scene ends with a wild surge of aggression between the two boys.

Pat has been having an affair with Lily, a bitter, acid-tongued actress, but she acknowledges to Pat that she is totally without feeling where men are concerned (or women either). She suspects that her sexual anaesthesia derives vaguely from her old love for her father, an actor; her great wish to play Cordelia is blocked because of her fear of failure in the part. Ann too, would try to win Pat back, but he is honest in admitting he can feel nothing for her with the dead Mary between them. Ann is in no way neurotic, and with keen insight realizes that she must help Pat find himself and abandon his death-wish. She plays the role of Pat's mother in a psychodramatic recreation of his return from England, and leads him to retch out to her the traumatic memory of the death of his sweetheart. Pat is able to work out his Oedipal hatred for his father with his too high standards of "Be Good at Everything." Agonized, Pat wishes he could let the dead girl know he did try to come back and claim her.

Ann's father, Stephen, comes to her aid now as the group therapy grows more complex. Ostensibly insane, he is brilliantly sane enough to serve as Barry's *raisonneur* and to try to counteract their death-wishes with a philosophy which is Barry's own reconciliation of Freud, Jung and Catholic immortality of the soul:

> Stephen: I have found out a simple thing: that in existence there are three estates. There is this life of chairs and tables, of getting up and sitting down. There is the life one lives in one's imagining, in which one wishes, dreams, remembers. There is the life past death, which in itself contains the others. The three estates are one. We dwell now in this one, now in that—but in whichever we may be, breezes from the others still blow upon us.

As the master therapist, Stephen knows that for each of them "there is a turning." For each of their frustrations there is an answer within themselves—for Tom's wish to return "to what I was," for Lily's yearning for her father, for Norman's yearning for something which he does not know, for Hope's wish for her home and children, for Pat's wish for Mary, and for Ann's wish for Pat. Tom tries to kiss his wife with erotic warmth and she is shocked and annoyed, refusing to permit him to arouse her, unable to fulfill the role of wife to him. Tom then slips into childhood again and turns to Stephen as his confessor, Father Francis. Why is his erotic desire sinful, he would know? For the conventional dogma of the church, which Tom can no longer accept, Stephen substitutes an insight based upon dynamic psychology with its optimistic prognosis for altering human behavior:

> Stephen: You are the sum of all your possibilities, all your
>   desires—each faint impression, each small experience—
> Tom:—But when it's *over?*
> Stephen: You will be what your spirit wants and takes of
>   them. Life is a wish. Wishing is never over. . . .
> Tom: —Then everything about me *has* a meaning!—Every-
>   thing I see and feel and think and do—dreams, even!

When Stephen begins to experience his own death pains, Tom would run for a drink of water for his Father Francis, but his way is blocked by Norman, who has regressed to his youth as a peddler with a Jewish accent, and Tom is unable, as in an anxiety dream, ever to finish running for the drink of water. Instead the psychodrama goes on with Norman's scene—showing Barry's mastery of dream structure. Frustrated in his efforts to sell the cheap fur pieces, Norman furiously quits and resolves to make money to serve as a buffer against the humiliation of being rejected by gentiles. Now Stephen is Norman's employer, who predicts that Norman will marry a gentile girl, a "shiksa." He promises with pride in his religion that he will not, and we see now why the mature and wealthy Norman has felt too guilty to accept as a marriageable equal, Alice, his current gentile mistress who pretends not to care. Now Norman has achieved wealth and wishes only to go away without Alice and without "giant mergers," to find time to think.

Alice is an uncomplicated woman, sensuous and capable of deep sexual arousal, for which she is envied and treated with cattish sneers by Lily and Hope. After Alice has been given a sleeping pill, she returns to the room in a sleep-walking trance, and we see that underneath her genuine love for Norman is a little girl's persecution fear that Norman is a man who has been following her.

Stephen next plays the role of Lily's actor-father, quickening the tempo of the group therapy as he knows his own time is running short. Lily reverts to a girl of thirteen, living in hotel rooms as her father tours in second-rate plays.. Through Stephen's omniscient playing, Lily comes to see her father as he was, not a great actor and a hero, but a drunken fraud with erotic-sadistic urges toward his daughter. When he comes home tired from the theatre he would force her to dance for him and to drink whisky. At last Lily sees him for what he was, and is freed of her incestuous pattern of Electra feelings for him..

Stricken and dying, Stephen, nevertheless, forestalls death long enough to recreate the episode in which Ann and Pat meet and fall in love. Mary still stands between them until Stephen assumes the role of Mary's father and converts the projection back to reality. As Pat regains the border dividing fantasy from reality, the emotional tranference is made—he speaks of Stephen as Ann's father rather than Mary's and finally of Ann herself as the girl he loves. Stephen helps him to see that it was not the loss of Mary he mourned but the loss of his own ideal image of himself. Suicide would be a weak escape, Pat realizes. Instead, he recovers his pride in himself and goes out to recover the real and present Ann who loves him.

All return to reality now, each retaining some insight and re-lease from the psychodrama. Each has found something that was missing. Lily will play Cordelia, Pat and Ann will marry, Tom will go on to Rome, Hope will go home, and Norman will take Alice into his heart. Although Stephen dies, it is a new birth for the others, who no longer have need for the omnipotent assistance of Stephen. As he had predicted, there need not be an ending with death, for he lives on in the new freedom he helped the group find through a psychoanalytic reenactment of the past and a purgation of uncon-scious fears, guilts and wishes. "Wherever there is an end," Stephen had said, "from it the beginning springs."

No bare synopsis of the plot can do justice to *Hotel Universe*. Its genius lies in the subtle interweaving of *leit-motifs,* a musical orchestration of the mingled yearnings and wishings of these com-passionately drawn, deeply understood characters (though it is true that Barry can naturally penetrate deeper into the childhood emo-tional constellation of his Catholic Tom than of the Jewish Norman). But all of Barry's people are suffused with his unique humaneness, slipping in and out of the multiple roles that make up a complex adult with effortless artistry. Stephen plays four roles, Tom's priest-confessor, Norman's employer, Lily's father and the father of Pat's sweetheart; rather it should be stated in the converse: four indi-viduals project their feelings toward the authority-figure onto Stephen. *Hotel Universe* is truly a drama of role-playing, and if it was misunderstood in 1930 surely it deserves to be re-staged today and evaluated in the light of modern applications of role-playing and psychotherapy.

Hotel Universe evokes the child within the adult, flowing from past to present, from conscious to dim unconscious with consummate skill. The dramatist gives his characters the opportunity not often afforded outside the psychoanalyst's office to return to childhood, to play "Under the Piano," and reevaluate past experiences in the light of reality. Effecting its catharsis on audience as well as on participants, the play is fantasy not because it is fantastic —for it is not—but because its pattern compresses many lifetimes into one mosaic and permits characters to act and speak without the reality-testing censorship of the ego. It may be called psychoanalysis transmuted into a work of art, dramatized on a far deeper level than literal efforts such as Flavin's *Tapestry in Gray*. To the Freudian theme of finding oneself by a regression to the past, Barry adds his own special whimsy, his generous feeling for people and his poetic certainty that there is continuity to human life. With the warm humor lacking in *Mourning Becomes Electra* and the subtlety lacking in *Strange Interlude*, Barry created in *Hotel Universe* possibly the masterpiece of the psychoanalytic drama.

The third of what might be called Barry's "regression-fantasies" was *Here Come the Clowns*, which in 1938 left the critics as bewildered as if there had been no *Hotel Universe* or *In a Garden*. The intervening years, however, made certain differences notable. *Here Come the Clowns* was born of a mature playwright and thinker's perturbation about the meaning of life and the value of religion. Subjective and relatively plotless, it anticipated *The Time of Your Life* and *The Iceman Cometh* and has many similarities to the O'Neill play; both ask the question: Can man face himself without illusions? With a struggle that must have been as agonizing for the author as for his characters, Barry rejects religion, which fosters dependency, in favor of an active free-will. Man must be active in forming his own destiny, which he can only do when he is able to see the truth about himself clearly. This essentially psychoanalytic conclusion is not presented in Freudian terms; nor is the ending unequivocal in its meaning, so that it is not difficult to see why the reviewers disparaged the play with the epithet "philosophical."

In the same general form as *Hotel Universe* (although this time with intermissions), Barry assembles a grotesque, almost Toulouse-Lautrec collection of vaudevillians on the periphery of show business. In a café owned by a former female impersonator, a man named Ma Speedy, there is a ventriloquist and his dummy, a dwarf, a chronic drunk, a magician named Max Pabst, and a young couple who fear to marry because he is a foundling. There is also Clancy, a gentle, wonderfully kind, deeply suffering Irishman who had lost his beloved daughter and had gone away, returning after many years to a wife who doesn't love him. He free associates on a carnation, bringing to consciousness the repressed memory of a lemon tree and his mother who had taught him that carnations were the flower of God.

Max, an "illusionist" rather than a magician (for he shows truth rather than tricks), proceeds to show each of them the truth that he or she has been evading. In a group-therapy session, Barry again uses a kind of psychodrama as Max leads each of them back to the repressed truth, stripped of all ego-defenses or rationalizations. The ventriloquist uses his dummy to say for him the things that are too painful for him to vocalize—that his wife is a Lesbian and gets mash notes from girls in the audiences at the theatre. The truth for her is to leave her husband.

The truth for the dwarf is that he has had a normal child by a midget; the young foundling fears that he is this child and hence dares not marry. The truth for Clancy is that he has been unconsciously searching for ". . . no less a personage than . . . Than God himself." He projects his God-image (at first a father-image) onto a Mr. Concannon who owns the theatre and always wears a carnation. The bitterest truth for Clancy, however, is that the wife he so idolized only married him because she was pregnant by someone else, and that the daughter whose death had wrecked his life wasn't even his. Painfully the parts of these broken lives are fitted together under Max's super-conscious direction. Max next impersonates Mr. Concannon and through suggestion the group is ready to believe that he is God—a tremendously theatrical moment achieved through psychological projection of the unconscious wish to find the father-image. The chronic drunk carries a gun for suicide and accidentally shoots Clancy (trying to get the magician); Clancy dies happy, recognizing at last that he had been loved all along, not by his faithless wife but by her sister. Smelling lemon trees in a surge of symbolic return to the womb through death, he dies knowing that we cannot blame God for not looking after each of us when He gave us a Will to take care of ourselves.

The conventional answers of religious dogma which Max gives as he impersonates the God-like Mr. Concannon fail to satisfy, and although Clancy finds his catharsis, some of the others, notably the dwarf and the ventriloquist, do not; they are not in fact happier without their illusions than they were before.

As does Stephen in *Hotel Universe*, Max knows more than any one ego could know and as such represents the playwright—or The

Divine Playwright. If there is an inherent weakness in this bizarre group psychotherapy which Barry puts upon the stage, it is that the collection of characters is a motley one and cannot elicit the degree of empathy which one or two more fully developed roles might have. In that respect, the form of *In a Garden*, with its concentration on one individual's re-living his past, was more successful than the other two plays. The characters in *Hotel Universe* were more universal, more recognizable and sympathetic, while the Barry of *Here Come the Clowns* was in the bitter mood of the Munich years, and had to turn to a less savory and more warped assortment of human specimens. Clancy, who was potentially a great character, is given much less chance to grow to full tragic stature than Harry Hope, in O'Neill's comparable play. But his final awareness is greater and clearer than Hope's, for Clancy sees as he dies that in self-knowledge lies the road to freedom for the individual.

Although hardly apt to be a popular theatre piece, *Here Come the Clowns* is an important philosophical drama in which Barry predicates the only kind of religion which is acceptable to him—that which does not reduce man to a state of unconscious dependency. The device of the ventriloquist who uses his dummy to talk out the agonized confession that is too painful for him is a brilliantly original attempt to solve the same problem of duality for which O'Neill used masks, asides and two actors. If Barry's symbols seemed mordant—if humanity seemed to him only a side-show of clowns, ventriloquists, dwarfs and Lesbians, the play must be taken in the light of 1938 when the hope of the world was at a low ebb.

CHIT-CHAT

Barry is popularly known not for his philosophical plays, however, but for his sparkling high comedies of manners. *Paris Bound* (1927) contains little that is specifically psychoanalytic, but makes a plea for a more tolerant attitude toward infidelity. *White Wings* (1926) was a spoofing tribute to the dignity of the profession of street-cleaners and a satire on man's resistance to change; *Spring Dance* (1936) was a surface treatment of college life. With *Holiday* (1928), however, Barry achieved perhaps his most characteristic work, a delightfully heart-warming, bantering slice of society life. In this play, Barry records the revolt of a younger generation against all that is stuffy, conservative, conformative and frustrating in the life of the wealthy. Johnny Case is a poor young man with sufficient integrity to know what he wants—which is to "make a pile" and then to retire when he is still young enough to enjoy it. He and Julia Seton are in love, but Julia's idea is for him to settle into the rigid rut dictated by her successful and overbearing father. Her brother, Ned, finds his revolt against the father in alcohol. Julia's sister, Linda, is also a rebel against their father's rigidity and is naturally attracted to Johnny. When he breaks with Julia, Linda dashes off to get him.

Characteristic of Barry as early as *The Youngest*, and stated most clearly in *Holiday*, is his yearning to regress to a happier period —childhood. Linda keeps her old playroom upstairs just as it was when they were children. At moments of stress and frustration, she retreats up there, to the only room in her father's elegant mansion that she feels is her own, her home. There she feels a close bond with her dead mother. At Julia's engagement party, Linda retreats with a few friends to her playroom, calling her regression, "Me and my little what-d'you call it—defense mechanism—so pathetic. Yes, I'm just chock-full of pathos, I am."

If *Holiday* appears to strain for "cuteness," and if Johnny and Linda perhaps oversimplify the alternatives of regimentation versus *Gemütlichkeit*, the play is nevertheless one of the important comedies of the twenties, a record of the double-barreled rebellion against both the economic and the psychological inhibitions to self-fulfillment. The speech of Linda's friend, Nick Potter, mocking the legend of the self-made American business man is a classic and epitomizes Barry's bantering irreverence for the almighty dollar.

In *The Animal Kingdom* (1932), Barry treated with deepening maturity the same theme of the conflict in the younger generation between cloying conventionality and the search for self-realization. The Ned of *Holiday* becomes the hero Tom of *The Animal Kingdom* —minus the liquor. He is still the ambivalent son of a rich and dominant father who means well but tries to buy the boy's individuality and fails completely to understand his son's yearning for a literary career. Tom is an excellent portrait of an Oedipal, passive-dependent male, striving for self-assertion and saying, "Mother was the prize; you missed something there. Father means well, but you have to stand him off."

Tom is torn between two women—the conventional and beautiful Cecelia who would have him make peace with his father and settle down to his social position, and Daisy, his old mistress, a painter and a free-spirit. When he believes Daisy has gone to Europe no longer caring for him, he marries Cecelia and permits himself gradually to be reduced to dismissing an old butler to whom he was attached. But when Daisy returns from Europe still caring, they fight their love for three acts and finally succumb to it; they go off together to the freer atmosphere of the artists' world where they won't be submerged in money, social position and convention. As in *Holiday*, Barry depicts his characters with a lightness of touch, an elfin grace and a warmth of humanity. Tom explains his trouble to Cecelia:

> Tom: I'm not hard enough. All my life I've been trying to harden. I was born soft, that's the trouble with me.
> Cecelia: You soft!
> Tom: Yes, born it.—And then brought up to refuse to face any truth that was an unpleasant truth, in myself or anyone else—always be the little gentleman, Tommy—charming and agreeable at all costs—give no pain, Tommy.

The title as well as the theme of *The Animal Kingdom* suggests that beneath the surface of Barry's glittering dialogue was a richly perceptive psychologist who understands with psychoanalytic awareness the various strivings of his characters to reconcile their spiritual cravings within the animal kingdom.

RELIGION AND PSYCHOANALYSIS

Guilt feelings over Barry's rejection of the conventional dogma of the church apparently played considerable part in his life. He attempted to work them out in a routine and undistinguished Biblical drama, *John* (1927), and again used Biblical inspiration for *Tomorrow and Tomorrow*. We have seen the search for God-head figure as a principal theme in *Here Come the Clowns*, and the godly figure of Stephen dominates the development of *Hotel Universe*. In *The Joyous Season* (1934), Barry was most successful, however, in finding a common meeting ground on which psychoanalysis and religion could be reconciled. The common ground he proposes is, once again, regression to childhood.

Christina, a nun—memorably played by Ethel Barrymore—returns to her rich Back Bay Boston family for Christmas to find them a cynical, bitter lot, full of neurotic tensions and deep unhappiness. She sets about to straighten out their lives. Monica is a flippant smark aleck who is in love with her sister's husband, and quips upon learning that nuns travel in pairs: "A nun—gay! How ghastly—." Terry is unhappily married to Francis and wishes she could die. Reminiscent of Behrman's *The Second Man* is her lament:

> Terry: Why is it that when I count the people in a room I always count myself as two people?
> Francis: There are more of you than that.

Terry: And you don't care for any of them——
Francis: A few.
Terry: I might kill off the others.

A brother is a radical, while the oldest brother is a successful Back
Bay business executive, in love with his secretary but not daring to
marry her because she is beneath his caste. It is soon apparent that
it is not the cloistered nun but her entire family who have been
running away from life and dodging their own inner wants.

Christina's remedy for them all is characteristic Barry: she persuades them to return to their childhood country home for Christmas
dinner. Symbolically named Good Ground, the old house helps
them recover for a day their happy youth—not Back Bay but good
"shanty Irish." The reminiscences are aided by the return of a repressed childhood song. Christina concludes: "Here you seem to lean
on each other—you who used never to lean. Tell me: don't you
think all of you—secretly, maybe—maybe without even knowing it—
don't you think all of you long for Good Ground again?" Under the
influence of reliving the past, each of the family comes to face his
own inner needs for the first time. Francis realizes that he wants to
teach rather than practise law. His wife Terry sees her husband in
a new light, and can now stop ridiculing him: "I have a pleasant
sense of meeting a terribly nice man for the first time." Even Monica
is free of her hard defense mechanism when her love for Francis
can be admitted and purged. Francis and Terry enter marriage
anew, for their previous marriage had been with reservations which
made it void in the eyes of the Church. John decides to take a big
job in New York and to find happiness by marrying his secretary
although it violates the snobbery code of the Boston Brahmins.
Christina can leave her family knowing that she has helped them—
without any conventional moralizing or talk of theology—to find
themselves and to resolve the inner splits which were leaving them
neurotic and warped. Christina summarizes at the end her philosophy of self-realization through insight:

> I think I came here to you half expecting it would be a re-
> turn to my childhood. I've found that it's not possible to re-
> turn there and that it's well that it is not. Ahead is the only
> way,—ahead, but with a difference! (Then softly to herself.)
> Who are you? What are you? Where are you bound for?—
> What do you want of life? Who are your heroes?—Do you
> know anymore? You must—you must find out again! And
> there's so little time—no time, but for the best.

If there is a weakness in The Joyous Season, it is precisely that "there's so little time——." The speed and simplicity with which these character-changes are effected in this neurotic family strain both dramatic credulity and clinical practise. It is too easy—in fact, miraculous. Perhaps Barry intended it as such.

Even in 1941 when Barry was perturbed over the world political scene, he wrote in *Liberty Jones* an allegory of this nation's growing into maturity through a regression to childhood and a birthday party presided over by an old Irish nurse. What may be good Freud seemed, however, naive politics as Barry applied it to the ills of the world.

THE NEW PROPHET

Somewhat in a class by itself among Barry's work is *Tomorrow and Tomorrow* (1931). A serious modern drama, its theme is derived from the Biblical story of Elisha and the Shunammite woman (Second Kings, IV), in which a barren woman is made pregnant by the magic powers of Elisha and her son later restored to life by the prophet.

In Barry's version the new prophet is a psychiatrist, Dr. Nicholas Hay, who comes to teach a summer course at Redman College and stays at the home of the wealthy but immature grandson of the founder of the college, Gail Redman, and his gracious wife, Eve, who after six years of marriage have no children. Eve and the psychiatrist fall in love, although not until his last evening do they admit it to each other. Eve had nursed her father in his later years, and grew afraid of facing life and its overpowering emotions. Once, when she was fifteen, she came upon a laurel bank blooming at night, so breathtakingly beautiful that she has not dared to go back since. Hay sees the symbolism in her fear of facing life—fear that if she went back she might be disillusioned. He calls Eve "an artist without an art" and concludes that they ". . . must do something about life, with it, to it—or else——" What he does about it is to take her out to the laurel bank and accomplish by natural methods what Elisha was reputed to have achieved miraculously.

Eight years later Gail is raising his supposed son in his own image, forcing his love of horses upon the boy and making the lad believe he is "yellow" for shying at a jump. Eve is an over-protective mother and lavishes her son with tenderness. To prove he is not yellow, the boy sneaks out before he is well and takes the hurdle, then faints and is carried home in a coma. When nothing brings him back to consciousness, Eve thinks of calling Dr. Hay, whom they have heard on the radio preaching the Jungian gospel:

Who does not know the power of small things to recapture
lost emotions?—The sight of a green lawn curving beneath
chestnut trees—the rush of water running past—the smell
of certain flowers—Lost, did I say?—But they are never lost.
. . . Emotion is the only real thing in our lives; it is the person, it is the soul. . . . So if we earn the right, we may
trust emotion over it (reason), confident that in it we have,
somehow, the whole experience of the human race to draw
upon.

The conventional family doctor is unable to bring the boy out of
the coma, leaving with a neat bit of unintended irony as he says, "I
don't think in all my experience I've ever known a happier family."
But Eve knows that her son, like herself is ". . . Painfully,
agonizingly anxious to be what people want him to be." Dr. Hay
arrives and spends several days trying to get through to the unconscious boy, knowing that his trouble centers around his Oedipal
fear and hostility for his supposed father. Finally the boy snaps out
of the coma, under Hay's offstage ministrations, which are left unde-
fined. Learning that the boy is his, Hay is overwhelmed with his old
longing for Eve, and they have a tortured love scene, wanting to go
off together with the boy, but seeing how much the son means to
Gail and how his loss would wreck his life. Thus Barry has trapped
his psychiatrist and makes him eat his words—Hay cannot trust to
his emotions and find fulfillment wherever the archaic urges of the
race would lead him; there are still the ethics that require suppression and deflection of the emotions when someone else's happiness
is at stake. It is Barry's neat rebuttal to psychoanalysis: without
being satirical he puts the psychiatrist in a position where it is impossible to follow his own generalizations about trusting to the
emotions.

Tomorrow and Tomorrow is in many ways comparable to
Strange Interlude; the husband of each play bases his happiness
upon a child which he believes to be his and which his wife has
had by another man; in each there is the sacrifice of the lovers for
the husband's happiness, and in each the Oedipal rivalry of father
and son. Compared with O'Neill's masterwork, however, *Tomorrow
and Tomorrow* seems disappointingly inadequate to grasp all the richness latent in the theme. What kind of mother will Eve be, lavishing
so much displaced emotion on her son? What was the deep root of
the son's coma and the doctor's technique in bringing him out of it?
Hay, too, is a little unclear in his motivation, apparently having had
no deep love in the eight intervening years. But in his ability to

write deeply felt love scenes between sensitive, responsive people, Barry was incomparable.

WITHOUT LOVE

Another group of Barry's plays fall under the thematic title, "Without Love." They include the play of that name as well as *The Philadelphia Story* and *Bright Star*. The latter play (1935) was one of Barry's least successful, telling the story of Quin Hanna, a political and social reformer, who returns to the New England town of his bitter childhood and tries to make something worthwhile of his town. He has married the town's richest girl who loves him deeply, but he gradually learns that he himself has no capacity for love. After the loss of their unborn child and his deepening insight into his own emotional frigidity, Quin observes: "I've found out a funny thing— you have to have a heart to love, all right. But you don't need one to suffer. The inability to love is just about the finest torture there is." He leaves Hope, whom he feels he has cheated of her right to love.

In *The Philadelphia Story* and *Without Love*, however, it is the heroine who is emotionally frigid, perhaps with better theatrical results. *The Philadelphia Story*, as played by Katherine Hepburn in the high comedy style of *Holiday*, was Barry's most successful play. Just before her second wedding, Tracy Lord is told by three different people that she seems to be a virgin goddess, cool, chaste and untouchable. The first who tells her this is her former husband, C. K. Dexter Haven, who remembers that once after a champagne party she climbed out naked on the roof and stood there wailing to the moon like a banshee—with no recollection of it next day. Similar erotic sleep-walking and moon gazing, as we have seen, also formed the plot of Martin Flavin's play, *Children of the Moon*, and was the subject of a psychoanalytic study by Dr. J. Sadger.

C. K. Dexter Haven believes that their marriage failed because of Tracy's frigidity, because she was in fact a "married maiden," never having been aroused to love anyone but herself. Her fiancé inadvertently uses the same expression, and finally her father, who in his loneliness without Tracy is having an affair with a dancer of whom Tracy is furiously jealous, makes the third reference to her emotional blockage.

Concluding that she wants to be loved rather than worshipped on a pedestal, Tracy proceeds to get drunk on champagne, go swimming nude with a radical young reporter, Mike, and get carried to bed by Mike too drunk to be taken advantage of. She remembers nothing of it in the morning, but her little sister squeals, and her fiancé is ready to break off the marriage. A new and womanly Tracy, aroused out of her shell of frigidity, finds that she still wants her first husband, C. K. Dexter Haven, and sends the fiancé packing.

Beneath the smart sophistication of the dialogue, Barry's understanding of unconscious motivation is deep in this play, which even includes a lecherous old uncle whose passion is pinching girls' posteriors. *The Philadelphia Story* illustrates the growth of maturity in the New York playgoer's understanding of psychoanalytic concepts by the end of the thirties—to the extent that a playwright need only suggest the Freudian implications while telling with subtlety, zest, and affection for his characters, a story that is essentially psychoanalytic in its theme. Tracy Lord is a charmingly "normal neurotic" with whom the audience can empathize as it watches her grow into maturity. This quality of identifiability of the leading characters seems a conspicuous difference between the recent psychoanalytic drama and the period of violent psychoneurotics in the plays of the twenties.

The third of Barry's treatments of the frigidity theme, *Without Love* (1942), shows, like *Liberty Jones*, Barry's concern for the future of his country during world crisis. His hero, Pat, is perturbed because Ireland won't give bases to Britain to use in the struggle against Hitler; he would conduct a one-man crusade to bring Ireland into the war against fascism. Although there are some flashes of sardonic wit in Pat's makeup, the play is a humorless and unhappy one—not characteristic Barry. Pat has deeply loved a girl in Europe, Lila, and when he meets Jamie, a girl who also loved once and whose husband was killed—they decide to marry without love, with only a respect and enjoyment of each other. Jamie, Pat analyzes, is the kind of girl ". . . who has kept a lot of precious things locked up for many precious years." Jamie admits that her background was strict New England:

> Jamie: Miss Jennings, my governess, I always secretly hated, and I hate her now. She made me terribly shy with people and frightened the life out of me about God and Purity.
> Pat: You probably had a good healthy reaction.
> Jamie: No. The fact is I never did. By gum, I'm still scared. I pray for guidance and I blush when I get it.

Jamie breaks out of her repressed emotionality, however, and falls in love with Pat. When his old sweetheart, Lila returns from Europe, Jamie elaborately contrives a dinner party in order for Pat to meet and face Lila—to overcome her hold on him by facing her as she is today. But for once Barry switches the Freudian formula—Pat doesn't even need to see Lila, and goes off with Jamie for six days *with* love before he goes into the Navy.

SEMANTICS

The scene that never takes place between Lila and Pat in a sense becomes the plot of Barry's next play, although the sexes are reversed. In *Foolish Notion* (1945), Barry's theme again is, "Face the past to release its hold on you." The play is in the fantasy style of *Hotel Universe* and *Here Come the Clowns*—imaginative in its conception, original in its treatment and non-realistic in its structure.

Jim Hapgood has been abroad for five years, having been a drunkard and an unsuccessful husband to Sophie, a famous actress. During his absence, Sophie has had an affair with her leading man, Gordon Roark. As the play begins, Sophie has had the courts declare Jim legally dead and is about to marry Gordon, leaving her twelve-year-old daughter, Happy, with a tutor named Florence. Then the hints begin to pile up that Jim is not dead but returning. The plot of the play consists of four imaginary scenes as each of the leading characters fantasies what Jim will be like when he returns—bending the outcome as each unconsciously wishes it. The fifth scene, his real return, is unlike any of the imagined ones. He had said he was bringing Flora with him—and each of the Floras is also different— each a projection of the wishes of the person doing the fantasying. Thus *Foolish Notion* might be called a play of semantics—a study of the mechanism of projection and the difference between objective and subjective reality. There is Jim_1, Jim_2, Jim_3 and Jim_4, and finally Jim as he is to himself, Jim_5.

Fantasy Number One is as Gordon would have Jim's return. He is still a drunkard and Gordon deliberately plies him with drink. He is such a derelict, however, that he still wins Sophie away from Gordon by pity.

Fantasy Number Two is as Sophie's father, Horatio, sees it. Horatio is a retired professor of drama, and he sees the return with theatrical flourishes. Jim masquerades as a Scotch Highlander, complete with a Scottish accent, a Scotch name, and a case of amnesia. Over-dramatizing the event, Horatio sees him recovering his memory through playing the harp and being sentimentally reunited with Sophie. Flora becomes the new maid who arouses Horatio's erotic impulses—but he is too old and this is mere wish-fulfillment; Flora waltzes off with Gordon.

Fantasy Number Three is as Happy, the daughter, sees her father's return. True to the Freudian formula, she fantasies herself in the midst of a perfect Agamemnon-Clytemnestra-Aegisthus triangle—almost a burlesque of *Mourning Becomes Electra*. Sophie tries to give Jim poisoned pills, but Happy prevents it. Jim had entered doing his old trained seal act, walrus mustache and all, with which he used to amuse her as a child (again the regression motive). He is portrayed as a loving and gentle recollection of a dear father. Flora this time is Florence, her tutor and childhood friend. Jim kisses Flora in a friendly way—she had been seventeen when Jim went away and, we know, had been in love with Jim. In Happy's twelve-year-old mind she has her father tell Gordon off as she would do it:—"Nuts to you, meatball." Next Gordon and Sophie try to give Jim a poisoned drink, which Happy also foils. Gordon finally shoots Jim melodramatically and the lovers flee leaving Happy singing a distracted ballad over her father's body in the best Ophelia style.

Back to reality after the fantasy, however, Barry effectively dramatizes the cathartic effect of reliving Happy's repressed Electra-rivalry. After accusing Sophie of wanting Jim dead, Happy says:

Happy: Anyhow, I know you *do* . . . you want him dead.
Sophie: Oh, Happy, . . . you don't give me half a chance.
Happy: . . . And besides, you want to send me back. I
    know! I wish you'd never got me.
Sophie: Happy! Happy! Do you really think those things of
    me?
Happy: (After a moment, turns front) I did. But I don't any
    more. I . . . I think I've thought them out of me.

Happy is thus reconciled with her mother.

Fantasy Number Four is as Sophie sees her husband's return. Her old rival was a famous actress, Lily Spring, whom she thought Jim loved. To her the Flora is Lily, returning after having loved and mothered her Jim. Sophie first fantasies Jim as horribly maimed, with herself as the gallantly suffering heroine. Then Sophie's death-wish takes over, and she fantasies Lily bringing in the ashes of Jim; Sophie tragically sends Gordon away so that she can properly suffer as a tragic heroine.

After the four charmingly tongue-in-cheek projections, Barry finally shows us the reality of Jim's return. Happy's fantasy was nearest to the truth. To him Flora was Florence, whom he had loved all along, and who was the cause of his leaving for Europe five years ago. Florence had been seventeen and the romance seemed impossible then. Sophie is utterly suprised to learn of Florence's love for Jim. Jim is unlike any of the projections of him. He is mature, sobered and wise. He had fought during the war and hidden out with the Maquis in France after being cut off from his outfit. Finding himself needed and on his own for the first time, Jim had grown into manhood, learning, as he says, to live in the present instead of the past. Like O'Neill's Lazarus, he says, "Maybe it's because at last I've learned to say 'yes' to life, instead of nay, nay, nay."

Realizing that Florence had more than just a seventeen-year-old's crush on him, Jim claims her now. Sophie feels what Happy described earlier in the play as the way her dad wanted her to grow up—"uninhabited." He and Sophie are able to talk maturely and dispassionately about their marriage and its failure. He had loved "the idea of her" but they were clearly incompatible. He had retreated to liquor because he couldn't compete with her success in the theatre. Just when Gordon is about to be unselfish and leave, he realizes that Sophie is free of Jim and needs him. They go off on their starring tour, leaving Jim, Florence and Happy as a joyous threesome.

Throughout the play there is the Barryesque repartee of verbal twists—as for example, when talking about their love Jim calls it:

> Jim: A great thing, when recognized and granted. Then it means the interest never flags.
> Sophie: Flag the Southbound Interest. This is a station-stop. . . .

Or again, the childish word-pun game played by Happy and her father, a verbal romp which seemed to delight the naive Barry ever since *Holiday*:

> Gordon: Dead. Dead. The fact is, you really do belong to the morgue.
> Jim: And thou? And thou?
> Gordon: And what have we got?
> Jim and Gordon: (together) Morgenthau!

Foolish Notion is a challenging play, reflecting Barry's truly original powers as a dramatist. He builds his plots out of thematic concepts, in this case the psychoanalytic *leit-motif* of the return of the past. His dialogue is sharply bantering, brittle without being superficial. Rather there is underlying the hard surface warm love for his characters and compassion for their wont to mix up their lives. Even Gordon, who is not depicted entirely with sympathy, turns out to be just another confused little man who became an actor because he hated to get up early in the morning and found he could be paid for showing off. *Foolish Notion*, the title of which is derived from Robert Burns' famous quotation on insight into ourselves as "ithers see us," is a play built out of the rosy memory of a childhood full of freedom to fantasy and to free associate. Our subjective images of ourselves, derived from ego-defenses and distortions of reality, are truly foolish notions, and the sooner we can see through them the better.

OUR REVELS NOW ARE ENDED

Second Threshold (1951) was Barry's last play, revised after his death by Robert Sherwood. It is surely more than mere hindsight that makes it seem the swansong of a playwright of youth who has grown old. The author must have felt death approaching, and his mood here is that of Schnitzler in *The Lonely Way*—the gay wit grown old and feeling his guilt. A touching and finely wrought play, it fuses at once his bantering *Holiday* mood and an infinitely sad overtone of melancholy that is free of the cynicism of *Here Come the Clowns*. Again it is more than a coincidence that the daughter's name is Miranda. This is Barry's *The Tempest*, and his lonely hero, Josiah Bolton, standing upon the second threshold between middle and old age, all but proclaims, "Our revels now are ended . . ."

The psychoanalytic meaning of *Second Threshold* is outlined in clear hints. Bolton has been successful as a lawyer, but is now divorced and lonely. His life is "without love." His daughter Miranda, with whom he has been close—too close—all her life is about to sail for England to marry a rich and elderly man, a contemporary of her father's. Watching this occur causes so strong a return of repressed wishes for his daughter and jealousy of the father-image she is marrying—that he undergoes extreme anxiety and mental disturbances—seeming to hear voices in the garden and talking to them. A young Dr. Toby Wells, son of Josiah's physician, calls and, remembering a summer flirtation with Miranda, is attracted to her anew.

At their parting Miranda and her father are hostile and sarcastic with each other—defenses against their strong emotion. With acid comments, Josiah refuses to give his blessings to Miranda's marriage, calling his daughter, "Mentally, very advanced, I'll admit. Emotionally, still in the egg."

> Miranda: The hell with emotion. It's sloppy and messy and
>   to my mind it's completely——
> Josiah: To your mind. What about your heart?

Miranda then breaks down and cries, the first time since she was five. "Oh, God, dear God," she sobs, "how I hate the ones who blubber." Here is Barry again at his old "without love" theme—emotional impoverishment, denial and repression of emotion—the sterile triumph, Freud would have said, of *ego* over *Id*. To Toby, also, Miranda denies any father-fixation:

> If you're leaping to the obvious conclusion that there's ever been anything Freudian in this family—then you'd better go right back to Johns Hopkins and specialize in osteopathy. There was never anything like that. As a matter of fact, it was the exact opposite. We were friends—companions. Nothing emotional. We were close to each other because I was the only member of the family he could trust *not* to be emotional. . . .

The lady doth protest too much, however. Miranda is the frozen virgin, Tracy, of *The Philadelphia Story*, but the dynamic causes of her reaction-formation are more clearly suggested than were Tracy's. When Miranda calls her brother Jock to help with her father, he arrives admitting frankly he doesn't love his father; from Jock's point of view Josiah is the same unsympathetic father as in *Holiday*, but we have already come to empathize with him, whereas *Holiday* was the children's play and told from their perspective. In Jock's Oedipal bitterness, he says of his father: "He had a God complex . . . thought he could create me in *his* image." Josiah had set too exacting standards for his son, with the result that he flunked out of law school.

Realizing the seriousness of her father's breakdown and suicidal broodings—he has had two nearly fatal accidents which may not have been accidental—Miranda postpones her voyage and tries to apply mental hygiene to help her father. She has had some psychiatric training in a hospital—though it apparently gave her little insight into her own problems. With her smattering of psychoanalysis she would verbalize and dismiss an erotic memory of Toby as, ". . . related to the essential *Id* and its desire to preserve its sphere of activity." As with many individuals, however, she can help others where she cannot help herself. She perceives that her father needs to feel loved and wanted again, and persuades Washington to urge him back to his old job, persuades her divorced mother to invite him out to California to visit her—and most significantly, encourages the pert little nineteen-year-old Bennington freshman named Thankful Mather to flirt with him in the hope of restoring his will to live. The latter device works so unexpectedly well that Josiah sings a song he once wrote for a college musical and takes Thankful dancing, while Miranda concludes, "A little knowledge is dangerous. A little psychiatry—is disaster."

The *leit-motif* of regression to childhood echoes here too, as Miranda curls upon a sofa with Toby, and asks him to tell her a baby bedtime story. "Anything—just a story. You're an animal— tell me—an animal story. . . ."

The discovery that she and Toby love each other happens through a Freudian blurting out of the denied emotion—she has threatened her father that if he takes his life she will follow, much as she might want to live:

> Because—for all the awful things about it and all the jams I get into, I love living, love it—and—oh, if only *you* would again—because I love you too—and I couldn't stand to see you go that way, and me not having been able to—and I'm so crazy about Toby that I don't know where I'm at and— (Suddenly she stops, looks appalled, turns to Toby). What did I say just then?

With a dazzling burst of tragic awareness, Josiah sees his neurotic life-pattern and accuses himself as a lawyer to a jury:

> Desperately afraid of all human relationships and of his own and others' emotions, he finally starved them out, scared them off—fearful, of course, that they might take from him something of himself . . . he deliberately allowed her (his daughter) to identify herself with him—fostered this relationship until they became almost as one person. . . . Then when the cruel, inevitable necessity came to break the bond, he stupidly wondered at the fact that, from the vacuum in which he left her, she went on to another, perhaps less benevolent despot, and quite as suave, ruthless and cynical as he—and two years older than I am.

When Josiah discovers that he and Thankful love each other, and that his daughter "doesn't want her father to die," he is revitalized, and kisses Miranda brusquely, sending her to England to break with the elderly suitor and return to marry Toby. Thankful, too, will sail and he will await her return with something to live for. Life is only meaningful, Barry seems to say, when there is love— full and accepted—not withered or distorted. The irony escapes him that he is condemning Thankful to the same alliance with an older man from which he has just freed his own daughter. At any rate, he is released from his hallucinatory voices, and dismisses them.

Although it is quiet and unspectacular, *Second Threshold* is a tightly knit piece of playwriting. Only fifty-three at his death, Barry seemed to have been vouchsafed, Moses-like, one last long look into the deep and profound dynamics of personality which motivate human beings—a look to a depth known to Ibsen, and Chekhov, perhaps Schnitzler—and precious few others. *Second Threshold* should leave no doubt that Barry was profoundly indebted to psychoanalytic insight, transforming it with his own particular background and outlook into something individual, fresh and subtle, infinitely rich and gentle. As a humanitarian, Barry was impatient with the defense mechanisms that whittle people down to a smaller than life size and deprive them of the fullness of love.

The themes that recur throughout the work of Philip Barry and which relate to Freudian psychology are: reliving the past in order to be free of it (*In a Garden, Hotel Universe, Here Come the Clowns, Foolish Notion*); regression to the security of childhood (*You and I, Holiday, Hotel Universe, The Joyous Season, Liberty Jones*); frigidity or the impoverishment of emotion: (*Bright Star, The Philadelphia Story, Without Love* and *Second Threshold*); and finally, the search for self-realization or emotional maturity which is somehow related to the "victory over his own family"—in all of his work.

Certainly it falls far short to dismiss Barry as a witty writer of high comedy of manners, bantering, facile and superficial. He was that and more. Beneath his flippancy and his "chit-chat" was a sensitive and deeply spiritual writer coming to grips with the psychology of his times and expressing a yearning for maturity and emotional wholeness. No other American playwright was able to transmute the raw elements of unconscious life into a work of art so delicate, so subtly ingratiating, and so fresh in form, as did Philip Barry. If these are the criteria of greatness, *Hotel Universe* belongs among the great plays.

CHAPTER IX

Shifting Psychology in the Thirties

JUVENILE PROBLEMS

The thirties were significant as a transitional decade in American history, and no less crucial as a transition in the American drama. The most conspicuous shift was from an interest in isolated aspects of individual psychology to group-centered problems. With the changed attitude, however, the influence of psychoanalysis did not diminish. Rather the insights of psychoanalysis were variously applied to social problems as related to prisons, schools, labor and management, poverty, juvenile delinquency, fascism and radicalism. Eyes newly opened to social and economic pressures saw with the perception afforded by dynamic psychology.

Credit for the first psycho-social study since the early effort of Theodore Dreiser in *The Hand of the Potter* (whose greatness was that he was ahead of his time) should be given to Martin Flavin, who as early as 1929 wrote a psychoanalytic study of frustration in prison, *The Criminal Code.*

Following *The Criminal Code* came a number of plays dealing with reform schools and the general subject of juvenile delinquency, finally branching off into more general explorations of adolescent psychology. T. C. Upham's *Lost Boy* (1932) was a grim tragedy of a boy who is delinquent at school because of the influence of his domineering, ignorant mother and his helpless, hysterical father. Arrested for attempting to wreck a train when he had actually been trying to prevent the wreck, the boy concludes that the world is against him, and turns to petty thievery. A State psychologist is on the way to gaining his confidence and rehabilitating him through woodcraft when a vindictive reform school superintendent brings new charges against the boy and he is hopelessly lost in a hostile adult world.

Other plays reflecting the new awareness of the childhood etiology of criminalism and society's responsibility in preventive psychiatry include *Incubator* (1932) by John Lyman and Roman Bohnen, and *Little Ol' Boy* by Albert Bein (1933). The former shows the reform school itself as the incubator where future criminals are bred, and includes a homosexual relationship in the sexual maelstrom which surges within a reform school. The boy effects his release by discovering the matron and a guard in a compromising position, but he too by then is a lost boy. Bein's *Little Ol' Boy* is naturalistic reporting, in which a slatternly, indolent wife of a guard befriends a sensitive young inmate, who develops an Oedipal relationship with this mother-image. Her husband is an ". . . effeminate looking man, fat and fuzzy of face, with a small sensitive nose, browless eyes, long slicked-back hair, broad shoulders and with an overly developed bosom." There is, however, no overt treatment of any homosexual relationship with the boys. The plot concerns the gradual toughening of the boy and his acceptance by the gang whom he hero worships. They make a break but are captured when the pleasure of riding a new bicycle delays their escape. He dies in the arms of his buddy who has tenderly looked after him and delayed their escape because he could not swim.

Two military school plays, *Bright Honor* (1936) by Henry R. Misrock and *So Proudly We Hail* (1936) by Joseph M. Viertel added little new to the study of juvenile psychology but made the same point that military schools, like reform schools, are brutalizing forces, suppressing sexual curiosity, regimenting the pupils and fostering gang loyalty at the expense of individual growth. Its feminine counterpart, *Schoolgirl* (1930), showed the unfortunate results of suppressing sexual curiosity in a girls' school.

An adolescent in love with his school teacher formed the basis of *Remember the Day* (1935) by Philo Higley and Philip Dunning, which includes the use of an inner voice speaking out of the man's childhood to remind him to be kind to the old schoolteacher he once loved.

Perhaps the most effective psychological study of the inner world of childhood during the thirties (and one which Moss Hart's recent *Christopher Blake* could not surpass in the depth of its insight) was Leopold Atlas' *Wednesday's Child* (1934). Atlas takes a psychoanalytic point of view in depicting the devastating effects of divorce upon a sensitive eleven-year-old. Bobby has seen his mother kiss another man while her husband is away. When her husband returns unexpectedly, she has to tip off her lover, and kisses her husband reluctantly, causing Bobby to blurt out in a surge of Oedipal jealousy, "Don't do that!" Bobby has been starved for his mother's affection and identifies himself with his father in the betrayal by his mother. Bobby goes to bed that night praying to God to "Kill the other man!" He then has a fitful dream in which Atlas uses offstage voices mocking Bobby for his mother's infidelity, chanting, "You don't know who your father is." This is one of the few applications of subjective techniques of dramaturgy during the thirties.* Suddenly Bobby is awakened by voices in the next room, and he sits up in bed to see the silhouettes of his parents quarreling, his mother striking his father and the father returning the slap. The most traumatic shock for the child is to hear his mother admit that having him was a mistake; he was unwanted and interfered with his mother's career. The mother walks out on her husband and Bobby follows her to her lover's apartment, where his anxiety is further increased by witnessing his mother with the other man.

The judge at the divorce tries to make Bobby betray his mother by testifying against her, but he refuses. Bobby is awarded to his mother, with the father permitted to see him during the summer. He is miserable with his mother and his new step-father, however, and cannot wait for the summer with his dad. Whatever sympathy the father had up to this point is lost when he promises the boy a two weeks' fishing trip and then reneges because his mistress wanted to go away with him during those weeks. Bobby's defense mechanism against his feelings of rejection is to pull farther within himself; he grows sullen and then develops a psychosomatic fever with no organic cause. He is finally sent to a military school, and although his parents occasionally visit him, he soon learns to take the advice of an older boy there and forget about them. He won't be hurt again.

---

* Atlas also named several of his motion picture scripts as intentionally using dramatic devices to explore the unconscious—"superimposed motion-pictures on living characters in *He Sat on a Wall*—counterpointed dream scenes—conscious wish scenes and actuality in *Nocturne*—nightmare scenes—*Wednesday's Child* . . . Dream projection in *So Long*."

Atlas has written in his questionnaire to the present author that he was familiar with "quite a number" of Freud's works, including his *Basic Writings, The Problem of Anxiety* and *Moses and Mono-theism* as well as the works of Deutsch, Reik (whom he especially liked), Brill, Menninger, Horney, and Jung. It is thus no accident that *Wednesday's Child* demonstrates a considerable depth of understanding of the conflicting emotions in a disturbed child, growing out of Oedipal jealousy centered on the primal scene, feelings of ambivalence and rejection. Nevertheless, Mr. Atlas wrote in his questionnaire of the danger to the creative writer of substituting arbitrary dogma for original intuition:

> May I suggest another avenue of approach. Been thinking of it for some time. Will suggest it telegraphically. The negative influence (deleterious) of Freudism on Creative writing—Formerly writers searched their own insights and revelations—now the use of Freudianism as a crutch—a handy cliché—with overtones of pseudo-profundity—Become dependent on authoritarian research rather than their own insights and understandings—Psychiatrists formerly sought for corroborations of their findings and theories in authors—Note the quote-studded texts with references to Dostoevski, Shakespeare, Goethe, the Greek playwrights etc. (How in the world did they ever get along without Freud?) Today the reverse is true—authors are constantly dependent on statements by Freud, etc. to replace their lack of individual insight. . . . This is not to say writers should divorce themselves from studies of psychiatry—the reverse—Every field of knowledge is important to a writer— But instead of using psychiatric theories as a Fundamentalist might a Bible, they should use it for flights (even iconoclastic) of their own in the probing of the human heart and mind. In other words I would call on writers to reassert and regain their rightful position on the forefront of insight and revelation, independently.

Mr. Atlas' admonition does not apply to *Wednesday's Child,* however, which seems to possess genuine creative insight and fresh theatrical power.

Atlas wrote one other drama on the effects of environment upon children. In *But for the Grace of God* (1937), however, the factor is poverty rather than divorce which is decisive in the life of the young boy. The father has been out of work for two years, the older brother has tuberculosis, and Josie, the younger brother is forced to rob and kill to get money. There is bitter hostility between the boy and his father, who sarcastically calls him Mr. Rockefeller because he supports the family. The stage directions in Atlas' play often contain more psychoanalytic comment than the drama itself, as when Atlas describes Josie's resentment of Rosie, a girl who dreams of a better life for herself than her sister's career of prostitution, in terms of "a mad, sadistic desire to shatter the scaffold of false dreaming she has erected; to rub her nose in reality, to make her face facts." So Josie proceeds to try to seduce her with the help of his gang.

When Josie is finally arrested for murder, the police officer says, "We know the boy's not solely to blame. Environment, education. What he probably needs is a good doctor, a psychiatrist to—." The father interrupts:

> A full stomach's what he needs, not a doctor. An end to for-ever worrying about where the next penny's coming from, that's what he needs. You fellers need the doctors. You and your whole rotten set-up.

The emphasis placed by modern psychology upon the critical influence of childhood indicted poverty and emotional insecurity so decisively that American society's guilt feelings were aroused during the depression as they had never been by previous periods of economic distress, giving rise to the remedial social legislation of the thirties.

By contrast with the serious approach to the problems of juvenile psychology by Atlas, the first comic treatment of child psychology was a superficial British import, Lesley Storm's *Billy Draws a Horse* (1939), which mildly satirized self-expression in children without psychological perception, although the wife does realize that her son's drawing of a horse, rear end foremost, on the wall of his father's office, is somehow a displacement of hostility for the pompous father.

HOMOSEXUALITY

As is apparent from *Incubator* and *Little Ol' Boy*, the subject of homosexuality was treated with considerably more frankness during the thirties than previously. We have seen Lesbianism treated sev-eral times during the twenties. It was to be developed most fully in Hellman's *The Children's Hour* (1933), which was anticipated the year before by an adaptation of Christa Winsloe's German play, *Girls in Uniform*. Male homosexuality was less frequently depicted, until George O'Neil in his epic of an American family, *American*

Dream (1933) traced a dynasty from fanatic Puritans through rene-
gade pioneers down to the present cynical and disillusioned generation complete with parlor pinks, nymphomaniacs, and a homosexual who exclaims hysterically to another man just before shooting himself: "You're all I've got to hang on to. That makes me a
homosexual hero-worshipper, I guess. Yes, I'm a fairy, then. A
pansy." In the bleak thirties O'Neil could see only neurosis and disintegration as the legacy of the American dream.

The two most successful Broadway treatments of inversion during the thirties, however, came from England (which is something
of a reversal in that the London censor has been traditionally more
severe than New York critical tastes). In 1933 there were two such
British imports, the first a delightful comedy written by Noel Coward
especially as an acting vehicle for the Lunts and himself. In *Design
for Living*, the situation was based upon a "menage à trois," of
which the psychoanalyst, Dr. A. A. Brill wrote:

> The dramatis personae consisted of two men and a woman.
> The men loved each other and both loved the woman. . . .
> I do not know whether the author of the play knew our
> psychological concept of homosexuality, but all the essen-
> tial factors of it were cleverly depicted. The narcism was
> expressed by making the two men look and dress almost ex-
> actly alike; they even kiss each other. The overvaluation of
> the penis . . . (is reflected in the line:) "But don't forget,
> it's in the *London Times*—it's the organ of the nation."

At the beginning of the play, Gilda has been living with Otto, until
the return of Leo complicates their lives. As Leo explains their entangled relationship to Gilda: "The actual facts are so simple. I
love you. You love me. You love Otto. I love Otto. Otto loves you.
Otto loves me. There now! Start to unravel from there."

Otto becomes jealous, however, and in a scene described by Leo
as "fully charged with a hundred-per-cent feminine emotionalism,"
Otto walks out. After a year or so of living together, Gilda and Leo
both miss Otto, and on his return Otto proves virile enough to reclaim Gilda. Now it is Leo's turn to be petulantly jealous, and when
both men find Gilda has walked out on them, they get very tearfully
drunk together and end up crying amusingly on each other's
shoulders. At the end, the happy triangle is restored, however, and
Otto expresses a rationale for their unconventional lives to answer
the charge of "moral degeneracy" which the strait-laced might voice:

> But the whole point is, it's none of their business. We're
> not doing any harm to anyone else. We're not peppering

the world with illegitimate children. The only people we could possibly mess up are ourselves, and that's our lookout. It's no use you trying to decide which you love best, Leo or me, because you don't know! At the moment it's me, because you've been living with Leo for a long time and I've been away. A gay, ironic chance threw the three of us together and tied our lives into a tight knot at the outset. To deny it would be ridiculous, and to unravel it impossible. Therefore, the only thing left is to enjoy it thoroughly, every rich moment of it, every thrilling second——

This the "menage à trois" proceeds to do, laughing joyfully as the curtain falls. Coward's characters have found a solution which fulfills their ambivalent needs for masculine and feminine identifications. Their frank acknowledgment of inversion is at least less damaging to the personality then repressed homosexuality, which Freud has called the basis of paranoia. By projection, the paranoid denies his homosexuality by this formula: "I love him . . . no, I hate him . . . because he persecutes me."

In the second British play of 1933, the absence of a virile father is shown as a factor in the son's latent homosexuality. Mordaunt Shairp's *The Green Bay Tree* is a more serious study of a triangular relationship in which a girl and an older man are rivals for the possession of the young man. Julian had been adopted as a boy by the rich sybarite, Mr. Dulcimer, when his own alcoholic father was unable to support him. Mr. Dulcimer has raised Julian in his own image, effete, sensual and helpless.

Dulcimer had not known a father either, but had adored and identified with his mother, ". . . the only woman who ever meant a thing to me." The play becomes Mr. Dulcimer's sinister, cat-and-mouse efforts to prevent Julian's marriage to a normally feminine girl (though he shortens her name Leonora to the masculine Leo) by dangling an allowance over the otherwise penniless man. The inner conflict in Julian is between passive dependency and masculine self-reliance. Though he tries valiantly to study veterinary medicine (of all unsuitable professions), he finally succumbs to the blandishments of Mr. Dulcimer and his epicurean luxuries.

To save him, Julian's own father, who had reformed, tries to reclaim Julian; he shoots and kills Dulcimer, but it is to no avail. Even in death Dulcimer wins Julian, for his fortune goes to Julian, the father goes to jail, and Leonora gives him up in disgust, leaving him placidly making a flower arrangement at the final curtain of this incisive portrait of male inversion.

Although *The Green Bay Tree*, which ran for 166 performances with Laurence Olivier as Julian, was the most adult and understanding treatment of the theme during the thirties, it also entered Osborn's *Oliver Oliver* (1934), J. R. Ackerly's *Prisoners of War* (1935), *Reprise* (1935) by W. D. Bristol, and Chester Erskin's *The Good* (1938). Malicious and false insinuations of inversion against a professor formed the plot of Francis Bosworth's *The Fields Beyond* (1936). But as Brooks Atkinson pointed out in reviewing one of these dramas, "Such themes need deeper clarification today. They are no longer fascinating in themselves."

SEX IN THE DEPRESSION

The pendulum had swung sufficiently far by the thirties so that the single standard of sexual freedom was no longer daring nor shocking. Where the flaming flappers defied convention in order to test the bounds of freedom and to defy their Victorian elders, their children in the thirties turned to sex as an escape from a turbulently insecure world and because the economic barriers to marriage had so drastically increased.

No playwright better expressed the changed attitude toward sex in the generations between the two World Wars than did Mark Reed in *Yes, My Darling Daughter* (1937). Reed bridges the gap between 1918 and 1937 by having the mother of the play, Ann, a former flaming young poetess who had an affair in the Greenwich Village of the generation which was avidly reading its Freud and producing Edna St. Vincent Millay and Susan Glaspell. Now, however, Ann has happily married a conventional business man and their daughter, Ellen, has reached the same dangerous years of decision. Whereas the mother in her day felt the necessity of flaunting Puritan convention and living openly with her lover, her daughter merely plans to go quietly off with her young man for a weekend before he has to go overseas. (His going to Europe, taken for granted a few years later, seems contrived in this pre-war year). The mother's perplexity as to whether she can withhold her blessings on this weekend escapade of her daughter's without being a hypocrite is complicated by the return to her life of her old Greenwich Village lover. When Ellen realizes who he is from her research into her mother's past, Ann has no choice but to send Ellen off to join her young man, conceding her daughter the same rights for which she had crusaded so militantly a generation before. The famous curtain line of the second act expresses the mother's exasperation: "Oh, goddamn sex anyway!"

Ann's sister-in-law, Connie, has not outgrown the restless sexual anxiety of the twenties. She is thrice divorced and still in search of love, offering herself casually to Ann's old lover, only to be rejected. While at Reno the last trip, she explains:

> I've found myself. At last I know what I want and why I haven't been happy. From now on I'm going to simplify my life . . . I've analyzed myself. I've dug deep into my character with knives. I'm a very affectionate person at heart.

Reed's problem is not dissection of motives, however, but rather to debate the rightness of pre-marital experience. After tittilating his audience for two hours with the prospect of an affair condoned by the mother, Reed has the father insist that his daughter be made an honest woman by getting married before the boy sails. Reed thus begs the very question which the play raises. There is in *Yes, My Darling Daughter*, however, a compassionate treatment of very human beings caught in the essential moral dilemma of their generation.

Although Reed indicated in his reply to the questionnaire that he had read a few books on psychoanalysis, his reply to the query relative to discussing plots and characters with a psychoanalyst evoked an emphatic, "God, no!" Reed's general comment reflected the same caution concerning psychoanalysis as did Leopold Atlas:

> It is my feeling that a playwright, if he is interested in human nature, should forget Freudianism and psychoanalysis. Start with a frustration or a neurosis and it dominates your characterization. A dozen very varying people can have the same inferiority or Oedipus complex. After the playwright's people are on the stage let the audience and the critics find Freudian complexes if they want. I say all this in face of *The Cocktail Party* which I thoroughly enjoyed.

Similarly valuable as a reflection of the sexual standards of the upper classes during the thirties is the work of Clare Boothe Luce. The kaleidoscopic Miss Boothe has been editor of *Vogue*, playwright, Congresswoman and foreign diplomat; some have assumed that she provided the model for Fay Kanin's *Goodbye, My Fancy*. Following her divorce from George Brokaw early in the thirties, Miss Boothe underwent psychoanalysis, hoping that it would "shake off her psychic angularities" and make her a "happy woman again." The imprint left by psychoanalysis upon her plays is at a relatively superficial level, however, consisting more in the use of terminology than in deep level insights.

Miss Boothe's first play, *Abide With Me* (1935) is the sort of play Mark Reed must have had in mind when he wrote his caution: "Start with a frustration or a neurosis and it dominates your characterization." Miss Boothe started with the neurosis of sadism, and depicted a young, wealthy alcoholic who loved to squash bugs as a child, and as an adult ingeniously tortures his long-suffering wife. The reason for his sadism Miss Boothe traces to his father, who was diabolically inhuman, this in turn the result of his wife's infidelity. The young wife finally has an affair with her doctor (the transference motif) and becomes pregnant by him, to the delight of the husband who refuses to give her a divorce and looks forward to torturing the child. He is mercifully done away with in a manner that is made to look like suicide. *Abide With Me* makes amply clear the principle that psychological penetration and dramatic vitality are not necessarily concomitants.

Clare Boothe's most famous play was *The Women* (1936), which captured with biting humor the speech and manners of upper class women whose pastimes are sex, gossip and psychoanalysis. A story of a divorce as seen entirely through the eyes of women, this play shows a variety of female attitudes towards sex, from Crystal's exploiting of herself for economic advantage, to a young girl's exclamation that she is ". . . what nature abhors. I'm a virgin—a frozen asset." A rich and no longer young countess who has bought herself a young husband, Buck (her fifth) finally decides, "First I thought it was gin interfering with his libido—But now I think Buck is deceiving me." Those who are not promiscuous derive vicarious satisfaction from endless gossip about those who are. Mary Haines, a generous woman caught in this sea of superficiality and brittle defense-mechanism against unfulfilled lives, loses her husband as they approach middle years. Her own mother had faced the same situation and had learned to understand infidelity as man's urge for change when he gets tired of himself:

> And the urge usually hits him hardest just when he's beginning to lose his hair. No, dear, a man has only one escape from his old self: to see a different self—in the mirror of some woman's eyes.

Psychoanalysis becomes a fashionable fad for these wealthy women, satisfying their need for attention, flattery and someone to listen to their malicious chatter. Sylvia Fowler takes up analysis after her divorce, and interprets the developments of Mary's divorce through the words of her analyst, who, it is apparent, must be cajoling and catering to Sylvia rather than attempting to lead her out of her immaturity. Some of her psychoanalyst's quotes, however, provide the most incisive humor of the play:

> Sylvia: He says men of Stephen's generation were brought up to believe that infidelity is a sin. That's why he allowed Mary to divorce him, and that's why he married you, Crystal. He had to marry you just to convince himself that he was not a sexual monster.
> Crystal: Yes? Well, if Stephen is a sexual monster, psychoanalysis is through.

Or again, her comment concerning a blackmailing doorman: "I asked my psychoanalyst about him and he said blackmailers are really perverts who can't think of a good perversion."

Clare Boothe's later two plays, *Kiss the Boys Goodbye* (1938) and *Margin for Error* (1939) did not reflect deepening psychological powers but rather indicated the author's growing concern with political and social questions, which ultimately led to her entry into public life. The influence of psychoanalysis diminished to an occasional use of terminology or a "crack" such as this from *Kiss the Boys Goodbye:*

> Rand: Oh, let's not analyze it, dear. Fine theme song for moderns. (singing) Let's not analyze. . . .
> Leslie: I know why I love you. . . .
> Rand: (singing) If you know why you love me, I'm a-Freud that you don't, dear. That's the chorus.

But with *The Women* Miss Boothe achieved, in the best high comedy tradition, a devastating picture of the role of psychoanalysis in the lives of idle, pampered women.

FATHERS—PASSIVE AND OTHERWISE

The conventional father, either preoccupied and disinterested in children as in *The Women,* blusteringly moral in preserving his daughter's virtue as in *Yes, My Darling Daughter,* or pompous and crass as in Philip Barry's satire, was destined for a set-back during the depression years when economic circumstances vastly reduced the prestige, security and authority of the male in the home. One of the first comedies to express with delightful contrast the changing attitudes toward the role of the father was *Fly Away Home* (1935), by Dorothy Bennett and Irving White. The young people here are precociously flip and saucy, having been taught the facts of Freud by a professor of anthropology who lives next door and who is going to marry their mother when she is free of "the mother's husband," a stuffy and conventional father. The professor has told the children about the research of Malinowski in the Trobriand Islands (where the father is subservient to the mother), thereby reinforcing the children's disrespect for their father. Of parental authority, the professor says: "My researches have shown it to be chiefly a hunger for power." The children have picked up the psychoanalytic lingo and the sixteen-year-old tells her housekeeper, "You're frustrated." In the end however, it is the conventional father, not the "modern" professor who wins out, buying off the son's mistress, getting his daughter safely married, and recovering his wife's affection.

The matriarchal family with a dependent father, described by Malinowski in primitive cultures, became one of the recurrent *motifs* in the American drama of the thirties. Odets depicts in a number of plays the passive-dependent father and the masculine-aggressive mother. *The Warrior's Husband* (1932), by Julian Thompson, also treats this theme of the reversal of the roles of the sexes, deriving good farce humor from an Amazonian society where the women rule and the men, without being effeminate, are the sheltered creatures who remain at home during a war. Franken's *Another Language* is perhaps the classic indictment of matriarchy. Dr. Karl Menninger, the distinguished psychiatrist, points out in *Love Against Hate* that the popularity of Crouse and Lindsay's *Life With Father* (1939) is significant of the growing matriarchy of our socio-economic culture:

> . . . the fact that a play portraying the head of the house
> being consistently defied and outwitted by every member of
> his family was the most popular play on Broadway in 1940
> suggests the rarity and obsolescence of the masterful father.
> For better or for worse, the dominance of the male is un-
> doubtedly passing.

But while the bellowing Clarence Day at least deceived himself into thinking that he was master of his home, many of the stage fathers of the thirties were resigned to their chimney corner. For example, in *After Tomorrow* (1931), by Hugh Stange and John Golden, the young depression sweethearts, Pete and his girl, Sidney, have been saving for four years in order to get married. Each of them is Oedipally attached to a parent, Pete to his possessive, giddy mother who is merely empty-headed rather than malicious; Sidney to her sweetly ineffectual father whom she fusses over, runs bath water for, and defends against the mother's constant insinuations about his inability as a provider. He would have been more effectual in business, the daughter asserts, if he had had tenderness and ego-satisfaction from his wife. Sidney's mother is a shrew and a hypochondriac, perpetually complaining of a nervous headache. Finally the mother blurts out to her daughter:

> Elsie: You've always been so much in love with your father you never stopped to think of all the suffering and pain that I went through from the night you were born.
> Sidney: I didn't ask to be born—
> Elsie: And I didn't want you.

When the mother runs away with another man and the father has a stroke, all the money Sidney and Pete have saved goes for medical expenses. They manage to marry Pete's mother off to a widower, but just when it looks as though the marriage can proceed, the girl's father has a final heart attack and dies.

If the ending of *After Tomorrow* is unsatisfying, the resolution of *Best Years* (1932) by Raymond Van Sickle presented such a problem that the author provided the reader with three solutions from which to choose. The mother in this play is even more insidious than her counterpart in *After Tomorrow;* for she uses whining self-pity and hypochondria as the club over her daughter, Cora's head, keeping her from marrying the man she has loved for years and making her into a resigned spinster. The family doctor understands just enough psychology to know that, "The woman actually . . . feeds on you. . . . She's a neurotic, of course. You'll have to handle her with gloves." He advises Cora to stand up to her and defy her with regard to her sweetheart. Cora does assert herself and this time the mother actually does have a stroke. Cora is overwhelmed with guilt, although the doctor assures her that the stroke would have happened in any case. Cora feels that she cannot leave her sick mother to marry, and lets the man go out of her life. After he has left, Cora sits reading to her mother as the mother dies. This was apparently the version played on Broadway although the printed text gives two alternate endings, one in which the mother lives and Cora goes on being her slave, and one in which Cora finds out her mother was only malingering and goes to join her man. One may take his choice. But the author's indecision indicates the weakness of the drama and the lack of inevitability in the motivation.

The catalogue of insidious mothers should also include Hugh Stange's *Mother Sings* (1935) in which the mother poisons her son's mind against normal relations with women to the extent that he finally is driven to a brutal murder of a woman who aroused him. The extent of recent sex murders suggests that some deep unconscious force may be at work as Stange implies, but in regard to the handling of the theme, Brooks Atkinson wrote, "Mr. Stange . . . has taken the worst features of *Desire Under the Elms, The Silver Cord* and *Tobacco Road* and combined them in psychopathic guignolism. . . ." The silver cord was still holding fast by 1940 when Andrew Rosenthal's *The Burning Deck* depicted a father trying to rescue his son from a mother about whom someone says, "They strangle their sons with umbilical cords."

Passivity in the male, although this time not in a father, received no more delightful treatment than in *The Male Animal* (1940) by James Thurber and Elliott Nugent. Nugent was already co-author of one comedy of passivity and inferiority in the male, *The Poor Nut;* somewhat the same formula of "the worm turns" was employed in this collaboration with Thurber, who invested the play with the whimsical overstatement for which his cartoons are enjoyed. Thurber stated in his questionnaire to the present author that he had read a few works on psychoanalysis, including the *Basic Writings of Sigmund Freud* and Jung's *Fragmentation of the Personality.* In reply to the question, "Have you ever sought for dramatic devices or techniques to dramatize for the audience the workings of the unconscious?" Thurber replied that he had in one or two scenes and lines in *The Male Animal.*

The scene to which Thurber undoubtedly referred, and one of the most amusing in all modern comedy, occurs when Tommy Turner, a quiet, easy-going young English professor who looks like "a puzzled spaniel" finds his academic life at a crisis because of pressure from the university trustees over a letter by Vanzetti which he plans to read to his English classes, and his marital life at a crisis over the return of his wife's former sweetheart, a hulking all-American football player, who is accustomed to taking what he wants. Under the influence of ample amounts of Scotch whiskey, Tommy and the student journalist responsible for his notoriety quietly work out their feelings of passivity and rouse themselves to masculine aggressiveness. Tommy draws upon Jungian concepts of the collective unconscious to convince himself he must fight for his wife:

Tommy: Let us say that the tiger wakes up one morning and finds that the wolf has come down on the fold. What does he——? Before I tell you what he does, I will tell you what he does not do.
Michael: Yes, sir.
Tommy: He does not expose everyone to a humiliating intellectual analysis. He comes out of his corner like this—

(Assumes awkward fighting pose, fists up—rises—sits quickly). The bull elephant in him is aroused.
Michael: Can't you stick to one animal?
Tommy: No, that's my point. All animals are the same, including the human being. We are male animals, too.

The combination of Jung and Scotch arouse Tommy sufficiently to recapture his wife's affection and to lead her in dancing—apparently this skill was the other man's chief appeal. *The Male Animal* extracts fresh humor from the cry of the male beast in the civilized breast of a passive modern, and without resorting to preaching makes telling comment upon the need for academic freedom.

THE PSYCHO-MELODRAMA

One of the most influential new tendencies of the thirties was the use of psychoanalytic motives and types in the murder melodrama. This form of popular theatre (and more recently, television) has found Freud so useful in the concoction of suspense and the suggestion of the imminent eruption of criminal impulses that a short course in psychoanalysis seems a prerequisite for mystery writing today. Hypnotism, of course, has been invaluable to the mystery writer ever since *The Case of Becky*. The twenties applied Freudianism in melodrama by using naive psychological tests to catch criminals, as in Owen Davis' *The Haunted House*. Perhaps the first melodrama to use psychoanalytic insight in tracing criminal impulses to their unconscious source was *Killers* (1928), by Merling and Bisch. Rice in *The Adding Machine* (1923) had shown the forces which can make a murderer out of an innocuous Mr. Zero when under sufficient emotional pressure, and Sophie Treadwell's *Machinal* made a comparable study of a girl driven to murder by irreconcilable unconscious conflicts. By 1931 the formula had been found by Howard Comstock and Allen Miller in *Doctor X* for a gruesome "shiver, shriek and shudder" melodrama based on the use of a lie detector and a series of psychic shocks effected by a re-enactment of the crime.

Whether or not the depression caused the public to demand more sensation in the theatre, the number of psycho-criminal melodramas increased during the thirties, became a definite "genre" of playwriting during the forties, and has threatened to monopolize theatre, film and television melodrama by the fifties. One of the first murder melodramas of literary distinction was *Nine Pine Street* (1933) by Carlton Miles and the co-author of *Rain*, John Colton. This play—as well as the recent ballet, *Fall River Legend*—takes as the subject for psychological probing a brutal slaying such as the Lizzie Borden murder case of Fall River, Massachusetts, some forty years ago.

The murderess in *Nine Pine Street* is Effie Holden, an intensely religious and sensitive girl, who is in love with a young preacher and about to marry him and go to China. When her mother, with whom she has close identification, dies of a heart attack, Effie is the only one who knows that a neighbor lady who had set her cap for her father deliberately knocked over the mother's medicine, thus causing her death. The neighbor lady marries the widowed father, and Effie puts off her trip to China in order to stay home and make her step-mother's marriage as miserable as possible (the Hamlet situation in reverse). Although Effie is not depicted as particularly affectionate with her stern father, it is apparently her father-fixation and unconscious jealousy of her step-mother which makes of her a morbid, hysterical woman who ultimately smashes her step-mother's head with a flat iron and then does the same to her father. Although acquitted through the pressure brought by her church, Effie remains alone in her old house for twenty years; a young reporter comes to interview her in the last scene, saying he believes that she stayed in the old house for "some funny New England conscience idea of punishing yourself for something—even though you had been acquitted—it was just as though you had put yourself in prison. . . ." It had been only a year and a half since Lavinia Mannon had masochistically locked herself in a similar prison.

Crimes of sudden, psychotic eruption such as Effie's do not provide the theatrical suspense of premeditated crimes. In *Double Door* (1933) by Elizabeth McFadden, the crimes are the product of a malevolent and coolly possessed brain. As memorably played by Mary Morris, Victoria Van Bret is a dominating older sister who attempts to destroy her younger half-brother, Rip's marriage and to break him psychologically by using childhood memory and guilt feelings as a weapon. She keeps their parents' ashes in urns in the living room (a striking embodiment of *super-ego*) and Rip remembers that when his father died, his sister put the body where Rip had to see it and feel the cold dead eyes watching him. The play hinges upon a melodramatic contrivance—a secret vault in which Victoria once locked her sister to punish her. No one else knows of the room, and when she tries to lock Rip's wife in there, her plan almost succeeds. Instead, however, Victoria is left alone at the end gloating over her cache of pearls in a psychotic state, the result of her obsessive striving for superiority.

It was not a year until other tyrannical sisters were prowling Times Square. Carlton Miles, co-author of *Nine Pine Street*, had another try in *Portrait of Gilbert*, and Leigh Wells in *Allure* depicted one sister pushing the other down the stairs, making her a cripple for life. The sadistic sister grows more demonic in revenge for the hostility of the family, and it is only Dr. Koppel, "a famed psychiatrist from Vienna," who enters in time to expose the sister's cruelties and cure the younger sister of her fear as well as her paralysis, thus leaving her free to marry while the older sister shoots herself. The wonders of third-act psychiatry!

A more credible and subtle treatment of female insidiousness was *The Old Maid* (1935) adapted by Zoe Akins from Edith Wharton's novel. A ruthless woman is shown denying the man who loves her; when he has a child by another woman, she contrives to obtain possession of the child, raising her as her own and teaching her to think of her real mother as a crabbed old maid aunt. Without insight into unconscious motives, the play was nevertheless an effective, sentimental treatment of the frustrated impulses of mother love.

There were numerous examples of melodrama derived from psychiatric sources—hallucination, obsessions and delusions of persecution: *The Night Remembers* (1934) by Martha Madison; *A Room in Red and White* (1936) by Roy Hargrave; *Goodbye in the Night* (1940) by Jerome Mayer and *At the Stroke of Eight* (1940) by Percy Robinson. In *Steel* (1939) by Harold Igo, a huge Polish immigrant becomes obsessed with steel as a religion for today's world and when he loses his job for union activity, sacrifices himself in the crucible of molten steel.

The best of the psychiatric crime melodramas of the thirties, however, was James Warwick's *Blind Alley* (1935), which reflects a considerable knowledge of unconscious mechanisms and uses them credibly for the build-up of strong theatrical suspense. It is set in the tranquil home of a psychologist, Professor Shelby and his wife. A hunted ganster, Hal Wilson, breaks in with his moll and trigger men. While they hold Professor Shelby prisoner and wait for their getaway boat, they kill a student. The professor's only defense is to apply his knowledge of psychoanalysis. He first gains Hal's confidence by showing him that circumstances over which he had no control made him what he is; he urges him to talk about his dreams, his boyhood and his fears. His father was hypocritical and his mother a drunk whom he hated. Soon, however, Shelby has him realizing that he also loved his mother and deeply resented her going with another man and finally marrying him. His mother-fixation and Oedipal hatred for his step-father forced him as a child to earn money by luring girls for a white-slaver and to give the money to his mother as a bribe to stay away from the step-father. Hal's one obsessive recurrent dream is of a pillar of stone swinging threateningly behind him. The pillar has the face of a girl—Tiny, his step-sister by his mother and step-father. Mazie, Hal's moll would stop this probing, but Shelby goads him on until he mistakes Mazie for Tiny and shoots her. Then Shelby uncovers the fact that as children Hal played erotic-sadistic games with Tiny, beating her with a switch for her enjoyment. Tiny had become the image of their mother, and he was projecting his erotic impulses for his mother onto Tiny. Hal finally accounts for his hallucination of a swinging pillar of stone—he had killed Tiny, leaving her swinging from a rope. Stripped of all his ego-defenses, Hal sees himself now as if in a mirror—he is a paranoid with an obsessive mother-fixation. Shelby saves his own life by showing Hal that his only path is suicide.

Never was a psychoanalysis conducted under such tense circumstances as in *Blind Alley*, where the slightest miscalculation of the criminal's anxiety would have resulted in the professor's immediate death. The play is a brilliant *tour de force* and achieves genuine suspense through the valid—though theatrically condensed—application of insight into the complicated set of defenses that operate within a criminal personality.

PSYCHOSIS

As is evident from *Blind Alley*, the psychoanalyst became a more respectable figure in the drama of the thirties. Compared to the twenties, there were fewer plays which satirized the psychiatrist as a comic-opera, bewhiskered Viennese—often neurotic himself (as in Joseph Anthony's *A Ship Comes In*, in which the great psychiatrist himself suffers from obsessive fear of women and can't bear to be left alone with one). At least twenty-two stage psychiatrists crossed the Broadway boards during the thirties, often as the *raisonneur* or *deus ex machina*, whose solutions of the plot complications were—more or less—psychoanalytic. Louis K. Anspacher, for example, showed in *The Rhapsody* (1930) a psychoanalyst called in to cure a war veteran who is obsessed by a desire to avenge himself on a sergeant who had brutalized him and killed his best friend during the war. Although a successful musician, the veteran disappears for weeks and attacks every stranger who resembles the sergeant. The psychoanalyst's therapy is to confront the veteran with the sergeant and let him shoot the sergeant (with a gun from which the doctor had carefully removed the bullets). A woman psychiatrist was called into the proceedings in A. J. Minor's *Masks and Faces* (1933) to rid the heroine of the hallucination that a "phantom lover" comes between her and her husband. The psychiatrist in Paul Treichler's *Cure for Matrimony* (1939) has troubles of his own when he hypnotizes three men and three women (including his own wife) to determine experimentally whether man is unconsciously monogamous or polygamous.

When a physician turns to playwriting, more authentic material might have been expected than was to be found in Dr. Louis S. Bardoly's *Case History* (1938). After watching the jumbled plot in which a doctor condemns his patient for calling in a Christian Science practitioner for appendicitis but permits one to be called for insanity, Brooks Atkinson made the delicious comment:

> If Dr. Bardoly is going to take up playwriting seriously, the Dramatists' Guild will have to assign one of its most skillful men to take over his practise in Cleveland.

More authentic use of psychiatric material was to be found in Hardie Albright's *All the Living* (1938), which was adapted from Victor R. Small's book, *I Knew 3000 Lunatics*. A naturalistic study of conditions in a state insane asylum, it makes an indirect plea for psychoanalytic as well as preventive psychiatry; for it shows a devastating picture of the stalemate and helplessness of official state psychiatrists to effect cures. The doctors merely classify the inmates and when one is disturbed, follow the standard formula: "two drams of paraldehyde and put her in seclusion." They refer to Kraepelin rather than Freud, and the director is a pompous autocrat who refuses to permit a neurotic young doctor to experiment with a new cure for dementia praecox. The young doctor is about to break down with delusions of persecution when a co-worker comes to his aid; they apply a form of psychodrama and a new drug to a speechless patient and he is finally motivated to talk. But the general impression of this asylum is bureaucratic indifference to patients, overcrowded conditions, incompetent staff and lack of modern techniques for psychotherapy. How accurate a picture of our state mental institutions was presented in *All the Living* raises the same issue hotly debated in 1952 over *The Shrike*. One can only hope in the name of humanity that both plays are grossly exaggerated. But one fears they are not.

The question of just what is a "lunatic" and "who is crazy?" has been raised before in the drama, most recently in *Behold This Dreamer* and *Johnny Johnson*. The sanity of the insane has nowhere been more ironically expressed than in Wilbur Daniel Steele and

Anthony Brown's dramatization of Steele's short story, *How Beautiful With Shoes* (1935), in which a shy and lovely young country girl is about to marry a brutish lout of a man. During the wedding preparations a "dangerous lunatic" escapes from the asylum and abducts the girl. He turns out to be a mild soul, obsessed only by a search for beauty. He finds it in the girl and loves her. He is captured and shut in jail, but sets fire to it and escapes; they find him on top of a mountain with the girl, reciting to her of his love in the language of the "Song of Songs": ". . . How beautiful are thy feet with shoes, O Prince's daughter. . . ." The lunatic is shot but the girl has had a glimpse of a more ecstatic love than her lout of a bridegroom offers, and she will have none of him.

Modern psychiatry has dropped the term "lunatic" in favor of the less opprobrious term "psychotic," meaning out of touch with reality. The thirties saw a growth in understanding of the psychoses, and a gradual narrowing down of terminology until three main categories of psychoses were recognized: schizophrenia or split personality, manic-depressive psychosis and paranoia. Susan Glaspell's incisive portrait of a manic-depressive in *The Verge* has yet to be equalled, but the theatre of the thirties saw effective illustrations of the other two types, schizophrenia and paranoia.

Robert Ardrey in *Thunder Rock* (1939) depicts an idealistic young liberal, disillusioned with the world of his day and withdrawing from it to be a lighthouse keeper on Lake Michigan. Although the primary thesis is ideological rather than psychiatric, the author's penetration of a mind that lives with its own ghosts is an interesting artistic expression of the schizophrenic state. At first the ghosts of immigrants who came to America a century ago are only tools of Charleston's will, but as the play progresses, they become more and more real; they make it clear to Charleston that the world of 1849 was just as full of despair as that of 1939 and that there was no easy solution even then. Charleston almost falls in love with the creation of his brain, Melanie, as did his schizophrenic brother in *Berkeley Square*. At the end, however, he rallies himself and returns to reality, going to China to help resist Japanese aggression. Without being psychologically profound or theatrically stirring, *Thunder Rock* makes its thematic attack against withdrawal into ivory or lighthouse towers.

A play which offers a much more unusual exploration of the psychotic world is *Thunder on the Left* (1933) by Jean Black, from Christopher Morley's novel. A fantasy predicated on a ten-year old's wish that he could know what he and his friends will be like when they grow up, it permits the ten-year old to walk through adult situations with the body of an adult and the mental and emotional reactions of a child—the equivalent of a psychotic. The only person among the adults whom the child doesn't like is the one who represents what he himself will be in twenty years. The startling effect of seeing a grown man ask a woman (who fancies herself being seduced) to come and kiss him goodnight and turn out his light indicates the originality of this play. By the end, the boy-man is happy to unwish his wish and return to ten years of age. Seeing adult life was too painful an experience.

Paranoia proved more popular with playwrights than schizophrenia, perhaps for the reason that paranoid symptoms are more often apt to erupt into criminal acts than do the withdrawal symptoms of schizoids. Elmer Harris and Philip Stern studied the psychology of *The Man Who Killed Lincoln* (1940) and found in the disordered mind of John Wilkes Booth a "Brutus complex" or desire to be a martyr based on the paranoiac idea that the nation was being oppressed by the tyranny of a Caesar.

The most effective case of theatrical paranoia during the period, however, was in the British writer Emlyn Williams' *Night Must Fall* (1936), with its charming young Danny insinuating himself into the affections of the invalid Mrs. Bramson while carrying with him a hatbox containing the severed head of his last victim. Danny is haunted by delusions of persecution and is constantly "acting"; in his own inner world he is "somebody special." It is this compulsion to prove his specialness to the world which causes him to murder Mrs. Bramson in a memorably terrifying night scene, and to go jauntily off with the police when he is finally caught. The paranoid Danny proved to be one of the choice actor's roles of the decade.

DEFENSE MECHANISMS, ASSORTED

Paranoia need not always lead to homicide, however. One paranoid reaction which is often used as a defense mechanism in normal behavior is that of projection, that is, of attributing to others the impulses within ourselves; paranoids attribute to others the hostility within themselves and conclude, "Everybody is against me." The Rorschach "ink blot" test provides a provocative but neutral stimulus into which the individual can project or "see" various shapes and forms, whatever his individual psychology determines. Similarly, George M. Cohan provided American playgoers with a whimsical kind of theatrical Rorschach test, *Pigeons and People* (1933). The grand old showman wrote and played in perhaps his most literate drama in this Pirandelloesque study of the power of suggestion in human relationships. What, asks Cohan, is the truth about a person? His leading character, Parker, is an eccentric who sits on a park bench talking to the pigeons because he prefers them to people. He is brought home by a friendly, well-intentioned man, Heath, but in two minutes Parker has Heath believing that he is a dangerous criminal, wanted for murder. Heath immediately calls the police. When Heath's friend arrives with two girls, Parker offers to kiss them and dances with one of them. He tries to bribe a servant to open Heath's safe, and when the servant refuses, compliments him on his loyalty, saying it was just a test. He suggests to Heath's secretary that they have an affair; when a doctor and nurse arrive he proposes to the nurse that they blackmail the doctor. When she refuses, he also compliments her on her loyalty; in the same way he tests the police detective who arrives. Parker ends up by confusing everyone, and each is sure that he is one or another of the possible roles which he has suggested to them. The detective who takes him away later telephones Heath to tell him that he has found out who Parker really was. Heath laughs as he hears Parker's identity over the phone, and the curtain falls. Who was he? Cohan plays a neat trick on his audience and maddeningly refuses to tell. But it does not matter. Each may project onto Parker whatever personality he chooses, may make of him either saint or sinner, blackmailer or loyal friend, depending on how strongly the impulse to treachery or loyalty is in the person doing the projecting. Or is that the meaning Cohan had in mind? Is this interpretation only a projection as well?

Another play in which audiences were able to project their own personal interpretation was Emmet Lavery's *The First Legion* (1934). Among a group of Jesuit brothers, Lavery depicts one who has been paralyzed from shell-shock during the war. When he suddenly finds himself able to walk, a physician believes that emotional and psychological explanations are sufficient to account for hysterical paralysis; but when others come to the priests as to a shrine and are also cured of their illnesses (including a boy with polio), the most skeptical Jesuit becomes convinced that the doctor was wrong and that it is a miracle wrought by God. Lavery thus reopens the provocative question of faith healing—the crossroads at which religion and psychotherapy come closest together.

An earnest Catholic, Lavery has played a significant role in the revival of interest in religious drama. He wrote the present author that he had known a few psychoanalysts and psychiatrists and had read, over the years, a few books on the subject. While not finally committing himself as to whether the cures in *The First Legion* were miraculous or psychosomatic, Lavery remarks on the parallel lines of religion and psychiatry:

> I have always been aware of the close relationship—at certain points—of religion and psychiatry but I have no theories to offer. In his effort to observe and to understand human behavior, a dramatist may use one set of tools or techniques—a psychiatrist another. (Some may use the same.) I think most dramatists make an honest effort these days to look at man whole—to report (rather than to correct, desirable though some correction may be) the man in relation to his complete environment,—and by environment I mean anything in a man's past, present or future—or his family's past, present or future—that is likely to illuminate his hopes, his despairs, his ambitions. In this connection I find Cardinal Newman's *Grammar of Assent* a very timely book.

Another metaphysical attempt to "look at man whole," and to deal with the true identity of a person was Benjamin M. Kaye's *On Stage* (1935), in which a playwright believes that he knows all about his dramatic characters because he models them on friends whom he knows well. But he goes to sleep and dreams a fantastic dream in which his characters do not behave at all as he thought they should, but instead turn out to have all kinds of seething unconscious problems which he failed to detect. "Kindly Dr. Gleason," whom he modeled on his friend Gilman, turns out to be an erotic sadist who has a girl undress in his office, gives her knock-out drops and whips her. In the playwright's dream, there is some use made of wish-fulfillment, distortion and secondary elaboration, as well as anxiety when a curtain falls between him and his girl, cutting him off from reality.

Sadism, premeditated and conscious, was more thoroughly explored by Alexander Woollcott and George S. Kaufman in *The Dark Tower* (1933), which restored the now-almost old fashioned subject of hypnotism to the theatre. It depicts a famous actress, Jessica Wells, who is under the hypnotic influence of her sinister, sadistic husband. When they had thought him dead, he returns to plague Jessica, her actor-brother and her producer-fiancé. The husband intimates an incestuous brother-sister attachment as the reason they resent him, a rationalization of his own impotence to feel any emotion save cruelty for his wife. She is somnambulistic, responding to his every whim until the brother is forced to disguise himself and carry out a carefully plotted murder of the husband. The greatest acting of his career succeeds completely but may never be revealed for public applause. When she learns of the murder, Jessica suffers amnesia, blocking out the week of the murder from her consciousness. A doctor explains it as, "Defense mechanism, I think they call it. It's just an inner necessity for her to forget what had been an intolerable experience. Of course it's not a rare phenomenon. We doctors run into it often." Her fear that she had killed her husband proves to be the cause of her amnesia, and further acting by her brother is necessary to absolve her of her guilt feelings in time for a happy ending. Apparently hypnosis could still be given theatrical credibility (with even a hint of extra-sensory perception).

After his early period of collaboration with Marc Connelly which produced *Beggar on Horseback* and his period of collaboration with Moss Hart which produced *You Can't Take It With You,* the versatile George S. Kaufman showed little interest in the psychoanalytic drama except where it might occasionally provide targets for his satiric wit. In *Stage Door* (1936), written with Edna Ferber, the heroine's father is a physician for whom business has dropped off because of psychoanalysis, causing him to offer this *reductio ad absurdum:*

> Well, it seems just being a medical man isn't enough these days. If you had a cold, we used to just cure the cold. But nowadays, the question is, why did you get the cold? Turns out, it's because, subconsciously, you didn't want to live. And why don't you want to live? Because when you were three years old the cat died, and they buried it in the back yard without telling you, and you were in love with the cat, so naturally, forty years later you catch cold.

The Man Who Came To Dinner (1939), supposedly modelled on Kaufman's ex-collaborator on *The Dark Tower,* Alexander Woollcott, became a comic classic with its portrait of the salacious, bawdy reprobate, Sheridan Whiteside, whose dialogue was liberally sprinkled with epithets such as, "Don't look at me with those great cow-eyes, you sex-ridden hag."

After his collaboration with Moss Hart ended, Kaufman treated Freudian concepts seriously only once, in *The Small Hours* (1951), written in collaboration with his wife, Leueen MacGrath. *The Small Hours* seems precisely the kind of play a number of playwrights such as George Kelly had in mind when they wrote of the dangers of literal or text-bookish use of Freudian dogma as the basis for drama. In this story a neurotic family has a multitude of psychoanalytic complexes, all of which seemingly derive from theory rather than observation. Laura Mitchell, the wife of a rich publisher, is a plain, not-too-bright woman who cannot keep up with her husband and is terrified of the smart dinner parties she must attend. Her husband is having an affair with an authoress in order to be able to publish her books, the daughter coldly and calculatingly marries without affection, and the son is a marijuana addict who goes to prison after a narcotics raid. Laura suffers hysterical paralysis as she asks her husband for a divorce. A prison psychiatrist apparently analyzes the son offstage. When the husband loses his business, the frigid daughter her husband and the son returns from prison coolly announcing, "I'm a latent homosexual," Laura feels needed and necessary, and is able to walk again. Though the situations in *The Small Hours* are both psychologically valid and potentially tragic, they fail to carry emotional empathy for we have not participated in the deeper strivings of the characters, in the inner dynamics that make inevitable the authors' ready-made conclusions.

PSYCHO-ECONOMIC FRUSTRATION

The most characteristic new genre in the playwriting of the thirties was the fusion of psychological and socio-economic themes brought to focus by the depression. This is not to suggest that the whole of the proletarian drama of the thirties was psychoanalytic. There was a considerable segment of sociological writers who did not care to do psychological analysis and were content with simple, uncomplicated tintypes of "the worker," "the struggling young lovers," "the capitalist." But the more enduring playwrights of the thirties retained the insights of the psychoanalytic movement in their treatment of the new themes of war, unionism, economic frustration, fascism and crime. In the work of Lillian Hellman, John Howard Lawson, Sidney Kingsley and particularly Clifford Odets, the ideological theme found its happiest union with characterization based upon genuine feeling for the motives of human beings; and in upper class drawing room comedy, S. N. Behrman was able to assemble a group of significant individuals whose unconscious motives illuminated some of the central problems of his time.

A number of other writers attempted this combination of psychological and sociological themes with varying success. Gertrude Tonkonogy, a "one-play playwright," created in *Three-Cornered Moon* (1933) a delightful comedy about a zany and irresponsible family which meets the problems of the depression in a humorously psychotic way. The forerunner of the Vanderhof family of *You Can't Take it With You*, the Rimplegars of this play all do the unexpected and the irrational until they lose their money in the stock market crash. Their young doctor moves in with them to help with the rent. The daughter, Elizabeth, has a boy friend, Donald, who is a "writer" and "can't bear the thought of earning a living." When last he held a conventional job, he explains, "Somebody in the office would say something wrong or do something wrong and I'd go cold. I'd break —right in the middle, I'd get black spots in my brain." Similarly, Mrs. Rimplegar meets all the crises of life by going upstairs and lying down. The young doctor proceeds to bring the family into closer contact with reality and to win Elizabeth away from the writer. *Three-Cornered Moon* is an amusing example of post—Freudian comedy based upon charmingly irrational responses to the problems of the depression. In Arthur Kober's *Having Wonderful Time* (1937), too, the characters face bleak economic reality with good-humored, amatory zest and a racy vocabulary of Freudian terminology.

But of all the plays of the depression, none is more famous than *Tobacco Road* (1933). Adapted by Jack Kirkland from the novel by Erskine Caldwell, *Tobacco Road* depicts a segment of society at the lowest possible level of both economic and psychological frustration, with each interplaying upon the other until the will to meliorate has atrophied. Without attempting to use psychoanalysis, the play shows that at the animal level to which the Jeeter Lesters have been reduced, the sexual impulses found repressed in the unconscious of civilized man by Freud are freely and openly expressed. There is evidence of father-daughter incest between Jeeter and his girls, Pearl and Ellie May. Sister Bessie, the evangelist, believes that the Lord, knowing of Jeeter's sinful impulses, made Ellie May with a hare-lip to keep him from touching her. Out of the degenerate and loathsome conditions of their life, it is little wonder that the beautiful daughter, Pearl, has developed a complete abhorrence of sex and refuses to consummate her marriage to the clod, Lov Bensey, who comes complaining to his inlaws: "You tell her to stop sleeping on that durn pallet and get in the bed. . . ." Lov has a sack of turnips and while the hare-lip girl grovels in the dirt to seduce Lov, the wily Jeeter steals the turnips. Jeeter's half-wit son, Dude, marries Sister Bessie in order to get to drive her car. With something more primitive even than voyeurism, Jeeter and the two daughters all peep as Dude and the libidinous woman preacher begin to consummate their marriage. Emotional impoverishment serves as an effective defense mechanism, however—nothing further can perturb the genial cracker, Jeeter; not the fact that his mother dies out in the fields—he'll go look for her some day; not the fact that the bank takes over his farm; nor the fact that Dude and Bessie run over his wife and kill her (her last act was to bite Jeeter to make him release Pearl so she could escape from Lov and flee to Augusta). Jeeter sits on the sagging porch of his house and rubs the Georgia dirt through his fingers, the last of this dynasty of derelicts that had once been human.

Such a play as *Tobacco Road* would not and could not have been staged in New York until the traditional taboos had been cleared away during the twenties—largely as a result of Freudian influence which rendered incest and sexual perversion a clinical fact rather than an unspeakable anomaly. There is no question but that *Tobacco Road* was written as a humanitarian protest that such conditions could exist in the United States. Jeeter was played at first by Henry Hull with a deep feeling for the tragic implications of the story. But as the run of the play progressed, other Jeeters took over and began to heighten the comic "hokum" as well as the shock value of the sexual behavior, until *Tobacco Road* became the theatrical sensation of the decade. It achieved the longest run of any play on Broadway, 3182 performances (later surpassed by *Life With Father*).

There were of course imitations, or at least other efforts to employ the gross naturalism of *Tobacco Road*, but as a rule without success. *Jackson White* (1935) by David Balch depicted equally primitive *mores* in the hills of New York State, where a father seduces his son's wife. There was *Weep For the Virgins* (1935) by Nellise Child, in which the mother of an impoverished family dreams of a rosy future in Hollywood for her daughters, and is determined to keep them in ignorance of sex. As a result, one of the girls gets pregnant by a sailor, one is arrested for "rolling" an amorous transient, and the one who had been forced to diet for Hollywood marries an old man in exchange for a few trinkets and the promise she can eat all the sweets she wants. *Washington Heights* (1931) by Vincent Lawrence was an even more lurid tale of sexual frustration among the poverty stricken tenement dwellers of New York. *Soliloquy* (1938) by Victor Victor showed a frustrated bookkeeper making the same revolt made by Rice's Mr. Zero and Kaiser's cashier in *From Morn to Midnight;* it was unusual in this decade of naturalism in that the unspoken thoughts of the hero were heard by the audience from a sound track, an interesting variation of O'Neill's *Strange Interlude* technique.

If most of the naturalistic dramas were depressing rather than elevating, it was because they lacked the single element of man's struggle to rise above the repressive forces—within and without. The nobility of Greek tragedy lay in the exertion of man's will—even against predetermined destiny. But in a *Tobacco Road* there is little if any struggle—only the mother makes some effort at retaining human dignity. It took some years for the naturalistic playwright to find a solution to the problem of seeking tragic greatness within squalor and human degradation. Odets found the solution in *Golden Boy*, Anderson in *Winterset;* and in the entire decade of the thirties, perhaps the most successful solution was John Steinbeck's tragedy of migratory workers on a California ranch, *Of Mice and Men* (1937).

In *Of Mice and Men*, George and Lennie embody the wish of the human spirit to better itself and grow to fulfillment. While George is reality-oriented, his companion Lennie has the feeble mind of a lovable little child. He has a strong erotic attachment for little animals but is psychotically unable to control his erotic-sadistic impulses toward them. He pets mice or rabbits until he squeezes them to death. He is totally dependent upon George, who reluctantly accepts his responsibility, even passing up visits to the local "cat house" to save his money. Together they plan to "roll up a stake" and buy a ranch where they can raise rabbits and "live off the fat of the land!"

The best laid schemes of mice and men, however, often fail to take into account the tragic convergence of inner and outer flaw. On the ranch is the sexually frustrated wife of the owner's son, Curley, who is a short man with compensatory meanness and resentment at his inadequacy as his wife's sexual partner. She looks hungrily at the ranch hands and, by accident, she and Lennie find themselves alone in the barn with their guilts—she running away from her husband, he hiding a dead puppy he has killed. There is a superb scene of free association almost in the *Strange Interlude* manner as Curley's wife reminisces about her life, her experiences with her drunken, lecherous father and his promise of taking her off to live with him. Lennie does not listen to her but in contrapuntal manner free associates from his own unfulfilled wish for the rabbit ranch and for soft things to pet. When Curley's wife invites him to feel her soft hair, destiny closes in. Soon Lennie's hands are around her neck; as she gets panicky and struggles, Lennie is unable to let go, and strangles her.

George finds his pathetic charge hiding on a riverbank and to keep him from the posse that is hunting him down, knows that he must shoot him. He pulls the trigger as Lennie talks of the place with the rabbits where they can live off the fat of the land. Lennie's tragedy is the universal experience of the human race. Aspiring to peace and security, man seems helpless to understand and discipline his own unconscious impulses to destruction. To know and channel these chaotic impulses has been the goal of psychotherapy. But until the understanding of man is translated into political, economic and sociological realms, man will continue to seem from time to time a great, loutish child, seeking only "to live on the fat of the land" but carrying within him and unknown to him the seeds of destruction.

SURREALISM—STEIN AND SAROYAN

When Freud first opened the doors of *super-ego* and *id* to the *ego* of the world, the artist had two choices: either he could make the descent into his own unconscious life and upon his return exert his most conscious ego to mould his materials into an art-form that would be meaningful to others who had not participated in his private experience—or he could remain at the unconscious level and produce his art-work from there. The vast majority of novelists, playwrights and musicians chose the former path. Many painters, sculptors, poets and a few playwrights made the latter choice and followed James Joyce into free-association. E. E. Cummings, (correction, e. e. cummings), Edmund Wilson, John Dos Passos, Em Jo Basshe, William Saroyan and Gertrude Stein are among those who have created plays from a deep level of unconsciousness with a minimum of direction from the ego.

Freud showed the value of free-association as a method of diagnosis and therapy; the surrealists seized upon it as an art-form. Its technique is invitingly easy and does not require the exertion of rigorous discipline: merely suspend conscious control and report everything and anything that rises to consciousness, letting one idea produce its own associations along whatever pathways the unconscious chooses to go. There is no evidence in the writings of Freud that he saw value to this as art *per se,* merely as a clinical aid in resolving a person's psychological conflicts. But Freud became the unwilling patron saint of surrealism.

The name *surrealism* was taken from the subtitle of a French play by Guillaume Apollinaire, *Les Mamelles de Tirésias* (1917), which although never played on Broadway has recently been made into an opera. Beginning in France during and after the first World War, surrealism was actually in protest not only against traditionalism but also against the *dada* movement, with which it was frequently linked. While the dadaists insisted on the futility of all meaning, the surrealists sought to record the inner meaning of the unconscious. André Breton stated the manifesto of surrealism:

> Assuming that the image is the irreducible minimum of art, the surrealist wishes to protect the imagery he finds in dreams and in other expressions of the unconscious, to reproduce it with as little interference as possible from the

conscious mind. What results may be intelligible or not; its intelligibility is not an important matter; rather, its fidelity to the poet's experience is the test it must pass, and no one but the poet can judge of that success.

The "automatic writing" which Breton advocated had interested psychologists since the 19th century work of Garth Wilkinson and Ludwig Börne, the latter a favorite author of Freud's who may, Dr. Ernest Jones suggests, have unconsciously influenced Freud's discovery of free association as a clinical technique. Automatic writing was first introduced to American playgoers by George Cram Cook in his curious play of 1921, *The Spring*. But surrealism in the drama remained essentially a French expression, meeting the needs of the restless, post-war artist in a war-torn country which was disillusioned with conventional standards, weary of order and distrustful of reason. The plays of Jean Cocteau, Fernand Crommelynck and Roger Vitrac which came out of this movement were not seen on Broadway and had little influence upon the American psychoanalytic drama.

Among Americans, the notable literary critic, Edmund Wilson, has twice tried to extract drama from the unconscious world. The first, *The Crime in the Whistler Room* (1924) was summarized by a fellow critic, Kenneth Burke:

> In a dream play by Edmund Wilson, *The Crime in The Whistler Room*, there are two worlds of plot, with the characters belonging in the one world looking upon those in the other as dead, and the hero of this living world taking a dream shape as werewolf. The worlds switch back and forth, depending upon the presence or removal of a gateleg table. In this instance I think we should not be far wrong in attributing some such content as the above to the table when considering it as a fulcrum upon which the structure of the plot is swung.

More recently in *The Little Blue Light* (1951), Wilson created a fantastic nightmare-projection into the political future of the United States. While the country is menaced by a foreign enemy, a science-fiction writer is more obsessed with the menace of Shidnats Slyme, a character of his own creation who is brute Evil incarnate. There is a gardener who, dreamlike, speaks first with an Italian accent, then an Irish, Scotch and Russian accent. At the end, Shidnats Slyme proves unexpectedly to be the young wife who is the monster of Evil because she is neurotic and frigid, unable to love her husband and therefore killing his faith in himself rather than see him succeed. She had been obsessed with transplanting hydrangeas, and the science-fiction writer says:

It's so obvious they're sexual symbols. . . . You can't bear to have those handsome flowers flourishing in front of the house, just because you want to castrate the men.

Though there is considerable psychoanalytic validity in Wilson's suggestion that the ultimate evil may be "the woman that won't be a woman," the woman who desires to compete with men rather than to love them, *The Little Blue Light* was presented in a strange, psychotic form which mystified rather than illuminated.

A few other literary notables followed Wilson into the unconscious—novelists more often than dramatists perhaps because of the influential pioneering of Joyce. (Interestingly enough, however, Joyce himself sensed the impossibility of doing for the stage what he had done for fiction, and his one drama, *Exiles* (1917)—a triangular design for living in which a man masochistically urges his wife to betray him with his best friend—was structured in the realistic form.)

John Dos Passos in *Airways, Inc.* (1929) employed the *Strange Interlude* technique of suspended motion and stream-of-the-unconscious soliloquies which the other characters on the stage do not hear —achieving at times an arresting and powerful effect. Em Jo Basshe tried in *Adam Solitaire* (1925) to capture in expressionistic form an anxiety dream of a young man who tries to die but cannot commit suicide, try as he will, until he has fulfilled a prophecy. E. E. Cummings in *Him* (1927) created the most incoherent and Joycean drama of the Freudian twenties, completely based on subjective symbols and associations. All three of these serious attempts to achieve in drama the freedom from objectivity which Joyce achieved in the novel were mercilessly rejected by the metropolitan critics. Dos Passos, Wilson, Basshe and Cummings apparently found that the avenue into the unconscious is a perilous street down which to lead a spectator in the theatre, with the risk ever present that the production of one individual's unconscious will not be meaningful to any other individuals without considerably more intermediary comment than is possible in the creative arts. By its very nature, the theatre presupposes that a number of individuals sitting in orientated rows of seats will necessarily respond to approximately the same stimuli on the stage. Breton's dictum that "only the poet can judge of that success" would render these seats superfluous. His manifesto, taking the image as the "irreducible minimum of art" is inadequate for the theatre, where the irreducible minimum is the character. The important Freudian playwrights, O'Neill, Elmer Rice, Arthur Miller, John Howard Lawson, Philip Barry and Kaufman and Connelly in *Beggar On Horseback*, reveal their free associations through their

individual characters and retain to varying extents a conscious ego
and a disciplined theatrical awareness to organize the chaotic unconscious and at times to interpret it. As Allardyce Nicoll has pointed
out, if the manifesto of surrealism were literally adopted, ". . . then
anybody's dream is as good as anybody else's, and . . . hence the
position of the 'artist' becomes imperiled. . . ." Valuable as the
surrealistic experiments were in opening closed doors and enriching
theatrical potentialities, they may be likened to a psychoanalysis
which is broken off prematurely. The regression to the past is not an
end in itself and the therapy is not over until the patient is brought
back to conscious reality with a mature insight into the meaning of
his unconscious life. Similarly, the playwright has the obligation of
sending his spectator out of the theatre more aware and less bound
by his own anxiety because of his theatrical exploration into the unconscious. Pure surrealist drama would be of interest not to the playgoer but only to the clinician, as in the case of Pablo Picasso's
recently published play, *Desire*, which is no play at all but the associational images of a disturbed mind obsessed by sex, pus and mussed
bed sheets. (In this case there may be special interest for the art
critic in shedding light on the painting of Picasso.)

Of all playwrights, the one who apparently set out to suppress
the conscious as rigidly as the pre-Freudians suppressed the unconscious was Gertrude Stein, who has been represented on Broadway
only by the opera, *Four Saints in Three Acts*, (1934), with music by
Virgil Thompson. Opera or ballet may be a more suitable sphere for
her texts than the theatre, for Miss Stein's plays read like the psychotic mumblings of a patient in a ward for the severely disturbed.
She plays with words and sounds, caressing them, repeating them,
developing them as a musician does notes, as in fact Bach does with
contrapuntal motifs. To call them nonsense is of course untrue and
unjust. There is sense to the words, but the sense is known best to
Miss Stein and can generally be illuminated only with reference to
her own association. At times, however, there is painfully poignant
sense and sanity which emerges and strikes the reader out of pages
of word-fugues; and, at other times, it is as if a psychoanalyst's notes
on which he had recorded the dreams and free associations of many
patients had blown off the desk and been picked up in random order.
As others have pointed out, *Four Saints in Three Acts* is neither
about four saints nor in three acts. The saints split, multiply, vanish
as in a dream. But whereas most dreams are largely of visual images,
Miss Stein's imagery is aural and deals with word sounds such as an
infant or a psychotic babbles in pure delight at vowels and conso-
nants. This is the closing scene of *Four Saints:*

Who makes who makes it do.
Saint Therese and Saint Therese too.
Who does and who does care.
Saint Chavez to care.
Saint Chavez to care.
Who may be what is it when it is instead.
Saint Plan Saint Plan to may to say to say too may and
    inclined.
Who makes it be what they had as porcelain.
Saint Ignatius and left and right laterally be lined.
All Saints.
    To Saints.
Four Saints.
    And Saints.
Five Saints.
    To Saints.
Last Act.
Which is a fact.

Where many of the unconscious productions of modern painters
and poets are at least charged with personal emotional content which
gives some definite impression to the audience, Miss Stein's stream-
of-the-unconscious is generally a cold and emotionless one—almost
suspiciously full of super-ego. There is nothing about herself, no
lyrical expression of emotion, no tangible relationships to people,
animals or things.

   An Exercise in Analysis plays havoc with both psychoanalysis
and the drama, labelling each line a different Act or Part, in what
Thornton Wilder believes to be her "satirical jab at pedantry and
formalism in general, her way of saying, 'Don't fence *me* in!'" There
is considerably more emotion and reality-orientation in *Yes Is For
A Very Young Man* (1944-5) which is somewhat in a class by itself
and has seen a production at the Pasadena Playhouse. Miss Stein
apparently had a practical motive in writing it: ". . . it is complicated and simple, and I hope it will make you feel the French as they
really were during the long years of the occupation." She has, therefore, attempted to capture the endless repetition of everyday dialogue, the inane statements, inability to deal with powerful emotions, divergent streams of consciousness by which people can talk
to each other and not hear each other. But any power that the play
achieves—and there is more than a little—comes from its theme and
its one character presented under a strong and vividly expressed
emotion.

   Gertrude Stein was disassociated from the mainstream of drama,
and there are those who believe that she was only playing a great

joke on a gullible public, conditioned by Freudianism to accept the irrational and incoherent, afraid to be called "old-fashioned" by rejecting it but deriving from it neither aesthetic pleasure nor psychiatric benefit.

Unlike the pure subjectivism of Gertrude Stein, William Saroyan represents a compromise position between the demands of the practical theatre and the cry of Breton for automatic writing. A buffeted young man who was raised in an orphanage, Saroyan describes his insecure youth in his whimsical autobiography, *Bicycle Rider in Beverly Hills*. His defense mechanisms against the uncertainties of his childhood proved to be an exuberant zest for living, an early identification with and love for the common man and an early and unswerving love for William Saroyan as an uncommon man. Where Gertrude Stein was apt to see life compulsively as a crazy unreality, Saroyan tried hard to laugh at life's incongruities. In reply to the present author's questionnaire about works of Freud, Jung and other psychoanalysts he had read, Saroyan answered, "I read around in all of them that were at the Fresno Public Library 1920-1925. (Read around in everything there, though.)" He has elsewhere stated that his favorites of the Fresno days included Gertrude Stein, Shaw, Mencken, Schopenhauer, Whitman, Andreyev, Chekhov, Gorki and Hemingway. From this avid reading and his native fluency, Saroyan developed an amazing, semi-poetic rhetoric and an abundant, ever-eloquent verbalization of emotion which critics have from time to time called a maddening infatuation with the sound of his own voice. But critics have been Saroyan's Achilles' heel—the only group of his fellow men for whom he does not feel unbounded love. His defense against feelings of inferiority is apparently to assume the bumptious role of a literary Peck's bad boy, to announce that all his plays are irreproachably great, and to turn with hostility upon anyone who criticizes them.

Saroyan's early one-act plays tended to have the surrealistic, free-associational quality of a dream. The title of one of these one-acts, *The People With the Light Coming Out of Them*, might well be taken as the collective theme of the group. There is a kind of illumination, of radiance coming out of the common men and women in Saroyan's innocent idealization of them. *Subway Circus* (1935) is a cross-section of the day-dreams of the little people who sit silently on a subway train. The child dreams of confounding his teacher with wise answers; others dream of riches, sex, respect, superiority. In this early play, too, the first of Saroyan's many Postal Telegraph messenger boys makes his debut, a segment of Saroyan's childhood experience that remains very much alive and unrepressed.

Elmer and Lily again deals with the private wishes and dreams of the humble. Elmer is the perennial failure who conducts a schizophrenic debate with himself, half derogatory and half starry eyed. His efforts to sell a twenty-five cent novelty (which he cannot make work) become a surrealistic nightmare—a man chasing a girl multiplies into two men and the girl multiplies until there are six. A rival salesman makes the gadget work and Elmer spends his last quarter to buy one. Other scenes, however, are unrelated and rambling. Saroyan's favorite character seems to be a precocious, free-associating child who asks questions adults cannot answer. Elmer ends up at a kind of psychoanalyst's (who has a fantasy-pantomime of his own secret life), and with dream-condensation the doctor writes everything on the board as if he were a school teacher. Though Elmer dreams of Lily, he himself cannot even get into the dream. A mad, chaotic finale interrupts the analysis, but the doctor buys the twenty-five cent gadget and Elmer can win Lily. *Elmer and Lily* contains effective elements of dream distortion, wish-fulfillment, secondary elaboration, condensation and the doctor's fantasies of masochism and self-pity. Though Saroyan retold this basic dream many times, *Elmer and Lily* is one of its most effective realizations.

Again, in *The Great American Goof*, a ballet-play created for and danced by Eugene Loring, there is the little man, the inept failure who tries all through the play to woo the beautiful lady but without success. Each of the ways the goof tries to find himself proves disappointing, and he proclaims, "I resign." At the end the girl smiles on him, and the goof asserts he'll change the world—if it takes six or seven thousand years. The girl had uttered what might well prove to be the explanation for all of Saroyan's one-acts:

> I do understand everything. Everything is dreamed. Everything is *supposed* to be dreamed.

But the dream requires interpretation and is not necessarily an artform, as the surrealists found out; even some dreams have more structure than most of Saroyan's little vignettes: *The Poetic Situation in America Since Alexandre Dumas, Opera Opera, The Ping-Pong Players, Coming Thru the Rye, Talking to You* and *Across the Boards on Tomorrow Morning*. Only in *Hello, Out There* did Saroyan lay aside surrealistic sketching to create a tightly-plotted, powerfully realistic and yet lyrical story of a man falsely imprisoned for rape.

The most effective and fully realized of Saroyan's one-act fantasies, and the first to bring Saroyan to the New York stage (under the auspices of the Group Theatre) was *My Heart's in the Highlands* (1939), which has the subjective, dreamlike unreality of

the earlier plays. It is life viewed through childlike eyes, and all
the characters partake of childish qualities; it is wish-fulfillment
objectified—if only life could be such a fairy-tale world where the
neighbors and the grocer all produce food in order to feed the old
actor who plays haunting melodies on his bugle. The world is
responsible for feeding its artists and givers of beauty, the symbolism
declares. The preoccupation with food in this play might be interpreted by a psychoanalyst as an "oral regression." Curiously enough,
Saroyan is said to have objected to the stylization of the Group
Theatre production and defended the play's realism.

After the critical acclaim for *My Heart's in the Highlands,*
Saroyan is purported to have turned out his first full-length play in
six feverish days of writing. Had he spent longer, *The Time of Your
Life* might have proven a masterpiece of the American drama. As it
is, this play (for which he refused the Pulitzer Prize) contains much
original characterization and compassion for the frustrations of the
common man and woman. In his San Francisco waterfront dive,
Saroyan assembles an ingratiating collection of humanity: Joe is a
man with unlimited financial resources who gives away money to
help people find happiness; his slow-witted friend, Tom, is, like
Steinbeck's Lennie, a child-man; Kitty, the prostitute, is "one of the
few truly innocent people," and the policeman hates the police
force but doesn't know what else to do; there is an Arab who
mutters, "No foundations. All the way down the line," and there is
a pin-ball maniac, a pathetic vaudevillian who can't make people
laugh, a philosophical longshoreman, a kindly bartender, and other
assorted tragic-comic figures. There is a bare minimum of plot,
which consists of Tom's mute love for Kitty and Joe's efforts to help
them find a better life. Blick, a sadistic vice-squad officer, has been
hounding the prostitutes and when he would arrest Kitty, he is
mercifully killed by a wonderfully loquacious old coot named Kit
Carson. *The Time of Your Life* is pervaded by Saroyan's dream of
innocence, his sentimentalized feeling that the little people are spiritually beautiful. The childish wish-fulfillment again prevails—Joe is
a magic dispenser of all good, a father-image if not The Father. Joe
illustrates by his actions the theme of the play, stated at the beginning in an eloquent stage direction:

> In the time of your life, live—so that in that wondrous time
> you shall not add to the misery and sorrow of the world, but
> shall smile to the infinite delight and mystery of it.

All ends happily with Saroyan condoning murder if necessary to
prevent people from adding to the misery of the world.

In his orientation to reality, Saroyan has not again approached *The Time of Your Life*, but instead has gradually returned to the surrealistic, subjective style of the one-acts but with a deepening cynicism. *Love's Old Sweet Song* (1940) is a rather smart-aleck satire on the Oakies and on young radical writers who want to dramatize them. A son of the Oakies kills his father with a brutal blow of a club on the head because he wanted to rest his head in his mother's lap and the father wouldn't let him; but whether Saroyan is taking his Oedipus complex seriously or not is hazardous to say. The familiar Saroyan trade-mark of "a little child shall lead them" is apparent in this play—the young Postal Telegraph messenger who memorizes the collect messages to save people paying for them turns out to be the *deus ex machina* and hero of the play. As a paean to love, however, the song Saroyan sings here is too *scherzo* to be affecting.

The Beautiful People (1940) enlarges the theme of *My Heart's in the Highlands* and again shows the wish for the beautiful people to have the material necessities somehow provided for by exceptional if not supernatural means so as not to interfere with the things of the spirit. In this case the magic manna comes in the form of pension checks intended for a previous tenant who is dead. The insurance adjuster who comes is so enchanted with the beguiling way of life of these child-adults (the brother writes novels consisting of one word and the sister befriends the mice who spell out her name in flowers) that he stays and lets the checks continue. In spite of some moments of exquisite feeling—the young girl's radiant, "I met a man today," speech—the play adds little to Saroyan's previously established feeling of passive-dependency and faith in a fairy-tale world.

The last of Saroyan's plays to be seen on Broadway was *Get Away Old Man* (1943), which was Saroyan's satirical jab at Hollywood. Following Samson Raphaelson's kidding of his obsession for glorifying the "little man" in *Jason* (1942), Saroyan is here able to kid himself and to show in his obviously autobiographical character of Harry Bird an eccentric, mad-cap writer, brought to Hollywood because of his "compassion for little people," but obstreperously throwing darts in his office, ordering pianos sent up, yelling at actresses out the window and generally offering unsolicited and caustic analyses to people. Harry is employed by an egomaniac movie mogul who wants him to dramatize his life story for him—it turns out, for a psychoanalytic reason. He wants to be purged of his great hatred for women, resulting from his memory of worshipping an angelic girl when he was eight years old—only to have

her spit on him. Since then his tenderness to women has been converted into sadistic hatred. "In my heart I spit at *them*," he confesses.
But Harry cannot write it because it is not *his* experience, and
instead dashes off to make love to an actress onto whom he projects
(even though she is a tramp) all the innocence and spiritual beauty
of womanhood. The plot of *Get Away Old Man* is more developed
than is usual for Saroyan, but it does not crowd out his love for
juxtaposition and incongruity.

Since 1943 Saroyan has to all intents and purposes said "Get
Away Old Man" to all Broadway producers by his growing tendency
to subjectivism. But he has continued to write for the theatre, and
some of these later plays have been attempted by the more courageous of university theatres. In *Sweeney in the Trees* (1946) he vents
himself of much hostility for the finances of the bourgeois world and
the merchant mentality. A character happily and childishly kicks
money around the stage thinking it is not real, but at the end it
proves to be real and all is well. Passive-dependency and infantile
resentment of the material world, whimsically stated in *My Heart's
In the Highlands, The Time of Your Life* and *The Beautiful People*,
here grows humorless and perilously close to psychotic.

Of all Saroyan's excursions toward the *dada* world of Gertrude
Stein, his most extreme is *Jim Dandy* (1947) in which the author says
of the leading character, "He knew the truth and was looking for
something better." At one point the characters contemplate putting
on a play within the play, and Jim Dandy says, "Then let him close
his eyes to this play and open them to the play on the stage of
his sleep." This is the only advice that can enrich our understanding of *Jim Dandy*, which is totally without plot, totally "creative" in
that each symbol is a purely personal one to the author, conceived
as a dream-play with elements juxtaposed in fantastic unreality. The
mood is bitter, sardonic, oppressive—until the end where the joy is
equally compulsive and manic. Like Jim Dandy, Saroyan had
proven himself able to depict objective reality and "was looking for
something better."

The setting is a transparent eggshell (Freudian symbol of
fertility?), inside which are ruins symbolizing civilization in collapse
after a decade of war and madness. Out of the shadowy outlines
emerges an inner setting, the public library (Saroyan's spiritual home
in childhood). The librarian is a frustrated and somewhat batty
spinster with an enormous cash register for the payment of fines
which clangs, honks, grinds and shifts from time to time—reflecting
Saroyan's childish love of toys. The collection of characters here has
none of the ingratiating quality of *The Time of Your Life*, but con-

sists of Fishkin, a melancholy introvert, an old peasant woman who occasionally throws off her black rags and becomes a wonderful dancer, a prisoner in jail, a young boy and girl fearfully hugging at the edge of a cave like some nineteenth century painting of Paul and Virginia, Gibbon, half-man and half-ape, and Jim Dandy, an escaped convict followed by his Negro *factotum*. This motley group says and does wildly unpredictable things, occasionally with impassioned eloquence. Gibbon, the ape, would learn about the human race, but the others dissuade him. Fishkin wants only to read and think, but that is not permitted in the Public Library. A priest-like young man is searching for the Holy Grail but instead finds the frustrated librarian and they go off together ecstatically. Of man's need for dreams Fishkin speaks in a burst of Jungian eloquence:

> At night they light fires, or candles, or lamps or turn on electric lights, but it's no use. The dream returns to carry on its secret work. The speechless fall down to sleep, and sleeping speak, using every device of breath and lung, jaw and mouth, tongue and teeth, and all the words of races dead and gone, the words for father and mother, sister and brother, son and daughter, neighbor and friend. And all the numbers of things, and all the signs. In the light of day, while they are awake, the speechless stutter and lisp and wait for night again, and then they say oh and ah, hello Ma, hello Pa, hey Jenny, hey Joe, ha ha and ho ho, ah-ah and alas. Alas, alas. The night is parent and home, school and church, starting point and destination.

After this flash of unconscious poetry they ask who spoke, and Fishkin is sure it wasn't he. Then a loaf of bread appears, and Saroyan returns to his theme of oral fixation. As in a dream, they all break off and eat a piece of bread but the loaf does not diminish. Sharing and eating from the same loaf has a symbolic ritual significance for Saroyan, and after it the characters seem purged of their neurotic wants. The man in jail is set free and the play ends in Wagnerian ecstasy. Fishkin proclaims, "*I* never knew until this very instant how wrong I've been to hate my father, and my mother, and myself—and *all* the sons of *all* the fathers and *all* the mothers." All sing and dance for joy and the cash register goes into its act of honking, groaning and spewing coins forth in a fountain. For all the play's moments of intensity and lucid translation of the unconscious world, however, the catharsis of Fishkin can hardly be shared empathically by the mystified and frustrated reader of *Jim Dandy*.

Of his next play, *A Decent Birth, A Happy Funeral* (1949), less need be said. Saroyan here grows preoccupied with death and writes a symbolic play without being particularly surrealistic. Although there are a few affecting and humorous moments, the play is largely Saroyan's naive delight in the obvious. Reflecting the author's unhappy experience in the army, the plot concerns an Ernest Hughman who is taken into the army and who makes his friends (also named Hughman—"human") promise to give him a happy funeral. The macabre funeral for a moment suggests the clinically familiar dream of seeing one's self in a coffin, but the perennial Western Union messenger arrives at the end to announce that Hughman is still alive.

Even more bitter toward the war and the army was *Sam Ego's House* (1949). The cast of characters leads one to anticipate a Freudian play: Ample Urge, Inner Urge, and Outer Urge are the three sons of Utmost Urge and the mother Yester Urge. But the symbolism is superficial and does not go much farther. An old house, formerly belonging to Sam Ego (who is now in the insane asylum) is being auctioned off; it is bought and moved away by Utmost Urge, a junkman. (Also in the insane asylum, says irreconcilable ex-private Saroyan, was a Brigadier-General, but the excitement of war restored his mind and he was given command of three divisions in Italy.) Where Moss Hart, Maxwell Anderson, Robert Sherwood and Arthur Miller found their wartime experiences an enriching opportunity to make contact with the common man so admired by Saroyan, morbid hatred for the military crops up in Saroyan's post-war plays. The three sons of Urge are all wounded veterans—one fell out of a taxi while drunk, one got cut in a saloon fight and one had a nervous breakdown in Paris. Sam Ego escapes the asylum and is hunted in his old house, now used as a retreat for lovers. A little boy smuggles food to the old man, reminiscent of *My Heart's In the Highlands.* A crochety and amusing old church sexton develops a Boy Scout-phobia as the children help hunt for the old man. The last scene depicts the end of the war and the wild hysterical abandon of the girls who kiss the house-movers and cry with incredible tastelessness: "Oh, Hiroshima." "Oh, Nagasaki." At this point, Sam Ego recovers his sanity and doesn't have to go back to the asylum but will live in peace with the Urges—a Freudian parallel for mental health. The inevitable Western Union Messenger brings news of the sons' return; the most poignant moment is their return, total strangers to their parents, walking casually into the house where nobody greets or pays attention to them. One wants a bed, one a comfortable chair, and one doesn't know what he wants. At the end, as they go to dinner, one boy finally hugs his mother.

A more recent play published in *Theatre Arts*, *The Slaughter of the Innocents* (1952) expands the theme of hatred for militarism and the police state into a full-blown nightmare. Pushing the unconscious drama almost as far as Strindberg and Gertrude Stein, Saroyan here uses subjective elements—distortion and secondary elaboration grotesquely arranged in a kind of grim warning of the potential implications of regimentation—whether of Soviet or McCarthy brand he does not specify. The scene is a bar taken over by the inquisitors as a drumhead court to try and execute all of the accused. The bar owner tries to stomach the brutality until a child is brought in, his crime that of hating his father and mother. A kindly, detached old lady who never quite realizes that this is a bloody court, takes the child upstairs for a nap and he returns purged of his hatred for his mother and father. In production some of the scenes would be tedious and repetitious and some so overwritten as to verge dangerously on the burlesque. The fault of *Slaughter of the Innocents* is the weakness of all Saroyan's plays—the apparent inability to view the script with some objectivity and to ask: "What does my dream mean?"

Of all Saroyan's closet dramas, however, perhaps the most powerful and most deserving of at least experimental production is *Don't Go Away Mad* (1949). Reminiscent of Schnitzler's *Last Masks* in its morbid preoccupation with death, the play is laid in the sun room of a city hospital where a number of patients await death from some incurable disease. The form here is not surrealistic but brutally photographic; the plot structure, after some wordiness in the second act, becomes tense and stageworthy. The symbolism of this modern *Everyman* is clear—the title is Saroyan's admonition not to die with unresolved hostility for mankind. An old man blind in one eye and losing the sight of the other says:

> We ain't the only people who're dying, you know. The whole human race is—Starvation, homelessness, exhaustion, fear, anger, anxiety, despair, nervousness, overwork, worry.

The patients include Poseyo, a Greek who loves Mozart, Greedy Reed, one of the richest Negro characterizations of our theatre, Andy Boy, a Chinese who is the only one among them who can read, and Buster, a new patient whose son did not recognize him when last he saw him. Each of them faces death in his own way. But Greedy discovers a kind of therapy for them all. He has Andy Boy read the dictionary to them, word by word beginning with A. In a poignant scene, Greedy relishes each definition, particularly the one pointing out the prevalence in many languages of the vowel *a* in the words for *mama* and *papa*. Their education is interrupted, however, when Andy Boy is taken away by the doctor for an operation that may relieve his pain. As they wait for his return, Georgie gives all his money to the new patient to go out, see his son and hold him in his arms once more before he dies. When they realize Andy Boy has died, Greedy knows that to purge himself of his hatred he must kill the doctor who operated on Andy Boy. This killing is made unnecessary when they read in the paper that the bartender who took Buster's wife and son away from him has been mysteriously killed the night before. Greedy proudly realizes that he has outlived that bartender, and they touchingly agree to stick by Buster and not betray him for killing the bartender—for he is now the only one who can read the dictionary to them. Each of the words he reads seems pertinent now to these dying men as the curtain falls on ". . . abide . . . ability. . . ."

The same theme as *The Time of Your Life,* that men of good will must sometimes kill, is here carried one step farther and the caution added that they should then purge evil from their hearts and not go away mad. In spite of the unrelieved morbidity of the slice of life Saroyan presents, there is at the end a kind of catharsis and spiritual feeling that these men have found how to die with dignity. Education, symbolized by the dictionary, proves to be the satisfaction of the spirit which sustains them; feeling needed and necessary once more releases them from bitterness and self-pity.

For the first time, in *Don't Go Away Mad,* Saroyan's common man has dignity and self-respect. In most of his early work, the common men and women prove to be buffoons, goofs like the mawkish lover, Dudley R. Bostwick, the helpless moron, Tom, the fatuous Oakies, the addle-brained Elmer, and the various passive-dependent poets. Nowhere in Saroyan does a character solve his problems through his own initiative—more often they are solved by the *deus ex* Postal Telegraph. Although during the late thirties Saroyan was hailed by the proletarian movement as the poet of the little man, it is not difficult to see beneath that surface an unconscious contempt for the common man. Saroyan has yet to create a major play, as Steinbeck has done, in which a little man is a tragic hero.

In a recent letter refusing Columbia University permission to produce *The Slaughter of the Innocents,* Saroyan turned with singular ingratitude against the educational theatre which had been keeping his plays alive when Broadway would not. Equating himself with O'Casey and Wilder, he reiterated that all of his plays are good, and took the professional theatre to task for not recognizing the merit of them. Little wonder that Raphaelson in *Jason* appraised him as half charlatan and half genius, exasperatingly gifted and able to breathe humanity into his characters, yet unable or unwilling to detach himself from his work and view it dispassionately. To the present author's question concerning the value of discussing plots or characters with a psychoanalyst, he wrote, "I do not have plots. Never discuss any work not finished." His comment upon the value of Freudianism in general was:

> No value at all unless a playwright (I mean a playwright, not anything else) writing a play is involved and then no more value than anything—everything—else.

And yet the work of Saroyan remains of particular interest for the psychoanalytic-minded, with its recurring *leit-motifs* of child-like passive-dependency, naive wish-fulfillment for a better world, hostility toward money, oral regression, free associational dream distortion, the absence of a mature man-woman love relationship in favor of sentimentalization of the loose woman, and finally the justification of killing in order to live the time of your life without inflicting pain on one's fellow man.

Saroyan's only recent rival in the surrealist drama has been Tennessee Williams in *Camino Real*. But Saroyan has been largely alone in the American drama in the relative emphasis he puts upon the stream of unconscious association and the minimal attention he pays to conscious structure and integration. From the psychological point of view, Saroyan might be called the poet of immaturity.

CHAPTER X

Freudian Fraternity of the Thirties

THORNTON WILDER

The one playwright in American drama who appears to have found a means of straddling the two worlds of Joycean unconscious writing and the conscious orientation of the commercial theatre is Thornton Wilder. Sharing with Saroyan a dislike for the mere depiction of surface reality and a desire to enlarge the scope of the theatre, Wilder brings to his free fantasy, however, a mature mind and a craftsman's awareness of effect. Where Saroyan repeats himself, Wilder is eclectic and refuses to be categorized; where Saroyan is bound by a limited perspective, Wilder is cosmic in his point of view and draws effortlessly upon European literature, archaeology and psychology; where Saroyan's common people are drawn from eccentric walks of life and prove to be trivial, foolish and incompetent, Wilder's common people are extracted from the very heart of American family life and strike a universality which eludes Saroyan.

Three times Pulitzer prize winner (for the novel *The Bridge of San Luis Rey*, and his two plays, *Our Town* and *The Skin of Our Teeth*), Wilder has also done a number of adaptations from foreign drama* and early in his career wrote the one-act plays, *A Happy*

* *Lucrece*, adapted from the French of André Obey, *A Doll's House* from Ibsen, *The Merchant of Yonkers* from Nestroy, and a novel, *The Woman of Andros*, based upon a play of Terence.

255

Journey and *The Long Christmas Dinner,* which are not only theatre classics but which contain the germ of the theatricalist style later to flower in *Our Town.* Abhoring the well-made, contrived play of "door bells and telephones," Wilder has sought for pure theatre by denying the audience any easy empathy and frequently jolting them back to the realization they are in a theatre.

Wilder's admiration for James Joyce and his friendship with Gertrude Stein are better known than his familiarity with Freud. He stated in a letter to the present author that he had read much of Freud and the "classical" psychoanalysts, and was fascinated by Jung. He became a personal friend of Freud and wrote of a significant conversation with Freud on the subject of psychoanalytic material in literature:

> I knew Freud and used to call on him on Sunday afternoons in Grinzing. One afternoon he seemed to me to sum up the essence of what you are after:
>
> "My friends—Werfel, Arnold Zweig, Stefan Zweig, and so on—have been using psychoanalysis in their works. It still appears in them, however, as schematization and as conscious organization. I think it will be a hundred or two hundred years before the *Dichter* can assimilate it at so deep a level of knowing that they will not be aware that they are employing it: it will have to them the character of self-evidence."
>
> That is it. He spoke too hastily, however; at that moment the greatest living writer was using it with a mastery that far surpassed book-learning—with humor, ease, and boundless insight: James Joyce in *Finnegan's Wake.* And certainly Kafka had employed it consciously and magnificently in *The Castle.* Another time: when I expressed surprise to Dr. Freud at why psychoanalysis had appeared so late in human culture he said gently: *"Ja, aber die Dichter haben das immer gekannt!"* *

Wilder too used psychoanalysis with such ease and boundless insight that audiences which streamed misty-eyed from productions of *Our Town* were very likely unaware that at least one scene was consciously derived from Freudian concepts. The play has as its objective to record for some hypothetical archaeologist who might open a time-capsule a thousand years from now just what daily life, marriage and death meant in a New England village early in our

---

* "Yes, but the poets have always known it!" Kafka, incidentally, has been represented on Broadway only in the French language production of *The Trial* by Jean-Louis Barrault in 1952.

century. Its story—or rather lack of story—and its fanciful use of the
stage manager as narrator and property man substituting for scenery
in the manner of the Chinese theatre, are too well known to need
retelling. Not so well known, however, is the fact that there is one
scene, according to Wilder's letter to the present author, which was
written, "with conscious use of psychoanalytical material—but it
didn't have to be: any born *Menschenkenner* could have done it
from the sheer observation of life and I hope I could have." The
scene to which Wilder refers is the wedding scene, just before Emily
and George walk up to the minister. The external action stops while
George and Emily each have a resurgence of their old Oedipal attachment to their parent of the opposite sex. Mrs. Gibbs has been a
most normal mother, fussing protectively over George, making him
wear overshoes and an umbrella in the rain on his wedding morning;
at the moment of finally severing the silver cord, George cries out
almost in stream-of-unconscious verbalization:

> George: I wish I were back at school . . . I don't want to
>   get married.
> Mrs. Gibbs: George, what's the matter?
> George: Ma, I don't want to grow *old*. Why's everybody
>   pushing me so?
> Mrs. Gibbs: Why, George . . . you wanted it.
> George: Why do I have to get married at all? Listen, Ma, for
>   the last time I ask you——
> Mrs. Gibbs: No, no, George . . . you're a man now.
> George: Listen, Ma, you never listen to me. All I want to
>   do is to be a fella . . . why do——

In much the same way, Emily free associates to her father as
the infantile Electra dependency is rearoused at the occasion of
entering upon her sexual role as a woman:

> Emily: I never felt so alone in my whole life. And George
>   over there, looking so . . . ! I *hate* him. I wish I were
>   dead. Papa! Papa!
> Mr. Webb: Emily! Emily! Now don't get upset . . .
> Emily: But, Papa,—I don't want to get married . . .
> Mr. Webb: Sh-sh—Emily. Everything's all right.
> Emily: Why can't I stay for a while just as I am? Let's go
>   away.
> Mr. Webb: No, no, Emily. Now stop and think.
> Emily: Don't you remember that you used to say,—all the
>   time you used to say that I was *your* girl. There must be
>   lots of places we can go to. Let's go away. I'll work for
>   you. I could keep house.

Mr. Webb: Sh . . . You mustn't think of such things.
You're just nervous, Emily. Now, now,—you're marrying
the best young fellow in the world. George is a fine
fellow.

These two brief scenes poignantly dramatize the deeply rooted
Oedipal attachments which the individual must and normally can
grow out of if a marriage is to be successful. As Wilder expressed it,
". . . people are so put together that even at a good wedding there's
a lot of confusion way down deep in people's minds and we thought
that that ought to be in our play, too." The theme of *Our Town* is a
kind of distillation of psychoanalytic wisdom: to regress to the past
and to relive your childhood crystal-clear and undistorted while
watching yourself live it would be too painful an experience to bear
—as it was for Emily Webb. The alternative is to realize the fullness
of life *as it is lived*—every, every minute. *Our Town* is an antidote
for anxiety.

Wilder's most controversial play, combining elements of Joyce,
Stein, Freud and Jung in a startling effect which left many conventional playgoers baffled if not downright belligerent, was *The
Skin of Our Teeth*. With Joyce's feeling for making one word bear
many meanings, Wilder lets his family, Mr. and Mrs. Antrobus, their
two children and the maid, Sabina, stand for the entire human race.
Written in 1942 as Wilder's expression of wartime faith that the
human race would somehow pull through "by the skin of its teeth,"
the play is surrealistic, dream-like, outrageously distorted in form;
but, unlike Gertrude Stein and Saroyan, there is a strong conscious
mind guiding it to make its final philosophic statement. It might be
called purposive surrealism. The realistic walls of the set go up into
the fly gallery as, little by little, we are made to feel the emergence
of the archaic past of the human race. Sabina complains that the
author can't decide if the setting is New Jersey or a cave during the
Ice Age. To Wilder, it is both—compacted in the manner of the
dream. Mr. Antrobus is both a harassed commuter and Freud's
primal father. His son, Henry, emerges as the eternal Cain, Oedipally
hostile to his father through five thousand years. Sabina becomes
Eros, or the eternal temptress, but she is destined to lose Mr.
Antrobus to Mrs. Antrobus, who is Jung's "Earth-Mother," living
for her children, ". . . and if it would be any benefit to her children
she'd see the rest of us stretched out dead at her feet without turning
a hair . . ." Sabina, whom Mr. Antrobus raped and brought home
from the Sabine hills, has to be content with domestic work, milking
the mammoth, shooing a baby dinosaur off the front lawn, and
periodically protesting to the audience about the absurd dialogue

she has to speak. There is panic in the north, for the Glacial Wall is moving down upon New Jersey. But Antrobus is confident that the human race can survive. He has just invented the wheel and discovered that ten times ten makes one hundred—"consequences far-reaching." Refugees fleeing the ice wall come in—Homer, Moses and others each reciting in their native tongue, and by the end of the act they are burning furniture to keep warm and asking the ushers to hand up chairs from the audience.

In Act II, the Antrobus family has pulled through that crisis and is now at Atlantic City at a delightfully burlesqued fraternal convention, of which Antrobus has been elected president, while Mrs. Antrobus is acclaimed a "gracious and charming wife, every inch a mammal." The one occasion when Wilder uses Joyce's peculiarly compacted language with its association of unconscious meanings is when Sabina strolls by as a beauty contest winner, exuding sexual invitation to Antrobus and he greets her—answering his wife's demand to know who that was with: ". . . just a solambaka keray."

Another crisis arises, this time the deluge, and it finds Antrobus about to be seduced by Sabina, while his daughter has dressed up like Sabina in red stockings and has identified herself Electra-like with the eternal feminine to please her father. The Fortune Teller advises them to get into a boat, taking two of each species of animal with them, and they do; but they are unable to leave behind Sabina with her irrepressible sensuality or Henry-Cain with his uncontrollable aggression, both deeply and inevitably a part of the Freud-Jung-Wilder conception of the family anthropos.

In Act III, the human race has just emerged from another devastating war like the one raging in 1942. Gladys is now a mother, Antrobus a fighter and Sabina a camp follower, while Mrs. Antrobus has sustained the home. There is an absurd rehearsal of a scene in which the Planets and Hours march across the stage—in which Wilder, borrowing from his early one-act, Pullman-Car Hiawatha, deliberately irks his audience with an amateurish view of a backstage crisis.

Henry returns from the war sullen and defeated. He has been the Enemy, the Führer. He has been looking for his father to kill him—"I've spent seven years trying to find him; the others I killed were just substitutes." The pent-up frustration of a people like the Germans Wilder sees as a displacement of the original Oedipal hatred for and yet ambivalent need for the authoritarianism of the father. The seeds of war Wilder thus shows as being sown in the infantile relationship of father and son and therefore amenable to cultural mutation.

The quarrel-scene between Henry and his father is psycho-analytically significant, and as Wilder stated in his letter, was written with a more subtle handling of Freudian psychology than the wedding scene in *Our Town*. "I doubt," writes Wilder, "whether I would have expressed it that way without the reading in Freud." This is an extraordinarily honest statement from a great writer who did not feel that his claim to original creativity would be diminished by an acknowledgment of indebtedness.

Cutting through Henry's bluster and belligerency, Wilder shows him whining that nobody cares about him. He protests:

Henry: I don't want anybody to love me.
Sabina: Then stop talking about it all the time.

He soon falls asleep under the gentle ministrations of his mother; but when he wakes, Antrobus confronts him accusingly and the undisguised hostility of father and son flares again. To the father, Henry stands for "strong, unreconciled evil," and he will go on fighting him ". . . as long as you mix up your idea of liberty with your idea of hogging everything for yourself. . . ." Now the conflict becomes so real that Sabina has to stop the scene, for the previous night the actor playing Henry almost strangled his father at this point. The actor, however, is immediately apologetic:

. . . something comes over me. It's like I become fifteen years old again. I . . . I . . . listen: my own father used to whip me and lock me up every Saturday night. . . . It's like I had some big emptiness inside me,—the emptiness of being hated and blocked at every turn.

Sabina says that she knew his father and that he had not whipped the boy. The actor had fantasied it, much as Freud found his patients fantasying scenes of seduction by a parent as an expression of Oedipal wish-fulfillment. This scene, with its interruption and drama-within-a-drama, is a brilliant visualization that beneath the layers of artificiality of the theatre is the actor's own humanity with its own unconscious life.

The final scene rises to superb illumination as Wilder's theme emerges out of Joycean juxtaposition. Mr. Antrobus' books have been saved and are unpacked. Lying in the trenches during the war, he had tried to extract a faith from all the past experience of the human race, and had named the hours of the night from the great minds who seemed to illuminate the present—Plato, Spinoza, Aristotle, the Bible—the books the human race considers worth cherishing.. The quotations spoken by the actors whose mawkish rehearsal we had watched earlier now are infinitely significant as they summarize Wilder's faith: ". . . I saw that all the objects of my desire and fear were in themselves nothing good nor bad save insofar as the mind was affected by them."

Mrs. Antrobus finds her faith in the family, Mr. Antrobus in knowledge, and even Sabina is willing to go on, although she may need to go to the movies occasionally to calm her nerves. The end of the play isn't written yet, Sabina tells the audience. "We have to go on for ages and ages yet. . . ." But the Antrobus family is full of confident plans for the future, and Sabina sends the audience out of the theatre knowing that Wilder has managed to change what seemed at first like a surrealist trick upon the audience into a deeply moving expression of faith in the mind and will of man to fathom his own dark impulses and to build a better world.

CLIFFORD ODETS

Faith in the progress of the human race is also implicit in the work of Clifford Odets, although his early expressions of it were more buoyant and politically dedicated than Wilder's. Odets was perhaps the most original and yet characteristic playwriting talent which the American drama produced in the thirties. He began as an actor with the Group Theater, and it is significant that he wrote, as did Shakespeare, Molière, Chekhov and O'Casey for specific actors and a specific playing style. His first play to be produced was *Waiting for Lefty* (1935), a sociological one-act which defended and attempted to explain the forces causing a New York taxi drivers' strike. With the other taxi drivers hovering in the shadows as a kind of Greek chorus, each hack acts out his reason for voting to strike. Of all the episodes only two seem today to have flesh and blood characters, the scene with Joe and his wife, Edna, who goads him into striking by threatening to leave him for another man, and the scene between the young hack and his girl. The other episodes are written with the mawkish zeal of a young propagandist. It is characteristic of Odets, however, that he could not be content with easy social-political formulas and there is in his work visible progression away from left-wing stereotypes toward insight into the complex human dynamics that lie behind social and political events.

Odets' answer to the questionnaire is the best evidence of this progression, and makes clear his position with regard to orthodoxy, be it Freudian or Marxian:

My method of writing is to bring to characters and situations whatever fullness of psychological awareness and experience I have on my own. Let the psychologist beware, not the artist, is my belief! I suspect writers who consciously bring psychological principles to their work. . . .

If a writer is really creative, let him write as fully as possible what he is and what he knows. *After* that let the psychologists, the religionists, Communists (or what you will) bring their analysis to bear. But the other way around is sterilizing and deodorizing, and is a position that I for one would fight as vigorously as possible.

Odets stated that he has not been psychoanalyzed, nor has he discussed his characters with psychoanalysts, but that both experiences might prove enriching if the analyst were not an orthodox Freudian. Asked if he had sought for devices to dramatize the workings of the unconscious, Odets the realist replied, "No, a thousand times no!!!" He did state, however, that he had read a large number of books by the Freudians. Rejecting Freud's instinct theory and the Oedipus nexus, Odets felt that his most mature evaluation of Freud reached him through the William Alanson White Institute of Psychiatry and the work of Erich Fromm and Harry Stack Sullivan.

Odets concluded his questionnaire with perhaps the most eloquently expressed appreciation of Freud yet written by an American playwright:

The best of Freud is already so deeply in creative writing that it is bootless to stop for examination of where one always knew or where Freud opened up knowledge of self or others. Freud seems to me great in the discovery of the "Unconscious" motivation, the analytic situation and its resultant therapy and the big matter of "transference." As for the rest, I don't give a hang, except for Freud's greatness of spirit, his human nobility as it were.

It is not bootless, however, to examine the plays of Odets in the light of psychoanalysis, tracing the remarkable way in which he has paralleled Freudian insights with his own. Whether it is "where one always knew" from personal experience or "where Freud opened up knowledge of self or others," *Awake and Sing!* (1935) is rich in observed detail which falls into psychoanalytic patterns that are never forced, never "textbookish," never orthodox.

All of the characters in *Awake and Sing!*, Odets has stated, "share a fundamental activity: a struggle for life amidst petty conditions." A lower middle-class Jewish family in the Bronx, they are dominated by the mother, Bessie Berger, who is not only the mother but the father as well. Her husband, Myron, is a sweet, passive-dependent, ineffectual little man who calls his daughter "Beauty," who lives in a dim distant past and who remembers Teddy Roosevelt with affection. As both cause and result, Bessie is a high-strung, neurotic mother whose life is charged with pressure and economic frustration. Her son, Ralph, is a serious-minded young man whose inferiority feelings, based upon a wretched childhood, are laid bare pathetically near the surface. Odets' characters free associate readily, and Ralph remembers: "I never in my life even had a birthday party. Every time I went and cried in the toilet when my birthday came." He knows too the importance which little repressed episodes assume as they are recalled: "It's crazy—all my life I want a pair of black and white shoes and can't get them. It's crazy."

Now Ralph has a girl, but his mother opposes the romance with curt and sarcastic antagonism which is as much Oedipal jealousy as it is realistic awareness of the economic obstacles to Ralph's marriage. Rudely, Bessie prevents Ralph from getting his girl's telephone call, and says of Ralph's girl: "Before she'd ruin a nice boy's life, I would first go to prison. Miss Nobody should step in the picture and I'll stand by with my mouth shut."

The most prosperous member of the family, Uncle Morty, is too preoccupied with his own sensual comforts to sense the imminent tragedy in the family and has no sympathy for Bessie's anxiety over Ralph's romance:

Bessie: Morty, I didn't say before—he runs around steady with a girl.
Morty: Terrible. Should he run around with a foxie-woxie?

Bessie is equally abrupt and compulsive when she learns that her daughter, Hennie, is pregnant. "You were sleeping by a girl from the office Saturday nights?" she cries, "you slept good, my lovely lady. You'll go to him . . . he'll marry you." When she learns that the man cannot be located, she immediately decides that her daughter must marry the hopelessly neurotic and lonely immigrant, Sam Feinschreiber, who says of himself, "I'm so nervous—look, two times I weighed myself on the subway station."

Jacob, the old grandfather, is a superbly realized character, a liberal old barber with his Caruso records and his wish that "human life should have some dignity." To help the family to "awake and sing, ye that dwell in dust," Jacob makes out his insurance to Ralph and jumps off the roof. Hennie finally summons up courage to leave her pathetic husband, Feinschreiber, and go away with Moe Axelrod, a bitterly hostile and defensive war veteran with a crippled leg and a desire for Hennie which he describes as "a yen for her and I don't mean a Chinee coin." Ralph at the end sees something of the vision of a better life for which Jacob died, and grows from boy to mature man.

The dialogue of *Awake and Sing!* is electric with a racy Jewish folk idiom and a wealth of humor which is a defense against frustration. The Berger family, as all of Odets' characters are to be, are eloquent in their inferiority feelings, expressive of their frustrations and universal in their human impulses. Particularly in the richly sympathetic performance of the Group Theater, *Awake and Sing!* became a classic of American drama of the middle class seeking a way out of the dead end of economic and psychic depression.

There is little humor, however, in Odets' *Paradise Lost* (1935); it is an angry, bitter protest at the desperate economic plight of the middle class. It is perhaps his weakest and most plotless piece of writing and contains a collection of neurotic characters, not analyzed with any great psychological insight but rather assembled to show the depth to which the middle class was sinking. The son of the family, Julie, has sleeping sickness from which he loses his mind at the end of the play. His sister, Pearl, is a high-strung, neurotic pianist whose boy friend leaves to find work elsewhere; she broods alone in her room with the piano, "the white keys banked up like lilies and she suckin' at her own breast." Ben, the older brother, is an unemployed ex-athlete who knows that Kewpie, a taxi driver, has been supporting him and sleeping with his wife. The family is less matriarchal than in *Awake and Sing!* and the father, Leo, a kindly and liberal small business man, tries somehow to hold his head above water. His business partner, Sam Katz, however, is willing to set fire to the business to collect the insurance. Sam is depicted as impotent and smoking eighteen cigars a day—perhaps an implied phallic symbol; his wife confesses, "We have upstairs a closet full of pills, medicine, electric machines. For seven years Sam Katz didn't sleep with a girl."

An old friend of the family, Gus Michaels, best expresses the frustration and the wish-fulfillment of the times; having seen Marlene Dietrich in the movies, he says:

> Marlene, I got her in the harem of my head . . . I have my troubles, Mrs. G. Be surprised how often I think about it—taking my life by my own hand . . . But I turn on the radio instead of the gas . . . Ha, ha, ha.

In addition to wish-fulfillment, Gus, like Myron in *Awake and Sing!*
regresses to the past as a defense against the emptiness of the
present: "I can't explain it to you, Mr. G., how I'm forever hungerin'
for the past. It's like a disease in me, eatin' away . . . some nights I
have cried myself to sleep for the old Asbury Park days. . . ."

Paradise Lost ends as Leo, the father, "sees the light" of world
revolution against the oppressive forces of capitalism. In 1935 Odets
could apparently find no other solution for the hopelessly neurotic
and sick family he arbitrarily created. He shows as little interest in
the economic causes of their plight as he does in the dynamic childhood forces which made them impotent to deal with their environment. They are sick because they live in a sick world. Neurosis is
here used for symbolic rather than psychological value, but the symbols are overwrought and unrelieved.

After *Paradise Lost* Odets seems to have parted company with
the Marxist commitment and to have dedicated himself only to
writing "as fully as possible what he is and what he knows." His
next play, preceded by a hiatus in Hollywood, is perhaps his greatest.
Golden Boy (1937) made the fortune of the Group Theatre as that
organization had earlier helped to make and shape the special genius
of Odets.

Golden Boy is one of the few important tragedies in American
drama. It tells the story of Joe Bonaparte, a sensitive, shy violinist
who has cross-eyes and a deeply rooted inferiority complex. His
defense mechanism against the hostility of the world is aggression,
to fight back blindly when he has been hurt:

> People have hurt my feelings for years. I never forget. You
> can't get even with people by playing the fiddle. If music
> shot bullets, I'd like it better.

Loaded with hostility, Joe becomes a prize fighter, but he is split
between the desire to win fame in the ring and the fear that he will
damage his hands and never play the violin again. He loses one fight
because an old man carrying a violin case passed him that day. His
manager, Moody, sends Lorna, his blonde young mistress, to find out
why Joe is holding back in the ring. Their scene is a superb character
study of inferiority feelings. "This is the anatomy of Joe Bonaparte,"
Lorna proclaims, and proceeds to analyze with considerable as-
tuteness:

> You're a miserable creature. You want your arm in *gelt* up
> to the elbow. You'll take fame so people won't laugh or
> scorn your face. You'd give your soul for those things. But

every time you turn your back your little soul kicks you in the teeth. It don't give in so easy.

The sight of expensive automobiles whizzing by, and the prospect of having a mistress like Lorna lead Joe to make the fateful decision to fight to win.

His sternly dignified old Italian father has bought him an expensive violin and urges him to be careful of his hands. When Joe asks for "the word" to go ahead, Mr. Bonaparte refuses to give his blessings on a fighting career, but comes to sit ominously in the dressing room, an objectification of Joe's conscience. For all his guilt feelings, however, Joe has made the decision compulsively and cannot turn back. By contrast with Joe, his sister, Anna, and her husband, Siggie, are Odets' most delightfully happy couple, Anna finding perpetual reason to giggle at her husband's good-natured kidding. "Come to bed, Siggie," she has been urging him, to which he replies:

'Come to bed, come to bed!' What the hell's so special in bed. (Anna's answer is a warm prolonged giggle.) It's a conspiracy around here to put me to bed.

Joe becomes a successful fighter and with his new confidence wins Lorna. When she decides to marry Moody because he has the greater need for her, however, Joe's old hostility surges up so furiously that he breaks his hand while boxing. For him it is the beginning of the world, releasing him from his guilt feelings over abandoning the violin and the ideals of his father. Now Joe has no choice but to fight. A new promoter, Eddie Fuseli, who buys "a piece of Joe," is characterized as a racketeer with a homosexual fascination for his fighters, for whom he buys sensuous silk shirts. Ultimately Joe kills an opponent and is so overwhelmed by what he has made of himself that he asks Lorna: "What will my father say when he hears I murdered a man? Lorna, I see what I did. I murdered myself, too! I've been running around in circles. Now I'm smashed! That's the truth." Joe and Lorna go off together to forget everything but their love and to burn up the roads in his new car. The last scene brings to Mr. Bonaparte and the family the news that Joe and Lorna have been killed in a crash. Mr. Bonaparte speaks the memorable final lines: "Joe . . . Come, we bring-a him home . . . where he belong. . . ."

On the symbolic level, *Golden Boy* is a universal drama of man's search for fulfillment which, as in *Faust*, requires him to sell his most precious self to his baser self. On the ideological level it suggests that the price a man must pay for integrity under the economic pressures of our society is too great. On the psychological level, it is a richly rewarding character study of inferiority-feelings and compensatory aggression. The ending is not contrived but inevitable in terms of Joe's character and the unconscious effect of speed and rich motor cars upon him. It is, at least, no less contrived a death than Euripides used in *Hippolytus* for a similarly disturbed young man. Even on the autobiographical level, *Golden Boy* is meaningful, for Odets had been accused by his fellow Group Theatre actors of "selling out to Hollywood" during the two years he was there. From Hollywood, Odets sent back money to help the Group Theatre, married Luise Rainer, wrote the film *The General Died at Dawn*, and came back with *Golden Boy*, the story of a man and his guilt-feelings.

Odets' next play was *Rocket to the Moon* (1938) which depicts another matriarchal marriage and passive-dependent male. This time he is a dentist, Ben Stark, whose wife, Belle, has a thinly disguised contempt for him which requires her to dominate him. Belle is aware, however, that her own childhood made her what she is. "The way Poppa and Momma were always quarreling?—My nerves mincemeat? The way I felt when I married you, I'd have married a shoemaker almost." Ben aspired to be a great orthodontist, but instead is trapped as a poor neighborhood dentist. He avoids clash with his wife, however, and prefers to churn inside. Belle has lost a child and is unable to have another; in the first act she is bent on persuading Ben not to accept her father's offer of an office in an uptown neighborhood, lest it make them beholden to her father, which she fears will turn Ben against her.

Mr. Prince, Belle's father, is a brilliantly depicted older man of charm, humor and self-importance, a Jewish actor who is accustomed to getting his own way. It is his opinion that ". . . the universe is governed by a committee; one man couldn't make so many mistakes." Mr. Prince is mildly interested in the view outside Ben's window of a disreputable hotel across the alley—he might come and peep some night. Knowing the wretchedness of Ben's marriage, Mr. Prince tells him that his daughter has ". . . got you where she wants you. . . Like an iceberg, three-quarters under water. . ." (Freud had used the same image to describe an individual with a larger part of his personality under repression.) Mr. Prince virtually goads his son-in-law to have an affair with Cleo, his dental assistant. Having had the latent wish of his unconscious mind brought to awareness, Ben proceeds to fall in love with her; but he is inept and reluctant to declare himself, while Mr. Prince is unabashed and frontal in his proposition that Cleo live with him. Cleo grants him a date which serves the useful purpose of inflaming Ben's jealousy and giving her the chance to tell him she loves him. She had to take the initiative, however, while passive Ben waited.

Cleo is a lonely and inhibited girl who is given to telling little lies about her family wealth and connections. Ben forgives her petty lies, saying, "Everyone tells little fables, Cleo. Sometimes to themselves, sometimes to others. Life is so full of brutal facts . . . we all try to soften them by making believe." Their turbulent love affair during a hectic summer of New York heat is punctuated by the entrances and exits of the other doctors in the building—a dentist who can't make a living, and a foot doctor who fancies himself an amateur psychologist and cautions Cleo rather perceptively about Ben: "And like millions of others he constantly feels worried, depressed and inadequate. But!—His unhappiness is a dangerous habit of which he is not fully aware—it may make him bust loose in some curious way. . . ." He knows too that "Love is no solution of life! Au contraire, as the Frenchman says—the opposite. You have to bring a whole balanced normal life to love if you want it to go!"

Belle senses that she may lose Ben to Cleo and comes to make a plea for him. Remembering her mother sitting by the window crying for ten years, she would not be similarly cast off. But Ben wants to know, "What do you know about *my* needs?" Mr. Prince assures Cleo that Ben won't leave Belle, that ". . . they're attached underground by a hundred different roots." He himself offers her maturity and marriage, ". . . a vitalizing relationship: a father: counselor, lover, a friend!" The scene, as the two men bid for Cleo, is one of electric tension. Cleo does not love Mr. Prince and cannot win Ben. She walks out of the office a free woman, leaving the two men with new understanding of themselves. Ben feels himself freed, released from guilt and fear of his wife for the first time in years. He will go back to Belle, and will "never take things for granted again."

If the ending is somewhat disappointing and inconclusive, it is because the dilemma of the ambivalent Ben is so fundamental that glib denouements would be untruthful. Odets suggests that for Ben and Belle to go on living together is perhaps a more devastating tragedy than divorce. Passive-dependency in the male is so deeply rooted in Oedipal wishes that, as Cleo was to find out, a man is not apt to break these hundred unconscious roots with which his wife holds him. The tragedy is that not one of the hundred is warm physical love.

Night Music (1940) formed a transition in the work of Odets. The coming of war in Europe marked the end of the era of easy left-wing panaceas and left many liberals disturbedly groping for a new set of beliefs. In *Night Music,* Odets turns from the predominantly social problem to the predominantly individual problem, with the social theme running in contrapuntal fashion against it. In the plays to come the balance is to continue to shift toward individual psychology until with *The Country Girl* Odets, for the first time, writes a purely individual study.

Night Music is the story of the emotional re-education of Steve Takis, a belligerent, hostile, inferior-feeling first cousin to Joe Bonaparte who is arrested while escorting a shipment of monkeys to Hollywood. He is thrown together with Fay, an actress out of work, and their relationship is at first as much hostility as it is attraction. Like most of Odets' characters, Steve free associates easily from his unhappy childhood: "Didn't sleep much on the plane. . . There's like a smell of geraniums an' I hear my mother say, 'Go to bed, Stevie, tomorrow's another day. . . .'" But Steve does not tell us enough of his childhood to justify his neurotic hostilities, and he remains an unsympathetic hero.

There is a little man in the park who is one of Odets' most characteristic forgotten people . . . what Dr. Stark might become in a few years. He talks to Fay, wishing he had courage to separate from his wife: "I'm the man nobody knows. I'm very bold, but some nights I'm gripped by unbearable shame and shyness. . . Had my tonsils out. On top of that, neuritis is stabbin' every nerve. The saddest part is when you go to the doctor and he says, 'It's your imagination, five dollars please.'"

Steve and Fay spend one night together in her hotel room and another on a park bench, but there is no physical expression of their suppressed attraction until Steve has been reawakened and freed of aggression at the end of the play. The man largely responsible for this catharsis is A. L. Rosenberger, a philosophic detective who is retiring with cancer and who knows that, "Lying is a certain form of cheering yourself up." After serving as good angel and Saroyanesque mentor to keep Steve out of worse trouble, Rosenberger sums up his understanding of the psychology of Steve:

There are two ways to look, Mr. Takis—to the past or the future. We know a famous case in history where a woman kept looking back and turned to a salt rock. If you keep looking back on a mean narrow past, the same can happen to you. You are feeling mad. Why shouldn't you feel mad? In your whole life you never had a pretzel. You think you have to tell me it's a classified world? There is an old saying, 'A hungry man is an angry man.' We understand that. But your anger must bear children with him. Why should two bald men fight about a comb? You have the materials to make a good man. But stop breaking things with your fists. Look ahead, Mr. Takis. What did the doctor prescribe for

society? Boys like you! God gave you a fine head—use it,
dear boy. (an afterthought) Sincerely yours, A. L. Rosenberger, your old Dutch Uncle. . . .

With this appeal for maturity and the new confidence which Fay's
love gives him, Steve is able to outgrow his inferiority feelings; the
play ends with the sense of the exhilaration of self-discovery, as
Steve says to Fay: "You have a Steve Takis Club? I'd like to be a
member."

Night Music was found disappointing by most of the critics, but
represents in Odets' development a growing awareness that to vent
spleen against society and to convert childhood frustration into
contempt for one's fellow man is both futile and neurotic.

More powerful in its integration of themes was *Clash by Night*
(1941), a study in dependency and impotent rage at man's helplessness, set in the torrid summer heat which, as in *Rocket to the Moon,*
seems to heighten sexuality. Analytically, Odets penetrates the surface of his sexual triangle, which consists of Mae Wilenski, a restless,
lusty woman, her passive-dependent husband, Jerry, a blundering,
guileless boy who loves his wife and child with clumsy passivity, and
Earl Pfeiffer, a flashy fellow-worker whom Jerry idolizes with the
latent homosexuality often associated with passive-dependency. Earl
is a sensualist with sadistic impulses which Jerry fails to comprehend
—Earl says, ". . . the day's past when I wanna cut up every beautiful woman I see." At Jerry's naive urging, Earl becomes the Wilenskis' boarder, much against Mae's wishes. While Jerry is away at
work, Earl and Mae stalk each other about the house, unnerved by
their desire. Earl confesses that he too, is lonely and wants to feel
that he belongs to someone. "How can I help you. . . ?" Mae asks.
They find the answer in a tempestuous love affair.

Gradually Jerry's slow mind grasps the truth, in spite of his resistance to believing it. Jerry confronts the guilty lovers in jealous
fury when they return from a hotel, and Mae coldly and deliberately
admits guilt, trying almost sadistically to goad Jerry into manhood
by announcing, "I'm sleeping in Earl's room tonight." Jerry rages impotently, "weeping and writhing, unnerved, unmanned, shapeless,
struck down." But he does not try to stop her from sleeping with
Earl. Instead of a virile fight to hold Mae, Jerry's reaction is to regress
within himself. He free associates to his father of his childhood:

We had those Christmas cards when I was a boy—a little
warm house in the snow, yellow lights in the windows . . .
remember? It was wonderful . . . a place where they told
you what to do, like in school . . . You didn't have to have

no brains—he told you what to do. (Beginning to cry) I
wished it was like on the Christmas cards again, so nice an'
warm, a wonnerful home . . . No, I wished I never grew
up now.

This eloquent expression of man's wish for dependency parallels
Erich Fromm's *Escape from Freedom*, a socio-psychoanalytic study
(which appeared the same year as *Clash by Night*) of man's unconscious wish for a "magic helper" or a regression to the security which
authoritarianism represents to a passive-dependent individual. As
Fromm sees the psychological basis for the Nazi and Fascist movements in man's guilt feelings of isolation and fear of responsibility, so
Odets shows in *Clash by Night* the overwhelming impotence of this
man who confesses the deep unconscious wish for "a place where
they told you what to do. . . ." Even Jerry's Uncle Kress, a significant minor character, illustrates the conversion of frustrated sexual
impulses into latent Fascism. He had accumulated a roomful of erotic
pictures, had been caught as a *voyeur*, and now goes about cadging
drinks and mumbling warped, anti-semitic rationalizations of his inability to get a job. It is he who plays the Iago role and for his own
vicarious satisfaction leads Jerry to discover his wife's infidelity.

Jerry follows Mae to the movie theatre where Earl works as a
projectionist and in a fantastic scene with the garbled sound from
the film orchestrated in the background, strangles Earl while Mae
pounds on the door. The homosexual theme now is clear: man kills
the thing he loves. In this case, Jerry kills Earl, not Mae, for he felt
betrayed by the man whom unconsciously he had loved and revered
as a "magic helper."

Although the contemporary judgment of *Clash by Night* was not
favorable, it may well be that this was only a reflection of Marxian
disappointment that Odets was turning away from ideological writing. Re-examination suggests that *Clash by Night* is a powerful and
original American drama, showing Odets' ever-deepening mastery of
psychoanalytic insight into unconscious motivation, his ability to
draw identifiable and rounded characters with racy, charged dialogue and to create theatrical tension. The portrait of the gentle,
passive child-man, Jerry, assumes considerable scope in both its psychology and theatrical vitality.

In *The Big Knife* (1949—titled *A Winter Journey* in London),
Odets returns to the *Golden Boy* theme of "unto thine own self be
true." After a stint in Hollywood, filmland again symbolizes to Odets
a "selling out" of the artist's integrity. His hero is a famous movie
star, Charlie Castle, superficially suggesting John Garfield who
played the role. He is at a crisis in his marriage, with his studio, and

over the problem of concealing the fact that he once killed a man in a hit-and-run accident when drunk and at the persuasion of the studio had let his publicity man, Buddy, go to jail for him for ten months. An adventuress named Dixie Evans was in the car with him at the time, and the studio has given her a contract to keep her quiet; but all live in perpetual fear that she will blabber when she is drunk.

Like Jerry Wilenski, Charlie free associates back over his childhood, remembering the aunt and uncle who raised him:

> They were awfully poor, my aunt and uncle. I made money too late to be able to help them. I regret that . . . (Softly, pausing) We're homesick all our lives, but adults don't talk about it, do they?

Ridden with guilt feelings, Charlie is forced to sign a fourteen-year contract with the studio; with the killing to hold above his head, the chief of the studio, Marcus Hoff, owns Charlie body and soul. Sex to Charlie is a way of loathing himself—he so despises his lack of integrity that he masochistically cheapens himself by sordid affairs with Dixie and with Connie, the wife of the man who went to jail for him. There is the added motive of wanting to hurt and defy his wife, who had struggled up from poverty with him and who reminds him of his own loss of integrity.

When Charlie learns, however, that the studio had planned to kill Dixie with poison gin, he at last balks and tries to rediscover what he himself represents. He stops the poisoning but Dixie is by then so drunk that she is hit and killed by a police car, no less. Then Charlie goes upstairs to kill himself in the bathtub with a razor.

Odets depicts men better than he does women, and there are remarkable portraits in *The Big Knife*. There is the egocentric, driving and yet shrewd producer, Hoff, and his keen Irish assistant, Coy, the gentle, warm-hearted agent, Nat Danziger, whom Odets and Charlie love and who cries as he embraces Charlie. There is, in fact, considerable latent homosexual feeling among the men.

The play holds interest because the characters are all created in white heat. But it would have been stronger to show dramatically the night of Charlie's crucial decision to let Buddy go to jail for him. The situation from then on grows so atypical that we cannot empathize fully with Charlie, whose problem is that he sees life in a semantic "either-or," "all or nothing"—either complete integrity and no Hollywood career, or complete concession and no integrity whatever. In a materialistic world, the characters of Odets seem unable to find the middle road toward self-realization.

An exception to that statement, however, is Odets' recent play,

The Country Girl (1950), which in many ways is his most mature and satisfying work. What began in the first draft, curiously enough, as the story of a "destructive, bitchy woman," ended in the final version as Odets' most affectionate portrait of a compassionate, maternal image. *The Country Girl* also marks Odets' first complete departure from a sociological in favor of a psychological evaluation of people.

The play is again the triangle of two men and a woman. Frank Elgin is a down-and-out actor who has become an alcoholic. His wife, Georgie, is about to leave him when he gets a tremendous opportunity at a comeback through the faith a young director, Bernie Dodd, has in him. Much like Jerry Wilenski, Frank is another remarkable study of a passive-dependent man, so used to relying upon his wife and so sure of his own inadequacy that when offered the leading role in the new play he says to his wife, "I can't do it, can I?" But Georgie knows that she was attracted to marry Frank because she saw so little of her own father and says of him: "Frank's brought out the mother in me." Frank and Georgie have lost a child and endured poverty together, but just why his need for alcohol or a wife-mother is so great, Odets does not tell us. His feelings of guilt and insecurity are deeply rooted however, and he is potentially manic-depressive in the degree to which little incidents can trigger him from moody stupor to top-of-the-world exhilaration—as when he has a dream that all goes well with his play and that people are laughing in the street.

During the rehearsals, however, an insidious sparring takes place between Bernie and Georgie with Frank helpless between them, trying desperately to learn his lines and stay off the bottle. By a subtle example of projection, Frank has convinced Bernie that it is Georgie who is suicidal, alcoholic and jealous of his success. Bernie is lonely and mentally disturbed over the breakup of his own marriage; his defense mechanism is arrogance and rudeness; he rationalizes that Georgie is an evil influence on Frank and actually wishes him to hit the bottle again. Bernie is unconsciously motivated, however, by a desire to have Georgie himself and all that she represents in maternal strength and security. Unconsciously, he would pry Frank away from her, even at the jeopardy of the play to which he is consciously dedicated.

Frank helplessly pleads for "the word," as did Golden Boy from his father, sure by now that Georgie and Bernie want him to fail. When Georgie and Bernie, half-hostile and half-fascinated, grow so tense in their relationship that Bernie orders her back to New York, Frank hits the bottle in an all night bout. With almost paranoiac suspicions, Bernie is convinced that Georgie must have gotten him the bottle, projecting onto her his own wish for Frank to drink himself out of the triangle. It takes a sight of Frank's scars on his wrists to make Bernie realize that all his suspicions of Georgie were false. Bernie has to play humble for the first time before Georgie and return Frank to her if he is to save his play. By opening night in New York Frank gives a great performance, and Bernie knows that he has lost any chance of winning Georgie, the country girl, away from the father-husband-child to whom she is tied. Although Georgie's future life with Frank will not be enviable, she emerges at the end as something of a superb figure, surely the finest woman in all of Odets' drama.

Odets shows, too, his insight into the psychology of acting, derived in part from his experience with the Group Theatre's use of the Stanislavski method of improvisation. When Frank feels himself unwanted, he is so carried away in his role onstage that he uncontrollably slaps the ingénue, knowing with a sudden flash of awareness how the man he was playing must have felt at being rejected by his grandchild.

Although it lacks the rich folk idiom and humor of the Bronx milieu, *The Country Girl* reflects Odets' most mature understanding of human psychology. He has built theatrical suspense masterfully (of course, the easiest kind of suspense is to put a reformed alcoholic on one side of the stage and a bottle on the other.) But Odets has done more. He has created an absorbing human relationship and finely etched characters; he has captured the backstage excitement of the theatre, and above all, he has dissected with psychoanalytic understanding the ambivalence of hate and love by which a director could compel himself almost to wreck his play in a struggle to win a man away from his wife's maternal ministrations because he himself unconsciously could not bear to be without such attention.

Although it is true, as Odets has said, that "it is bootless to stop for examination of where one always knew or where Freud opened up knowledge of self or others," an understanding of dynamic psychology is an essential tool in the full appreciation of the rich and complex characterization in the plays of Odets. The psychological themes which appear recurrently in Odets are passive-dependency in men coupled with a hint of latent homosexuality and the wish to return to the security of childhood; the matriarchal family pattern; childhood inferiority feelings converted into adult aggression and hostility; the search for psychological integrity and the struggle with guilt over "selling out"; and, finally, the devious conversions of suppressed sexual energy into sadism, Fascism, alcoholism and *voyeurism.* To ascribe psychoanalytic influence to the plays of Odets, however, is not to detract in any way from his own powers of creative observation and his intuitive feeling for people. His embattled Joe Bonapartes and impotent Jerry Wilenskis and Frank Elgins, yearning to regress to childhood, are significant representatives of the times in which Odets lives.

ROSE FRANKEN

The classic picture of the matriarchal American family and its passive-dependent males given by Odets in *Awake and Sing!* was equalled only once during the drama of the thirties—in Rose Franken's *Another Language* (1932). Here the family is free of the economic pressure that aggravates the neurosis of Odets' people, and the picture is, therefore, all the more insidious. Miss Franken's Hallam family is presided over by a strong-willed, indomitable mother who rules by the devotion she exacts from her sons.

Miss Franken had shown her interest in psychoanalysis in an early novel, *Pattern,* and in *Another Language* she exposes the Freudian pattern of the Hallam family in terms that are psychologically perceptive without resorting to obvious analytic terminology.

Mrs. Hallam's husband is a mild, lovable little man who is resigned to matriarchy, and the sons sublimate in their business lives. All of the Hallam wives are sexless, emotionally sterile creatures, one finding release in eating constantly, one in gossiping, one in accumulating jewelry, none in love with their husbands because the Hallam males are incapable of love except for their mother. The oldest couple have a son, Jerry, whom they are forcing into business although he wants to be an architect. The chief target of gossip is Stella, the wife of the youngest son, Victor, who is going to art school. Stella and Jerry discover that they speak "another language"—two sensitive people in a family of quarrelsome, petty, snobbish Philistines, held together only by a species of family loyalty which is shown up for the evil thing it can be when used as a weapon to insure conformity.

Victor, who once wanted to be an artist himself but preferred to conform, resents his wife's interest in Jerry, and Mother Hallam is hostile to Stella for taking her youngest son away from her. Typical of the Hallam mentality which ridicules what it does not understand is Victor's remark about Jerry: "A boy of that age oughtn't to be hanging around art galleries. What do you want to do, make a fairy out of him?"

When Stella urges Mrs. Hallam to let Jerry study architecture,

Mrs. Hallam develops a fainting and sick spell, using hypochondria as a neurotic club over her children's heads. Jerry is left alone with Stella, whose own marriage has reached a crisis, and they console each other with love. When the repercussions begin the next day, Stella realizes that Victor cares less about his wife's infidelity than about covering up for the family. Mrs. Hallam tries to restore her control but Stella has made Victor see the spineless thing he is, and he comes in the end to a new evaluation of his marriage and manages to shake off the hand of Mother Hallam. Jerry will get to architecture school as the curtain falls on this devastating picture of a matriarch ruling over her clan of Oedipally fixated males, inadequate husbands to frigid wives. Commented Brooks Atkinson in reviewing *Another Language*:

> Labelling "Another Language" as a psychoanalytical drama is classifying it accurately, but the charlatans have given psychoanalysis in literature so odious a name that Miss Franken's sensitively written drama of family tyranny deserves a more appreciative description.

Like Lillian Hellman with her Hubbards, Miss Franken was reluctant to abandon a family which was so fertile for psychological probing and which had existed for 433 performances on Broadway. In 1948 she continued this family chronicle in *The Hallams*, which, however, is not as varied or interesting a play as *Another Language*. In fact the bickering Hallam family begins to get on our nerves as they do on each other's. Stella has died during the intervening years, and the oldest son's wife has taken up a faith-healing religion. Her son Jerry has had tuberculosis; Victor has taken to living on a boat to escape the family; but Mrs. Hallam remains the same cold and grasping matriarch, not having apparently aged at all. The new themes introduced are anti-semitism and the psychosomatic basis of tuberculosis.

Jerry is recovering from TB when he meets and marries a recovered patient, Ken. The family's vicious and uncivil treatment of Ken forms most of the plot. To show them his love for her, Jerry lifts her up and suffers a hemorrhage. He is ambivalent over whether to stay with Ken or go home to his mother's to die; true to the Hallam pattern he ultimately chooses the latter.

Recent research has found evidence to indicate that emotionally disturbed individuals have more than average susceptibility to tuberculosis. Ken tells Jerry that he had to pay a price for years of not doing what he wanted. Even Grace, with gall-bladder attacks, was asked by her physician, "Was I mentally disturbed over anything?" The woman whose son is to die of tuberculosis, ironically insists "Infection has no reality." Another Hallam daughter (who unfortunately never enters) has apparently gotten interested in Freud, prompting her father to comment:

> Walter: Didn't you know family feeling went out when
>   Freud came in?
> Grace: Yes, Nancy has a whole room full of books that tell
>   you what happens to you when you love your mother.
> Mrs. Hallam: (firmly) I would not permit it.

Nancy is in love with a Jewish doctor, and outrages the Hallams by marrying him. They had maintained that "A Hallam always marries his own kind"—but the Jewish boy's mother is equally hurt that her son would marry into such a family as the Hallams. Victor objects to the way the family tries to protect everyone from facing life—all bad news is kept mysteriously hidden as long as possible. "It's time our family stopped this cotton wool stuff. What's the matter with us that we can't stand what other people stand?" By this time the audience knows the answer only too well. Miss Franken's Hallam neurosis of mother-fixation and incapacity to love has become transparent.

When Miss Franken turned her psychoanalytic probing from thoroughly unpleasant to thoroughly pleasant people, the result was one of the most popular comedies of the decade, *Claudia* (1941). Crisp and bright in dialogue, incisive in characterization, the play tells the story of Claudia's emotional growing up from mother-fixated girl to mature wife. Claudia is married to David, who is somewhat older, and on their wedding night had said to him: "David, you couldn't be more darling to me if you were my own father." David's comment is: "And the damndest part of it was, I felt like her father." Claudia sees sex all around her on the farm they own, and says of a large egg, "If I were a rooster, it'd give me an inferiority complex." But she is fearfully naive of her own sexual role, and provokes a flirtation with a wolfish Englishman in order to test her sex appeal. She gets into further difficulties by trying to sell their farm in order to assert herself and disprove her dependency. Her childish habit of listening in on telephones brings her the first real shock of her life when she learns that her mother suffers from an incurable disease. David stands by her understandingly and tries to help her grow out of her anaclitic feelings. Like the Hallams, Claudia and her mother are used to hiding painful truths from each other. David gives Claudia good psychoanalytic advice:

I wish you had the strength to put your arms around her and say, 'Look, let's not go on pretending. I know. And I can face it . . .' It would release her, utterly. It would release you, too. Because when you face a thing, you cease to fear it.

Claudia applies the advice, and the end of the play finds her mature enough to begin living her role as woman—and mother-to-be.

Two of Miss Franken's other plays also deal with maturing interpersonal relationships, although with relatively little depth of analytic insight. *Doctors Disagree* (1943) shows a male doctor attempting to overcome his prejudice against women doctors. *Soldier's Wife* (1944) treats the post-war adjustment necessary when a dependent wife has, during her soldier-husband's absence, learned to make her own way emotionally and financially. A return to a deeper level of character-analysis is represented in *Outrageous Fortune* (1943), which is a sensitive and delicately handled study of neurosis and homosexuality. As a play it is static and plotless, but as psychological character study it is astute.

The mother of this family is the exact antithesis of Mrs. Hallam; she knows that her children must find their own way without parental domination. Her two sons are depicted as complex individuals, perhaps without sufficient cause. The older son is the unresponsive husband of a woman who is becoming neurotic from sexual hunger. The younger son, Julian, who has always worshipped his older brother, gradually becomes aware of his own latent homosexual tendencies. He is engaged to a healthy young girl who realizes somewhat hysterically that Julian is incapable of loving her physically and is neurotically devoted to a man with whom he is writing a musical comedy. This man is also a homosexual but with less guilt feelings over it. He is the only son of a mother whose whole life he became after the death of his father. But this explanation is insufficient for Julian, and his inversion remains but ". . . the slings and arrows of outrageous fortune." They have a house-guest, an older woman who is notoriously promiscuous. She reveals that she is dying of an incurable disease, and through her will to enjoy life to the fullest, she helps the whole family adjust to a new understanding of themselves. The play is handled with the highest taste, restraint, and compassion for the characters. It lacks only dramatic momentum. The great play which will explore and analyze the tragedy of homosexuality remains yet to be written—though the recent Goetz dramatization of Gide's *The Immoralist* is a significant approach.

LILLIAN HELLMAN

The most famous American play to deal with the outrageous fortune of the homosexual was written by another woman playwright, Lillian Hellman. Since this first play in 1934, Miss Hellman has contributed at least three of the most grim, trenchant and tightly constructed studies of human evil in the modern drama.

Like Eugene O'Neill, Clare Boothe Luce and Moss Hart, she has herself undergone psychoanalysis. Her reply to the present author's questionnaire, however, was only a brief apology for her inability to answer specific questions, each of which she felt raised so large a point that a quick answer would be a distortion. Miss Hellman concluded, "You absorb what is of your time to absorb." Nowhere is this more applicable than in her own case. Her time was of the turbulent thirties and the war-torn forties, and she absorbed not only a psychoanalytic insight into unconscious motives but a predilection for the bitter themes of rapacity, human evil, Fascism, blackmail and diplomatic duplicity.

Few Broadway playwrights have been fortunate enough to have their first play run for anything like 691 performances, but such was the history of *The Children's Hour* (1934). As the dowager playgoer in *The New Yorker* cartoon discovered to her chagrin, *The Children's Hour* was anything but a play for children. Its frank handling of Lesbianism, however, was free from sensationalism or self-consciousness. Yet Miss Hellman tells in a recent interview in connection with the 1952 revival of *The Children's Hour* that it was difficult to cast the original production because prominent actresses were afraid to take part. It had only been seven years since the New York police closed Bourdet's *The Captive,* and even Professor William Lyon Phelps of Yale, a member of the Pulitzer Prize committee, refused to attend *The Children's Hour;* the prize that season went to a comparatively tepid study of the relationship of two women, *The Old Maid.*

The germ of the idea for *The Children's Hour,* Miss Hellman states, came from a Scottish book describing the case of "a malicious child who said that the two headmistresses at her school had 'an inordinate affection' for each other." To motivate such a situation, Miss Hellman created the incisively drawn character of a neurotic adolescent, Mary Tilford, of whom the author later said:

> On the stage a person is twice as villainous as, say, in a novel. When I read that story I thought of the child as neu-

> rotic, sly, but not the utterly malignant creature which play-
> goers see in her. . . . It's the result of her lie that makes her
> so dreadful—this is really not a play about lesbianism, but
> about a lie. The bigger the lie the better, as always.

At a boarding school, Mary is shown as a lonely, disturbed girl with sadistic hostility, a persecution complex and feigned heart attacks. She is about to run away from school when she hears a bit of significant gossip from another girl who has been eavesdropping on the two women who run the school. Karen Wright is engaged to marry Dr. Cardin, and the child has heard the other woman, Martha Dobie, accused by her aunt of resenting the marriage:

> Martha: I'm very fond of Joe, and you know it.
> Mrs. Mortar: You're fonder of Karen, and I know that. And
> it's unnatural, just as unnatural as it can be. You don't like
> their being together. You were always like that even as a
> child. If you had a little girl friend, you always got mad
> when she liked anyone else. Well, you'd better get a beau
> of your own now—a woman of your age.

With only the vaguest idea of the implications of this, Mary runs away from school to her grandmother and in a wild chance tells her grandmother of the "unnatural relationship" in the hope of not being sent back to school. Without stopping to verify the accusation, the grandmother is quick to spread it among the mothers, and Martha and Karen find the children being taken out of school. Although Karen and Martha deny the relationship vehemently, Mary terrorizes another girl into supporting her lie. Lacking the flighty aunt's testimony, Karen and Martha lose their libel suit; they are then ostracized and deserted. Although Dr. Cardin would still marry Karen, she forces him to admit that even he is unsure and wants to know just how true the accusations were. Karen knows their marriage could never succeed with this between them, and sends him away. In a delicate and superbly handled scene, Martha finally realizes that she *had* unconsciously loved Karen with an unnatural affection, although Karen had never suspected it and is revolted now to learn it. Martha takes her own life just too soon to know that Mary's grandmother finally learned the falsity of the charges and comes, guilt-ridden, to offer to make it up to them as best she can. Karen goes away and the ending implies that there is some hope for her and her fiancé.

Although there is no reference to the psychodynamics which are responsible for Martha's latent inversion, *The Children's Hour* is nevertheless a daring step forward in the theatre's humanizing power to create understanding and empathy for unconscious deviation as a tragic flaw rather than a loathsome anomaly. Only a playwright as skillfully restrained and impatient with sentimentality as Miss Hellman could have handled such a theme successfully. In all her selfish fatuousness, the publicity-shy aunt who failed to show up at the trial is as responsible for the tragedy as the paranoid child; but Miss Hellman does not attempt to account for the aunt's perversity. To excoriate the inexplicable malignancy of the human soul seems Miss Hellman's special gift.

Her next play, *Days to Come* (1936) was a play of labor strife, told not in the simple realism of Sklar, Maltz or even Galsworthy, but interwoven with the complicated, neurotic lives of the industrialists themselves; as such it is perhaps a clearer illumination of the forces from which strikes grow than would be bare socio-economic photography.

Andrew Rodman is a kindly and decent factory owner in a town where he has known most of his workers and their families all his life. Andrew's maiden sister, Cora, is a pathetic psychotic who acts like a child, fussing with the servants, hating her brother's wife with an incestuous jealousy, and knowing so little of sex that she thinks Caesarian operations are when the woman is under age.

Andrew's wife, Julie, is a neurotic, unsatisfied woman who married without love and has had an affair with Andrew's business partner, Henry Elliott. Now as a strike looms, Andrew is so ineffectual and so indebted to Henry that he permits him to bring in professional strikebreakers. Julie meets the union leader, Whalen, and falls in love with him. When a strikebreaker is murdered and the body dumped outside Whalen's house to pin the murder on him, Julie is the only one who can clear him; for she had been there with him that night. Andrew is so broken up over the death of a striker's child that his wife's infidelity is secondary; at the end there is a new kind of awareness between Andrew and his wife.

The play is strange and jerky in its construction, curt and telegraphic in its dialogue. The characters are cold and unsympathetic, even Andrew who might have ingratiated himself as a humanitarian business man caught between a venal partner and an unfaithful wife. With her insatiable drives and her restless seeking for sensation, Julie had, as she tells the union leader, been trying to find "something I could be." She is Hedda Gabler without even the compassion that Ibsen evokes for his neurotic heroine. Although *Days to Come* illustrates the fusion of socio-economic themes with psychoanalytic treatment of motives in this post-Freudian period, it failed to satisfy either as labor relations, as psychological analysis, or as theatre.

Miss Hellman's next play, set within the framework of historical rather than contemporary business practice, undoubtedly remains her masterpiece. *The Little Foxes* (1939) is a sombre study in the psychology of evil. Although there are unmistakable psychoanalytic touches, the play is more concerned with describing and dramatizing evil than in explaining it. There is more financial intrigue than there is penetration into the childhood of this family of foxes. The animal nature of these predatory humans suggests nothing in drama so much as Ben Jonson's *Volpone, or The Fox*, but in a dramatic structure superior to anything achieved by the rare Elizabethan for all of his devotion to Plautus and Terence.

The Hubbards are Southern reconstruction business men who have made their fortune exploiting the poor white "trash" and the Negroes. The only aristocrat in the family is Birdie, whom Oscar married in order to acquire her family plantation, Lionet. Birdie is desperately frustrated and quietly drinks by herself to deaden her memories of a gentle, lovely mother at the old plantation. Cruelly indifferent to her, Oscar finds an outlet for his sadism by going hunting every morning, having only missed one day in eight years— but he will not permit the starving Negroes to shoot animals for food.

Oscar's brother is Ben, a bachelor and a combination of driving planner and shrewd charmer. Their sister, Regina (so memorably created by Tallulah Bankhead), has married a banker, Horace Gidden, but their marriage is like Birdie and Oscar's, a desecration. Regina used to pray at night that Horace wouldn't come near her, and has refused to have sexual relations with him for many years (although she accuses him of having "fancy women"). She has identified herself so completely with the male Hubbards that she expresses a hint of Lesbianism by her curiosity over the lovely women in Chicago. When Horace returns from Johns Hopkins with a heart condition, their daughter Alexandra (the most sympathetic character in the play) is tenderly solicitous of her father in the Electra pattern. Alexandra is being pushed into a marriage with Leo, son of Oscar and Birdie, because it will increase Oscar's share of the cotton mill. Birdie loves Alexandra enough not to want her to marry Leo and live as she has lived.

The central plot concerns the brothers' efforts to get Horace to invest in one of their schemes, and their prompting Leo to steal his bonds when he refuses. When Horace discovers this, he tells Regina the bonds are to be her only legacy; but before he can change his will, Regina antagonizes him into a fatal heart attack and callously stands by without giving him his medicine. The male Hubbards would now rapaciously outwit Regina, but she is a match for their avarice and is able to gain the upper hand in their cynical game of wits. At the end, Regina gaily leaves for Chicago and would take Alexandra; but the latter rebels at last against the entire family of foxes, saying, ". . . there were people who ate the earth and other people who stood around and watched them do it."

After two intervening plays, Miss Hellman returned to the Hubbard family with *Another Part of the Forest* (1946), which is the prologue to *The Little Foxes* and takes place 20 years earlier. The play's dedication is "For my good friend, Gregory Zilboorg," a psychoanalyst and author of *Mind, Medicine and Man* as well as the English translator of Andreyev's *He Who Gets Slapped*. Whether or not it represents Zilboorg's influence, Miss Hellman digs deeper into the background of her sadistic, predatory Southern family and here shows the psychodynamics motivating the Hubbards. With her former mastery of suspense, she shows the rise of the family fortunes beginning with Marcus Hubbard, a driving, ruthless carpetbagger who makes a huge profit in black-market salt during the Civil War and increases it by foreclosing on loans. As a defense against his guilt feelings, Marcus has turned to music and Greek literature. The masculinity of Regina is illuminated now by her attachment to her father, which assumes more significance than her affair with Captain John Bagtry, an emotionally disturbed Civil War veteran, who was happiest during the war and longs for another one. To get away from Regina's possessiveness, he contrives to go to Brazil where there is fighting.

Marcus' wife, Lavinia, is out of touch with reality and has a fuzzy memory and judgment. Out of her overwhelming sense of guilt, she has taken up the religion of the colored and goes to church with her servant, Coralee. She wants to go off with Coralee and open a school for Negro children. Marcus has given out that she is crazy, and treats her with utter contempt and indifference—just as their son Oscar was to treat his wife in *The Little Foxes*. Even Ben and Oscar are treated as hired help by their father, who pays them a pittance and shows no respect for their opinions. Little wonder, then, that Oscar and Ben found it necessary in the other play to release their Oedipally engendered hostility on whomever they could find as substitutes for their autocrat father.

In *Another Part of the Forest* Oscar is shown as a pathetic weakling, in love with a prostitute, Laurette Sincee, in the pattern of Freud's comment on "love for a harlot." But even she considers herself better than the carpetbagging Hubbards whom the townspeople despise. The aristocratic Bagtrys also scorn the Hubbards, but being penniless, the daughter Birdie is forced to come and ask Ben to arrange a loan to save the plantation, Lionet. Ben sees a way to pry some money from his father's tight fists, and arranges for a $10,000 loan of which he plans to give Birdie only $5,000. But Marcus finds out and cancels the loan. Oscar has been riding at night with the Ku Klux Klan and his father has to bail him out of that difficulty, deducting it from his pittance of a salary. He and Laurette plan to run away to New Orleans, and Regina is planning a trip to Chicago with Bagtry, both trips displacements of hostility for their father.

As in *The Little Foxes*, the crucial reversal centers around a character's learning a piece of information which can be used as a lever against the rest of the family in this never ending competition for superiority. Here Ben learns accidentally from the psychotic chattering of his mother that Marcus had guided Yankee troops to ambush a Confederate encampment. Rather than give his father over to the townspeople to be lynched, Ben uses his information to break Marcus' power over the family. Marcus is forced to surrender the business to Ben, who calls off Regina's trip to Chicago, permits his mother to go free with Coralee to her Negro school, forces Oscar to marry Birdie and Regina to marry an older man, Horace Giddens, whom she despises. The little trollop flees to New Orleans and Bagtry to Brazil, well out of the Hubbard web of evil. Thus in one terrifying act, the later destinies of this family of foxes are determined, and the sequel seems now to stand out in bold illumination.

With psychoanalytic perception Miss Hellman shows that evil begets evil through family dynamics—the influence of parents upon children and the creation of pressures within the family that require outside release. There is a kind of malevolent magnificence in the scenes in which brothers, sister and father pit their wits and unbridled aggression against each other, devoid of humanity or affection. As in *The Little Foxes*, Miss Hellman seems uninterested in drawing sympathetic characters or generous human emotions. But she can create theatrical suspense and sharply etched characters who fascinate in their malignancy. Miss Hellman has said that she is planning a third play on the Hubbard dynasty. Apparently her alternatives will be either to reach back into the early life of Marcus and discover the reasons for his original sin of total ruthlessness, or to push forward past the end of *The Little Foxes* and trace the future of Regina, searching for release in Chicago while the vulture minds of Ben and Oscar turn over and over the strange circumstances of Horace's sudden heart attack and death. If the third play equals the craftsmanship of the other two, the Hubbard trilogy cannot help but be one of the superb works of art in American drama, exploring deeply the origins of human evil with an understanding derived from psychoanalysis: the sadist is an individual who, having been hurt himself, must hurt others. The big fox, Marcus Hubbard, could not have had a family of anything but little foxes.

The Nazi regime in Europe seemed to Miss Hellman part of the same picture of evil and sadism in the human spirit. *The Little Foxes* was followed in 1941 by *Watch on the Rhine*, which deals with a characteristically isolationist and self-centered American family that gradually awakens to the facts of European life as Kurt Muller, a refugee from Nazi brutality, comes to stay with them, bringing his wife and three children. As in the Hubbard plays, evil consists not of stupidly inhuman acts but of keen-minded Renaissance plotting so as to use information to advantage. In this case, Teck de Brancovis, a somewhat mysterious and penniless Roumanian count who is also staying with the family immediately senses the marketable value of Kurt Muller and his locked brief case; with his paranoiac ability to project evil everywhere, he also suspects that his wife is in love with the son of the family. He manages to unearth the fact that Kurt is an active anti-Nazi and carries money in his brief case to be used in underground work. When one of his colleagues is captured by the Nazis, Kurt knows that he must return to Germany and try by bribing guards to free him. Teck's price for silence is $10,000. He believes that there is in the German characters, "a pain-love, a death-love." Although Freud's "death-wish" and sado-masochistic dependency were believed by Erich Fromm to form the basis of the Nazi psychology, they are far from Kurt's motives for returning to Germany. When there is no other alternative, Kurt quietly and with dignity goes about the business of killing Teck in order that he may go on with his work of fighting Hitlerism. He parts with his wife and his wonderfully precocious children in a scene of almost unbearable poignancy, and returns to the underground fight for a world where men need not kill one another. Although *Watch on the Rhine* permits crime to go unpunished, there was never a man audiences were happier to see die than the paranoid Teck de Brancovis. To Miss Hellman's restraint and precise ability at characterization, she adds for the first time a warm emotional feeling within the family which makes *Watch on the Rhine* one of the finest plays to come out of the war years.

Miss Hellman's next play, *The Searching Wind* (1944), again deals with the family of an American diplomat, this time an attaché at Rome during the rise of Mussolini and Hitler. With keen awareness of the interaction of psychological and political factors, the author shows our isolationist foreign policy during the thirties as an inevitable expression of the personal escapism of the men who made the policy. Through the play, which covers a number of years, runs the triangular love story of two school chums, Emily and Cassie, for the rising diplomat, Alexander Hazen. Ambivalent and confused as to his own emotions, he marries Emily but continues to have an affair with Cassie, who has the revealing habit of dropping something whenever she is nervous or trying to conceal emotion.

Alexander has a significant interview with a Nazi ambassador who appreciates psychoanalysis, although he draws a cynical conclusion from it:

> Von Stammer: I have little faith in men influencing other men. Each of us goes the way he goes, and that way is decided early in a man's life. I have read a little Freud. (Carefully, as if to a child:) Sigmund Freud, the Jewish Viennese psychiatric physician.
> Alex: I know his name. We have a few printing presses in America now.

Cassie reveals considerable psychoanalytic wisdom in her summary to Alexander of their generation's behavior:

> You know, when you don't think you're bad, then you have a hard time seeing you did things for a bad reason, and you fool yourself that way. You don't do anything for just one reason. It gets all mixed up and—maybe the hardest thing in the world is to see yourself straight. The truth is, I was haunted by Emily, all my life. . . . I wanted to take you away from Emily; there it is. It sounds as if I didn't care about you, but I did and I do. But I would never have done anything about you if I hadn't wanted, for so many years, to punish Emily . . . It's too bad that all these years I saw it wrong—Oh, I don't want to see another generation of people like us who didn't know what they were doing or why they did it. You know something? We were frivolous people. All three of us, and all those like us—Tell your son to try—

This speech illustrates the tendency of the thirties to view socio-political events with Freudian insight into misplaced motives and substitutions. *The Searching Wind* is thus a scathing indictment of a generation of smug American indifference to Hitlerism, brought poignantly home when Alex and Emily's son, who has lost a leg in the war, soberly castigates his parents' frivolous, snobbish world which is responsible for his personal tragedy. To ignore powerful undercurrents either in politics or in emotional life, Miss Hellman seems to say, can only bring later devastation upon the society or the individual. Defense mechanism and rationalization in personal life can only make for an ostrich-like national and foreign policy. If there is a weakness in *The Searching Wind,* it is that the plot construction is not of the tense cat-and-mouse battle of minds that made Miss Hellman's Hubbard plays memorable. Charmingly weak characters are more difficult to deal with dramatically than wilfully sadistic ones.

Miss Hellman's most recent play, *The Autumn Garden* (1951) is at the same time her most ineffectual, her most baffling and her most psychoanalytic. Although Freudian interpretation can help to explain it, it cannot give the play the dynamic plot development which it lacks. *The Autumn Garden* is a muted, obscure play with the characters moving through decadence, sterility and emptiness as in Chekhov's world, but without the Russian's warmth and affection for his characters. A more appropriate comparison is perhaps with Schnitzler's autumnal play of approaching death, *The Lonely Way.*

The scene is an aristocratic Southern summer boarding house, but without any local color of the South. The assembled characters have little dynamic connection with each other, except that each is in search of some kind of meaning for his empty life: General Griggs, a retired officer, is married to a scatterbrained and flirtatious wife whom he wants to divorce; Edward Crossman, who had loved Constance but never married her, is now a cynical book publisher who remarks that, "Medical statistics show that sixty-one percent of those who improve have bought our book on Dianetics and smoke Iglewitz cigarettes." Constance brings her niece, Sophie, over from Germany and tries to get her married to Frederick Ellis, a passive dependent youth with a dominant mother. Frederick develops an attachment instead for a Mr. Payson, and wants his mother to pay Mr. Payson's passage to Europe with them. His homosexuality is on the unconscious level, however, and he is deeply hurt to learn Mr. Payson's true motives. Frederick's grandmother is a perceptive old lady who knows that her daughter ". . . will never want him to marry. And she will never know it."

Constance's former lover, Nick, returns to her life with his wife, Nina, and Constance would resume her love for him. But he proceeds to get sardonically drunk and tries to seduce Sophie. He passes out mumbling his love to a Julie who must have figured somewhere in his past. The next morning Nina and Nick quarrel and almost split up over his behavior; but they are tied together with unconscious bonds which will reconcile them.

The relationship of Nick and Nina is astutely depicted as that of a weak, passive-dependent man, destined always to be unfaithful and to return repentant to his wife, whose unconscious masochism requires just such a man-child. As Fred's old grandmother observes to Nick, shaking his hand off her shoulder, "You're a toucher. You constantly touch people or lean on them. Little moments of sensuality. One should have sensuality whole or not at all. Don't you find pecking at it ungratifying? There are many of you: the touchers and the leaners. All since the depression, is my theory." The grandmother's theory of the leaner or toucher suggests the psychiatric concepts of Harry Stack Sullivan.

The most sympathetic character up until now has been Sophie; but even she is doomed to betray a sour side of her nature. She would use Nick's attempted seduction as an excuse to blackmail him for $5000 with which to return to Germany. Miss Hellman seemed determined to remind us that the human personality is composed of sadistic and aggressive as well as tender and generous impulses in a subtle balance. With her back to the wall in a hostile, foreign land, Sophie uses her wits to advantage, a familiar trademark of Hellman's characters.

The resolution is as inconclusive as these lives have been. Nick and Nina are reunited and will pay Sophie her blackmail money. Griggs cannot leave his wife when she announces that she has a serious heart condition; he isn't even sure that he doesn't welcome the doctor's verdict, as it helps rationalize his own ambivalence and indecision. Disturbed as he faces the end of his unfulfilled life, he finds himself wishing to see his sister again—a regression to Oedipal infantile emotions:

> Griggs: I really want to see her because she looks like my mother. The last six months I've thought a lot about my mother. If I could just go back to her for a day. Crazy at my age. . . .
> Crossman: I know. We all do at times. Age has nothing to do with it. It's when we're in trouble.

Constance is left alone as all of her guests go their ways in a scene of disintegration reminiscent of the end of *The Cherry Orchard*. All the moments of crisis and decision have been missed. Even Crossman, whose unfulfilled love for Constance has warped his life, does not want to marry her now; he apologizes:

> Crossman: Sorry I fooled you and sorry I fooled myself. And I've never liked liars—least of all those who lie to themselves.
> Constance: Never mind. Most of us lie to ourselves, darling, most of us.

The Autumn Garden is a poignantly sad play of the discovery of the lies or rationalizations by which a group of people have lived—

only to learn in the autumn of life that their ego-defenses were only excuses for not doing what they could not or would not will. With profound psychoanalytic perception, Miss Hellman has laid bare the dependency of humans upon each other and upon various rationalizations. If the material somehow eludes Miss Hellman's customarily tight dramaturgy, and if she gives us no single character with whom we can fully empathize, nevertheless *The Autumn Garden* is a masterful attempt to look deep into tragic, empty lives which lacked only self-awareness.

The *Autumn Garden* marks a step forward in psychology for Lillian Hellman, enlarging her grasp of unconscious motivation beyond the sado-masochism which permeated the Hubbard plays. The theme of latent inversion, too, is suggested in a number of her plays. The task of bringing together in one play the complex and deeply perceived motives of *The Autumn Garden* and the superbly structured theatrical tension of *The Little Foxes* remains the task which Miss Hellman's talents give promise of fulfilling.

MOSS HART

Like Lillian Hellman, Moss Hart achieved his psychological insight in part from personal psychoanalysis. Hart, moreover, was willing to state in the present author's questionnaire that he had been psychoanalyzed and that it had influenced his playwriting. He has read, "Almost all of Freud—None of Adler or Jung," and finds it valuable to discuss his plots or characters with a psychoanalyst "sometimes—not always." Hart believes the theory of the unconscious to be the most influential of Freud's concepts upon his work and specified *Christopher Blake* as well as *Lady in the Dark* as reflecting the influence of Freudian psychology—the latter play resulting from a conscious search for techniques to dramatize for the audience the workings of the unconscious. In his remarks on Freud's influence, Hart wrote: "The writer's debt to Freud—any kind of writer—playwright, novelist—is enormous."

Maurice Zolotow has given credit to psychoanalysis for freeing Hart from a neurotic dependence upon his collaborator, George S. Kaufman. If that is correct, it indicates the slowness of psychoanalytic therapy; for Hart has stated that his analysis began in 1934, and it was after this time that he and Kaufman collaborated on their most successful light comedies, *You Can't Take It With You* (1936), *I'd Rather Be Right* (1937), *The Man Who Came To Dinner* and *George Washington Slept Here* (1940). It was not until 1941 that Hart emerged on his own as a successful playwright, though it was with the subject of psychoanalysis itself that he made the break with Kaufman.

It is interesting to note, however, that 1934 was the date of Kaufman and Hart's first serious study of characterization, *Merrily We Roll Along*, which is a panorama of the loose and flaming twenties as a background for the struggle of a young playwright wrestling with the temptation to "sell out" to the brash and easy money of the period. What would have been an otherwise undistinguished play achieves some dramatic irony by the novelty of proceeding backwards in chronology so that we see first the cynical, successful and wretched man of middle age and only at the end the young man of ideals setting forth with his concept of integrity which was destined for a jolt.

Reversing this picture of despair in 1936, Kaufman and Hart contributed their great essay on integrity and fulfillment which has become a classic of American comedy, *You Can't Take It With You*. Here the characters actually do roll merrily along, oblivious to the competitive pressures that motivate their countrymen. Grandpa hasn't worked for years because he realized one morning on the way up in the elevator that he wasn't getting enjoyment from life—so he rode down the elevator again to begin a new life of delightfully zany, whimsical fulfillment. Though he has no money and has ignored the notices from the Income Tax Bureau, he can proudly tell a grumpy, unsatisfied business man, "I haven't taken a bicarbonate of soda in thirty-five years."

Jung's old association of ideas test, which has sporadically cropped up in the drama since *Good Gracious Annabelle* in 1916, is used here by Kaufman and Hart for some hilarious situations at the expense of the pompous business man and his frustrated wife. As the bird-brained mother reads the answers, Mrs. Kirby's entire life with Mr. Kirby becomes transparent:

Kirby: Will you go on, Mrs. Sycamore? What was the next word?
Penny: (reluctantly) Honeymoon.
Kirby: Oh, yes. And what was Mrs. Kirby's answer?
Penny: Ah—'Honeymoon—dull!'
Kirby: (murderously calm.) Did you say—dull?
Mrs. Kirby: What I meant, Anthony, was that Hot Springs was not very gay that season. All those old people sitting on the porch all afternoon, and—nothing to do at night.
Kirby: That was not your reaction at the time, as I recall it.
Tony: Father, this is only a *game*.

Kirby: A very illuminating game. Go on, Mrs. Sycamore!
Penny: (brightly, having taken a look ahead). This one's all
right, Mr. Kirby. 'Sex—Wall Street.'
Kirby: Wall Street? What do you mean by that, Miriam? . . .
Mrs. Kirby: (Annoyed) Oh, I don't know what it means,
Anthony. It's just that you're always talking about Wall
Street, even when—(She catches herself.) I don't know
what I mean . . . Would you mind terribly, Alice, if we
didn't stay for dinner? I'm afraid this game has given me
a headache.

Although the Vanderhof solution to the problems of our complex society by simply ignoring reality and Federal law is hardly
Freudian but rather Hart and Kaufman's tongue-in-cheek bit of
wish-fulfillment, the basic theme of You Can't Take It With You is
the search for self-realization and mental health.

On his own for the first time, Hart turned in 1941 to a less whimsical aspect of this same theme and wrote Lady in the Dark, the
first musical drama based upon psychoanalytic therapy itself. With
the incomparable Gertrude Lawrence as Liza Elliott, Lady in the
Dark ran for 467 performances and was considerably effective in
popularizing psychoanalysis to a musical comedy public. Dr. Otto
Fenichel wrote in his authoritative book, The Psychoanalytic Theory
of Neurosis that the play illustrates the mechanism of repression of
the exhibitionistic impulse. Another psychoanalyst who found the
psychology of Lady in the Dark valid was the anonymous "Doctor
Brooks" (very likely Hart's own analyst) who wrote in the preface to
the play: "As a case history this is wholly accurate; and at the same
time it could be the document of almost any human life."

In Act I, Liza Elliott comes fearfully to the office of Dr. Brooks
for her first psychoanalytic session. She is disturbed because she
has thrown a paperweight at Charley Johnson, her assistant on the
fashion magazine of which she is editor. She is experiencing a nervous breakdown just as she reaches the pinnacle of her career. Dr.
Brooks accounts for this by pointing out that while she was still
struggling to rise, "she could always tell herself that the next step
would bring her the ease, peace, security and reassurance which
would mean happiness." Now that she has achieved the security and
success without the accompanying happiness, she has been thrown
into a new panic of insomnia and anxiety; her old rationalizations
are now inadequate and "rage, depression and terror below the
smooth surface of her life" threaten to break through from the unconscious. Lisa has the natural resistance to psychoanalysis which

Dr. Brooks has learned to expect, but he soon has her relaxed on the couch and recounting a recurring memory of a childhood song.

In the first flashback into Liza's subjective world, she sees herself as a glamorous and worshipped lady courted by a male chorus. The psychoanalyst interprets this fantasy as significantly the opposite of the role Liza plays in life—that of a severely dressed, mannish business executive.

At the office of her magazine are a delightfully Kaufman-and-Hartish collection of characters—an effeminate photographer, Russell (Danny Kaye), Maggie, an acidulous confidante, Charley Johnson, a heavy-drinking cynic who pinches the models, and a promiscuous "sleeping beauty." Liza's life is thrown into further panic when her married lover, Kendall, who founded the magazine for her, comes to announce joyfully that his wife has consented to divorce him at last. Now Liza realizes that perhaps she doesn't love Kendall, who is an older man, but has looked upon him as a father-image which offers security and reassurance. In her next fantasy, Liza sees herself marrying Kendall, with Charley Johnson as the jewelry salesman selling the ring, and the chorus accusing her of not loving Kendall in spite of her protests that she does.

Dr. Brooks now attempts to interpret Liza's fantasies: "I wonder if your scorn and hatred of other women is because you are afraid of them." He suggests that perhaps her severe dress is a protective armor against having to compete as a woman; therefore the prospect of having to hold Kendall as his wife increased her anxiety. Liza is unable to assimilate this interpretation and turns her hostility upon Dr. Brooks in transference, terminating the analysis.

After Liza has kept the staff waiting all day because she cannot make a decision on whether to have a circus cover or an Easter cover for the next issue, Charley resigns and she throws a second prop at him. A handsome movie star, Randy (Victor Mature), asks Liza to dinner and she accepts, glamorizing herself in a borrowed model's gown.

Subjectively, Hart uses offstage voices to reproach Liza for her indecision. As she mulls over the cover and the three men in her life, she fantasies a circus scene with Russell as ringmaster. In true dream condensation, however, the circus soon becomes a court where Liza is tried for not being able to make up her mind. Charley is the prosecuting attorney now, and Randy her counsel. Liza's defense is to sing the memorable "Saga of Jenny," which might be called the first Ballad on Fixation:

Jenny made her mind up when she was three
She, herself, was going to trim the Christmas tree.
Christmas Eve she lit the candles—tossed the taper away.
Little Jenny was an orphan on Christmas Day.*

Jenny's saga goes on to tell that Jenny shocked Vassar because ". . . in twenty-seven languages she couldn't say no."

Liza returns to her analyst and tells him of her "bad feelings," the origin of which she traces back to a traumatic experience when she was three or four and her father compared her unfavorably with her beautiful mother, calling her "a plain child." Most traumatic of all her childhood memories, however, is her mother's death, when Liza put on her mother's cape and posed in it before a mirror, eager to assume the role of her beautiful mother. When her father discovered her, he ripped off the cape furiously; Liza interprets this as total rejection by her father. Even in adolescence she was unable to compete with beautiful girls and remembers a boy deserting her for a more attractive girl. These episodes, Dr. Brooks believes, have produced as a defense, ". . . rebellion—rebellion at your unfulfillment as a woman." The repression of this exhibitionistic impulse has resulted in a professional sublimation—the career of glamorizing other women by her fashion magazine.

When Randy, envy of a million women, comes to propose to Liza, she realizes that underneath his handsome exterior he is a frightened and dependent child, needing strength from a woman which Liza is not in a position to give. Kendall too comes to her, pleading pathetically for her not to leave him. Even Charley comes to her at last and she realizes it is he she loves; she is able for the first time to be a woman with him and not a competitor, and offers to share the running of the magazine with him.

Lady in the Dark has psychological flaws, of course. In the preface "Dr. Brooks" points out that Liza's insight happens much too quickly and that the analyst's technique is at fault in asking too many leading questions which precipitate anxiety and an interruption in the therapy which might have been avoided. Liza's dream fantasies are hardly dreams at all but rather rococo musical comedy "production numbers" which seem rather tame compared with the dreams in *Roger Bloomer, Beggar on Horseback* or Strindberg's *The Dream Play*. Except for the conversion of the circus into the court and the identification of characters from Liza's daily life, there is little distortion, symbolism, or sexual undercurrent. The psycho-

---

* Music by Kurt Weill, lyrics by Ira Gershwin.

analyst does not come back after Act II, and the final scene of Liza's
finding herself happens apparently without the analyst's help; somehow Liza is purged of mother envy offstage. But by then we have
been deluged by such brilliant spectacle and music that these weak-
nesses are hardly apparent in the theatre. As other dramatists have
also found, it is easier to portray a lady in the dark than in the light.
Lady in the Dark was a "big musical" based upon a serious theme
which is handled with integrity; it became a milestone in American
musical comedy as well as in the story of the influence of psychoanalysis upon the drama.

After a wartime tribute to the Air Force in *Winged Victory,*
Hart returned to subjective fantasy in *Christopher Blake* (1946),
which might be termed "Child in the Dark"—but in a serious, non-
musical form. Christopher, a child of twelve, is faced with the decision as to whether he wants to live with his mother or his father
after their divorce. Less distorted and expressionistic than those
in *Lady in the Dark,* the fantasies which occur in Christopher's mind
are "flash-forwards" or projections. His fantasies of self-pity, self-
aggrandizement and revenge on his parents are at times relatively
prosaic. As the play opens, Christopher fantasies himself receiving
the highest medal of the land from President Truman for inventing
both a super atom bomb and a workable peace plan. But when the
President asks his parents to step forward, Christopher breaks down
and reveals his parents are divorcing. Overcome with masochism,
Chris shoots himself as the President intones, "Now he belongs to
the ages!" The effect of the scene is weakened, however, by our not
meeting Christopher in reality before we are led into his free association of self-pity.

The actual scene is the judge's chambers as the mother and
father wrangle with lawyers over the settlement of the divorce. The
father has had a mistress for which the mother cannot forgive him.
Mrs. Blake is a frigid woman who has known since the second year
of their marriage that it was loveless, having been entered into only
for security and escape from loneliness. Mr. Blake is depicted more
sympathetically—he is repentant and willing to give up his mistress.
The scene in which the father attempts to explain to his son what
infidelity means is one of considerable effectiveness.

Chris' second fantasy is of himself as a great playwright who invites a strange couple (that turns out to be his parents) to watch a
dress rehearsal of his play dealing with the son of a divorced couple
who is left at a boarding school and sent away at Christmas when
the school closes. With no place to go, the child is finally chased by
a policeman at the end of this fantasy within a fantasy.

The third projection grows out of Chris' effort to deal with his Oedipal hostilities. He sees his parents as charity cases in the county poorhouse with a villainous superintendent starving them. Chris arrives as a millionaire from South America and instead of saving his parents from starvation he merely introduces them to his foster parents who have befriended him and with whom he leaves, saying that he hates his real parents. The final free-association is what Chris imagines the court and judge to be. There is here a little more of the anxiety and fear of which many dreams are compounded. In the real court, however, the judge is kindly and understanding, and Chris breaks down and cries. Finally, he chooses to stay with his father; for it is apparent that his dad needs him and that his mother will get along well without him. The Judge tells him that grown-ups sometimes feel as lost as children.

The poignant and deeply troubled inner world of this child of divorce is somehow not entirely captured nor his relationship to his parents fully explored. Hart has apparently been at some pains to make Christopher a normal, healthy, mature lad—at a sacrifice of the intensity that is found in Atlas' *Wednesday's Child*. The parents fail to arouse empathy, and Chris would have engendered more if we had felt his ambivalent love for his parents as well as his hatred and self-pity. The choice to remain with his father is made without agony or reawakened Oedipal strivings toward his mother. His fantasies are, in fact, unrelated to this choice and provide little insight into it. Without music to reinforce the emotion, the rambling construction and diffuse handling of material seem more of a weakness in *Christopher Blake* than in *Lady in the Dark*.

The brittle world of conscious ego and bawdy repartee proves more manageable than the turbulent life of the unconscious, and it was to this level that Hart returned with his next play, *Light Up The Sky* (1948). Here he salutes the mad folk of the theatre, particularly a Billy Rose like figure who can't lose money no matter how wild a flier he takes in the theatre. The only reference to psychoanalysis comes when the leading lady, as pampered and self-dramatizing an extrovert as ever trod the boards, is telling of a bad dream which she has had. In her play she doesn't speak a line during the first act, but while taking a nap on the afternoon of the opening performance, ". . . suddenly I was dreaming that I was on the stage and the curtain was going up. Everything was exactly as it is—absolutely real. And then *I* began to speak. I took the lines from all the other actors and nobody spoke but me. I couldn't stop. It was horrible." The cynical playwright who understands the actress replies quietly: "What a really great man Freud was." Whether this dream was wish-fulfillment or anxiety must be left to those who have studied the psychology of actresses.

After a two years' interim during which Hart ". . . found nothing that excited or pleased me enough to write . . .," he discovered *Shadows Move Among Them*, a novel by Edgar Mittelhölzer, which he dramatized as *The Climate of Eden* (1952). The subject matter gave him the opportunity ". . . to explore and set down my own feelings on what I can most easily and quickly term 'a Utopia of the heart.'" The physical setting for this Utopia is a remote mission in the savage jungle of British Guiana. The missionary, Reverend Gerald Harmston, has created a kind of ideal civilization here, based upon an ethical code, hard work, wholesome play, and frank sexual love. Swimming nude is encouraged even for the Reverend's daughters, and he announces in church that a new supply of contraceptives has arrived.

Into this lush tropical Eden comes a characteristic product of the neurotic pressures of a more "civilized" society. The nephew of the Harmstons, Gregory, arrives from England, drinking heavily and suffering such extreme guilt feelings over the suicide of his wife that at times he feels that he has killed her. He has paranoid hallucinations of being watched and hated by his wife, and the frequent clenching and unclenching of his hands is one of his neurotic symptoms.

The two daughters of the Reverend are both attracted to Gregory. Mabel, the beautiful nineteen-year-old, at first conceals her emotion, but her fourteen-year-old sister, Olivia, is delightfully outspoken about the erotic impulses Gregory has aroused. Akin to Carson McCullers' Frankie Addams in *Member of the Wedding*, Olivia is a roundly characterized adolescent, profane, uninhibited, precocious, self-dramatizing, curious and unbearably eager for sexual experience. Her adult wisdom exceeds her vocabulary, and she says that she loves her brother but ". . . not in an infestuous way." She soon analyzes Gregory's disturbance as "shittsophrenia."

In the eerie jungle mood, the appearance of Gregory with a bloody razor convinces them that he has murdered someone; but it proves to be only a chicken which Gregory substituted when he felt the uncontrollable death-wish against his wife. Invited to go swimming nude by Mabel and aroused even more by meeting the native boy who has been Mabel's lover, he succumbs briefly to a compulsive desire; psychotically identifying Mabel with his dead wife, he forces her to kneel and begin to undress at the point of the razor. Before he does violence, however, he is brought back to reality and collapses sobbing in Mabel's comforting arms.

Later Gregory improves and loses all memory of the episode with the razor. Olivia is obsessed with jealousy of her sister, and her premonitions of disaster heighten the pervading sense of jungle foreboding. Olivia tries to slash her wrists, less anxious to commit suicide than to dramatize herself. Sibling rivalry and its conversion into dreams was never more eloquently expressed than Olivia's confession:

> I had a dream last night, too. I dreamt I used the razor to slice off your breasts! I hate you, Mabel! I don't want to— but I hate you like chicken-gall! He called me a little girl! Just because my chest is flat! I'm so jealous my head is swaying like a tower . . . !

Olivia is forced to turn to masochism for release, and begs the cook to hit her as hard as she can. There is a scene of powerful tension as Mabel goes to Gregory's room and gently offers herself to him— interrupted by a note thrown in at the window by Olivia reading, "My flat chest burns for you." Gregory cannot accept Mabel on these frank terms, neurotically fearing that he is destined to hurt all those who love him. When her mother also urges intimacy with Mabel in order to discover if they really love each other enough to marry, Gregory flees from this Eden in a panic of guilty sexual anxiety. He is about to embark on the steamer when he purges himself by confessing to the Reverend that he hated his wife not because she had a lover but because of his own shameless infidelities: ". . . I saw my own failure mirrored in her eyes—in her pity—in her love for me." With the Reverend as his father-confessor, he finally arrives at the psychoanalytic wisdom:

> I can see myself as though it were someone else—the brilliant young man who never quite made it—who suddenly stopped dead—and faced out his failure in other women's beds . . . Perhaps love gets mixed up with the business of success, Reverend—the daily battle of getting and needing approval—of proving through others that you're all right. And if you fail—and you're to survive—and you must survive —the burden is shifted—the burden of your guilt and your failure is shifted to the one who loves you.

With her adolescent fantasy Olivia announces that Mabel has been bitten by a bushmaster and is dead. When it proves to be a native who was bitten and Mabel returns, Gregory is able to overcome his neurotic blockage and passionately draws Mabel to him. The reverend will not marry them, however, until they have lived together and Gregory has had a chance to prove his love for her. They go off together in trust, leaving Olivia to face the wrath of the Reverend for her sadistic prank. Although she confesses wanting to see the pained expression on Gregory's face when he heard of Mabel's death, the Reverend is in a benign mood and there is a tender scene between father and daughter as he realizes, "You arrive at your womanhood." He knows that the Electra-bond between father and daughter must be broken. To answer her fear at being left by her father, the Reverend says:

> Not leaving you Olivia. I'm returning the gift you gave me—
> the miracle of yourself. It's yours now—to discover alone—
> without any of us. Your mother and I have nothing greater
> to give you.

Olivia's poignant soliloquy of farewell to her girlhood brings down the curtain on this stirring and provocative play.

Little wonder that with his psychoanalytic experience Hart found Mittelhölzer's novel irresistible. Although he undoubtedly fails to reduce all of the materials of the novel to a tight dramaturgy, he has devised a fluid, almost cinematic script which moves from place to place in and out of the house, surrounded by the ominous jungle. The Freudian theme of the play is the contrast between the neurotic, guilt-ridden "civilization" that creates shame over sex, and the healthy, pagan acceptance of sex which permits the full development of the individual. There is implicit in modern, dynamic psychology such a promise of a utopia of mental health, in which each parent, educated by preventive psychiatry to understand the causes of neurosis, raises his children free of unconscious conflict and able to pursue self-realization. Yet there are curious inconsistencies in this otherwise perfect Garden, stemming from the personality of Reverend Harmston. Brooks Atkinson has pointed out that he is potentially a more significant dramatic character than the neurotic Gregory. He uses stern authoritarianism and brutal physical punishment with the natives, yet holds his own family together with love and dignity. He practises a rational, undogmatic religion, yet tells Gregory not to seek scientific answers to all questions. Although Gregory is made considerably more sympathetic than Eugene O'Neill's tortured heroes, it is true that the Reverend Harmston, with his compassion for humanity and his deep intuition into unconscious life, could have become a dramatic character of major proportions. If *The Climate of Eden* had only qualified success in New York, it, nevertheless, cannot be dismissed lightly.

Hart's interest in psychoanalytic drama is apparently undiminished. He has recently permitted the first act of an unfinished drama, *The Nature of the Beast*, to be shown on the *Omnibus* television program. It is an exploration of the inner world of a married man who reaches middle age and asks, "Is this all?" Now that his children are grown, he wants freedom to discover that vital part of himself that was left by the wayside during the anxious years of parenthood. To escape he pretents to have amnesia; but an astute nurse sees through the pretense, and he ends the first act stretched out as though on the analytic couch confessing himself to the nurse. With this provocative beginning and Hart's old ability at deft wit, there is promise of fresh insight into *The Nature of the Beast*.

TWO NATURALISTS—KINGSLEY AND HECHT

The avenue toward uninhibited language in the theatre—as used by Hart's adolescent in *The Climate of Eden*—was paved by Sidney Kingsley's daring use of profanity in *Dead End*. It was Kingsley's particular genius to combine a documentary naturalism in observing the picturesque in metropolitan society—a hospital, a steam-laundry, an East River slum, a police station—with more than a little psychological perception. The truest naturalist our theatre has produced, Kingsley manages to give more than a Zola "slice of life," for his slices generally include psychological depth as well as environmental breadth.

His first play, given a notable production by the Group Theatre, was a picture of the frustrations and conflicts in the lives of physicians in a busy hospital. In *Men in White* (1933) a young interne, driven to a choice between medical research and his society-minded fiancée, turns in his despair to an evening's affair with a lonely student nurse. Although the language of the doctors is not yet interlarded with talk of psychosomatics as it would have been a few years later, it is made clear that the doctor's affair, which ends tragically in the nurse's death from abortion, is only a displacement of rage at his selfish fiancée.

Dead End (1935) is not only the high-water mark of American naturalism but is credited with significant sociological influence in calling attention to the need for slum clearance. Taking a step beyond *What Price Glory?* Kingsley's play employs a frankness of language which would not have been possible a few years earlier. The "dead-end kids," with their "Frig you," and "Ah, yuh muddah's cooch," shocked the public into a realization that these slums were breeding the potential criminals of tomorrow. With the uninhibited sadism of young savages, the boys "cockalize" or befoul the genitals of new members of the gang (a castration substitute). Against the background of these prematurely hardened children whose profanity and sexual games have the same unconscious roots as those described by John Dollard in "The Dozens," we see a gangster and killer, the product of this degrading neighborhood, return to visit his old mother, only to be repudiated and slapped by her. He looks up his old sweetheart but she is now a diseased prostitute. A sensitive and frustrated young architect, Gimpty, turns the gangster in to the FBI, but afterwards is gnawed with guilt. Talking to his sweetheart, a rich man's mistress living in the wealthy apartment juxtaposed in ironic contrast to the slums behind them, Gimpty free associates back to a childhood memory as he stares at the black, swirling sewer water; talking "faster and faster, trying to push back into his unconscious the terror that haunts him, to forget that afternoon if only for a few seconds," he remembers his childhood wish that he could fall into the beautiful, swirling dirty sewer—which he has symbolically done by betraying a childhood companion. He sees clearly the forces that have made the man into a killer; when one of the dead-end kids is arrested for beating up the rich, sissified boy who lives in the elegant apartment building, Gimpty pleads with the rich father not to press charges, telling him what a decent, courageous, clean-cut boy even this killer was until the neighborhood and the reform school brutalized him. But the boy is nevertheless arrested and the wheels of injustice again set to grinding.

Kingsley's second play of depression slums, *The World We Make* (1939), was based on a novel by Millen Brand and showed the combined pressures of catastrophic world conditions and perilous emotional instability as the cause of psychosis. The heroine, Virginia, is seen in a prologue at a private sanitarium under a psychiatrist's care for her melancholia and paranoid reaction to the death of her brother. She dreams of going down a long corridor carrying a doll, wanting to scream and being unable to. She accuses her hostile and unsympathetic parents of killing her brother. When the psychiatrist leaves for a moment, Virginia escapes the sanitarium and begins her precarious climb back to reality.

Virginia finds a job in a steam laundry—a perspiringly real piece of stage naturalism. A worker, John, befriends her and takes her home with him to his wretched little cold-water flat where she collapses. But in his absence next day, she pitches happily into the housework. Although at first she cannot bear a man to touch her, she soon finds herself in love with John and gains security by living with him. When John wants to marry her, she feels compelled to confess that she is insane. He needs her, however, and urges her to stay; but when he asks her to have a baby, she is thrown into panic; anxiety over death and the war in Europe forces her to phone for the psychiatrist to come for her. For the pain this will cause John she cries masochistically to him, "Hit me! Slap my mouth. Hurt me!" Then John's younger brother, Jimmy, dies of tuberculosis, and John takes the shock badly. Even the psychiatrist is disturbed because his mother is in the war zone in Poland; but he shows Virginia that people must go on living and trying to be socially useful. Her own guilt feelings over her brother's death are re-lived and purged by her emotional participation in the death of John's brother and she realizes that to mourn indefinitely is unrealistic. At the end she is able to offer John the strong hand he needs. *The World We Make* is an effective clinical study of a neurotic who finds readjustment by being loved and needed, by helping to make the world instead of being passively buffeted by it.

The depth of psychoanalytic insight shown in *The World We Make* carried over into Kingsley's next modern play (following a sensitive historical play, *The Patriots*). In *Detective Story* (1949), he returns to his *Dead End* naturalism, capturing the wealth of detail of a busy New York police precinct station. Beyond naturalism, however, *Detective Story* is a character study of a police detective who does his job too well, who hounds the suspects with a self-righteous passion which Kingsley understands as sadistic and derived from unconscious, childhood sources.

The assorted individuals who come to the police station include a sweetly paranoid old lady who believes that she is being watched by foreigners with radar and atomic vapor; a sad little spinster-girl who compulsively shoplifts—which is about the only way she can get any male attention; a young, mixed-up veteran who has stolen to get money to woo his expensive girl friend; and a man suspected of being an abortionist. Tromping heavily among this ailing humanity is detective James McLeod, who is warned by his lieutenant to stop badgering people:

> Your moral indignation is beginning to give me a quick pain
> in the butt. You got a Messianic complex. You want to be
> the judge and the jury, too.

Ostensibly outraged at the abortionist for butchering girls, he confesses to a newspaper reporter-friend that his fervor comes from a childhood in which his father abused his mother. "I saw that sadistic son-of-a-bitch of a father of mine with that criminal mind of his drive my mother straight into a lunatic asylum." Now convinced he is helping rid the world of such criminal minds, McLeod third-degrees the abortionist until he collapses and suffers internal injuries.

There have been hints that McLeod had personal motives in persecuting the abortionist, and the lieutenant runs down every lead to find out the truth. He uncovers more than he bargained for—McLeod's idolized wife, Mary, had had an affair before her marriage and had gone to this abortionist for help. When McLeod learns this, he is violently unforgiving and calls Mary a whore. The young veteran becomes the victim of McLeod's displaced hostility for his wife, and is to be prosecuted even though the employer from whom he stole is willing to give him a second chance because of his fine war record.

Mary decides to leave her husband but even then he cannot "be a little human"; instead he cries out:

> How, how? How do you compromise? How do you compromise, Christ!—convictions that go back to the roots of your childhood? I hate softness. I don't believe in it. My mother was soft; it killed her. I'm no Christian. I don't believe in the other cheek. I hate mushiness. . . .

Before she leaves, Mary brings McLeod to a kind of insight about himself, and he realizes that he has become the very image of his sadistic father: "I built my whole life on hating my father—and all the time he was inside me, laughing—or maybe he was crying, the poor bastard, maybe he couldn't help himself, either." This is a vivid dramatization of the mechanism of introjection, by which parental attitudes are unconsciously incorporated; in McLeod's case the repressed wish for his mother's softness was converted into the defense-wish, to avoid softness at any price. Only when he is dying from a pistol shot from an escaping burglar who has felt the sting of McLeod's brutality does he for the first time become soft, and his dying gasp is an order to let the young veteran go free and have his second chance.

Detective Story is a tense, theatrical melodrama with a leading character whose motives are psychoanalytically sound. Although in such a kaleidoscopic picture there is little time for the details of McLeod's childhood reaction-formation, there is, nevertheless, an understanding, incisive cross-section of the multitude of human forces brought to focus in a precinct station—the sexual frustrations and mixed emotions that force decent people to crimes they don't understand, and the deeply compulsive drive toward sadism that might make a man either a criminal or a police detective, depending on circumstances. As in *Dead End*, Kingsley is particularly anxious for misguided and maladjusted youth to have a second chance, and as in *The World We Make* he gives a character that second chance to find himself.

Kingsley's more recent play, *Darkness at Noon* (1951), was

adapted from the novel by Arthur Koestler, one of the most psychoanalytic-minded of modern novelists. More Freudian in its form
than its content, *Darkness at Noon* explores the mind of an old
Bolshevik, N. S. Rubashov, whose story was so prophetic that it
might be that of Beria. As he lies in his prison cell awaiting trial for
bourgeois deviation, he free associates, and the forgotten memories
of his life return to him—the many times he has employed ruthless
force and inhuman cruelty because the end justifies the means in
Soviet ideology. The strikingly effective setting represented a number of cells in which prisoners endlessly tap messages to each other,
while out of the surrounding darkness materialize the scenes of
Rubashov's stream-of-the-unconscious and into which he walks to
re-enact his role. Although the free associations are not of Rubashov's childhood, they are in most cases associated with his guilt
and are subtly brought back to his consciousness by Kingsley with a
respect for the workings of the mind which was not often found in
the older flash-back plays. Luba, the girl he loved and lived with,
recurs to him when an old Czarist prisoner taps out, "When did you
last sleep with a woman . . ?" Even Luba, Rubashov recalls grimly,
was liquidated with his tacit consent. In the end, Rubashov calls
his sadistic torturer, "My son," realizing that he lacks any of the
older generation's contact with humanizing western civilization and
is in fact the son and product of the philosophy Rubashov taught.
"That's the horror. The means has become the end; and darkness
has come over the land."

Like Kingsley, Ben Hecht made his theatrical fame with documentary naturalism—in this case the world of newspaper reporters.
Hecht had manifested some interest in psychology since 1922 when
he wrote *The Egotist,* which showed the amusing conflict in a man
who conceives of himself as "a great lover" but who when made
to eat his words is left frightened and hapless, fleeing from the appointed romantic rendezvous. In collaboration with Charles Mac-
Arthur, Hecht wrote the classic comedy of journalism, *The Front
Page* (1928), in which newspaper men use psychoanalytic terminology in a tongue-in-cheek, breezy, superficial way. One of the reporters has a dirt-phobia and fears that he will be infected if other
men use his telephone; another has a theory of dual personality concerning the escaped convict. Hildy Johnson, the brash reporter,
says of his boss, "Tell that paranoiac bastard to take a sweet kiss for
himself . . ." The escape of Earl Williams is caused by Dr. Max J.
Eglehofer, a noted alienist from Vienna, who naively gives Williams
a gun to let him recreate his crime in psychodrama. Of Eglehofer,
a reporter says:

He's one of the biggest alienists in the world. He's the
author of that book, 'The Personality Gland.'

McCue: And where to put it. . . .

Murphy: Them alienists make me sick. All they do is goose
you and send you a bill for five hundred bucks.

From *The Front Page,* with its raucous picture of police reporters with a smattering of psychology, Hecht turned in 1937 to a
more serious psychological theme, and created in *To Quito And
Back* one of the most perceptive studies in the drama of unconscious
motivation. His leading character is an American novelist of left-
wing tendencies, Aleck, who arrives in Ecuador with his mistress,
Lola, just when a revolution is breaking out under the leadership of
the radical, Zamiano. Aleck and Zamiano become friends when he
wins the rebellion, and Lola is deeply happy in her love for Aleck.
But Aleck suffers from guilt feelings because he has a wife in the
states whom he cannot bear to hurt. He feels that his affair with
Lola is merely an escape, a futile running away from his own psychic
inadequacy. "We both kept dramatizing ourselves—for the other's
benefit. And talked ourselves out of reality, out of New York—
into Ecuador and pure fiction." When Lola asks him if he wants to
go back to his wife, he replies, "No. I want never to have left her."
Yet he senses his inadequacy as a husband, knowing that his trouble
is psychic impotency—"always wanting to love and never loving."

An erotic and cynical old countess knows that Aleck unconsciously enjoys his suffering—a psychic masochist, as Bergler was to
call his type—and tells Lola to stop accusing him:

It's like catching smallpox to argue with those mental
types. The moment you accuse them of anything—they
confess . . . twice as much! You can't get anywhere with
them . . . they're too proud of their faults.

The revolution is later put down and Aleck faces deportation to
the United States by the Fascists. Lola realizes that he will not divorce his wife; and so she makes Aleck send his wife a wire saying
that he is returning. But when he tries to write the telegram, he forgets his own home address—"A rather Freudian lapse, isn't it?"
When he remembers, the pen blots, and he manages to stall until
Lola, seeing that he is incurably indecisive, walks out on him. When
Zamiano is trapped by the Fascists, Aleck goes out to die with him,
calling himself, "One second-hand Hamlet—a hollow heart and a
woodpecker mind . . ." He writes Lola a farewell note saying, "It
seems to me I am more than a guilt complex running amok. . . ."
and dies with an expression of faith in the future of mankind and

its revolution against the forces of Fascism. The countess says of his death: "In a pinch they all turn into children—and figure out something heartbreaking—and useless."

Although Hecht does not round out the portrait by exploring the causative factors that could make an Aleck, he has depicted with rare insight a chain of causality starting with psychic inadequacy and ambivalence—which produces strong feelings of guilt—which can only be assuaged by further masochistic behavior which confirms the guilt—and from which the only escape is suicide. Aleck had said he was not a neurotic—"I'm too clever to have complexes, too clear-minded to hide inside neurosis . . ." but in him neurotic behavior had actually become so deeply rooted that it assumed the nature of a "character-neurosis." Aleck is a remarkable portrait of a man who could sacrifice himself to a cause such as Communism—a martyr not to the glory of the masses, but to his own guilt-feelings.

Hecht's subsequent contributions to the theatre have been sporadic. In 1942 he brought forth *Lily of the Valley* which was a highly original allegory which deserves a resurrection from the quick burial Broadway gave it. Set in the county morgue, the play brings back to life strange samples of human driftwood who tell their stories and project their feelings for God onto a half-mad mission preacher. There were powerful moments in Hecht's poignant drama of "lower-depth" characters—as when a defunct longshoreman tries to organize the dead into a union to bargain with God for a better life.

Hecht's most recent effort in psychological drama, *Swan Song* (1946), written with Charles MacArthur, was, like *To Quito And Back*, a clinical study of neurosis—this time with criminal tendencies. A young pianist is obsessed with jealousy of his musical rivals. He has destroyed his sister who overshadowed him as a pianist, and almost kills another girl pianist before he is finally thwarted. This time, however, Hecht and MacArthur's combination of suspense and psychology made for only moderate success, and with little encouragement from Broadway, Hecht has gone on working outside the drama.

WESTERN FREUDIANS—TOTHEROH AND RIGGS

Dan Totheroh and Lynn Riggs have a number of qualities in common—an interest in western themes, a feeling for the lyricism of rude speech, and a clear conception of unconscious motivation. Both writers, too, have been somewhat slighted by Broadway.

Totheroh's first play attracted the attention of those who hoped that in the wake of O'Neill a whole new generation of native American playwrights would emerge (as indeed they have). Included in Burns Mantle's *Best Plays of 1924-25, Wild Birds* is a sensitive though immature play of sexual ignorance and suppression—*The Awakening of Spring* with a mid-west accent. A seventeen-year-old girl and a boy escapee from a reform school fall in love and run away together when the girl's tyrannical father to whom the boy is bonded refuses to let them get married. When the father finds out she is pregnant he whips the boy to death in a sadistic frenzy based, as is hinted, upon his incestuous desire for his daughter. The implications of this theme are evaded, however, by having the girl's true father turn up at the end.

In 1932, Totheroh wrote an imaginative study of a strangely obsessed neurotic woman in *Distant Drums*. As a covered wagon caravan moves across the western prairie toward Oregon, the sadistic leader, Captain Wolfhill, drives his wife into the arms of a young man on the expedition. They sneak off to watch Indian dances, and aroused by this primitive frenzy find release together. She has prophetic dreams and the superstitious caravan people believe she is a witch and responsible for the cholera which plagues the expedition. When the wagons lose their way, Captain Wolfhill's only choice is to bargain with the Indians to lead them to the pass. The Indians claim his wife in exchange and she is strangely exhilarated and willing to go to her fate with them, having felt all along the mystic call of the savage. Totheroh leaves the interpretation of the play ambiguous—it could be viewed as a study of the unconscious sexual appeal which the Indians had for this masochistic woman with a strong martyr complex, or it could be interpreted simply as a portrait of a prophetic woman who felt her destiny and selflessly sacrificed herself to it. Even Jung's call of the collective unconscious might prove to be the key to *Distant Drums*. Each interpretation finds some basis in the evidence supplied by the playwright.

Totheroh leaves less room for speculation as to the Freudian interpretation of his next play, *Moor Born* (1934), a study of frustration in the famous Brontë family. Whether biographically accurate, it seems psychologically valid in characterization. The three Brontë sisters, Emily, Charlotte and Ann, live in isolation from men, suppressed under the shadow of their brother, Branwell, whom their father believes to be a genius. The father, Reverend Brontë, is a warped fanatic himself, firmly believing in his own genius. While the other two sisters make some adjustment in their lives, Emily is the brooding, untamed creature who turns to the moors and the wind as a sublimation, calling the moors "a wild mother to us three." Branwell becomes addicted to alcohol and dope after a frustrated love affair with a woman twenty years his senior—an image of his dead mother; Emily is the only one who can handle him, mothering him until he is like a child with her. He recalls a repressed child-hood memory of a traumatic shock—being left all alone on the moors and so frightened that he could not scream. Emily gives Branwell money knowing he will buy dope with it, and he ". . . throws his arms violently around her, and kisses her savagely on the face and neck." The narcotics finally destroy him and he dies babbling in the arms of Emily, his mother-surrogate in this inverted sister-brother attachment. Gradually the sisters win fame in the literary world under male pseudonyms and the critics are sure Emily's *Wuthering Heights* was written by a virile, coarse man who "seems to have a sense of the depravity of human nature." After Branwell's death, Emily goes into a morbid melancholia over her guilt-feelings. Finally, she writes a farewell poem naming Branwell as the author of *Wuthering Heights* in a last gallant effort to give her brother some recognition. But when Emily dies, Charlotte sees that the poem is de-stroyed so that nothing might detract from the fame of Emily Brontë, who had said with true insight that her inspirations ". . . come to me from some unknown source." *Moor Born* contains some of the mysti-cal elements of *Distant Drums* in the fascination of the wild moors, but, in addition, is a perceptive Freudian biography of genius and neurosis.

Totheroh's latest play, *Live Life Again* (1945), fared very badly on Broadway and was withdrawn after two performances. A verse attempt to retell the *Hamlet* legend in terms of a Nebraska farmer's family, it dealt with a youth haunted with his dead mother's voice and obsessed with the idea that his father murdered her.

Like Totheroh, Lynn Riggs reflects Freudian orientation in his themes of inversion, and like Totheroh he has not had the recogni-tion on Broadway which a serious-minded and authentic writer war-rants. His main material distinction lies in having his *Green Grow the Lilacs* made into the musical *Oklahoma!* by Rodgers and Hammer-stein. In his reply to the present author's questionnaire, Riggs wrote that he had read a few of Freud's works, including *Moses and Mono theism, Totem and Taboo* and *The Interpretation of Dreams*. To the question of discussing plots with a psychoanalyst, Riggs replied: "No. An analyst once said to me: 'You're doing the same thing I am.' In a way, I suppose that is so of any writer whose concern is with the nature and meaning of people." Riggs was one of the writers who indicated that he had sought for dramatic devices to dramatize the workings of the unconscious: "Yes—in several plays—in which I use 'subjective scenes.'" He named as his plays which were most influenced by Freudian psychology *The Cream in the Well, All the Way Home,* and *Out of Dust,* and made this general comment on the contribution of Freudianism to the drama:

> Freud is part of our heritage. Everyone ought to know his work—and most people do. Like an artist—for he is that too—he illuminates, stimulates, *reminds.*

Riggs' early plays on Broadway included the lusty *Roadside,* a comedy of a pair of high-spirited, unconventional westerners. Then, in 1931, he wrote *Green Grow the Lilacs,* an exceptional play of authentic Americana. The principal obstacle to the happy love of the wholesome pair, Laurey and Curley, is Jeeter Fry, a neurotic, sex-obsessed farm-hand who lives in a filthy room and keeps obscene French postcards to look at. Since Laurey once touched him, Jeeter has been in a frenzy of desire for her. He talks to Curley of murder and death, taking sadistic delight in newspaper accounts of brutal sex-slayings. Curley compares him to a rattlesnake that crawls up in his hole and festers with poison. During the shivaree this poison spills forth and he is killed trying to knife Curley. Curley escapes a murder charge and gets to spend his wedding night with his bride, however, thanks to the contriving of Aunt Eller and the good people of Oklahoma.

The "subjective scenes" Riggs referred to occur principally in his unique play, *The Cherokee Night.* Although never seen on Broadway, this remarkable mystical drama of the Cherokee Indian people is a strange and haunting experience, subjective in form and non-chronological in structure. Suggesting Jung's concept of racial memory, the play depicts the Indian of today as a tragic figure, obsessed with disturbing memories of his racial past as well as insecurity and violence in his own childhood past. "Night has come to our people," the Cherokee proclaims, and Riggs illustrates this through flash-backs and flash-forwards into the past and future lives of a group of mixed-breed descendants of the tribe—one is a prostitute, one a stutterer, one very rich, one a murderer and one an obsessed old Indian who digs up graves to find arrowheads. A magnificent, full-blooded old Cherokee proclaims that the trouble with today's descendants is not "too much Indian blood" but too little.

In *Russet Mantle* (1936) Riggs returned to a more objective dramatic form in a psychological study of depression-bred disillusionment which is comparable to Sherwood's *The Petrified Forest.* To the New Mexico home of a retired man and woman come her empty-headed sister and her independent young daughter Kay, who spends her first night there in bed with a cowboy. John, a sensitive young poet and seeker after self-realization, comes needing a job and is hired to tend chickens. Kay spends the second night with him. But he sees through her pose of worldliness and shrewdly interprets her attempt to escape from herself as a defiance of her parents:

> So now—to hide what you are, even from yourself—you erect defenses. You're sullen, brash, unfeeling, crude, armored with disdain, harsh, iconoclastic—and a little stupid. Behind those defenses, you are killing yourself, little girl. You are dying by your own hand . . . you became a very torrent of defiance. You spouted and steamed and spurted. You did things you thought revolting just to insult them. You became so good at it, you've forgotten what you were actually supposed to be.

The young lovers are disturbed to learn of the hypocrisy and compromise of the older generation, represented by the miserable, loveless marriage of the retired couple. Kay is determined to have a better life than this sterile wife "with no joy in her at all—only a thin little stirring of the senses sometimes—and the blood stream cold as ice!" John learns by the end of the play that "there's a place for love—and a need for love—no matter where a man's going or what he's searching for." When he acknowledges himself the father of Kay's expected child, the older man is furious and would drive him off the place; John understands his motive with sudden lucidity:

> You couldn't help driving me off like this. I see that. You were troubled before—now I've just made it worse for you. If you dared, you could say, 'God bless you' to us both. *If you dared.* (To Kay) But their whole world would collapse if they said that. They can't do it! That could break your heart if you'd let it.

The rigidity of reaction-formation, Riggs knows, is so strong that the whole adjustment of the personality depends on keeping up the denial, the ego-defense and the self-deluding lie upon which it is founded. Riggs thus achieves in *Russet Mantle* a strong awareness of unconscious motivation and the mechanism of ego-defenses by which one set of behavior is only a way of warding off the opposite— a good illustration of post-Freudian dynamic psychology in the drama.

Riggs has acknowledged the Freudian influence upon *The Cream in the Well* (1941), his most mature and penetrating study of personality. A tragedy of an inverted farm family, *The Cream in the*

Well attempts to come to grips with the smouldering unconscious pressures which destroy the individual. Ibsen-like in its retrogressive exposition, the play is not particularly theatrical nor complicated by plot invention. Riggs depicts an old part-Indian couple, the Sawters, who have homesteaded in Oklahoma. Their only son, Clabe, has gone off to be a sailor, leaving behind two sisters, Bina—a normal but not particularly bright nor attractive girl who does the housework, and Julie—a high-strung neurotic of whom the stage directions say: ". . . something is gnawing at her, something darkly troubling and dangerous. She too, however, like her mother, is full of a deep, controlled cynicism; she usually means much more than she says."

Clabe had left the farm suddenly at Julie's urging because he found himself engaged to a girl he didn't want to marry—Opal, from the farm across the lake. Opal then married Gard Dunham, who used to be fond of Julie and as we first meet him, still is. When Opal and Gard come to dinner, Julie sadistically goads Opal into a depression by showing pictures of Clabe and giving them Clabe's room to sleep in when a storm arises. Even as a child Julie had been cruel, once killing a kitten by hanging. Now she tortures the poor Opal, whose mother is insane, until from fear of insanity Opal rushes out to drown herself in the lake. Gard recovers his wife's body and would sit up with it all night, but Julie comes to the room and tries to seduce him. Gard's fever for her is undiminished, and she gives herself to him not because she loves him but because she loathes herself so much that she wants to be defiled. "Because I don't care what I do now, do you understand. *Just so it's filthy and disgusting.*"

Later Julie marries Gard and proceeds to drive him to drink by her frigidity and sadism. Clabe finally returns from the sea and confesses to his sister Julie that he has a dishonorable discharge from the Navy after having done every disgusting thing he could find to do in Oriental ports—including being a prostitute for male hire. He has the same soul sickness as Julie, the same desire to destroy himself in masochistic punishment. Riggs breaks into poetry as the brother and sister talk to each other. "Give in to what you are," Clabe urges, and the thing gnawing at them is soon made clear:

> Let's say it out plain, and see if it can hurt us. We're in love with each other. We always have been. It's taboo, they say. Who says so? It's happened like that. We fought it, both of us, fought each other, turned our sickness and disgust at ourselves toward others . . . .

Julie goes out to drown herself in the lake and only the fact that the family needs him on the farm keeps Clabe from joining her.

The Cream in the Well is a compacted study of the destructive furies of incestuous love and psychic masochism designed to alleviate guilt-feelings. Its morbidity is without redeeming features, however, and only Bina has any ingratiating quality with which the audience can empathize. The parents have only a patient understanding of the evil in their family and at the end, somehow, rise above it to the serenity of Colonus.

Riggs, like Totheroh, has shown himself to be a perceptive analyst of unconscious motives—particularly inverted sexual drives. If their plays leave something to be desired in theatrical effectiveness and richness of palate, they are nevertheless distinguished attempts to plumb the depths of the human personality and to find drama along the twisting labyrinths which Freud explored.

PAUL GREEN

More successful than Totheroh or Riggs in capturing for the stage the simple, eloquent poetry of native, rural folk was Paul Green. Born and raised on a farm in North Carolina, he studied playwriting at the University of North Carolina under Professor Frederick Koch, who played a significant role in the development of the indigenous regional drama independent of Broadway, exhorting young playwrights to "Write what you know." Like his fellow alumnus, Thomas Wolfe, Paul Green wrote what he knew of the human mind and its conflicting impulses, and gave the American drama folkplays that were rich in their authenticity and compassion for the inner and outer struggles of the common man.

No white American in the arts—surely no Southerner—has done more to champion the cause of the Negro than Green. His one-act plays range from such sensitive and masterful studies of frustration in Negro life as *The No 'Count Boy* and *White Dresses* to angry, naturalistic protest such as *Hymn to the Rising Sun*. With his first full-length play on Broadway, *In Abraham's Bosom*, Green won the Pulitzer Prize in 1926. A profoundly stirring tragedy of a Negro's efforts to bring education to his people, *In Abraham's Bosom* is more than an attack upon white injustice. Green understands that frustration and suppression such as Abe suffers at the hands of Colonel McCranie, a former slave-owner whose own illegitimate mulatto son he is, instills in a Negro one of two defense mechanisms—either fearful, docile subservience as Abe's fellow workers show, or a blind, uncontrollable hatred for whites. Abe is depicted with keen insight as he wrestles with his hostility for his white father and for the Colonel's arrogant white son, Lonnie. After a brutal whipping by the Colonel for striking Lonnie, Abe takes refuge in sexual consolation with his sweetheart, Goldie. After he marries her, however, his efforts to set up a Negro school are constantly thwarted and he rails bitterly against the religion of his superstitious race which keeps them in ignorance. Before the Colonel dies he gives Abe some land and a school, but ironically it is Abe's own ungovernable temper, born of displaced hatred for whites, that causes him to whip a Negro pupil until the parents withdraw their children and wreck his school.

For years Abe moves from town to town trying to found another school, raising his son in the familiar Oedipal pattern of too-severe standards. The son grows up to be a contemptuous, guitar-strumming idler, consumed with hatred for his father and for his father's ambitions. Forbidden to return home by Abe, the son ultimately betrays his father to the whites, who keep him from delivering the passionate plea for education he had prepared for the opening of his school. Staggering wounded down the road, Abe comes upon Lonnie and kills him, the final expression of displaced hatred. Fleeing the inevitable posse in a daze, Abe has dream-fantasies reminiscent of *The Emperor Jones*. Emerging from shadows he sees the memory of a lynched Negro whom he once buried, and identifies himself with the lynched Negro. He then fantasies a projection of the primal scene of the Colonel going into the bushes with his Negro mother to beget him. Abe is shot, a victim of the converging hostilities of intolerant whites, Oedipally hostile son, and his own emotional burden.

Pervading most of Green's plays is the conflict between aggressive social protest, as reflected in *In Abraham's Bosom*, and a guilty, almost masochistic Christian piety. Out of this agonizing ambivalence came one of his most powerful plays, *The Field God* (1927). Here Green creates a deeply felt portrait of a white Southern farmer, Hardy Gilchrist, a virile man who believes in his own inner adequacy and ability, loves his fellow man and shows Christian devotion to his old farm hands. But because he cannot accept the evangelical, hymn-shouting gospel religion of his neighbors, he is called an atheist. He is married to Etta, a pathetically sterile woman who is unable to give him children or affection. Religion is her entire sublimation, as it is to so many of the economically depressed in the "Bible Belt."

When Rhoda, a strapping and passionate young niece of Etta's, comes to live with them, it is inevitable that Hardy should fall in

love with her. When Etta discovers their love, she dies of the shock.
Rhoda and Hardy marry and are supremely happy in their physical
love. But the neighbors and relatives assume the proportions of the
Greek Erinyes or chorus of the super-ego. Led by his Aunt Margaret
who had raised Hardy, they try to make him feel guilty for his
happiness bought by the death of Etta. A young farm hand kills
himself for love of Rhoda, the farm animals die of cholera and there
are other signs which make Hardy feel that he is actually cursed
for having married her. Rhoda too, is barren and begins to feel remorse. When the neighbors, who had been ostracizing them, come
to pray for their souls, Hardy is soon brought to his knees in a
hysterical prayer-meeting scene (such as Green had skillfully depicted in earlier one-acts). Hardy admits to Aunt Margaret, his
mother-image, that he feels mixed up but cannot accept their sin-
ridden concept of religion. Rhoda, however, is carried away by her
sense of shame and guilt and leaves Hardy, unable to have intimate
relations with him until he admits his sin and is saved.

Hardy begins to lose his rational control, mumbling, "Where is
Etta?" In a magnificent scene of free association, repressed childhood memories return to him. But when his ego control is secure
again, he can explain all the evil omens as natural phenomena, and
cries out against superstition, refusing to repent because he does not
believe that he has sinned. "Why should man be afraid of that which
is right and got pleasure in it—make him a bed of nails to sleep
upon?" When Rhoda finally comes back "saved," pale, passionless,
hypnotically detached from reality, it is too late—Hardy has killed
himself, a victim of the apparently hopeless conflict between reason
and psychic guilt feelings reinforced with the loss of love. *The Field
God* is one of the truly tragic and Aeschylean works in American
drama.

In 1931, Paul Green's *The House of Connelly*, rejected by the
Theatre Guild, became the first production of the Group Theatre,
which was to make a distinguished contribution to the American
stage. Critics have compared Green's study of the smouldering frustrations of a decadent Southern family with Chekhov's *The Cherry
Orchard;* and the Stanislavski method of acting, used both in the production of *The Cherry Orchard* and *The House of Connelly*, seemed
ideally suited to psychological penetration and quiet dissection of
motives.

Like the landed gentry of Russia, Green's aristocratic Southern
family is virtually bankrupt, trying almost psychotically to pretend that the old regime still exists. The two maiden aunts are
warped and frigid because in the plantation days no men were good

enough for them. The young man of the family, Will Connelly, is
the weak and ambivalent son of a domineering mother. Petulant
and indecisive, he finally marries a poor white farm girl who brings
new vigor and directness of purpose to the introverted family (although Will has merely substituted one mother-image for another
in his choice of the girl). His Uncle Bob is a degenerate old Gaiev,
inept and incompetent, cavorting in drunken, lecherous revelry with
two big, sexual Negresses who act as a kind of Greek chorus to
symbolize the fertility of the earth which must be renewed through
physical power if the Connelly plantation is to survive. If not consciously Freudian, *The House of Connelly* is nonetheless rich in
psychoanalytic meaning and is an important socio-psychological
analysis of the South in transition.

   With Europe again resounding to marching men in 1936, Green
wrote a biting anti-war satire with music, *Johnny Johnson*. Perhaps
influenced by the German expressionistic drama, *The Good Soldier
Schweik*, Green depicts in Johnny a simple, common man, so naive
as to believe that the good people of this earth don't want war.
By applying somewhat too literally this idea, Johnny wins over a
German soldier and almost stops World War I. But when he confronts the high chiefs of staff with his simple pacificism and humanity, he is declared insane. Act III in a state mental hospital is a cruel
satire on psychiatry. Dr. Mahodan, who examines Johnny, is himself
caricatured as crazy. He sings a song of the history of psychiatry,
from the ages primitive, when witch doctors did the healing, down
to modern times:

> Today psychologists agree
> The insane man is only sick,
> The problem is psy-chi-a-trick,
> See Jung and Adler, Freud and me,
>   And we will analyze.
> And though it hurts, we probe the ruts
> Of mental pain that drives men nuts
> And heal their lunacies.
> And from their devils being free,
> They all take up Psychiatry.

Dr. Mahodan is so preoccupied with his own problems that he
constantly forgets Johnny Johnson's name, and the scene ends as the
doctor calls his patient, "Dr. Mahodan."

   Against his protest, and without any tests to verify insanity,
Johnny is kept in a "house of balm" where the inmates have a debating society modelled on the League of Nations. An old bearded

gentleman named Dr. Frewd insists that Johnny is President of the United States. Although they are role-playing and out of touch with reality, the insane behave with dignity and purpose. The incisive pacifist theme is reinforced with irony as the group persuades the recalcitrant Hiram Johnson of California to vote for the League of Nations, and the one dissenter is finally psychoanalyzed into acceptance by Dr. Frewd. Johnny concludes: "Think how much happier all of us are since we started to work at something that interested us. We've forgot our own troubles and we eat better, sleep better. And besides if we don't take up these big troubles, who will? In the outside world they don't seem to be interested any more." With his illness diagnosed as "peace monomania," Johnny is finally released from the institution, a broken and gently wise man who sells toys on a street corner and watches the indifferent and war-mad world go by him—including his former girl friend, her now-rich husband—and their son who wants to be a soldier.

Green's satire of psychiatry is only incidental to his main theme of indignation at the insanity of war itself in this most shattering of modern anti-war plays. The scene with the psychiatrist in *Johnny Johnson,* ludicrous as it is, had in fact been discussed with a psychoanalyst during the writing, as Green wrote in his answers to the present author's questionnaire. He stated that he had read "a large number" of books by psychoanalysts, "Especially Freud's book on dream interpretation—since dreams and visions are rich material for drama from the days of Aeschylus." In answer to the question as to whether he had sought for dramatic devices to dramatize the workings of the unconscious, Green's reply was, "No. I have enough trouble with the 'Conscious'." Concerning which of Freud's theories were most influential upon his work, he replied, "Freud has interested me most by way of Joyce's *Ulysses.*" Green's general comment on the importance of psychoanalysis for the playwright is significant:

> Freud's pioneer work no doubt is of world stimulating effect, but if the dramatist fails to pass beyond Freud into the realm of freedom and self-responsibility then I for one think he would likely be a half-baked dramatist. But the style of treatment could well determine the outcome.

The two plays mentioned by Green in the questionnaire as influenced by Freudianism, "vicariously, I suppose," were *Tread the Green Grass* and *Shroud My Body Down.*

Called by the author "A Folk Fantasy in Two Parts, with Interludes, Music, Dumb-Show, and Cinema," *Tread the Green Grass* is brilliant and original symbolism, straining the limitations of the theatre with the proportions of *The Oresteia, Faust* and O'Neill's *Lazarus Laughed.* The influence of Freud is here at a deep philosophical level where he, along with Nietzsche, postulated the two rival principles of the universe: the ecstatic or Dionysian acceptance of life—physical, sexual, emotional—which he called the "pleasure principle," contrasted with the denying, repressive force of sin, guilt and super-ego which rejects the physical, symbolized as in *The Field God* by the evangelical, sin-obsessed religion of the superstitious tenant-farmers of the South. Caught between the demands of the two forces is Tina, the young farm wife who dominates *Tread the Green Grass.*

In the opening scene, Tina flings herself upon the ground and embraces it with the fervor that Peer Gynt feels for the joy of life in the opening of Ibsen's drama. She hides from her prosaic clod of a husband and makes herself a bed in the earth, suggesting Otto Rank's "return to the womb" motif in her lyric expression:

> Let the leaves pour down over me. Let it snow them out of the sky over me, hiding me away, keeping me in sleep —warm sleep—leaves—and no spring to melt them from my hair and eyes. Ring around the rosie—hush, hush, we'll all tumble down. (Her voice trails off). Pretty birdie—ba—

As she sleeps we see her fantastic dream of masked and grotesque figures of an old man and old woman who beckon to her and almost spirit her away before she is awakened and led home by her husband, who believes her "not herself" since the death of her child.

In the next scene, Tina goes to the cottage of the mysterious couple of whom she had dreamed. They are thought to be witches, and their son, Young Davie, is a curious folk-evocation of the spirit of Pan or Dionysus. He is a goatish satyr, with his face set in a devilish mask which seems saintly to Tina; he does almost as much laughing as O'Neill's hero in *Lazarus Laughed.* Davie's brother is the Young Reverend, a detached, spiritual young man whom Davie mockingly calls "Jesus Christ" and who turns out to be a Christ-image, as much a stranger to the holy-rollers who profess to worship Him as he is to His Dionysian brother, who runs out into the forest to make love to Tina.

To the village folk Tina is "cursed," and she herself has little awareness of her unconscious motives, which she has learned to explain in terms of folk-lore, witches, and evil spirits. Fearing that some sin of hers caused their child's death, her husband calls in the preachers to pray for Tina's salvation. In a macabre dinner scene written in indignation, Green shows the medieval superstition and coarse degradation of evangelism, as represented by Brother Caders (who eats with a ravenous, Chaucerian appetite) and his three assistants, ". . . middle-aged, with sickly ignorant faces marked by long nights of prayer, periods of gluttony, fasting and flagellations," who sit mumbling catch-phrases from the gospel and stuffing themselves. The Young Reverend sits apart, unable to enjoy the meal.

Young Davie makes a shambles of their prayer session, tearing up Bibles and mocking the preachers until they are sure they can see horns under his curly hair. Caught between the ribald abandon of Davie and the pious platitudes of the preachers, Tina turns for help to the Young Reverend, but he is impotent to restrain his brother. The husband arrives with a gun and captures Davie, but the spirit of sensuality is not long held imprisoned, as Freud had so frequently to remind the world. Davie easily breaks down his prison bars and escapes, going to the church where he continues to wreak havoc on the frightened congregation, breaking up a prayer meeting by arousing the lusty passions of the young on the sinners bench until the girls bare their breasts and dance around the church with their men in a wild Dionysian orgy of released emotion. (This is the dumb-show referred to in the sub-title.) The young couples rush out into the grove (the word suggests the sacred Greek counterpart) while Davie burns down the church.

The final scene shows Tina gently relaxed and at peace in Davie's arms, calling him Jesus in her adoration—until Davie runs playfully away and leaves her in panic. She is repentant and remorseful now, and The Young Reverend leads her by the hand to the edge of a precipice where Tina finds the familiar figure of her dead brother, sees Davie now as a goatish-faced Jack-muh-Lantern climbing from tree to tree in evil, satanic animalism, and projects in her feverish imagination the Crucifixion of the Young Reverend by a ghoulish group of little goblins. Tina sees herself kissing the bleeding feet of the Young Reverend as he stretches out his arms to her calling, "Mother." As the scene vanishes, left behind in the real world are the husband and the preachers, who curse the devil and pray for Tina in their helplessness; but Davie's smiling face mocks them from the very sun itself.

Tragedy for Green, as for Freud, lay in the denial of the totality of life, which includes physical release as well as spiritual security. Green appears troubled that Christianity is unable to resolve the conflict, and his portrait of the Young Reverend, who must suffer and watch Tina but cannot help her is a conception born of disturbing doubts. *Tread the Green Grass*, a *Goat-Song* of the South, is one of the most original and powerful works of the imagination by an American playwright. Out of the superstitious and hysterical religion of the rural Southerner, Green has fashioned a drama of Man's eternal conflict between sensuality and mortification—between the yea-saying and the nay-saying. Pagan *id* clashes with an almost Hindu asceticism. If the dilemma seems unnecessarily insoluble, it is only because each is defined by the other's standards—Pan or Young Davie as a moralist sees him and the fatuous preachers as seen through unbelieving eyes. The modern psychiatric resolution of the conflict between the *ego* and the *id* is not as hopeless as Tina's dilemma; but Green knows the distance that the sin-obsessed religionists of the South have to travel to a synthesis of body and spirit, to the day when mental health and unrepressed acceptance of life will seem like the sun—with the shining face of the irrepressible satyr.

Mentioned by Green along with *Tread the Green Grass* was a play not seen on Broadway, *Shroud My Body Down* (1935). A companion piece in many ways, it is also a folk fantasy with a poetic feeling for the suppressed and inarticulate. Again the leading character is a young girl strangely unable to accept the commonplace life around her, yearning for emotional fulfillment and developing a "Christ Complex" based upon sublimated sexual urges for a "beautiful young man." Her young farm-hand suitor is too prosaic a clod, and she finds companionship instead with a grinning, impish Negro boy of ten who in some ways is the counterpart of the animalistic young Davie.

In the preface to the play, Green appears cognizant of the static and experimental nature of the play, which is a search for suggestive moods rather than plot. In defense, however, he points out:

> The secret and pervasive malady which possessed and finally destroyed the unhappy Grahams without benefit of psychiatry was such as to demand that sort of story-telling out of me. As for the experimental nature of the piece, the modern Spanish dramatists also would find it all too obvious.

The Spanish dramatists referred to bring to mind Benavente, and specifically his *La Malquerida* (*The Passion Flower*), in which an incestuous father-daughter relationship is treated. For that is part of the "secret and pervasive malady" suggested in *Shroud My Body Down*, although Green was reluctant to treat the theme as frankly as did Totheroh or O'Neill.

An old folk-seer, Tapley, who is the Teiresias of this tragedy, senses something ominous in Oscar Graham's strange anxiety to get his daughter, Lora, quickly married to a farm-hand as soon as she is seventeen. The father's own emotional life was warped by the sudden and mysterious breaking of his engagement to Lady Jane in favor of a cold-eyed and unresponsive woman with a face of an Indian mask. Lady Jane hovers through the play, her mind out of touch with reality, begging Oscar to come back to her.

The reason for Lora's evasion of her marriage is ultimately clear—her beautiful brother Edward returns and in a fierce love scene the brother and sister glory for a brief moment in their intense and inverted passion. Lora, who was destined to love only two men, her brother and the image of Jesus, identifies the two as one and wildly cries out to her brother, "You are Jesus, the light of this world." The father overtakes them and would shoot the brother, but he grabs the pistol and performs the deed himself. Graham hangs himself and the broken Lora is led away by Lady Jane, as Tapley proclaims, "Lady Jane has got a child by Oscar Graham at last."

Tapley provides the unity for this unfortunately static play, claiming to be able to interpret dreams. There is considerable discussion of the meaning of dreams, but Tapley is too laconic to suggest any theory of interpretation, Freudian or otherwise. Rather he is content to suggest that in general the dreams of Graham and his daughter presage evil for their cursed house. Lora dreams of giving herself to "somebody like Jesus," and of her two dead sisters who appear to her in masks—and who, it is hinted, may also have been killed by their father. This is truly a cursed line, this tobacco-stained house of Atreus. If Green's attempt to evoke suggestive poetry out of the darkly troubled waters of the unconscious was less successful than *Tread the Green Grass*, it was, nevertheless, a notable experiment—although one that did not lead Green to further lyric exploration of Freudian metaphysics.

It was with Negro material that Green returned to realistic drama. With his distinguished record of insight into Negro life, he was the logical choice to dramatize Richard Wright's novel, *Native Son*, which was brought to Broadway in 1941 by Orson Welles. In the tradition of Dreiser's *The Hand of the Potter*, *Native Son* is indignant social protest based upon psychological insight. There is here no mystic Jungian racial unconscious as in O'Neill. Green and Wright attribute the tragedy of Bigger Thomas directly to the environment in which he had been raised—which included the trauma of watching as a child while a Southern lynch mob killed his father for trying to protect a fellow Negro from violence. After this his mother, sister and brother moved to Chicago where they were forced to live in wretched, degrading poverty—to the extent that killing a huge rat in their kitchen provides the theatrical sensation of the first scene.

The Negro slums of Chicago are owned by a rich white philanthropist, Mr. Dalton, who tries to help Bigger by giving him a job as chauffeur on a social worker's recommendation. But Bigger has already been moulded by unconscious motives deep in his childhood and it is too late; Bigger is warped by murderous hatred for white people, derived from his feeling of guilt and inferiority. There is a remarkable scene near the beginning as Bigger and his Negro pals wait for time to stage an armed robbery of a white man and let their minds free associate to airplanes and flying, the symbol to them of power and rising above their environment. They mockingly imagine themselves Secretary of State and President, and sarcastically project into the make-believe their conviction that these officials must spend all their time trying to keep the Negro in his place.

It is tragic irony that Bigger's first day as chauffeur places him in the one situation where as a repressed welter of conflicting drives he dare not find himself—in a white woman's bedroom. The Dalton daughter is a spoiled, heavy-drinking, pseudo-intellectual fellow-traveller of the Communists. She asks Bigger to drive her to a workers' rally and shocks Bigger by treating him as an equal. But she passes out from drinking and Bigger has to carry her up to her bed. In a sloppily drunken way she tries to show him that she is not prejudiced, but the effect is paralyzing on the Negro alone with her in the bedroom. Almost inarticulate, he keeps begging to be allowed to go, but she chatters stupidly on until her blind mother walks in; Bigger is in such panic at being discovered there that he holds a pillow over the girl's face until the blind woman leaves. When he finds that he has smothered her, his complete hysteria is symptomatic of the conditioning he has received—that to be caught in a white woman's bedroom is the ultimate crime. He frantically burns the girl's body in the furnace he tends.

Gradually he breaks down from guilt under the goading of an alert reporter who needles him into shaking down the ashes of the furnace. Bigger escapes and hides out in a deserted warehouse with his sweetheart. But her arrival brings the police and he almost kills her in fury. At last, he is captured, and the trial scene is a stirring indictment of a society that permits a Bigger Thomas to grow up hostile to whites, frustrated and fearful, needing only the most accidental of situations to permit an eruption of dangerously dammed up impulses. In a touching scene with his lawyer as he awaits his execution Bigger explains how he felt after killing the girl:

I was my own man then, I was free. Maybe it was 'cause they was after my life then. They made me wake up. That made me feel high and powerful—free! That day and night after I done kill her—when all of them was looking for me—hunting me—that day and night for the first time I felt like a man. (Shouting) I was a man!

The defense attorney sums up to the jury the authors' socio-psychological insight into the mechanism of conversion:

With one part of his mind, he believed what we taught him—that he was a free man! With the other he found him-self denied the right to accept that truth. In theory he was stimulated by every token around him to aspire to be a free individual. And in practise by every method of our social system, he was frustrated in that aspiration. Out of this con-fusion, fear was born. And fear breeds hate, and hate breeds guilt, and guilt in turn breeds the urge to destroy—to kill.

Native Son made for stirring theatre, based on the fusion of psychoanalytic and sociological insights. Since then, however, Paul Green has not pursued documentary naturalism any further, but turned to another of his early and life-long interests, the symphonic music-drama. In 1934 he had written *Roll Sweet Chariot*, a sym-phonic drama of the Negro race, and with the gathering of war-clouds in Europe, Green returned to the pageant form. In 1937 his first epic drama of American history, *The Lost Colony* was pre-sented at Manteo, North Carolina, with the cooperation of the Fed-eral Theatre Project. In subsequent years Green has continued his interest in outdoor, regional productions in which drama, music, dance and poetry become a civic celebration, until they now include: *The Highland Call* (Fayetteville, North Carolina), *Faith of Our Fathers* (Washington, D. C.) and *The Common Glory* (Williamsburg, Virginia). His loss to Broadway has meant the enrichment of the areas in which he has worked. Whether his material has been his-torical epic or fresh observation of rural Americana, Green's feeling for his people is honest and compassionate. Without systematic or orthodox application of Freudian *motifs*, Green wrote what he knew of human ambivalence and man's dream of freedom from repression —whether racial, economic, sexual or religious. Unless he returns to Broadway, theatre-goers may remember him best for *The Field God*, *In Abraham's Bosom*, *Johnny Johnson* and the one-acts, but *Tread the Green Grass* retains its special significance as one of the most imaginative distillations of Freudian psychology in the drama.

CHAPTER XI

Drawing Room Freudians—
Behrman, Osborn, Raphaelson

☆ ☆ ☆ ☆

S. N. BEHRMAN

Samuel Nathaniel Behrman's contribution to the psychoanalytic drama ranks in importance with that of O'Neill and Barry. Although he consistently employs the comedy of manners form rather than expressionism, Behrman possesses a mature awareness of the complexity of unconscious motivation and has been able to reflect this in a number of timely and delightful plays.

Behrman's mastery of psychology is no accident. He attended Clark University, Worcester, Massachusetts between 1912 and 1914 and majored in psychology. Sigmund Freud had made his influential trip to Worcester for a series of lectures in 1909. Behrman wrote the present author that he had heard much about Freud from the head of the psychology department, ". . . his personality, the aura which emanated from him, his effect on his listeners and on his colleagues." Behrman also told of sitting at the feet of Dr. G. Stanley Hall, President Emeritus of Clark, who had invited Freud to America:

> I read Hall's 'Adolescence' and he was very patient (I blush to think how I pestered him) when I bombarded him with questions about Freud.

322

Behrman was then at work on a book of reminiscences in which he hoped to include these impressions of Freud in America.

Although he has not been psychoanalyzed, Behrman wrote that he has many friends in the profession:

> I have lived (as one can scarcely fail to do nowadays) in an atmosphere where most of my friends were undergoing psychoanalysis, and I have had long and exhaustive talks with practitioners. It was not that I was consciously trying to gain information. It was merely that impulses which I have felt stirring since childhood demanded elucidation. I feel that whatever you may discover in my work of a psychological nature is not due to constant study but to introspection!

After a course with George Pierce Baker and an M.A. at Columbia, Behrman first achieved success on Broadway with *The Second Man* (1927). Several years before O'Neill's *Days Without End, The Second Man* dealt with an *alter ego*, a secondary or inner self—although not developed as visually as O'Neill was to do with John Loving. Establishing his smart drawing room comedy style, Behrman depicts a young writer, Clark Storey, who is loved by two women—a wealthy widow and a vivacious twenty year old, Monica, described as "really an innocent. A Tennysonian *ingénue* with a Freudian patter." Even as he makes love to Monica, he confesses that there is a second man within him that mocks his ideal of love and urges him to marry for money:

> Storey: There's someone else inside me—a second man—a cynical, odious person, who keeps watching me, who keeps listening to what I say, grinning and sophisticated, horrid . . . He never lets me be—this other man . . . Even now he's looking at me. He's mocking me. He's saying: 'You damn fool, talking nonsense to this girl— pretending you want her above everything . . .'

The cynical *super-ego*—a defense mechanism against the fear of disillusionment—wins out, and Storey marries the rich widow at the end of this polished comedy of the duality of man and the ambivalence of self-esteem and self-derogation.

Behrman's brilliance in depicting the manners of high society was first crystallized in an adaptation of Enid Bagnold's novel, *Serena Blandish* (1929), which is as near to a Restoration comedy as has been written since the close of that period. Serena is a calculating adventuress who rises in London society by her physical attraction and shrewdness. Like Storey, she would like to combine wealth and sexual satisfaction in her marriage, but when she cannot, she reverses Storey's decision and runs off to be the mistress of a fellow-fortune-hunter rather than the wife of a rich old man.

Just before the stock market crash ended an era of aggression in business, Behrman wrote a study of the superiority complex, *Meteor* (1929). His powerful character of Raphael Lord believes himself destined for big things, in contrast to his good friend, Douglas, who lacks self-confidence. Raphael wants to marry Douglas' sister, Ann, and ruthlessly disposes of her other suitor. He floats a big oil development in Latin America, fomenting a minor revolution there to further his ends and calling upon the U.S. Marines to protect his interests. He confesses to his wife that psychological pressures have made him the egocentric genius that he is—his poverty-stricken youth in the slums and his contempt for weaklings and those who endure their environment. Lord's confidence in himself is based upon an uncanny sixth sense of foreseeing the future—an almost auto-hypnotic belief in his own powers. Once this fails him and a rival syndicate breaks him. Ann hopes now that he will admit his fallibility and grow humble, but he is unregenerate at the end even though she leaves him. As a study of a self-made man, *Meteor* is perhaps less compelling than Lawson's *Success Story* but it does reveal considerable insight into the compensatory nature of the aggression drive.

With *Brief Moment* (1931), Behrman began a series of thoughtful comedies of American manners in which the characters are wise in the terminology of Freud and sophisticated in their understanding of human motives—others' if not their own. *Brief Moment* is a study of an ineffectual, passive-dependent playboy son of a millionaire father. Rod is a dilettante in the arts and is inseparable from his fat, Rabelasian friend, Sigrift, played by (and very likely modelled after) Alexander Woollcott. Rod falls desperately in love with Abby Fane, a torch singer in a night club, the owner of which has assumed the role of father-image to Abby and says, "I think most everything a man does he has some little girl in the back of his mind. Don't you?"

Rod understands that his feeling of being "highly dispensable" was caused by his overbearing father who demanded too early in life that Rod prove himself. After he marries Abby his sense of inferiority grows even worse as Abby begins to excel him. She quickly takes to drawing room society and gives large dinner parties for the celebrities, including eminent psychoanalysts, one of whom Rod overhears ". . . talking to Abby—on the dance floor, mind you—about bed-wetting and thumb-sucking in infants." Sigrift advises Rod to see the psychoanalyst: "He'll tell you in sixty lessons. Wonderful discovery, psychoanalysis! Makes quite simple people feel they're complex."

Abby's former lover returns and would renew their affair. Rod's passivity blocks him from jealousy and he laments to Sigrift, "My indignation vanishes. My hate simmers down. That's abnormal, isn't it, to feel like that?" Like Odets' heroine in *Clash by Night*, Abby is so disappointed in Rod's inability to make a fight for her that she does go off with her old lover as revenge on her weakling husband. This proves the trauma that awakens Rod. When Abby returns unhappily, she finds him sure of himself and self-reliant for the first time:

Abby: Roderick Deane, what's come over you?
Rod: Maturity.

Rod has come to see that his marriage failed because "it was based on a false assumption, that one can derive from some one else a strength that one hasn't oneself." Abby finds new respect for him and a new and workable marriage begins.

In his next play, Behrman introduces a character for whom he shows a rather special insight. Since the depression the young meteors like Raphael Lord could no longer take the business world by storm, and instead turned to political radicalism and personal bitterness. Such a young man Behrman dissects with masterful perception in *Biography* (1932). He thrusts the cynical, hostile young intellectual, Richard Kurt, into a world totally different from his own, one centering around Marion Froude, a charming and impulsively generous person who has found fulfillment. She has been all over Europe, has painted portraits of many celebrities, and has had many affairs. She is writing her biography for the magazine of which Kurt is editor when an old sweetheart, Bunny Nolan, comes to have his portrait painted. When he hears of the forthcoming autobiography, he tries to prevent its publication, as he is running for Senator with the backing of a powerful publisher, Kinnicott, and would have his spotless reputation damaged if it were known he had philandered with Marion. But Marion assures him that he wasn't the first: "I suspected in myself a—a tendency to explore, a spiritual and physical wanderlust that I knew would horrify you once you found it out." She is reluctant to give up her biography, the writing of which is proving a catharsis for her in the Freudian sense:

One is perpertually reborn, I think, Dickie. Everyone should write one's life, I think—but not for publication. For oneself. A kind of spiritual Spring-cleaning.

When Kinnicott comes to force Marion to suppress her story, he ends up with a date to dine with her, while his daughter, Slade, an unhappy rich girl, breaks up with Bunny.

It is Kurt, however, who is the most complex character. He is immediately belligerent to Bunny for being patronizing to Marion: "When a man starts worrying out loud about unprotected women you may know he's a hypocritical sensualist." Uncompromising and unwilling to see two sides to a question, Kurt is on the defense against Marion's probing. She is forced to justify him to Feydie, an old European composer-friend of hers on his way to Hollywood:

> Marion: Underneath his arrogance I suspect he's very uncertain.
> Feydak: Oh, now, don't tell me he has an inferiority complex!
> Marion: Well, I think he has!
> Feydak: This new psychology is very confusing. In my simple day you said: 'That young man is bumptious and insufferable' and you dismissed him. Now you say: 'He has an inferiority complex' and you encourage him to be more bumptious and more insufferable. It's very confusing.

Kurt passionately hates Marion's charming detachment from the burning socio-political issues that arouse him. She finally draws out of him the admission that he had to watch his father beaten to death by the militia during a strike riot. After unburdening himself, Kurt is in Marion's arms at last, lonely and disarmed, as she murmurs, "Dickie—Dickie—Dickie—Why have you been afraid to love me?"

Their love is tempestuous, however, and Kurt is disappointed that Marion wins Kinnicott over rather than fight with him. Marion suspects him of a martyr complex and a paranoid wish to be a dictator:

> Marion: You know, Dickie, I adore you and I'm touched by you and I love you but I'd hate to live in a country where you were Dictator. It would be all right while you loved me but when you stopped. . . .
> Kurt: It wouldn't make any difference if I stopped—I shouldn't be that kind of a Dictator. . . .
> Marion: I see you've thought of it. . . .

Bunny comes back ready to tell off his prospective father-in-law, and to marry Marion, but she sends him away and burns her biography rather than cause people pain. She must also break with Kurt, whom she loves, saying: "Studying you, I can see why so many movements against injustice become such absolute—tyrannies." He cannot forgive her that she has so deftly stripped him of his defense mechanisms, and he parts with her furiously, telling her what it is he has learned from her:

> Why the injustice and the cruelty go on—year after year—century after century—without change—because—as they grow older—people become—*tolerant!* Things amuse them. I hate you and your tolerance. I always did.

Marion has dismissed all three of her prospective suitors but with her capacity for finding happiness she is anything but a lonely figure at the final curtain. A telegram comes from Feydie in Hollywood with the offer of a job, and she is off for the coast.

Biography is a devastating portrait of the dedicated mentality, with its inner necessity to hate deriving from childhood feelings of frustration and inadequacy. During the thirties Marxians often accused Freudians of teaching the individual to adjust to the world as it is rather than to remake it. In his original way, Behrman dramatizes that dichotomy without ridiculing the impulse to make the world better. He merely depicts a woman so generous in her love for humanity and so at peace with herself that she could never accept a humorless "movement" which required blinking at the means for the ultimate end. She understands that much of the fervor expended in the radical movement derives from unconscious pressures of martyrdom and inferiority as well as conscious ideology. *Biography* is perhaps Behrman's finest play and one of the most provocative attempts to apply psychoanalysis to the understanding of the temper of the frustrated thirties and the types it produced. It represents the maturing of the psychoanalytic drama, a second phase in which literal Freudianism has been superceded by post-Freudian insight into psycho-social dynamics.

As conditions grew more grim in Nazi Germany, Behrman began to examine with more sober awareness the forces making for intolerance and fanaticism. Although *Rain from Heaven* (1934) retains the charming banter of poised people, there are more serious implications in the collection of characters Behrman has assembled in Lady Lael Wyngate's British drawing room. From this distance Behrman makes some pertinent observations about neo-Fascism in the United States. Among Lady Lael's guests are Hobart Eldridge and his younger brother, Rand; the former is an American Fascist business man who would organize a Youth for Fascism League; the latter is an explorer hero returned from Polar regions. Another house guest is a German music critic, Hugo Willens, who had to leave Berlin because he was partly Jewish; disillusioned because a great playwright (such as Hauptmann) went over to the Nazis, he has written a pamphlet championing the Jews:

Hugo: I began to ask myself whether subconsciously, I hadn't written the pamphlet to defend my antecedents.
Lael: But—how absurd! Really, do you have to go Freud to explain an act of simple humanity? You wrote the pamphlet because you are a generous human being. Don't you think—don't you really think—that the subconscious has been done to death and that it's high time someone rediscovered the conscious?

Rand and Hobart of course find Hugo objectionable, particularly because they know he is in love with Lady Lael and they suspect (wrongly) that she is his mistress. Rand, the "clean-cut American hero type," is soon revealed as a sexually obsessed and desperately frustrated man. He is driven by morbid curiosity to know if Lael has had affairs. He is under the influence of his older brother whom he fears, and feels so guilty that he cannot bear praise. He recalls that when he was being paraded as a hero in New York, a childhood memory returned to him of sneaking out, climbing a mountain, and being spanked severely for it when he returned—only to be feted now for following the same impulse. Rand destroys Lael's love for him when in an outburst of jealousy he calls Hugo a "dirty Jew."

Trying to justify himself, Hobart has a maudlin drunk scene in which he tells how money was his only compensation for all the things he has missed in life—including a faithful and loving wife. As he grows amusingly tearful for the plight of the poor capitalists, Lael realizes that his hostility toward Jews is not simple hatred:

Lael: He doesn't hate you. He's afraid of you. Suspicion and fear. They're suffocating the world.
Hugo: How're you going to get rid of them? Through some cosmic psycho-analysis?
Lael: Through understanding.

Although Hugo calls her humanism ". . . A self-hypnosis. A wish-fulfillment," he, too, behaves as if he believes it; for he gives up his newly found love for Lael and returns to Germany to fight in the underground. Lael sends Rand out of her life, knowing that his utter intolerance stands between them; even Rand has realized this although he doesn't see the unconscious basis of his prejudices:

Rand: I know now, Lael—whether he goes or stays—there's some awful fence in my mind and in my spirit, and you're on the other side, and no matter what I do I'll never be able to break through to you—never.
Lael: We're all shut in behind our little fences, Rand——

CURTAIN

Behrman has struck upon a vivid image for the psychological conception of reaction-formation and the insulation of the mind against threatening ideas. The little fences which create hatred between peoples are the unconscious fears, suspicions and insecurities which derive from denied and converted emotional energy. Compensation is the illuminating principle as it is in many of the other plays of Behrman.

Social historians studying the temper and mood of the American mid-thirties will find a valuable transcript in *Rain From Heaven* and Behrman's companion piece, *End of Summer* (1936). The two comedies are similar in that they compress a number of the significant types of the times in a drawing room situation and permit them to express themselves with eloquence and wit. Lady Lael's counterpart in *End of Summer* is an American hostess, Leonie Frothingham, more charmingly helpless and guileless than the astute Lady Wyngate. Leonie's houseguests include two young radicals just out of college and unable to find jobs, the son of a famous Russian writer who is writing his father's biography, and a psychoanalyst, Dr. Kenneth Rice, who was invited to help the Russian. Dr. Rice soon discerns that Boris is not writing any biography at all and that he does not worship his father's memory as the world believes, but hates him with a fierce Oedipal jealousy. Rice calls Boris' difficulty "Shadow Neurosis," a sensation of existing only in someone else's shadow, and advises him to go ahead and write the book truthfully to purge himself (as did Marion Froude). He also advises Leonie not to marry Boris as again he would feel himself in another's shadow.

Dr. Rice's ambition is to have a clinic of his own, and Leonie offers to buy it for him, falling gaily and giddily in love with him. There is a mocking scene as Dennis, one of the radicals, satirizes psychoanalysis and wonders, "Who analyzed Sig Freud himself? Whom does he tell his repressions to? Why, the poor guy must be lonely as hell!" He goes on to assert that, "We Catholics anticipated both Marx and Freud by a little matter of nineteen centuries . . . As for Dr. Rice, he offers confession without absolution. He is inadequate." Even Leonie's mother has misgivings about Dr. Rice, conceding that psychoanalysis may have behind it a profound and healing truth yet wondering how one may evaluate a particular doctor and thereby recognize "where his knowledge ends and his pretensions begin."

The plot of *End of Summer* centers around these pretensions of Dr. Rice. Raised in a foundling home, he had searched through the encyclopedia for the names of famous bastards with whom he could identify. Now his compensation is to make money as fast as he can, proclaiming glibly, "The poor have tonsils but only the rich have souls." He is soon infatuated with Paula, the daughter of Leonie, who loves one of the radical boys and is herself a new convert to the movement. Paula accepts Rice's love only on condition he make a clean break with Leonie. This he cruelly does when Leonie comes romantically floating in wearing her mother's wedding dress. Leonie is crushed, but Paula reveals that she did it only to show up Rice for his duplicity. Although he tries to recover Leonie's affection, she, too, is through with him and sends him away. Paula was, he concedes as he beats a humiliating retreat, his last miscalculation. As all the houseguests leave at the end of summer, there is a pervading, Chekhovian sadness. Her daughter marries and Leonie is left with her last remaining friend, Dennis, who gets her to invest her money in his radical magazine.

Behrman stated in his letter to the present author that he received a flood of correspondence, much of it angry, because he made the character of Dr. Rice a "charlatan psychoanalyst."

> I certainly did not want to throw away the baby with the bath; it merely suited my dramatic purposes to have a pseudo instead of a genuine psychoanalyst in this particular play. But I remember with pleasure that a very distinguished psychiatrist, Dr. Mayer, was all on my side, and felt there was a need to indicate the danger of not fully qualified 'healers' in practise. He made my play the subject of an official talk before the Psychiatric Association and sent me the pamphlet of his remarks.

There was no danger of throwing away the baby with the bath; for Behrman had drawn too heavily upon psychoanalysis for it to be discredited along with Dr. Rice. Its wisdom transcends its practitioners—who are not entirely immune from the same unconscious pressures as their patients.

Little of Behrman's more recent work has equalled the brilliance of *Biography, Rain from Heaven* and *End of Summer*. In *Wine of Choice* (1938) he dips deeper into the psychology of the radical mind. The Communist, Chris, is a hard-hitting writer of sociological fiction which is "well dipped in Freud." The play revolves around a stunning model named Wilda who is being turned into a movie star by Ryder, her loving admirer, a super-patriot running for Senator. She is struggling hard to find herself and to think out her mixed-up emotions after a disastrous marriage, an affair with Ryder, and a growing love for Chris. Watching a screen test of herself, she feels that to each of these men she is a different woman: "I've always instinctively reflected what people wanted me to be . . . I myself have never been anything—not really."

The rotund Woollcottian character first introduced in *Brief Moment* recurs in *Wine of Choice* and has the role of the somewhat sardonic but always psychoanalytically perceptive *raisonneur*. He is not the only analyst in the cast, however; when Chris rejects Wilda's offer to go away with him, Ryder proceeds to dissect Chris:

> Nothing about you is so horrifying to me as your rejection of Wilda. You love her but you deny her because she won't fit into your scheme. You are locked deep in the cold fastnesses of theory—on that surface nothing can take hold, nothing can take root, nothing can flower—neither love nor friendship nor affection. I see now how people like you can condemn to death their best friends—because equally well you can condemn yourselves to lovelessness, to abnegation, to death.

Recent psychoanalysts have paralleled Behrman's insight into the radical psychology, with its strong components of unconscious sadomasochism, the impulse to torture, flagellation and martyrdom. Yet, in spite of its psychology, *Wine of Choice* is a discursive and rambling play, without the humor or ingratiatingly human set of characters that distinguish Behrman at his best.

No play of the late thirties better reflects the impotence of the liberal movement at the ascendancy of Hitler and the inevitability of war than Behrman's *No Time For Comedy* (1939), which makes up for all that *Wine of Choice* lacks in warmth and plot interest while retaining its depth of psychological awareness. Gay Esterbrook is a lightweight playwright who faces what Edmund Bergler has named "writer's block"; although he wishes he could come to grips with the political world around him, he cannot. His obsession to create an important contemporary play comes from his new love, Amandah, who gives him the uncritical admiration which he does not get from his wife, Linda, a famous actress. Learning that Gay is working on a socially significant play about Spain, Linda confronts her rival, saying: "Sleep with him if you like but for pity's sake don't ruin his style."

Behrman's affection for Freud is indicated by an anecdote related by Linda:

> I was told a charming story the other day about Sigmund Freud in Vienna. An old man, eighty-two and mortally ill. One afternoon people walked into his little apartment and

cleared it out—money, gold and silver ornaments, passports, bank-books, everything. When they left he turned to his family and said: 'Well, those fellows earned more in this one visit than I make in a year of fees!'

The motives of this triangle are anything but simple. Linda has a powerful hold over Gay, a kind of "unconscious censorship" which she exerts so that even when he is seducing another woman she becomes his "second man," and he hears ". . . her silent laughter reducing my ardor to platitude." In the end, Linda persuades him that his play on Spain represents a running away from himself and the things that he can write best—besides, it has no role in it for her. He stays with her and writes a play about two women, one of whom massages a man's ego and the other of whom is critical and makes him exert himself. Gay has learned: "Perhaps one expresses oneself in spite of oneself. One manages to—your unconscious forces you to. One's expression, I imagine, is what one is—no more, no less."

Katherine Cornell as Linda in *No Time For Comedy* was one of the parade of leading ladies who have appeared in the Behrman comedies—Jane Cowl, Ina Claire and Lynn Fontanne. After endearing herself in *End of Summer,* Ina Claire returned to the stage in Behrman's *The Talley Method* (1941), playing Enid Fuller, a spinster engaged to a distinguished surgeon, Dr. Talley, whose sublimation is in surgery and who is too busy to understand his two children: Avis, a beautiful and left-wing minded young girl who is active in the American Youth Congress which had been so boisterous in front of the White House, and Philip, a weakling who flunked out of medical school because he couldn't stand corpses and who has been a great disappointment to his father who comes from a long line of doctors. Philip is in love with a Greenwich Village strip teaser, and Avis with an older man, an Austrian refugee, named Manfred Geist. Enid tries to win over the two youngsters, as well as a cynical and flip young radical named Cy Blodgett. Through Avis, Behrman makes an effective statement of the motives of the young left-wing generation who scorn their parents' ideals and displace Oedipal hostility into contempt for the world's values: if they can't win their father's love they can at least strike back and hurt him. Radicalism is thus seen as a converted defiance of father-authoritarianism.

Enid convinces Dr. Talley that he is an inadequate father, and in two pathetic scenes Dr. Talley tries to mend his ways, but he cannot communicate with his children on their terms. He ends up fighting with them both. Manfred, meanwhile, has fallen in love with Enid and when she discourages him, he commits suicide. Philip agrees to return to medical school, for his father's approval means more to him than anything else. By then, however, Dr. Talley has revealed his own emotional impoverishment and coldbloodedness, and Enid breaks her engagement—though leaving in the best *Doll's House* tradition with the door on the latch for a "major operation" which would reform Dr. Talley. *The Talley Method* is the method of denial of basic life responses and ascetic sublimation in discipline and career. The Behrman method is a frank acceptance of human needs and a search for fulfillment—lest a nation's mental and political health be jeopardized when too many people displace and disguise their drives. A people secure against warped feelings of hostility would be in no danger of succumbing to Fascist or Communist propaganda.

The Lunts, who first played Behrman in *The Second Man* and later in his adaptation, *Amphitryon 38*, returned in his next play, *The Pirate*, which was an adaptation of Ludwig Fulda's *Die Seerauber*. In an otherwise conventional romantic comedy of 19th century life, Behrman spoofs with his psychoanalytic-minded audience and lets his characters speak in anachronisms such as: "I have no inferiority complex, Trillo. . . ." Serafin, a dashing mountebank, arrives at a little town, recognizes the town's leading benefactor, censor and richest citizen as a retired pirate, Estramudo, and falls in love with his young wife, Manuella, who although technically faithful, lives in a fantasy world of erotic wish-fulfillment. Serafin must resort to Mesmerism to win Manuella, and asks her under hypnosis to name the one she most wishes for—reminiscent of Schnitzler's *Anatol;* Manuella says, "I am not a pure soul. I am an unhappy love-starved woman. You can't be pure when you're frustrated." Her silly mother giggles back, "It's even hard when you're not frustrated." In the end Serafin gets the girl and has Estramudo recognized as the pirate and arrested.

The Pirate was Behrman's first play of the war years, apparently a time for comedy. But Behrman's reaction to the war also produced *Jacobowsky and The Colonel* in collaboration with Franz Werfel, in which a humble Jewish refugee and a haughty Polish officer are placed in juxtaposition as the Nazis pursue them, with the resultant humanizing of the officer. Since the war, Behrman has done two adaptations, neither of them notable nor conspicuously Freudian: *Jane*, from a Somerset Maugham story, and a vehicle for the Lunts entitled *I Know My Love* (Marcel Achard's *Aupres de ma blonde*), which although lightweight, plays some amusing tricks upon a family chronology by showing first the old grandfather of the clan retaining such an authoritarian hold that his son at fifty is still a

frustrated underling, while we later see in flash-back that the grandfather also began as a frustrated underdog of his wife's proud family.

Of Behrman's post-war plays his most psychoanalytic is *Dunnigan's Daughter* (1945). His leading character, evolved from *Meteor*
through *Biography* and *Rain from Heaven*, becomes Clay, a modern
robber-baron, a Fascist-minded American entrepreneur living in
Mexico and getting rich through exploitation of Mexican resources.
He is married to his third wife, Ferne, young enough to be his
daughter, but who is the daughter of Dunnigan, who died in prison
—framed by Clay and his father. Clay's own daughter by a previous
marriage is Zelda, who has the most serious father-fixation since
Lavinia Mannon. She is willing to sleep with Jim Baird, a diplomat
from the U.S. State Department, but she cannot bring herself to
marry him because, as she says, "Dad made him seem ridiculous.
Somehow he manages to do that with every man I get interested in."
Also staying at Clay's home is a Mexican painter, Miguel Riachi, who
is a colorful figure of whom Zelda says:

> Zelda: Always asking you pointed questions. He psycho-
> analyzes you without making you lie down.
> Jim: Well, don't give up hope—that will come later.

Ferne confides to Jim her frustration at being treated by Clay only
as an exquisite possession:

> Did you ever have a horrid dream of trying to climb a
> mountain with a shining, slippery surface—and you can't get
> a foothold? You keep slipping back all the time. Well, that's
> how I am. How is it with you?

Jim is discouraged by the ruthlessness of American exploiters who
create so much ill-will for the United States in Mexico, but Ferne
encourages him not to resign, confessing she really wishes Jim would
defeat Clay if only to humble him a little.

In a scene of original power, Clay sits at the piano improvising
arpeggios as Ferne tries to dig to the bottom of his emotions. With
ironic musical punctuation, he states his philosophy that two emotions more powerful than love are acquisitiveness and revenge.
Ferne sees that fear is at the root of his aggressiveness and his
Fascistic belief that to the ruthless belong the spoils. Fear of losing
a possession like Ferne causes Clay to get drunk and to make cutting
remarks to her, saying he'd be amused if she had an affair. This
suggestion arouses him to sudden passion and he tries to kiss his
wife fiercely. When she resists, he says, "For a girl whose father died
in jail you're awful proud." For this Ferne decides to leave him.

To hold her he sadistically denies money as his last string over her, but when that fails, he breaks down and whimpers, pleading with her not to leave him. For the first time Ferne sees him humanized and almost weakens. Miguel knows that "this man is tortured."

> Ferne: Why must he torture other people?
> Miguel: Because it is impossible to suffer in a vacuum—The trouble with the world is caused not by happy people but by frustrate people. There are, unfortunate, very few happy people.
> Ferne: What do you suggest we do—psychoanalyze the world?
> Miguel: It would be cheaper than destroying it.
> Ferne: Perhaps we economize on the wrong things.
> Miguel: Nevertheless this Freud, I think, is closer to the truth, much, than this Karl Marx.

Both the daughter and the wife desert Clay in the end, finding they must leave him to assert their own individuality. Jim helps Ferne to make the break, telling her that it was Clay who caused her father, Dunnigan, to commit suicide in prison. Clay has thus married the daughter of the man his father hated in order unconsciously to spite his pious tyrant of a father. Miguel had expressed the author's psychoanalytic wisdom when he comments upon all these disguised motives: "All the miscalled loves—the loves that masquerade pity, that masquerade gratitude, that masquerade revenge."

Dunnigan's Daughter is one of Behrman's least satisfying plays, as though his brilliant perception of unconscious motives had matured beyond his dramaturgic skill in handling such epic material—which includes a revolt of the peasants against Clay, Jim's effort to win the State Department to see Clay's insidiousness, and the whole episode of Dunnigan in prison for crimes Clay's father instigated—which according to the title should have assumed greater importance. Nor is it clear how Zelda is able to break so easily with her father and leave him without any inner misgivings when he is in trouble—merely because Ferne sets the example. But there is much sophisticated banter in Behrman's best style while his characters are whistling in the dark. As with Philip Barry, wit and charm become defense mechanisms against emotional chaos.

Behrman's work has been a rather profound catalogue of the devious ways in which the motives of the "frustrate people" referred to in *Dunnigan's Daughter* are disguised and displaced: fear of failure is converted into the defense mechanism of cynicism in *The Second Man;* the superiority complex is seen as a compensatory drive in *Meteor* and to a lesser extent in *Dunnigan's Daughter;* an over-bearing father causes the son's inadequacy in *Brief Moment, End of Summer, No Time for Comedy, I Know My Love* and *The Talley Method;* Behrman explores the psychology of the contemporary American radical with considerable perception in *Biography, End of Summer, Wine of Choice* and *The Talley Method,* showing the conversion of paternal hostility and inferiority feelings into rigid, masochistic denial and displaced fervor for overthrowing political authority; Neo-Fascism in America comes in for Behrman's scrutiny in *Rain from Heaven* and *The Talley Method* and he finds that the anti-semite and the hater in general is "sex-ridden," shut in behind the little fences of fear and insecurity; in *Brief Moment, No Time for Comedy* and *I Know My Love* infidelity serves the disguised purpose of breaking the hold which the wife has upon the husband and permitting him to assert his individuality.

Behrman thus typifies the post-Freudian playwrights of the thirties who directed their psychoanalytically sharpened observations away from the individual in isolation and toward the socio-centered problems of Fascism, radicalism, racial intolerance and greed, which are best understood in terms of the unconscious pressures causing them. Behrman's compassion for humanity and his generosity toward human foible keep his work from ever becoming didactic. His deft sense of comedy banter makes his characters ingratiating and refreshing. Yet nothing could do Behrman a greater injustice than to dismiss him as a writer of surface comedies of manners. True, his characters tend to verbalize rather than solve their conflicts in action. But it is brilliant verbalization and consistently psychoanalytic in its wisdom—although Behrman has as little use for the dedicated, unquestioning acceptance of Freudian dogma as he has for the other "isms." His wistful, civilized evocations of the tragi-comic in the human drama—even during the thirties and forties when other writers were apt to see only despair—is Behrman's greatness as a writer. Kurt, in *Biography,* aptly summarizes the understanding which pervades Behrman's work: ". . . as they grow older—people become tolerant! Things amuse them. . . ."

PAUL OSBORN

Like Behrman, Paul Osborn studied playwriting with George Pierce Baker and with his comedy of manners bridges the gap between the twenties and the fifties, reflecting the mutations in the psychological concepts derived from Freudianism. Osborn's first Broadway play, *Hotbed* (1928), introduced what was to be a consistent theme in his work, a dislike for suppression and false modesty concerning sex. It shows a bigoted preacher obsessed with the idea that our colleges are hotbeds of immorality; he hounds a young instructor out of his job only to find that the girl found in his room was the preacher's own daughter.

Although produced in 1930, Osborn's *The Vinegar Tree* is one of the most delightful and typical high comedies which reflect the point of view of the twenties concerning sex and Freud. Laura Merrick (played by Mary Boland) is a scatterbrained matron whose sister is having an affair with Max Lawrence—the man whom Laura loved as a girl and whose memory she has clung to as a wish-fulfillment all these years. Her daughter, Leone, is a high-strung, vivacious modern, bubbling over with Freud and worried for fear that she is *cold*. Her fiancé, Geoffrey, isn't sure he wants to marry her because she is inexperienced in sex. So Leone determines to end her state of virginity in a hurry, and selects Max with whom to experiment. She explains to him:

> Leone: I'm very cold, you see.
> Max: Of course I didn't know.
> Leone: You might have guessed. I'm cold because I'm suppressed.
> Max: Are you—? That's too bad.
> Leone: I think about sex all the time. But I shouldn't. I want to put it in its proper place so that I'll have time to think of other more important things.

Max tells Laura that he wants to elope and Laura coyly assumes that he means with her. When she learns it is her daughter, she exclaims, "Incest—that's what it is. Incest." In the end, Leone is reunited with her young man, Laura makes up with her husband, and Max bows out gracefully. Then Laura remembers that her first love was not Max Lawrence at all but Lawrence Mack.

An even more brilliant comedy of manners in the high style of the Restoration is Osborn's *Oliver Oliver* (1934). Like the hero of *March Hares* and Noel Coward's plays, Oliver is a charmingly rude, passive and utterly feminine young man who cannot bear the thought of work. Constance, his mother, is like Laura, a scatterbrained, giddy creature. As they are penniless, mother and son each urge the other to marry for money—Constance wants him to marry Phyllis, a daughter of her oldest friend (whom she constantly insults as only old friends can), and Oliver wants his mother to marry a wealthy old banker, but objects to the idea of a woman for himself, to which his mother replies:

> Constance: Oh, that's all tommyrot. I've met a great many

more men than you have, Oliver, and I can assure you
there's not *one* of them that isn't after some woman.
Oh, that is—unless he's a——
Judith: A what?
Constance: Oh, you know. Artistic.

After three acts of amusing Freudian banter—Oliver for example
suspects Judith of having a "camel complex" because she is so often
thirsty—it turns out that Oliver and Phyllis are really in love with
each other, which solves both romantic and financial problems.

More recently Osborn has entered upon a period of adaptation
from novels, and has contributed at least three memorable plays
with psychiatric interest. *On Borrowed Time* (1938) from Lawrence
Watkins' novel, uses fantasy to make some fundamental points about
child psychology. When his parents are killed, Pud, a young lad, is
left in the hands of his old Gramps. Gramps is able to stave off Mr.
Brink (Death) by getting him up a tree and not letting him down.
Gramps permits Pud a healthy, unrepressed, spontaneous existence
—hunting rocks, discussing sex freely, swearing a normal amount,
and satisfying his intellectual curiosity. The maid, Marcy, is even
encouraged to bring her fiancé home instead of necking in the park,
because: "How the hell's Pud gonna learn about kissin' if he don't
never see any of it?" Pud wishes that Granny would knit two bumps
on the front of his sweater like Marcy has on hers.

The threat to this pagan, Rousseau-like existence is an old maid
aunt, Demetria, a frustrated, rigid Puritan with a severe reaction-
formation against sex. She would dismiss Marcy, put Pud in a strict
school, and break his fine spirit—for which Pud calls her a "pissmire."
She almost succeeds in having Gramps committed to an asylum because he insists Mr. Brink is still up the tree. Though they finally
are able to scare Demetria off, Pud falls off the fence in trying to
reach the tree, and Mr. Brink has to claim him too. He and Gramps
go off together at the end of this ingratiating Freudian fantasy.

Without a novel as source material, Osborn then went on to
create a highly original play in a psychological pattern. *Morning's
at Seven* (1939) depicts a family of oldsters—the youngest is Homer,
a bachelor of forty who can't bring himself to marry because his
mother takes such good care of him at home. Homer's father, Carl,
has schizophrenic spells, which begin when he says that he wanted
to be a dentist all his life but failed; in a kind of katatonic stupor, he
leans against a tree as if holding it up with his forehead; when the
attacks get severe he loses awareness and cries out, "Where am I?
What's happened to me?"

After being engaged seven years, Homer finally brings Myrtle home to meet his mother, but can't force himself to propose. The mother, in her sixties, cries at the thought of Myrtle buying Homer's underwear after they are married. The plot is largely based on family intrigue concerning a house where Homer and Myrtle might live if they marry; Myrtle finally is able to give Homer courage to propose by announcing she is pregnant. Although *Morning's at Seven* contains fine characterizations and structure, it somehow fails to enlist vigorous empathy with its collection of bland, petty oldsters.

A Bell for Adano (1944), one of the more meaningful plays to come out of the war, applies psychological insight to the understanding of conquered people and their needs. It was followed in 1951 by another adaptation, John P. Marquand's *Point of No Return*. In the manner of Philip Barry, the hero of this play is made to return to the past and relive part of his youth in order to free himself of its hold on him. Charley Gray is wretchedly unsatisfied with his present life as a bank assistant, hoping for a vice-presidency but having to "creep" and lick boots to win it—under pressure from his wife, Nancy. Charley is sent back to his home town on a bank errand and on the train he has a chance to re-evaluate his life and the supine creature he feels he has become.

In contrast with the authentic stream of associations with which Willy Loman returns to his past, Charley's memories are structured into a logical and developing act in which he sees the girl he loved, Jessica, and her possessive, rigidly severe snob of a father, of whom a Freudian-minded anthropologist says, "Her father is in love with her, of course . . . Of course, basically, Jessica is equally in love with him. It's a standard pattern, as old as the first decadent civilization."

The anthropologist friend warns Charley that in primitive tribes a man is severely punished for trying to change his class or violate the taboos; but Charley will not heed him, and keeps trying to win Jessica by making himself acceptable in the eyes of her father. When Charley's father loses his money in Wall Street, Jessica dutifully breaks off her engagement as her father orders.

Back home in the present with his Nancy, Charley does a poor job of "creeping" when they have the boss and his wife for dinner; when he believes he has lost his chance for the vice-presidency, he feels free for the first time. The boss offers it to him anyway, and Charley accepts it only on the condition that he is through "creeping," and will not have to join the boss' country club or do any other little meaningless rituals that do not express himself. By his trip to his past, Charley has learned that he had been striving for acceptance unconsciously to prove himself in the eyes of Jessica's father, to win compensation for his own feelings of inferiority long after he had gotten over Jessica and married Nancy. Charley is through projecting onto his boss an image of Jessica's father. He has found his own integrity at last. If *Point of No Return* lacks a little of the white heat of emotional searching and followed too pat a structure in its return to the past for psychologically attuned audiences, it nevertheless made a pertinent comment upon an aspect of our society, in which "creeping" is so often more lucrative than self-realization.

Osborn, whose work clearly reveals its kinship with the psychoanalytic movement in drama, stated in his questionnaire that he had read a few books by the Freudians, and that he had sought for devices to dramatize for the audience the workings of the unconscious. His reply to the request for general comment on the influence of Freudianism is as follows:

> I don't know. I feel, in general, a playwright should understand 'Freudianism' instinctively. After all some of the greatest plays were written before Freud. In fact, he may have obtained information from them. Not that 'Freudianism' couldn't help anyone *personally*.

Like Behrman and Raphaelson, Osborn has enriched the drama with sparkling comedies of manners—*The Vinegar Tree* and *Oliver Oliver,* but he has also utilized the fantasy form in *On Borrowed Time* and an almost clinical realism in *Morning's At Seven* to make penetrating psychological observation. The contrast between the self-conscious preoccupation with sex in *The Vinegar Tree* and the mature self-searching in *Point of No Return* illustrates the extent of American drama's assimilation of Freudian psychology within two decades.

SAMSON RAPHAELSON

Comparable in many ways to Behrman, another playwright who knows his Freud, knows his dramatic craftsmanship and is able to bring the two together in ways that are authentic, subtle and original is Samson Raphaelson. He stated in his questionnaire that he had read a large number of psychoanalytic books, "much of Freud," as well as the collected works of Stekel and some by Jung and Adler. He had once or twice, he stated, discussed his plots or characters with a psychoanalyst, and was aware of searching for dramatic devices to dramatize for the audience the workings of the unconscious. He believes that almost all of Freud's theories were influential upon his work, and named *Hilda Crane, The Perfect Marriage, Jason* and *Accent on Youth* as plays of his which contained Freudian influence. Raphaelson eloquently expressed his point of view as to the significance of Freudianism for the writer:

> Very valuable to learn and forget; and write about people as the mysteries they still are, creatures to be described with wonder and humility and analyzed hardly at all.

Raphaelson made his Broadway debut with *The Jazz Singer* (1925), a vehicle for George Jessel which dramatized the conflict in the son of an orthodox Jewish Cantor between his desire to be a jazz singer and his father's ambition for him to be a Cantor. When his father is dying, the boy leaves a musical show and returns to the religious fold. The same theme of "Be true to your origins" was restated in a later Raphaelson play, *White Man* (1936), which showed the tragedy of a man with Negro blood who attempted to conceal it from his white wife.

Raphaelson's first psychoanalytic play, however, was *Young Love* (1928), which, in contrast with all the superficial "flapper plays," is one of the most tender and intimate explorations of the emotions of the flapper generation faced with a conflict between idealism and skepticism toward the sanctity of marriage. Fay and David are young lovers who have just spent their first night together. David is going away and wants Fay to marry him, but she is haunted by an inner fear of her own ability to be faithful in marriage because of the divorce of her parents when she was ten, a divorce which "did a lot of things" to her.

Among the things it did were to give her an unconscious compulsion to destroy love as her parents did—destroy it before the infidelity of the one she loves can destroy her. (The same theme was treated by O'Neill in *Welded* and *Days Without End*.) Before she dares marry David, Fay feels that she must test their love. Nancy and Peter Bird, a delightful couple, who apparently have been happily married for ten years offer the opportunity, and Fay decides to have an affair with Peter and to encourage David to do the same with Nancy—to see if their love can survive.

Only Peter and Fay go through with the experiment of changing partners, however. David is so shocked at Nancy's sensuality that he leaves her, but later returns and Fay and David are reunited in a superb scene of erotic sado-masochism:

> David: You're not my equal. You're not even fit to be my slave—or even one of my women.

Fay: I'll gladly be anything for you, David.
David: Gladly? You're never going to be glad again! I'm
    going to use you when I want you, and when I don't
    you're going to sit in a corner.
Fay: That's all I want, David.

As long as Fay had David dangling on a string and had the
power to hurt him, she had used that power. Now, however, the
balance of power is shifted by David's demonstration that his love
was surer than Fay's, and she feels the security of being dominated.
Her punishment has been masochistic humiliation equal to her own
inner sense of guilt, and she goes off happily with David to what
promises to be a cohesive marriage.

Raphaelson has called *Young Love* a "tragifarce" of the young
people of the twenties as he knew them, "free about sex, mentally
avid, spiritually intense, romantic." He writes interestingly in *The
Human Nature of Playwriting* of his own enlarged insight which
came about as a result of the condemnation of *Young Love* in Chicago and Philadelphia by enraged moralists, while Robert Benchley
in New York called it, "a nice, clean little comedy about adultery."
Raphaelson concludes that the prudes could accept *Rain* because it
dealt with a prostitute, but were outraged by *Young Love* because
Fay was "a nice girl," a recognizable daughter of the middle-class
couples who filled the audience. Even worse—Raphaelson had committed the unpardonable sin of letting David and Fay marry and
live happily. The sentimental tradition still required a philandering
heroine to be punished—as in Michael Arlen's British drama, *The
Green Hat*, three years before. *Young Love* might have had a longer
run if it had ended with chastisement for Fay, Raphaelson specu-
lates, but because it did not it remains one of the fine works that have
come out of the psychoanalytic writing of the twenties.

Raphaelson's use of psychoanalytic material might be called
"post-Freudian," in that it is never literal or text-bookish, but gives
the audience credit for more than a little psychoanalytic insight itself. In *Accent on Youth* (1934) he uses the familiar and potentially
trite situation of a young girl in love with an older man, a father-
image. But in Raphaelson's skillful hands the play avoids the obvious
and builds upon a residuum of insight into unconscious motivation.
Linda is the secretary to a famous playwright, Steven Gaye, and in
love with him although he is old enough to be her father. Whatever
the forces were in Linda's childhood relationship to her own father
which make her prefer the company of an older man, Raphaelson
does not dwell upon them; instead he contrasts the older man,
Steven, who is charming and affectionate, with the young man who

loves Linda, and who is a vain, narcissistic, physical-culture-minded simpleton. Steven is about to go on a trip with an old actress flame of his when Linda blurts out her love for him. Raphaelson understandingly probes his tortured misgivings based on the fear of the discrepancy in their ages; and Cyrano-like he coaches the young man, Dickie, how to woo Linda. This he does and Linda marries him. But Dickie proves a most unsatisfactory husband and Raphaelson is again daring in his ending by letting Linda leave Dickie and return to Steven with whom there is a love and rapport that transcends age differences.

Skylark (1939), which was tailored for the talents of Gertrude Lawrence, is a conventional treatment of the problem of a big business man who is in love with his job, who sublimates his affections and "commits adultery with a business." *Jason* (1942), however, is one of the four named by Raphaelson as influenced by Freudian psychology. It proved something of a departure for Raphaelson in that it attempted to satirize a hypothetical writer such as William Saroyan, a brash, blustering poet of the common people. The Saroyan-character, Mike Ambler, walks into the life of a chilly snob, an effete drama critic named Jason Otis, and tries to win him over to a love for the common man in art and life. Jason is newly married to Lisa, and Mike doesn't need long to uncover the fact that their marriage is at a crisis. Lisa has been living a lie, pretending that she is from a refined old Virginia family whereas she is actually a "linthead" from the "poor white trash" of South Carolina whom Ambler would idealize as "the beautiful people." Lisa is deeply perturbed by his play and calls these people vile and sordid, struggling to suppress her own memory of that life. She blurts out to Mike that she saw enough poverty first hand, having run away from a drunken father and a stupidly overworked mother when she was fifteen. She is in Mike's arms soon after she has unburdened.

Jason becomes completely won by Mike (as George Jean Nathan was by Saroyan after *The Time of Your Life*) and gives a party for some of the "common people" whom Mike invites—some amusing types who fail to reflect the spiritual beauty Mike expected to show Jason. Lisa and Mike confront each other again and their attraction for each other is fraught with sado-masochism. She orders him out of the house, and he roughly makes her take off her high heels and go barefoot while he analyzes her. She slaps him and he returns the slap, which arouses her strangely in a sexual way. Lisa is fascinated yet terrified by Mike's perception, and is about to let him kiss or slap her when they are interrupted by the "characters" Mike has invited. Mike suffers while Jason is out reviewing the opening of his new play, and Jason is faced with the necessity of trying to judge Mike's play objectively, knowing he is taking Lisa from him.

Jason first dictates a glowing praise of Mike's play—then when he sees his wife leaving him with Mike changes it to a scathing denunciation of Mike as a phony and a poseur; when he wins Lisa back by being aroused to a new male jealousy, however, he writes a synthesis of the two reviews, appraising Mike as both a genius and a charlatan, part phony and part prophet (which is a fairly discerning evaluation of Saroyan).

Jason reflects Raphaelson's earlier theme of "Be true to yourself —don't deny your past." He does not attempt to psychoanalyze the forces that make a phenomenon such as Saroyan, but creates a full-dimensional figure in Lisa, whose masochistic need for sexual domination resembles Fay's in *Young Love*. Although an unpretentious comedy, *Jason* contains some astute psychological observation.

The Perfect Marriage (1944) proved imperfect as drama, although it was potentially a provocative analysis of marriage. It begins as a couple, Jenny and Dale Williams, celebrate their tenth anniversary with a quiet evening at home. As in *Welded*, the husband is about to carry his wife off to bed when a friend drops in— and he bears his frustration a little more maturely than did O'Neill's hero. But each keeps accusing the other of being bored, each afraid to admit that he is projecting his own boredom onto the partner in the form of extra-solicitous concern for the other. When Dale stifles a yawn in the midst of love-making recriminations begin and by morning Jenny is convinced their love is dead and is ready for a divorce.

There are poignant moments as they tell their daughter, eight, about the impending divorce. She is a sophisticated juvenile who has been raised by modern psychology, and looks forward to the divorce because her friends who are the product of broken homes have told her how the parents vie for the child's affection with extra toys and candy. Dale reads in a book on modern psychology that, "Marriage can thrive on a healthy hostility between the sexes . . .", and he and Jenny are reunited, knowing that "the other man" or "other woman" is more often than not merely a symptom, not a basic cause of marital conflict, and that a perfect marriage must be based on keeping each other intrigued as a sexual partner. But just why Dale and Jenny's marriage will have any better prognosis than before, Raphaelson does not show. The husband and wife seem too trivial to command great respect.

Hilda Crane (1950), on the other hand, is a moving study of a modern woman told with compassionate understanding of defense-mechanisms. Vibrantly in love with life, Hilda has been twice married and divorced by thirty-three—for which she blames the twentieth century, saying half seriously that women must return to a previous century to find security. But Raphaelson in his questionnaire summarized Hilda's dilemma in more psychoanalytic terms: "Mother didn't love husband, hated daughter, father died, daughter (Hilda) morally without anchor."

Hilda returns now to the little college town where her mother lives. She is "on a desert island," having lost her job in New York, and feels suddenly like returning to childhood and putting her head on her mother's lap. She remembers how her father had pushed her as a gifted child and groomed her for a career, wishing now he hadn't. Looking up her old English professor, Charley Jensen, she picks up where they left off eleven years ago, ". . . Freud and Kafka, T. S. Eliot, D. H. Lawrence and Cole Porter . . . I think that's what I came home for."

Henry Ottwell, a substantial business man who has long admired Hilda, comes to ask her to marry him. But Henry is stuffy and under the thumb of his mother, a big, overdressed, and uncouth person whose inspection of Hilda is so brutal that Hilda is ready to return to New York.

The professor has also kept his desire for Hilda during the years she was away and now would make love to her. But there is in him an immature element of sadistic revenge toward Hilda for having rejected him years ago, and his dream all these years has been to sleep with her once to show her what a tragic mistake she made. He does not propose now, fearing Hilda would not be content on a professor's salary and that she would still be promiscuous. He offers her only an evening's affair, and Hilda's dilemma is poignant—wanting emotional security and a decent marriage with Charley she gets only a pass from him but a generous offer of marriage from a man who arouses no desire. She is cornered, and has no choice but to accept Henry, crying to her mother, "I don't think it matters at all that I don't love him." The mother shocks Hilda by replying that she didn't love Hilda's father either. Hilda is in panic—the wild generation of *Young Love* now facing middle age with nothing to cling to. That Hilda's dilemma is a real one for contemporary audiences is indicated by the fact that during the intermission following the act in which Henry listed all of the stocks, bonds and insurance policies he would give Hilda if she married him, more than one woman in the lobby was overheard to say, "I'd take it."

Only the day before the wedding does Charley come to Hilda—but it is too late. Henry's mother has a fierce scene with Hilda, trying

with a combination of Oedipal possessiveness and moral condemnation to make Hilda give up Henry. But Hilda is challenged by this
and now determined to go through with it.

Raphaelson mercifully kills off the mother during the honeymoon, and Hilda and Henry have a child. But like Hilda's nemesis,
her *id* objectified, Charley comes back now to teach summer school,
and their need for each other is undiminished. Hilda goes with
Charley to a little country inn for the night, but after Charley's ardor
is spent, he must hurt her by calling her "a classic figure, a courtesan,"
and Hilda sees flash before her eyes the image of Henry's mother
calling her a whore. Her belief in her own dignity shaken, Hilda returns home, gives her child to her mother to be raised by a wiser
woman, and takes sleeping pills to die. *Hilda Crane* is the tragedy
of two people caught in a life-long passion which neither had the
emotional maturity to consummate—Charley because his own super-
ego was so strong that he could only look on Hilda as beneath him
even while urgently desiring her, and Hilda because she was raised
to be discontent with dependency and unable to find enough love to
balance her unconscious feeling of being unloved. If *Hilda Crane* is
perhaps a woman's play, it is, nonetheless, a persuasive study of the
plight of modern woman. Hilda summarizes her life in the words of
Edna St. Vincent Millay:

> With him for a sire and her for a dam,
> what should I be but just what I am?

Raphaelson depicts women with perhaps greater insight than he
does men, and most of his women have a streak of sado-masochism in
them. But he combines a firm mastery of the theatre with considerable psychoanalytic understanding of the relationship between the
sexes in modern society. *Young Love* and *Hilda Crane*, and to a
lesser extent, *Jason* and *Accent on Youth*, reflect their times with ingratiating humor, honesty and an un-stereotyped application of
Freudian patterns of motivation. If Behrman has a more sparkling
wit, a more polished style and a broader political awareness, and if
Osborn takes advantage of greater freedom in his selection of theatrical forms, Raphaelson brings to the theatre a rich, humane feeling for his people; and all three playwrights have found the drawing
room comedy a flexible vehicle for psychological unmasking.

CHAPTER XII

New Freudian Blood

☆   ☆   ☆   ☆

ARTHUR LAURENTS

As we reach the third generation of psychoanalytic writers, we find
a group of young talents, many of them with wartime service, who
are very much aware of the socio-political pressures in the contemporary world and who are able to interpret them in the light of
unconscious motivation. Subtly and with personally created symbols
they are able to apply psychoanalytic insights to such various problems as race relations, juvenile delinquency, and the American occupation of conquered countries. If there is a difference between the
post-war group and their sociological-minded predecessors in the
thirties, it is the disappearance by now of doctrinaire political
theories to explain the world's troubles, in favor of a psychological
substructure of unconscious conflict within the inter-acting individuals who compose the social and political masses.

One of the most important and promising of the younger playwrights is Arthur Laurents, who comes to the theatre like Arthur
Miller with a background in radio, where he learned to use the flash-
back and stream-of-consciousness techniques to give fluidity and
depth to drama. After a start with the Columbia Workshop and a
number of Army broadcasts including "The Man Behind the Gun"
and "Assignment Home," Laurents won considerable critical attention and a $1,000 grant with his first Broadway play, *Home of the
Brave* (1945).

In his questionnaire, Laurents stated that he has been psycho-analyzed and that his attitude toward characterization and motiva-tion has been thereby affected. He acknowledged the influence of psychoanalysis upon *Home of the Brave,* and indicated that he had read a few books and articles on Freudianism, but preferred not to discuss his plays with a psychoanalyst except in cases where a techni-cal expert was required.

Home of the Brave treats the fears of soldiers in combat, com-plicated by the additional pressure of anti-semitism. Like *The Hasty Heart,* the scene is a hospital base, but unlike Patrick's play the Army here has assigned a psychiatrist to duty with these jumpy, over-wrought troops who have been in the South Pacific two years. The commanding officer, a twenty-six year old Major, too inexperienced to have earned respect, calls for his four best men to land on a Japa-nese-held island and map it for invasion. An arrogant, outspoken anti-semite, T.J., a Jewish boy, Coney, his close friend, Finch, and Sergeant Mingo are the men selected.

When the men return from the Japanese island, Coney has de-veloped amnesia and hysterical paralysis of his legs. The psychiatrist uses narcosynthesis in an effort to help him walk again. The "truth serum," sodium pentathol, is injected and Coney is asked to count backwards from 100 until his sluggish counting indicates the drug has taken effect. Then the psychiatrist questions Coney and uses role-playing, identifying himself with the others on the mission so that Coney can work out the traumatic memories. He reveals that during the mapping of the island under the eyes of the Japanese, T. J. had called him a "lousy yellow Jew bastard." Coney associates this with childhood memories of intolerance that have contributed to his hyper-sensitivity and unconscious feelings of being unwanted and "different." Even his best friend, Finch, who had left the precious map case and had to go back for it, exploded furiously at Coney and then caught himself: "I'm not asking you to stay, you lousy yellow —jerk." From shame at his own mistake, he had unconsciously struck Coney at his most vulnerable point. Then Finch had been shot and had sent Coney back with the maps; Coney later confesses to the captain his guilt feelings at leaving Finch. Waiting to be taken off the island, Coney had heard Finch's screams as the Japanese tortured him. Finally, Finch had crawled back to Coney to die in his arms, after which the sobbing Coney found that he could not walk.

Probing more deeply with the sodium pentathol, the doctor helps Coney trace his "bad feelings" back to a momentary sensation of gladness when Finch was shot after almost calling him a "Jew bastard." Believing that Coney's paralysis can be cured as it was caused—by shock—the doctor suddenly shouts him an order: "You lousy, yellow Jew bastard, get up and walk." The surge of hostility does bring Coney to his feet and the paralysis is broken. After this the doctor discontinues narcosynthesis and uses as psychotherapy discussion and evaluation, trying to help Coney see that he need not feel guilty over the death of Finch; his momentary gladness was the normal and natural reaction which soldiers experience when a buddy falls—a feeling of relief that it was not he. When Mingo confirms this by his own experience, Coney is purged of his guilt and, though shaky, is whole again. Mingo, whose wife had written him a "Dear John" letter and who had lost an arm on the mission, becomes the substitute for Finch. "Coward, take my coward's hand," is the theme for the moving ending as Coney and Mingo help each other back to the States and emotional restoration.

Home of the Brave contains compelling scenes, authentic in their handling of psychotherapy and in the language and character-ization of GI's. Laurents' understanding of the conditioning which makes Jewish children tend to respond to rejection and intolerance by hyper-sensitivity and unconscious guilt feelings is poignantly dramatized. The childhood conditioning and defensive hostilities of the anti-semite, T.J., are less fully developed; but even the guileless Finch, who had said he didn't know what Jews were before the war, in an unguarded moment makes the Freudian slip of responding to the conditioning he had received from T.J., indicating the extent to which individuals under pressure tend to seek a common target for hatred. The film version of *Home of the Brave*, substituting the parallel problem of prejudice against the Negro for that of the Jew proved to be equally powerful as drama and psychological insight. By contrast with *Home of the Brave*, Elsa Shelley's *Foxhole in the Parlor*, earlier the same year, was a contrived and mawkish jumble that included a psychoneurotic veteran, truth serum, compulsive dreams, the world peace movement, and sex.

In his questionnaire, Laurents suggested that while psycho-analytic study might enrich an author's understanding of human mo-tives, there was a great danger of over-simplification, settling for the easy cliché that would resolve evil on the basis of being "unloved in childhood," just as a previous sociological generation of writers ex-plained it on the basis of poverty. Laurents believes that Freud's teaching points to the fact that there are many motives for what ap-pears to be a simple action, and that the playwright should use psy-choanalytic insight to help himself in creating character rather than to expose it directly to the audience.

In his next work, *The Bird Cage* (1950), Laurents seems to have applied this maxim; for the play is a grim, naturalistic picture of the sordid defense mechanisms to which a collection of human beings can be forced. Like Barry in *Here Come the Clowns* and O'Neill in *The Iceman Cometh*, Laurents orchestrates his variations on the theme of frustration in a bar, here called The Bird Cage to symbolize both prison and security for its inmates. They prowl through the back bar of the night club where they work as if it were a jungle where the primitive drives of sex, power, and group "belongingness" are obsessive. Each person has his private illusion or defense mechanism: Wally, the owner is an egomaniac who is blatantly aggressive, uncouth, ruthless, and believes that The Bird Cage is the world and that he is God of it; his partner, Ferdy, is a sweet, gentle, Odetsian character whose child was born deaf and dumb— God's punishment, he believes, for his conniving with Wally to blackmail the previous owner out of his night club. Ferdy's pathetic efforts to clear his conscience and restore his child's hearing by urging Wally to pay back the former owner convince Wally that he is out of touch with reality and he destroys him. When Wally is unable to seduce one of the showgirls, he arranges for his son to be alone with her in his backstage bedroom, that Wally may vicariously enjoy her degradation. But the son is a frightened child and confesses to the girl his hatred for his father. In a charged scene, father and son confront each other; Wally learns that his son is in trouble at school and that the father's money could not buy him friends; like Willy Loman, Wally suffers traumatic shock at the collapse of his one ideal—his son. Although Wally would cling to his club which gives him the satisfaction of having people dependent on him, he is finally forced to sell it and to pay the former owner his just share. Psychotically unable to bear the loss of the club which has become identified with his own ego, he locks himself in and burns down the building.

The Bird Cage is a tough, gamy view of human nature. With all its crudities, it gives promise that Laurents will one day write a masterpiece. Often static and murky in its progression, its characters merely come in to tell their feelings but in dialogue that has compression and crisp realism. As with T.J. in *Home of the Brave*, the compulsive drive to trample on the feelings of others is shown as a substitution, the "hurt or be hurt" component of paranoia; Wally had an embattled childhood, his first sexual relations at twelve, and had lost the one woman he loved—Joe's mother—in childbirth. But consistent with Laurents' theory of avoiding obvious explanations, Wally's ruthlessness is not explained away; he remains cynical egotism personified.

Apparently purging himself by this grim exploration of the human jungle, Laurents turned in his next play to a more sunny but none the less psychoanalytic study. In *The Time of the Cuckoo* (1952) he deals with warm-hearted, generous people in search of emotional fulfillment. Two approaches to this search are compared— the American with its survival of Puritan moral attitudes toward sex, and the Italian with its pagan acceptance of sex as a natural body hunger. "The Cuckoo is a summer visitant to the whole of Europe," Laurents observes. "It proclaims its arrival by a cry heralding the season of love . . ." He proceeds to depict a summer visitant to Italy, crying for love. She is Leona Samish, an American spinster secretary who naively searches for romance and finds it in the person of Renato Di Rossi, a charming middle-aged Venetian—who woos her with expensive garnets, old world charm and simple honesty. When Di Rossi sends his son to say he will be late for a date, Leona is perturbed to learn that he is married. Torn between her desire for him and the fear of being taken in by a playboy, she finally succumbs to him.

At the other extreme from Leona and her complicated battle of *super-ego* and *id* is the cynical landlady, Signora Fioria, middle-aged and able to take sexual pleasure where she finds it—which proves to be with the young American painter who is staying at her pensione with his wife. Suffering from "painter's block" and quarreling with his wife because she blindly tries to hold him with a sweetness that lacks understanding, he turns to Signora Fioria coldbloodedly and casually. Afterwards, his wife is obsessed to know if he has been unfaithful and he kiddingly says that he has.

By now deeply in love with Di Rossi, Leona learns that he owes money on the gifts he has given her; when she pays for them with money he has exchanged for her, it proves to be counterfeit. Fearful that Di Rossi, too, is something counterfeit which she had to buy for herself, Leona breaks with him and gets very drunk, making allusions to the painter's infidelity for his wife to hear—a displacement of her guilt feelings over her own affair with a married man. Laurents has called this mechanism a particularly American device—to cover up and disguise emotion. Signora Fioria astutely berates her for her shabby treatment of Di Rossi:

> You know why you threw out Di Rossi? Because he is not your dream of perfection. That dream, that ideal does not exist, Miss Samish. It never did, it never will.

At the end, Di Rossi returns to say goodbye; although poor he is easily wounded with the insinuation that he can be bought with

American dollars. Laurents' political commentary is a significant overlay upon the psychological pattern. Europe needs our money but we need equally her traditions of emotional honesty and personal adjustment. Di Rossi leaves Leona, saying that although he is used to frustration with his obese wife and family, he cannot take the complications that Leona presents: "With you—cara Leona, with you the complication is you yourself and—it is too much!" Like Elmer Rice's heroine in *The Grand Tour*, Leona returns a wiser but still single woman. Laurents has vividly dramatized his theme of contrast between two ways of dealing with emotion:

> Americans, while seeming so practical, realistic and down to earth, are actually romanticists in comparison to Italians, who seem so romantic, lyrical and careless but are actually realists.

The Time of the Cuckoo is an important modern comedy which deals entertainingly with the psychoanalytic concept of denial and concealment of emotion, disguise of motives and guilt over sex. Avoiding a dogmatic thesis, Laurents is true to his characters and permits audiences to draw their own conclusions as to the respective merits of permissive and restrictive *mores*. He does not over-simplify to make a case: there is implied criticism of some aspects of Italian culture—its poverty, its dependence upon American tourist dollars, the cynical sensuality of Fioria and the precocious mendicancy of Italian children; balanced with it is a delicious satire of American tourists who race through Italy on a guide-book itinerary. But above all, Laurents depicts in Leona and Di Rossi endearing, recognizable humans in search of fulfillment in ways that are characteristic of their time and place.

WILLIAM INGE

Comparable in some respects to Arthur Laurents, another talent to emerge since the war and give promise of becoming a major American playwright is William Inge. Like Laurents he has undergone psychoanalysis and is able to utilize its insights without following outworn literary patterns. Influenced in his first play by *The Glass Menagerie*, the work of a fellow resident of St. Louis, Inge's *Farther Off From Heaven* (1947) has not been seen in New York, but his second play, *Come Back, Little Sheba* (1950) proved to be a remarkably well motivated drama with fine suspense and considerable Freudian influence. (Several psychiatrists read and approved the manuscript before it reached production.) It was helped to Broadway success—

as was Laurents' *Time of the Cuckoo*—by the glowing acting of Shirley Booth.

Come Back, Little Sheba is also a study in contrasts—between the erotic satisfaction of the young lovers, Marie and Turk, and the bleak frustration which is all life offers the middle-aged couple, Doc and Lola, with whom Marie rooms. Doc is a quiet, gentle person who had wanted to be a physician but had dropped out of medical school to marry Lola when she became pregnant. Now he is a chiropractor and a former alcoholic who has been helped by Alcoholics Anonymous. Like Marie, Lola was herself a sought-after beauty in high school, but her strict father would not permit her to go out with boys. Her first date was Doc, and since their affair her father has never permitted her to return home. Having lost the child and had no others, there is a gnawing loneliness now in Lola's life, and she substitutes a dog, Sheba, in her affections; but Sheba has wandered off and wistfully Lola calls for Sheba to come back; Lola has an anxiety dream in which she walks so fast Sheba gets lost. Like Sheba, youth and romance have just disappeared from Lola and Doc, and one cause of alcoholism is clearly indicated: disillusionment.

Doc repeats the prayer of Alcoholics Anonymous, which might well be taken as the motto of the entire mental health movement:

God grant me the serenity to accept the things I cannot change, courage to change the things I can, and wisdom always to tell the difference.

The thing Doc can neither change nor accept is the courting of Marie by Turk, a tall athlete who poses in his shorts for Marie's sketching. Doc, an only child and "sortuva Mama's boy," idealizes Marie as he had his own mother; he resents Turk with fierce moral indignation without being conscious of his desire for Marie—merely for his own lost youth and medical career. Lola too finds substitute outlets for her emotions, spending her mornings in an unkempt house listening to the radio and overwhelming the mailman and milkman with friendliness. (Both Turk and the milkman are muscular, athletic male animals who foreshadow the character of Hal in *Picnic*.)

His anxieties aroused unbearably by the sight of Turk sneaking out of Marie's bedroom, Doc hits the bottle and returns early the next day roaring drunk. In a scene of curdling power, Doc unburdens his accumulated resentments of Lola, her grammatical ignorance and her slovenly housekeeping. Calling both Marie and Lola sluts, he goes after Lola with a hatchet and implies that he would like to castrate Turk. He is subdued with the help of his Alcoholics Anonymous friends and taken to the city hospital. When he returns again sober and in control, Lola tells him of a dream she has had of Turk throwing the javelin; the man in charge of the athletics was her father, and Turk kept changing into others and finally into Doc. Doc threw the javelin so high it never came down and her father disqualified him. Then she dreams Sheba is dead, and Lola comes to realize that Sheba, like her own lost youth, is irretrievably gone. With new maturity she and Doc draw together, resolved to stop looking to the past and to accept what they cannot change. Audiences that smiled knowingly at the Freudian dream symbol of the javelin thrower were moved by the integrity of Inge's ending and his insight into the pressures causing alcoholism.

As in *Come Back, Little Sheba*, it is a half-undressed young male who upsets the emotional defenses of the characters in Inge's next play, the Pulitzer-prize winning *Picnic* (1953). In this play, however, it is an exclusively feminine world, protective and serene on the surface. Wrote Inge, "I was fascinated to find how . . . the women seemed to have created a world of their own, a world in which they seemed to be pretending men did not exist. It was a world that had to be destroyed, at least for dramatic values." The male who arrives to do this is Hal Carter, a vagabond with a muscular physique and little else; he is the rooster that manages to arouse this whole barnyard colony of hens. Handled as romantic comedy with a Chekhovian orchestration of the various characters' frustrated lives, *Picnic* is an intimate and powerful handling of the emotional needs of a group of women in a small, monotonous Kansas town.

The dumpy, middle-aged lady, Mrs. Potts, who is burdened with her senile mother (who once forced her to annul her marriage), takes in the penniless young Hal and gives him breakfast, lets him do chores for her and finds her outlet in mothering him. In the house adjacent lives a widow with two daughters: Millie at sixteen is a wiry adolescent who seems to have stepped right out of the work of Carson McCullers, whose *Ballad of the Sad Café* Millie is currently reading. She swears and dresses like a boy, and, as does the girl in *Climate of Eden*, fiercely resents her sister, Madge, for her beauty and success with boys. Madge, who works in a dime store, takes her beauty for granted, finds it less satisfying than a train whistle which suggests wonderful faraway places, and is often embarrassed by her good looks, lamenting, "What good is it to be pretty?" Her wealthy fiancé, Alan, respectfully hero-worships her and his kisses leave her unaroused; not overly bright, she is ill at ease with Alan's wealthy friends. She is thus more than ready for Hal. Also boarding with the widow and her daughters is an old-maid school-teacher, Rosemary, whose defense mechanism is to reiterate that although men want to marry her, "I don't have time for any of 'em when they start gettin' serious on me."

Hal, who has been in reform school, suffers extreme inferiority feelings: his father died in jail from alcoholism, his mother attempted to declare him insane to get his property, and his fraternity brothers in college lorded it over him for his crudity. He tells Alan of his having been picked up by two girls, taken to a motel and held as prisoner until both had been satiated. The only thing Hal has is his frank virility, reinforced by such little devices as boots. The women all become conscious of Hal working around the yard with his shirt off, and are both repelled and intrigued by his brash male braggadocio. The Labor Day picnic provides the occasion for the eruption of the awakened sexuality of the women. Hal's whisky breaks down Rosemary's inhibitions and she screams at a piece of garden hose, fearing it is a snake—or a phallic symbol. Hal and Madge finally come together in a dance which ". . . has something of the nature of a primitive rite that would mate the two young people." Rosemary wants to dance that way too, but must settle for a middle-aged storekeeper, while Millie, who wears her first feminine frock, gets nauseated from Hal's liquor. Instead of going on the picnic, Hal and Madge find each other in a powerful surge of desire after Rosemary had fiercely upbraided him for his rottenness. The aftermath of the picnic for Rosemary is intimacy with Howard, the store-keeper, after which they return, drained and weary. But Rosemary becomes hysterically insistent and in a tremendous scene, not fully realized in the production, she browbeats him into a promise of marriage. Hal and Madge return too, ashamed and trying to fight their desires for Alan's sake. Hal must flee town because Alan has reported his car stolen when they stayed out all night, but he wants Madge to come to Tulsa and meet him. Her mother, who sees a repetition of her own marital failure, tries valiantly to keep Madge from going to Tulsa; but it is clear that she must go—her deepest emotional needs have been answered by Hal with his combination of aggressive virility and small-boy self-pity; Hal, too, has found compassion and tenderness for the first time. Though the ending is painful from the mother's point of view, Inge seems to suggest that the marriage of Hal and Madge has a fighting chance, for it is based upon a deep-level satisfaction of mutual needs. Perhaps all of the vagabond, maladjusted, delinquent Hals need only to find themselves through being loved.

Picnic illustrates the most mature level of the American drama in the fifties, able to draw upon Freudian insights without succumbing to the obvious or the trite, able to extract ever fresh and original patterns of human relationship from contemporary life and to view with psychological as well as aesthetic perception the life around us. Inge ably summarized his own approach to psychoanalytic drama in his questionnaire:

> I'll put it briefly—Freud has deepened and expanded man's own awareness of himself. Any writer, inwardly involved with his own time, can not help but reflect the feelings and viewpoints that Freud has exposed in us. Yet, I cannot point out any specific plays (of my own or of other playwrights) that intentionally serve to illustrate Freud. Rather I feel that the understanding and sympathy expressed for human character in such plays as "The Glass Menagerie," "All My Sons," "Golden Boy," "A Streetcar Named Desire," "The Shrike," "Skin of our Teeth," "Death of a Salesman" come about as the result of Freud's discoveries, even though the authors of these plays may not have read Freud, or any of the psychoanalytic writers since.

Inge's two naturalistic dramas have quickly found their way to the company of these plays he mentions and have earned him a conspicuous place among the new playwrights.

MARY CHASE

In our predominantly realistic theatre Mary Chase has brought a refreshing sense of fantasy which links her to the earlier American drama of wish-fulfillment—*The Poor Little Rich Girl, The Willow Tree, His Majesty Bunker Bean, Barbara,* and *Lady of the Rose.* Her style is ingratiating whimsy but beneath it there is the soundly motivated psychology of hallucination.

After an unsuccessful realistic play, *Now You've Done It* (1937), Mrs. Chase brought to New York in 1944 the now-immortal *Harvey,* in which she explores the inner world of Elwood P. Dowd, a charming bachelor who is to all intents and purposes the most rational person in the play except for his persistent hallucination of a large white pookah rabbit, Harvey. Elwood drinks a good deal, upsets his scatterbrained sister, Veta, and responds to people who anxiously ask if they can do something for him with his disarming, "What did you have in mind?" When Veta attempts to have Elwood committed to a private psychiatric sanitarium, it is she who is committed and forcibly given hydrotherapy. Veta manages to extricate herself and returns comically indignant at the attendant, who she is sure is a white slaver, and the doctor, who asked her a lot of questions, ". . . all about sex-urges—and all that filthy stuff. That place ought to be cleaned up." It is not long until the psychiatrist himself is sure that he sees Harvey, for as O'Neill pointed out in *Where The Cross Is Made,* the root of belief is in all of us. By the end of the second act, even the audience is ready to believe that it has seen Harvey cross the stage and open the door of the psychiatrist's office. The doctor himself unburdens to Elwood that he wishes he, too, could escape reality, his private wish being to go to a cool grove outside Akron with a strange young woman who would just stroke his head and say, "Poor thing! Oh, you poor, poor thing." All men apparently need their private Harveys, their ideal creatures to console them and minister to their wants. Few are as frank as Elwood in admitting that need. As Elwood explains to the doctor, "I wrestled with reality for forty years, and I am happy to state that I finally won out over it." When the psychiatrist is about to administer an injection to cure Elwood of Harvey, Veta finally stops him. Neither she nor the audience really wants Elwood any different than he is. If he is happy with Harvey, it is no one else's business; and as the two of them go out together, leaving behind the neurotic, hyper-tense, anxious ones who live in reality, we wonder, as at the end of *Button Button* and *Behold This Dreamer,* just who is crazy?

Mrs. Chase's next play, *The Next Half Hour* (1945), ran only a little longer than its title suggests; utilizing wish-fulfillment again it lacked the happy union of whimsy and humanitarianism that endeared *Harvey*. An Irish woman can foretell the future by listening to the wail of the banshees; she tries to save her eldest son, "a silver-cord" boy, from an affair with a married woman and succeeds only in getting her precious younger son shot by the jealous husband. Mrs. Chase went on, however, in her next play, *Mrs. McThing* (1952), to treat the fairy world of witches with somewhat greater success. Here she depicts a never-never-land as it might be imagined in the fantasy of a child, Howay Larue, a poor little rich boy who has all the luxuries except affection, boyhood roughhouse, and companionship. When Howay begins to behave with suspicious perfection, coming in clean and neat, dutifully kissing his mother's guests and refusing candy because it would spoil his dinner, it becomes apparent that a witch, Mrs. McThing, has spirited Howay away and substituted a stick—a child's projection of the impossible ideal mothers would like their children to be. The true Howay turns up at a low dive, the Shantyland Pool Hall, and Mrs. Larue is forced to go there in search of him.

The gang of bad men is also conceived through a child's mind —a mind saturated by comic books and radio programs. The meanest member of the gang goes around looking for an old lady to push

under a street car; the cook whimsically refuses to take an order
unless he likes the name of the customer; and the boss of the gang is
dominated by his old mother who marches in and slaps him for staying out last night. Howay cross-examines his mother to learn if she
prefers the stick to him, and decides to stay with the gang. Mrs.
Larue becomes a drab scrub woman at the pool hall, while a stick
takes her place at home also. The gangsters plot a robbery of the
Larue house but are caught by the police, who search them but find
no guns, only comic books, Wheatena box tops and bubble gum.
Mrs. Larue saves the day by telling the police the boys are her guests,
and wins back the good will of the witch by accepting the little girl
Howay had wanted to play with. *Mrs. McThing* has amusing moments but is somewhat too heavy a dose of whimsy and witchcraft.
If it leaves something to be desired as theatre it is, nonetheless, rewarding in its understanding of the inner logic of the child's world.

With her next play, *Bernardine* (1952), Mrs. Chase steps from
the child's world to that of the teen-ager and tries to help the public
understand the gang-centered boys, confused, frustrated, sexually
eager, who all too often are branded as "juvenile delinquent." They
are shown in their native habitat, a back-room of a beer joint, "a
world with its own set of rulers, values, dreams, and cockeyed edge
to laughter. Here no adult can enter fully—ever." Mrs. Chase captures the strong drive of "belongingness" which motivates boys to
seek acceptance by the gang, whose be-bop music, private jargon
and talk of sex are rituals of initiation. Mrs. Chase's boys are not
vicious, merely keen-minded, imaginative and desperately anxious to
express superiority to the adult world in which they are such novices.
The leader of the gang, Beau, strives to be blasé, saying of his father,
"I barely know the man." Each of the boys has a slogan in terms of
a verb—similar to the Stanislavski system of analyzing roles in a play.
For one it is "I scheme," for others, "I bull," "I conquer," "I laugh,"
and for the boy rejected by the gang, "I stink."

The boys also have a creature of wish-fulfillment like Harvey.
An objectification of their erotic wants, she is called Bernardine
Crudd and is a little older and "beat up looking" but blond, dreamy,
and her eyes flash a message. She knows only one word—"yes." The
sex-mad member of the gang is Wormy, whose mother is over-
anxious to be a companion to him. The boys try to get Wormy dates
but he is too fast for the girls. He has to be home by ten o'clock, so
"Where's the time for technique?" The boys project an ideal world
where Bernardine lives, at Sneaky Falls, on the banks of Itching
River:

Up there the mothers have to come to the boys for spending

money and permission to leave the house. (Now turns and
faces an imaginary mother, placing arms akimbo) So, you
say you're going downtown to lunch with women friends
and need five bucks? Who are these women? How do I
know they're not bums? Go back upstairs. You're not leaving
this house and take off that dirty old fox fur.

In search of the mythical Bernardine, Wormy happens upon a stunning blond in a hotel lobby. There is a near-riot in the lobby and
they would be arrested but for Beau's glib talking. Wormy ends up
in the blond's hotel room, to the envy of the gang. In a hilarious
scene, Wormy tries to seduce her but grows frightened when she
offers no resistance. The shock of learning that the girl is an old
friend of his mother's chills his ardor and he leaves with her gentle
reassurance that he will find a nice girl his own age. When he stands
up to his mother and announces that he is joining the Navy to escape
home, his mother experiences a new emotional awareness, realizing
the meaning of their club and their gang outlets. She sees that she
had expected and demanded too much of her son:

> Oh, what's the matter with us? Nothing in creation is good
> enough for you—nothing and no one. We don't want you to
> live the way we've lived, love the way we've loved, or die
> the way we'll die. We want the miracle! We want you to
> walk into the future a brand new way—over a bridge of
> rainbows.

Wormy finally manages a date with the teen age girl he admires and
the play ends with an epilogue in which the gang leader, now an Air
Force flyer, pays tribute to the gang and points out the psychological safety valve which it provided for the boys. It was the gang which
understood Wormy better than his own mother and provided him
with a steadying force until he could grow to maturity. In *Bernardine*, Mrs. Chase reveals more insight into adolescence than has
any other playwright in our theatre today. She dramatizes her insight
with the mechanism of projection—the fantasy of imaginary characters and situations that meet the needs of the individual. In spite of
its knockabout farce situations, *Bernardine* must not be underestimated as a major contribution to the drama of juvenile psychology.

JOHN PATRICK

Among the younger psychological playwrights, John Patrick has recently come to the fore with his highly successful *Teahouse of the
August Moon*. Like Arthur Laurents, he has had both service experience during the war and radio training as a writer. His first Broad-

way play, *Hell Freezes Over* (1935), was an unsuccessful attempt to draw drama from seven survivors of a dirigible crash at the South Pole. After that Patrick spent a number of years in Hollywood as a film writer, and returned to the theatre in 1942 with a psychoanalytic drama, *The Willow And I*. An atypical, theatrical contrivance, it depicts a girl, Mara, suffering complete amnesia on her wedding day when she suspects her fiancé of loving her younger sister, Bessie; she and her sister wrestle over a gun which goes off. There is a jump of forty years, a difficult theatrical feat at best, and we learn that the fiancé married Bessie, had a son, and died. The son now resembles him so much that the walking ghost, Mara, mistakes him for her former sweetheart. Mara recovers her faculties during a thunderstorm and tries to piece together the fragments of her life. Her old doctor, with a blend of Freud and Aesop, explains:

> You know how nature has equipped the 'possum to deal with fear. In the face of danger—animation is suspended. Well—sometimes the mind follows the same fugitive pattern. An overwhelming threat to happiness—an unbearable truth the mind can't accept—and it retreats into a protective loss of memory.

The reason for her amnesia proves to be her fear after the gun-shot that she had killed the sister whom she had unconsciously wished to kill. Her consolation is that Bessie's husband remained true to his love for Mara. *The Willow and I* characterizes Mara too sketchily before her blackout to permit the audience to experience her inner conflict. The result was a lifeless case history.

In addition to Patrick's handling of amnesia and Laurents' version in *Home of the Brave,* amnesia motivated several other plays including Armstrong's *Ring Around Elizabeth* (1941) and Walling's *Manhattan Nocturne* (1943).

The same problem of recovery from psychological withdrawal formed the basis of Patrick's next and far more successful play, *The Hasty Heart* (1945), which has proven to be one of the more enduring of war-time dramas. It depicts a group of soldiers from many nations recovering in a field hospital, into which is brought a young Scotsman who does not know that his one remaining kidney will soon become infected and cause his death. The other men in the ward are forewarned and make every conceivable effort to befriend Lachlen; but he is surly and paranoiacally suspicious of generous motives. He has never formed a warm human attachment, having been illegitimate and forced to battle for his bit of land that is now almost paid for. Projecting evil motives into every effort to warm up to him, he suspects the nurse of trying to marry him for his land.

Learning of his birthday, the men chip in to buy him the set of kilts
he has always denied himself, but he accepts the gifts ungraciously
and refuses to wear them. Gradually, however, the men's patient and
persistent kindness begins to thaw his defenses and he finds himself
accepting cigarettes and talking with the men. Once his repressed
longing for human relationships is cleared, he goes to the other extreme and becoming almost manic or compulsive in his desire to talk
with the men, haranguing them against the British and unable to
stop himself. To atone for his hostility, he is compelled to invite each
of the men to come to his Scottish farm after the war—though none
accepts him. Feeling "a terrible need tae help," he is reached lastly
by Margaret and proposes marriage to her, the fulfillment of his repressed wish that was earlier expressed as suspicion of her motives.
Finally he wears his kilts, permits himself to be photographed, and
is well on the road to adjustment with Margaret to help him, when
the medical officer is forced by inept regulations to inform him that
he has not long to live. He suffers a violent regression to his paranoid
defenses, sure now that all of their kindness has been only pity.
About to leave alone for his solitary farm, he finally comes to realize
that he had made true friends here and stays with them. *The Hasty
Heart* is an engaging play with a keen and perceptive insight into
psychological dynamisms.

Again in *The Curious Savage* (1950) Patrick showed interest in
the problem of withdrawal from reality. An amusing whimsy, it is
based upon the contrast between the "sanity" of the psychotic and
the insanely money-and-sex-mad behavior of the "rational." Mrs.
Ethel Savage is committed to a private mental institution because
she has insisted on quietly selling out her family's financial posses-
sions and using the cash to set up an endowment trust for people to
do the foolish things they have always wanted to do. An ingratiating
notion, it proves upsetting to her family, a judge whose verdicts are
the most reversed in history, a Senator who is the most hated in
Washington, and a social butterfly who is much divorced. Mrs. Savage is sweet and gently rational, and the inmates are delightfully and
kindly portrayed without satire. Mrs. Paddy is a psychotic who has
not spoken since her husband told her to shut up twenty years ago,
except to recite a long list of hates:

> I hate everything in the world but most of all I hate light-
> ning, skunk cabbage, custard, mustard, spiders, blisters. . . .

Fairy is a little wisp of a woman who obsessively wants everyone to
tell her she is loved. There is a statistician whose mind cracked, and
a woman who clutches a doll, believing she has had a child while

in the asylum. Another patient is a former flier who lost his reason when his plane was shot down during the war; he does not recognize his wife, who has become a nurse at the sanitarium to be near him.

Mrs. Savage manages to make her family look considerably foolish going on wild goose chases for her negotiable bonds, which finally prove to be hidden inside the teddy bear she always keeps with her. Though she is tempted to remain in this sheltered place where she has found love and generous human relations, Mrs. Savage realizes sadly that the inmates are all preoccupied with their irrational releases and that she can do more good with her money in the real world. She goes back to find ways to help people express themselves.

Two of Patrick's plays showed little psychological depth—*The Story of Mary Surratt* (1947), which dramatized the trial and execution of a woman innocently implicated in the murder of Lincoln, and *Lo and Behold* (1951), a throw-back to the twenties when farces about ghosts and spiritualism were in vogue.

Patrick's most recent work, adapted from a novel by Vern Sneider, is the Pulitzer Prize-winning *The Teahouse of the August Moon* (1953), which is one of the most delightful and yet psychologically provocative of recent plays. Sneider, who served in the Allied military government, writes of the American occupation of Okinawa; he contrasts two cultures, the relaxed, patient acceptance of the Orient with the high-powered, often short-sighted logic of the west. Captain Fisby finds himself with the thankless assignment of rehabilitating the impoverished village of Tobiki. He arrives armed with a voluminous "Plan B" prepared in Washington for the handling of occupied countries, including orders to build a schoolhouse in a pentagon shape and to organize the women into a "Ladies League for Democratic Action." But Plan B fails because it is not based upon the wants and needs of the occupied peoples. Instead of a pentagon-shaped school (they have no five-sided children) they want a teahouse. The natives make Captain Fisby a present of a geisha girl, something not covered in Army regulations. The housewives, organized into their Ladies League for Democratic Action, want most of all to be given lessons in dancing and cosmetics by the geisha girl. Unable to sell the natives' handicraft work, Fisby discovers that they know how to make an excellent sweet-potato brandy; with American marketing methods he proceeds to build up a thriving trade with all of the Army and Navy installations in Okinawa, making the village prosperous and grateful. When Fisby's progress reports stray farther and farther from Plan B, an Army psychiatrist is sent out to look into the matter. But he, too, succumbs to the charm of Tobiki's way of life, and the Colonel finds him out of uniform, comfortably in sandals giving vent to his suppressed passion for growing things. Threatened with an investigation by Washington, the natives are forced to dismantle their teahouse and their brandy stills; but Washington has the wisdom to hail the Tobiki experiment as a fine example of rehabilitation based upon an understanding of local needs. The stills weren't destroyed, and the teahouse can be reassembled instantly (before the eyes of the audience) in the enchanting final scene. The Okinawans, who had withstood invasions from China and Japan, were not going to succumb to this invasion from America. As interpreted by their spokesman, Sakini, (memorably played by David Wayne) pithy comments of Oriental wisdom are used to introduce each scene and form the narrative framework of the play. Like A Bell For Adano, Patrick's play makes the point that conquerors rule best by psychological understanding, and like Steinbeck's The Moon is Down Patrick shows the conquerors gradually conquered by the simple dignity of the life they have come to reorganize. As Sneider points out for the benefit of any future occupation officers, ". . . if he looks to the wants of the people under him, then tries to satisfy those wants, he will have very little need for barbed wire and guards armed with rifles."

RODGERS AND HAMMERSTEIN

There have been musical comedies utilizing dreams and psychoanalytic ideas since Tillie's Nightmare (1910), Judy Forgot (1910), and Nothing But Love (1919), but it remained for Moss Hart, Ira Gershwin and Kurt Weill to give Broadway its first serious approach to musical theatre based upon psychoanalysis—Lady in the Dark (1941). Hart has shown no further interest in musical comedy and the gifted composer, Kurt Weill, died in 1950 after doing the score of Maxwell Anderson's Lost in the Stars. The most significant influence upon the musical theatre, therefore, and one which pointed it in the direction of modern psychology, must be credited to Richard Rodgers and Oscar Hammerstein II. Their collaboration has brought musical comedy and operetta up-to-date and has rendered thoroughly old-fashioned their forerunners in operetta—Rose Marie, The New Moon, The Desert Song—all three, by the way, with librettos by Oscar Hammerstein II.

Rodgers had employed psychoanalytic motives in musical comedy as early as 1926 with Peggy Ann, but his then-collaborator, Lorenz Hart (as Cecil Smith has observed) had a brittle wit which did not match the tender, flowing melody of Rodgers. In 1937, Rodgers and Hart brought teenagers to the musical stage in *Babes In Arms,* which included one of the earliest dream ballets. Oscar Hammerstein II had also shown an early affinity for psychoanalytic themes, introducing a curious form of psychodrama into *Gypsy Jim* (1923). When Rodgers and Hammerstein were brought together to adapt Lynn Riggs' play, *Green Grow the Lilacs,* a revolution in musical theatre occurred and the new American music-drama based upon the psychology of mental health was born. Significant, too, was the contribution of Agnes De Mille in evolving a fresh American style of choreography based on a working acquaintance with Freudian motivation.

Oklahoma! (1943) deals with the courting and wedding of a spirited farm girl, Laurey, and her cowboy sweetheart, Curly. In place of the stereotyped operetta baritone-villain, the obstacle to their love is Jud, a sex-obsessed, disturbed man with immodest French postcards on the wall of his room—postcards which provided Agnes De Mille with the motif for a satirically bawdy ballet. In her dream-ballet Laurey is torn between the two men, Curly and Jud, and violence flares between them, requiring her to give herself to Jud to save Curly. Such a clash develops in actuality and on his wedding night Curly fights with Jud, who falls on his own knife and dies; the good folk of Oklahoma quickly clear Curly of charges so that he can honeymoon properly. Ado Annie, too, gets her man by her honest and irrepressible lustiness, which she confesses in the delightful song, "I'm jist a girl who cain't say no."

Continuing the pattern of adapting mature psychological drama for the musical stage, Rodgers and Hammerstein turned to Molnar's *Liliom,* and, changing its setting to New England, created one of the masterpieces of the modern musical theatre, *Carousel* (1945). When it was revived in 1954, Atkinson commented that it seemed in retrospect the most eloquent and enduring of the Rodgers and Hammerstein hits. *Carousel* has no villain in the conventional sense— Jigger is at worst only an evil influence on Billy Bigelow, whose own inner ambivalence and fear of failure as a parent is the true antagonist. The exuberant good spirits of the music carry the romance of Billy Bigelow, the tough carnival barker and idol of a thousand chambermaids, with Julie Jordan, a quiet, "queer one." The exhilarating song, "June is bustin' out all over" might be called a kind of rural New England paean to Dionysus and the spring festival of returning fertility:

> June is bustin' out all over!
> The saplin's are bustin' out with sap!
> Love hes found my brother, junior—

And my sister's even lunier!
And my ma is gettin' kittenish with pap!

When Billy learns that Julie is pregnant, he sings the stirring ode to parenthood, projecting his hopes for his boy, Bill—then realizing with a start that it might be a girl. The ballad is sound in terms of modern psychology, suggesting that Billy wants the best for his child but will let him choose his own goals rather than select them for him: "I don't give a damn what he does, As long as he does what he likes." Billy only makes one reservation: "And I'm damned if he'll marry his boss's daughter, a skinny-lipped virgin with blood like water . . ." At the contemplation of a daughter he feels a surge of Electra affection:

> She has a few
> Pink and white young fellers of two or three
> But my little girl
> Gets hungry ov'ry night
> And she'll come home to me!

Unable to do anything but live by his physical charms, Billy tries to provide for his child by robbing, is caught and takes his own life. He goes to Molnar's whimsical heaven, and fifteen years later is allowed his wish to go back to earth to see his child—a girl who suffers from inferiority feelings (which she expresses in Agnes De Mille's dance movement) because of the aspersions cast on her father. As an unknown traveller, Billy restores her faith in her father and she is released from her fears. The ending, bitter-sweet in Molnar with the wisdom that "You can hit someone and hit them and never hurt them at all," is enlarged in *Carousel*, as Rodgers points out, ". . . to make it clear that the little girl had actually derived a measure of strength from her father's weakness." The new finale takes the audience to her high school commencement where the orator enjoins the young people not to be held back by their parents' failures or to lean on their successes but to stand on their own feet. Billy's spirit urges her to believe this and the stirring "When you walk through a storm, keep your chin up high. . . ." brings *Carousel* to its catharsis.

The farthest that Rodgers and Hammerstein have gone toward the creation of new forms for the psychological music play was in *Allegro* (1947). There is no external antagonist at all here, only the growing inner conflict in the mind of a young doctor, Joseph Taylor, whose career is traced from the day he is born until the day he returns home to find himself. The subjective singing chorus is used to express the unspoken and often unconscious feelings of Joseph, beginning with his googling at rattles and reacting to the over-sized grown-ups: "It's a funny place. And all those things with the big heads don't help to clear things up." The first Oedipal stirrings begin in infancy when he notices mother paying attention to father, and discovers that he can interrupt that by wailing. The chorus brilliantly dramatizes the sensation of learning to walk in the song, "One Foot, Other Foot." The ballet then depicts his growing up with his girl friend, Jenny, who uses femininity as a defense against fear of failure as a tomboy. Through the chorus we hear him suppressing his fear of death and wishing he had the courage to kiss Jenny. Joe is touched by the lasting love between his parents, described in the ballad, "A Fellow Needs A Girl." In college he remains true to Jenny, though he is sorely tempted on a date arranged by his friend Charlie. As his English professor reads "The Eve of St. Agnes," two girls come into his erotic fantasy and undress. But he resists the blandishments of the other woman, who laments, "We Have Nothing to Remember, So Far." Jenny loses her campaign to keep Joe from becoming a doctor, and persuades him to become a fashionable city doctor rather than practising with his father in the country. There is a flare-up of mother-daughter-in-law jealousy which causes the mother's stroke and death. Joe suffers guilt feelings as he leaves his father's country practice and goes to the city, where he is made wretched treating rich people with their interminable "Yatata yatata yatata." Yearning for the sick who need him rather than the wealthy hypochondriacs who can make or break a doctor over the dinner table, and discovering his wife Jenny in an infidelity, Joe is visited in fantasy by his mother's image singing "Come home, come home," and finally by his grandmother's image, singing "One Foot, Other Foot." The chorus now represents Joe's roots, his unconscious memories. Turning down an appointment to a society hospital, Joe discovers that his loyal nurse is in love with him, and together they go back to his home, to the unrestrained joy of the chorus singing "One Foot, Other Foot." Although the run of *Allegro* was shorter than the other Rodgers and Hammerstein music-dramas there is much that is rewarding here both musically and psychologically. Its chorus, with its subjective stream-of-the-unconscious, is indebted to O'Neill and ultimately harks back to Greek tragedy, but its introduction in musical comedy was a courageous step taken by Rodgers and Hammerstein.

A similar stream-of-the-unspoken is introduced early in *South Pacific* (1949), which Rodgers, Hammerstein and Joshua Logan adapted from Michener's *Tales Of the South Pacific*. Nellie Forbush, who is a "cockeyed optimist" about life, finds herself attracted to the worldly planter, Emile De Becque. The only villain which stands between them is racial intolerance, which keeps her from condoning Emile's two Polynesian children by a native mistress. There is a racial barrier too between the "saxy young Lootellan" and the lovely Polynesian girl, Liat, whom he possesses first and then falls deeply in love with. The lieutenant sings of the childhood conditioning which is the only basis for racial intolerance:

> You've got to be taught to hate and fear,
> You've got to be taught from year to year . . .
> Before you are six or seven or eight,
> To hate all the people your relatives hate—
> You've got to be carefully taught.

But the lieutenant is killed on a mission to a Japanese-held island, which sidesteps the question of his marriage to Liat. Nellie had tried to wash Emile right out of her hair and life, but when he returns from the mission safely, she realizes that her reservations were "piffle," and *South Pacific* ends with a joyful reunion.

The richly inventive musical score of *South Pacific* has become familiar, but, unlike many operettas the words are not merely nonsensical excuses for melody. "Bali Ha'i" tells of a special island which, although real for Liat and the lieutenant, is merely wish-fulfillment for most individuals.

> Mos' people live on a lonely island,
> Lost in de middle of a foggy sea.
> Mos' people long for anuddor island
> One where dey know dey would lak to be. . . .

On Bali Ha'i there are pagan ceremonial rituals, and the comic Seabee hints that everyone drinks coconut liquor, the women dance with bare breasts, "and everybody gets to know everybody pretty well." The seabees sing a raucous expression of their sexual longing, "There is nothing like a dame." The lyrics of Bloody Mary's song to urge the "Lootellan" to marry her daughter, Liat, are sound mental hygiene:

> Happy Talk.
> Keep talkin' Happy Talk!
> Talk about tings you'd like to do.
> You got to have a dream—
> If you don' have a dream
> How you gonna have a dream come true?

This combination of exquisite melody and lyrics which convey meaning for modern, psychologically aware audiences is apparently the secret of Rodgers and Hammerstein's popularity.

They also begged the question of interracial love, however, in their next work, *The King and I* (1951), which was adapted from Landon's novel, *Anna and the King of Siam*. When Anna threatens to leave Siam and humiliates the king for his sadistic whipping of one of his concubines, the king suffers a deep psychosomatic shock and dies just as Anna realizes her love for him. *The King and I* included the charming song of courage, "I Whistle a Happy Tune," and Anna's gracious "Hello, Young Lovers," in which she rejoices that others find love because she has known a love of her own. The enchanting ballet, "The Small House of Uncle Thomas," a version of Uncle Tom's Cabin done in the manner of the Oriental theatre proved the climax of this thoroughly satisfying musical play.

Rodgers and Hammerstein's most recent work, *Me and Juliet* (1953) proved to be the least successful of the group, a regression to a pre-*Oklahoma!* brand of psychology where there is a simple triangle with the girl, the rejected and the successful suitor. There are several subjective devices, however, as when the chorus of voices in the heroine's mind persuades her, "You can do better than him, Jeanie." The backstage romance is integrated with a musical play the company is staging, in which there is a symbolic psychological character named ME who is externalized by various people for whom he has a different existence. Juliet represents the tender aspect of love, "Marriage type love," while Carmen symbolizes the sensuous seductress. The hero observes astutely that Juliet will undoubtedly be more passionate when she is aroused by the man she loves than is Carmen. The story is the weakest of the Rodgers and Hammerstein repertoire, and suggests that adaptation from literature has played a significant part in the revolution which Rodgers and Hammerstein have effected in the musical theatre.

Awareness of modern psychology has not been the exclusive property of Rodgers and Hammerstein, although they have become most adept at its use. The year after *Oklahoma!*, Sheldon, Kilgallen and Roberts collaborated on a musical for Vera Zorina entitled *Dream With Music* and based upon wish-fulfillment. Alan Jay Lerner and Frederick Loewe were more clearly indebted to psychoanalysis for their moderately successful musical, *The Day Before Spring* (1945), in which a wife who has been married a decade returns to her college campus and meets her old lover. When she cannot make up her mind whether to run away with him, she turns to three campus statues for advice—Plato, Voltaire and Freud. "Plato advises her to keep her love platonic," commented Burton Rascoe, "Voltaire to eat her cake and have it too, and Freud to drop her inhibitions and run away with her lover." Freud himself, who appeared on Broadway almost half a century after his influence began to be felt, goes with the lovers, but in the end the woman returns to her husband. Anthony Tudor created two dream-fantasy ballets which contributed to the effectiveness of *The Day Before Spring*.

Broadway is nothing if not trend-conscious, and another Freudian dream musical quickly followed *The Day Before Spring*. In Gladys Shelly's *The Dutchess Misbehaves* (1946) an art gallery attendant is knocked unconscious and dreams he is Goya making love to the Duchess of Alba. Three musicals in 1948 utilized psychiatric material: *Inside U.S.A.*, with the torrid dancing of Valerie Bettis, who leads her analyst to the precipice and nudges him over it; *Small Wonder*, in which skits by George Axelrod glorified "The Normal Neurotic"; and Charles Gaynor's *Lend an Ear*, which included an uproarious slapstick skit entitled "Neurotic You and Psychopathic Me." The most successful musical comedy song based on psychoanalysis was by Jo Swerling and Abe Burrows; the latter, according to Zolotow, has been psychoanalyzed, and in *Guys and Dolls* (1950) provided the lyrics for "Adelaide's Lament," a delightful impression of psychosomatic medicine, which observes that from feeling insecure or frustrated, "a person can develop a cold."

The musical theatre now parallels the non-musical drama more closely than it had during the twenties and thirties, thus illustrating the ingenious and varied ways in which the basic tenets of dynamic psychology may be sung, danced and dramatized. Although not "new blood" themselves, Richard Rodgers and Oscar Hammerstein II exerted the strongest influence in this direction by their collaboration beginning in 1943.

In the non-musical drama, there is a highly promising group of new playwrights, many bringing with them an easy working familiarity with psycho-dynamics, and some, like William Inge, Arthur Laurents, and George Axelrod enriched by a personal psychoanalysis. Mary Chase and John Patrick show particular skill in fantasy and in the psychology of withdrawal and wish-fulfillment. There is an encouraging number of other writers, too, whose command of psychology is notable—Arnaud D'Usseau and James Gow, Carson McCullers, Samuel Taylor, Ruth and Augustus Goetz, Jane Bowles, Horton Foote, Robert Anderson, Mignon and Robert McLaughlin, Truman Capote, N. Richard Nash, George Tabori, and Herman Wouk. If anything, the American drama presages a healthier future than ever before. One fact, however, has already emerged—the mantle of O'Neill, Barry and Behrman as leaders of the psychological drama has already settled snugly upon the shoulders of Tennessee Williams and Arthur Miller.

CHAPTER XIII

Tennessee Williams and
Arthur Miller

☆ ☆ ☆ ☆

SHELTERED SOUTHERNERS

Of all the younger American playwrights, none is more characteristic of his generation, more psychoanalytic-oriented, or more provocative of popular controversy than Tennessee Williams. To many, his name is synonymous with sex on the stage; it is true that he can dramatize the fierce hunger of passion, but he can also create gentle and poetic imagery with a unique feeling for the frustration of loneliness. A product of the South which he has analyzed with devastating effect in several plays, he has a special insight into the mental processes of withdrawal and disguise. It is not so much his treatment of sex that has aroused the anxiety of some playgoers as it is his blunt scorn for squeamishness and the emotional dishonesty which distorts the sex drive.

Like O'Neill, Williams received his apprenticeship both in university drama courses and in a turbulent adolescence of vagabondage. Like O'Neill, too, he began with one-act plays, some of which foreshadowed his major work. Shortly before it disbanded, the Group Theatre gave Williams a cash prize for his one-acts which included *Mooney's Kid Don't Cry*, *The Case of the Crushed Petunias*, and

370

Ten Blocks on the Camino Real—all destined to be developed into more mature restatements. He had written four youthful tragedies before his first professional production, which was *Battle of Angels* (1940). In discussing the play, Williams tells that it contains a large amount of autobiography. His grandfather had been a clergyman in the Delta region of Mississippi and in making the rounds with him he had met the frustrated woman of shimmering glass who recurs in his plays. Like the hero of *Battle of Angels*, Williams knocked about for five years, wrote poetry on shoe box lids, and then returned to St. Louis to write *Battle of Angels* "as a katharsis for myself."

Bringing him not only emotional purgation but a Rockefeller Fellowship, the play was tried out in Boston and then abandoned. It deals with a neurotic girl, Myra, (forerunner of Alma Winemuller) who is hyper-tense and verges on hysteria as a result of a childhood emotional disaster. Married to an invalid husband, she runs a mercantile store in the deep South and gives a job to a young vagabond, Val, who makes the fitting of women's shoes an erotic caress. As in *Picnic*, the arrival of the male has various effects upon the females of the community—a haughty aristocrat with nymphomaniac tendencies (the forerunner of Blanche DuBois) who says that the women in town suffer from "sexual malnutrition," and a stout middle-aged woman who paints religious and mystic paintings and uses Val's face as the model for Christ. There is a brutal hostility between Val and the nymphomaniac when he rejects her offer to drive up to the cemetery where, as in *The Case of the Crushed Petunias*, the "dead people give such good advice . . . just one word—Live!" There is an ominous Conjure Man who glides mysteriously through the play as in *The Rose Tattoo*. There is finally the trembling hunger for Val which Myra denies and converts as long as she can and then succumbs to in a scene of white-hot eagerness. But in his last act, Williams seems to have borrowed a page from Saroyan's *Hello Out There*, and a woman turns up who has accused Val of raping her because he would not marry her. Coincidence and over-wrought melodrama weaken the ending, in which Val, hounded by a posse because he defended a Negro, rejects the chance to flee with Myra, who is then shot by her clod of a husband. Val, with a childhood phobia of fires, is lynched with a blowtorch in the flaming store. *Battle of Angels* thus is an interesting preface to Williams' major work, and in spite of its immature and awkward elements, led Gassner to predict that with rewriting it might prove successful. Williams has recently followed Gassner's suggestion and his latest play, *Orpheus Descending*, is apparently the result of this revision.

At the New School for Social Research, where Williams studied playwriting with John Gassner and Theresa Helburn, he also worked with the noted German director of "epic theatre," Erwin Piscator, whose influence may be seen in Williams' next play, *The Glass Menagerie* (1945), which vaulted Williams into the front rank of American playwrights. One of the finest and most poignant dramas of our times, it states the major theme in Williams' work: the tragedy of the individual who is out of touch with reality. The lives of the Wingfield family are all unfulfilled, and each finds his own way of dealing with frustration—by a variety of escape-mechanisms. The father has literally escaped long ago, ". . . a telephone man who fell in love with long distances." The son, Tom, escapes to the movies and by writing poetry on the lids of shoe boxes at the warehouse where he works; his sister, Laura, who has a slight limp, escapes into a fantasy world peopled by the figures in her glass collection. The mother, Amanda, lives in the past, escaping to the rosy memory of a time when she had seventeen gentlemen callers courting her. Being a "memory-play," as recalled and narrated by Tom, it is at times hazy and ephemeral, with gently recurrent melodies. After the fragmentary opening scenes, however, the play is structured and progresses toward its climax more directly than does a free association memory.

In developing his theme of living in the past, Williams borrows from Piscator the non-realistic theatrical device of projected images and sub-titles fading in and out on a screen above the actors. The memory-projections are intended to give an added dimension by commenting upon the action, by illuminating the characters' subjective stream-of-unconscious associations: blue roses are the unconscious image of Laura; for Amanda, who constantly compares Laura's failure with boys to her own successes, seventeen gentlemen callers are the recurrent image. Although the projections were not used in the New York staging, the device is worthy of being tried in a production.

Amanda neurotically persists in projecting an obsolete pattern of life, a gracious Southern plantation existence, onto the dismal reality of life in a St. Louis alley flat. From this Tom rebels while Laura retreats farther into her dream-world. Tom is passive-dependent, and unable to communicate successfully with his mother. He calls her "an ugly, babbling old witch," but apologizes next morning. He is touched by his sister's plight but equally unable to make contact with her. Laura is so fearful of the real world and so deeply convinced of her own inferiority after years of comparison with her mother that she cannot face even typing school, and suffers a vomiting hysteria at her first speed test. To avoid further pain, she escapes to the floral gardens while her mother thinks she is at business college, and the scene when her mother discovers the deception and plays the wounded martyr is a masterpiece.

Amanda confiscates a book Tom had been reading by "that insane Mr. Lawrence," and Tom defends his movie-going in words D. H. Lawrence might have used:

> Tom: Man is by instinct a lover, a hunter, a fighter, and none of those instincts are given much play at the warehouse!
> Amanda: Man is by instinct! Don't quote instinct to me! Instinct is something that people have got away from! It belongs to animals! Christian adults don't want it!

With an ominous sense of social awareness, Williams knows that the war, then germinating in Spain, Italy, and Germany will soon provide the adventure that the lost generation of Tom Wingfields could not find at home.

The goal of finding a "gentleman caller" for Laura becomes an obsession with Amanda. "Like some archetype of the universal unconscious," Tom says in language borrowed from Jung, "the image of the gentleman caller haunted our small apartment." In a desperate bargain for his own freedom, Tom promises to bring a man home from the warehouse to meet Laura. The tragedy becomes devastating as the family grows more and more dependent upon this outside figure, this unreal object of their wish-fulfillment.

When the gentleman caller finally arrives, in the person of Jim O'Connor, Williams shows Amanda absurdly bedecked in an ancient dress in which she once led cotillions; her fussing over the bewildered Jim, flirting with him herself in a coy, girlish regression, is pathetically out of touch with the reality of the situation. This competition with her mother and the shock of recognizing Jim as a boy she had a secret crush on in high school prove too much for Laura and she becomes ill. After dinner, there is a superb scene as Jim, sensing that he was invited to be attentive to Laura, tries to break down her shyness and draw her out. Jim is an amateur psychologist and is ready to psychoanalyze Laura:

> You know what I judge to be the trouble with you? Inferiority complex. Know what that is? That's what they call it when someone low-rates himself! . . . Yep—that's what I judge to be your principal trouble. A lack of confidence in yourself as a person. You don't have the proper amount of faith in yourself . . . You know what my strong advice to you is? Think of yourself as *superior* in some way!

To convince her that her limp is hardly noticeable, Jim dances with her, and finally kisses her. But symbolically, the little glass unicorn which was Laura's favorite has been knocked over in the dancing and has lost its horn. Jim, too, soon falls from his pedestal as he reveals that he is engaged to a girl and only accepted the dinner invitation because she was out of town. Gentle Laura, as fragile as her glass menagerie, is also broken and can hardly speak as she presses the unicorn into Jim's hand as a souvenir. To Amanda, the sky falls, and her whole unreal world crashes; she turns upon Tom, projecting her failure onto him:

> You don't know things anywhere! You live in a dream;
> you manufacture illusions!

Tom has no choice now but to leave Amanda and her dream world, following his father's roving footsteps, "attempting to find in motion what was lost in space—." His closing narration eloquently tells of his later life, forever haunted by the memory of his sister: "Oh, Laura, Laura, I tried to leave you behind me, but I am more faithful than I intended to be!" The tender image of womanhood which Tom carries is not his mother—she had become ludicrous—but Laura, symbol of everything pure and fragile in a violent world. Tom will go on—travelling, escaping, drinking, or perhaps writing a play as exquisite as *The Glass Menagerie.*

"That insane Mr. Lawrence," whose books Amanda could not tolerate, is the writer whom Tennessee Williams most admires; through him he has apparently absorbed the Freudian concept of sex as "the primal life urge," and the repression of it as a distortion for the individual or society. Lawrence was hailed as the most Freudian of novelists for his *Lady Chatterley's Lover* and *Sons and Lovers;* he later broke with Freud and went off on what Williams has called "tangent obsessions," publishing two books criticizing psychoanalysis for bringing sex into consciousness—instead of remaining in the unconscious as "a great affective-passional function and emotion." Williams expressed his admiration for Lawrence in a one-act play, *I Rise in Flame, Cried the Phoenix,* in which he imagines the death of Lawrence as a kind of symbolic seduction of the primitive male sun-god by the harlot of darkness—only to rise again as the principle of virility is perpetually reborn. His martyr complex Williams expresses in a line as electric as this:

> Frieda: You can't stand Jesus Christ because he beat you
> to it. Oh, how you would have loved to suffer the *original*
> crucifixion!

In collaboration with Donald Windham, Williams paid further tribute to Lawrence by dramatizing his short story, *You Touched Me!* (1945). By then Broadway had caught up with sex, and Lawrence's story was hardly a shocker, but rather a pleasant and delightful comedy of what might have been the fate of a Laura had she been fortunate enough to meet a kindred spirit who was not already engaged. The young girl, Mathilda, lives with her father, a bibulous, lusty, profane old sea captain who lost his papers for getting drunk and foundering his ship, and who has converted a room in his house, like O'Neill's Captain Bartlett, into a ship's cabin. His home is supervised by his spinster sister, Emmie, who symbolizes for Williams "aggressive sterility," a bundle of misdirected libido which at first is half laughable but which grows more sinister as the play progresses. She has kept the house hedged in by a double row of petunias, which to Williams symbolizes, as in his one-act, *The Case of the Crushed Petunias,* a walling out of all that is living, virile, and passionate in favor of all that is frigid, neat and orderly.

Hadrian, whom the Captain has adopted, returns from the war and finds himself in love with Mathilda but aware that he must awaken her emotions and break down her reaction-formation. She is painfully shy, insecure and under her aunt's domination. Mathilda's father shocks her with a bawdy story about being shipwrecked so long that even a female porpoise seemed desirable, and breaks up Emmie's solemn tea party with her one matrimonial prospect, the local preacher, a prissy little man who wants only a spiritual marriage in which he and his wife would spend quiet evenings with books, meeting again at breakfast refreshed (an "ecclesiastical capon," the Captain calls him).

Having been an orphan, Hadrian knows his own unconscious need: "I grew up reaching for something that wasn't there any more —maybe the breast of my mother. . . . Something warm and able to give me comfort—I guess that's what I'm still reaching for. To be warmed—touched—loved." It is Mathilda who touches him, by accident, when he has been given the Captain's bed for the night and Mathilda comes in the dark to kiss her father goodnight. Her tender touch brings Hadrian to propose next morning, but Mathilda virtually swoons at the thought. The prospect is loathsome to Emmie whose sexual jealousy is apparent; she tries immediately to block the marriage. (She had shot the rooster by mistake for the chicken the night before, and Hadrian says of her, "Well, at least she succeeded in reducing the net amount of masculinity on the place.") Eager to have Hadrian breathe new life into "the poor clay figure"

Emmie is making of his daughter, the Captain explains to Hadrian that he must proceed cautiously:

> Captain: Mathilda is a virgin.
> Hadrian: That I know.
> Captain: My sister is also a virgin.
> Hadrian: That I suspected.
> Captain: But there is a difference in their cases. Emmie's virginity is congenital.
> Hadrian: Isn't that mostly the case?
> Captain: No, no, no, a total misapprehension. Virginity is mostly the consequence of bad environment an' unfavorable social conditions. But Emmie's is congenital, and so firmly entrenched—that dynamite couldn't remove it.
> Hadrian: So——
> Captain: In Emmie's opinion, any threat to virginity is a threat to existence. Why, to me it's surprising that Emmie Rickley will even put a teaspoon in a cup.
> Hadrian: How about the Parson's?
> Captain: No threat!—not even a teaspoon.

When Emmie calls the police to accuse Hadrian of rape, the Captain finally takes command and puts a stop to Emmie's malicious efforts to thwart the marriage. But Hadrian knows that his opposition is not only external in Emmie but introjected as a defense mechanism within Mathilda. Gently he tells her of his need for her, and cautions her of the consequences of denying sexual fulfillment:

> There is only one danger for you—the horrible noiseless danger of locked up places . . . the world is only dangerous when it is locked out.

Mathilda walks around all night, gaining new awareness of herself, and matures enough to whisper when Hadrian says he wants her: "What's stopping you, you fool?" She embraces him warmly at the end, and her conversion seems genuine—at least it fulfills the audience's wish for her to find love.

MOST FAMOUS OF STREETCARS

After creating the Laura-Mathilda character who is all chaste and unawakened emotion, Tennessee Williams went on to explore her later destiny, as the Blanche-Alma character to whom sex comes too violently after too long a period of suppression.

Of all recent dramas, *A Streetcar Named Desire* is the quintessence of Freudian sexual psychology. Anyone familiar with Williams' one-act plays has seen clearly foreshadowed the development of Blanche DuBois of *Streetcar*. *The Lady of Larkspur Lotion* shows what a Blanche might have become if she had not met her nemesis in Stanley Kowalski—a derelict prostitute living on delusions in the French Quarter; a writer across the hall gives what might be the rationale for all the Blanches: "Is she to be blamed because it is necessary for her to compensate for the cruel deficiencies of reality by the exercise of a little—what shall I say?—God-given imagination?" Williams' *Portrait of a Madonna,* is another one-act which shows an old and still virginal version of Mathilda or Blanche manufacturing illusions—fantasies of rape and pregnancy—until she is taken away by the same doctor and nurse who come for Blanche when the *Streetcar* reaches the end of its tragic line.

A *Streetcar Named Desire* (1947) depicts characters who are volatile, colorful, deeply real for our times. With a mastery no playwright has equalled in this century, Williams arranges in a compelling theatrical pattern the agonized sexual anxiety of a girl caught between *id* and *ego-ideal*. Blanche DuBois arrives at her sister's squalid, dilapidated home in the French Quarter of New Orleans unconsciously playing a role, that of the gracious, refined lady of the old South—the same ego-ideal which Amanda held for herself. It is a sincere role, for it is the only one a sheltered Southern belle was raised to know. Blanche finds her sister, Stella, married to the shirtless Stanley Kowalski, a superbly original character who would have delighted D. H. Lawrence. "Since earliest manhood the center of his life has been pleasure with women, the giving and taking of it, not with weak indulgence, dependently, but with the power and pride of a richly feathered male bird among hens." Stanley immediately finds himself challenged and baffled by Blanche, whose "airs" are a defiance to his manhood and unconsciously dare him to conquer her. Blanche is overcome by his sensuality and almost vomits. She has met her match, and the play becomes an unconscious sexual battle between the two—although the principal battlefield is within Blanche herself.

Her sister, Stella (for Star) is anything but a star. She is a healthy housewife, adjusted to reality, expecting a child, and serenely happy in her physical relationship with Stanley. With unconscious jealousy, Blanche tries to split them apart and convince Stella that Stanley is an ape, "something sub-human, thousands of years old, a stone age cave man." In spite of Stanley's explosive temper, however, their violent quarrels always end in passionate reconciliation, and for Stella it is the "things that happen between a man and a woman in the dark" that make her life in the slums of New Orleans worthwhile.

It is this relationship that keeps Blanche in sexual anxiety, which she keeps in check with hot baths and shots of whiskey. Her almost hysterical drive is to find protection and security, which in the Southern chivalric code could only come from a gallant gentleman. She believes that she has found such a man in Mitch, a friend of Stanley's. With him Blanche is all coyness and charm, shielding a naked light bulb with a little colored lantern—which Williams makes the symbolic theme of the play: people who cannot face reality try to pretty it up with the colored shades of illusion. Her efforts to play the lady with Mitch irk Stanley until he spills to Stella the scandal which he has been motivated to dig up on "Dame Blanche": she had been a prostitute in Laurel and had been thrown out of the worst hotel in town. Stanley's ironic tale of her nymphomania, complete with soldiers from the nearby army camp and the loss of her position as a schoolteacher for seducing a 17-year-old boy, is told contrapuntally against the giddy singing of Blanche in the hot bath —"It's only a paper moon . . ." In fact, Williams throughout *Streetcar* has orchestrated the sounds of the French Quarter with a superb musical feeling—its sexual throbbing, its sensual "blue piano" playing, the voices of Mexican women, the violent fights of the couple upstairs, and the hallucinatory return of the Varsouvienne music to Blanche as she recalls the tragic story of her love for her husband. Only to Mitch is she able to reveal the details of her marriage to a sweet-faced, poetic boy who turned out to be a homosexual and who shot himself after she had found him with a man. Mitch in turn confides to her of his sick mother, and betrays himself as a boy with an Oedipus complex, wanting to escape his mother yet loyally worshipping her. In their mutual loneliness, Blanche and Mitch embrace passionately, and there is in this scene promise that marriage might be a salvation for them. But the tragedy for Blanche is that she has already whetted the appetite and sadism of Stanley, and now he becomes her *Ate* who tells Mitch about her past and destroys his illusion of her. Instead Mitch comes, drunk and vindictive, to seduce Blanche. His mother-attachment blocks what might have been a solution for him—Blanche now "isn't clean enough to bring into the house with his mother." He tears the colored lamp shade off to hold the naked bulb up into Blanche's haggard face. Unable to seduce Blanche as he hoped, he leaves and Blanche packs in a state of shock, deluding herself that she is going for a moonlight swim with spectral gentlemen callers. When Stella is rushed to the hospital in labor, Blanche is left alone in the house with Stanley; if ever there were an *obligatory scene* in the drama, this is it. Although she tries to defend herself with a broken bottle, Stanley quickly disarms her and rapes her, saying, "We've had this date with each other from the beginning."

When Stella comes home from the hospital with her baby, Blanche is again having a hot bath, and has mentally withdrawn from reality. She believes that an old gentleman caller whom she wrote is coming to take her away. Stella and Stanley summon the doctor and nurse from the state mental asylum, although Stella feels guilt over commiting her sister and does not accept Blanche's story of Stan raping her. Though she does Blanche a technical injustice, it cannot alter her psychological destiny. Blanche is too psychotic now to be helped by the Kowalskis, and has transferred all her life-hope from Mitch to the illusionary gentleman caller whom she is sure will phone her. When the doctor arrives, she seems aware at first that he is not the gentleman caller, but when the doctor uses charm and gentleness instead of force, Blanche goes off with him at the end humbly grateful for his solicitous attention.

In *A Streetcar Named Desire,* Williams has depicted profoundly the origins and growth of schizophrenia. He has shown Blanche struggling to master her conflicting drives of sex and *super-ego,* to live up to an inner image of a belle of the old South while living in circumstances in which it is an anachronism. At first she is in rebellion against her own nature but in touch with reality. As the various doors of escape are closed to her and she finds Stanley across her one remaining path, her mind is unable to cope with this impossible conflict. She closes the door to reality and escapes to a psychotic world where gallant gentlemen will give her shelter.

There were some critics who considered Blanche as fit only for a hospital but not the tragic stage. Edward Chodorov, for example, questioned in his letter to the present author whether *Streetcar* met the requirements of tragedy. The director of the Broadway production, Elia Kazan, takes issue with Chodorov's position and in an astute analysis calls the play a poetic tragedy:

> We are shown the final dissolution of a person of worth, who once had great potential, and who, even as she goes down, has worth exceeding that of the 'healthy,' coarse-grained figures who kill her.

It is not merely an academic issue to test a play such as *Streetcar* by the classic, Aristotelian standards, for with it much of the modern drama may stand or fall. As Kazan points out, Blanche is a character of some dignity who strives to rise above her circumstances. In the love scene with Mitch she lifts the play to universality, and Williams achieved the tragic irony of Sophocles in the discrepancy between reality and Blanche's distorted impression of it. Aristotelians balk, however, at the fact that Blanche achieves no insight, and to the contrary regresses until her final exit is made with no sublime tragic awareness of the forces that determined her destiny. But there is an escape from the dilemma—modern psychoanalytic psychology suggests a reinterpretation of Aristotle that restores *Streetcar* to the rank of tragic drama and at the same time confirms the universal insight of the observant Stagirite. It is simply that although Blanche closes her mind to any awareness as she escapes to psychosis, the insight happens *to the audience*. Williams is able to depict with his raw power the growth of psychosis out of simple defense mechanism, to show the conflict in a sensitive spirit between ugly reality and the quest for beauty. Blanche's tragedy is that of the individual unable to integrate the sex drive, to reconcile the physical hunger with tender and spiritual yearnings. Because of her sheltered background she cannot find security by other means than sexual ones. Thus she has as little free will to choose her destiny as had Oedipus. By illuminating Blanche's sickness, by dramatizing the dark unconscious forces with which Blanche grapples and by which she is defeated, the dramatist, like the psychoanalyst, makes it possible for others to be purged of guilt and fear, to say "There, but for the grace of whatever mental health I have been able to achieve, go I." To understand and participate in Blanche's fate is to escape it. Williams must be credited with a psychological masterpiece; *Streetcar* is powerful naturalism but also infinitely more—it affords a clear perception into the pressures that degrade, both the social forces which make for an environment of brutality and the individual's unconscious forces which make him a psychic cripple helpless to deal with his environment. Blanche is no less a tragic figure than Antigone or Medea—whether she is literally destroyed or whether it is only her mind seems but a technicality. It is a tragic experience in the theatre to participate in the disintegration of a personality.

As if to answer the critics who thought Blanche too special a case, Williams shows in his next play a small Southern town where the forces that nurtured Blanche are at work. *Summer and Smoke* (1948) is a kind of prologue, an Advance Section of the *Streetcar Named Desire*. Before her marriage to the poetic boy with homosexual tendencies, Williams seems to suggest, Blanche might have been like this girl, Alma Winemuller, delicate, refined, sensitive, interested in the "finer things of life"—yet strongly sexual (although this is largely unconscious). As a defense mechanism against her sexuality she develops a kind of prissiness, nervous laughter, prudery, and somatic symptoms as well: fast heartbeat, the sensation of her fingers being frozen when she is in panic, and swallowing air which gives her indigestion. Alma's mother is a psychotic who has regressed to a petulant childhood, demanding ice-cream cones like a spoiled child as her price for staying out of her husband's way. Alma is prematurely spinsterish because she has had to substitute for her mother at her father's rectory. The preacher has been overly strict with his daughter, objecting even to her singing; we see within Alma at the beginning the seeds of the same devastating conflict between physical desire and a stern *super-ego* which overwhelmed Blanche DuBois.

Alma's childhood neighbor and friend is John Buchanan, son of the town doctor and himself a doctor but frustrated in the stagnant town and unable to find outlets other than sexual dissipation for his powers.

He and Alma are attracted to each other, but there is a constant tug of war between them. He knows that Alma's swallowing air is "a little trick that hysterical women get into." Her *doppelgänger* is irritated, John tells her. John must choose between invitations to anaemic evenings at the rectory with Alma and dates with erotic-sadistic Rosa Gonzales, whose father runs a roadhouse of questionable reputation. Where all was violent eruption in *Streetcar* the mood here is muted and handled with charm. Alma comes over to John's at two in the morning, suspecting that he has Rosa there. She is in hysteria and is frightened of her heartbeat. John tells her to unbutton her blouse so he can listen to the stethoscope, but her fingers are frozen. All John can hear through the stethoscope is a little voice saying "Miss Alma is lonesome." His prescription is a date with her for Saturday.

On the date he takes her out near the questionable roadhouse, and tells her:

> Under the surface you have a lot of excitement, a great deal more than any other woman I have met. So much that you have to carry these sleeping pills with you.

Alma kisses him, but they are chaste kisses. She insists that a man must respect a woman whom he will want to be the mother of his children. John, however, tells her that on his anatomical chart of the human body, there is no area marked "soul." (Alma is Spanish for Soul, she has pointed out.) "There's other things between a man and a woman besides respect. Did you know that, Miss Alma?" When he offers to show her what they are, she is so offended that she calls a taxi and goes home alone.

John, thereafter, makes other adjustments for his sexual needs. He has a torrid party with Rosa during his father's absence, while next door Alma is in such a jealous panic that she calls John's father to come home. John meanwhile comes sobbing to Alma's maternal lap while his father returns, orders Rosa's drunken father out of his house, and is shot by him.

After the death of his father, John goes away and finds maturity, while Alma goes into a decline. John returns to marry Nellie, the little coquettish daughter of the town "merry widow." When Alma learns of their engagement, she goes to John in a touching scene and humbly offers herself to him now on any terms he wants. She has come over to his way of thinking now—she had looked up *doppelgänger* and found that it means "another person inside me, another self." Alma has now laid to rest the other self, the prudish self: "she died last summer . . . suffocated in smoke from something on fire inside her." But now it is too late, as it was for Blanche and Mitch. John too has changed, and ironically has accepted Alma's thinking. He tells her he knows now it was her purity and tenderness which he craved—the projection of yearning for maternal affection which has been frustrated in him. Now John has found Nellie, who somehow manages to combine for him the duality of sensual (Rosa) and tender (Alma) impulses. Alma lost him because she won the argument about the chart. She has become identified now as his mother-image. Even if she had let him at the Casino, he exclaims, "I wouldn't feel *decent* enough to touch you." Alma is utterly bereft, and in a state of shock goes off to pick up a travelling salesman as Nellie's mother was reputed to have done. To atone, she condemns herself to do promiscuously what she missed doing for love with John. At the end of *Summer and Smoke* she has entered the phase of her life where Blanche DuBois was before her escapades forced her to leave Laurel and come to New Orleans. The character of John is hardly the equal of Stanley Kowalski, and the play is restrained and delicate where *Streetcar* is explosive and raw; but *Summer and Smoke* is a fine and revealing portrait of the hysterical repression of sex into conversion symptoms in the South—which to Williams symbolizes the last stronghold of unrealistic, ostrich-attitudes.

BREAKING THE MOLD

To confute his critics who said that Williams had only one string to his violin and could create only portraits of sexually stifled Southern belles, he selected the florid, passionate Sicilian peasants of the Gulf Coast for the subject of his next play, *The Rose Tattoo* (1951). As in *Summer and Smoke*, the set is a skeletonized view into two rooms, but this time it is surrounded by the richly orchestrated overtones of Italian folk *mores;* peasant neighbors form a kind of menacing chorus of Greek Furies, there is a witch with the Malocche (Evil Eye), and a wealth of other detail that frames this lusty romance.

The leading character, Serafina Delle Rose, is a monumental figure. She is the first of Tennessee Williams' women who cannot be said to be in any way "repressed." She is impulsive, out-going, intensely emotional, childlike in her simple faith. She has had a satisfying sex life with her husband, and is now pregnant. With peasant superstition she is convinced that at the moment of her recent conception the rose her husband has tattooed on his chest was transferred to her breast. She soon learns, however, that her husband has been killed while smuggling narcotics under his truckload of bananas. How Serafina endures the traumatic loss of her loved one and her unborn baby as well forms the main action of the play.

For three years Serafina remains secure and happy in the memory of her life with her dead husband. She keeps his ashes in an urn in the living room, although it is against the priest's orders. To the two floozies who give her work as a seamstress, Serafina speaks with religious eloquence of her sexual fulfillment:

> When I think of a man I think about my husband. My husband was a Sicilian. We had love together every night of the week, we never skipped one, from the night we was married till the night he was killed in his fruit truck on that road there . . . I count up the nights I held him all night in my arms, and I can tell you how many . . . I *know* what love-making was. And I'm satisfied just to remember . . . I'm satisfied to remember the love of a man that was mine—*only Mine!*

But the two floozies prattle about her husband's mistress, and Serafina collapses in a state of shock, praying to the virgin for a sign to confirm or deny the gossip. Serafina's adolescent daughter, Rose, has in the intervening years matured enough to date a sailor, and this, too, has thrown Serafina into such a frenzy that she keeps the girl locked up in her room naked. After Rose tries to slash her wrist, the schoolteacher persuades Serafina to let Rose go to her graduation, but first Serafina talks to the sailor and makes him swear on his knees to the Virgin that he will not take the virginity of Rose.

The second act takes as its motif: "Oh, Lady! Give me a sign," and is as tight and breathtakingly constructed as the first act was loose and episodic. Serafina tries to browbeat the priest into telling her if her husband had confessed an affair to him, and eloquently tells him what she thinks of frigid women who put their big bed in the basement and get twin beds after age thirty:

> They make the life without glory. Instead of the heart they got the deep-freeze in the house. The men, they don't feel no glory, not in the house with them women; they go to bars, fight in them, get drunk, get fat, put horns on the women because the women don't give them the love which is glory.—I did, I give him the glory. To me the big bed was beautiful like a religion. Now I lie on it with dreams, with memories only.

Serafina lets herself become slovenly and unkempt, almost animal-like, from depression over the loss of her ideal image of Rosario. Then into her life comes another Sicilian truck driver, Alvaro Mangiacavallo (Eat-a-Horse), a lonely little bachelor with three dependents. He resembles her husband in body but his face is that of a clown. To overcome his sense of inferiority and woo her, Alvaro has tattooed on his chest a rose similar to Rosario's. That and the Oil of Rose in his hair are too much for Serafina. She smashes the urn of Rosario's ashes and spends the night with Alvaro.

In the early dawn, Rose and her sailor return. He has respected his vow, and idealistically worships Rose. But at fifteen she is all hot desire and provokes him unbearably. She would like to meet him in New Orleans and go to a hotel with him, but he will not let her. Then she goes to sleep on the sofa. Later Alvaro is drunkenly leaning over her to admire her when Serafina discovers him and chases him around in a jealous fit. Rose is shocked to find that her mother hypocritically spent the night with a man after denying the same outlet to the young lovers, and there is a subtly handled resurgence of the Electra jealousy of mother and daughter:

> Serafina: Don't look at me like that with the eyes of your father!
> Rose: Yes, I am looking at you with the eyes of my father.
> I see you the way *he* saw you. Like this, this *pig*.

In disillusion, Rose determines to meet her sailor in New Orleans. Serafina finally sends Rose off with her blessings: "How beautiful—is my daughter! Go to the boy!" and is herself radiant, believing she has conceived because she saw the rose tattoo again on her breast. She has been freed of the past by smashing the urn, and now is released to take up a new life with Alvaro.

After three plays decrying the idea of living an illusion or "life-sustaining lie," *The Rose Tattoo* might be called Williams' *Wild Duck*. Perhaps Serafina needed never to know about Rosario's affair with another woman. But at the end we see that even this truth must be faced. Serafina will have a fuller life with Alvaro than if she had remained alone with her dead husband's ashes and image. And, certainly, this time she has fewer illusions about Alvaro; he is only a little man who needs her, and who found the way to break through her defenses with a rose tattooed on his chest. *The Rose Tattoo* is less complex from the psychoanalytic point of view and more of a folk play than Williams' previous work. At times, the actual drama fails to equal the emotional intensity Williams calls for in the stage directions. He has taxed the resources of the theatre to a new limit ,and yet the form of the play remains imperfect. There is in *The Rose Tattoo*, however, a growth of the poetic feeling for character with which Williams writes and which had been muted since *The Glass Menagerie*; there is genuine power and compassion as Williams extracts drama out of a fresh and ingratiating set of characters. Most of all there is one further illustration of Tennessee Williams' main theme—of the central power of sex in human life.

The Rose Tattoo meant breaking out of a mold for Williams, and in his next play he went much further, creating his most subjective and surrealistic play-form. Based upon an early one-act, *Ten Blocks on the Camino Real*, the idea is said to have come to Williams when he was sick and despondent in a desolate part of Mexico. In *Camino Real* (1953) he expands this image into a full-fledged dream play, in which the town square of a little Latin-American village becomes the world in microcosm, a kind of symbolic dead-end for the traveler who is Man. The published version adds a prologue which sets the play up as the dream of Don Quixote, legendary tilter with windmills, who comes from the back of the auditorium to motivate the action. As a gate like a frontier barrier is lowered across the proscenium, Don Quixote proclaims the beginning of his fantastic dream: "And my dream will be a pageant, a masque in which old meanings will be remembered and possibly new ones discovered, and when I wake from this sleep and this disturbing pageant of a dream, I'll choose one among its shadows to take along with me in place of Sancho . . ." The dream symbols are universal and literary rather than personally related to Don Quixote, and when Williams was asked in an interview to give the key to his symbols, he felt that the play did not require explanation:

> We all have in our conscious and unconscious minds a great vocabulary of images, and I think all human communication is based on these images as well as our dreams are based on them, and a symbol in a play has only one legitimate purpose which is to say a thing more directly and simply and beautifully than it could be said in words.

To Williams the people of *Camino Real* were ". . . mostly archetypes of certain basic attitudes and qualities, with those mutations that would occur if they had continued along the road to this hypothetically terminal point in it." His symbols include the eternal lover, Jacques Casanova, the sentimental courtesan with tuberculosis, Marguerite, the brilliant poet in search of an ideal, Lord Byron, the Baron who is an erotic-sadistic homosexual, the little man, Kilroy, who is perhaps autobiographical, and a sinister authoritarian, a God-image who holds a white cockatoo named Aurora on his wrist and manipulates the destiny of the town with a Fascist police force. It is he who announces the blocks or episodes as they occur on the Camino Real.

Kilroy had been a boxer in America until his heart went bad and he had to give up boxing and sex. Everywhere he finds vice, cruelty, leering depravity, and death on the Camino Real. His image of himself changes to that of a clown or Patsy, and he is chased as in an anxiety dream. He finds a kindred spirit in Esmerelda, the daughter of a gypsy who announces that at the full moon the virginity of her daughter will be restored. This takes place in a kind of primitive village rite of fertility, a Fiesta of the Coronation of the King of Cuckolds. When an unscheduled airliner lands, there is frantic struggle to get passage, and, again as in dream-anxiety Marguerite can never get on board. When a wealthy old man collapses of heart failure, the two inevitable street cleaners, Death, come to take his body away. Though Marguerite would have left without Jacques, he stands by her now as she is failing, and speaks persuasively of the power of love as a defense against betrayal—the opposite of Marguerite's betrayal as a defense against love. Kilroy is alone at last with the gypsy girl after her mother has extracted ten dollars from him, but the experience leaves them both disillusioned. Finally the streetcleaners come for Kilroy and he meets them swinging blindly: "Come on, you sons of bitches! Kilroy is Here! He's ready!"

Camino Real does not end here, but goes on to become a gruesome nightmare as a Medical Instructor conducts a post-mortem of Kilroy and extracts his solid gold heart. Kilroy runs after his heart, seizes it and is pursued around the theatre. He would pawn his heart to buy jewels for Esmerelda but she falls asleep disinterested. When he would utterly despair, Quixote advises Kilroy, "Don't! Pity! Your! Self!" and Kilroy goes on with Quixote in place of Sancho. There is new hope for himself and the others—for Jacques whom Marguerite finally embraces and for mankind. There was an escape after all from this dead-end, though it is through a bleak desert. Kilroy, who was dead, has been reborn. Williams has celebrated the death and resurrection of Man, with his allegory played not on medieval pageant wagons but in a brothel, a pawn shop, and a flophouse.

Camino Real has many powerful moments and startling effects. Though the anxiety dream determines its form, the content is philosophical and even a little platitudinous. The characters have little inter-relation and the plot generates little suspense. The subjective dream perspective does not remain with any one character but shifts bewilderingly. The final theme is not hopelessness, however, but one of hope through human tenderness and brotherhood. As Saroyan has discovered, there are dangers in surrealistic playwriting, and Williams has not entirely escaped them; in some respects his shorter, one-act version is more effective than its expansion to a larger pattern which is not always illuminating. Mr. Williams has written that he felt "a new sensation of release," in working on *Camino Real*, and hoped to transfer this to his audience:

> My desire was to give these audiences my own sense of something wild and unrestricted that ran like water in the mountains, or clouds changing shape in a gale, or the continually dissolving and transforming images of a dream. This sort of freedom is not chaos nor anarchy. On the contrary, it is the result of painstaking design, and in this work I have given more conscious attention to form and construction than I have in any work before. Freedom is not achieved simply by working freely.

That Williams did not entirely succeed in imparting these wild images to his Broadway audiences was apparent, but the play inspired a stream of hotly defensive as well as hostile letters to the *New York Times*. Two barriers stood between Williams and his audience—his unrelenting pessimism and cynical view of modern life, and his use of psychoanalytic dream symbols instead of direct statement. Dreams at best require interpretation—and a cosmic dream of universal degeneracy and depravity proved more than a little disturbing for playgoers.

Camino Real represents a mid-point in the artistic development of Williams. He apparently felt it necessary to break out of the mold of his early naturalistic and psychoanalytic studies of suppressed spinsters unable to face reality in a sexual world. He has demonstrated in *Streetcar* and *The Rose Tattoo* his ability to create vigorous, earthy, uninhibited portraits, and in *The Glass Menagerie* his gift for dealing sensitively and poetically with human frustration. If he perceives that surrealism, like the Camino Real, may prove to be a dead-end and returns to psychological realism, there is little doubt that Williams will maintain his position beside Arthur Miller —the two most important American playwrights of mid-century.

FATHERS AND SONS

Arthur Miller, the author of what many consider to be the most important drama yet written by an American, brings to a climax the psychological drama thus far in the twentieth century. By comparison with Tennessee Williams, Miller is more objective, more sociopolitical in his orientation, less poetic, better able to depict men than women, and more systematic than intuitive in his play construction. From his plays and the comments on his questionnaire it would seem that Miller, of all American playwrights, comes the closest thus far to illustrating Freud's prediction that ultimately writers will assimilate psychoanalysis ". . . at so deep a level of knowing that they will not be aware that they are employing it: it will have to them the character of self-evidence."

Although it was a Broadway failure, Miller's first play, *The Man Who Had All The Luck* (1944), is interesting for its foreshadowing of his major theme—that of the relationship of fathers and sons. In this connection Miller stated in his reply to the questionnaire on Freudian influence: "Have never identified any ruling idea of mine with Freud, although the struggle of father and sons (which of course antedates Freud) seems to be central to his theories." He did not, however, know which of Freud's theories were most influential on his work, and had never discussed his characters with a psychoanalyst. He said that he had "dipped into a few" books by psychoanalysts "but could never finish one."

It is the sons who most interest Miller in *The Man Who Had All The Luck*. The older son, David, is the man who has more luck than sense—in winning his girl, in business, and in his family. The younger son, however, has none of this luck. Their father had, like Willy Loman, raised him to be the apple of his eye, to believe in his own great destiny, and to train for a career as a big league baseball player. The scene in which a baseball scout for the Dodgers tells him that he will not be hired was apparently a particularly effective one, as was the moment when the father confesses that he too was lucky—he got a military citation in 1918 because the roof of a brothel fell in on him.

As David's luck grows, he feels not confident but guilty, knowing that his capacities far from equal his success and that others who have worked harder have had less reward. In the end, David wishes for misfortune as punishment for a luck that he cannot comprehend. Some of the critics were not sure as to Miller's theme, but others commented on his understanding that fathers may warp their sons' lives by instilling false ambitions and unrealistic goals which can only lead to failure and "bad luck." Burton Rascoe, Louis Kronenberger and John Chapman were among the critics who saw genuine merit in Miller's first play.

Miller, who studied drama at the University of Michigan, wrote a diary of his experiences during the war gathering material at various army camps (an old football injury kept him out of service); this material was used in the film *The Story of G.I. Joe.* His first novel, *Focus,* dealt with anti-semitism in an American town, and he contributed a number of worthwhile radio scripts, including the delightful *The Pussycat and the Expert Plumber Who Was A Man,* and a historical father-son conflict, *William Ireland's Confession.* It was 1947 before Miller returned to the theatre with one of the most meaningful plays to come out of World War II, *All My Sons.*

Although the theme in *All My Sons* deals with social responsibility and business ethics during the war, the play contained the elements of Miller's psychology which was to be enlarged to major proportions in *Death of a Salesman.* The son here has devotion, even worship, for his father rather than hostility; but the feelings of father as a God who can do no wrong is in itself a denial and a compensation for the earlier Oedipal hostility—a way of absolving guilt by saying in effect, "How could I have ever hated him—he's great." At the moment of crisis in both plays, when the father is shorn of his infallibility and reduced to human size, the old Oedipal hatred flares so intensely that the sons are at their fathers' throats.

The son in *All My Sons* is Chris, who has come back from the war to work with Keller, his father, in their business, and who says of his warmhearted, richly human father:

Chris: Isn't he a great guy?
Ann: You're the only one I know who loves his parents!
Chris: I know. It went out of style, didn't it?

The other son, Larry, has been missing in áction, but it is the mother's psychic, almost obsessive conviction that he is still alive. This theme of the missing son's return is intricately interwoven with the other theme of the father's company having shipped defective airplane engines to the Air Force, causing the death of twenty-one fliers—for which Keller's foreman went to prison. Now the foreman's daughter, Ann, returns to marry Chris, but this presents two hazards —Ann had been Larry's girl and the marriage would violate the mother's conviction that he is still alive; secondly, Ann's imprisoned father will be bitter and unforgiving for Keller's insistence in court that he was sick the day the fateful decision was made to ship the cracked cylinders. With a mastery of compression equal to Ibsen, the latter theme gradually takes control of the play as Ann's brother, convinced of Keller's guilt, comes to prevent Ann's marrying Chris.

Chris becomes a significant figure, struggling with his sense of integrity and attempting to clarify his thinking about his father; he tries at first to suppress any suspicion that his father was guilty, lest it make a mockery of the entire war and the death of his own buddies:

I got an idea—watching them go down. Everything was being destroyed, see, but it seemed to me that one new thing was made. A kind of . . . responsibility. Man for man. You understand me? . . . I mean you can take those things out of a war . . . you've got to know that it came out of the love a man can have for a man, you've got to be a little better because of that. Otherwise what you have is really loot, and there's blood on it.

Chris' hero-worship of his father must not be tampered with, be-cause unconsciously rooted in it lies all of his conscious ideals and humanitarianism. The final "love that man can have for man" is the love of father and son.

But Chris is haunted into agonized uncertainty by a careless slip of the tongue his mother makes—Keller, who is supposed to have been too sick to go to the plant when he knew of the cracked cyl-inders, "hasn't been laid up in fifteen years." In a scene as electric as anything in the modern theatre, Chris demands of his father: "Explain it to me. What did you do? Explain it to me or I'll tear you to pieces!" (These words might suggest to a psychoanalyst the Freudian *Totem and Taboo* in which the sons literally tear the father to pieces and devour his flesh ceremonially). Keller's explanation is inadequate and, in fact, a confession; but it is an eloquent defense of a philosophy which is not unfamiliar: "I'm in business, a man is in business; a hundred and twenty cracked, and you're out of business; . . . Chris, I did it for you, it was a chance and I took it for you. I'm sixty-one years old, when would I have another chance to make something for you?" Chris answers:

> What the hell do you mean, you did it for me? Don't you have a country? Don't you live in the world? What the hell are you? You're not even an animal, no animal kills his own, what are you? What must I do to you? I ought to tear the tongue out of your mouth, what must I do? (*With his fist he pounds down upon his father's shoulder. He stumbles away, covering his face as he weeps.*) What must I do, Jesus God, what must I do?

In a state of shock at the collapse of his ideal image of his father, Chris drives around most of the night, while Keller has time to prepare a kind of rationalization—to the effect that no business man did anything for the war effort until he got his price. Chris answers "*I know you're no worse than most men but I thought you were better. I never saw you as a man. I saw you as my father.*"

Ann brings both themes to crisis when she reveals the last letter Larry had written her, in which he had just learned of the scandal at his father's firm and had been so enraged that he said he could kill his father. His ideal also smashed, he had written Ann he was going on a suicide mission. Now the mother knows he will not return and the father knows that he has lost the respect of all his sons. He has no alternative but to take his own life.

The father-son relationship is shorn of extraneous plot complications and brought superbly to realization in the Pulitzer-Prize-winning *Death of a Salesman* (1949). No son ever depicted a more epic father with all the characteristically American ambitions and frailties of fatherhood than did Miller with Willy Loman. Where the dramaturgy in *All My Sons* was realistic and retrogressive in Ibsen's tradition, in *Death of a Salesman* it is subjective, free-associational and deeply psychoanalytic. Enriching our theatre with a fresh use of the stream-of-unconscious technique which Miller must have mastered as a radio writer, his characters do not return to the past—rather the repressed past returns subtly to the present, gradually to take possession of the deteriorating mind of Willy. We first see Willy past the age of sixty, coming home exhausted, unable to complete his trip, carrying his two huge (and symbolic) salesman's cases which

weight him down. Willy's car had been going off the road as he day-
dreamed "such strange thoughts," brought on by the return of Biff,
his thirty-four year old son, who is still a wanderer and failure. Biff
had come home the day before and the old hostility between father
and son had flared immediately. Willy is volatile, impulsive, emotionally trigger-sensitive, and ambivalent toward Biff. He calls him a lazy
bum one minute and "he's not lazy" the next. Willy is a quixotic
dreamer, wanting greatness for his sons, Happy and Biff. Willy's
tragedy is that his dreams for Biff are totally out of touch with the
reality of Biff's deeply rooted feeling of inferiority. Happy, the
younger son, suffers none of Biff's insecurity and is nearer to following in his father's footsteps, working in a store, keeping a car, an
apartment and women who are like bowling—"I just keep knockin'
them over and it doesn't mean anything." Both boys wish they could
find a nice girl like Mom and get married, but neither makes any
effort in that direction.

More and more, the past returns to Willy, his old red Chevy of
1928, his memory of the open horizon before apartment buildings
hemmed in their home. As his hallucinatory free associations are
visualized, the realistic lighting fades, a projected pattern of remembered sunlight through the leaves surrounds his skeletonized Brooklyn home, and flute music is heard (we learn later Willy's father was
an itinerant maker of flutes). Willy's first regression is to Biff's young
manhood when he simonized the car and was captain of the high
school football team, for whom the cheering section goes wild yelling
"Loman." Willy even found excuses for Biff's petty thievery in his
headlong wish-fulfillment for him to be great.

Bernard, the son of his old friend, Charley, next door, would
help Biff study, but Willy's ambitions for Biff do not run in that direction. Willy's motto is, "Be liked and you will never want." Willy's
ideal is a salesman who at eighty-four could pick up a phone and
make a living getting orders. He visualizes himself as a likeable,
witty, high-powered huckster, a go-getter, a "man-with-contacts."
But to his wife, Linda, he confesses that selling isn't as easy as he tells
the boys, that it actually comes hard to him and that he has a perpetual fear—almost paranoid—that people are laughing at him. Even
as he tells Linda how much he loves her, he remembers a woman
in Boston who came up to his hotel room and brought him a brief
respite from the pressures of mortgage, insurance and refrigerator
payments, the life of bills which he shared with his wife. As Willy
tries to concentrate on a card game with Charley, he is haunted
by the memory of Ben, Willy's older brother, who has just died and

who symbolizes for Willy all the material success he never achieved. Willy barely remembers his father, "just Mamma's lap and a man with a big beard." So Ben has become a father-image to Willy, and has given Willy the same feelings of unsureness and inferiority that he has given Biff. Ben has made his fortune in Africa and Alaska, and perpetually chants the leit-motif, "William, when I walked into the jungle I was seventeen. When I walked out I was twenty-one. And by God, I was rich!"

While Willy is engrossed in his inner world, the boys and the mother are shocked at his mental deterioration; but Linda loyally insists that the boys respect him. She gives the play its universal social pertinence when she cries out:

> But he's a human being, and a terrible thing is happening to
> him. So attention must be paid. He's not to be allowed to
> fall into his grave like an old dog. Attention, attention must
> be finally paid to such a person.

Realizing that his father is suicidal and has been hiding a section of rubber hose near the gas pipes, Biff agrees to stay home and try to live up to Willy's expectations. He renews a contact with a former employer who might help him (even though he had once stolen some basketballs from his store).

The next day Biff goes to see the man, hoping for a big loan which would enable him to go in business with Happy. Meanwhile Willy is in high spirits—the house will be paid for in one more installment—and he goes to his boss, the son of the man who employed Willy for many years, to ask for a transfer to a job that won't require travelling. The young boss, depicted not as a villain but merely as disinterested in Willy and preoccupied with a wire recorder of his child's voice, not only does not transfer Willy but fires him altogether. Willy cries out to Ben in his daze—"How did you do it? What's the answer?" Still seeking an answer and a meaning for his misdirected life, Willy goes to Bernard, now a successful attorney, and learns a crucial fact: it was after Biff came to see Willy in Boston that his attitude changed, he gave up high school and entered on his path of failure. "What happened in Boston, Willy?" Bernard asks, "that made Biff lose his ambition?"

After the big interview, Biff and Happy plan to meet Willy and treat him to a meal. But Biff had been curtly brushed off by the employer and had compulsively stolen a fountain pen off his desk. Willy joins them and they order drinks, a magnificently ironic feast of the failures. With a trumpet note jarring Willy, he hardly hears Biff tell of stealing the fountain pen; he staggers to the washroom in panic, reliving the moment in Boston when Biff, coming up to get Dad to "fix" his flunk in math, surprised Willy with the other woman in the hotel room, and suffered a traumatic, dizzy loss of illusion about his father. Shocked to learn his father is a sexual human and not a God, Biff's Oedipal disillusion centers around Willy's giving the woman stockings he should have given Linda. Willy is left yelling to Biff on the floor of the washroom as the boys desert him for two wenches they have picked up.

As Willy clarifies in his mind what he must do, he feels a need to leave his seed behind him in a worthier form than his sons, and is found out in the dark, planting in the garden. Even contemplating his own funeral his ideas are grandiose—buyers from all over New England will come and Biff will see how well liked his father was. Biff comes to say goodbye to Willy, planning to go away for good, convinced that he is doomed to failure. Willy still has a paranoiac conviction that Biff is doing this merely to spite Willy, and refuses to shake his hand. But now Biff has come to an awareness of himself, to insight into the forces that made him what he is. "We never told the truth for ten minutes in this house!" he realizes. He is able to confess that he has been in jail, a compulsive kleptomaniac who stole his way out of every job, unable to endure not being a big shot. The father and son are at each other's throat viciously, and then Biff sobs in Willy's arms. Willy is elated that Biff loves him and cries out to his imaginary Ben, "Oh, if I could kiss him, Ben!" Willy imagines how great Biff will be with the $20,000 he can leave him from his insurance policy, and staggers out to be run over and killed by an auto.

His funeral is a quiet little postscript, to which no buyers swarm, merely his sons, his wife, and old Charley, who knows the meaning of Willy's tragedy: "He had the wrong dreams. All, all, wrong . . . He never knew who he was."

Dr. Daniel Schneider, author of *The Psychoanalyst and the Artist,* has written a provocative psychoanalytic interpretation of *Death of a Salesman.* Paying eloquent tribute to the deep level of insight into unconscious forces which this play, like *Hamlet,* achieves, Schneider points out that the full power of Miller's work can only be assessed by noting what the play would be if the hallucinations were deleted. Without them the play is a routine bourgeois "death of a Babbitt." But with the "inner logic of his erupting volcanic unconscious," the play becomes a lucid experience. "It is visualized psychoanalytic interpretation woven into reality."

Schneider points out the symbolic nature of the three men's meeting in the restaurant—the eons-old Freudian totem-feast in which the sons make peace with their father over sexual rivalry. When the results don't turn out as Willy hoped, however, and he learns that Biff has stolen the employer's fountain pen (a psycho-analytic symbol for castration, as were the stolen basketballs), Willy is forced to rush into the wash-room in a castration-panic. Willy is deserted in favor of the "babes" and is left babbling impotently at the sexual, competitive assertion of his sons. Willy, himself a younger son and "low-man on a totem-pole," has a deep, guilty hatred for Ben who made the grade; he could have gone to Alaska under Ben's patronage, but he had to stay and out-do Ben. He is finally over-whelmed with his own guilt, although he cannot admit even to him-self that he destroyed Biff by disillusioning him in Boston. Schneider concludes that, "It is one of the most concentrated expressions of aggression and pity ever to be put on the stage. If Arthur Miller's *All My Sons* was aptly named, then this work is All Our Fathers."

In the questionnaire to Miller, he was asked if he agreed with Dr. Schneider's Freudian interpretation of the play. His comment was:

> He made several extremely fascinating observations; I can-not vouch for some of the interpretations; some of them are anthropological—(the "Totemic" idea). Impossible to "agree" or "disagree," because I do not know my subconscious well enough.

Miller reflected throughout his questionnaire a great respect for Froud's ideas and a humility toward the unconscious sources of his own creative power. When asked if he had ever sought for tech-niques to dramatize for the audience the workings of the uncon-scious (an academic question to the author of *Death of a Salesman*) he replied, "Always. The externalization of conscious but repressed, and unconscious thoughts and motives is the basic problem of dra-matic structure."

To the question of which play most reflected Freudian psy-chology, Miller replied, "*Salesman,* I suppose. But again, for good or ill, am not conscious of using Freudian ideas, but am told that is what I do!" His general comment on the value of Freudian attitudes for the playwright is succinctly expressed:

> Whatever I have received from Freud has come "through the air." It is part of me; I could not therefore evaluate it separately. All I can say is that analysts and analyzed people find corroboration in my plays from time to time and so I assume I have been "influenced." If so, it is a good influence.

I know enough to say, however, that the schematic use of Freud in art is disastrous. The problem of art is not to dramatize Freud, to 'prove' him, but rather to go beyond and discover the total truth of the making of man—the interaction of his inherited nature with the Society in which he must struggle to mature—and to so symbolize the disparate as to create 'beauty,' which is the ultimate organization of reality.

Death of a Salesman may prove to be the finest American tragedy thus far in the twentieth century. Certainly it is the one which best succeeds in compressing deeply understood psychological relationships into a form that is vibrantly alive in the theatre. Its success must indicate that there are enough Willy Lomans and sons among our playgoers to give universality to the subject. Its blinding flashes of insight into modern American standards make it the most overwhelming playgoing experience of our times. Gassner has called it "one of the triumphs of the mundane American stage," although he interprets it as *drame bourgeois* rather than genuine high tragedy. True, there is no *anagnorosis*, no recognition by the tragic hero of the reason for his downfall. Willy goes to his death sure that his way of raising Biff was right and that Biff would be great. But the *anagnorosis* is there, and is given instead to Biff, who is purged of his father-hostility when he comes to see his father for what he is. Naively bungling through the parent-child relationship, Willy never knew where Biff got his inferiority feelings—nor where he got his own. But he dedicated himself to a high ideal, that of raising his sons well, and his ambitions are those of every man for his children. The final dignity is given to Willy by his wife, by the majesty with which she endows him. Coupled with Miller's profound understanding of the emotions of sons and fathers is a sure social point of view which sees the falsity of the "hail-fellow-well-met," "don't get caught at it" standards which the Willy Lomans hold up for themselves and their children. Finding oneself for Miller implies both psychological insight and social integration. The glib, false-front salesman, ". . . way out there in the blue, riding on a smile and a shoeshine," cannot help but be a tragic figure when viewed through the eyes of all his sons.

HISTORY AND PSYCHOANALYSIS

In his most recent work, Miller turns away from family relationships (one hopes only temporarily) to express his social and moral indignation over an incident in American history which could have dangerous analogy in our contemporary era of McCarthyism. *The Crucible* (1953) is a powerful historical recreation of the 1692 witch-hunt of Salem, Massachusetts and a stern illustration for all Americans of the need for church and state to be kept forever separate.

Although Miller's purpose is socio-political, he cannot help but view history with his deep insight into unconscious motives. The facts are known—his purpose is to explain the "why" of history. The little band of Salem Puritans, as Miller writes in his lengthy introduction to each character, ". . . carried about an air of innate resistance, even of persecution. Their fathers had, of course, been persecuted in England. So now they and their church found it necessary to deny any other sect its freedom, lest their New Jerusalem be defiled and corrupted by wrong ways and deceitful ideas." Their spiritual leader, Reverend Samuel Parris, clearly suffered from a persecution complex, a form of paranoia.

The plot of *The Crucible* shows how the various pent-up, frustrated individuals use the witch-hunt to vent their personal spleen and vengeance, to obtain a neighbor's land by accusing him, to derive the vicarious sexual pleasure of testifying publicly that a woman (a witch) entered a man's bedroom at night and sat on his chest, and in the case of Abigail, to get rid of her married lover's wife. The sadistic witch trial thus becomes a kind of mass catharsis for the village, a volcanic eruption from deep psychic sources in a rigidly repressed community.

As a consequence of their stern denial of sex, the first step toward hysteria is a surreptitious meeting of some young girls in the forest for a harmless outlet of adolescent sensuality—dancing naked, and encouraging a superstitious Jamaica Negress, Tituba, to try and work a spell. When the Reverend Parris abruptly surprises the pagan romp, the girls are thrown into a kind of shock, and several of them become sick with a mysterious psychosomatic illness which resembles unconsciousness. Abigail, a wide-eyed young dissembler, had instigated Tituba's incantations in the hope of making John Proctor's wife die—she had worked for the Proctors and John Proctor had succumbed once to his desire for her, then had gotten control of himself and dismissed her. When caught, Abigail denies dancing naked in the forest and with a sinister power reminiscent of *The Children's Hour*, gets the other girls to corroborate her lie.

Reverend Hale, a nearby preacher who specializes in witch-hunts, is called in and immediately begins to look for and find signs that the Devil is in Salem. Abigail has had dreams and awakened to find herself naked in the open doorway—which she blames on

Tituba's spells. When Tituba is about to be punished as a witch, she is needled into admitting that she saw two Salem parishioners with the Devil. Abigail hysterically confirms that she, too, saw them in traffic with the Devil, and adds another name. Each of the other girls adds a name in a swelling climax of ecstatic, contagious release as the girls hysterically realize they have found scapegoats who will absolve their own guilt.

John Proctor is portrayed as a fine, keen-minded, virile Puritan man, struggling hard to suppress his desire for Abigail and to reassure his ailing wife that he has returned to her after his temptation. Their present serving girl, a dim-witted dolt named Mary Warren, who was one of the girls implicated with Abigail, testifies in court and interprets simple psychosomatic conversion such as a choking sensation as the work of witches. To pass the time in court, she makes a doll or poppet, and leaves it in the Proctor's home. John is bewildered by the alarming growth of mob madness and would go to his best friend, but instead the friend comes to arrest his wife, Goody Proctor, who was "named" in the trial by Abigail as one of those in league with the Devil. The presence of the poppet proves it, and Goody Proctor is carried off. Mary Warren even admits that she made the poppet, but that no longer matters. "The accuser is holy now," and anyone named for any malicious reason is guilty until proven innocent. They are guilty by wish-fulfillment—their accusers unconsciously wish and need them to be guilty. In a new scene added after the original Broadway production, Miller strengthens Proctor's resolve to save his wife and shows Abigail's perverted motives—accusing indiscriminately as she had been accused of looseness. At times she psychotically believes in her own inventions of witchcraft and then craftily concedes that her wish is to destroy Proctor's wife and possess him.

The third act is a bloodcurdling courtroom trial as the townspeople are confronted one after the other by trumped up evidence of the Devil and led off to their execution with holy, self-righteous zeal. There can be no witnesses to defend them, says the incredibly dogmatic judge, Deputy Governor Danforth, because witchcraft is itself invisible. Mary Warren testifies that the girls were all improvising, but Reverend Parris must violently refute her or see his entire crusade undermined. Goody Proctor is temporarily saved because she is pregnant, but in trying to clear her, John Proctor becomes entangled himself because his attendance record at church was less than perfect. Even Reverend Hale balks now and would give Proctor a chance to obtain a lawyer, but there can be no turning back for such violent mob sadism as has been liberated in Salem. Mary Warren is the one witness that must be discredited and this Abigail and her friends do in a frighteningly powerful scene in which Abigail hypnotizes Mary into seeing visions of a yellow bird (a symbol of sexual anxiety, Freud believed) until Mary is reduced to a whimpering, hysterical tool who finally accuses John Proctor and causes his arrest.

The final act in prison, like that of *Saint Joan*, extracts high emotional power from the efforts to break John Proctor's spirit and make him confess. Even Reverend Parris has now protested at the mass murder, but Deputy Governor Danforth remains implacable. Abigail has vanished now, leaving the witches' brew she stirred for others to cool (Miller says in a footnote that historically she was thought to have ended up as a prostitute in Boston). John turns to his wife for advice, but she cannot advise him to confess. He is even brought to sign the confession, but finally balks at implicating anyone else and like Joan, tears up the paper. He goes to his hanging with grim courage, a powerful, tragic figure with the insight into his destiny which Willy Loman lacked.

The Crucible opens up what may prove to be a new avenue for the drama—the psychoanalytical interpretation of history and current socio-political events. After intensive research, Miller attempted to read human motives, deep and unconscious, into historical fact. Whether or not Miller's projections are historically correct, he has in any case created in *The Crucible* a stinging commentary for our times and a grim lesson in the value of civil liberty. If the play evoked some critical disappointment, it is only because it is demanding a great deal for an author to "top" *Death of a Salesman*. True, Miller does not get his analytic scalpel as deep into the emotional roots of John Proctor, Goody Proctor and Deputy Governor Danforth as he does into his sons and fathers. But *The Crucible* is an important contribution, synthesizing historical and psychoanalytic insight into moments of memorable power.

CHAPTER XIV

War and Post-War Neurosis

☆   ☆   ☆   ☆

NEUROSIS IN THE RECENT DRAMA

Many of the major plays of the forties and fifties have been discussed in connection with their individual authors. In attempting an overview of the drama of the last decade, however, one fact is most impressive: the drama now regularly turns to psychoanalytic psychology for source material. In the hands of master playwrights the result is illumination. In the hands of those without either intuitive understanding or personal psychoanalytic experience, the result is apt to be a kind of "superficial depth," the substitution of the names of complexes and neuroses for the deeper exploration of cause and effect; it was the latter which so many playwrights deplored in their questionnaire replies. There can be no doubt that we live in a neurotic era; the sensitive playwright who is aware of his times must observe the pressures and defense-mechanisms of a fearful atomic age. And yet the cry is now commonly heard in some quarters to spare us "these neurotic plays" and get back to wholesome drama. But Freudianism can hardly be made to bear this guilt. The theatre has always had trashy plays—before the complex there was the missing letter or the foreclosed mortgage. Rather the cry should be to get us back to works of stature by playwrights of broad perception. The great dramatic heroes and heroines of classic drama have all in a sense been "neurotic." The difference is that today there is available to both audiences and authors a vocabulary and a system, a set of symbols and a wealth of clinical data. This has made playwriting at once easier and more difficult.

Some authors chose to concentrate upon the development of one clinical case, while others assembled a varied cross-section worthy of a psychiatric clinic. Among the latter were Bercovici's adaptation of a Thomas Mann story, *Gabrielle* (1941), in which neurotic and sexually frustrated patients in a tuberculosis sanatorium make life unbearable for each other, and Joseph Hayes' *Leaf and Bough* (1949), in which a farm family is involved with alcoholism, kleptomania, incest, and nymphomania. Several plays attempted to understand the neurotic complications of the returning war-veteran, including Maxwell Anderson's *Truckline Cafe* (1946) and Bessie Breuer's *Sundown Beach* (1948), the latter depicting maladjusted service men with mother-attachments, inferiority complexes, homosexuality, paranoia and schizophrenia. The problems of the returning veteran, curiously enough, were generally avoided by playwrights, and the few which were successful limited themselves to an intensive study of one veteran's reintegration into a post-war situation. Perhaps the most forceful and mature explorations of the impact of the soldier's return were Arthur Miller's *All My Sons* (1947) and *Deep are the Roots* (1945) by Arnaud D'Usseau and James Gow; the latter concentrated upon the ironic situation of a Negro Army officer who returns to an intolerant South where he is a second-class citizen. As the title suggests, D'Usseau and Gow recognize the deep unconscious level where prejudice is rooted, but do not penetrate psychoanalytically to that level. They show that the white girl and the Negro's hopeless love is based upon childhood associations and bonds, and that the sister's outburst of intolerance which turns him over to the sheriff was unconsciously based upon jealousy of her sister. D'Usseau and Gow understand a lynching as an ecstatic perversion of lust, a form of erotic sadism. The bitter frustration and betrayal of the Negro at the hands of the Southern senator was the most powerful indictment of intolerance since Green's *In Abraham's Bosom*.

After *Tomorrow the World* and *Deep are the Roots*, Gow and D'Usseau apparently parted company, and D'Usseau collaborated with Dorothy Parker recently on *Ladies of the Corridor* (1953), another of the assorted-neurosis plays, with its naturalistic picture of the pathetic widows and divorcees who lead empty lives in hotels. Included are a chattering Southern lady who gives vent to minor kleptomania, an alcoholic who is separated from her erotic sadist husband and throws herself at a bellboy and finally at an open

window, a recent widow who is hurt by a love affair in which she
cannot control her jealousy and fear of loneliness, and a ruthless
cripple who keeps her son in subservience as a companion because
she can blackmail him concerning his last job which he lost for a
homosexual advance. Some of Miss Parker's old satire is directed
toward the daughter-in-law of the widow who raises her allergic,
asthmatic child as an over-protected example of too much psychology. *Ladies of the Corridor* proved unsatisfying, however, because
it was diffused by too many stories, none of which were sufficiently
engaging. Although the women's dependence on petty gossip,
needlework, movies, lending libraries, kleptomania and even arth-
ritis is understood as compensation for the loss of sex and the fear
of loneliness, *Ladies of the Corridor* does not go deep in its analyses.

John Van Druten's *Old Acquaintance* (1940) limited its study
of middle-aged loneliness to two women, and was thus able to cut
more deeply into the ambivalent elements of hostility and affection,
cattiness and loyalty, jealousy and self-sacrifice, which compose
friendship. As in Hellman's *The Searching Wind,* the relationship of
Van Druten's "good friends" was based upon childhood insecurity,
resentment of the other's success and the unconscious wish to identify with the other. But of all recent studies of the friendship of
women, none is more devastating than *In The Summer House* (1953)
by Jane Bowles, who has been termed one of the most original and
promising of the new playwrights. She depicts two mothers and their
relationship with their daughters. Mrs. Eastman-Cuevas oppresses
her daydreaming daughter with taunting criticism. The other mother
feels rejected and unloved, turning to drink as solace. The latter's
daughter, who is uninhibited and aggressive, tries to insinuate herself into the affections of Mrs. Eastman, only to be accidentally
killed by Mrs. Eastman's frightened, jealous daughter. When Mrs.
Eastman's second marriage fails, she tries to break up the marriage
of her daughter—into which she had pushed her—by using the death
as a blackmail threat. In the ironic ending, the dominating mother
is deserted by her submissive daughter, at the urging of the weak
mother. To Mrs. Bowles, wife of Paul Bowles, a composer, the summer house was symbolic:

> The people in my play are all covering up something about
> themselves. Each of them has her summer house. A summer
> house is a flimsy construction with no foundation. It is an
> invention of those who seek escape from themselves or
> reality, a sanctuary, a haven from the terrors which haunt
> them.

Although critical reaction to *In The Summer House* was mixed, there was little doubt that Mrs. Bowles had an uncommon psychological insight into unconscious motives and a subtle, suggestive style likened to Chekhov and Tennessee Williams. But there was a plea for clarification and for a more universal frame of reference than merely the particulars of individual neurosis.

Turning from the drama of assembled neuroses to the concentrated study of one neurotic hero, there are again ample examples from the theatre of the forties and fifties. The distortion of sexual pressure into religious hysteria was the subject of *Comes The Revelation* (1942) by Louis Vittes; its conversion into sadism was treated in Green and Feilbert's *The House In Paris* (1944), in Claiborne Foster's *Pretty Little Parlor* (1944), in Orin Jannings' *Hear That Trumpet* (1946), and in Elsa Shelley's *With a Silk Thread* (1950). A more successful case history in "bitchery" was *Guest In The House* (1942), by Hagar Wilde and Dale Eunson. Here the young heroine uses a heart condition as a neurotic weapon and gradually disrupts the household that has given her sanctuary. She has paranoid tendencies, projecting her sexual wishes as suspicions of infidelity in a happily married couple and almost succeeding in parting them. Her repressed eroticism takes the form of running to the local minister to accuse her host of rape. Her obsessive fear of birds brings her to death from hysterical fear that a bird is loose in the room. A melodrama rather than a psychoanalytic study, *Guest In the House*, nevertheless, illustrates the use of clinical detail in contriving effective theatrical suspense.

One of the neurotic manifestations seen frequently in recent drama—in *In The Summer House* and a number of other plays—is passive-dependency. Odets proved himself a master in depicting the passive-dependent male during the thirties, and more recently William McCleery has attempted in two plays to construct family comedies around the amusing situation of a male who believes that he is master of his destiny only to find that his wife, armed with a knowledge of psychoanalysis, has been ". . . manipulating her husband as if he were a damned puppet!" The wife's rebuttal, in McCleery's first play, *Parlor Story* (1947), is that ". . . it's men behaving like rag dolls that brings out the puppeteering instinct in women, generally speaking." In the sequel, *Good Housekeeping*, which has not been seen on Broadway, McCleery's puppeteering wife guides her husband even higher in the political world, interpreting his every action, including a flat tire on an auto, as unconsciously motivated. Although the wife considers it only "good housekeeping" to use her knowledge of psychoanalysis and psychosomatic medicine to guide the emotional health of her family, it is clear at the end that she has herself been compensating for her feelings of being unnecessary. As in Barrie's *What Every Woman Knows,* a passive-dependent husband can go far if he has the right wife behind him; the humor, however, is thin and the insight superficial.

The most successful play to dramatize passivity in the male was Thomas Job's *Uncle Harry* (1942), in which the sweet and meek brother, blocked in marriage by his two sisters, finally gives vent to his murderous hostility and contrives the death of one sister, putting the blame on the other. Even though Uncle Harry finally confesses, no one ever believes him capable of such a crime. Other Uncle Harrys, dominated by women and seeking outlets in devious ways, occurred in Hugh White's *Little A* (1947), Telfer and Jamerson's *Oh, Mr. Meadowbrook!* (1948), and in two plays by Horton Foote; the first, *Only The Heart* (1944) shows a Southern matron whose deep fear of the give-and-take of a healthy love relationship warps the lives of her husband, her sister, and her daughter; the family's lack of resistance, however, gives the play a flabby quality in spite of its promising characterizations. Foote's more recent play, *The Trip to Bountiful* (1953), shows an old lady living wretchedly with her daughter-in-law and her passive, weakling son. She yearns to return to the past and finally does go back to her childhood home, deriving enough spiritual refreshment to help her endure the present. A similar faith to go on living comes at the end of Terence Rattigan's *The Deep Blue Sea* (1952), a restrained British treatment of a potentially turbulent subject, in which a woman seeking a full love relationship falls in love with a passive, psychically impotent male who finds himself cloyed by her demands and deserts her for a kind of sexless drifting. A prissy neighbor tells her that the physical side of life is really not important, and she finds herself poignantly between the devil and the deep blue sea. The irony of mismated human relationships is somehow tamely handled in contrast with Raphaelson's *Hilda Crane.*

The wish to return to the past, delicately dramatized by Foote in *The Trip to Bountiful,* was one of Philip Barry's recurrent motifs, and has been treated by other playwrights as well—Osborn in *Point of No Return,* Fay Kanin in *Goodbye, My Fancy* (1948), and Irving Elman in *The Brass Ring* (1952). Mrs. Kanin's play shows a famous Congresswoman returning to her college and its president whom she has loved since her undergraduate days. Learning that he has become a supine "educaterer" she discovers that she must outgrow her undergraduate crush, and goes off with a more vigorous male who had branded her romanticizing of the past as "an overwhelming desire to return to the womb." A successful comedy which makes pertinent comment on the subject of academic integrity, *Goodbye, My Fancy* moves effortlessly and pleasantly through a psychoanlytic concept. The same theme of growing out of the fancies of the past which stand in the way of emotional maturity was treated by Irving Elman in *The Brass Ring*. Mr. Elman's hero is a successful business man who is bound to a routine job and a routine wife. He has been mentally unfaithful with his youthful sweetheart and wishes he had taken the daring road to Paris with her instead of the prosaic path to family responsibility. In the technique of *Dream Girl* and *The Seven Year Itch*, the play penetrates his dream-world and shows his nightmarish image of himself, put in a strait-jacket as a young man by his parents. Seeing his son and daughter following the pattern toward stuffiness, the father is about to fly to Paris when he meets the former sweetheart—now a dumpy middle aged drudge—and awakens to the ludicrousness of his pursuit of the illusive brass ring on the merry-go-round of youth.

The relationship of mother and son, so thoroughly explored in the drama of the twenties, has not entirely been abandoned by American playwrights. Two new young playwrights of the forties brought authentic folk material to the theatre, both suggesting the matriarchal pattern of the immigrant family. Alexander Greendale's *Walk Into My Parlor* (1941) dealt with an Italian-American family held together by the mother, who resorts to passing counterfeit money, while her tough son seduces his brother's wife and then burns his hand masochistically with hot coals in punishment. In Arnold Sundgaard's Norwegian-American comedy, *The First Crocus* (1941), the mother also pushes her family and weak husband to the point where their child cheats and disgraces the family. In both plays the crises stem from the mother's compulsion to hold the family together at all costs. Few of the Oedipal mother plays of the forties and fifties proved successful—with the exception of Van Druten's *I Remember Mama* (1944); the figure has become dangerously obvious by now. Garrett's *Sleep My Pretty One* (1944) and Davis Snow's *The Long Days* (1951) took their sinister mothers seriously, while Rosemary Casey in *Late Love* (1953) and Don Appell in *Lullaby* (1954) found humor in the struggle of the son to uncoil himself from the silver cord.

There were fewer examples of father-daughter relationship, but they proved to be more successful in the theatre—not counting Gustav Eckstein's awkward *Christmas Eve*, in which a neurotic Irish girl overcomes her father fixation and aversion to young men only when she witnesses her mother giving birth to another child.

Among these folk-studies in family life, the most effective was Philip Yordan's *Anna Lucasta* (1944), written with a Polish-American milieu but altered in the production to a Negro family. Anna has become a prostitute when her fanatic father catches her with a man and banishes her from home. It is soon clear that his hostility to Anna is a defense against his own desire for her. His wife believes that he has a "sly-cosis" (psychosis) as a result of her catching him having "tid-bits" of infidelity and serving him a love-letter cooked in his stew. Now he gets headaches, loses every job, and has an ungovernable temper. When an old friend of his sends his young son north with $800 to find a good wife, the greedy-son-in-law contrives for him to meet Anna. She returns and the boy falls sincerely in love with her. Wanting to dance, Anna pulls her father to her and he screams "Let go of me," running out of the house in obvious sexual panic and returning blind drunk. He does what he can to block Anna's wedding, with the help of a waterfront lover of Anna's who is introduced somewhat gratuitously. As in *Anna Christie*, the audience wants the reformed prostitute to have her second chance at a decent life with a man who loves her, and Yordan suggests at the end that this will transpire.

The unconscious motives of such a father are more fully explored in *The Heiress* (1947), an adaptation by Ruth and Augustus Goetz of Henry James' novel, *Washington Square*, which Dr. C. P. Oberndorf called a "penetrating study of the effect of an unconscious, perhaps incestuous father-daughter relationship." The authors astutely trace the young daughter's neurotic shyness and feelings of inferiority to her father's constant comparison with her beautiful and accomplished mother who died when she was born. Remaining a widower, the father had transferred all his wishes for feminine affection to his daughter and demanded of her that she follow an impossible pattern. The daughter, as a result, grows up feeling unwanted and unloved, turning with pathetic hunger to the young fortune-hunter who makes love to her. The father's motives in disinheriting the girl are as much realistic awareness that she is being used as they are unconscious desires to hold her for himself. Abandoned when her fortune is diminished, the girl finds a way to exact a cruel revenge on the suitor some years after her father's death, and remains alone in the old home with her fortune if not her mental health intact. The team of Ruth and Augustus Goetz, here as well as in their most recent play, *The Immoralist*, give evidence of having one of the best working commands of psychoanalytic insight among the newer dramatists. They had treated the father-daughter theme once previously, in *One-Man Show* (1945), a play which just missed fire although it depicts with sensitivity a father keeping his grown daughter attached to him while they run an art gallery. She is about to give herself to a wealthy older man who promises to endow the father's gallery when a young man arrives who diagnoses her trouble as father-fixation and proceeds to win her for himself. The Goetz' interest in this theme was rewarded when they found the Henry James story and made it into one of the hits of the 1947-8 season.

THE TRAGEDY OF INVERSION

America in midcentury has learned from Freud to view without anxiety the devious ways in which the sexual drive may express itself. Homosexuality has interested modern dramatists since the days of *March Hares, Roger Bloomer* and *The Great God Brown.* Aspects of the problem were treated with growing frankness during the thirties in such works as *The Children's Hour, Design for Living, Oscar Wilde*, and *The Green Bay Tree.* With the war and the great uprooting of population, the emergence of women into war industries and the services, the existence of inversion became known to many to whom the term had been previously taboo. The findings of Kinsey indicated the prevalence of homosexuality on a scale wider than had been generally believed—more than a third of men studied and more than ten per cent of the women studied. Inevitably the theatre, relatively free where the motion pictures, television and radio are not, would reflect an interest in this aspect of human behavior and would examine it whenever audiences were ready to do so without guilt feelings.

We have seen the unconscious homosexuality that Odets suggests between many of his gentle male characters and which Hellman suggests with some of her brittle, aggressive women. Rose Franken's *Outrageous Fortune* valiantly attempted to find the tragic implications in homosexuality, and Moss Hart used the swishing male for comedy in *Lady in the Dark.* Similarly, Wolcott Gibbs' *Season in the Sun* (1950) used the homosexual as a recognizable comic type; two boys who chatter and go for dips together cause their landlady to comment: "I take the window screens off so's they can *fly* in and out." Most of the handlings of the subject, however, have indicated a greater awareness of and empathy for the tragic implications of homosexuality.

One of the early war plays suggested the existence of Lesbianism in the armed services. In *Cry Havoc* (1942) by Allan R. Ken-

ward, the accused girl is large and mannish, having been raised in
a lumber mill camp. She likes to hold hands with and fondle girls
but is unconscious of the meaning of the term Lesbianism; she is
thrown into anxiety when she is accused of being different from
the others. The melodrama does not, however, explore her problem,
but makes a patriotic retreat with the suggestion that it is un-Ameri-
can to question the girl's motives and that, faced with death, she
should be allowed the life-sustaining illusion of normality.

Lesbianism was more sensitively developed by Dorothy and
Howard Baker in *Trio* (1944), in which a brilliant woman professor
is the rival of the young man for the affections of the girl whom
she has lived with and dominated as a lover. The triangle, the reverse of *The Green Bay Tree*, ends in the suicide of the older
woman. The attempt by the Shubert interests to exert censorship by
refusing to book *Trio* in New York indicated a cultural lag which
was finally overcome when the play ran sixty-seven performances in
a non-Shubert-owned theatre.

The other significant play of the decade to treat Lesbianism was
Jean-Paul Sartre's *No Exit* (1946), which was not so much a psychoanalytic study of cause and effect as a philosophical commentary:
man seems to exist only for the purpose of serving as the torturer
for his fellow man; Hell consists of any room in which humans with
irreconcilable desires are trapped to torment each other for all time
—as are this man, woman and sadistic Lesbian. Powerful theatre
resulted from Sartre's handling of this theme.

The fusion of sadism and homosexuality was found in the male
as well. In *Gayden* (1949) by Mignon and Robert McLaughlin, the
hero is not a criminal but a social sadist who wrecks the lives of
those he comes in contact with from deliberate malice. Gayden is a
type familiar in psychoanalytic literature: his latent homosexuality
makes him aloof and cold with women, yet compels him to seduce
them calculatingly and hurt them wantonly. He and his mother
move in a rarefied social and intellectual plane, and have perfect
mutual understanding. Witty, charming, effete, he causes at least
one woman and one boy to commit suicide on his account. His inadequacy in sex and his inability to form a love attachment are indicated by his observation of women:

> If you ignore them, you're heartless. But if you're nice to
> them just once, they're all over you like love-starved pup-
> pies. And, like puppies, they make a mess, so you have to
> get rid of them.

Gayden must hurt where he cannot love. The girl who falls in love
with him is cruelly disenchanted and leaves Gayden alone at the

end with his mother, a modern Mrs. Alving and son. The mother admits that she did not love her husband, was glad when he died, and drew her son to her over-possessively. Without being spectacular in the theatre, *Gayden* is among the more powerful and perceptive psychological studies of the period.

The close relationship between homosexuality and paranoia was shown in several other plays, including Mel Dinelli's *The Man* (1950) and *The Dancer* (1946) by Milton Lewis and Julian Funt, the latter play a study suggested by the life of Nijinsky; in the story a sinister patron and a selfish wife each make demands upon the psychotic dancer until his pressures erupt in several murders including that of his homosexual benefactor.

A pre-Freudian novelist's ability to imply deep and subtle human undercurrents made it possible for Louis O. Coxe and Robert Chapman to dramatize successfully for a modern audience Herman Melville's *Billy Budd* (1951). A study in absolute good and evil, the sadistic Master-At-Arms, Claggart, is pitted against the guileless, sweet-faced Billy Budd. Unable to believe evil of anyone, Billy nevertheless stutters badly when under pressure from authority. The unmistakable hint of homosexuality comes when Claggart, who had been comfortable in the knowledge that all men hate him, is ruffled by Billy's friendliness. "Do you—like me, Billy Budd?" he asks searchingly, and when Billy picks up the whip Claggart had dropped, Claggart stares at Billy and then exclaims, "No, No! Charm me, too, would you! Get away!" Claggart has no choice but to destroy Billy, and when he tells the Captain that Billy is inspiring a mutiny, Billy stutters so badly that he cannot answer the charge but instead strikes Claggart dead. The subsequent trial of Billy for mutiny assumes little of the tension of *The Caine Mutiny Court-Martial,* but instead becomes a dialectic to establish the need for Billy's death. In pointing out the significance of Melville's work, Dr. C. P. Oberndorf has indicated that a psychoanalytic interpretation of *Billy Budd* may not be amiss:

> We cannot leave our discussion of the psychoanalytic slant in Hawthorne and earlier American literature without a reference to his friend and neighbor in the Berkshires, Herman Melville. Melville idolized Hawthorne and judging from certain of his letters to Nathaniel it may be inferred that his adulation of Hawthorne's work was over-determined. At all events Melville found in him a kindred spirit, struggling wildly with God and the perplexities of life. Like their brilliant contemporary, Edgar Allan Poe, both suffered from periods of despondency and depression.

It is likely that playwrights seeking material for today's psycho-analytic-minded playgoers will turn more and more to the muted, intuitive psychologists of the last century, Henry James, Melville, and Hawthorne.

Not unlike the innocent hero of *Billy Budd* in a hostile male world, the boy in a preparatory school has also interested a number of playwrights. The preparatory school has, in fact, come off rather badly in plays dealing with homosexuality. Two new playwrights made their debut in 1953 with dramas of boys' schools: the first, Calder Willingham, shows in *End as a Man* a brilliant, sadistic, wealthy boy who uses his father's position as a benefactor of the school virtually to wreck the school and some of the pupils, one of whom is a boy of homosexual tendencies. The second and more important treatment of the theme was by Robert Anderson in *Tea and Sympathy*, which recalled to more than one critic an important predecessor by Van Druten, *Young Woodley* (1925). The same ingredients were present in Van Druten's sensitive study of the suppression of sex in a British preparatory school, which was banned by the British Lord Chamberlain and brought the author to America where his talents have taken root. Young Roger Woodley is shown by Van Druten as a brooding, poetic young boy preoccupied with sex. One of his classmates boasts that he has had sexual experience with the town tart, but Woodley is revolted by this and is too shy to kiss the sweet young girl. The wife of a teacher shows sympathy and appreciation for his poetry and they find themselves, in spite of their age discrepancy, in a love born of loneliness. When the teacher surprises them together and Woodley manfully says, "I am in love with your wife," the master contemptuously ridicules his mawkish love-making and tries to get him expelled from school. Like his counterpart in *Tea and Sympathy*, Woodley ultimately seeks the town tart to prove his manhood, and is expelled for attacking with a knife a boy who cast an aspersion on the master's wife. Though the master would imply abnormality in young Woodley, his father learns the truth and takes the boy out of school, his chances for the university blighted. Van Druten's fine and perceptive study of the perturbations of adolescence dealt a forceful blow to the pedagogical theory that would limit sex education in adolescence to the slogan, "Keep yourself pure in thought, word and deed."

Anderson's *Tea and Sympathy* some thirty years later can afford to be specific where there were only implications in *Young Woodley*, and to probe the character of the teacher, his marital relationship and the boy's background with considerably greater psychoanalytic insight than did Van Druten. In Anderson's play the boy is also in love with the wife of his teacher and also perturbed about his essential manhood. One instructor has been dismissed for homosexuality and Tom Lee has been seen swimming with him. In the mentally ill mind of the master, circumstantial evidence begins to add up: Tom enjoys "long-haired" music and is "artistic," he walks in a bouncy manner and is playing a female role in the school play. In this era of trial by insinuation, Tom is clearly "off-horse" and the master is convinced that he is a homosexual. He breaks the news to Tom's divorced father, who is virtually a stranger to the boy, but is pathetically eager for Tom to prove himself "regular." Anderson makes it clear that the master's projection of guilt onto the boy is a warding off, a defense, against the recognition of his own impulses of latent homosexuality. His wife has been aware of the growing emptiness of their marriage, and is disturbed to see Tom hounded into leaving the school by the blustering pseudo-virility of her husband. When Tom tries to prove himself a man with the town tart only to fail in disgust, he is ready to accept the master's verdict that he is abnormal. To prevent this and to restore his belief in his own normality, the wife goes to Tom and offers herself in as breathtaking a closing scene as a Broadway play has ever had. There is ample evidence in *Tea and Sympathy* that Anderson (no relation to Maxwell) has the ability to create fully dimensional characters, to sustain interest in a plot of some scope, and to explore perceptively the unconscious motives of a self-righteous crusader for virility and conformity. Memorably played by Deborah Kerr, *Tea and Sympathy* proved to be the most mature and important play of the 1953-54 season. (The same season another instructor was dismissed for an alleged homosexual advance in Parker and D'Usseau's *Ladies of the Corridor*.)

Van Druten has an especial affinity for the delicate, civilized comedy-drama which, as he indicates in his *Playwright at Work*, is based upon his own intuitive feelings and needs rather than upon any systematic approach to psychology. In 1928 he had worked out his feelings toward his father by *Diversion*, in which a motherless son is neurotically attached to his father, passive-dependent in his relationship with women and finally wanted for the murder of a mistress who denied him. To save him, his physician-father gives poison—the ending of *Ghosts* transposed. The son, like young Woodley, had sobbed in the arms of a more mature woman, a mother-image. Van Druten's emotional connection with mothers was worked out in a number of plays, first unsympathetically in *After All* (1931), then more flatteringly in *The Distaff Side* (1934), and ultimately with sentimental affection in his adaptation of Kathryn Forbes'

novel as *I Remember Mama* (1944). Van Druten was at his best in his
warm-hearted comedy of mature sexual behavior during the war,
The Voice of the Turtle (1943). After the war, he returned to a
second psychological study of a British boys' school, *The Druid
Circle* (1947), a powerful, tightly constructed study of sexual impotence and the resultant reaction-formation in an intellectual
drudge who teaches in a small college. Professor White discovers a
passionate love letter one of the students has written his sweetheart,
in which he fantasies that he is intimate with her. In his privately
conducted inquisition (a magnificent scene), the sadistic Professor
makes the boy read the letter aloud to him in front of the girl, who
goes into a state of shock from her guilt-feelings and tries to commit
suicide. The professor is finally forced to resign, after the boy
accuses him of deriving vicarious satisfaction from the letter—the
only level of satisfaction open to him. British schools are the better
off for the departure of this professor at the end of *The Druid Circle*.
A similarly dessicated school master's emotionless heart is restored
to human feeling, however, by a pupil's impulsive generosity in
Terence Rattigan's *The Browning Version* (1949).

A British study of sex in a boys' school which focused on the
teachers rather than the pupils was Keith Winter's *The Rats of Nor-
way* (1948). Although overwrought and lacking Van Druten's compression, there are effective moments in Winter's analogy drawn
from the lemmings who swim out to their death toward an island
that has long since sunk beneath the sea. The sunken island here is
homosexuality, and although the young instructor tries valiantly to
reciprocate the love of a young girl, it is a man to whom he is irresistibly drawn—a man who has fought and lost his own battle
against his desire for the wife of the headmaster.

In Van Druten's *I Am A Camera* (1951) as in *Tea and Sympathy*
there is no specific evidence of homosexuality. But Van Druten's
hero, unlike Anderson's, is a gentle, introverted man, mixed up and
blocked as a writer, who is able to live in a tender and mutually
understanding relationship with the promiscuous Sally for a considerable period of time with no manifestation of physical desire
between them. Much wry humor is derived from the mother's natural
conclusions that her daughter and Chris have been lovers. His passive-dependency is so great that he is willing to be taken around the
world as a kept man by the wealthy playboy whose mistress Sally is.
Deserted by their mutual "sugar daddy," Sally and Chris are sustained by the genuine friendship between them, and Chris in the
end finds his fluency as a writer. Their final embrace is with a kind
of love, but, as Chris observes, ". . . it's so damn stupid that that's

not enough to keep two people together." Such love also proved insufficient to keep two people together in Williams' *Streetcar Named Desire*, where Blanche's discovery that her refined young husband is a homosexual marks the beginning of her neurotic search for illusion. So, too, the heroine of Anouilh's *Mademoiselle Colombe* (1954) finds her petulant, mother-fixated husband unsatisfying. Demanding of her lover just what power his kisses have that won her, the husband himself kisses the lover in a fierce identification with his own wife, seeking the male strength which he himself lacks.

George S. Kaufman and Leueen MacGrath dabbled with a Freudian case-history in *The Small Hours* (1951) and learned that it is not sufficient to have a character announce his neurosis in such words as: "I'm a latent homosexual." The empathic identification between audience and characters was missed by the Kaufmans, but another man and wife team, Ruth and Augustus Goetz made considerable progress toward finding it in their adaptation of André Gide's autobiographical novel, *The Immoralist* (1954). Called by Atkinson ". . . an admirable piece of work. The tragedy is austere, crushing and genuine," Gide's story apparently meets two of the requirements of psychoanalytic drama: it depicts the spiritual agony of the struggle of a man to achieve wholeness in spite of unconscious forces pulling him in other directions, and it suggests the childhood etiology of the problem. Although some of the original scenes were deleted for the Broadway production, *The Immoralist* was an unvarnished story of a young man who makes what Freud termed the "flight into marriage" in the hope of curing his aberration. The girl, too, has been blocked sexually and proposes to the man because he is the only man who doesn't frighten her. They go to North Africa and try to make their marriage work. But there are Arab men who find him desirable—one a mature professor who was expelled from his university and now advises frank acceptance of one's sexual nature—and the other an insidious houseboy who quietly taunts him into consummating his marriage. Faced with the mysterious challenge of the houseboy, the husband and wife cling together in confusion. The wife takes to drink and the husband finally is ready to acknowledge his deviation and follow the professor's caution against trying to live in two worlds. But the wife ironically is pregnant now and the end of the play finds them together again attempting to find "a middle way," as Gide himself had spent a lifetime in doing. *The Immoralist* was a courageous play and its respectable run of ninety-six performances indicates the psychological maturity of the Broadway theatre by the mid-fifties.

OUT OF THIS WORLD

Plays of wish-fufilling hallucination such as *Smilin' Through* flourished during and just after the first World War. The second World War and its aftermath of atomic pessimism manifested itself in a noticeable rise in the number of plays in which escapism took the form of an affectionate glance at psychosis or toward an unreal world to which the mind might retreat—for example, *Harvey* and *The Curious Savage*. The most outstanding and successful of the psychosis plays, however, was one which made excruciatingly funny farce out of criminal insanity—*Arsenic and Old Lace* (1941). It is a curious commentary on the times that this play which finds hilarity in mayhem and good clean fun in corpses has been an all-time favorite among high school drama groups. The author, Joseph Kesselring, is said to have intended the play seriously and to have been excluded from rehearsals while the producers, Crouse and Lindsay, proceeded to burlesque it. Kesselring apparently takes the old hereditary view of insanity, for his Brewster family of Brooklyn is composed of madmen. The two sweet old ladies, Aunt Abby and Aunt Martha, are known and loved in the neighborhood and the church, and rent rooms to old men whom they help out of their loneliness by murdering them with poisoned elderberry wine and burying them in the basement. Their nephew Teddy suffers from the delusion that he is President Theodore Roosevelt and provides comic relief with his bugle charges and mock attacks up San Juan hill. Another nephew, Jonathan, who resembles (and was played by) Boris Karloff, arrives with his criminal friend, Dr. Einstein. The only sane member of the family (and he is a dramatic critic) is Mortimer, who discovers a body in the window seat, then the twelve buried in the basement (in the "locks" dug by Teddy for the Panama Canal), and finally becomes the target for Jonathan's murderous plans, only to be saved accidentally by a policeman who wants to tell him the plot of the play he has written. Mortimer's fiancée is the daughter of a preacher who learned about sex in the choir loft, and Mortimer says to her, "I'll explain that to you sometime, darling—the close connection between eroticism and religion." Mortimer finally gets Teddy committed to an institution and the aunts willingly go with him to keep him company. Caught by the police, Jonathan's only regret is that his aunts tied his score of twelve murders, but they pull ahead of him in the home stretch by offering their elderberry wine to the asylum director at the fall of the curtain. Although there is a hint that Jonathan's murders were all vicarious attempts to kill his brother for whom he has had a lifelong hatred, there is little time for psychological analysis in this outlandish joke on criminal insanity.

From here the line splits into two directions—plays dealing with psychopathic killers and those dealing with the non-criminal or withdrawal psychoses. Among the latter was Ketti Frings' *Mr. Sycamore* (1942), which deals whimsically with a man who wants to be a tree and succeeds in rooting himself and growing into a spreading sycamore under which his wife and friends sit in the shade. In *Land's End* (1946) the results were more tragic for the young waitress in Cornwall who develops an Isolde-complex and identifies herself with the passionate heroine. Scott Michel's *Angels Kiss Me* (1951) tried to make it clear that insanity was not generally inherited. A demented lady has something of a peacock-complex in Jean Anouilh's *Cry of the Peacock* (1950), a savagely bitter fable with a pair of children who mock romance while a pair of lovesick hunchbacks symbolize the distortion of love. "Few plays," wrote Richard Watts, Jr., "have managed to make sex seem so undesirable."

Two of the most psychotic theatrical worlds were created by European playwrights, Giraudoux and Bridie. Adapted by Maurice Valency, Giraudoux' *The Madwoman of Chaillot* (1948) uses the cloak of insanity to make pertinent observations on political and moral issues of our day. The madwoman is a tragi-comic figure, dressed in an 1885 outfit and collecting bones to feed the dogs and cats of Paris. Learning of a secret trapdoor to the sewer under her cellar apartment, she brings a strange collection of types there in search of oil. In a fantastic trial scene, four madwomen and a mad ragpicker try the evil people of the world, the financiers, the press agents, the prospectors, the ladies. All are summarily condemned and marched off into the sewer from which there is no escape—a charmingly childish and unrealistic political solution. Although Giraudoux' purpose is social satire rather than a psychological study, he does take time to suggest the cause of the madwoman's breakdown—for the love of one Adolphe Bertaut who never asked her to marry him. All these years she has fantasied that he is alive, and projects him onto a dazed man who attempted suicide. In a poignant scene, she urges the young waitress to kiss the young man who had tried to commit suicide, so that she won't end up a madwoman. The cause of insanity is thus suggested to be the discrepancy between the individual's need for love and the painful facts of reality which deny it.

The Scotsman's view of psychosis is less flambuoyant and sardonic than that of Giraudoux. James Bridie, in *Daphne Laureola* (1950), also has a madwoman who frequents a café, but she is a more psychologically complete case of cyclothymic psychosis. Alternately rational and irrational, she comes during her irrational cycle to the café where she attracts attention by free associating loudly on her memories of childhood, her father and mother, God and sin. A psychiatric attendant finally arrives to take her away, but only after she has invited all the guests to her estate. At the country home her husband explains to a man who would make love to her that her trouble stems from the death of her father and her Puritan conscience which inhibits her desire for extra-marital experience. Some months later she returns to the restaurant without remembering it. Her husband having died, she has married her attendant, which upsets the young swain, who visualizes himself as rescuing her from the ogre. But she gently lets him down by saying that she was ". . . too old to play these games, and she married the ogre and settled down." She is rational and content as she leaves, having put forth tree-roots like the legendary Daphne. The symbolism is murky in Bridie's strange fable, and the psychological insight, although real enough in its clinical picture, leaves the reader dramatically disinterested.

A more whimsical use of dry, tongue-in-cheek humor was in Elaine Ryan's adaptation of a Ludwig Bemelmans novel, *Now I Lay Me Down To Sleep* (1950), in which an insatiably lecherous old general spends a lifetime pursuing chambermaids while the real love of his life, like her sister of Chaillot, grows psychotic, melancholy and suicidal from denial. Frigid and stern, she remains with the general as a "governess," but has never permitted him to touch her. Yearning to return to England to die, she keeps a coffin with her in anticipation of the blessed event. Overwhelmed with guilt since she deserted a child as a young governess and found him killed, she is a complex clinical figure. She ends up relinquishing her coffin and wish to die in England, remaining abroad to raise the child of the general and one of his many paramours; her return to reality is motivated by being needed.

One of the most sensitive and original treatments of the psychotic evasion of reality was Truman Capote's *The Grass Harp* (1952). A fifty-year old spinster, Dolly, lives in a harmlessly psychotic child-world. Her sister is a cruel and calculating woman who takes away from Dolly her secret gypsy herb formula and markets it commercially. With two companions, a garrulous Negress and her adolescent nephew, Dolly withdraws from the world and goes to live in a tree house (perhaps a symbol for the unconscious wish to retreat to the womb). They are joined by a retired judge, and these unwanted "little people" find themselves and regain their essential dignity in the security of their retreat. Escape from reality is made to seem inviting, and the realists thoroughly sordid. Dolly is won back to reality, however, when her sister is deserted by her unscrupulous lover and in her loneliness needs Dolly. Atkinson filed a minority report, calling *The Grass Harp* the most creative play of the 1951-2 season.

A similar theme occurred in N. Richard Nash's *See the Jaguar* (1952), in which an insane old lady raises her son a complete prisoner in an ice-house so that he would know nothing of the cruelty of the world. Nash's play was a quick failure in New York, but it is the irony of our theatre that such a powerful experiment can find no hearing in the hit-or-flop economy of Broadway. The play was not entirely clear in its symbolism, which contrasted good and evil, the indecisive lovers pitted against the cruel, driving tyrant. The caged jaguar and the imprisoned boy finally are liberated as in Werfel's *Goat Song*. The tangy folk poetry of the dialogue, however, and its psychological theme of the need for cages to be opened gave the play distinction.

Escape from reality assumed a more inviting appearance in Joshua Logan's adaptation of Chekhov's *The Cherry Orchard* set in the old South and renamed *The Wisteria Trees* (1950). Here the genteel aristocrats have not become psychotic but grow perilously close to it as they regress to the nursery to play Frog and Mousie to amuse the colored children while the estate is being auctioned off.

COPS AND PSYCHOTICS

Of all the psychoses, the ones that prove to be the most commercial in the theatre are those that lead to psychopathic homicide. We have seen the *genus* of psycho-melodrama grow important during the depression, beginning with *Nine Pine Street, Double Door, Blind Alley,* and the British thriller, *Criminal at Large*. Much of the credit for the technical mastery of the psychological murder melodrama, in fact, goes to the British. As early as 1929, Patrick Hamilton began with *Rope's End* to hold audiences aghast with psychologically motivated crimes; in this play two unstable young men, reminiscent of the Loeb-Leopold case, murder a boy for the thrill of it and invite his family for tea served from the chest in which the body is hidden. Hamilton's most famous thriller, *Angel Street* (1941), was more subtly insidious, with the sadistic Mr. Manningham attempting to convince his wife she is insane. Edward Percy and Reginald Denham in collaboration or individually turned out a number of suspenseful plays, some effective and others only straining for effect. *Ladies in Retirement* and *Suspect* made the most use of psychological concepts; in the former there are two sisters bordering on psychosis and a third willing to kill to protect them; in the latter an Oedipally over-protective mother blocks her son's marriage and is suspected of being the notorious ax murderess who slew her father and step-mother from "emotional frustration"—the same situation as in *Nine Pine Street* except that the authors manage to exonerate her in the end. Psychopathic killers do away with assorted women in Hoey's *The Haven* (1946) and Green's *Gently Does It* (1953). It is only the psychological implications which keep Agatha Christie's *Ten Little Indians* (1944) from seeming outlandish, as the author assembles ten individuals with assorted guilts on their consciences and pro-ceeds to kill them off. A British thriller which had all the ingredients —tightness of plot and psychoanalytic motivation—but somehow failed to come to life was Aldous Huxley's *The Gioconda Smile* (1950). The pre-fabricated plot involves a woman who feels such an uncontrollable passion for a married man with an invalid wife that she secretly feeds the wife arsenic. After the wife's death she pants to him, "Take me," but he prefers to take someone else, and then is arrested for his wife's murder. The true murderess ultimately breaks down because of her phobia of lightning and thunder and a doctor's use of truth serum. Huxley's thesis is that man has found many ways to disclaim responsibility for his misdeeds—by devils, for example, in the middle ages:

> The other way, the more modern way, is to call the devils traumas and complexes, and say it's all your mother's fault for having weaned you too early. And perhaps she *did* wean you too soon, and perhaps there *are* devils. But, there's also such a thing as free will.

Although Huxley raises the pertinent question of the changing re-lationship between law and psychiatry, his characters neither prove the thesis nor ring true in themselves. He seems, instead, to have thrown the psychology book at his audience.

American writers have been quick to follow the British lead, although not always with equal subtlety. In Marie Baumer's *Little Brown Jug* (1946), a slightly psychotic little man with a compulsive wish for "belongingness" blackmails a widow and her daughter into providing him a permanent home. In *Portrait in Black* (1947) Ivan Goff and Ben Roberts make glib use of psychoanalytic terminology while weaving a skillful web which involves a guilty pair of lovers in a series of crimes to conceal crime. The daughter is in love with a man she terms "The Erotic-Compulsive-With-Dominant-Id Type," because he would not buy a pipe or marry a woman he could not sample before buying.

Sex slayings, with their unconscious component of heterosexual inadequacy, have interested a number of playwrights, and the timeliness of the subject suggests that dramatists are attempting to keep pace with the developing psychiatric knowledge of the problem. After Dreiser's masterful *The Hand of the Potter* (1921), authors skirted the subject until Charles K. Freeman and Gerald Savory collaborated on *Hand In Glove* (1944), in which the sexual maniac is fearful that he is impotent with women and obtains his sexual release by slashing and mutilating them. The metropolitan reviewers, however, were not ready to accept this particular treatment of the subject, however valid it may have been psychologically. Even less successful was A. B. Shiffrin's attempt to analyze a sex slayer in *Twilight Walk* (1051), which was billed as a "psychiatric thriller" but proved to be neither very psychiatric nor very thrilling. The heroine is a young authoress who was "weaned on Kinsey and Freud," and offers to be a decoy for the police and prove her theory by sitting on a park bench to trap the rapist-slayer. The latter is a gentle, passive, charming young man with a mother who paws him, makes decisions for him and wards girls away from him. In all his criminal attacks, the rape is not consummated and he kills in rage at his own impotence. Unconsciously, he is striking back at his mother and at the same time destroying the evidence against him. The author tries to make a case against police lethargy and ultra-conservative "shoot-to-kill" methods which fail to make use of psychiatric aid to rehabilitate the criminal. But unlike Kingsley's *Detective Story*, Shiffrin's characters are mouthpieces and the plot concocted. A semi-documentary treatment would have been preferable.

The most fully developed case of theatrical paranoia in recent melodrama was in Mel Dinelli's *The Man* (1950), a masterfully constructed shocker in the tradition of *Angel Street* and *Night Must Fall*. A friendly young man comes as a day laborer to clean the boarding house of Mrs. Gillis, and gradually the author reveals unmistakable signs of paranoia—his phobia against dirt, his effeminate interest in the curtains and the room, his violent hatred for the dog and his suspicion that the dog hates him, his painful erotic memory of being rejected by the army and having to walk back through the line of naked, laughing men. By the end of the first act, Mrs. Gillis realizes that he is a psychopath and handles him cautiously. In the second act it becomes clear to her that she is his prisoner, and she attempts in vain to get a message out. Once he suffers complete amnesia concerning his violent phase, but when she finally gets a telephone linesman to call the police, he takes her upstairs and quietly strangles her. *The Man* is a brilliant example of building theatrical suspense out of deep-level psychological awareness.

In writing about such psychiatric melodramas, William Hawkins observed: "Not too long ago, the thriller was referred to as a who-done-it. Now that psychiatry explains everything from hatchet murder to fingernail biting, a thriller should be called a what-done-it-to-him." The play to which Hawkins referred was Alexander Knox's *The Closing Door* (1949), which deals with a father who gradually develops manic-depressive symptoms with melancholic and suicidal tendencies. Knox, who played the role himself, stated that he came in contact with case histories such as this one while a member of the California Citizens' Committee for Mental Hygiene, Inc. Pointing out the alarming discrepancy between the percentage of hospital beds in the United States which are occupied by mental cases (50 per cent) and the percentage of the nation's doctors who are psychiatrically trained (2 per cent), Knox built his story around the obsessive fear of being committed to a state insane asylum—a fear which is rational enough and which can best be eradicated by making out-patient psychiatric aid accessible to far more individuals than are now being helped. In *The Closing Door* the family physician can only prescribe an expensive private clinic or the state asylum for Vail Trahern when his wife discovers him keeping a gun under his pillow, shying hysterically at a camera flash bulb, and reliving events from his disturbed past. His fear of the state asylum and the reluctance of his rich brother to pay for the private one provoke the crisis, the suspense of which is theatrically heightened by a red light which flashes on to indicate an elevator ascending to their apartment. Brilliantly contriving several tricks to evade the clinic, Vail returns and almost strangles his wife before he blacks out, awakening rational and purged of oppressive memories by the belief he has killed his brother. He free associates from his childhood, out of which suddenly emerges the realization that a compromising picture of himself and his sweetheart taken with a flashbulb was actually the work of his brother, who blackmailed him and kept him from going to college. Hatred for his father is identified with hatred of his brother, and both are released by projection onto his son, whom he has struck on the head during his manic phase because the boy carried a camera. The suspense grows unbearable as the wife patiently and skilfully tries to lead him back to reality and to recognize the unconscious but still living body as his son rather than his brother. *The Closing Door* carries an imperative message for our times, in desensitizing the public to the idea that to seek psychiatric aid is not to admit to "insanity." Many crimes of violence, as psychoanalysis has discovered, are in fact unconscious retaliations against the memory of a parent or sibling. The prognosis for the Vail Traherns is growing more hopeful in the light of the discovery of new drugs such as LSD 25, mescaline and reserpine. But there is an overwhelming gap between custodial institutions and expensive private sanitaria which must be filled for the mental health of the nation. Knox's clinical picture is not only psychologically accurate but terrifyingly alive in the theatre—certainly among the best of the studies of psychosis. It deserved better treatment than it received at the hands of the metropolitan critics.

The literature on the criminal psychoses by psychoanalysts and psychiatrists is a growing field. Theodor Reik's *The Unknown Murderer* was one of the early attempts to view psychoanalytically the criminal impulse. More recently the work of Dr. Frederic Wertham, director of psychiatric services for Queens General Hospital in New York, has served to popularize the psychiatric understanding of the criminal. His *Dark Legend* is a brilliant development of a matricide's case history in terms of its parallels with Orestes and Hamlet. Wertham's *The Show of Violence* attacks the problem of the confusions and ambivalence in the law as it relates to psychiatry and our woefully inadequate facilities for preventive therapy. It is not too much to predict that in this era of *Dragnet,* the Broadway stage needs and undoubtedly will presently have a serious, documentary study based upon such case histories as Wertham presents, in order to bring up to date our knowledge of the causation of crime and to stress the urgent need for society to protect itself by making psychiatric aid available *before* the crime is committed.

BETWEEN THE DARK AND THE DAYLIGHT

The most significant new development in the post-war theatre is the discovery of the child's world as a subject for adult drama. This appears to be an outgrowth of the discovery of the childhood origin of adult neurosis by Freud and the subsequent development of child analysis by his daughter, Anna Freud and Melanie Klein; by the application of permissive rather than authoritarian psychology to education by John Dewey and his followers in the twenties; by the widespread popularization of the child's needs and unconscious motives by such groups as The Child Study Association of America, parent-teacher associations, and mental health associations. Freud is said to have destroyed the "little angel" theory of childhood and to have introduced the concept of childhood sexuality. Dewey destroyed the "little lady and gentleman" concept of education and removed the repressive force of authority in the classroom. Recent psychiatric studies such as Axline's *Play Therapy* and Baruch's *One Little Boy* are having their influence felt in the theatre and film—the notable documentary motion picture, *The Quiet One*, being a case in point, as well as in other far-reaching fields, from interior decoration to psychosomatic medicine. The disturbed child is the criminal, the neurotic, the psychotic, the suicide, the alcoholic, the narcotic addict of tomorrow. Such children are the product of disturbed parents and disturbed homes—by a process not hereditary but no less inevitable. Dynamic psychiatry has made accessible the causes of the disturbance; it is the tragic irony of our century that professional psychiatric clinicians are too few and often legally powerless to alter the child's environment for him.

It is curious that the child should have been discovered so late in dramatic literature. A hundred and sixty years B.C., it is true, the Roman comic genius Terence was writing his "progressive education" comedy, *The Brothers*, in which he contrasts a harsh and a permissive parent to prove his thesis:

> This, indeed, is the part of a father, to accustom his son to do what is right, more from his own choice, than any fear of another; and here chiefly lies the difference between a father and a master. He who can't do this should admit that he doesn't know how to bring up children.

Shakespeare showed little interest in the child, but Molière restated Terence's theme in his comedy of the adolescent gaily outwitting her authoritarian parent, *The School For Husbands*. The nineteenth century idealized childhood as a period of uncomplicated innocence, although Ibsen stood on the verge of penetrating the child's world when he permitted the son in *Pillars of Society* to attempt to run away to America as a rebellion against his pompous authoritarian father—who at the end experiences a catharsis and agrees that his son will not have to be a pillar of society when he grows up but may be whatever he chooses. Shaw, Chekhov, Schnitzler, and O'Neill made little effort to depict children, with the exception of the latter's prologue to *All God's Chillun Got Wings*. Hauptmann's *Hannele* was the first to explore the feverish projections of a child's mind, and the influence of psychoanalysis was seen in the early dream plays, *The Poor Little Rich Girl*, *Barbara*, and *Jonathan Makes A Wish*. In the twenties there were only sporadic attempts to penetrate the child's world—for example, in Connelly's *The Wisdom Tooth*. Interest in the thirties shifted to a sociological view of the child's environment and produced a number of significant versions, climaxed by Kingsley's now immortal *Dead End* kids. The most psychoanalytic-minded writer to treat the child's world during the thirties was Leopold Atlas, followed by Moss Hart's less successful attempt to analyze his child in the dark, *Christopher Blake* (1946). Saroyan, of course, wrote often of children with adult intuition, but actually he represents a regression to the nineteenth century romantic conception of childhood as the innocence to which the adult would return.

The forties saw a number of serious studies of school life and the complicated emotional problems that come to crisis during these years. *Hickory Stick* (1944) by Frederick Stephani and Murray Burnett was an earnest study of a child with psychopathic hatred which culminates in murder, in spite of the teacher's efforts to get psychiatric aid for him in the face of the school's official indifference. The rehabilitation of a delinquent child—and the question of whether evil is native or environmentally acquired—received its best treatment of the decade by James Cow and Arnaud D'Usseau in *Tomorrow The World* (1943), in which a twelve year old Nazi boy is brought to the liberal, enlightened home of his uncle, an American professor working on secret war work and engaged to marry a Jewess. The boy's outbursts of vicious destructiveness and his sinister efforts to spy upon the professor provoke serious discussions as to whether the indoctrinated Nazi can be saved or will respond only to whippings. He finds a natural ally in the professor's sister, a neurotic spinster who suffers headaches at the thought of her brother's marriage. The boy's belligerence is finally broken down and he is seen to be a fearful child haunted to know if his father was a coward and betrayer of Germany, as he has been taught, or a liberal hero, as his uncle believes. Even after he has viciously struck the little girl who adores him, the family patiently decides to feed him before they re-educate him, and finally reach him by way of his need for love and security. After his repressed memories of torture at the hands of the Nazis are revived and expunged, he finds his father a hero and through that finds himself.

The same bitter barrier erected by children against the adult world was shown in Arthur Goodman's *Seeds in The Wind* (1948), in which the children who survive the Lidice massacre make peace within their own community but look upon all adults as enemies. Another child living under a middle-European police state was the focal point of George Tabori's *The Emperor's Clothes* (1953), in which an imaginative child who gratifies his need for vicarious power by fantasying that he and his father are a cross between Hoot Gibson and the Scarlet Pimpernel gets his father in serious difficulties with the secret police. The father learns a lesson in the meaning of integrity and the child in the difference between reality and fantasy in Tabori's original and often powerful work.

Children whose maturity is greater than that of their parents are becoming a familiar type on Broadway. A child solved her parents' problems in Whitfield Cook's *Violet* (1944); in John Van Druten's *Solitaire* (1942), based on a novel by Edwin Corle, a precocious and ingratiating little girl is driven by her mother's lack of understanding to form an idyllic and completely innocent attachment to a philosophical tramp who inhabits an arroyo near her home. In B. Harrison Orkow's *Star Spangled Family* (1945), the son's Oedipal resentment of his stepfather is neurotically encouraged by the grandmother, and in Victor Wolfson's *Pride's Crossing* (1950) it was a neurotic attachment between an old widow and her grandson's governess which blocks the child's normal development. In *Sunday Breakfast* (1952) by Emery Rubio and Miriam Balf, it takes a nine-year-old girl, who runs away from her neurotic, wrangling family, to teach them a badly needed lesson in mental health. Nathaniel Benchley shows in *The Frogs of Spring* (1953) that parents may make themselves ludicrous planning things for children which are scorned by the youngsters. While finding Mr. Benchley's play weak and disorganized, critics praised it for its keen observation of the basic hostility and bewilderment that characterizes the parent-child relationship. The most skillful theatrical attempt to penetrate the child's inner world, however, was Mary Chase's *Mrs. McThing* (1952) with its parent receiving a thorough punishment in fantasy for her failure to appreciate the needs of her son.

Paul Osborn assembled a beguiling group of children in *The Innocent Voyage* (1943) and placed them in an oppressive situation as prisoners on a pirate ship. One loses her mind and one is driven by hysterical fear to murder an innocent man. When the pirate captain is brought to trial for the crime, the girl is overwhelmed with guilt and confesses—but no one believes her capable of murder, and the gentle-hearted pirate must die for a crime he did not commit. Before he is led away, however, he takes pains to absolve the girl of her guilt-feelings.

In the midst of an otherwise insubstantial play such as *Season in the Sun* (1950) by Wolcott Gibbs, there is a little child who free associates in remarkably psychoanalytic style. Improvising a song which is half-Calypso and half confession, she projects her defiance of parental regimen onto a fictitious child:

She will not do anything at all.
She will just sit there in the noonday sun.
And when they speak to her, she will not answer them,
Because she does not care to.
Oh, she will stick them with spears and put them in the
    garbage.
And put the cover on.
Ooooh, she will not go out in the fresh air, or make wee-wee
    for them. . .
And she will get thin as a marble.
She will just sit there in the noonday sun. . . .

At the other extreme from this delightful deep-level perception
of the child's world is an inane farce such as *A Young Man's Fancy*
(1947) by Harry Thurschwell and Alfred Golden, which attempts
to show the influence of psychoanalytic psychology upon modern
summer camps. One of the co-owners would rule out all competitive
sports including baseball, because of the inferior feelings engendered
in the losers, but the other co-owner prevails and it is baseball
which rehabilitates the sissified, over-protected child whose parents
bring him there on the recommendation of the psychoanalyst. The
discrepancy between theory and practice in child psychology also
formed the basis of *King of Hearts* (1954) by Jean Kerr and Eleanor
Brooke, with more amusing results. An egocentric cartoonist adopts
a child in order to get material for his childhood comic strips, only to
find that his desire to "piece together a mosaic of reality" for the
lad requires a little more tolerance and self sacrifice than he is
willing to make. His long-suffering fiancée and his assistant finally
rebel against his heartless pretensions and go off together with the
boy, leaving the comic artist alone with his delusions of being a
champion of the nation's youth. The critics found that the insubstantial plot was more than compensated for by the sparkling
dialogue and called *King of Hearts* one of the most hilarious
comedies of the 1953-4 season.

The demand for child actors must have become acute by April
of 1954, when *King of Hearts* was followed in rapid succession by
Anniversary Waltz and *The Magic and the Loss*. Jerome Chodorov
and Joseph Fields' *Anniversary Waltz* showed a familiar American
couple finding marriage somewhat disillusioning after fifteen years;
their precocious youngster finds nothing shocking in the fact that
mother and father were intimate before marriage, and proceeds
to reveal this fact on a television quiz program. Father thereupon
made Broadway history by smashing in the television set.

The Magic and the Loss, by Julian Funt, is the story of a disturbed child of divorced parents; his mother is having an affair with another man, is striving for a vice-presidency at her business office and is startled to learn that her son despises her. The boy's father seems withdrawn to her because he is content with a college professorship. The mother's lover tries in vain to win over the rebellious son, but finding he cannot, leaves the mother, who loses her chance for the vice-presidency. The son too deserts her when he learns that she has been intimate with the other man, and goes to his father. Critics felt that Funt had dwelt upon the mother's self-pity rather than upon the moving plight of the son, and this "case history in child psychology" failed to come off.

With children introduced to the adult world on Broadway, it was inevitable that they would find their way into the suspense-melodramas. Children have been solving adult crimes since *Seen But Not Heard* (1936) by Marie Baumer and Martin Berkeley. In *The Secret Room* (1945), Robert Turney sets up a secret room which is known only to two little girls. Into their house comes a tragic refugee from Nazi Germany, having experienced enforced prostitution and the loss of her child. She murders the old doctor who befriended her, attempts to turn the two children against their mother and is about to kill the mother before she is apprehended— all psychotic expressions of her thwarted mother-love. If the children in *The Secret Room* were innocent bystanders, such was not entirely the case in William Archibald's *The Innocents* (1950), an adaptation of Henry James' story, *The Turn of the Screw*. Two interesting and conflicting interpretations have been presented for James' story: one suggested by Edna Kenton and elaborated by Edmund Wilson in "The Ambiguity of Henry James," is a Freudian explanation—that the "ghosts" exist only as projections in the mind of the governess, Miss Giddens. A psychoanalyst, C. P. Oberndorf, praised the insight of Henry James (brother of the psychologist, William James, who early expressed interest in Freudian theory), calling him ". . . a novelist who wrote like a psychologist, and at times like a psychoanalyst." In his dramatization of the James story, however, William Archibald preferred to rule out the subjective interpretation and play for the utmost ghost-story suspense. He neglects the attraction which the governess feels for her employer and presents the dead lovers, the valet, and the former governess as ghosts complete with a high-frequency oscillation in the air when they appear. Archibald frankly handled his material "for reasons of drama and for reasons of drama alone," letting the audience decide for itself if the two children, Flora and Miles, are innocents with a guileless imagination or if they are young Machiavellis with adult instincts. He shows Flora's infinite eight-year old wisdom, and then Miles' mysterious return from a school which expelled him for unknown reasons. In this eerie, empty house the governess, Miss Giddens, grows fearful and anxious. The intimate giggling of the children might imply some sinister secret or it might represent the lonely woman's paranoid projection. Gradually, she learns from the housekeeper that her predecessor was having an affair with the valet, and that the children knew of it and were used as a cover for their illicit meetings. The valet also took Miles on long walks and—it is implied—seduced him or at least introduced him to "vile things." The ghost of the valet walks the garden—or is it the wish-fulfillment of the frustrated governess? Ambiguous, too, is how the governess knew the appearance of the valet—or converted her image of her employer into the valet. In the most eerie scene in many a day the children dress up and play make-believe. Somehow Miles at twelve makes Miss Giddens "feel obscene"—is it the valet's spirit in him or is it her own unconscious sexual wish? She contrives to be alone with him at last and he sneers at her until she breaks down his defense and makes him admit that the dead man's presence comes to him. As the dead man returns, Miles collapses of shock and dies in Miss Giddens' arms. He is free now and the ghost disappears. The ending is deliberately ambiguous—has a child been freed from a dead man's hold by death, or has a neurotic governess literally frightened him to death? It is curious that the dramatist would deliberately sidestep the psychological implications in the story, for without them what remains is psychical hocus-pocus. As theatre suspense, however, *The Innocents* curdled the blood of Broadway audiences for 141 performances. Perhaps it is the mark of Henry James' insight that he was able, writing before the psychoanalytic movement began, to create a story of such subtle and ambivalent rovertones.

In the same year, a very similar play reached Broadway, but one that did not take its ghosts quite as seriously as did Mr. Archibald. Maurice Valency's adaptation of *The Enchanted* by Jean Giraudoux proved to be a truly enchanting play, using fantasy as a license to make some trenchant comment upon this life. The adapter in this case saw and sought to bring out psychological significance in the French legend, interpreting it as "the biography of a moment in the life of a young girl, the moment when she turns from girlhood to womanhood, from the love of mankind to the love of a kind of man." The mayor in the play is disturbed because everything in his town is topsy-turvy as a result of a ghost—dogs bite men when beaten, and children leave home when mistreated. "The women have quietly left their husbands and gone off with more attractive men." In their annual census people list as children their cats, dogs, birds and rubber plants, "the things they really love and consider part of themselves." Under "spouse" they list movie stars, heroines of fiction and occasionally the name of an auto or boat. Everything has a delightfully two-edged explanation in this fantasy-world. Two old spinsters—one who is deaf and misunderstands everything repeated to her—find the diary of a spiritual young girl, Isabel, and discover she is in communication with the ghostly young man. An investigating committee quickly decides she is subversive. The mayor has the ghost shot but he rises again. The only way he can be laid is for Isabel to transfer her affections to a real man, and this she ultimately does in a charming scene in which she is won by the Supervisor, a kindred spirit. He has taught the children frank biological facts that shock the elders, and he has defended as one of the glories of France the lusty Madame Lambert (whose charms are most apparent when she bends over). Giraudoux thus makes his psychological point through the medium of comedy, irony and fantasy, as he did with *The Madwoman of Chaillot*, and later with the Broadway hit, *Ondine* (1954), based on the medieval legend of the water nymph who comes to land and falls in love with the Knight who is doomed to destruction if he kisses her. Into this shimmering tale brought to life by the enticing Audrey Hepburn, Giraudoux reads the deeper psychological truth that ideal love cannot but come to disillusionment.

Giraudoux' symbolic effort to lead a child into adolescence is part of an important movement in playwriting, harking back to Lawson's *Roger Bloomer* (1923). Lawson's authoritarian parent has in the intervening years become almost extinct in the American theatre. It is now rare to find a heavy-handed father—Patterson Greene's *Papa Is All* (1942) is an exception (framed in the quaintness of Pennsylvania Dutch folk *mores*); Greene shows the suppressed wishes of the family entertainingly released by the supposed death of the tyrannical papa. But such sadistic martinets as this club-footed father literally haven't a leg to stand on in a modern psychological milieu. After the pendulum has swung to the other extreme of complete permissiveness, the parent of today is trying to find the middle ground, recover some of his lost prestige in the family, and keep up with his irrepressible youngsters.

Chodorov and Fields in *Junior Miss* (1941) and F. Hugh Herbert deserve the credit for discovering that juveniles could be "commercial" in our theatre. Creator of Corliss Archer with her articulate growing pains over sex ("Ever since I had to wear brassieres my family has been watching me like a hawk"), Herbert's *Kiss and Tell* (1943) depicts the modern adolescent at a surface level. His *For Keeps* (1944) is more perceptive in its analysis of the effects of multiple divorce upon a lonely fifteen-year old who is shuttled from parent to parent; she drinks Martinis and swears valiantly—her defenses against feelings of rejection. Her supercilious father has just married his fourth wife when she comes to stay with them and falls in love with a young man. They are left alone all night with ample liquor and opportunity. But the lad flees in panic when he learns the girl's age. She ultimately charms her way into the heart of her new step-mother and finally is invited to make a home with them, finding the security she had so urgently needed. Wise beyond her years, she had observed that her step-father has ". . . taken to patting my fanny in what he calls a fond, paternal way . . . Only I think it's more fond than paternal . . ."

Herbert's tremulous teen-ager, advanced in her sexual vocabulary but entirely virginal in her behavior, went on to test the breaking point of various males in *For Love or Money* (1947), *The Moon is Blue* (1951), and *A Girl Can Tell* (1953)—the latter with a flash-back to mother's adolescence which was as provocatively innocent as daughter's. Other efforts to tittilate audiences with teen-age sex exonerated by third-act respectability were less successful—there was Mary Orr and Reginald Denham's *Wallflower* (1944) with its tasteless picture of a shy adolescent girl whose inferiority complex leads her to offer to "neck in the nude;" similarly *The Bees and the Flowers* (1946) by Frederick Kohner and Albert Mannheimer pokes fun at the precocious youngster who spouts Freud (a prototype from the twenties), and her boy-friend, a seventeen-year-old sophomore, who is studying to be a psychiatrist. So-called "progressive schools" generally received the blame for the "precocious brats" in these plays—overlooking the fact that such children were generally products of broken homes, were rejected or left with servants, were unloved in childhood even though materially overindulged, and subjected prematurely to the adult world's sophistication. In *Edward, My Son* (1948) by Morley and Langley, for example, the overindulgence of the father is purely a rationalization to mask his own unscrupulousness.

Even the relative restrictiveness of a parochial school proves no barrier to the blossoming of womanhood in Jean Kerr's *Jenny Kissed Me* (1948), especially when the metamorphosis from dowdy child to eligible woman is begrudgingly and amusingly presided over by a crochety priest. An even more startling transformation occurred in *Time Out For Ginger* (1952) by Ronald Alexander, which was a latter-day extension of the "suppression of youth" comedies of the twenties. The plot, little more than a *reductio ad absurdum,* revolves around a wide-eyed adolescent tomboy who is full of rebellion at the inequality of the sexes. Prompted by her own father's theories, she decides that if permissive psychology is the order of the day, she will do what she most wants—to play on the boys' football team. She throws the school into pandemonium but ends up making a spectacular touchdown. Her father, however, had wanted a boy and makes the fatal Freudian slip of saying to her after the game,"Welcome home, son." Wounded that her father unconsciously rejects her as a girl, she has a serious talk with him and he is able to convince her that he wouldn't trade her for any boy in the world. Freed of her unconscious pressure to be a boy for her father's sake, she relinquishes her place on the football team and changes to a frilly formal gown, while the father at the end takes his wife upstairs in the hopes of yet begetting a son. Although the principal of the high school may be right in believing the father "a full grown juvenile delinquent," his theories of letting youth grow to maturity with a minimum of restraints that would infringe upon their essential dignity have not been disproved by *Time Out For Ginger.*

Perhaps the most significant contribution to the psychological drama of adolescence was Mary Chase's *Bernardine.* It was not alone, however. *Picnic, End as a Man, The Climate of Eden, Tea and Sympathy* and *Take a Giant Step* all made pertinent comment upon the inner conflicts of adolescence. The latter, the first play of a promising playwright, Louis Peterson, depicts the added complications which are involved in the adolescent who happens to be Negro. The young man is expelled from high school for talking back to his teacher about slavery in the Civil War. His parents want him to accept a secondary role and not speak back to whites, but his old grandmother urges him to be proud rather than subservient. Suddenly threatened with isolation from his white high school friends as they reach marriageable age, he goes on a bender and seeks out a prostitute, only to return home disgusted. After the death of his grandmother he introjects her dignity and comes of age—he will take the giant step and cut off his white friends before they can cut him off. Peterson has caught the anxieties of youth and their preoccupations with sex; the boy amusingly fears that he will die a virgin, and yet restlessly raps himself with a stick to control his sexual anxiety.

Guilt feelings over minority group identification were also effectively treated by N. Richard Nash in *The Young and Fair* (1948). In a fashionable girls' school, he assembles a seriously disturbed kleptomaniac, an anti-semitic bully, and a Jewess who has been made to feel guilt over her religious difference. Although the characters are authentic and the emotional conflicts perceptively drawn, the plot complications of the school owner's concern for the good will of the rich and reactionary trustee has all too hackneyed a ring to it. As in *The Children's Hour*, the hostile girl uses every available weapon to force girls to substantiate her lie.

The seriously maladjusted girl was the subject of several other plays. A. B. Shiffrin in *Love on Leave* (1944) presupposes that it might be amusing to have the daughter of an expert on child psychology run away and conduct her own rebellion with a sailor. A more elaborate attempt to analyze juvenile sexual misconduct was Elsa Shelley's *Pick-Up Girl* (1944), a crude and meretricious picture of a Children's Court. The girl of fifteen has had an abortion and syphilis by the time she reaches the "understanding judge" who, nevertheless, gives her a most unsympathetic sentence and blocks her one chance at rehabilitation. The judge sternly condemns the parents, but fails to call in psychiatric aid. Either the author or the Children's Court of New York is far behind the times. It is to be hoped it is the former.

The impossibility of writing a psychological play today without an understanding of psychoanalytic mechanisms and psychosomatic illness was further illustrated by Viña Delmar's *The Rich Full Life* (1945), in which over-protective parents keep their adolescent daughter from the "rich full life" until mother permits her to attend the big prom with a boy and—just as the father predicted—she catches a severe illness.

The psychological study of the lonely, sexually eager and verbally eloquent adolescent girl reached its highest point to date in Carson McCullers' *The Member of the Wedding* (1950). Unsatisfied with a previous dramatization of her novel, Mrs. McCullers is reported to have undertaken the adaptation herself at the urging of her friend, Tennessee Williams (although she had no previous playwriting experience and had seen only two Broadway plays). The result was a play whose appeal lay in its fresh and incisive characterizations and whose weakness lay in its flabby plot structure. It is fragmentary, static, repetitious. Mrs. McCullers chose not to sacrifice her characters' integrity to a well-made plot, but lacking this her play was forced to depend upon brilliant star performers to hold its audience—Ethel Waters as the patient, maternal, perceptive Negress, Berenice, and Julie Harris as the gangling, imaginative twelve-year old tomboy, Frankie—to say nothing of the child actor, Brandon De Wilde as John Henry. The three of them spend most of the play together in the rambling kitchen of the home where Frankie lives with her widowed and stodgy father. Frankie's soldier brother comes

home with his fiancée to announce he is going to be married, and
Frankie displaces her need for love and family security into an obsessive desire to go with her brother and his bride on their honeymoon. She is too naive to understand why this is impractical, as her
knowledge of sex is limited to a suspicion that men and women
"look at each other and peepee or something." Scorned by the neighborhood girls, Frankie vents her spleen upon John Henry, her cousin,
but Berenice knows, "When folks are lonesome and left out, they
turn so mean." Frankie speaks an eloquent soliloquy on "belongingness" at the end of the first act:

> The trouble with me is that for a long time I have been just
> an "I" person. All other people can say "we." When Berenice
> says "we" she means her lodge and church and colored
> people. Soldiers can say "we" and mean the army. All
> people belong to a "we" except me . . . I love the two of
> them (her brother and his fiancée) because they are the we
> of me.

The day of the wedding, Frankie suffers tantrum and shock
when she learns she cannot be a member of her brother's wedding.
Deprived of her "we," she is also somewhat gratuitously parted
from John Henry, whom the playwright kills off unexpectedly of
meningitis; Frankie compensates as Berenice knew she would—she
develops a sudden crush on a girl whom she previously despised. At
the end, Frankie is deep in fresh fantasies, dramatizing herself on a
world-cruise with her new friend.

Contrapuntal to Frankie's isolation is the mature and more
poignant loneliness of Berenice. She deeply loved her first husband,
Ludie (such a synthesis of sensual and tender love is treated more
fully in Williams' *The Rose Tattoo*). When he died, Berenice married several other times, but each only because something about the
others suggested her first husband. "What I did was to marry off little
pieces of Ludie whenever I come across them. It was just my misfortune that they all turned out to be the wrong pieces." Her foster-
brother is a hostile, bitter young man taking marijuana and hating
whites. After he kills a white man he feels, as did Paul Green's
Native Son, suddenly free for the first time:

> I know now all my days have been leading up to this min-
> ute. No more 'boy this—boy that,'—no bowing, no scraping.
> For the first time, I'm free and it makes me happy.

He hangs himself in jail to save the white people the trouble. It is
evident that what little plot there is is sudden, violent and insuffi-

ciently motivated. But the richness of the three main characters and their freshness of speech makes *The Member of the Wedding* one of the notable modern American psychological plays, a superb portrait of the baffling years between childhood and womanhood. Frankie Addams has a secure place in the annals of adolescence. There is more than a touch of Frankie in Moss Hart's Olivia of *The Climate of Eden* and Inge's Millie of *Picnic*.

We have seen that some of the major plays of the forties and fifties have dealt either comically or seriously with the disturbing emotions of adolescence—anything but a happy time for most children. Contrasted with these guilty wrestlings with hostility, sex, and the need for group identifications, one play stands out as a positive picture of parents seeing their son into adolescence with love, with understanding and with unified family loyalty. This is Samuel Taylor's *The Happy Time* (1950). It depicts an effervescent family of French Canadians all ingratiatingly in love with life and sex, from twelve-year old Bibi who is just entering "la puberté" to old Grandpa who may die of high blood pressure making love to the Widow La-Touche but who asks, "The one who knows of a better way to die, will he step forward? Allons!" Maman, being Scotch, is the one sobering influence in the happy-go-lucky family. Though she struggles to keep order and objects to the raffish Uncle Desmonde's giving Bibi a copy of "La Vie Parisienne," it is clear that this is basically a secure marriage. Grandpa charmingly explains puberty to the curious Bibi:

> It is a matter of the glands. . . It gives pleasure, like eating, but also gives children, which eating does not do. . . It is when you have the knowledge to use the glands and the heart and the mind, together, correctly. Tu comprends, Bibi? To be truly a man one must know love, one must know truth.

When Mignonette, an attractive young lady, is brought into the home as a maid, both Bibi and his more experienced Uncle Desmonde fall in love with her. After holding hands with her at a Rudolf Valentino movie, Bibi steals Mignonette's nightgown, believing this to be Valentino's way of seeing women undressed. Desmonde is accused and Maman grows upset for fear Bibi will turn out like Desmonde. Meanwhile another uncle, Louis, has retreated from all marital responsibility and lounges around, drinking wine from a water-cooler; he rallies himself, however, to interview a prospective suitor for his daughter and proceeds to get the suitor drunk on the "water." The crisis of the play is the result of Bibi's trouble at school over the issue of "La Vie Parisienne." Falsely accused by the principal of making an obscene drawing, Bibi is defended by the three brothers, who rally with family pride and march off to convince the smug, authoritarian, and sexually frustrated principal that his might does not make right. In the end, the nightgown is returned and Bibi recognizes the "truth and love" between Desmonde and Mignonette. Reluctantly, he relinquishes his first adolescent crush, as his father tells him an old French saying, "Le coeur a ses raisons, que la raison ne connait point." Explaining why the principal was evil and cruel, Papa relates it to universals in a keen and Freudian way:

> It is because he has been brought up to believe that the desire is wrong. And since he himself has the desire, he is even more mixed up than we are. He has been brought up in a world where the desire has been used so badly, so badly, believe me, that now it, itself, is thought to be bad. And this is wrong. It is wrong, Bibi. And the reason for this condition? It is because so many people are without love.

The Happy Time depicts adolescence as the happy time it should be, and treats sex with healthy, unrepressed interest that is free of nastiness. It is one of the most entertaining and yet meaningful of modern comedies. After this notable beginning, Taylor's second play, *Sabrina Fair* (1953) which depicts a girl choosing the man who can dominate her rather than the ones whom she dominates, proved somewhat thin and disappointing.

It is amply evident, however, from the foregoing that one of the most significant trends in the American drama of the forties and fifties is a new interest in childhood and adolescence, crucial periods newly illuminated by psychology.

PSYCHIATRISTS CAN BE PEOPLE

The psychoanalyst, who emerged in the drama of the twenties as a kind of *deus ex machina,* has by the fifties lost his aura of infallibility as well as his comic-opera whiskers but retains his importance in the American theatre. More and more today stage psychiatrists are eclectic as to the therapies employed. In Jan De Hartog's first Broadway play, *This Time Tomorrow* (1947), for example, he uses hypnosis as therapy for a tubercular and sex-hungry girl; narcosynthesis is employed in Laurents' *Home of the Brave* and Shelley's *Foxhole in the Parlor,* dream analysis in Kingsley's *The World We Make,* a drug to cure schizophrenia in *Jupiter Laughs,* and projective tests such as the Rorschach in *The Shrike.* The orthodox Freudian couch is used in *Oh, Men! Oh, Women!* and in Louis Paul's *The Cup of Trembling* (1948), in which a psychoanalyst and Alcoholics Anonymous combine to help an alcoholic woman suffering from unconscious father-hatred (this is the play Kronenberger called a "side-car named desire"). Other plays with psychiatrists among the *dramatis personae* include *The Walking Gentleman* (1942) by Grace and Fulton Oursler, Henry Misrock's *A Family Affair* (1946), and Lesley Storm's *Black Chiffon* (1950). The latter British melodrama deals with a society matron who compulsively shop-lifts a black chiffon nightgown just before her son's wedding. The psychiatrist uncovers her deep attachment to the son but causes such a shock reaction when he confronts her with the interpretation that she prefers to plead guilty and go to prison rather than use the defense of an "abnormal" relationship. The weakness of the play is the psychiatrist's permitting the woman to make such a decision—itself the final proof of her attachment to her son.

Comic and satiric jibes at psychoanalysis were much more prevalent during the twenties than they have been since. Freud's theories have withstood the test of ridicule, and Walter Kerr pointed out in reviewing *Faithfully Yours* (1951) that the authors seemed "totally unaware that psychiatry is not precisely a new field for comic investigations." Based on Jean-Bernard Luc's *The Philemon Complex* and adapted by L. Bush-Fekete and Mary Fay, *Faithfully Yours* derives its fun from a phony rather than a legitimate psychoanalyst, one who intrudes upon a happy marriage and tries to woo the wife by convincing her that this "fidelity neurosis" is itself abnormal and that she must help her husband find other women. It may be that France is twenty years behind this country in its applications of psychotherapy, for *Faithfully Yours* has about it the familiar stamp of the twenties—but for that matter so does Alfred Golden's American comedy, *Lady, Behave!* (1943) with its equally fraudulent psychoanalyst. And there were a few survivals—almost anachronistic—of foolish farces such as Conrad and Gabel's *Horse Fever* (1940), in which a man tries to hide a horse in a hotel room and apply psychoanalysis to cure its neurotic balking at the post, or *Eight O'Clock Tuesday* (1941) by Wallsten and Eberhart, in which the detective applies psychoanalysis to catch the criminal. Even more inane is *Be Your Age* (1953) by Reginald Denham and Mary Orr, with its college professor making love with a psychiatric text as guide.

The quack psychoanalysts and sophomoric satires were far less common by the fifties, however, than the mature play which depicts psychiatrists realistically both in their professional work and in their private lives. Philip Barry, with *Tomorrow and Tomorrow* and Robert Sherwood with *Reunion in Vienna,* both in 1931, may be said to have begun the "psychoanalysts can be people" school of play-writing. Noel Coward carried the concept one step further in his group of *Tonight at 8:30* one-acts, and showed in *The Astonished Heart* (1935) a distinguished psychiatrist himself suffering from a nervous breakdown and committing suicide. Possessing little psychoanalytic wisdom, the doctor proves to be another of Coward's passive-dependent lovers who go to pieces when denied their mistresses' affection. So far has the trend toward humanizing psychiatrists gone that by the time *The Teahouse of the August Moon, The Caine Mutiny Court-Martial, The Seven Year Itch* and *Oh, Men! Oh, Women!* reached Broadway, Walter F. Kerr exclaimed: "It's getting so no Broadway show can afford to be without one." He went on to point out that the psychiatrists are an unstable lot—one goes native in *Teahouse,* two of them are made to look foolish by the attorney in *Caine Mutiny,* the one in *Seven Year Itch* confesses to a repressed wish to murder his wife, and the harassed analyst in *Oh, Men! Oh, Women!* spends the entire play trying to control his flighty fiancée. Kerr suggests that playgoers' attitudes by the mid-fifties are no longer satirical of psychoanalysis but neither are they entirely awesome:

> Our comedies aren't exactly harsh with the bumbling ana-lysts; they seem to have a certain wry affection for them, perhaps even a hope that someday they'll amount to some-thing. But they do seem to be saying that psychiatry, as a science, is still a little unsure of itself.

Certainly no moment in recent drama made a more telling commentary upon the personal pressures of a psychoanalyst than when at the end of an arduous session in T. S. Eliot's *The Cocktail Party* the analyst collapses in exhaustion upon his own couch. The Missouri-born Eliot, a Britisher by adoption, has manifested a curious interest in fusing psychiatry and poetry, although it may be observed that *The Cocktail Party* (1950) is neither very poetic nor very psychiatric. The first act is brilliant drawing room comedy, in which an Unidentified Guest at a cocktail party proves to be the psychoanalyst, Sir Henry Harcourt-Reilly. Most of the humor of the first act stems from the fact that the host cannot remember that the Unidentified Guest is drinking Gin and Water. In the second act in Sir Henry's consultation room, we learn that the elaborately contrived cocktail party was for the purpose of getting three individuals who need therapy to seek it: Edward, his wife Lavinia, and his mistress Celia. No reputable psychoanalyst would intrigue so mysteriously to get reluctant patients into his office. When Edward comes, his problem proves to be indecision. "I have ceased to believe in my own personality," he announces, but Sir Henry cuts him short and discourages any recollections of childhood, dream analysis or free association —an incredible action for a modern psychiatrist. Instead, he proceeds to behave even more fancifully and even unethically by confronting Edward with his wife and exposing his affair with Celia. The wife knew of it all along, but Edward did not know of her affair with an effete young hot-house plant named Peter Quilpe. By his heavy-handed blundering and insistence upon making deeplevel interpretations with little to go on and in spite of the patients' protests, Sir Henry so enrages Edward and Lavinia that they are driven together again and leave with Sir Henry's poetic benediction: "Go in peace. And work out your salvation with diligence." (Or, one is tempted to add, find legitimate psychiatric help.) Next Celia arrives suffering from a sense of sin and solitude. The analyst summarily sends her to his private sanitarium and he and his two old friends who have called him on this triangular case drink a mystic toast which appropriately brings down the curtain on this dubious therapy. In the third act, two years later, Edward and Lavinia are happily reconciled, but Ceila has been killed off by Eliot during the intermission. She died in the south seas, where she had gone to atone for her sense of sin by joining a nursing order. Crucified near an ant-hill, her death had been apparently satisfyingly masochistic, and the psychoanalyst observes, "If that is not a happy death, what death is happy?" *The Cocktail Party* thus toys with psychoanalytic themes in an aura of mystery created by withholding information as to who and what the author intends his people to represent. The play provoked much serious discussion and managed to command sizeable audiences with its glittering performances and polished verbal elegance. Some critics believed Sir Henry to be an allegorical figure of God or Christ, and others, such as William Hawkins, insisted that audiences were being taken in by an outrageous parody. One or the other interpretation must surely be correct, for the psychoanalyst bears no resemblance to anything known and sanctioned by psychoanalytic societies.

Eliot has a propensity for playing tricks upon his audiences. In *The Family Reunion* (1939) his family is never reunited, and his leading figure, haunted by Conscience in the form of a chorus of the Eumenides, is sent out to seek his salvation much as in *The Cock-*

tail Party. The father-image of Eliot's most recent play, *The Confidential Clerk* (1954), has found his salvation—in making pottery—but the rest of Eliot's people do not know who they are, and the play becomes a grand scramble to find parents. The secret son of Sir Claude cannot marry the girl he is attracted to when he learns that she, too, is Sir Claude's illegitimate daughter, but in the end Sir Claude and his wife, Lady Elizabeth, fighting to claim the boy as a son, find that he is neither of their's and that Lady Elizabeth's true son is a common young man whom she cannot abide. Eliot's theme is apparently that heredity will tell after all, for the son goes off to follow his true father's calling as an organist. There is occasionally in *The Confidential Clerk* a pungent line such as, "If you never knew either of your parents, you can't understand what loathing really is," but in the main Eliot merely flirts with psychology. By the time all the mistaken identities are straightened out, one has the impression that by comparison *Twelfth Night* and *The Importance of Being Earnest* are realistic documentaries. *The Cocktail Party* and *The Confidential Clerk* seem to be deliberately vague, pretentious, thoroughly artificial—but often amusing. Although Eliot moves glibly through psychoanalytic terminology and implies a psychological profundity ("If you haven't the strength to impose your own terms upon life, you must accept the terms it offers you"), there is insufficient reward for taking the pains to penetrate his brilliantly enameled, craftily tooled surfaces.

A very different point of view on paternity from Eliot's was suggested by John Steinbeck, who returned to the theatre with *Burning Bright* (1950). Although hardly more than a skeleton of a play, it contains the superbly characterized figure of an old acrobat who grows obsessed with the desire to have a child to carry on his line. His wife conceives a child by a younger man as an act of love for her sterile husband, and he ultimately comes to accept it as his own. All men are fathers to all sons, Steinbeck concludes, and by raising the child and shaping his environment the old man will be more truly a father to him than the callow young man who sired him.

A British compatriot of Eliot, A. J. Cronin, who happens to be a physician, offers reassuring evidence that psychiatry in Britain is not in the alarming state one might assume from *The Cocktail Party.* In *Jupiter Laughs* (1940), Cronin depicts a neurological clinic where doctors are at work on a new drug to cure schizophrenia and find themselves under the same nervous pressures as the public at large—a theme previously treated in *All The Living.* A more recent picture of institutional psychiatrists at work proved highly controversial and elicited an emphatic "tain't so" from at least one psychiatrist. In Joseph Kramm's Pulitzer Prize winning *The Shrike* (1952), a patient is brought into the city hospital, having attempted suicide with an overdose of phenobarbital. His wife devotedly waits by his bed as he recovers, but gradually the audience realizes her sinister intent. We learn that Jim has been separated from his wife and in love with a girl named Charlotte. First the wife suggests to the doctors that he should not keep an appointment for a job—although his financial failure had brought him to the attempted suicide. He is transferred to the "Psycho ward" for observation and given a Rorschach and association word test; but the latter is hammered at him as though it were a police third-degree. The psychiatrists take the wife's word that Jim was often violent at home, exclude Charlotte from visiting or giving information, and gradually permit the wife to make a prisoner of her husband, who faces permanent commitment unless he agrees to the wife's terms—to return to her and give up the woman he loves. Like the shrike, a bird which impales its prey on thorns, the wife has fiendishly employed his mental illness for her own selfish motives. The staff psychiatrists permit this to happen apparently from disinterestedness. They have ample time to talk to the wife but not enough, apparently to discover that the husband is perfectly rational. The result in the theatre is a breathlessly tight work of suspense, but the degree to which *The Shrike* accurately depicts conditions in modern mental hospitals has been challenged by Dr. Lawrence Kubie, Professor of Psychiatry at Yale, who points out a number of fallacies in the play, including the absurd way that the psychiatrists close their eyes to possible sources of information about their patient and take only the wife's biased interpretation:

> To portray all psychiatrists as ignorant or destructive is hardly calculated to dispel fear among people, so many of whom may some day have to face or deal with mental illness. Is it really too much to ask that when the stage attempts to deal seriously with matters which are essential to human progress, the playwright and the director should understand deeply and fully the subject which they are portraying?

Although Kramm has not defended himself against Dr. Kubie's charges, he wrote in *The New York Times* an evaluation of Freud's contributions to medicine. Pointing out the parallel between the Stanislavski method of acting and actor training and psychoanalytic methods—a parallel shown by Odets in *The Country Girl*—Kramm believes that Freud's theories, "based on monumental research, intense observation, original thinking, and a study of literature," were not so much a new psychology as a new vocabulary, just as Stanislavski's method was only a new vocabulary for analyzing the problems of acting. Kramm would minimize the effect of psychoanalysis upon the theatre, which he believes to depend upon the author's instinctive psychological insight:

> Neither Stanislavski in the theatre, nor Freud in analysis, lay claim to originating psychological thinking in their respective fields. What to do with it, yes; how to apply it, yes; how to make it serve their purpose, yes. Only spurious disciples claim for them original birth—the masters never claimed this for themselves.

It is unfortunate, however, that in *The Shrike* Kramm did not find ways to sustain his suspense without making all of the psychiatrists tools of the venal wife. One can only hope in the name of humanity that his picture of city psychiatric hospitals is not accurate, although the antiquated methods described in Dr. Wertham's *The Show of Violence* confirm the need for a re-examination of our legal handling of criminals and potential criminals.

The state of official psychiatry in the armed forces also came in for implied criticism in *The Caine Mutiny Court-Martial* (1954) by Herman Wouk. Unlike *The Shrike,* Wouk's theatrical suspense is gained because of rather than in spite of his valid handling of psychological detail. Wouk calls Captain Queeg a paranoid and then proceeds to prove it by gradual introduction of clinical symptoms. This masterful technique permits the audience to participate as in a board of review—it is in fact the jury. Two Navy psychiatrists both make positive statements that Captain Queeg was sane and competent to command, and then proceed under cross-examination to betray overwhelming evidence that Queeg had lost control of himself and that his junior officer, Lieutenant Maryk, was justified in assuming command of the Caine during the typhoon. Queeg's childhood problems are brought out by the first psychiatrist—his inferiority feelings caused by his parents' divorce, his school and financial problems—aggravated by his short stature—which has caused him to compensate by a strong identification with his role as a Naval officer. Shrewdly the defense counsel leads the psychiatrist to admit that Queeg was a perfectionist, suspicious of subordinates, unable to admit failure, a stickler for detail. "You might say," the psychiatrist concedes innocently, "he revises reality in his own mind so that he comes out blameless." The term for these symptoms, he admits, is a paranoid personality. The second psychiatrist, a smug young

Freudian, confirms this diagnosis but quibbles over terminology, preferring to call Queeg an "obsessive personality with paranoid features." In this psychiatrist's theory, a person can compensate but can never *adjust* without undergoing psychoanalysis. He points out Queeg's compulsive rolling of two steel balls in his hands—and its Freudian symbolism. He is soon amusingly backed into a corner and must admit that he cannot define "sick." The prosecution abruptly dismisses him still insisting that Queeg was not incompetent to command—even though the psychiatrist has never been to sea and has been in the Navy only five months.

Queeg is finally called to the stand and proceeds to confirm all the allegations of paranoid behavior—his persecution of the men for minor infractions, his cowardice under fire, his lying under oath, his offer to falsify the log if Maryk would relinquish command, his projection that all the officers hated him, his outbursts of temper which he controls by rolling his two steel balls, and even his subtle insinuation of homosexuality between two of the men who testified against him. Wouk has revealed his deep insight into a paranoid personality by the time he has reduced Captain Queeg to a twitching, writhing psychopath, and the court acquits the officer who took command of the ship. In an epilogue, however, Wouk rebuilds Queeg's prestige. The Jewish defense counsel points out that our nation had to depend upon regular Navy officers to stop Hitler from invading the democracies, and that it was their deeds, done as best they knew how, which held off the enemy while the future young officers were studying their psychology books in college. The epilogue is no whitewash of the Queegs but rather a footnote which places this superbly written play in its historical perspective, freeing the author of the charge that he had written an indictment of the Navy.

The most recent point of view about psychoanalysts, and one of the funniest plays of its kind, is Edward Chodorov's *Oh, Men! Oh, Women!* (1953). Unlike *Reunion in Vienna* or *Tomorrow and Tomorrow,* the purpose is not to make the psychoanalyst eat his Freudian words, but merely to suggest that the analyst is human and may be permitted an occasional moment of helplessness at the irrationality of the human race, particularly as represented by his fluffy screwball fiancée who taxes his theoretical understanding of human motives to the breaking point. The poised young analyst, as played by Franchot Tone, is about to go on his honeymoon when his last two patients assume the reclining position and reveal disturbing information about his fiancée, Myra. First a wretched young man with a compulsive hand mannerism needs help in getting over his affair with Myra—a detail she had neglected to tell her fiancé; then a married woman who has been fighting with her alcoholic husband comes for help because he has had an affair—also with Myra. Each of the patients plays a long scene on the couch—almost monologues which are both funny and at the same time painfully embarrassing in their flippant treatment of intimate personal unhappiness. In the second act, the psychoanalyst reproaches his fiancée —not for the affairs but for not being honest in revealing them. The doctor has to exert all his insight—with the help of his own wise old analyst, to deal with his flighty fiancée whom the other men would still try to win away from him—one by force and one by an excruciatingly funny alcoholic retelling of Ibsen's A Doll's House.

The third act proves somewhat anti-climactic, with the doctor forced to assert himself in a way that he might have done without studying Freud. No greater wisdom emerges from the play than the thought that men and women can never get along, because they want different things—"men want women and women want men." It can hardly be called a satire on psychoanalysis—rather it is a comedy about psychoanalysis to be enjoyed by audiences to whom psychoanalysis is familiar and who find it reassuring to watch a good-natured psychoanalyst prove himself human and face his problem just about like everybody else.

Chodorov's previous plays reflected little psychoanalytic influence, and in his questionnaire, four years before Oh, Men! Oh, Women! he pointed out that a number of playwrights have been thrown into a "fine confusion" because of psychoanalysis—growing self-conscious about their work, blocked as writers now that they know the self-revealing nature of creative writing. Psychoanalysis, he felt, could not substitute for original creativity:

> . . . poetic feeling and thought—the inherent ability to express the inexpressible or the difficult—these I must confess I feel arise from a combination of experience, observation and reading—reading Freud if you like!—plus the knack and desire to say it with dialogue.

Chodorov observed, too, that such heroines as Blanche in A Streetcar Named Desire seemed sick and pathetic, but not tragic. Perhaps he has had a change of heart during the writing of Oh, Men! Oh, Women!—for if the neurotic is unworthy to be a tragic figure, is it any more logical to make of him a comic figure? And this Chodorov has assuredly done with infinite skill and hilarious results in Oh, Men! Oh, Women!

THE MIND'S EYE

Subjective techniques of staging, so popular in the twenties, had all but disappeared during the thirties, but now threaten to make a comeback under the influence of the musical drama and revue which has in the interim seized upon them. The thirties were apparently not a period for spoofing or spooking, and American playgoers of the forties seemed willing to accept their ghosts only if they were set in a tongue-in-check framework such as Noel Coward achieved in *Blithe Spirit* (1941), or if the hallucinations could be given psychological rationale, as in Archibald's *The Innocents* or thematic significance as in *Thunder Rock* and *Bury the Dead*. Most of the latter day explorers of the world of poltergeist discovered to their sorrow that audiences were too sophisticated to take their ghosts straight —witness the unsuccessful *Lo and Behold* (1951) by John Patrick, Kaufman and MacGrath's *Fancy Meeting You Again* (1952), *The Scene of the Crime* (1940) by Frank Gould, *The Lady Who Came to Stay* (1941) by Kenneth White, and Paul Vincent Carroll's *Kindred* (1939). Only John Cecil Holm managed to make ghosts moderately lucrative at the box office, in *Gramercy Ghost* (1951). Van Druten whimsically asked playgoers to accept—for an evening at least—the existence of witches in his *Bell, Book and Candle* (1952), and it required a similar frame of mind to visit Mary Chase's *Mrs. McThing*. The possibility of the transference of a dead man's impulses through his hands was apparently taken seriously in Mary Bell's British play, *Duet for Two Hands* (1947), and the transference of souls after death was mixed up with psychiatry and hypnosis in *A Boy Who Lived Twice* (1945) by Egbert and Tubby. One of the more effective —albeit tear-jerking—use of ghosts was in a wartime fantasy, *The Wind is Ninety* (1945) by Ralph Nelson, in which a dead soldier sits on stage with a buddy and watches his family take the news of his death. Each of the family fantasies him as he wishes to remember him, and the ghost finds consolation in the fact that for his family he is a living memory that can give them a faith by which to live.

Hallucinations based upon subjective pressures are a more acceptable technique to the psychoanalytic-minded audience of today. *The Gambler* (1952), adapted by Alfred Drake and Edward Eager from the Italian of Ugo Betti, showed a man who has caused his wife to be murdered (though he is technically innocent) suffering obsessive guilt feelings until he begins to see his dead wife in visions all over his house or sitting on her own grave. He craves the judgment of God and substitutes the old station-master as his judge.

There were also hallucinatory visions in a play dealing with faith-healing, *Touchstone* (1953) by William Stucky.

One of the most entertaining of recent comedies to deal with the individual's inner world, distorted and altered by psychological pressures, was *Happy Birthday* (1946) by Anita Loos. A genial comedy of wish-fulfillment, it shows the rebirth of a mousy librarian into a sexually desirable woman. Addie, frustrated and morally prim, comes into a bar for the first time in search of her father, stays in this "sanctuary of the spirit" because her bank clerk—whom she unconsciously loves—is there with his fiancée, and ultimately gets amusingly tight on Pink Ladies. Then the bottles on the bar begin to glow, to bubble and make lovely sounds which only Addie sees and hears. As she emerges from her shell of timidity and orders drinks from a bottle that had called "yoo-hoo" to her, she discovers that the people in the bar need love just as much as she does, and by the end she has made fast friends with a number of lonely creatures, danced a tango, and won the bank clerk from his callow and frigid mistress. When Addie's drunken father turns up at last, he is proud of her for the first time, and at the end everything lights up again, not from drink but from love. Although psychiatrists have found that moderate amounts of alcohol may in fact contribute to the mental health of hyper-tense and introverted individuals, there is no evidence that one good "binge" effects such a complete personality change as Miss Loos depicts in her lightweight comedy.

Other subjective techniques—less original than the fluorescent whiskey bottles—were occasionally used, as in Ernest Pascal's *Peepshow* (1944), which harks back to O'Neill's *Days Without End* in its use of two actors to play one man and his conscience, here with farce results as the hero manages to get the girl into the bedroom and to exclude his conscience. Donald Ogden Stewart went Pascal one better by having two *alter egos*, a man named Mind and a beautiful girl who struggles with Mind in *How I Wonder* (1947). Another and more daring use of subjective devices was Charles Schnee's *Apology* (1943), which should rightly be called Epic Theatre, reflecting the influence of Erwin Piscator in its use of projected scenery, lantern slides and didactic narration directly to the audience, as well as its employment of actors doubling in psychologically identified roles. The stream-of-consciousness monologue, another of the theatrical techniques of the twenties, was restored by Arnold Manoff in his play, *All You Need Is One Good Break* (1950), the story of a neurotic and frustrated little man who dreams expressionistically of great achievements when his big break comes. The discrepancy between his imaginary triumphs and the facts of reality finally drive him to mental breakdown.

As in Manoff's play the dream device so beloved by playsmiths of the twenties and earlier still proves its worth from time to time— unsuccessfully in *A Strange Play* (1944) by Patti Spears, but with rare imagination and charm by Peter Ustinov in the British fantasy, *The Love of Four Colonels* (1953), which gave the conscious control to surrealist free-association which Williams' *Camino Real* lacked. A combination of modern psychology and the Gothic *doppelgänger* motive, the Wicked and Good Fairy struggle to possess the four army colonels, French, British, American and Russian, who meet at a disputed border town in the middle of Europe. Characteristically enough, the American has a psychoanalyst, but the Britisher says, "We can't afford them, thank God." The Good and Wicked Fairies arrive, their destiny being eternally to torture mankind into a choice between them (if not for this inescapable task the Good and Wicked Fairy could find happiness, as they love each other—symbolic of Freudian wholeness, the synthesis of *id* and *ego*). They lead the four Colonels to a Sleeping Beauty, and four psycho-dramas are enacted, with the Wicked Fairy serving as a kind of Stage Manager. Each projects onto the sleeping girl his wish-fulfillment of ideal woman-hood. To the Frenchman, she is a lady in an 18th-century comedy of intrigue and his love for her is foiled by the Good Fairy role-playing not as his wife but as his mistress. To the Englishman, she is a Shakespearean heroine, an "Illyrian nun" who represents a conversion of the Yugoslavian girl he had seduced. The Good Fairy blocks this romance disguised as the virgin's mother. To the Ameri-can, Beauty is a prostitute in a Grade B movie—suggested by *Rain* —complete with the preacher who tries to seduce her. Disguised as his psychiatrist, the Good Fairy orders the American to relax, inter-preting the girl as "Illusion, my dear. Just a superimposition of the mother image onto you." To the Russian, Beauty appears as a gen-tle, ineffectual Chekhov heroine. All four of the colonels fail to kiss Beauty and free her. Now their four wives arrive, a scene of delicious satire. The American wife is a busy career woman, editor of three magazines, *Urge*, *Wife* and *Think*. Armed with Kinsey-like statistics on sex, she makes a survey and finds that the four wives average 1.25 infidelities or "outlets" a year. The American colonel is shocked to learn that his wife has had one more outlet than he. The British wife cannot bring herself to discuss sex at all, and the Russian has had a child by another man in her husband's absence. Two husbands re-turn to their wives, the British and Russian, while the American and

French couples separate and go on alone in the quest of eternal beauty. All four wonder if they did the right thing. Ustinov thus combines psychology with fairy tale and subtle satire which, while not robust theatre, is, nevertheless, keen cerebral comedy.

Another exploration of man's erotic fantasies was given a much less subtle and more robust American handling in the tradition of *Beggar on Horseback* and *Dream Girl,* proving to be one of the funniest of the Freudian comedies—*The Seven Year Itch* (1952), by George Axelrod. Axelrod, who has been psychoanalyzed, began by writing radio and television plays and skits for Broadway musicals, in one of which, *Small Wonder* (1948), his comic hero named "The Normal Neurotic" was played by Tom Ewell, who went on to create Axelrod's famous example of a normal neurotic, Richard, in *The Seven Year Itch*. He has been married seven years and the itch develops as his wife goes away with their son for the summer, leaving him alone in his apartment which has a blocked-up stairway to the floor above. The play consists of the adventures, part real and part fantasy, of Richard, who has promised his wife not to drink or smoke but who finds himself distracted by a woman undressing across the court. Once when he boasted to his wife that he was attractive to women she had mocked him with "Name one." Now he begins to recall all the sexy girls he has known, all of whom throw themselves at him. The girl in the apartment above drops a tomato plant which almost kills him, but provides him the opportunity to invite her down. Waiting for her, he is in a tizzy of sexual anticipation and fantasies himself as a debonair Noel Coward hero pouring her cocktails. Before the girl arrives, he is interrupted by an ingratiatingly distraught psychoanalyst, Dr. Brubaker, whose book Richard is publishing. Brubaker has come one night early for his appointment, and interprets this as an expression of a repressed wish to kill his wife. Richard gets rid of him in time to receive the real girl, a charming and genuine miss who has modelled and posed for nude photography. She is glad Richard is married as she finds married men the safest. Irked because she thinks him old enough to have seen Sarah Bernhardt, Richard carries on inner debates with his other self, his *alter* or *super-ego*. Their first meeting ends with his taking her in his arms on a piano bench so awkwardly that they fall off. The next night Richard unburdens to Dr. Brubaker (in spite of the latter's efforts to discourage Richard's subtle maneuvering onto the couch), and confesses his guilt feelings over his "criminal assault" of the girl on the piano bench. To Richard's threat to kill the girl if she reveals anything to his wife, Dr. Brubaker makes the classic retort: ". . . until you are able to commit a simple criminal assault, I strongly advise that you avoid anything so complex as murder. One must learn to walk before one can run." There is next an expressionistic scene as all the girls in Richard's erotic life appear together at a tea party in various states of undress, clicking their tea cups in unison as they gossip to Richard's wife about him. To counteract these guilt feelings Richard has a projection in which he fantasies his wife also unfaithful with a notorious wolf. Later Richard takes the girl to dinner and as they settle down cozily at his apartment afterwards each has a fantasy scene of unspoken thoughts. The girl's inner voice urges her to go ahead with the affair and chides her for not being a virgin anyhow. They are in each other's arms with the blessing of their respective inner voices. The next morning, however, while she is still asleep, Richard suffers extreme guilt feelings, imagining the many possible outcomes—tearful pleading, scandal, threatened blackmail, murder, and finally his own death at the hands of his wife. Dr. Brubaker discovers him in this state and diagnoses it as an "extreme state of sexomasochistic excitement bordering on hysteria"; observing that masochists enjoy their guilt feelings, he leaves with a cheerful: "Enjoy yourself." Dr. Brubaker does, however, suggest that the young lady whose nude picture he admires should be referred to him if she is in need of psychoanalysis. Finally, the girl emerges and none of the fantasied scenes take place. Instead, she is thoroughly adjusted and happy, going blithely to work with none of the guilt feelings of the girl in *Time of the Cuckoo* or in Van Druten's *I've Got Sixpence*. She has, however, come to realize that perhaps a husband of her own would ultimately be desirable. Richard, too, has worked out his guilts by the end and is off for the country to see his wife. Although no great depth of insight nor originality of expressionistic devices is involved, *The Seven Year Itch* is a thoroughly hilarious exploration of the private fantasies of a "normal neurotic," the domesticated male. Mental sickness is, as the psychiatrist in *The Caine Mutiny Court-Martial* insisted, a relative term, and audiences are only too happy to identify themselves with Axelrod's thoroughly normal fantasies of sex and guilt.

CHAPTER XV

Freudian Drama in Perspective

In the first half of the twentieth century the American drama grew from gawky adolescence to worldly maturity. The remarkable distance it has traversed in fifty years has no parallel in theatrical history unless we go back to the decades preceding Shakespeare. From *The Girl With the Green Eyes* to *The Rose Tattoo,* from *The Great Divide* to *The Time of the Cuckoo,* and from *The Witching Hour* to *The Crucible,* American playwrights have learned their psychology well and through it have found their voice in the theatre of the modern world.

We have seen that the first signs of "change of voice" in the adolescent coincided with the arrival from Paris and Vienna of the "new psychology" in the first decade of the century. Augustus Thomas, David Belasco, Charles Klein, William Vaughn Moody, and Edward Locke sensed that the "subconscious" contained implicit dramatic values, but they were not sure how to deal with them. Lumped with the subconscious were all of the psychic phenomena of hypnosis, transference, telepathy, and faith healing, from which gradually emerged Freud's scientific technique for the exploration and treatment of mental illness.

After Freud's visit to America in 1909, the change began, gathering momentum after the first World War. In spite of the anxieties and hostilities it aroused, psychoanalysis played a central role in our changing standards of sexual conduct, family relations and social

448

sciences. It was Arthur Hopkins who apparently first managed to create serious drama out of the concepts of Freudian psychiatry. His obscure play, *The Fatted Calf* (1912) proved to be the harbinger of the new intellectual climate. Audiences that were not ready for paranoia flocked to the dream plays, while the more *avant-garde* playgoers were enjoying *Suppressed Desires* and *Overtones*. By the time World War I ended, the first great period of fruition in the American theatre was ready to begin, using Freudianism as one of its most pervasive subject-matters.

By 1921, Eugene O'Neill, Susan Glaspell, and Theodore Dreiser were pointing the way toward a serious psychological drama based upon an understanding of character rather than upon the old contrivance with plot. By 1923, their ranks had been joined by the authors of *Rain*, *The Adding Machine*, *Icebound*, *Roger Bloomer*, and *A Square Peg*. The sudden outcropping of genius in our theatre during the twenties seems to have been the result of the previous conditioning of the literary soil by serious fiction and the impact of Freudian psychology.

We have seen how the first generation of Freudian playwrights dealt with the themes suggested by psychoanalysis: the dethroning of motherhood and the liberation of children from possessive parents, the consequences of sexual suppression, inferiority and guilt feelings, and compensatory mechanisms. Howard's *The Silver Cord* was only one of many attacks upon the mother who uses her children for her own unconscious gratifications, while Dodd's *The Changelings* was the first of many comedies to reflect the dazed reaction of parents suddenly confronted with their "flaming youth," kicking over the traces of parental authority with the words of Freud on their lips and bootleg gin on their breath.

A few playwrights saw the humorous implications in the new world charted by Freud, and in *Beggar on Horseback*, *The Wisdom Tooth*, and *The Vegetable* a fresh and ingratiating style of dream-comedy was created. There was little humor, however, in the anguished drama of Eugene O'Neill. It was he who gave the American drama its first body of serious psychological work, and the vogue he established for experimental techniques, neurotic protagonists and sexual symbols had a considerable influence upon the other playwrights of his era. In *Diff'rent*, *The Great God Brown*, and *The Iceman Cometh*, O'Neill anticipated Tennessee Williams in the discovery that tragedy lies in the discrepancy between the ego-ideal and the real. Much of O'Neill's early work, as we have seen, was influenced not by Freud but by Jung's less scientific and more poetic concepts of the racial unconscious, masks, and The Earth-Mother.

When O'Neill brought his most mature psychoanalytic powers to bear, the results were the masterpieces of the twentieth-century drama—*Desire Under the Elms, Strange Interlude, Mourning Becomes Electra* and (although this is yet to be confirmed by a Broadway production) *A Moon for the Misbegotten*. In retrospect, O'Neill will perhaps be most remembered not for the subtlety of his handling of psychoanalytic motifs, but for his dazzling vitality in the theatre, his ability to extract agonizing emotion from his characters, and his use of fresh forms to dramatize Man unconsciously in conflict with himself.

His influence upon his contemporaries was inestimably great. If O'Neill could use Freudianism to give the drama dignity and serious art-form—and moreover make it pay at the box office—then this clearly was the direction for the drama to move. From Owen Davis, with his generally superficial dabbling in psychoanalysis, to the powerful socio-psychological plays of Elmer Rice and John Howard Lawson, a whole generation of young American playwrights used Freudian insights in a variety of ways and with original variations in form. Some of the most perceptive writers of this group have been lost—a few, like Sidney Howard and Philip Barry by death, and others, like Martin Flavin, Dan Totheroh, Lynn Riggs and John Steinbeck to other forms of literary endeavor. Next to O'Neill, Philip Barry seems to have realized most deeply the implications of psychoanalysis and to have articulated them in personally experienced emotion. Re-living the past in order to re-evaluate it and free oneself of its shackles was Barry's most persistent theme, resulting in at least one great play, *Hotel Universe*, and several others of major importance.

By the thirties there were a considerable number of serious artists working in the American drama and reflecting a depth of insight which before Freud was available only to a Sophocles or a Shakespeare. Robert Sherwood, Thornton Wilder, Paul Green, Moss Hart, and Sidney Kingsley each saw a particular frame of reference in Freudian-Jungian-Adlerian psychology and countless recent modifications thereof. Among the socio-political writers of the thirties, Clifford Odets was one of the few to avoid the pitfalls of ideological writing by breathing life into his characters and perceiving with rare analytic feeling the unconscious responses of individuals under social pressure.

Women play a major role in the entire psychological movement —from which they had derived much of their new freedom—and the drama is the richer for the work of Susan Glaspell, Rose Franken, Sophie Treadwell, Mary Chase, and Lillian Hellman—the latter with her special genius for exploring the dark world of human sadism. Sophie Treadwell followed O'Neill into the unconscious life of a neurotic in *Machinal,* and contributed to the gradual removal of the taboo on such themes as homosexuality.

In the thirties the emphasis shifted from individual psychology to the study of interpersonal human relationships, the convergence of inner and outer tension. S. N. Behrman's unique gift for dealing with the socio-political scene in his civilized high-comedy style makes him a particularly valuable contributor to the Freudian drama. Some writers, like Saroyan, however, took too literally the writer's new freedom to "free-associate," and found that the tenuous link between communicator and communicatee can only be subjected to limited amounts of strain. But most of the experimentalists in form—Rice, Green, Hart, and Atlas retained the rationality of the irrational, the inner logic of one character's subjective distortion of reality.

By the forties, the drama had shown its ability to probe deeply into the life of the child, the adolescent, the soldier, the psychotic, the criminal, and the homosexual. In a war-time world with few remaining standards, maladjustment could for the first time be viewed with a new penetration into cause-and-effect. The theatre became once again a place for psychological illumination.

The third Freudian generation has further enriched the drama with plays that are more subtle, more individualized, and less self-conscious. Laurents, Inge, Patrick, Chase, McCullers, the Goetzes, Robert Anderson, Samuel Taylor, Herman Wouk, and George Axelrod all have made major contributions to the psychological drama and promise to enlarge its scope even farther. In the musical theatre, Rodgers and Hammerstein have reformed the old sentimental operetta into a vehicle sensitive to the undercurrents of emotional health. In the forties and fifties, two new figures of outstanding importance have emerged—Tennessee Williams and Arthur Miller, the former expressing the music of unconscious yearning and the latter penetrating the father-son relationship with unmatched brilliance. By the mid-fifties, it must be clear to the most worldly of drama critics that the United States need no longer apologize for its drama and look enviously to the British, French or Italian. Quicker to assimilate Freudian psychology than many European countries (a condition which caused Freud himself no little alarm), the United States has been able to integrate it into its literature and arts, its educational structure and its social agencies during the years when it was relatively free from the burdens of two post-war reconstructions. This integration is as yet far from complete, but the history of American culture since 1900 is an overwhelming testimony to the influence of the new psychology.

The individual playwrights who generously replied to the present author's questionnaire have made a valuable summary of the impact of psychoanalytic theory. Although many of the concepts of Freud and his successors permeate our attitudes without our being aware of their origin, American playwrights as a group are conscious of a great indebtedness to Freud, as well as of a great danger which he has created for them by making psychological perception too easy, too tempting a substitute for original understanding of themselves and their dramatic characters. As Arthur Laurents points out, human motives are never simple, and to ascribe all neurosis to being "unloved as a child" has already become as much a cliché as poverty was for the writers of the depression drama. Perhaps we are coming to the recognition that destiny is neither external nor internal but a synthesis of the two. The pendulum in psychiatry too is returning to a reëxamination of the organic aspects of mental illness as recent findings suggest that body chemistry, endocrinology, and vitamin deficiency may be factors in the origins of psychosis.

Of the playwrights who have written this half-century of America's theatrical history, a number are known to have been personally psychoanalyzed—including Eugene O'Neill, Moss Hart, Clare Boothe Luce, Lillian Hellman, Arthur Laurents, William Inge, George Axelrod, and possibly Arthur Hopkins. But others have been equally resourceful in applying psychological insight in their work. As Odets ably summarized it, "The best of Freud is already so deeply in creative writing that it is bootless to stop for examination of where one always knew or where Freud opened up knowledge of self or others." (Contrast this with the comment of Bernard Shaw, who, late in his career, begrudgingly took cognizance of the founder of psychoanalysis, referring to him as "an extraordinarily indelicate adventurer named Sigmund Freud.")

To illustrate the extent to which Freudian mechanisms are now at the command of authors dealing with such broad fields as global politics, there is the recent Lindsay and Crouse play, *The Prescott Proposals*, an otherwise vapid work in which the American delegate to the United Nations, seeking to find some evidence that the Russians cannot indefinitely repress the humanity of their people, discovers it in a crucial Freudian slip made by the coldly dehumanized Russian delegate which betrays his emotional conflict and gives hope that Russia, too, may ultimately grow to emotional maturity in the family of nations.

What then is the future of the psychoanalytic drama? In a world

of three-dimensional entertainment, James Gow and Arnaud d'Usseau predicted in their preface to *Deep Are The Roots* the direction
which the American drama will follow:

> . . . there is one dimension of drama in which Hollywood
> today cannot compete. This is a 'fourth dimension' having
> nothing to do with form. It is *depth of perception*. Percep-
> tion of human character, perception of life itself. Here lies
> the only direction in which the stage can expand, grow and
> flourish.

We have seen that in fifty years the entire form and content of the
American drama has been revolutionized as a result of the dissemina-
tion of the psychology of unconscious motivation and the childhood
origin of later neurosis. There is no evidence that this tendency is
diminishing. In calling for the drama to purge the spectator of the
emotions of pity and fear, Aristotle stated for all times the therapeutic value of the dramatic experience. And if, as some scholars insist,
Death of a Salesman and *A Streetcar Named Desire* fail to meet all
of Aristotle's requirements for tragedy, then it is clear we must define a new *genre* of playwriting to identify the modern drama. It
might be termed a form of theatre in which the author leads his
audience to participate emotionally in the hero's conflict with his
own unconscious drives. Whether the result is tragic or comic, the
essential ingredient is that the *audience* should achieve a *state of
awareness*, which implies both an intellectual perception of *wholeness* (which the hero may or may not have reached) and an emotional
release of repressed fears, wishes or anxieties which parallel those
of the characters on stage. When this is accomplished in comic terms,
we have a Billie Dawn in *Born Yesterday* being reborn into the responsible world, and when the author's viewpoint is serious we have
a Lola and Doc growing to emotional maturity in *Come Back, Little
Sheba*.

The drama is the most persuasive of art-forms and the most
satisfying of therapies. The complex, bewildering, ambivalent, groping human animal is still the only subject for the drama; his coming
to consciousness, his discovery of himself and his unconscious impulses, and his integration of them into a meaningful whole will
remain the great theme of the psychoanalytic drama—as well as the
principal motive for the playgoer to attend the theatre.

Perhaps this is too optimistic a prediction, but the entire mental
health movement is essentially ameliorative. Dynamic psychology
has replaced Schopenhauer's pessimism with a bright prognosis for
the human race. As we learn more from psychiatry about ways of

living at peace with ourselves and with each other, there is promise
that solutions can be found for the problems of crime, intolerance
and aggression within the family, the community, the nation and the
family of nations. To find these solutions is the imperative of our
century. Until they are found, there will be no shortage of material
for the dramatist—tragic or comic—whose curiosity runs to the question of human motivation.

In this era of "isms," there should be an "ism" to express this
goal of the drama and to set it along side of expressionism, surrealism, naturalism, and symbolism. If such a term might be coined
to describe much of the American drama since 1920, it would be
motivationism.

If realism answers "what," *motivationism* must answer "why."
The playwright's chief task remains to understand and illuminate
for his audiences the behavior of his fellow man. His task today is
infinitely more possible of realization because of the reunion of the
dramatist and the psychologist—a classic affinity which had somehow gotten lost during the centuries. The most significant fact in the
history of the modern American drama is its overwhelming indebtedness to the concepts of behavior developed and systematized by the
psychoanalytic movement, and most particularly by the genius of its
founder, Sigmund Freud.

Bibliography

CHAPTER I

Thomas Mann, *Freud, Goethe, Wagner*. New York: Alfred A. Knopf, 1937, p. 11.
Ernest Jones, *The Life and Work of Sigmund Freud*. Vol. I, New York: Basic Books, 1953, p. 329.
Sigmund Freud, "Dostoevsky and Parricide," *The Yearbook of Psychoanalysis*, II, 1946, p. 231.
Sigmund Freud, "The Interpretation of Dreams," in *The Basic Writings of Sigmund Freud*. New York: The Modern Library, 1938, p. 309.

CHAPTER II

Arthur Hobson Quinn, *A History of the American Drama From the Civil War to the Present Day*. New York: Harper and Bros., 1927, p. 294.
Sydney Kessler, "The Place of Clyde Fitch in the American Theatre," Unpublished Master's thesis, University of Southern California, 1948.
John Gassner, *Masters of the Drama*. New York: Random House, 1940, p. 339.
A. A. Brill, Introduction to *The Basic Writings of Sigmund Freud*, p. 6.
Josef Breuer and Sigmund Freud, *Studies in Hysteria*. New York: Nervous and Mental Disease Publishing Company, 1936.
A. A. Brill, *Freud's Contribution to Psychiatry*. New York: W. W. Norton and Co., 1944, p. 61.
Sigmund Freud, "A Difficulty of Psycho-analysis," *Collected Papers*, IV, London: The Hogarth Press and The Institute of Psycho-Analysis, 1950, p. 355.
Neue Freie Presse, Vienna, December 2, 1895; partly republished in *Psychoanalytische Bewegung*, IV: 73, 1932.
Ernst Kris, "Book Reviews," *Psychoanalytic Quarterly*, XV; 226, 1946.
Havelock Ellis, "Freud's Influence on the Changed Attitude Toward Sex," *American Journal of Sociology*, 45: 309, November, 1939.
Albert Deutsch, "The History of Mental Hygiene," *One Hundred Years of American Psychiatry*. New York: Columbia University Press, 1944, pp. 325-365.
A. A. Brill, *Freud's Contribution to Psychiatry*, p. 20.
Ralph Tymms, *Doubles in Literary Psychology*. Cambridge, England: Bowes and Bowes, 1949, pp. 92-95.
Augustus Thomas, *The Print of My Remembrance*. New York: Charles Scribner's Sons, 1922, pp. 403-4.
Walter Prichard Eaton, *The American Stage of Today*. Boston: Small, Maynard and Company, 1908, p. 36.
Review in *Current Literature*, 67: 427, October, 1909.

A. A. Brill, *Psychoanalysis: Its Theories and Practical Application.* Philadelphia: W. B. Saunders Co., 1922, p. 202.

The Basic Writings of Sigmund Freud, p. 308.

H. Addington Bruce, "Masters of the Mind," *The American Magazine*, LXXI, 71-81, 1910.

Celia B. Stendler, "New Ideas for Old: How Freudism was received in the United States from 1900 to 1925," *Journal of Educational Psychology*, 38:193-206, April, 1947.

Sigmund Freud, "Some Character-Types Met With in Psycho-Analytic Work," *Collected Papers* IV, 318-344.

Mark Kanzer, "The Passing of 'The Oedipus Complex' in Greek Drama," *Yearbook of Psychoanalysis*, V, 1949, p. 306.

William Winter, *The Life of David Belasco.* New York: Moffat, Yard and Co., 1918. Vol. II, pp. 387-393.

Walter Prichard Eaton, *Plays and Players.* Cincinnati: Steward and Kidd Co., 1916, p. 20.

CHAPTER III

New York Dramatic Mirror, Vol. 67, February 28, 1912.

Green Book Magazine, VII, May, 1912, pp. 1068-9.

Arthur Hopkins, *How's Your Second Act?* New York: Samuel French, 1948, p. 24.

Erich Fromm, *The Forgotten Language.* New York: Rinehart and Co., 1951.

John Jacob Weisert, *The Dream in Gerhart Hauptmann.* Morningside Heights, New York: King's Crown Press, 1949, p. 53.

Paul Schilder, "Psychoanalytic Remarks on *Alice in Wonderland* and Lewis Carroll," *Journal of Nervous and Mental Disease*, 87:2, February, 1938, pp. 159-168.

See also: John Skinner, "Lewis Carroll's Adventure in Wonderland," *Yearbook of Psychoanalysis*, 4, 1948, pp. 330-354.

Martin Grotjohn, "About the Symbolization of Alice's Adventures in Wonderland," *American Imago*, 4, 1947, pp. 32-41.

Current Opinion, LIX, 4, October, 1915, pp. 240-3.

Helen Deutsch and Stella Hanau, *The Provincetown: A Story of the Theatre.* New York: Farrar and Rinehart, Inc., 1931, p. 5.

Quoted in Frederick J. Hoffman, *Freudianism and the Literary Mind.* Baton Rouge: Louisiana State University Press, 1945, p. 69.

Bobby Edwards, *Quill*, XIII, 1923, p. 14.

Carl G. Jung, "The Association Method," *American Journal of Psychology*, XXI, April, 1910, pp. 230-35.

Smith Ely Jelliffe and Louise Brink, *Psychoanalysis and the Drama.* New York: Nervous and Mental Disease Publishing Co., 1922, p. 99.

Kenneth Macgowan, *The Theatre of Tomorrow.* New York: Boni and Liveright, 1921, p. 99.

CHAPTER IV

Heywood Broun, *New York Tribune*, January 14, 1920.

Alexander Woollcott, *New York Times*, January 20, 1920.

Theodore Dreiser, "Remarks," *Psychoanalytic Review*, 18, July, 1931, p. 250.

Susan Glaspell, *The Road to the Temple.* New York: Frederick A. Stokes Co., 1927, p. 297.

Daniel E. Schneider, *The Psychoanalyst and the Artist.* New York: Farrar, Straus and Co., 1950.

Ives Hendrick, *Facts and Theories of Psychoanalysis.* New York: Alfred A. Knopf, 1934, p. 159.

CHAPTER V

Philip Wylie, *Generation of Vipers.* New York: Farrar and Rinehart, 1942.

Robert Littell, *New York World,* November 19, 1929.

William Bolitho, "Matriarchy," *New York World,* March 20, 1930.

William G. King, "Berkeley Square's Peter Standish is Psychoanalyzed," *New York Evening Post,* April 12, 1930.

Karl A. Menninger, *The Human Mind.* New York: Alfred A. Knopf, 1949, p. 230n.

Alexander Woollcott, "The Stage," *New York World,* April 5, 1926.

Richard Lockridge, *New York Sun,* November 26, 1928.

CHAPTER VI

Barrett Clark, *Eugene O'Neill: The Man and his Plays.* New York: Dover Publications, 1947, p. 136.

Arthur H. Nethercott, "O'Neill on Freudianism," *Saturday Review of Literature,* May 28, 1932, p. 759.

Deutsch and Hanau, *The Provincetown,* p. 23.

Eugene O'Neill, in *New York Tribune,* February 13, 1921.

Beatrice M. Hinkle, *The Recreating of the Individual.* New York: Harcourt, 1923.

Clarence P. Oberndorf, *The Psychiatric Novels of Oliver Wendell Holmes.* New York: Columbia University Press, 1946, p. 113.

Carl G. Jung, *Psychological Types or the Psychology of Individuation.* New York: Harcourt, Brace and Company, 1926, p. 567.

Carl G. Jung, "The Conception of the Unconscious," in *Collected Papers on Analytical Psychology.* New York: Moffat Yard and Co., 1917, p. 457.

Eugene O'Neill, *Memoranda on Masks,* quoted in Barrett Clark, *op. cit.,* p. 103.

Eugene O'Neill, "The Playwright Explains," *New York Times,* February 14, 1926.

Edwin Engel, *The Haunted Heroes of Eugene O'Neill.* Harvard University Press, 1953.

Gregory Zilboorg, *Sigmund Freud: His Explorations of the Mind of Man.* New York: Charles Scribner's Sons, 1951, p. 78.

Brooks Atkinson, *New York Times,* January 31, 1928.

Eugene O'Neill, "Working Notes and Extracts from a Fragmentary Work Diary," reprinted in Barrett Clark, *European Theories of the Drama.* New York: Crown Publishers, 1947, p. 534.

Fritz Wittels, "Psychoanalysis and Literature," *Psycho-analysis Today,* Sandor Lorand, editor, New York: Covici-Friede, 1933, p. 347.

George D. Stephens, "The Narrative and Dramatic Poetry of Robinson Jeffers: A Critical Study," Unpublished doctoral dissertation, University of Southern California, 1953, p. 56.

Hiram Motherwell, "Tell Your Dreams," *The Stage*, 9, 11, June, 1934, p. 13.

Martin W. Peck, "A Psychiatrist Views the Drama," *Psychoanalytic Review*, 22, 1935, pp. 306-313.

Brooks Atkinson, "Eugene O'Neill," *New York Times*, II, 2, December 13, 1953.

CHAPTER VII

Sigmund Freud, *The Interpretation of Dreams*, in *Basic Writings*, p. 390.

John Howard Lawson, Preface in Playbill for *Nirvana*, quoted by Gilbert W. Gabriel, *New York Sun*, March 4, 1926.

From a letter by Mrs. John Howard Lawson in reply to the author's questionnaire, 1950.

Elmer Rice, quoted by Heywood Broun, *New York World*, March 29, 1923.

J. Sadger, *Sleep Walking and Moon Walking: A Medico-Literary Study*. New York: Nervous and Mental Disease Publishing Co., 1920.

Joseph Wood Krutch, *The American Drama Since 1918*. New York: Random House, 1939, p. 56.

Barrett H. Clark, *Intimate Portraits*. New York: Dramatists Play Service, 1951, p. 193.

John Gassner, *Twenty-Five Best Plays of the Modern American Theatre*, Early Series. New York: Crown Publishers, 1949, p. 294.

Carl G. Jung, *Modern Man in Search of a Soul*. New York: Harcourt, Brace, 1933, p. 233.

CHAPTER VIII

Gerald Hamm, *The Drama of Philip Barry*. Philadelphia: University of Pennsylvania Press, 1948, pp. 6-7.

Jacob L. Moreno, *The Group Method and Group Psychotherapy*. New York: Beacon House, 1931. Also see Joseph I. Meiers, "Origins and Development of Group Psychotherapy," *Sociometry*, VIII, Aug.-Nov., 1945.

Arthur Hobson Quinn, "The Meaning and Method of Hotel Universe," *New York Post*, May 2, 1930.

Alfred Korzybski, *Science and Sanity: An Introduction to Non-Aristotelian Systems and General Semantics*. New York: Science Press Printing Co., 1933.

CHAPTER IX

A. A. Brill, *Freud's Contribution to Psychiatry*. New York: W. W. Norton, 1944.

Sigmund Freud, "Psycho-Analytic Notes Upon An Auto-biographical Account of a Case of Paranoia (Dementia Paranoides)," *Collected Papers* III, p. 448.

Brooks Atkinson, *New York Times*, January 29, 1935, p. 24.

Faye Henle, *Au Clare de Luce: Portrait of a Luminous Lady*. New York: Stephen Daye, 1943, p. 33.

Karl Menninger, *Love Against Hate*. New York: Harcourt, Brace and Co., 1942, p. 53.

Brooks Atkinson, *New York Times*, November 13, 1935, p. 24.

Brooks Atkinson, *New York Times*, October 22, 1938, p. 15.

F. L. Lucas, *Literature and Psychology*. London: Cassell and Co., Ltd., 1951.

Frederick J. Hoffman, "From Surrealism to 'The Apocalypse'," *Journal of English Literary History*, 15, June, 1948, pp. 147-153.

Ernest Jones, *The Life and Work of Sigmund Freud*, I. New York: Basic Books, Inc., 1953, pp. 246-7.

Kenneth Burke, "Freud and the analysis of Poetry," *American Journal of Sociology*, 45, November, 1939, p. 401.

Allardyce Nicoll, *World Drama*. New York: Harcourt, Brace and Co., 1949, p. 774.

Thornton Wilder, quoted by Carl Van Vechten in Introduction to *Last Operas and Plays*, by Gertrude Stein. New York: Rinehart and Co., 1949, p. viii.

William Saroyan, *Bicycle Rider in Beverly Hills*. New York: Scribner's, 1952.

William Saroyan, Preface to *Razzle-Dazzle*. N.Y.: Harcourt, Brace and Co., 1942.

William Saroyan, "Some Frank Talk from William Saroyan," *New York Times*, January 4, 1953.

CHAPTER X

Erich Fromm, *Escape from Freedom*. New York: Farrar and Rinehart, 1941.

Brooks Atkinson, *New York Times*, April 26, 1932, p. 25.

N. Bryllion Fagin, " 'Freud' on the American Stage," *Educational Theatre Journal*, II, 4, December, 1950, p. 302.

Harry Gilroy, "The Bigger the Lie," *New York Times*, December 7, 1952.

Sigmund Freud, "Contributions to the Psychology of Love," *Collected Papers*, IV, p. 194.

Patrick Mullahy, *Oedipus: Myth and Complex*. New York, Hermitage Press, 1948, p. 281.

Maurice Zolotow, "To Couch or Not to Couch," *Theatre Arts*, 38, 2, February, 1954, p. 93.

Otto Fenichel, *The Psychoanalytic Theory of Neurosis*. New York: W. W. Norton and Co., 1945, p. 177.

Moss Hart, Preface to *The Climate of Eden*, reprinted in *Theatre Arts*, 38, 5, May, 1954, p. 32.

John Dollard, "The Dozens: dialectic of insult," *American Imago*, 1, 1939, pp. 3-25.

Frederick J. Hoffman, *Freudianism and the Literary Mind*, p. 307.

Edmund Bergler, *Neurotic Counterfeit-Sex*. New York: Grune and Stratton, 1951, p. 58.

CHAPTER XI

S. N. Behrman, *The Worcester Account*. New York: Random House, 1954.

Edmund Bergler, *The Writer and Psychoanalysis*. Garden City, N.Y., Doubleday, 1950, Chap. 6.

Samson Raphaelson, *The Human Nature of Playwriting*. N.Y.: Macmillan Co., 1949, pp. 221-2.

CHAPTER XII

Arthur Laurents, "A Theme on Variations," *New York Times*, October 12, 1952.

Milton Bracker, "Boy Actor to Broadway," *New York Times*, March 22, 1953.

William Inge, "The Schizophrenic Wonder," *Theatre Arts*, 34, 5, May, 1950, pp. 22-33.

William Inge, " 'Picnic' of Women," *New York Times*, Feb. 15, 1953.

William Inge, "From 'Front Porch' to Broadway," *Theatre Arts*, 38, 4, April, 1954, p. 33.

Harry Gilroy, "The Playwright of the August Moon," *New York Times Magazine*, November 15, 1953, p. 17.

Vern Sneider, "Below 'The Teahouse'," *New York Times*, October 4, 1953.

Cecil Smith, *Musical Comedy in America*. New York: Theatre Arts Books, 1950, p. 343.

Agnes deMille, *Dance to the Piper*. Boston: Little, Brown and Co., 1951.

Brooks Atkinson, "Eloquent Musical," *New York Times*, June 13, 1954.

Richard Rodgers, " 'Carousel' Returns," *New York Times*, May 30, 1954.

Burton Rascoe, *New York World-Telegram*, November 23, 1945.

CHAPTER XIII

Tennessee Williams, "The History of a Play," postscript in *Battle of Angels*. *Pharos Magazine*, Spring, 1945. Distributed by *New Directions*.

John Gassner, *Best Plays of the Modern American Theatre*, Second Series. New York: Crown Publishers, 1947, p. 3.

Hoffman, *Freudianism and the Literary Mind*, pp. 149-179.

Elia Kazan, "Notebook for *Streetcar Named Desire*" in *Directing the Play*, edited by Toby Cole and Helen Krich Chinoy. Indianapolis: Bobbs-Merrill, 1953.

Tennessee Williams, "On the 'Camino Real'," *New York Times*, March 15, 1953.

Daniel Schneider, "Play of Dreams," *Theatre Arts*, 33, October, 1949, pp. 18-21.

John Gassner, *The Theatre in Our Times*. New York: Crown Publishers, 1954, pp. 367-368.

CHAPTER XIV

Richard L. Coe, "Storm over 'Summer House,' " *New York Times*, Dec. 27, 1953.

C. P. Oberndorf, *A History of Psychoanalysis in America*. N.Y.: Grune and Stratton, 1953.

Donald Webster Cory, *The Homosexual in America*. New York: Greenberg, 1951.

Alfred C. Kinsey and staff, *Sexual Behavior in the Human Female*. Philadelphia: W. B. Saunders Company, 1953, p. 475.

Oberndorf, *op. cit.*, p. 30.

John Van Druten, *Playwright at Work*. New York: Harper and Brothers, 1953.

Brooks Atkinson, *New York Times*, Feb. 9, 1954.

Maurice Zolotow, "The Impossibility of Drama Criticism," *Theatre Arts*, 38, 7, July, 1954, p. 91.

Richard Watts, Jr., *New York Post*, April 12, 1950.

William Hawkins, *New York World-Telegram*, December 2, 1949.

Alexander Knox, "About the Play," *Theatre Arts*, 34, 5, May, 1950, p. 62.

Frederic Wertham, *Dark Legend*. New York: Duell, Sloan and Pearce, 1941.

Frederic Wertham, *The Show of Violence*. London: Gollancz, 1949.

Edmund Wilson, "The Ambiguity of Henry James," in *The Triple Thinkers*, New York: Oxford Press, 1948.

William Archibald, "The Quick and the Dead," *Theatre Arts*, 34, 6, June, 1950.

John Gassner, *Best American Plays, Third Series, 1945-1951*. New York: Crown Publishers, 1952, p. 174.

Walter F. Kerr, "Today's Play Can't Afford to Be Without a Psychiatrist," *Los Angeles Times*, June 13, 1954. IV, 2.

Lawrence S. Kubie, "Psychiatrist on 'Shrike'—Other Views." *New York Times*, X, 2, March 16, 1952.

Joseph Kramm, "Basic Equipment," *New York Times*, 2, 1, July 20, 1952.

CHAPTER XV

Bernard Shaw, *Buoyant Billions, Farfetched Fables, and Shakes Versus Shav*. New York: Dodd, Mead and Co., 1951, p. 62.

Arnaud d'Usseau and James Gow, Preface to *Deep Are The Roots*. New York: Dramatists Play Service, p. 6.

Index
of
Names and Titles

463